THE PAPACY 1073–1198

Before the middle of the eleventh century the pope was far from being the active leader of the Church that he is today: he restricted himself to the local concerns of the diocese of Rome and was virtually ignored by the outside world. This book is a study of the transformation of the role of the pope in the late eleventh and twelfth centuries, from which he emerged as monarch of the universal Church, dedicated to reform and to making the Church independent of secular control.

The most important role in the new model government was given to the cardinals, who henceforward were the principal advisers, agents and electors of the popes. These developments were accelerated by schism and political conflict: on three occasions the lawful pope was driven into exile by an antipope supported by a powerful secular ruler.

Professor Robinson's text emphasises the growing importance of the college of cardinals and the practical aspects of papal government. It offers the most detailed analytical study yet available of this key period in the history of the papacy.

Cambridge medieval textbooks

This is a series of specially commissioned textbooks for teachers and students, designed to complement the monograph series Cambridge Studies in Medieval Life and Thought by providing introductions to a range of topics in medieval history. The series combines both chronological and thematic approaches, and deals equally with British and European topics. All volumes in the series are published in hard covers and in paperback.

Germany in the High Middle Ages *c.* 1050–1200
HORST FUHRMANN
Translated by Timothy Reuter

The Hundred Years War: England and France at War *c.* 1300–*c.* 1450
CHRISTOPHER ALLMAND

Standards of Living in the Later Middle Ages
Social Change in England *c.* 1200–1520
CHRISTOPHER DYER

Magic in the Middle Ages
RICHARD KIECKHEFER

The Struggle for Power in Medieval Italy
Structures of Political Rule
GIOVANNI TABACCO
Translated by Rosalind Brown Jensen

The Papacy 1073–1198: Continuity and Innovation
I. S. ROBINSON

THE PAPACY 1073–1198

Continuity and innovation

I. S. ROBINSON

Associate Professor of History,
Trinity College, Dublin

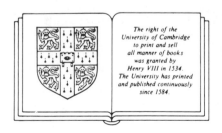

CAMBRIDGE UNIVERSITY PRESS

Cambridge
New York   Port Chester   Melbourne   Sydney

Published by the Press Syndicate of the University of Cambridge
The Pitt Building, Trumpington Street, Cambridge CB2 1RP
40 West 20th Street, New York, NY 10011, USA
10 Stamford Road, Oakleigh, Melbourne, 3166, Australia

First published 1990

Printed in Great Britain at Redwood Press Ltd.

British Library cataloguing in publication data

Robinson, I. S.
The papacy 1073–1198.
1. Papacy, history
1. Title
262'.13'09

Library of Congress cataloguing in publication data

Robinson, I. S. (Ian Stuart). 1947 Feb. 11–
The papacy 1073–1198: continuity and innovation / I. S. Robinson.
p.   cm. – (Cambridge medieval textbooks)
Includes index.
ISBN 0–521–26498–7 – ISBN 0–521–31922–6 (pbk)
1. Papacy – History – To 1309. 2. Church and state – Europe –
History. 3. Europe – Church history – Middle Ages. 600–1500.
1. Title. II. Series.
BX1210.R63 1990
261'.13'0902 – dc20   89–34126
CIP
68984
ISBN 0 521 26498 7 hard covers
ISBN 0 521 31922 6 paperback

CONTENTS

PREFACE

This is a study of the papacy and its relations with western Christendom in the period from the accession of Gregory VII to the death of Celestine III. In order to compress so large a subject into a relatively small book, my approach has inevitably been selective. I must, therefore, begin by explaining precisely which aspects of papal history are treated in this study. Firstly, my subject-matter is the papacy's relations with the churches and kingdoms of the *west*. To have included a survey of papal relations with Byzantium and the other neighbours of western Christendom would have made the book far too long and so I was obliged to omit this complex topic. The first part of my book presents the institutions of the papal government in action. Chapter one deals with the problems of governing the city of Rome and the lands of the papacy ('the Patrimony of St Peter'). The following six chapters examine the institutions by means of which the papacy sought to govern the western Church: the college of cardinals and the curia (chapter two), the papal council (chapter three), the papal legation (chapter four), papal judicial institutions and the pope's legislative authority (chapter five), the papal protection accorded to religious houses (chapter six) and papal financial institutions (chapter seven). All these institutions were either created or remodelled to serve the needs of the reform papacy in the later eleventh century. All survived the drastic rethinking of papal policy in the 1120s and 1130s (which some historians have called 'the end of the reform papacy') and greatly extended their operations in the course of the twelfth century. The second part of the book is devoted to the papacy's involvement in the secular politics of western Christendom. It is concerned with the political ideas of the papal curia (chapter eight), the papal role in the promotion of the crusade (chapter nine) and the two relationships which dominated papal political calculations in this period: that with the Norman principalities of southern Italy (chapter ten) and that with the empire (chapter eleven).

Each of these topics is examined from the point of view of the papal curia, as an aspect of papal reforming or political strategy; and the effect of this approach is necessarily to produce a study much narrower in its range than would be appropriate, for example, in a general history of the western Church. My treatment of the religious orders in chapter six provides an obvious illustration of this. One of the most important features of the history of the Church in the later eleventh and twelfth centuries was the development of new conceptions of the religious life and the foundation of new religious orders. In this major innovation in the life of the Church the role of the papacy seems often to have been a rather limited one, which provides an obvious contrast with the decisive role of the thirteenth-century papacy in the history of the religious life. The popes of the later eleventh and twelfth centuries appear in the history of the religious orders not as innovators but as protectors. They were urgently requested by the new religious houses and by their founders and patrons to use St Peter's legitimating authority on their behalf and to confer on the houses the powerful protection (*patrocinium*) of St Peter. My discussion of the papacy's relations with the religious orders, therefore, concentrates on these papal institutions – the legitimating role and *patrocinium* – rather than on contemporary monastic institutions. A similar case is that of heretical movements, another topic which would command considerable space in a general history of the western Church in this period. The eleventh- and twelfth-century popes did not respond to the problem of heresy in the decisive manner of their thirteenth-century successors. Their response remained largely on a theoretical level: the theory of the pope as defender of the catholic faith and the theory of the lay power as the 'secular arm' of the Church. These are consequently the aspects of the problem of heresy which are treated here (respectively in chapters two and three and in chapter eight). The enormous subject of the crusade is likewise treated here solely from the papal point of view (chapter nine).

Considerations of space have also prevented me from providing a full bibliography. However, readers who wish to make a more

detailed study of topics covered in this book will find in the footnotes
a guide to the extensive secondary literature on the papacy in the
period 1073–1198. The footnotes are intended also to give students
some impression of the range and character of the available primary
sources. These notes above all emphasise my indebtedness to the distinguished scholars who are currently working in this field.

The century-and-a-quarter covered by this book was the period in
which the popes ceased to be concerned exclusively with the narrow
affairs of their diocese of Rome and began to exercise that universal jurisdiction throughout Christendom claimed by the tradition of
the Roman church. That tradition was summarised *ca.* 1150 by
Bernard of Clairvaux for the instruction of his pupil, Pope Eugenius
III.

According to your canons, some are called to a share of the responsibilities,
but you are called to the fullness of power. The power of others is confined
within definite limits, but your power extends even over those who have
received power over others . . . [The pope] must rule not the people of this
or that city or region or kingdom, . . . not one people but all people . . . the
universal Church spread throughout the world, made up of all the churches.

The popes of the years 1073–1198 intended to use this unique authority to reform the Church. These years witnessed two successive
papal reform movements. The first of these, inaugurated in the
Roman councils of Gregory VII in 1074 and 1075, was the well-
known 'Gregorian reform' of the late eleventh and early twelfth centuries. The papal reform which had begun under imperial auspices in
the middle of the eleventh century was a movement dedicated to the
eradication from the Church of simony and clerical marriage. In the
early Church 'simony' had been defined as the sale of priestly ordination by a bishop; but the term had subsequently been extended to
cover all trafficking in holy things. In the eleventh century the term
'simony' was most frequently used for the sale of the office of bishop
or abbot by the secular ruler. It was regarded by the reform papacy
as the earliest and most dangerous of the heresies of the Christian
Church. By the time of the accession of Gregory VII in 1073 the
papacy had reached the conclusion that the most potent cause of
simony was the royal control over ecclesiastical appointments which
was characteristic of western Christendom in the eleventh century.
Bishops and abbots were usually elected in the king's presence and
must perform feudal homage to the king, from whom they received
the investiture of their office and the property attached to it. The

Gregorian reform was an attempt to end this secular control of ecclesiastical appointments and the resultant subordination of the priesthood (*sacerdotium*) to the royal power (*regnum*). The reformers' objective was, in Gregory VII's words, 'to snatch [the Church] from servile oppression, or rather tyrannical slavery, and restore her to her ancient freedom'. The reforming measures and the political strategy adopted by Gregory VII provoked a conflict with the most formidable secular ruler in the west, King Henry IV of Germany, which continued long after the deaths of the two antagonists. Historians have called this conflict 'the Investiture Contest' after the ceremony of investiture, which symbolised the traditional lay control of the Church. The second papal reform movement of our period was less dramatic than the Gregorian reform. Unlike Gregory VII's struggle for the freedom of the Church, it did not lead to conflict with the secular power. The new reform programme was introduced in Innocent II's council of Clermont in 1130 and it was elaborated in successive councils, culminating in the Third Lateran Council of Alexander III in 1179. The new programme was concerned not with the freedom of the Church, but with the discipline of the clergy and the inculcating of Christian standards among the laity. It was in order to reform the Church that the popes of the period 1073–1198 sought to communicate with the faithful throughout western Christendom by means of papal legates and papal councils. It was in the interests of reform that the papal government became more efficient and that papal judicial procedures were made more effective.

Reform is the first underlying theme of this study: the second theme is schism and its effects on the papacy. Three papal schisms dominated the history of the papacy in this period: the schism of the antipope 'Clement III' (1080–1100) and his short-lived successors (1100, 1102, 1105–11, 1118–21); the schism of 'Anacletus II' (1130–8); the schism of the antipopes 'Victor IV' (1159–64), 'Paschal III' (1164–8) and 'Calixtus III' (1168–78). Each of these antipopes was supported by a secular ruler powerful enough to drive the lawful pope out of Rome and into exile: 'Clement III' by Emperor Henry IV, 'Anacletus II' by King Roger II of Sicily, 'Victor IV' and his successors by Emperor Frederick I. The popes of the schism of the late eleventh and early twelfth century found refuge mainly in southern Italy; the popes of the later schisms found refuge in central and northern Italy and in France. These three schisms were not resolved in Rome: it was ecclesiastical and secular opinion throughout western Christendom which ultimately accepted the claims of the popes and rejected those of the antipopes and their secular champions. The aphorism in which Bernard of Clairvaux described the fate of Innocent II in the schism of the 1130s – 'he was expelled from the city and accepted by the world' – applied equally to the other popes who were driven out of Rome by antipopes at the end of the eleventh century and during the twelfth century. Urban II, Paschal II and Calixtus II in the first of these schisms, Innocent II in the 1130s and Alexander III in the schism of 1159–77 were ultimately victorious in their struggle against the antipopes because they were 'accepted by the world'; but they must first persuade princes and churchmen throughout the west of the legitimacy of their cause. These efforts at persuasion inevitably brought the papacy closer to the world outside Rome.

It was not only the three schisms of our period that forced popes to leave Rome. During the years 1073–1198 Rome became a dangerous residence because of the hostility of the Romans towards the pope. In the late eleventh and early twelfth centuries papal independence was threatened by the ambitions of noble families. After 1143 the threat was intensified by the foundation of a Roman commune which claimed jurisdiction over the city. The popes maintained their freedom of action by creating a system of government which made them independent of the Romans, by exploiting the resources of the papal territories ('the Patrimony of St Peter') and by means of their alliance with western princes. How far the popes succeeded in emancipating themselves from Rome in this period is evident from a glance at the origins of the nineteen popes of the years 1073–1198. Only five were Romans: Gregory VII, Innocent II, Anastasius IV, Clement III and Celestine III. Three were southern Italians: Victor III, Gelasius II and Gregory VIII. Eight came from central or northern Italy: Paschal II (Bleda), Honorius II and Lucius II (Bologna), Celestine II (Castello), Lucius III (Lucca), Urban III (Milan), Eugenius III (Pisa) and Alexander III (Siena). There was one Frenchman (Urban II), one Burgundian (Calixtus II) and one Englishman (Hadrian IV). The same impression of emancipation from Rome can be found in the college of cardinals during this period. The reform papacy of the later eleventh century gave an 'international' character to the cardinalate, which it continued to bear during the twelfth century. The appointment of French and above all of central and northern Italian cardinals reflected the importance of these regions for the twelfth-century papacy. The college of cardinals was by far the most important institution in the papal government of the twelfth century. The cardinals served the pope as his principal advisers, the chief administrators of his government, his most trusted legates; so that it is impossible to write a history of the papacy in this period without investigating the college of cardinals and its factions. This book is therefore as much a study of the cardinals as of the popes.

I should like to record my grateful thanks to Ms Gillian Maude and Mr William Davies of the Cambridge University Press for their valuable advice and tireless assistance. I owe a particular debt of gratitude to the staff of the libraries in which I have been privileged to work in recent years: to the staff of the Library of Trinity College, Dublin, especially Mr Roy Stanley; to the staff of the Lesesaal and Handschriftenabteilung of the University Library, Bonn; to the staff of the Library of the Monumenta Germaniae Historica and of the Staatsbibliothek, Munich; to the staff of the Herzog August Bibliothek, Wolfenbüttel. Important material was found for me by friends working in other libraries: Elizabeth Diamond-Rublack (Tübingen), Sheila Watts (Göttingen) and Niall ó Ciosáin (Florence). I was particularly fortunate in the support and encouragement of my colleagues, Professor Aidan Clarke and Dr Patrick Kelly. My family in Germany – Waldi and Werner Becker in Bad Godesberg, Dagmar and Walter Hammerstein in Nassau – generously provided me with an ideal environment in which to work. I record my grateful thanks to them and above all to my long-suffering wife, who must be extremely glad that this book is finished.

ABBREVIATIONS

The following abbreviations and short titles are used in the footnotes.

AHP	*Archivum Historiae Pontificiae*
Becker, *Urban II.*	A. Becker, *Papst Urban II. (1088–1099)* (Schriften der Monumenta Germaniae Historica 19/1, 2: 1964–88)
BISI	*Bullettino dell' Istituto Storico Italiano per il Medio Evo e Archivio Muratoriano*
Conciliorum Oecumenicorum Decreta	*Conciliorum Oecumenicorum Decreta* ed. J. A. Dossetti (3rd edition: Bologna, 1973)
DA	*Deutsches Archiv für Erforschung des Mittelalters*
Decretales Gregorii IX	E. Friedberg (ed.), *Corpus Iuris Canonici* 2: *Decretalium collectiones* (Leipzig, 1881)
EHR	*English Historical Review*
Gratian, *Decretum*	E. Friedberg (ed.), *Corpus Iuris Canonici* 1: *Decretum Magistri Gratiani* (Leipzig, 1879)
Gregory VII, *Registrum*	E. Caspar (ed.), *Das Register Gregors VII., Monumenta Germaniae Historica Epistolae selectae* 2

Hauck, *Kirchengeschichte Deutschlands*	A. Hauck, *Kirchengeschichte Deutschlands* 3–4 (6th edition: Leipzig, 1952)
HJb	*Historisches Jahrbuch*
HZ	*Historische Zeitschrift*
Italia Pontificia	P. Kehr (ed.), *Italia Pontificia* 1–8 (Berlin, 1906–35)
JL	P. Jaffé, *Regesta pontificum Romanorum ab condita ecclesia ad annum post Christum natum MCXCVIII* ed. S. Loewenfeld, F. Kaltenbrunner, P. Ewald 1–2 (2nd edition: Leipzig, 1885–8)
Liber Censuum	P. Fabre and L. Duchesne (ed.), *Le Liber censuum de l'Eglise romaine* 1–3 (Bibliothèque des Ecoles françaises d'Athènes et de Rome, 2. série 6: Paris, 1889–1952)
Liber pontificalis	*Le Liber pontificalis* ed. L. Duchesne and C. Vogel 1–3 (Bibliothèque des Ecoles françaises d'Athènes et de Rome, 2. série 3: Paris, 1886–1957)
Mansi, *Sacra Concilia*	G. D. Mansi, *Sacrorum conciliorum nova et amplissima collectio* 1–31 (Venice-Florence, 1759–1798)
MGH	*Monumenta Germaniae Historica:*
Constitutiones 1	*Constitutiones et acta publica imperatorum et regum* 1 (911–1197)
Dt. Ma.	*Deutsches Mittelalter. Kritische Studientexte*
Libelli	*Libelli de lite imperatorum et pontificum saeculis XI et XII conscripti*
SS	*Scriptores*
SS rer. Germ.	*Scriptores rerum Germanicarum in usum scholarum separatim editi*
MIÖG	*Mitteilungen des Instituts für oesterreichische Geschichtsforschung*
MPL	J. P. Migne, *Patrologiae cursus completus. Series latina*
MRIS	L. A. Muratori, *Rerum Italicarum scriptores*
NA	*Neues Archiv der Gesellschaft für ältere Deutsche Geschichtskunde*

Pacaut, *Alexandre III*	M. Pacaut, *Alexandre III. Etude sur la conception du pouvoir pontifical dans sa pensée et dans son œuvre* (L'Eglise et l'Etat au moyen âge 11: Paris, 1956)
QFIAB	*Quellen und Forschungen aus italienischen Archiven und Bibliotheken*
RHC Occ.	*Recueil des historiens des croisades, Historiens occidentaux* 1–5 (Académie des inscriptions et belles-lettres: Paris, 1841–95)
RHE	*Revue d'histoire ecclésiastique*
RS	*Rolls Series. Rerum Britannicarum medii aevi Scriptores*
Sb	*Sitzungsberichte*
Servatius, *Paschalis II.*	C. Servatius, *Paschalis II. (1099–1118)* (Päpste und Papsttum 14: Stuttgart, 1979)
SG	*Studi Gregoriani per la storia della riforma gregoriana (per la storia della 'Libertas Ecclesiae', 1972–)*
SMGBO	*Studien und Mitteilungen zur Geschichte des Benediktinerordens und seiner Zweige*
TRHS	*Transactions of the Royal Historical Society*
ZKG	*Zeitschrift für Kirchengeschichte*
ZSSRG	*Zeitschrift der Savigny-Stiftung für Rechtsgeschichte*
GA	*Germanistische Abteilung*
KA	*Kanonistische Abteilung*

BIBLIOGRAPHICAL NOTE

In addition to the specialised works mentioned in the footnotes, the following works provide a valuable introduction to the papal history of this period, together with advice on further reading.

G. Barraclough, *The medieval papacy* (London, 1968)

A. Fliche, *La réforme grégorienne et la reconquête chrétienne (1057–1123)* (Histoire de l'Eglise 8: Paris, 1946)

A. Fliche, R. Foreville and J. Rousset de Pina, *Du premier concile du Latran à l'avènement d'Innocent III* (Histoire de l'Eglise 9: Paris, 1948–53)

J. Haller, *Das Papsttum, Idee und Wirklichkeit* 2–3 (second edition: Stuttgart, 1951–2)

H. Jedin (general editor), *Handbook of Church history* 3 (English translation: New York-London, 1969)

J. Paul, *L'Eglise et la culture en occident, IXe–XIIe siècles* 1–2 (Nouvelle Clio. L'histoire et ses problèmes 15: Paris, 1986)

W. Ullmann, *A short history of the papacy in the Middle Ages* (London, 1972)

PART I
THE PAPAL GOVERNMENT

I

ROME AND THE PATRIMONY OF ST PETER

———— · ————

The bishop of Rome ruled over a diocese which in the period 1073–1198 must have been the most turbulent and ungovernable in western Christendom. The city was 'almost a ruin, broken down, reduced to ashes': Rome's decline from her ancient splendour was a favourite theme of visiting poets.[1] In the twelfth century a population of no more than 20,000 persons inhabited a city which at the height of her ancient prosperity had housed at least half a million.[2] No longer a thriving economic centre, the city derived her wealth from her churches. 'In place of the ruins of walls and ancient temples, there spring up every day innumerable buildings of churches or monasteries':[3] over 300 had sprung up by the end of the twelfth century. The pilgrims attracted by these churches and their relic collections provided an important part of the income of the Romans in the eleventh century. During the following century an additional source of income was provided by the litigants and petitioners drawn to Rome by the rapid expansion of papal government. It was Rome's parasitical attitude towards these strangers which prompted the well-known complaints of non-Roman historians and satirists about the avarice of the Romans. The English historian William of

[1] Hildebert of Lavardin, *Carmina* 63, *MPL* 171, 1409B; cf. no. 64, 1409D–1410A. See P. E. Schramm, *Kaiser, Rom und Renovatio* I (3rd edition: Darmstadt, 1962), pp. 296–305; G. Tellenbach, 'La città di Roma dal IX al XII secolo' in *Studi storici in onore di Ottorino Bertolini* 2 (Pisa, 1972), 693–6.

[2] K. J. Beloch, *Bevölkerungsgeschichte Italiens* 2 (2nd edition: Berlin, 1939), 1.

[3] Arnold, *Miracula sancti Emmerami* II.34, *MGH SS* 4, 567.

3

Malmesbury described Rome as 'a heavenly storehouse' inhabited
by 'a people drunk with insane fury'. They preyed on the pilgrims
and 'would shed the blood of citizens even over the bodies of the
saints, whenever they could not satisfy their lust for money'.[4] The
most effective predators were the noblemen, who supplemented the
income from their estates in the Roman countryside with tolls
exacted from visitors to the city. For example, Cencius Stephani
(Gregory VII's principal opponent among the Roman nobility) 'built
a tower of astonishing size on the bridge of St Peter and demanded
tribute from all who crossed the river'.[5]

The Romans also regarded their bishop as an important source of
income. The pope, as vicar of St Peter, received the offerings of the
faithful who wished to obtain the saint's good will; and the Romans
desired a share of the spoils. On his accession the pope was expected
to bestow gifts – known in the twelfth century as *beneficia* – on the
Roman people in order to buy their support. Similarly on certain
feast days he conferred gifts, called *presbyteria*, which were shared by
the Roman clergy and the secular officials of the city. These practices
were denounced in the mid-twelfth century by two distinguished
moralists from north of the Alps. Bernard of Clairvaux wrote to his
former pupil, the Cistercian pope Eugenius III: 'whom can you point
to in the whole of the great city who accepted you as pope without
receiving a penny or the hope of a penny?'[6] Gerhoch of Reichersberg
claimed that Hadrian IV on his accession (1154) 'spent 11,000 talents
on the Romans so that they would swear fealty to him'. The pope
should submit to exile, thought Gerhoch, rather than encourage the
avarice of the Romans in this way. It is not clear whether this is an
accurate sum or a rhetorical exaggeration: 11,000 talents was more
than a third of the annual income which the emperor claimed from
his Italian kingdom in the twelfth century.[7] During Hadrian IV's
pontificate the pope's confidant and compatriot, John of Salisbury,
informed Hadrian of the resentment felt by the rest of Christendom
about the papal gifts to the Romans. 'You wish to maintain control

[4] William of Malmesbury, *Gesta regum Anglorum* IV.353, *RS* 90/2 (1889), 409.
[5] Bonizo of Sutri, *Liber ad amicum*, *MGH Libelli* 1, 603. For Cencius Stephani see
below, pp. 6–7, 12, 21, 402.
[6] Bernard of Clairvaux, *De consideratione* IV.2, *MPL* 182, 774C.
[7] Gerhoch of Reichersberg, *Liber de investigatione Antichristi* c. 69, *MGH Libelli* 3,
388; cf. c. 49, p. 356. See K. Wenck, 'Die römischen Päpste zwischen Alexander
III. und Innocenz III. und der Designationsversuch Weihnachten 1197' in *Papsttum
und Kaisertum. Forschungen zur politischen Geschichte und Geisteskultur des Mittelalters
Paul Kehr zum 65. Geburtstag dargebracht* ed. A. Brackmann (Munich, 1926) p. 420.

of the city by means of the gifts of the Church': the offerings of the faithful were used by the pope to buy the loyalty of his subjects.[8] The only pope of this period who is known to have refused to bestow *beneficia* on the Romans was Lucius III (1181), the austere admirer of Bernard of Clairvaux. Contemporary chroniclers regarded this refusal as one of the causes of the conflict between the pope and the Romans which exiled Lucius III and three of his successors from the city.[9] When Clement III finally made peace with Rome, the treaty (31 May 1188) specified that henceforward the pope would pay 'the accustomed *beneficia* and *presbyteria*' to the Roman officials.[10]

The sources make it clear that besides the regular bestowal of *beneficia* and *presbyteria*, the pope was obliged to make additional gifts in order to secure the support of the Romans at moments of crisis. In 1083, for example, Gregory VII's ally, Duke Robert Guiscard of Apulia, 'sent more than 30,000 *solidi* to the Romans, so as to reconcile them to the pope'. The Romans had become disaffected partly because Gregory VII's conflict with the emperor threatened the Romans with an imperial siege of their city and partly because the pope's preparations for war had caused him to economise on gifts to the Romans.[11] In 1121 'the nobility and the generosity' of Calixtus II inspired the Romans to assist him in capturing and deposing the imperial antipope 'Gregory VIII' (Archbishop Maurice of Braga).[12] In 1149 the hostilities between Eugenius III and the Romans were temporarily forgotten when the pope returned from a visit to France and the Romans 'scented the gold and silver of Gaul'.[13] The need to bribe the Romans forced the pope to increase his demands on the faithful throughout western Christendom. This in turn contributed to the complaints of the greed of the Roman church which twelfth-century satirists gleefully elaborated. The relics to which the apostolic see was allegedly most devoted were those of the martyrs Albinus and Rufinus – white silver and red gold – which the pope had reverently interred 'in the treasury of St Cupidity, next to the con-

---

[8] John of Salisbury, *Policraticus* VI.24 ed. C. C. J. Webb 2 (Oxford, 1929), 71.

[9] *Gesta regis Henrici II*, RS 49/1 (1867), 308; Lambertus Parvus, *Annales*, MGH SS 16, 649.

[10] *Liber Censuum* I, 373–4. See below p. 16.

[11] Lupus Protospatarius, *Chronicon* 1083, MGH SS 5, 61; *Liber Censuum* 2, 171–4 (the customary papal gift on the Saturday after Easter). See below p. 245.

[12] Suger, *Vita Ludovici grossi regis* c. 27 ed. H. Waquet, (Les classiques de l'histoire de France au moyen âge 11: Paris, 1929) p. 205. See below p. 283.

[13] John of Salisbury, *Historia pontificalis* c. 21 ed. M. Chibnall (London, 1956) p. 51.

fession of her sister, the blessed Extreme Avidity, not far from the basilica of their mother, Avarice'.[14]

In the century before the establishment of the reform papacy the most powerful of the noble Roman clans – the Crescentii (960–1012) and the Tusculani (1012–44) – had controlled the election of the pope and had exploited the papal office and its wealth in their own dynastic interests. The first major achievement of the papal reform movement had been to bring to an end this aristocratic papal regime (*Adelspapsttum*). The reformers sought to make the election of the pope independent of the great Roman families by conferring the right of election solely on the cardinal bishops, who were the principal supporters of reform.[15] However, the great noble families continued to dominate their own areas of Rome and were still capable of challenging the reform papacy. The Crescentii retained their hold over the district of Sabina, where a branch of the family, the Octaviani, continued to exercise great influence into the later twelfth century.[16] The Tusculani remained powerful not only in Tusculum but also in Velletri and perhaps in Palestrina. A branch of the clan, the Colonna, continued to be formidable throughout the twelfth century because of their possession of the strategic fortress of Castel Colonna.[17] After a last vain attempt by the Tusculani in 1058 to regain control of the papacy, the great Roman clans of the old regime were forced to recognise that their resources were inadequate to overthrow the reform papacy and its secular allies. However, the outbreak of conflict between the papacy and the empire in the later eleventh century provided these Roman clans with a formidable ally of their own. Throughout the Investiture Contest the old Roman families supported the German kings and emperors Henry IV and Henry V and enabled them to set up imperial antipopes in Rome.

At the beginning of the pontificate of Gregory VII the leader of the noble Roman opposition to the reform papacy was Cencius Stephani of the Stefaniani, a branch of the Crescentian clan. On Christmas day

---

[14] *Tractatus Garsiae Tholetani canonici de Albino et Rufino c. 5, MGH Libelli* 2, 431. See P. Lehmann, *Die Parodie im Mittelalter* (Munich, 1922) pp. 43–69.

[15] See below pp. 36, 59.

[16] H. Schwarzmaier, 'Zur Familie Viktors IV. in der Sabina', *QFIAB* 48 (1968), 64–79.

[17] H. Stoob, 'Die Castelli der Colonna', *ibid.*, 51 (1971), 229; R. Hüls, *Kardinäle, Klerus und Kirchen Roms 1049–1130* (Bibliothek des Deutschen Historischen Instituts in Rom 48: Tübingen, 1977) pp. 256–7, arguing against the view of H. Hoffmann, 'Petrus Diaconus, die Herren von Tusculum und der Sturz Oderisius' II. von Montecassino', *DA* 27 (1971), 20–7.

1075 Cencius abducted the pope from the basilica of S. Maria Maggiore and held him prisoner, presumably intending to force his abdication. But Gregory's supporters rescued him almost immediately and Cencius was forced to take refuge at the court of Henry IV.[18] Thereafter Gregory maintained his hold over the city, despite growing opposition, until 1084. Yet once Henry IV had succeeded in installing his antipope 'Clement III' (Archbishop Wibert of Ravenna) in Rome, the antipope found sufficient support from the Roman nobility to retain control over a large part of the city until his death in 1100. Theobald, the son of Cencius Stephani, was his faithful adherent and was entrusted with the safeguarding of the antipope's treasure. Between 1091 and 1098 'Clement III' had possession of Castel S. Angelo (formerly the fortress of Cencius Stephani), which gave him control over both the Tiber bridge and the basilica of St Peter.[19] On the death of 'Clement III' his noble Roman supporters elected two short-lived antipopes, Theoderic (1100) and Albert (1102), to succeed him.[20] In 1105 'Sylvester IV' (the archpriest Maginulf) was elected antipope by a conspiracy of old Roman families, the most notable being the Corsi and the Baruncii.[21] The attempts of the reforming pope Paschal II to reimpose papal control over Rome precipitated a large-scale rebellion of the nobility in the autumn of 1108, led by Count Ptolemy of Tusculum, Peter Colonna and Stephen 'Normannus' of the Corsi family. Paschal II was able to regain control only through the military intervention of his ally, Duke Richard of Gaeta.[22] Finally in 1118 the Roman nobility assisted Emperor Henry V in electing the antipope 'Gregory VIII' (Maurice of Braga).[23] The concordat of Worms (1122), which ended the first conflict between empire and papacy and inaugurated three decades of peace, inevitably brought an end to the alliance of the old Roman nobility and the emperor against the pope. However, at the outbreak

---

[18] Bonizo of Sutri, *Liber ad amicum* (n. 5) pp. 606, 610–11. See G. B. Borino, 'Cencio del prefetto Stefano l'attentatore di Gregorio VII', *SG* 4 (1952), 373–440. See below, p. 402.

[19] P. Kehr, 'Due documenti pontifici illustranti la storia di Roma negli ultimi anni del secolo XI', *Archivio della Società Romana di storia patria* 23 (1900), 277–8; Hüls, *Kardinäle* (n. 17) pp. 259–64; C. d'Onofrio, *Castel S. Angelo* (Rome, 1971) pp. 136–40.

[20] Servatius, *Paschalis II.* pp. 70–1.

[21] *Annales Romani: Liber pontificalis* 2, 345. See Hüls, *Kardinäle* pp. 261–2.

[22] Servatius, *Paschalis II.* pp. 76–7; P. Partner, *The lands of St Peter* (London, 1972) pp. 142–3.

[23] G. Meyer von Knonau, *Jahrbücher des Deutschen Reiches unter Heinrich IV. und Heinrich V.* 7 (Leipzig, 1909), 64–5. See below p. 431.

of the second conflict of empire and papacy in September 1159 the
political situation in Rome was reminiscent of that in the late
eleventh and early twelfth century. A number of Roman families
joined Emperor Frederick I in supporting an antipope, 'Victor IV',
who was Octavian of Monticelli, a member of the ancient clan of the
Crescentii-Octaviani.[24]

The later eleventh-century and early twelfth-century papacy was
opposed by the older noble families of Rome, but received support
from the newer families: for example, the Boboni–Orsini, Malabranca, Papareschi, Parenzi, Scolari and Scotti. All these families
owed their prosperity and political prominence to papal patronage
and they remained closely associated with the papacy throughout the
twelfth century.[25] Indeed, of the five popes of our period who were
of Roman birth, four came from these new families. Innocent II was
the former Gregory Papareschi; Clement III, the former Paul Scolari;
Celestine III, the former Hyacinth Bobo. Anastasius IV came from
a family of the district of Suburra (the name of which is uncertain),
which emerged from obscurity in the second quarter of the twelfth
century.[26] However, the 'new' Roman families which most influenced papal history in this period were the Pierleoni and the Frangipani. Already in 1076 Gregory VII identified them as his allies: he
described Alberic Pierleone and Cencius Frangipane as 'our familiars,
brought up with us in the [Lateran] palace almost from ado-
lescence'.[27] The Pierleoni were descended from Jewish bankers in
Rome who converted to Christianity in the mid-eleventh century
and became important financial backers of the reform papacy.[28]
Their residence, situated between the theatre of Marcellus and the
church of S. Nicola in Carcere, was a place of refuge for the pope in
time of danger. It was here that Urban II died on 29 July 1099.[29] The

[24] Schwarzmaier, 'Familie Viktors IV.' (n. 16) pp. 64–79. See below pp. 78–83,
     471–4.
[25] P. Toubert, *Les structures du Latium médiéval. Le Latium méridional et la Sabine du IXe
     siècle à la fin du XIIe siècle* (Bibliothèque des Ecoles Françaises d'Athènes et de
     Rome 221: Rome, 1973) pp. 1049, 1132, 1323 n. 1.
[26] H. Tillmann, 'Ricerche sull'origine dei membri del collegio cardinalizio nel XII
     secolo', *Rivista di storia della Chiesa in Italia* 26 (1972), 325–34, 350–3; *ibid.*, 29
     (1975), 370–1 (but see Toubert, *Structures* p. 1132); P. Classen, 'Zur Geschichte
     Papst Anastasius' IV.', *QFIAB* 48 (1968), 36–63.
[27] Gregory VII, *Registrum* III.21, p. 288 (see also E. Caspar's note, p. 288 n. 1).
[28] Beno, *Gesta Romanae ecclesiae* II.9, *MGH Libelli* 2, 379. See P. Fedele, 'Le famiglie
     di Anacleto II e di Gelasio II', *Archivio della R. Società Romana di Storia Patria* 27
     (1904), 400–5; D. B. Zema, 'The houses of Tuscany and Pierleone in the crisis of
     Rome', *Traditio* 2 (1944), 169–75.
[29] Becker, *Urban II.* 1, 112.

house of the Pierleoni commanded access to the island in the Tiber, on which they also possessed property. Thanks to the Pierleoni, the island served as a refuge for Victor III in 1087, Urban II in 1088 and Paschal II in 1105 and 1111.[30] Equally necessary for the survival of the reform papacy in these years was the support of the Frangipani, a Roman family which is first mentioned in a record of 1014. The Frangipane residence near the Colosseum sheltered Urban II in 1094.[31] Members of the family can regularly be traced in the papal entourage from the late 1080s onwards, both when the pope was in Rome and when he was on his travels.[32]

Both the Frangipani and the Pierleoni owed their commanding position in Rome in the early twelfth century to the patronage of Paschal II. When Paschal set out for southern Italy in 1108, he left the city in the care of Leo Frangipane and Petrus Leonis, the head of the Pierleone family: an arrangement which helped to provoke the rebellion of the older Roman families in that year.[33] It is possible that Paschal II enhanced the power of these two 'new' families in a deliberate attempt to reduce the danger to the reform papacy from the older Roman families. Certainly Paschal succeeded in transforming Petrus Leonis into the single most powerful nobleman in Rome. The pope 'treated him as his familiar before all others. For this reason [Petrus Leonis] grew miraculously in stature and every day . . . his wealth, possessions and honours increased.' Paschal conferred on him the Castel S. Angelo and promoted his son, Peter Pierleone to the college of cardinals (where he became one of Paschal's most energetic supporters). Furthermore in 1116 the pope planned to confer the Roman prefecture, the principal secular office in the city, on a member of the family of Petrus Leonis.[34] The effect of Paschal's advancement of Petrus Leonis was to create a rift between the Pierleoni and the Frangipani in the final years of the pontificate. By 1117, when Emperor Henry V visited Rome, the Frangipani

---

[30] Hüls, *Kardinäle* (n. 17) p. 265; Becker, *Urban II.* I, 99–100; Servatius, *Paschalis II.* p. 81.

[31] Godfrey of Vendôme, *Epistolae* I. 8, *MPL* 157, 47BC. See F. Ehrle, 'Die Frangipani und der Untergang des Archivs und der Bibliothek der Päpste am Anfang des 13. Jahrhunderts' in *Mélanges offerts à M. Emile Chatelain par ses élèves et ses amis* (Paris, 1910) pp. 452–4.

[32] Hüls, *Kardinäle* (n. 17) pp. 266–7.

[33] Pandulf, *Vita Paschalis II: Liber pontificalis* 2, 299. See Servatius, *Paschalis II.* p. 82.

[34] *Historia Mauriniacensis monasterii* II, *MGH SS* 26, 40. See L. Halphen, *Etudes sur l'administration de Rome au moyen âge* (Bibliothèque de l'Ecole des Hautes Etudes 176: Paris, 1907) pp. 24–5; Hüls, *Kardinäle* (n. 17) pp. 225, 261.

had become supporters of the empire against the papacy. Their change of sides was presumably inspired by the hope that the emperor would assist them in overthrowing the Pierleoni.[35] Since twelfth-century emperors could never remain long enough in the city to effect permanent political changes, the Frangipani were obliged to think instead of contriving the election of a pope who would divert his patronage from the Pierleoni to the Frangipani. When in 1118 Gelasius II, who was suspected of Pierleone sympathies, was elected to succeed Paschal II, Cencius Frangipane kidnapped the new pope. Gelasius's release and his escape from the Frangipani and their ally, the emperor, were the work of Petrus Leonis.[36]

In 1124 the Frangipani at last achieved their ambition of controlling the election of the pope: an achievement which they owed to a change in papal policy. As we shall see, the papal regime of the 1120s reversed many of the policies of the pontificate of Paschal II and turned against many of the alliances on which the previous regime had depended. The popes of the 1120s increased the power of the Frangipani in order to hold that of the Pierleoni in check. The crucial step was taken by Calixtus II, who gave Cencius Frangipane the command of the knights of the papal household (*masnada*). It was this military support which enabled the Frangipani to dominate the papal election on the death of Calixtus II (1124) and to compel the electors to accept Honorius II.[37] The certainty that the Pierleoni would retaliate on the death of Honorius II by controlling the election of his successor provoked the schism of 1130, in which the opponents of the Pierleoni elected Cardinal Gregory Papareschi as Innocent II and their supporters elected Anacletus II, the former Cardinal Peter Pierleone.[38] The double election of 1130 has been interpreted, together with the papal election of 1124, as the consequence solely of the faction-fighting of the Roman aristocracy. The Pierleoni and the Frangipani, creatures of the reform papacy, exploited their usefulness to the pope by seizing control of the papacy.[39] A detailed analysis of the papal elections of 1124 and 1130

[35] F.-J. Schmale, *Studien zum Schisma des Jahres 1130* (Cologne-Graz, 1961) p. 19.

[36] See below pp. 65–6.

[37] Pandulf, *Vita Honorii II*: J. M. March, *Liber pontificalis prout extat in codice manuscripto Dertusensi* (Barcelona, 1925) p. 203. See below pp. 66–8.

[38] See below pp. 69–75.

[39] P. F. Palumbo, *Lo scisma del MCXXX. I precedenti, la vicenda romana e le ripercussioni europee della lotta tra Anacleto e Innocezo II* (Rome, 1942). See also *idem*, 'Nuovi studi (1942–1962) sullo scisma di Anacleto II', *BISI* 75 (1963), 71–103, which reviews

is presented in the following chapter, where it is shown that neither the Frangipani nor the Pierleoni acted alone in 1124 and 1130. Both acted as the allies of factions inside the college of cardinals. The Frangipani were the allies of the faction which supported the new papal policy of the 1120s, led by the papal chancellor, Cardinal Haimeric; the Pierleoni were the allies of the conservative faction, led by Cardinal Peter Pierleone. It was this division in the college of cardinals rather than the faction-fighting of the aristocracy which initiated the noble *coups* of 1124 and 1130.[40] No Roman family of the twelfth century was sufficiently powerful to control the papacy as in the days of the *Adelspapsttum* of the tenth and early eleventh centuries. But the Roman aristocracy certainly had the power to render Rome both ungovernable and uninhabitable.

The practical duties of government in Rome belonged to the ancient office of prefect, which combined the functions of chief of police and sole judge in criminal cases. The prefect was responsible for the arrest and imprisonment of brigands, murderers and disturbers of the peace and for maintaining security in the city. He took an oath to 'guard the streets, do justice and devote care and labour to the defence of the fortifications'.[41] This oath was taken to the pope, from whom the prefect held his office. 'The prefecture, greatest and most ancient of offices', according to the historian John of Salisbury, received 'from the Church its jurisdiction as far as the hundredth milestone and the power of the sword': that is, the executive power.[42] The pope was obliged to delegate the executive power, since a priest was forbidden to exercise 'the power of the sword' and to take judicial decisions which involved bloodshed. A text referring to the year 1178 underlines the dependent status of the prefect as an agent of the pope. When in that year Alexander III returned to Rome after a long exile, the prefect John, 'falling at the feet of Pope Alexander, was confirmed in his prefecture and became [the pope's] vassal'.[43] That the prefect was a papal functionary was demonstrated in papal processions through the city: the prefect 'rode next to the lord pope, by his side with no one between them'.[44] The expenses

two works offering a different interpretation of the double election: H.-W. Klewitz, *Reformpapsttum und Kardinalkolleg* (Darmstadt, 1957) pp. 207–59 and Schmale, *Schisma* (n. 35). On this interpretation see below pp. 48–9, 67, 70–3, 215–16.
[40] See below pp. 67–75, 381–2, 444.
[41] Oath of the Roman prefect Peter to Innocent III (*Registrum* 1.577): *MPL* 214, 529BD. See Halphen, *Etudes* (n. 34) pp. 16–27.
[42] John of Salisbury, *Historia pontificalis* c. 27 (n. 13) 59.
[43] Romuald of Salerno, *Annales* 1178, *MGH SS* 19, 459. [44] *Liber Censuum* 1, 291.

which the prefect incurred in the course of his duties were charged to the papal treasury. Hence the papal financial record of the late twelfth century which specifies payments due to the prefect: 'when they hang someone, five *solidi*; also when they behead someone, five *solidi*; when they blind someone, twelve *denarii* for each eye; when they cut off any limb, likewise twelve *denarii*'. These were the sums that the prefect had to pay to his executioners.[45]

However, although the prefect took an oath to the pope as a servant of the Roman church, the pope does not seem to have been able to control the appointment of the prefect. The staunch enemy of the reform papacy, Cencius Stephani (of the family of Crescentii-Stefaniani) was prevented from succeeding his father as prefect during the pontificate of Alexander II; but it was not the pope who prevented him. 'When he wished to obtain the office of prefect, he was rejected by all the Romans because of the ferocity of his temper and by common counsel the office was given to another Cencius, the son of the prefect John.' This second Cencius was a faithful supporter of the reform papacy: when in 1077 he was murdered by a brother of Cencius Stephani, Gregory VII regarded him as a martyr for the faith.[46] However, although he was the pope's preferred candidate, he owed his office not to the pope but to 'the Romans'. The most detailed twelfth-century account of the appointment of a prefect comes from the year 1116. On the death of the prefect Peter, a member of the clan of the Tusculani, Paschal II intended to give the office to a son of Petrus Leonis; but 'the Roman people raised [Peter,] the son of the deceased prefect to the prefecture' and 'sent to Pope Paschal, requesting that he would give his consent to their appointment and confirm it.' Paschal's refusal provoked a large-scale rebellion, which ended only when the pope recognised Peter as prefect.[47] Here again the prefect is described as being appointed by 'the Roman people'. The appointment of Peter in 1116 required the confirmation of the pope; but this papal right of confirmation clearly did not amount to a papal right of veto. The prefect was a servant of the pope, but a servant whom the pope could neither choose for himself nor dismiss.

---

[45] *Ibid.*, 2, 108.
[46] Bonizo of Sutri, *Liber ad amicum* (n. 5) pp. 603, 611. See C. Erdmann, *Die Entstehung des Kreuzzugsgedankens* (Stuttgart, 1935) p. 198. (See also the English translation of this work, *The origin of the idea of crusade* (Princeton, 1977), which does not, however, contain the important appendices in the original.)
[47] Pandulf, *Vita Paschalis II*: (n. 33) p. 302. See Halphen, *Etudes* (n. 34) pp. 24–5; Servatius, *Paschalis II*. pp. 79–81.

The rebellion of 1116 revealed the practical limitations of the pope's control over Rome. In the middle of the century the papacy faced a much more serious challenge, when the Romans rejected the claim of the pope to exercise secular authority over them. A rebellion against Innocent II in 1143 developed into a revolution: the Roman commune discarded the traditional government of the pope and his prefect and created a new form of government. 'The prefecture . . . was reduced to an empty name', wrote John of Salisbury. 'For the senators whom the people created on their own authority had seized all judicial and executive powers throughout the city.'[48] The Roman revolution of 1143–5 was part of a much larger development affecting northern and central Italy in the later eleventh and early twelfth centuries. The cities of Lombardy and Tuscany rejected the government of their bishops and feudal lords, transformed themselves into autonomous city-republics and extended their authority over the surrounding countryside (*contado*). In the case of Rome in 1143 the revolution was sparked off by the Romans' determination to conquer Latium and subject it to the city as the Roman *contado*. Their first objective was the conquest of Tivoli; but their plans were frustrated by Innocent II, who received the fealty of the Tivolese and assumed control of the town himself. The Romans therefore rebelled against the pope; they seized the Capitol and set up a senate, which in turn entrusted the government of the city to a dictator with the title of 'patrician' (1144–5).[49] John of Salisbury noted that the aristocratic faction-fighting of the early twelfth century asserted its influence on the politics of the commune. 'They appointed as their patrician Jordan, a very great man of the Pierleone family. In order to injure the lord pope they destroyed the palace of Cencius Frangipane, whose family always assisted the Church in her hour of need.' The Pierleoni seem to have been the only great Roman family prepared to identify with the Roman demands for autonomy, presumably regarding this as a means of enhancing their own power.[50] Hostility towards the commune kept the other great families loyal to the pope.

---

[48] John of Salisbury, *Historia pontificalis* c. 27 (n. 13) p. 59.
[49] Halphen, *Etudes* (n. 34) pp. 53–7; A. Rota, 'La costituzione originaria del Comune di Roma. L'epoca del Comune libero (luglio 1143 – dicembre 1145)', *BISI* 64 (1953), 41–63; R. L. Benson, 'Political *renovatio*: two models from Roman antiquity' in *Renaissance and renewal in the twelfth century* ed. R. L. Benson and G. Constable (Oxford, 1982) pp. 340–59.
[50] John of Salisbury, *Historia pontificalis* c. 27 (n. 13) p. 59. See Palumbo, *Scisma* (n. 39) pp. 198, 291.

In the years 1146–55 the Roman commune came under a strikingly different influence: that of Arnold of Brescia, radical reformer, popular preacher and critic of the contemporary Church. According to John of Salisbury, Arnold preached to the Romans that the college of cardinals 'because of its pride and avarice, hypocrisy and manifold wickedness, was not the Church of God but a house of trade and a den of thieves' and that 'the pope himself was not what he professed to be – an apostolic man and a pastor of souls – but a man of blood who preserved his authority by means of arson and murder, a tormentor of churches and oppressor of innocence, who did nothing in the world except indulge his body and fill his coffers by emptying those of other men'. (Arnold's characterisation of the pope as 'a man of blood' was probably inspired by his observation of the papal wars against the Roman commune.) Both John of Salisbury and his fellow chronicler Otto of Freising considered that Arnold of Brescia exerted a great influence on Roman politics. Recent historians consider these judgements exaggerated: they present Arnold as a religious reformer with no political interests. However, the conduct of the papacy and its allies towards Arnold of Brescia leaves no doubt that he was regarded as the pope's greatest enemy in Rome. The city was placed under an interdict to secure the banishment of Arnold and his followers. In 1155 Arnold was captured by the army of King Frederick I of Germany, who was marching to Rome for the imperial coronation. 'Finally he was hanged by the prefect of the city and his corpse was reduced to ashes on the funeral pyre and scattered in the Tiber, lest his body be held in veneration by the insane mob.'[51]

From 1143 until 1188 the papacy fought and negotiated to recover its former authority over the city. Meanwhile the senators in the Capitol, varying in number between twenty-five and fifty-six, exercised the executive and the judicial power, declared war, made treaties and dated their official documents 'in the year of the renewal of the senate'.[52] The senate was prepared to struggle as hard as the pope to obtain his recognition of the new constitution. In December

[51] John of Salisbury, *Historia pontificalis* c. 31: pp. 63–5. Cf. Otto of Freising, *Gesta Friderici imperatoris* II.28, *MGH SS rer. Germ.*, 1884, p. 107. See H. Grundmann, *Religiöse Bewegungen im Mittelalter* (2nd edition: Hildesheim, 1961) pp. 495, 498, 513, 516–22; A. Frugoni, *Arnaldo da Brescia nelle fonti del secolo XII* (Istituto storico italiano per il Medio Evo. Studi storici 8–9: Rome, 1954); R. Manselli, 'Grundzüge der religiösen Geschichte Italiens im 12. Jahrhundert' in *Beiträge zur Geschichte Italiens im 12. Jahrhundert* (Vorträge und Forschungen, Sonderband 9: Sigmaringen, 1971) pp. 15–16, 31–2.
[52] Halphen, *Etudes* (n. 34) pp. 61, 66.

1145 Eugenius III was obliged to reach a compromise with the Roman commune, the terms of which were recorded by the chronicler Otto of Freising. 'Eugenius made peace with the Romans on these terms: that they should abolish the dignity of patrician and accept the prefect in his former dignity and that the senators should hold their office by [the pope's] authority.' Eugenius demanded the abolition of the patrician's office, which had replaced the prefecture during the rebellion of 1144–5; and he demanded the restoration of the prefect as chief papal functionary in the city. But the pope accepted that it was impossible for him to abolish the senate and required instead that the senators should regard their office as conferred by papal authority.[53] This compromise solution formed the basis of each of the subsequent agreements which followed outbreaks of hostility between the pope and the Roman commune. In 1149 Eugenius III resumed his conflict with the senators, who were now defying his authority by sheltering the excommunicate Arnold of Brescia. The pope waged war against the commune with the help of the Tusculani and the Frangipani, but without success. In a stalemate peace (October/November 1149) it was agreed that the senators would swear fealty to the pope and Eugenius would make them a gift of 500 pounds of silver.[54]

During the third quarter of the twelfth century the conflict between empire and papacy offered the Roman senate the opportunity of gaining its independence from the pope. In 1167 the senators submitted to the victorious Emperor Frederick I; and although the imperial hold over Rome was short-lived, the senate continued to be loyal to the emperor.[55] Alexander III spent much of his long pontificate (1159–81) exiled from Rome. After making peace with the emperor in 1177, Alexander returned to the city and received 'the customary fealty and homage' from the senators. Only a year after his return, however, conflict had arisen between the pope and the commune. The cause was, as in 1143, the commune's ambition to transform Latium into the Roman *contado*. Roman designs on Tusculum were the principal occasion of the dispute between the senate and the papacy which exiled four successive popes from Rome

---

[53] Otto of Freising, *Chronica sive Historia de duabus civitatibus* VII.34, *MGH SS rer. Germ.*, 1912, p. 367. See Rota, 'Comune' (n. 49) pp. 93–101.

[54] Partner, *Lands* (n. 22) pp. 183–4.

[55] J. Petersohn, 'Der Vertrag des Römischen Senats mit Papst Clemens III. (1188) und das Pactum Friedrich Barbarossas mit den Römern (1167)', *MIÖG* 82 (1974), 308–16.

in the years 1183–8.[56] Peace was finally made in the treaty of Clement
III with the Roman senate (31 May 1188), the definitive agreement
between the papacy and the commune, which enabled the pope once
more to reside in Rome. Like the agreement of 1145 between
Eugenius III and the senate, the treaty of 1188 accepted the principle
that the senate derived its authority from the pope: the treaty
'restored the senate' to the pope. Every year the senators and their
successors must swear fealty to Clement III and his successors. However, the treaty also underlined the obligations of the pope to Rome.
He must make the customary gifts to the Roman officials and make
an annual payment of 100 pounds of silver for the upkeep of the city
walls. Above all, the pope was obliged to consent to the Roman conquest and destruction of Tusculum and also to promise that he would
not defend Tivoli, should the Romans wish to attack it.[57] This was
the price of peace between the pope and the commune after forty-
five years of conflict: the pope must give up his resistance to the territorial ambitions of the Romans.

From the moment that Gregory VII lost control of the city and
went into exile in 1084 until Clement III made his treaty with the
senate in 1188, papal control of Rome tended to be uncertain. The
insecurity of Rome and the hostility of the Romans exercised an
important influence on the system of government which the papacy
developed in the late eleventh and twelfth centuries. The papal
government of the tenth and early eleventh centuries was centred on
the 'sacred Lateran palace' (*sacrum palatium Lateranense*), its most
important functionaries being the seven palatine judges (*iudices palatini*), whose duties were administrative as well as judicial. This papal
government was a 'bureaucratic oligarchy', steeped in the traditions
of the aristocratic papal regime of the Crescentii and the Tusculani.[58]
Such a government could hardly serve the purposes of the reforming
popes, the enemies of the old Roman families. However, the reform
papacy did not dismiss the officers of the old regime, but attributed
their duties to other functionaries and left them with merely
ceremonial functions.[59] The reform papacy created a new system of
government; but the most important role in the new regime was

[56] Boso, *Vita Alexandri III: Liber pontificalis* 2, 446. See Pacaut, *Alexandre III* p. 214;
     Wenck, 'Päpste' (n. 7) p. 420; Partner, *Lands* (n. 22) pp. 213, 215.
[57] *Liber Censuum* 1, 373–4. See V. Pfaff, 'Papst Clemens III. (1187–1191)', *ZSSRG
     KA* 66 (1980), 263–5; Petersohn, 'Vertrag' (n. 55) pp. 289–337.
[58] Toubert, *Structures* (n. 25) pp. 1015–24, 1043–4.
[59] K. Jordan, 'Die Entstehung der römischen Kurie. Ein Versuch', *ZSSRG KA* 28
     (1939), 106–7.

given to an institution which had already had a long history of service to the Roman church: the college of cardinals. The novelty in this situation was that previous papal regimes had not used the cardinals for governmental purposes: their duties had always been liturgical in character. The reform papacy transformed the cardinals into the chief advisers of the pope and the principal administrators of his government. Since the cardinals were no longer recruited from the old Roman aristocracy – the college was increasingly acquiring an 'international' character – their dominant role in government served to free the papacy from aristocratic control.[60]

The new administration constructed by the reform papacy – the papal curia (*curia Romana*) – was reminiscent in its structure and its terminology of the governments of the northern European kingdoms. The pope's *curia* bore a striking resemblance to the *curia regis* of France, Germany and England. The term *curia Romana* was first used to denote the papal household, together with the whole apparatus of papal government, in the letters of Urban II.[61] Karl Jordan (1939) remarked that 'it is no coincidence that the first pope to speak of his *curia* or the *Romana curia* was Urban II, the descendant of a family of French knights, who as a monk belonged to the monastery of Cluny'.[62] It is impossible to decide whether Urban II's experience of the Capetian kingdom provided the model for the papal curia, or whether it is to be found in the close association of papacy and empire during the first generation of the reform papacy. What is certain, however, is that the papal curia first began to assume its characteristic appearance during the pontificate of Urban II. In 1088 Urban succeeded to a papacy without a functioning government. For in 1084 the chief papal administrators had deserted Gregory VII for his rival, the antipope 'Clement III' and during the long vacancy which followed Gregory's death and in the short pontificate of Victor III there had been no attempt to reconstruct the administration. During a pontificate the greater part of which was spent outside Rome, Urban II and his advisers were obliged to create a government with new personnel and without access to the traditions of the previous administration.[63] From the expedients adopted by

---

[60] See below pp. 47–56.

[61] Urban II, *JL* 5403, *MPL* 151, 304C (see Jordan, 'Entstehung' p. 127 n. 3); *JL* 5421: 317A.

[62] Jordan, 'Entstehung' pp. 125–6. See also J. Sydow, 'Untersuchungen zur kurialen Verwaltungsgeschichte im Zeitalter des Reformpapsttums', *DA* 11 (1954–5), 18–73.

[63] Sydow, 'Untersuchungen' pp. 41–4. See below p. 251.

Urban II *ca.* 1090 there developed the papal government of the twelfth century, which contained the three departments also found in contemporary secular governments: the *camera* (for financial administration), the chancery and the chapel. The papal chapel performed the liturgical duties of the papal entourage which the cardinals were now too busy to perform.[64] For the cardinals had acquired the role of 'the spiritual senators of the universal Church', serving the pope as counsellors, as officials of the curia and as legates.[65] It was not only in its three main departments of *camera*, chancery and chapel, but also in its domestic personnel that the *curia Romana* bore a clear resemblance to the *curia regis* of France, Germany and England. The pope was served by a steward (*dapifer*, later *senescalcus*), a cupbearer (*pincerna*), cellarers (*buticularii*), a constable (*comestabulus*) and his assistant marshals (*marescalci*).[66] However, it was in the ceremonial life of the papacy that the influence of secular models was most apparent.

The papal ceremonies elaborated in the later eleventh century were intended to demonstrate the dual character of the papal office, which involved both spiritual functions and secular lordship. The pope was 'a royal priest and an imperial bishop', the vicar of Peter, whom Christ 'made prince over all the kingdoms of the world'.[67] Gregory VII in his memorandum on the rights of the papacy, the *Dictatus pape* of 1075, referred to two such ceremonial usages: '[the pope] alone can use the imperial insignia'; 'all princes are to kiss the feet of the pope alone'.[68] The pope's use of the imperial insignia is immediately evident in the ceremonies which marked the beginning of a new pontificate. These are best known from the biography of Paschal II, which describes his accession in 1099 in considerable detail. Immediately after his election the pope was clothed by the electors in what seems to have been the most important of these insignia, the mantle of imperial purple (*cappa rubea*). (By the mid-twelfth century the clothing of the pope with the purple mantle – 'immantation' – had come to symbolise the assumption of the papal office: hence the

---

[64] R. Elze, 'Die päpstliche Kapelle im 12. und 13. Jahrhundert', *ZSSRG KA* 36 (1950), 145–204.

[65] See below pp. 90–120.

[66] Jordan, 'Entstehung' (n. 59) pp. 142–4.

[67] *Descriptio sanctuarii Lateranensis ecclesiae*, cited in H.-W. Klewitz, *Reformpapsttum* (n. 39) p. 20 n. 33; Gregory VII, *Registrum* 1.63, p. 92.

[68] Gregory VII, *Registrum* II.55a, p. 204. See E. Eichmann, *Weihe und Krönung des Papstes im Mittelalter* (Münchener Theologische Studien 3. Kanonistische Abteilung 1: Munich, 1951) pp. 36–40.

action of the antipope 'Victor IV' in snatching the mantle from his rival Alexander III in the disputed election of 1159.) After his election and 'immantation' the new pope proceeded to the entrance of the Lateran palace, where he sat in turn in each of the two 'official chairs' (*curules*) which were placed there. Seated in the first chair, he received a girdle from which hung seven keys and seven seals; in the second chair he received a sceptre (*ferula*). These were the symbols of the pope's lordship over the Lateran palace and the papal lands.[69] The other ceremony mentioned by Gregory VII, the kissing of the pope's feet, was imitated from the Byzantine imperial ceremonial of proskynesis. The ceremony was performed by the faithful when Urban II gained possession of the Lateran palace (which had been in the hands of the antipope 'Clement III' for most of his pontificate).[70] Abbot Hariulf of Oudenbourg, a litigant in the curia of Innocent II in 1141, performed the ceremony of proskynesis when he first came into the papal presence. It was an imperial scene: the pope seated 'on the judgement seat', a raised tribunal, with the cardinals on his right and the Roman nobles standing or sitting at his feet.[71] Accounts of a prince kissing the pope's feet, as stipulated by Gregory VII, are to be found in a contemporary report of the meeting of the emperor elect Henry V with Paschal II in February 1111; in Cardinal Boso's account of the imperial coronation of Frederick I by Hadrian IV in 1155; in Rahewin's description of Frederick I's acknowledging 'Victor IV' as pope after the council of Pavia (1160); and in Boso's description of Frederick I's reconciliation with Alexander III in Venice in 1177.[72]

The theologian Bruno of Segni, adviser of Urban II and Paschal II, commented that 'all the insignia of the Roman empire' belonged to the pope; 'whence in great processions the pontiff appears in all that

[69] Pandulf, *Vita Paschalis II*: (n. 33) p. 296. See Eichmann, *Weihe* pp. 33–5; H.-W. Klewitz, 'Die Krönung des Papstes', *ZSSRG KA* 30 (1941), 120; P. E. Schramm, 'Sacerdotium und Regnum im Austausch ihrer Vorrechte', *SG* 2 (1947), 442–4; N. Gussone, *Thron und Inthronisation des Papstes von den Anfängen bis zum 12. Jahrhundert. Zur Beziehung zwischen Herrschaftszeichen und bildhaften Begriffen, Recht und Liturgie im christlichen Verständnis von Wort und Wirklichkeit* (Bonn, 1978) p. 251. On the 'immantation' of Victor IV see below p. 83.

[70] Godfrey of Vendôme, *Epistolae* I.8: (n. 31) 48B. See Gussone, *Inthronisation* p. 255.

[71] E. Müller, 'Der Bericht des Abtes Hariulf von Oudenburg über seine Prozessverhandlungen an der römischen Kurie im Jahre 1141', *NA* 48 (1930), 102. See below pp. 94–5, 189–90.

[72] *Disputatio vel defensio Paschalis papae*, *MGH Libelli* 2, 660; Boso, *Vita Hadriani IV*: *Liber pontificalis* 2, 391; Rahewin, *Gesta Friderici imperatoris* IV. 80: (n. 51) p. 267; Boso, *Vita Alexandri III* (n. 56) pp. 439, 443.

magnificence which used formerly to belong to the emperors'.[73] The
most striking of the ceremonies which the reform papacy imitated
from imperial practice were the papal coronations and crown-
wearings. Three near-contemporary accounts from the twelfth
century – relating to Paschal II, Calixtus II and Alexander III –
describe how after the election and 'immantation' the new pope was
crowned with the tiara (also called *regnum* or *phrygium*). The biography of Paschal II describes how the pope 'was clad in a scarlet mantle
. . . and a tiara was placed on his head'. Subsequently, after taking
possession of the Lateran palace and after being consecrated in St
Peter's, the pope 'went back, crowned, into the city'.[74] In Paschal's
case, therefore, coronation immediately followed 'immantation';
but in the case of Calixtus II the papal coronation on 9 February 1119
in Vienne occurred a week after the election in Cluny.[75] Alexander III
'was solemnly crowned with the papal *regnum* according to the custom of the Church' on 20 September 1159, a fortnight after his disputed election.[76] Evidently, therefore, the papal coronation was not
the constitutive ceremony which conferred the papal office on the
pope elect. The crown symbolised only one aspect of the papal
dignity: the secular authority enjoyed by the pope. Hence in 1198
Innocent III distinguished the papal crown from the mitre, his
liturgical headgear, explaining that St Peter 'conferred the mitre on
me as a sign of spiritual things and gave me the crown as a sign of
temporal things; the mitre for the *sacerdotium*, the crown for the
regnum'.[77]

The papal crown was especially associated, as Bruno of Segni
observed, with 'great processions'. The crown-wearings are the
most frequently described papal ceremonies of the twelfth century.
In the *Ordines Romani* which he compiled *ca.* 1188 Cardinal Albinus
of Albano noted that there were eighteen festive occasions during the
year when the pope 'must be crowned': the feast of the four crowned
martyrs (8 November), of St Martin (11 November) and St Clement
(23 November), the first three Sundays in Advent, the Nativity, St

73 Bruno of Segni, *Tractatus de sacramentis ecclesiae*, MPL 165, 1108B.
74 Pandulf, *Vita Paschalis II*: (n. 33) p. 296.
75 Cuno of Palestrina, letter to the bishop of Nevers: L. D'Achery, *Spicilegium sive
   Collectio veterum aliquot scriptorum qui in Galliae bibliothecis delituerant* 3 (Paris, 1669),
   493. See Klewitz, 'Krönung' (n. 69) p. 98 n. 7.
76 Boso, *Vita Alexandri III*: (n. 56) p. 399.
77 Innocent III, *Sermo in consecratione* c. 3, MPL 217, 665B. See Klewitz, 'Krönung'
   (n. 69) pp. 105–6; W. Ullmann, *The growth of papal government in the Middle Ages*
   (3rd edition: London, 1970) p. 317.

Stephen's day (26 December), Epiphany (6 January), the fourth Sunday in Lent, the first and second days of Easter, the second Sunday after Easter, Ascension day, Whitsun, the feast of SS. Peter and Paul (29 June) and St Sylvester (31 December) and the pope's accession day.[78] The earliest extant reference to a papal crown-wearing refers to Christmas day 1075. Gregory VII, freed by the Romans from his overnight captivity in the castle of his enemy, Cencius Stephani, 'returned crowned to the [Lateran] palace with the applause of the bishops, cardinals and magnates'. On this occasion the crown-wearing was a reassertion of papal lordship over Rome after Cencius's attempted coup.[79] Many of the later descriptions of crown-wearings come from periods of papal exile from Rome, notably in France. Urban II was crowned 'in the Roman manner' in Tours on the fourth Sunday in Lent (25 March) in 1096, when he went in procession from the church of St Maurice to that of St Martin.[80] Likewise when Paschal II was in Tours for that Sunday (24 March) in 1107, he wore the *phrygium* 'as is the Roman custom'.[81] Hugh the Cantor, the historian of the church of York, recorded three occasions when Calixtus II appeared crowned, 'as Roman custom demands', during his sojourn in France in 1119–20: on Whitsunday in Clermont, on Christmas day in Autun and on the Epiphany in Cluny.[82] Abbot Suger of St Denis described a papal crown-wearing in St Denis on Easter day 1131. Innocent II wore 'a *phrygium*, an imperial ornament like a helmet, surrounded by a circle of gold'; he rode in a procession 'in great and remarkable pomp', mounted on a white horse.[83] In such instances the ceremony served a didactic purpose, teaching those of the faithful who were unacquainted with 'the Roman custom' something of the nature of the pope's authority.

Particularly striking were those processions in which the crowned pope was accompanied by a secular ruler, likewise crowned. For example, Innocent II's meetings with his ally, King Lothar III of Germany, in Liège on the fourth Sunday in Lent in 1131 and in Rome

---

[78] *Liber Censuum* 2, 90. See Klewitz, 'Krönung' p. 100; Eichmann, *Weihe* (n. 68) pp. 40–1.

[79] *Vita Gregorii VII: Liber pontificalis* 2, 282. See above p. 7 and below p. 402.

[80] *Chronicon sancti Martini Turonensis, MGH SS* 26, 461; Fulk IV of Anjou, *Historia comitum Andegavensium, ibid.* See Becker, *Urban II.* 2, 446–7.

[81] Suger of St Denis, *Vita Ludovici grossi regis* c. 10 (n. 12) p. 52.

[82] Hugh the Cantor, *The history of the church of York 1066–1127* ed. C. Johnson (London, 1961) pp. 66, 84.

[83] Suger, *Vita* c. 32: pp. 262–4.

on Whitsunday 1133 involved joint crown-wearings.[84] A similar
occasion was the meeting of Hadrian IV with Emperor Frederick I in
Rome on the feast of SS. Peter and Paul 1155, eleven days after the
imperial coronation. Cardinal Boso's account underlines the importance of this demonstration. 'In order that the Church of God and the
empire might shine forth in greater beauty, it was decided after joint
consultation that, to praise God and rejoice the Christian people, the
Roman pontiff and the emperor should both go crowned in procession to solemn mass that day.'[85] Such an encounter with a secular
ruler could prompt the pope to wear his crown even on days other
than those eighteen festivals on which he 'must be crowned'. When
on 25 October 1131 in Rheims Innocent II anointed the young Louis
VII to the kingship in the presence of his father, Louis VI of France,
the pope was 'clad in all his insignia and, as is his custom on great and
holy festivals, crowned with the *phrygium*'.[86] One particular
ceremony served to instruct the faithful about the relationship of the
papacy with secular princes: the ceremony of the golden rose on the
fourth Sunday of Lent. The first detailed description of this
ceremony was given by Count Fulk IV of Anjou, who himself
received the rose from Urban II on 25 March 1096 in Tours. The
pope 'was crowned and led in solemn procession from the church of
St Maurice to the church of Martin, where he gave me the golden
flower which he held in his hand'.[87] When the ceremony took place
in Rome, the pope usually conferred the golden rose on the prefect
of the city; when it was celebrated elsewhere, the rose was given to
the secular prince who was the pope's host and protector. Hence on
3 March 1163 Alexander III conferred the golden rose on King Louis
VII of France in Paris.[88] On the fourth Sunday in Lent (3 April) 1177
Alexander was in Venice, negotiating the settlement of the papal
schism. 'He went in procession, during which he carried a golden
rose, large and extremely beautiful, which according to custom he
gives to an emperor or a king; and when he had celebrated mass, he
offered [the rose] to the doge [of Venice] with his own hand.'[89]

The papal crown, the other insignia and the ceremonies were

---

84 H.-W. Klewitz, 'Die Festkrönungen der deutschen Könige', *ZSSRG KA* 28
    (1939), 56.
85 Boso, *Vita Hadriani IV* (n. 72) p. 393. See Klewitz, 'Festkrönungen' p. 66.
86 *Historia Mauriniacensis monasterii* II: (n. 34) p. 42. See Klewitz, 'Krönung' (n. 69)
    p. 105.
87 Fulk IV, *Historia* (n. 80) p. 461. See Klewitz, 'Krönung' p. 123 n. 86.
88 Hugh of Poitiers, *Liber de libertate monasterii Vizeliacensis*, *MGH SS* 26, 148.
89 *Historia ducum Veneticorum*, *MGH SS* 14, 84. See below p. 495.

manifestations of the trend which Ernst Kantorowicz (1958) called 'the imperialisation of the Church' and which he regarded as 'one of the outstanding features of the reform papacy'.[90] The trend was not, however, confined to the reform papacy: this 'imitation of empire' (*imitatio imperii*) continued to be an important aspect of the pope's ceremonial existence even when the pope no longer explicitly made the papal claims of the Gregorian papacy. The papal *imitatio imperii* constitutes the most important evidence of the influence on the eleventh- and twelfth-century papacy of the *Constitutum Constantini*: the 'Donation of Constantine' forged at some point between the mid-eighth and the mid-ninth century, probably by the Roman clergy.[91] As the learned Bruno of Segni explained, the pope wore a crown and used the purple 'because Emperor Constantine long ago handed over all the insignia of the Roman empire to St Sylvester'. He was echoing the claim that Gregory VII had derived from the forged donation, 'that [the pope] alone can use the imperial insignia'.[92] The reform papacy had recognised in the *Constitutum Constantini* a valuable 'authority' in support of the reformers' idea of the papal primacy: it was 'the edict of Emperor Constantine in which he establishes the principate of the apostolic see above all the churches in the world'.[93] As early as 1053 the reformers had evolved from the *Constitutum* the concept of 'the earthly and heavenly empire or rather the royal priesthood of the holy Roman and apostolic see'.[94] The forged donation made over to the pope 'the various imperial ornaments and every procession of the imperial majesty' and decreed that he should 'use the *phrygium* in processions in imitation of our imperial power'.[95] It was from this concession that the reform papacy elaborated the imperial ceremonial of the crown-wearings. Bernard of Clairvaux denounced this influence of the *Constitutum* on the papacy in the famous rebuke which he administered to his pupil,

---

[90] E. Kantorowicz, *Laudes regiae. A study in liturgical acclamations and medieval ruler worship* (2nd edition: Berkeley, 1958) p. 138.

[91] For the extensive bibliography relating to the *Constitutum Constantini* see H. Fuhrmann, 'Konstantinische Schenkung und abendländisches Kaisertum. Ein Beitrag zur Überlieferungsgeschichte des Constitutum Constantini', *DA* 22 (1966), 63–178 and the same author's edition of the *Constitutum Constantini*, *MGH Fontes iuris germanici antiqui* 10.

[92] Bruno, *Tractatus* (n. 73) 1108B. Cf. Gregory VII, *Registrum* II. 55a, p. 204.

[93] Peter Damian, *Disceptatio synodalis*, *MGH Libelli* 1, 80.

[94] Leo IX, *JL* 4302: C. J. C. Will, *Acta et scripta quae de controversiis ecclesiae Graecae et Latinae saeculo undecimo composita extant* (Leipzig-Marburg, 1861) p. 72. See Fuhrmann, 'Konstantinische Schenkung' (n. 91) pp. 122, 178.

[95] *Constitutum Constantini* c. 14, 16: (n. 91) pp. 88, 92–3.

Eugenius III *ca.* 1150. 'Peter is not known ever to have gone in procession adorned in jewels and silks, nor crowned with gold, nor
mounted on a white horse, nor surrounded by knights, nor encircled
by clamouring servants . . . In these respects you are the heir not of
Peter but of Constantine.'[96] It is possible that Bernard's rebuke was
prompted by an intensification of the papal *imitatio imperii* particularly associated with the pontificate of Innocent II. The 'great and
remarkable pomp' which Abbot Suger witnessed in St Denis on Easter day 1131 impressed other observers in the 1130s: it was presumably one aspect of Innocent II's propaganda campaign against his
rival, the antipope Anacletus II. This campaign culminated in
Innocent's victorious return to Rome in 1138, where 'processions
were solemnly celebrated from church to church', a triumph which
Bernard of Clairvaux himself witnessed.[97]

   The most significant example of Innocent's preoccupation with
'the imitation of empire' occurred at his meeting with Lothar III of
Germany in Liège on 21 March 1131. Here the king 'offered himself
most humbly as a groom and hastened to him on foot in the midst of
the holy procession. Holding in one hand the staff to defend him and
in the other the rein of his white horse, he led him as if [Innocent] was
his lord.' For this meeting with the future emperor Innocent II
revived the ceremony recorded in the *Constitutum Constantini*,
according to which Constantine I performed the office of groom
(*stratoris officium*) for Pope Sylvester I.[98] Innocent was also responsible for a mural in the St Nicholas chapel of the Lateran palace
presenting a highly tendentious version of his relationship with
Emperor Lothar III. 'Pope Innocent . . . caused to be painted on a
wall in Rome both himself seated on the papal throne and Emperor
Lothar in his presence with hands folded, bowing down to receive
the crown of the empire.'[99] Hence Josef Deér (1959) portrayed
Innocent II as a pope who placed a special emphasis on the imperial
splendour of the papacy. Deér identified two important ways in
which Innocent intensified the 'imperialisation of the papacy', both
of which relied on the symbolic character of porphyry, the purple-
coloured stone associated with the Roman emperors. The first of

[96] Bernard of Clairvaux, *De consideratione* IV.3.6: (n. 6) 776A. See G. Laehr, *Die
     Konstantinische Schenkung in der abendländischen Literatur des Mittelalters bis zur Mitte
     des 14. Jahrhunderts* (Historische Studien 166: Berlin, 1926) pp. 50–1.
[97] Ernald of Bonneval, *Vita prima sancti Bernardi* II.7, *MPL* 185, 296C.
[98] Suger of St Denis, *Vita Ludovici* c. 32: (n. 12) pp. 260–2. Cf. *Constitutum Constantini*
     c. 16: (n. 91) p. 92. See below p. 446.
[99] *Chronica regia Coloniensis*, *MGH SS rer. Germ.*, 1880, p. 93. See below pp. 452–3.

these measures concerned the two chairs of state at the entrance of the Lateran palace. At some point during the twelfth century the 'official chairs' (*curules*) mentioned in the biography of Paschal II were replaced by the 'porphyry thrones' (*sedes porphyreticae*) first described by Cardinal Albinus *ca*. 1188: that is, imperial thrones with panels of purple stone. Deér conjectured that Innocent II was responsible for this change.[100] For Innocent certainly appropriated the imperial stone of porphyry to his own use on a second occasion: namely, in the choice of his own tomb. Innocent was buried, according to Cardinal Boso, 'in the Lateran church in a wonderfully constructed porphyry sarcophagus': a tomb believed in the twelfth century to be 'the sepulture of Emperor Hadrian'. Innocent had caused it to be removed from the Castel S. Angelo to the Lateran basilica and had designated it as his tomb to his closest advisers, the chancellor Gerard of S. Croce (Lucius II) and Guido of Castello (Innocent's successor, Celestine II).[101] Innocent's appropriation of an imperial tomb in the symbolic colour purple was imitated by a number of his successors. Anastasius IV was buried 'in a precious porphyry tomb', 'in which Helena, mother of Emperor Constantine [I], had once lain'.[102] The tombs of Hadrian IV, Lucius III and Urban III seem to have had a similar symbolic significance.[103] Even in death, therefore, the popes continued to lay claim to the imperial purple conferred on them by the *Constitutum Constantini*.

Constantine I was revered by the reform papacy above all for the generosity which had created 'the royal priesthood (*regale sacerdotium*) of the holy Roman and apostolic see' by creating the 'papal state'. 'Constantine conceded to [Pope Sylvester I] in perpetuity the Lateran palace, which had hitherto been a royal residence, and committed to him the government of the kingdom of Italy.'[104] This *regnum* consisted of the territories of Roman Tuscany, Sabina, the county of Tivoli, the Roman Campagna and the Maritime Province, which first appeared as a single principality under papal lordship in the Carolingian period: 'the lands . . . which Emperor Constantine and Charles [the Great] gave to St Peter', as Gregory VII described

[100] J. Deér, *The dynastic porphyry tombs of the Norman period in Sicily* (Dumbarton Oaks Studies 5: Cambridge, Mass., 1959) pp. 144–6.
[101] Boso, *Vita Innocentii II: Liber pontificalis* 2, 385; Johannes Diaconus *De ecclesia Lateranensi* c. 8, *MPL* 194, 1552AB. See Deér, *Porphyry tombs* pp. 146–53.
[102] Boso, *Vita Anastasii IV: Liber pontificalis* 2, 388; Johannes Diaconus, *De ecclesia Lateranensi* c. 8. 1553B.
[103] Deér, *Porphyry tombs* p. 152.
[104] Peter Damian, *Disceptatio synodalis* (n. 93) p. 80.

them. This complex of territories was called 'the land of St Peter' or 'the Patrimony of St Peter' or, less frequently, the *regalia sancti Petri*.[105] The attempt to secure control of this patrimony was a central preoccupation of the reforming popes and their twelfth-century successors. They saw in 'the land of St Peter' their principal guarantee of papal independence. The patrimony symbolised the 'freedom of the Church' (*libertas ecclesiae*) for which the reformers were campaigning and was moreover 'a necessary condition for the survival of a free and active papacy'.[106] The preservation of this property was represented as a principal duty of the secular defenders of the papacy. It was a duty required, for example, of the Norman princes of southern Italy when they became the vassals of the reform papacy. The oaths of fealty sworn to Gregory VII by the princes of Capua, Richard I (1073) and Jordan I (1080), and by the duke of Apulia, Robert Guiscard (1080), contain promises to help 'to hold and acquire and defend the *regalia* of St Peter and his possessions' and 'neither to invade nor to occupy the land of St Peter'.[107] When in the last quarter of the twelfth century the Norman kings of Sicily resumed the practice of swearing fealty to the pope, the oath of William II to Clement III (1188) and that of Tancred to Celestine III (1192) included the clause: 'I shall help you in good faith to hold the Roman papacy and the land of St Peter.'[108]

The popes also tried to extract similar promises from their traditional defender, the emperor or emperor elect. Gregory VII included a guarantee of the independence of the territory 'which Emperor Constantine and Charles gave to St Peter' in the oath which he devised in 1081 to be administered to the new German anti-king.[109] In 1095 Urban II obtained such a guarantee from King Conrad, when the latter rebelled against his father, Emperor Henry IV. Conrad promised to help the pope 'to acquire and hold and defend the *regalia* of St Peter both inside and outside Rome'.[110] Paschal II, during his negotiations of February 1111 with Henry V of Germany, strove to obtain a promise from the emperor elect to

---

[105] Gregory VII, *Registrum* IX.3, p. 576. See Toubert, *Structures* (n. 25), pp. 935–60; J. Fried, 'Der Regalienbegriff im 11. und 12. Jahrhundert', *DA* 29 (1973), 507–23.

[106] Toubert, *Structures* p. 1039.

[107] Gregory VII, *Registrum* I.21a, VIII.1a, pp. 36, 515; Deusdedit, *Collectio canonum* III.289 ed. V. Wolf von Glanvell (Paderborn, 1905) p. 396. See below pp. 369–72.

[108] Oath of William II: *MGH Constitutiones* I, 592; oath of Tancred: *ibid.*, p. 593. See below pp. 394–5, 508.

[109] Gregory VII, *Registrum* IX.3, p. 576. See below pp. 410–11.

[110] *Urbani II et Conradi regis conventus*: *MGH Constitutiones* I, 564. See below p. 417.

'restore and grant the patrimonies and possessions of St Peter, as was done by Charles, Louis, Henry and the other emperors'.[111] Even after the failure of these negotiations – culminating in Henry V's use of force to impose on the pope a settlement of the investiture dispute – Paschal II still sought imperial assistance in securing control of the patrimony. He wrote to Henry V in May 1111 (less than a month after he had been released from imperial custody) that the inhabitants of five cities were resisting the papal lordship. 'Nevertheless we trust that through the intervention of your power we shall obtain both them and the counties of Perugia, Gubbio, Todi, Orvieto, Bagnorea, Citta di Castello, the duchy of Spoleto, the march of Fermo and other possessions of St Peter'.[112] The guarantees which had eluded Paschal II in 1111 were finally obtained from Henry V by Calixtus II in the concordat of Worms (23 September 1122), which ended the Investiture Contest. The imperial privilege promised: 'I restore to the holy Roman church the possessions and *regalia* of St Peter . . . which I hold and I shall faithfully help so that those which I do not hold are restored.'[113]

During the three decades of peace between papacy and empire which followed the concordat of Worms, the papal hold over the patrimony was threatened by two new dangers. The first was the insatiable ambition of the Norman prince Roger II of Sicily, who during the schism of the 1130s became the champion of the antipope Anacletus II. In order to gain control of the papacy and the patrimony Innocent II was obliged to summon Lothar III of Germany to fulfil the traditional imperial role of 'catholic advocate of the Church'.[114] The second danger to the Patrimony of St Peter was the communal revolution in Rome in 1143–4, which sought to replace the government of the pope by that of a senate. The new republican regime laid claim to the papal patrimony – 'all [the pope's] *regalia* both inside and outside the city' – 'saying that [the pope] ought to be supported only by tithes and the offerings of the faithful in the manner of the priests of old'.[115] The Roman senate was supported in these claims to the patrimony by the preaching of the radical reformer Arnold of Brescia. Arnold allegedly preached 'that clerks possessing property, bishops possessing *regalia* and monks with

[111] Agreement of S. Maria in Turri: *ibid.*, p. 137. See below pp. 426–7.
[112] Paschal II, *JL* 6295: *ibid.*, pp. 569–70.
[113] Concordat of Worms: *ibid.*, pp. 159–60.
[114] Boso, *Vita Innocentii II* (n. 101) p. 383. See below pp. 442–3.
[115] Lucius II, *JL* 8684: Otto of Freising, *Chronica* VII.31: (n. 53) p. 359.

possessions could by no means be saved'.[116] The papacy looked to
Frederick I of Germany for protection against the double threat of
Sicily and the Roman republic. Eugenius III concluded the treaty of
Constance with Frederick I (23 March 1153), in which the king
undertook to protect 'the honour of the papacy and the *regalia* of St
Peter', to assist in the recovery of lands taken from the Roman
church and to make peace neither with the Romans nor with Roger
II of Sicily without the pope's approval.[117] Hadrian IV, hardpressed
both by the Roman commune and by Roger's successor, King
William I of Sicily, hurriedly renewed the treaty of Constance early
in 1155. But Frederick I failed to provide the assistance which the
pope urgently needed and Hadrian was obliged to make peace with
the king of Sicily and to become his ally.

This papal volte-face provoked Frederick's anger and seems to
have inclined him to challenge the pope's rights over the land of St
Peter. In 1159 the emperor sent envoys to the patrimony, who
demanded there the right of forage (*fodrum*) due to the emperor's
servants from lands under imperial jurisdiction. Hadrian protested
to Frederick that 'all government there belongs to St Peter, together
with all *regalia*'.[118] The tensions of Hadrian's pontificate exploded
into open conflict with the accession of Alexander III in September
1159 and the outbreak of the papal schism. During the eighteen-year
schism the emperor's supporters occupied an extensive area of the
patrimony on behalf of the successive imperial antipopes 'Victor IV',
'Paschal III' and 'Calixtus III'. The propaganda of 'Victor IV'
mocked the claim of the exiled and impecunious Alexander III to
'govern the pontificate of the Roman church and the *regalia* of St
Peter'.[119] The end of the schism did not bring the immediate restitution of the papal patrimony. In the preliminary peace of Anagni
(November 1176) Frederick promised the pope the restoration of 'all
the *regalia* and other possessions of St Peter . . . which the Roman
church had from the time of Innocent [II]'. However, the final settlement of the conflict – the Peace of Venice of July 1177 – was more
ambiguous: the papal lands were to be restored 'saving every right of
the empire'. In the last years of Frederick's reign and during the reign
of his son, Henry VI, the imperial government continued to use the

---

[116] Otto of Freising, *Gesta Friderici* II.28: (n. 51) p. 106. On Arnold of Brescia see
above n. 51.
[117] Treaty of Constance: *MGH Constitutiones* I, 201–3. See below pp. 388, 461–2.
[118] Rahewin, *Gesta Friderici* IV.34: (n. 51) p. 220.
[119] *Dialogus de pontificatu sanctae Romanae ecclesiae*, *MGH Libelli* 3, 538.

Patrimony of St Peter as a bargaining counter in the relations of empire and papacy.[120]

In the late eleventh and twelfth centuries the papacy sought to use its most important secular alliances to secure papal control over the Patrimony of St Peter; but the performance of the Norman and the imperial allies often proved disappointing. The popes were obliged, therefore, to deploy their own limited resources to strengthen their hold over the patrimony. From the pontificate of Gregory VII onwards the popes regularly perambulated the lands of St Peter. Sometimes they did so under compulsion, having been driven out of Rome by hostile noble factions, by the emperor or by the Roman commune. At other times, however, their visits to the patrimony were voluntary: the personal tours of inspection by means of which all western European princes imposed their authority over their territories. Hence the portrait of Gregory VII as 'a faithful steward and a careful manager' of the papal patrimony, conceded even by a hostile witness.

As soon as he became bishop [of Rome] . . . he commanded all cities, villages, towns and castles to be defended, he arranged for all properties to be guarded and he strove to recover what had been lost or seized by violence. He recruited a troop of knights, not (as some thought) for the sake of empty glory, but in order to enlarge the Roman church . . . The knights of the lord Hildebrand . . . by their daily labours, their wars and skirmishes, drove off the enemy, recaptured castles and cities, subdued rebels . . . and none was so bold and rash that he did not fear to touch the property of Peter.[121]

Independent evidence of this military activity is found in the record of an agreement between Gregory VII and the inhabitants of the fortress (*castrum*) of *Albininum* near Narni. 'The Roman pontiff may, if he wishes, build a residence or a tower in that fortress and station knights there for the service of St Peter; and the townsfolk must aid them, as far as they are able, for love of St Peter.' The townsfolk of *Albininum* were also reminded that they owed the duties of 'faithful knights' to St Peter. The garrisoning of *Albininum* bears witness to the main strategical preoccupation of the reform papacy in the patrimony: the safeguarding of the most vulnerable points of the frontier by means of *castra* directly subject to the pope.[122] Papal control over the patrimony was shaken by the reversals suffered by the papacy in

---

[120] Pact of Anagni c. 3, *MGH Constitutiones* 1, 350; Peace of Venice c. 3: *ibid.*, p. 362. See below pp. 494–5, 497.
[121] Wido of Ferrara, *De scismate Hildebrandi* 1.2, *MGH Libelli* 1, 534; cf. 11 pp. 554–5.
[122] *Liber Censuum* 1, 349. See Toubert, *Structures* (n. 25) pp. 1072–4.

the 1080s and 1090s during the conflict with the empire; but there are
signs of recovery already in the final years of the pontificate of
Paschal II. A document survives recording the submission of the
men of Ninfa to the pope (1110–16), which emphasises the fealty
which they owed 'to St Peter and the lord Pope Paschal' and his
successors, involving the performance of military service and submission to the judicial authority of the pope.[123] During the 1120s
Calixtus II and Honorius II pursued a war of attrition against the
baronage of the patrimony south of Rome, culminating in the submission of the troublesome counts of Ceccano, whom Honorius
compelled to become vassals of St Peter.[124]

After the setbacks of the schism of the 1130s and the communal
revolution in Rome (1143–4) there followed a new and vigorous
phase in papal territorial policy. The years 1146–59 witnessed papal
activity in the patrimony on an unprecedented scale, as first
Eugenius III, then Hadrian IV acquired large numbers of fortresses
(*castra*) and provided them with garrisons. It was no longer merely a
question of guarding the frontiers: the acquisitions of the mid-
twelfth century created a dense network of papal fortresses throughout the patrimony. Most of these *castra* were obtained by purchase or
exchange from the nobility of the patrimony; some were received as
donations by pious noble families. In exceptional cases *castra* were
acquired by military operations against noblemen who resisted papal
lordship. These papal acquisitions were proudly recorded by the
biographer of Eugenius III and Hadrian IV, Cardinal Boso. As the
chamberlain (*camerarius*) of Hadrian IV, Boso played an important
part in extending papal control over the patrimony during the
pontificate; and as a biographer he was far from underestimating this
achievement. He related that Eugenius 'recovered Terracina, Sezze,
Norma and the fortress of Fumone, which had long been alienated
from the lordship of St Peter'. Hadrian

augmented the Patrimony of St Peter very much with great possessions and
buildings. He acquired the fortress of Corchiano from the Boccaleoni for
140 pounds . . . He received S. Stefano together with half of Proceno and
Repeseno from the counts [Hildebrand and Bernard, the sons of Count
Hugolinus of Calmaniare] in pledge for 148 pounds and five *solidi* . . . He also
received all the land of these same counts by their spontaneous donation as

---

[123] *Liber Censuum* 1, 407. See K. Jordan, 'Das Eindringen des Lehnswesens in das
Rechtsleben der römischen Kurie', *Archiv für Urkundenforschung* 12 (1932), 49–50.

[124] *Annales Ceccanenses* 1121, 1123, 1125, *MGH SS* 19, 282. See Toubert, *Structures*
(n. 25) p. 1074; Partner, *Lands* (n. 22) pp. 162, 165.

the hereditary property of St Peter . . . He also acquired all the land of Odo of Poli as the perpetual inheritance of St Peter. He built a round tower in the fortress of Radicofani, defended by towers and a deep ditch. In order to ensure the peace and security of that land, he resettled the deserted fortress of Orchia, which had become a den of thieves, and defended it with a wall and towers, not without great expense.[125]

The *castra* which Eugenius III and Hadrian IV acquired were given the status of 'special fortresses of the Church' (*castra specialia Ecclesiae*) and placed under the direct lordship of the pope. In a few cases, a garrison was installed under the command of a papal *vicarius* (as, for example, the *castrum* Monte Libretti, which Hadrian IV entrusted in 1158 to the papal chaplain Ingo).[126] More frequently the former lords of the *castra* were retained in their office with the new status of 'vassals of the Church'. It was in this context of the acquisition of the *castra specialia* in the 1150s that the papacy first made extensive use of feudal institutions as a means of consolidating its hold over the patrimony.[127]

The papal schism and the conflict of empire and papacy in the years 1159–77 witnessed a sudden reversal in papal fortunes in the patrimony. 'The imperial persecution of the Church waxed so great', wrote Cardinal Boso, 'that the whole Patrimony of St Peter . . . from Acquapendente as far as Ceprano . . . was seized by the Germans.' The lordship of Alexander III was restricted to the *castra specialia* and the papal vassals of southern Latium, near the frontier of his ally, the king of Sicily.[128] It was only in the last decade of the twelfth century, in the pontificates of Clement III and Celestine III, that the papacy could return to the task of converting the barons of the patrimony into 'vassals of the holy Roman church'. By 1198 the papacy had regained control of the *castra specialia* which had served Hadrian IV as military and administrative strongpoints throughout the patrimony. However, the political situation in the patrimony of the 1190s differed markedly from that of the 1150s. For Clement III and Celestine III, who belonged respectively to the Scolari and the

[125] Boso, *Vita Eugenii III:Liber pontificalis* 2, 387; *idem, Vita Hadriani IV*: ibid., p. 396. See Toubert, *Structures* pp. 1075–8; Partner, *Lands* (n. 22) pp. 183–4, 192–4. On Boso as chamberlain see below pp. 254–6.

[126] O. Vehse, 'Die päpstliche Herrschaft in der Sabina bis zur Mitte des 12. Jahrhunderts', *QFIAB* 21 (1929–30), 169; Toubert, *Structures* p. 1078.

[127] Toubert, *Structures* pp. 1098–102, 1127–30, arguing against the view of Jordan, 'Das Eindringen' (n. 123) pp. 38–9, 52.

[128] Boso, *Vita Alexandri III*: (n. 56) pp. 403–4. See Toubert, *Structures* pp. 1079, 1130–1.

Boboni–Orsini families – both families of the new Roman aristocracy which established itself in the twelfth century – combined papal
territorial policy in the patrimony with dynastic ambitions. Both
Clement III and Celestine III used feudal institutions not only to
strengthen the papal hold over the patrimony but also to enhance the
power of their own families. Both granted the *castra specialia* of the
Roman church to their nephews as fiefs. This assimilation of papal
with family interests is reminiscent of the aristocratic papal regime
(*Adelspapsttum*) of the tenth and early eleventh century. In one
instance indeed the territorial interests of the papacy were damaged
by dynastic ambition: the fortress of Vicovaro enfeoffed by Celestine
III to his nephews in 1191 was subsequently absorbed into the
allodial lands of the Orsini family and was lost to the Roman
church.[129] However, Vicovaro was an exceptional case: elsewhere
there is no evidence that papal interests were sacrificed to family
ambition. Unlike the *Adelspapsttum* of two centuries before, the
aristocratic regime of the 1190s used family connections in order to
consolidate the power of the Roman church. Clement III and
Celestine III enfeoffed *castra specialia* to their nephews so as to ensure
papal control and to avert for the future the disaster which had overtaken the patrimony in the 1160s and 1170s. Family ties were
intended to ensure the fidelity of the 'vassals of the holy Roman
church'. The regime of the Scolari and Bobone popes of the 1190s
thus anticipated the highly successful regime of the Conti pope,
Innocent III.

[129] Tillmann, 'Ricerche' (n. 26) 24 (1970), 458–9; Toubert, *Structures* pp. 1131–3.

2

THE COLLEGE OF CARDINALS

THE STRUCTURE OF THE COLLEGE

In the second half of the eleventh century the papacy broke away from the narrow preoccupations of the diocese of Rome and began to make good its claims to a universal jurisdiction throughout Christendom. Simultaneously, in the years 1050–1100 the Roman cardinalate ceased to be a local institution of the city of Rome and became an institution of the universal Church: the college of cardinals. Before this transformation took place, the functions of the cardinals had been purely liturgical.[1] The seven 'cardinal bishops' – the bishops whose sees were Rome's immediate neighbours – had the duty of performing in turn the weekly services of the Lateran basilica: hence the sources sometimes call them 'the Lateran bishops'

[1] On the early history of the cardinalate see H.-W. Klewitz, 'Die Entstehung des Kardinalkollegiums', *ZSSRG KA* 25 (1936), 115–221, here cited from the reprint: *idem, Reformpapsttum und Kardinalkolleg* (Darmstadt, 1957) pp. 11–134; S. Kuttner, '*Cardinalis*. The history of a canonical concept', *Traditio* 3 (1945), 129–214; M. Andrieu, 'L'origine du titre de cardinal dans l'Eglise romaine' in *Miscellanea Giovanni Mercati* 5 (Rome, 1946), 113–44; C. G. Fürst, *Cardinalis. Prolegomena zu einer Rechtsgeschichte des Römischen Kardinalskollegiums* (Munich, 1967); C. Lefebvre, 'Les origines et le rôle du cardinalat au moyen âge', *Apollinaris* 41 (1968), 59–70; K. Ganzer, 'Das Römische Kardinalkollegium' in *Le istituzioni ecclesiastiche della 'societas christiana' dei secoli XI–XII* (Miscellanea del Centro di Studi Medioevali 7: Milan, 1974) pp. 153–6; R. Hüls, *Kardinäle, Klerus und Kirchen Roms* (Bibliothek des Deutschen Historischen Instituts in Rom 48: Tübingen, 1977) pp. 3–38.

33

(*episcopi Lateranenses*). The title of 'cardinal' was also borne by the twenty-eight priests who presided over the titular churches within the city walls. They were responsible for the weekly services in the four patriarchal basilicas, seven cardinal priests serving in turn in each of the basilicas of St Peter, St Paul, S. Maria Maggiore and St Laurence within the walls: hence the sources call them 'cardinals of St Peter, of St Paul, of St Mary and of St Laurence'. The 'cardinal' title belonged also to nineteen (by the later eleventh century, eighteen) deacons: the seven *diaconi palatini* who served in the Lateran palace and basilica, consisting of the Roman archdeacon and the six palatine deacons, together with the twelve *diaconi regionarii*.[2] Our most important source of information about the liturgical functions of these cardinals is an anonymous treatise entitled *Description of the sanctuary of the Lateran church*, an account of the services in the Lateran and in the four patriarchal basilicas, composed between 1073 and 1100. This treatise emphasises the intimate connection of the cardinal bishops, cardinal priests and cardinal deacons with the liturgical duties of the pope.

When the pope, the vicar of St Peter, on Sundays and on special festivals celebrates mass on the altar of the holy Saviour in the Lateran church . . . the seven bishops must assist, together with the 28 priests presiding over the 28 churches within the walls of the city of Rome . . . The archdeacon of Rome with the six palatine deacons . . . and the other twelve regional deacons must also be there.[3]

Already at the time of composition of this *Description*, the relationship of these cardinals with the pope had been rendered closer by the assumption of other duties, to which these liturgical functions rapidly became secondary. By 1100 bishops, priests and deacons had come to form a single college of cardinals and had been assigned that role in the Church which continued to be attributed to them into the twentieth century. 'The cardinals of the holy Roman church constitute the senate of the Roman pontiff and assist him in ruling the Church as his foremost counsellors and helpers.'[4]

---

[2] Klewitz, *Reformpapsttum* pp. 24–31, 47–60, 79–97. On the problem of the origins of the cardinal deacons see Kuttner, '*Cardinalis*' pp. 178–98; Fürst, *Cardinalis* pp. 108–11; Hüls, *Kardinäle* pp. 14–19.

[3] *Descriptio sanctuarii Lateranensis ecclesiae*, quoted by Klewitz, *Reformpapsttum* p. 20 n. 33.

[4] *Corpus Iuris Canonici* canon 230: see K. Mörsdorf, *Lehrbuch des Kirchenrechts auf Grund des Codex Iuris Canonici* 1 (Munich-Paderborn-Vienna, 1964), 355.

This development occurred in two stages. The cardinal bishops emerged as the pope's principal advisers during the 1050s; the cardinal priests and deacons joined them in forming a single college during the last two decades of the eleventh century. The prominence of the cardinal bishops in the counsels of the pope dates from the inception of the reform papacy in the pontificate of Leo IX (1049–54). Even before that date the seven cardinal bishops had been figures of considerable prestige in Rome. To the cardinal bishop of Ostia belonged the honour of consecrating the pope. (His preeminence among the cardinals would eventually be acknowledged in the fourteenth century by the title 'dean of the sacred college'.) His colleagues, the cardinal bishops of Albano and Porto, also had an important role on the occasion of the papal consecration.[5] During the 1050s the cardinal bishops' ceremonial and liturgical functions were augmented by governmental duties; and with increasing frequency the office of cardinal bishop was conferred on reformers of non-Roman origin. The historian Bonizo of Sutri (writing in 1085) described Leo IX's first reforming measure thus: 'in Rome bishops, cardinals and abbots ordained through simoniacal heresy were deposed and others from various provinces were ordained there.'[6] The change in the role of the cardinal bishops was partly the result of a change in personnel. The new men promoted to the cardinalate in the 1050s – Humbert of Silva Candida, Peter Damian of Ostia, Boniface of Albano – were distinguished outsiders brought in to assist the pope in governing and reforming the Church. The practice of the 1050s – the promotion of eminent reformers (often monks), unconnected with the anti-reform aristocratic factions of Rome – was followed throughout the later eleventh century; and in this way the dignity of cardinal bishop became identified with the role of principal papal adviser. This identification is already apparent in the works composed in the late 1050s and early 1060s by Peter Damian, cardinal bishop of Ostia, whom Luchesius Spätling (1970) has described as 'the true theologian of the renewed Roman cardinalate'. Peter Damian wrote that the prerogatives of the cardinal bishops 'transcend not only the rights of any other bishops but even those of patriarchs and primates'. He was the first to draw an analogy between the papal advisers and the ancient Roman senate: the cardi-

---

[5] E. Eichmann, *Weihe und Krönung des Papstes im Mittelalter* (Münchener Theologische Studien 3. Kanonistische Abteilung 1: Munich, 1951) pp. 50–1.
[6] Bonizo of Sutri, *Liber ad amicum* v, *MGH Libelli* 1, 588.

nal bishops were 'the spiritual senators of the universal Church'.[7] The most important prerogative of the cardinal bishops, Peter Damian wrote in 1062, was that 'they principally elect the Roman pontiff'. He was alluding to the Papal Election Decree of 1059, which confers on the cardinal bishops the right to hold a preliminary election, in which the other cardinals and the rest of the Roman clergy were then expected to acquiesce. It is the most striking statement of the new status of the cardinal bishops: their authority in a papal election is represented as equivalent to that of a metropolitan in the election of a bishop.[8] By 1059 most of the cardinal bishops were reformers and non-Romans: the election of the pope – and the future of the reform papacy – could safely be placed in their hands. For a generation after 1059 the cardinal bishops constituted the solid core of the Roman reform party. They were the most reliable supporters of Gregory VII (only one of their number, John of Porto, was among the twelve cardinals who abandoned Gregory in 1084) and it was they who rallied the shattered Gregorian party in 1088 by electing Urban II.[9]

During the early years of the reform papacy the cardinal priests and cardinal deacons continued, with a few exceptions, to perform mainly liturgical functions. It was the Investiture Contest and the schism of Wibert of Ravenna (the imperial antipope 'Clement III') which gave them the opportunity of joining the cardinal bishops in performing the duties of 'spiritual senators of the universal Church'. There is clear evidence that the cardinal priests were already laying claim to such a role in the early 1080s: namely in two versions of the Papal Election Decree of 1059. One of these versions is a summary of the election decree included among the decrees of the Lateran synod of 1059, found in the canonical collections of the three principal Gregorian canonists, Anselm II of Lucca, Cardinal Deusdedit and Bonizo of Sutri. The other is the forged 'imperialist version' of

[7] Peter Damian, *Epistolae* I.20, *MPL* 144, 238D; *idem, Opusculum* 31, c. 7, *MPL* 145, 540B. See L. Spätling, 'Kardinalat und Kollegialität', *Antonianum* 45 (1970), 278; G. Alberigo, *Cardinalato e collegialità* (Florence, 1969) pp. 36–42; E. Pasztor, 'San Pier Damiano, il cardinalato e la formazione della Curia Romana' in *Atti del Convegno internazionale dedicato a san Pier Damiani = SG* 10 (1975), 317–39.

[8] H.-G. Krause, *Das Papstwahldekret von 1059 und seine Rolle im Investiturstreit = SG* 7 (1960). The most recent discussion of the decree (with edition and full bibliography) is that of D. Jasper, *Das Papstwahldekret von 1059. Überlieferung und Textgestalt* (Beiträge zur Geschichte und Quellenkunde des Mittelalters 12: Sigmaringen, 1986).

[9] Klewitz, *Reformpapsttum* (n. 1) pp. 35–6, 39, 115; Becker, *Urban II.* 1, 91–6.

the decree, which evidently originated among the supporters of Emperor Henry IV. In both versions the clause dealing with the electoral rights of the cardinal bishops is amended, the term *cardinales episcopi* being replaced by *cardinales*.[10] These two documents reveal an attempt, both in Gregorian and Henrician circles, to deprive the cardinal bishops of their exclusive right and to grant to the cardinals as a whole the right of electing the pope. It is worth noting that the two most outspoken critics of Gregory VII's style of government were cardinal priests. Hugh Candidus (who had been appointed to the cardinalate by Leo IX) abandoned Gregory early in his pontificate. He was responsible for the accusations made against 'the false monk Hildebrand' at Henry IV's synods of Worms (1076) and Brixen (1080); and he was the only cardinal to participate in the election of Henry's antipope Wibert.[11] Beno, cardinal priest of SS. Martino e Silvestro was one of the twelve cardinals who deserted Gregory VII for the antipope in 1084. His polemic, *The Deeds of the Roman church against Hildebrand*, was a defence of the renegades' conduct, alleging that Gregory 'removed the cardinals from the counsel of the holy see'.[12] Of the twelve schismatic cardinals, one was a cardinal bishop, eight were cardinal priests and three were cardinal deacons (including Archdeacon Theodinus). This suggests the possibility that a major issue of the 'internal pontificate' of Gregory VII was an attempt by the other two orders of cardinals to obtain a role in government equal to that of the cardinal bishops. A cardinal priest who remained loyal to Gregory, the canonist Deusdedit, included in his collection a number of texts which favoured the claims of his order. Similarly the anonymous author of the *Description of the sanctuary of the Lateran church* was an enthusiast for the rights of the cardinal priests, 'who possess the right of judging all bishops throughout the Roman empire in all councils and synods'.[13]

Gregory VII's attitude to the claims of the cardinal priests and

---

[10] Krause, *Papstwahldekret* pp. 246–7. Cf. Anselm of Lucca, *Collectio canonum* VI.12–13, ed. F. Thaner (Innsbruck, 1906) pp. 272–3; *Die Kanonessammlung des Kardinals Deusdedit* I.168–9, ed. V. Wolf von Glanvell (Paderborn, 1905) p. 107; Bonizo of Sutri, *Liber de vita christiana* IV.87, ed. E. Perels (Texte zur Geschichte des Römischen und Kanonischen Rechts im Mittelalter 1: Berlin, 1930) p. 156.

[11] F. Lerner, *Kardinal Hugo Candidus* (Historische Studien 22: Berlin, 1931) pp. 46–59.

[12] Beno, *Gesta Romanae ecclesiae* I, MGH Libelli 2, 370.

[13] Deusdedit, *Collectio canonum* II.40, 110, 161 (n. 10) pp. 205, 235, 268: see Kuttner, 'Cardinalis' (n. 1) p. 176; J. Sydow, 'Untersuchungen zur kurialen Verwaltungsgeschichte im Zeitalter des Reformpapsttums', *DA* 11 (1954/5), 36–7. *Descriptio*, quoted by Klewitz, *Reformpapsttum* (n. 1) p. 20 n. 33.

deacons is a matter of conjecture; but the attitude of his rival, the antipope Wibert, was undoubtedly positive. In order to retain the support of the renegades of 1084 the antipope conceded to them the role in papal government which they claimed. The evidence for their participation is found in the privileges of 'Clement III', which – in sharp contrast to those of Gregory VII – contain numerous subscriptions of cardinal priests and cardinal deacons. The term *diaconus cardinalis* is found for the first time in these Wibertine privileges.[14] In the prolonged struggle for the city of Rome at the end of the eleventh century control of the titular and regional churches was of vital strategic importance. This was presumably the motive behind Wibert's decision to admit the cardinal priests and deacons into the senate of the Roman Church. It was likewise the reason why Urban II was obliged to imitate the antipope's policy. Urban's privileges bore the subscriptions of cardinal priests and deacons. They also borrowed the designation 'cardinal deacon' from Wibert's chancery: Urban's chancellor, John of Gaeta, regularly described himself as *diaconus cardinalis* from 1089 onwards.[15] Wibert of Ravenna was thus the real architect of the college of cardinals. It was in order to compete successfully with the antipope for the loyalty of the cardinal priests and deacons that the reform papacy created a college of cardinals in which they were full participants. There are indications in the sources that a fourth order was poised to join them in the college in the pontificate of Urban II: that of the subdeacons of the Roman church (the seven palatine subdeacons, the seven regional subdeacons and the seven subdeacons of the *schola cantorum*). For example, the envoy whom Urban sent to Canterbury in April 1088 was described by the pope as 'our beloved son Roger, cardinal subdeacon of our church'.[16] However, for some unknown reason the twenty-one Roman subdeacons failed to find a place in the senate of the Roman Church. When the college finally emerged in its definitive form *ca.* 1100, it contained only three orders: seven cardinal bishops, twenty-eight cardinal priests (the late eleventh- and early

---

[14] P. Kehr, 'Zur Geschichte Wiberts von Ravenna (Clemens III.)', *Sb. der Preussischen Akademie der Wissenschaften* 1921, pp. 980–1; Klewitz, *Reformpapsttum* (n. 1) p. 89; Ganzer, 'Kardinalkollegium' (n. 1) pp. 163–4.

[15] L. Santifaller, 'Saggio di un Elenco dei funzionari, impiegati e scrittori della Cancellaria Pontificia dall'inizio all' anno 1099', *BISI* 56 (1940), 208–10; Ganzer 'Kardinalkollegium' (n. 1) pp. 163–5.

[16] Urban II, *JL* 5351, *MPL* 151, 287A. See R. Elze, 'Die päpstliche Kapelle im 12. und 13. Jahrhundert', *ZSSRG KA* 36 (1950), 153–4.

twelfth-century sources refer to them as *cardinales* with no further designation) and eighteen cardinal deacons.

During the period of the creation of the college, the idea of the cardinals' special status in the Church was confined to the writings of the cardinals themselves; but after 1100 this idea is increasingly to be found in the works of authors outside the college and far from Rome. The image of the *senatus*, first used by Peter Damian, frequently recurs. Archbishop Balderic of Dol spoke in extravagant terms of 'the senators who had obtained the principate of all apostolic authority'.[17] William of Malmesbury described the honour accorded to Archbishop Anselm of Canterbury by the pope 'in the presence of the senate'; and Orderic Vitalis recorded the prominent role played by 'the Roman senate' at the council of Rheims in 1119. Otto of Freising also referred to 'the sacred senate of the cardinals'.[18] The chronicler Balderic, describing Eugenius III's visit to Trier in November 1147, emphasised the distinction of the cardinals in his entourage. 'They were men honourable in their countenance, outward appearance and mien, in their knowledge and their morals and worthy of immortal memory for the high esteem in which they were held.'[19] The closest approximation to a treatise on the cardinalate in the twelfth century is found in the writings of Bernard of Clairvaux: in his letters to cardinals and in his work on the papal dignity and on the curia, *De consideratione*, addressed to Eugenius III (*ca.* 1150). Bernard told the cardinals: 'God has put you in a high place so that the more useful your life is to his Church, the more eminent will be your authority in [the Church].' The primary duty of the cardinals was the reform of the Church. 'There is no doubt that it behoves you especially to remove scandal from the kingdom of God, to cut down the thorns as they grow, to bring an end to lamentation.' Writing to the pope, Bernard described the cardinals as 'those who assist you every day, the elders of the people, the judges of the world', 'your comrades and helpers (*collaterales et coadiutores*)', 'your eyes' (an image also used by Peter Damian).[20] In one respect Bernard's views

---

[17] Balderic of Dol, *Vita sancti Hugonis Rothomagensis episcopi*, MPL 166, 1167A. See Sydow, 'Verwaltungsgeschichte' (n. 13) p. 64.

[18] William of Malmesbury, *Gesta pontificum Anglorum* I.52, RS 52 (1870), 97; Orderic Vitalis, *Historia ecclesiastica* XII.21, ed. M. Chibnall 6 (Oxford, 1978), 252, 254: cf. *Historia* XII.9, p. 210; Otto of Freising, *Gesta Friderici* I.60, MGH SS rer. Germ. 3 (1912), 85.

[19] Balderic, *Gesta Alberonis archiepiscopi* c. 23, MGH SS 8, 255.

[20] Bernard, *Epistolae* 188, 230, MPL 182, 352A, 417B; *idem, De consideratione* IV.1.1, IV.2.2, IV.4.9, *ibid.*, 772C, 773A, 778A; *Epistola* 243, *ibid.*, 439B: cf. Peter Damian,

on the cardinalate were ambiguous. He assured the cardinal bishops of Ostia, Tusculum and Palestrina (perhaps in 1143) that their authority was divinely ordained ('God has put you in a high place'). But to Eugenius III he wrote *ca.* 1150 that the cardinals 'have no power except that which you either give or permit them'.[21] Presumably Bernard saw no discrepancy between the statements that the cardinalate was divinely ordained and that the cardinals had no power save that granted to them by the pope.

Later twelfth-century references to the college tended to assume that the authority of the cardinals was independent of that of the pope. Gerhoch of Reichersberg wrote of 'the assembly of the lord cardinals which we understand to be the Roman church'.[22] Emperor Frederick I in 1159 described the cardinals as 'the immovable columns . . . by which the holy and universal Church is most firmly supported'.[23] After the mid-twelfth century there was no doubt about the cardinals' exclusive right to elect the pope. Bernard of Clairvaux had reminded Eugenius III of the cardinals 'whom you did not choose, but who chose you'.[24] In the papal election decree of the Third Lateran Council (1179), *Licet de evitanda*, the cardinals are assumed to be the sole electors of the pope.[25] The inaugural discourse of this council, delivered on behalf of Alexander III by the eminent canonist, Bishop Rufinus of Assisi, emphasised the exalted position of the cardinals in the Church. They were the *proceres*, the magnates who assisted the papal monarch in governing the Church; the archbishops were the consuls of their respective provinces; the bishops and abbots, the people of the Christian republic.[26] The fellow canonists of Master Rufinus, the Decretists of the later twelfth century, preferred an ecclesiastical analogy: the pope and cardinals at the head of the Church corresponded to the bishop and his chapter and the abbot and his monks.[27] The classicist Peter of Blois reverted to

Epistolae I.7: (n. 7) 211D. See B. Jacqueline, 'Saint-Bernard de Clairvaux et la Curie romaine', *Rivista di Storia della Chiesa in Italia* 7 (1953), 27–44; Alberigo, *Cardinalato* (n. 7) pp. 63–6.

[21] Bernard, *Epistola* 230: 417B; *De consideratione* IV.4.9: 778B.

[22] Gerhoch, *De investigatione Antichristi*, *MGH Libelli* 3, 308.

[23] Frederick I, letter to the German bishops: *MGH Constitutiones* 1, 253 (no. 182).

[24] Bernard, *De consideratione* IV.4.9: 778B.

[25] *Concilium Lateranense III* c. 1, *Conciliorum Oecumenicorum Decreta* p. 211.

[26] G. Morin, 'Le discours d'ouverture du concile général du Latran (1179) et l'oeuvre littéraire de Maître Rufin évêque d'Assise', *Memorie della Pontificia Accademia di Archeologia* ser. 3, *Memorie* 2 (1928), 116. See below pp. 141, 144–5.

[27] J. B. Sägmüller, *Die Tätigkeit und Stellung der Kardinäle bis Papst Bonifaz VIII.* (Freiburg/Br., 1896) p. 225.

the image of the senate of the universal Church: the cardinals were the 'conscript fathers'.[28] In these twelfth-century references to the authority of the cardinals no distinction is made between the cardinal bishops and the cardinal priests and deacons. The original version of the Papal Election Decree of 1059 identified the cardinal bishops as electors: the decree *Licet de evitanda* spoke only of 'the cardinals'. The three orders of cardinals had become absorbed into a single college: the term *collegium*, designating the cardinal bishops, priests and deacons as a single unit, first appeared in 1150.[29]

The college was to develop its corporate identity through the creation of its own institutions independent of those of the papal curia. The development of this internal organisation is well documented in the case of the thirteenth century, but has left few traces in the twelfth-century sources. The evidence which survives for the twelfth century relates to the finances of the college. By the end of the twelfth century the college possessed its own financial officer or 'chamberlain' (*camerarius*) in the person of Cardinal Cencius Savelli (the future Pope Honorius III), who had previously served Clement III and Celestine III as papal chamberlain. There is evidence from earlier in the century that two chamberlains were simultaneously at work in the curia, in records of the years 1101, 1123 and 1151; but there is no firm evidence for identifying one of these officers as the papal chamberlain and the other as the chamberlain of the cardinals.[30] Already in the early twelfth century it was clear that the incomes of the cardinal bishoprics and the titular churches were insufficient to cover the expenses incurred by the cardinals as the principal agents of the papacy. When they were employed as papal legates – during the twelfth century all the most important legations were entrusted to the cardinals – their expenses were covered by the recipients of the legation, through the exaction of 'canonical procurations'.[31] Their expenses in Rome could be met only by making inroads on the income of the pope. A possible instance of this development occurs in a treaty of 1121 negotiated by papal envoys with the city of Genoa. The Genoese committed themselves to pay a subsidy of 1,200 marks to the pope, 300 marks to the *curia* and fifty *unciae* to the clerks who negotiated the treaty.[32] It seems safe to assume that the term *curia*

---

[28] Peter of Blois, *Epistola* 126, MPL 207, 377B.
[29] Sägmüller, *Kardinäle* p. 92.
[30] See below p. 253.   [31] See below pp. 162, 267, 283–4.
[32] *Annales Ianuenses*, cited in K. Jordan, 'Zur päpstlichen Finanzgeschichte im 11. und 12. Jahrhundert', QFIAB 25 (1933–4), 87–8.

here refers mainly to the cardinals, in the light of the more precise information, likewise from the pontificate of Calixtus II, provided by the *History of Compostela*. According to this source, when in 1124 Archbishop Diego Gelmírez of Compostela sent to Rome a gift of 400 gold pieces – intended as the price of a permanent papal legation for the archbishop – the money was to be shared by the pope with the cardinals and principal officials of the curia. In 1126 Diego Gelmírez sent another gift of 300 gold *marabotini*, of which 220 were for Honorius II, 80 for the curia.[33]

In the pontificate of Alexander III pope and cardinals are found raising separate loans in France.[34] From this period onwards the financial records regularly specify the proportion of the papal income allocated to the college of cardinals. The cardinals received, for example, part of the *presbyteria*, the gifts distributed by the pope on certain feast-days, and part of the payment made by archbishops when they received their pallium from the pope.[35] The cardinals also received personal gifts from petitioners at the curia, who wished them to influence papal decisions in their favour. The importance of this source of revenue is suggested by the reform introduced by Gregory VIII in 1187, in the aftermath of the fall of Jerusalem. The cardinals were obliged to promise that until Jerusalem was reconquered from the Saracens, they would receive no more gifts from petitioners other than what was intended 'for their needs and sustenance'.[36] By the end of the twelfth century the cardinals' income had become a major political issue, figuring in the negotiations between the pope and the emperor concerning their rival territorial claims in central Italy. In 1184 Emperor Frederick I suggested that the papacy surrender its claims in return for an annual payment to the pope of one-tenth and to the cardinals of one-ninth of the emperor's Italian revenues.[37] A somewhat similar story was told by Giraldus Cambrensis of Emperor Henry VI. He proposed to relieve the Roman church of her poverty by granting the pope a prebend in each metropolitan church and each of the richer bishoprics of the empire

---

[33] *Historia Compostellana* II.64, III.10, *MPL* 170, 1117D, 1173B. See below p. 265.

[34] Alexander III, *JL* 11256, *MPL* 200, 406B. See F. Schneider, 'Zur älteren päpstlichen Finanzgeschichte', *QFIAB* 9 (1906), 13.

[35] R. Foreville and J. Rousset de Pina, *Du premier Concile du Latran à l'avènement d'Innocent III (1123–1198)* (Histoire de l'Eglise 9: Paris, 1953) p. 242. See above p. 4 and below p. 263.

[36] Peter of Blois, *Epistola* 219, *MPL* 207, 508C–509A (to Henry II of England). See below p. 364.

[37] See below pp. 248, 501–2.

and to the cardinals and other members of the curia prebends in the lesser bishoprics.[38] There is no other record of this proposal and it seems wiser to attribute the story to Giraldus' well-known powers of invention than to his superior sources of information. However, like the authentic story of the proposal of Frederick I, it is evidence of the growing realisation that the college of cardinals had become an independent power within the Roman church. The emperor was forced to include them in his calculations and by making a favourable offer, like that of 1184, he may well have hoped to turn the cardinals against the pope. Similarly, when in 1197 Henry VI's widow, Empress Constance, sought the recognition of the curia for the succession of her son, Frederick II, as king of Sicily, she offered one thousand marks of silver to the pope and one thousand marks to the cardinals.[39]

The financial evidence reveals the growing independence of the college of cardinals in the twelfth century. Evidence more difficult to interpret is that of the dwindling numbers in the college during this century. Theoretically the college contained fifty-three cardinals (seven bishops, twenty-eight priests and eighteen deacons); but in practice during the twelfth century the college was smaller than this, since the pope regularly left a number of cardinal churches vacant. The trend is clear enough, even though complete information is not available for each pontificate. On the death of Paschal II (1118) the college contained thirty-six cardinals; on the death of Calixtus II (1124) there were forty-four cardinals; or the death of Honorius II (1130) the number was forty-two and on that of Innocent II (1143), thirty-one. In the middle of the century there was a slight increase in the size of the college: at the end of Celestine II's pontificate (1144) the number was thirty-eight; after that of Lucius II (1145), thirty-six and after that of Eugenius III (1153), thirty-five. Since Anastasius IV created no new cardinals, on his death (1154) the college contained only twenty-seven members; and on the death of Hadrian IV (1159) the number was thirty-one. At the end of Alexander III's pontificate (1181) the number of cardinals was twenty-four; and on the death of Lucius III (1185) it was twenty-six. On the death of Gregory VIII (1187) the number had fallen to between eighteen and twenty, too small a number to fulfil the duties of the papal government, so that Clement III was obliged to create many new cardinals (perhaps as

---

[38] Giraldus Cambrensis, *Speculum Ecclesiae* IV.19, RS 21/4 (1873), 302. See below pp. 519–20.
[39] Roger of Hoveden, *Chronica*, RS 51/4 (1871), 31.

many as thirty). At his death (1191) the college contained thirty-one members, together with four 'external cardinals' (churchmen bearing the title of cardinal but not resident in Rome). On the death of Celestine III (1198) the number had fallen again to twenty-eight. In the first third of the century, therefore, the college contained between forty-four and thirty-six members; in the second third membership ranged between thirty-eight and twenty-seven; and in the last third membership ranged between thirty-one and eighteen to twenty. During the thirteenth century the college continued to decline in size: in 1216 (on the death of Innocent III) the number of cardinals was twenty-seven, which was also the number in 1227; in 1261 it had fallen to eight and in 1277 to seven.[40]

In the case of the thirteenth-century college it is well known that the decline in numbers was the result of the cardinals' own policy: they wished to concentrate the authority and the revenues of the college in a small and exclusive group. It is worth asking whether a similar motive was at work in the twelfth century and whether the cardinals themselves played a significant role in restricting the size of the twelfth-century college. Marcel Pacaut (1956) examined the marked reduction in the size of the college in the pontificate of Alexander III. He considered the possibility that this developmen signified an attempt by the pope to enhance his own authority; bu concluded that the shrinking size of the college was merely an accident, the effect of sudden mortality among the cardinals at the end of the pontificate.[41] Barbara Zenker (1964) in her analysis of the college in the period 1130–59 inclined to the theory of a deliberate papal policy: a 'systematic reduction' in the number of the cardinals in the interests of more effective papal government. The theoretical membership of fifty-three cardinals, determined by the original liturgical duties of the cardinalate, was too large to carry out governmental duties rapidly or efficiently. What the pope needed was 'a

[40] Klewitz, *Reformpapsttum* (n. 1) p. 100; C. G. Fürst, 'Kennen wir die Wähler Gelasius' II.? Glaubwürdigkeit des Kardinalsverzeichnisses in Pandulfs Vita Gelasii' in *Festschrift Karl Pivec. Zum 60. Geburtstag gewidmet von Kollegen, Freunden und Schülern* ed. A. Haidacher and H. E. Mayer (Innsbrucker Beiträge zur Kulturwissenschaft 12: Innsbruck, 1966) pp. 69–80; F.-J. Schmale, *Studien zum Schisma des Jahres 1130* (Cologne-Graz, 1961) pp. 32–3; B. Zenker, *Die Mitglieder des Kardinalkollegiums von 1130 bis 1159* (dissertation: Würzburg, 1964) pp. 197–8; V. Pfaff, 'Papst Clemens III. (1187–1191)', *ZSSRG KA* 66 (1980), 269, 280; *idem*, 'Die Kardinäle unter Papst Coelestin III. (1191–1198)', *ibid.*, 41 (1955), 84–93; J. Lulvès, 'Die Machtbestrebungen des Kardinalats bis zur Aufstellung der ersten päpstlichen Wahlkapitulation', *QFIAB* 13 (1910), 84.

[41] Pacaut, *Alexandre III* p. 271.

relatively small, carefully chosen and therefore well harmonised staff of fellow-workers', containing 'experts in every relevant area'. Barbara Zenker also considered it possible that in reducing the size of the college the pope intended to prevent the cardinals from interfering with his direct personal rule over the Church.[42] The explanations of the diminishing size of the college offered by Pacaut and Zenker are completely different, although not necessarily incompatible: membership had fallen below forty in the years 1130–59 because of the deliberate policy of the pope; it had fallen below thirty in 1181 because of the accidents of mortality. These explanations can only be tested by a detailed study of the system of recruitment to the college; and for such a study the materials are almost completely lacking.

There is no doubt that the appointment of new cardinals was a prerogative of the pope. As Bernard of Clairvaux reminded Eugenius III: 'if [the cardinals] are good or if they are evil, . . . will not the responsibility be yours, since you either choose them or keep them in their places?'[43] The appointment of cardinals is never described in detail in the twelfth-century sources. A characteristic report is that by a French local historian, Herman of Laon, of the promotion of Drogo of Rheims in 1136: 'Pope Innocent [II] compelled him, bound as he was by the bonds of obedience, to go to Rome and he consecrated him bishop of the city of Ostia.' Here the author's concern is with the virtuous reluctance of the cardinal rather than with the process of his recruitment; but another report from the same source is more instructive: 'Pope Innocent, on the advice of Bishop Drogo of Ostia, had consecrated Abbot Hugh of Homblières as bishop of the city of Albano, having summoned him to Rome and compelled him by the bond of obedience.' In the case of the promotion of Hugh of Albano in 1143 Herman of Laon attributed the initiative to his compatriot, Drogo of Ostia. It is possible, of course, that this account is distorted by a tendency to exaggerate the influence of the local hero, Drogo. The *Papal history* of John of Salisbury makes a tantalisingly vague reference to five appointments of Eugenius III in 1151. 'Roland . . . Gerard and Cencius . . . John Paparo and Octavian . . . were chosen to be promoted in the curia.' But the *History* adds that when John Paparo resisted the attempt to promote him from cardinal deacon to cardinal priest and Eugenius suspended him, it was the cardinals who made peace between them and persuaded

---

[42] Zenker, *Mitglieder* (n. 40) pp. 198–9.
[43] Bernard, *De consideratione* IV.4.9: (n. 20) 778A.

John to receive ordination as cardinal priest.[44] An explicit statement
that the college participated in the appointment of a cardinal is found
in two accounts referring respectively to 1149 and 1179. The historian Cardinal Boso recorded that in 1149 Nicholas Breakspear,
abbot of St Rufus in Avignon was appointed cardinal bishop of
Albano by Eugenius III 'with the common counsel of his brethren'.[45]
The second account – the appointment of Archbishop William of
Rheims as cardinal priest of S. Sabina at the Third Lateran Council in
1179 – attributes the primary role to the cardinals. William was promoted 'by the common election of the brethren, the supreme pontiff
Alexander conceding this'.[46] Because detailed information is scarce,
there is unfortunately no way of deciding whether the English
author of this report exaggerated the role of the cardinals in the
appointment of William of Rheims.

It happens that the most detailed twelfth-century document concerning recruitment to the college was composed just before this
appointment, on the eve of the Third Lateran Council: namely, a
letter of 1178 addressed to Alexander III by his legate in France,
Peter, cardinal priest of S. Grisogono. The pope had instructed his
legate to send him the names of French clerks distinguished for their
'morality, knowledge of letters and religion', who would be suitable
recruits to the college of cardinals. Cardinal Peter replied with a list
of names of religious and learned men, of whom two – Henry of
Marcy, abbot of Clairvaux and Abbot Bernered of St Crépin in
Soissons – were appointed to the college during the Third Lateran
Council.[47] In this instance the initiative in appointing new cardinals
was clearly taken by the pope, who considered that the college had
become too small. He was, however, dependent on the judgement of
the cardinal legate, who drew up the short-list on which the final
decision was based. The conclusions that can be drawn from the
twelfth-century evidence must be tentative. The pope may very
often have played the principal role in appointing cardinals. That is

---

[44] Herman, *De miraculis beatae Mariae Laudunensis* III.22, 23, *MPL* 180, 1005A, 1005B;
John of Salisbury, *Historia pontificalis* c. 36 ed. M. Chibnall (London, 1956) p. 71.
[45] Boso, *Vita Hadriani IV: Liber pontificalis* 2, 388. See J. Sydow, 'Il "concistorium"
dopo lo scisma del 1130', *Rivista di storia della chiesa* 9 (1955), 171.
[46] *Gesta regis Henrici II*, RS 49/1 (1867), 222. See K. Ganzer, *Die Entwicklung des
auswärtigen Kardinalats im hohen Mittelalter. Ein Beitrag zur Geschichte des Kardinalkollegiums vom 11. bis 13. Jahrhundert* (Tübingen, 1963) p. 11 n. 49.
[47] Peter of S. Grisogono, *Epistola: MPL* 200, 1370D–1372A. See W. Janssen, *Die
päpstlichen Legaten in Frankreich vom Schisma Anaklets bis zum Tode Cölestins III.,
1130–1198* (Cologne-Graz, 1961) p. 104.

the obvious explanation, for example, of the papal kinsmen who appeared in the college in the pontificate of Lucius II, Clement III and Celestine III.[48] But there is reason to believe that the appointment of a cardinal, like many other papal decisions, required the approval of the college and that the cardinals also had the right to propose new appointments. It is not impossible, therefore, that the cardinals themselves played a part in reducing the size of their college during the twelfth century.

The letter of Cardinal Peter of S. Grisogono to Alexander III indicates that during the last quarter of the twelfth century the papacy was still anxious to recruit cardinals from beyond the Alps. The process initiated by Leo IX *ca.* 1050, of transforming the cardinalate from a Roman into an international institution continued throughout the twelfth century. However, from the information available concerning the origins of members of the college – covering between three-fifths and three-quarters of the cardinals of the twelfth century – it is also clear that throughout this period a substantial proportion of the college was Roman in origin. The Roman cardinals were predominantly either members of important noble families or chaplains and subdeacons in the Roman curia. The former were presumably promoted in most cases for political reasons, the latter for their usefulness to the papal government. The former Roman chaplains and subdeacons constituted the largest single component of the twelfth-century college: more than thirty in all in the course of the century.[49] The principal qualification of the non-Roman cardinals must usually have been what Cardinal Peter of S. Grisogono called their 'morality, knowledge of letters and religion'. Their promotion was intended to maintain the reforming tone of the college: hence the practice of appointing members of religious orders, which continued throughout the twelfth century.[50] Nevertheless a number of non-Roman cardinals had aristocratic and even royal connections and they may well have been appointed for political as well as reforming reasons.

The structure of the college of cardinals in the first two decades of the twelfth century was determined by the appointments of Paschal II. Two of his appointees became the rival pope and antipope in the

---

[48] Zenker, *Mitglieder* (n. 40) pp. 41, 132; Pfaff, 'Kardinäle' (n. 40) pp. 86, 91, 92.
[49] Elze, 'Kapelle' (n. 16) pp. 164–7; H. Tillmann, 'Ricerche sull'origine dei membri del collegio cardinalizio nel XII secolo', *Rivista di Storia della Chiesa in Italia* 24 (1970), 441–64; 26 (1972), 313–53; 29 (1975), 363–402.
[50] See below pp. 213–23.

schism of 1130: Gregory of S. Angelo (Innocent II) and Peter
Pierleone of SS. Cosma e Damiano (Anacletus II). A third, Theobald
Boccapecus of S. Anastasia, became pope for a few hours on
16 December 1124; a fourth, Lambert of Ostia, replaced him as pope
(Honorius II) and a fifth, Conrad of S. Pudenziana, became pope as
Anastasius IV. During Paschal II's eighteen-and-a-half-year pontifi-
cate, he created sixty-six cardinals. The pioneering study of Hans-
Walther Klewitz (1936) attempted to establish the origins of the
three-quarters of these cardinals for whom some record survives. Of
Paschal's appointees, nine were former papal chaplains and one a
former subdeacon of the Roman church. Perhaps twelve cardinals in
all were of Roman origin; six came from the Patrimony of St Peter,
eight from imperial Italy, two from France, three from Germany.
Ten cardinals originated in that territory which *ca.* 1100 was of the
greatest strategic importance for the reform papacy: southern Italy.[51]
The college created by Paschal II underwent a partial transformation
in the years 1121–3. In September 1121 an epidemic carried off
'almost all the abler cardinals' and in the subsequent two years
Calixtus II appointed sixteen cardinals.[52] Those of his appointees for
whom firm evidence is available came from northern Italy and
France: Gerard of S. Croce in Gerusalemme (the future Lucius II) and
Peter Rufus of SS. Martino e Silvestro, both from Bologna; Hubert
of S. Maria in Via Lata from Pisa; Giles of Tusculum from Toucy
(near Auxerre) and the Burgundian Haimeric of S. Maria Nuova,
who seems also to have had a Bolognese connection, as a regular
canon of S. Maria in Rheno.[53] Similar appointments were made by
Calixtus' successor, Honorius II: Matthew of Albano from Rheims,
the Tuscan Guido of S. Mari. in Via Lata (the future Celestine II)
from Castello, Albert of S. Teodoro from Florence, Stephen of S.
Lucia from Venice.[54] Our information is incomplete; but the surviving evidence certainly suggests the conclusion drawn by Hans-

---

[51] Klewitz, *Reformpapsttum* (n. 1) pp. 101–5; but see Tillmann, 'Ricerche' (1970)
    pp. 442–6. For Theobald Boccapecus see below pp. 65–6, 69.
[52] Pandulf, *Vita Calixti II: Liber pontificalis* 2, 323 (see below p. 381). See Hüls, *Kar-
    dinäle* (n. 1) pp. 116–17, 142–3, 149, 152–4, 162, 164, 183–4, 193, 196, 199, 205,
    220–1, 225–6, 230–6, 238, 240–3; Schmale, *Schisma* (n. 40) pp. 47–51; L. Pellegrini,
    'Cardinali e curia sotto Callisto II (1119–1124)' in *Raccolta di Studi in memoria di
    Sergio Mochi Onory* (Contributi dell'Istituto di storia medioevale 2, Pubblicazioni
    dell' Università Cattolica del Sacra Cuore, Scienze storiche 15: Milan, 1972)
    pp. 507–56.
[53] Hüls, *Kardinäle* (n. 1) pp. 142–3, 162, 164, 193, 220, 236, 238.
[54] Schmale, *Schisma* (n. 40) pp. 52–6.

Walther Klewitz (1939) and Franz-Josef Schmale (1961): that Calixtus II and Honorius II appointed north Italian and French cardinals to act as a counterweight to the Roman and southern Italian survivors from the pontificate of Paschal II.[55] Klewitz regarded this change in the personnel of the college, coinciding with the concordat of Worms, which brought the end of the Investiture Contest, as a principal factor contributing to what he called 'the end of the reform papacy'. The new cardinals reacted against the strategies of the Gregorian papacy – alliance with the Normans of southern Italy against the empire, alliance with the monasteries against the episcopate – and sought to return to the traditional strategies, seeking protection from the emperor and cooperating with the bishops in the reform of the Church. The tensions in the college between the 'new' and 'old' cardinals, according to Klewitz and Schmale, first revealed themselves in the papal election of 1124 and subsequently caused the papal schism of 1130.

In the light of this theory it is instructive to examine the appointments to the cardinalate of the two rival popes in the schism of 1130, the successful Innocent II and the antipope Anacletus II, respectively (according to Klewitz and Schmale) the candidates of the 'new' and the 'old' cardinals in the college of 1130. During his pontificate (1130–8) Anacletus II created seventeen cardinals, of whom six can be accurately identified: all were former subdeacons of the Roman church. Innocent II, like his rival, was left with only half a college at the outbreak of the schism: by the end of his pontificate (1143) he had created approximately fifty cardinals and thereby completely remodelled the college. Of Innocent's cardinals none is known to have been a Roman subdeacon before 1130. Four came from Roman families (one of them from a great Roman family: Octavian of Monticelli, the future antipope Victor IV); seven came from northern Italy (two Lombards and five Tuscans, including Hubald Allucingoli, the future Lucius III); one came from Lotharingia; nine were French in origin (including seven members of religious orders).[56] The contrast seems obvious enough: Anacletus followed the 'conservative', Innocent the more 'innovatory', policy of recruit-

---

[55] H.-W. Klewitz, 'Das Ende des Reformpapsttums', *DA* 3 (1939), 372–412, here cited from the reprint: *idem, Reformpapsttum* (n. 1) pp. 209–59; Schmale, *Schisma* pp. 31–57, 79–80. See below pp. 67, 70–3, 215–16, 381–2, 444.

[56] Elze, 'Kapelle' (n. 16) p. 166; Zenker, *Mitglieder* (n. 40) p. 202; Tillmann, 'Ricerche' (1972) (n. 49) pp. 336–44; W. Maleczek, 'Das Kardinalskollegium unter Innocenz II. und Anaklet II.', *AHP* 19 (1981), 57.

ment. Anacletus, like Paschal II, looked to the lower echelons of the Roman clergy when reconstructing his college; Innocent, like Calixtus II and Honorius II, looked towards northern Italy and France. It is probable, however, that the appointments of both popes were governed more by necessity than by a conscious policy of recruitment. The obedience of Anacletus was confined to Rome, Latium and the Norman kingdom of southern Italy and his cardinals were inevitably drawn from this narrow area. The evidence suggests that the lesser Roman clergy remained in Rome with Anacletus rather than accompanying Innocent into exile, so that the latter was compelled to look elsewhere for recruits. The two areas which seem to have provided most of Innocent's non-Roman cardinals, Tuscany and France, were both areas where he spent a considerable part of his exile after 1130. It is worth noting that of his nine French cardinals, eight – Drogo and Alberic of Ostia, Stephen of Palestrina, Imar of Tusculum, Baldwin of S. Maria in Trastevere, Ivo of S. Lorenzo in Damaso, Chrysogonus of S. Prassede and Luke of SS. Giovanni e Paolo – had close ties with Innocent's most important champion in France, Bernard of Clairvaux.[57] Innocent's non-Roman cardinals were men whose reforming credentials and whose abilities had become known to the pope during his exile. Thus the circumstances of the schism of 1130 intensified the international character of the college and continued the development begun in the mid-eleventh century.

Writing to Eugenius III *ca.* 1150, Bernard of Clairvaux emphasised the importance of electing non-Romans to the college, in order to maintain the reforming character of the curia. 'You must summon from wherever you can elders, not young men, following the example of Moses (Numbers 11, 16) – that is, elders not in age but in morals . . . Surely they who are to judge the world must be chosen from the whole world?'[58] This advice seems to have been heeded. The twenty cardinals appointed by Eugenius III included two Frenchmen, one Lotharingian, four Tuscans – including three of his own compatriots from Pisa and the Sienese Roland of S. Marco (the future Alexander III) – two Lombards and one Englishman, Nicholas Breakspear (the future Hadrian IV). Eugenius also appointed two Romans and one Neapolitan. This last cardinal, John of SS. Sergio e Baccho, was perhaps the first southern Italian to be

---

57 Zenker, *Mitglieder* (n. 40) pp. 13–14, 19–20, 40–1, 45, 55, 78–9, 117, 136.
58 Bernard, *De consideratione* IV.4.9: (n. 20) 778BC.

promoted to the college for thirty years.[59] The largest single group among Eugenius' appointments was evidently that of the north Italians. This trend can also be seen in the appointments of his short-lived predecessor, Lucius II: one Roman (the nobleman Hyacinth Bobo, later Celestine III), one Frenchman, one Englishman (Robert Pullen, the first English cardinal), one Tuscan and two Lombards (the two papal kinsmen from Bologna, Guarinus of Palestrina and Hubald of S. Croce).[60] North Italians also formed the single largest territorial group among the appointments of Hadrian IV: two Tuscans and four Lombards. (He also appointed four Romans, one cardinal from the southern part of the Patrimony of St Peter, three south Italians and one Frenchman.)[61]

Altogether between 1130 and 1159 twenty-five north Italians – twelve Tuscans and thirteen Lombards – were appointed to the college, compared with nine Romans and seventeen non-Italians, of whom thirteen were Frenchmen. Pisa and Bologna were of particular importance, the former providing six cardinals and the latter three: both cities indeed were continuously represented by cardinals for most of the twelfth century.[62] The relatively large number of northern Italians in the mid-twelfth-century college presumably reflected the growing economic, political and intellectual importance of northern Italy in this period. In the 1130s the papacy obtained the lordship of lands in Tuscany, which were a significant source of papal revenues. (These Tuscan lands remained a central preoccupation of the papacy for the rest of the century.)[63] In addition the Tuscan cities of Pisa and Genoa were major sea-powers, whose fleets played a significant part in the papal history of the twelfth century. The Lombard city of Bologna was important as a centre of intellectual and spiritual life. The Bolognese schools were the principal European centre of secular and canon law studies, whose graduates began to be recruited to the college in the second quarter of the twelfth century. The Bolognese house of regular canons, S. Maria in Rheno, was one of the most influential Italian centres of the religious life, producing a pope and at least five cardinals during the twelfth century. The Tuscan congregation of S. Frediano in Lucca (also regular canons) was likewise influential as a religious centre and pro-

---

[59] Zenker, *Mitglieder* pp. 21, 148; 179; 20, 92, 96, 85; 112, 171; 36; 67, 80; 156.
[60] *Ibid.*, pp. 161–2; 104; 91; 134; 41, 132.
[61] *Ibid.*, pp. 23, 149–50; 56, 157, 118, 107; 48–9, 64, 95, 154; 168; 126, 73–4, 140; 180.
[62] *Ibid.*, pp. 199–202.
[63] On the 'Matildine lands' see below pp. 246, 449, 497, 501–2.

duced a pope and four cardinals in the course of the century.[64] In appointing north Italians to the college the pope was no doubt responding to these new intellectual and spiritual currents, just as he responded to the growing influence of the French schools and French religious houses by appointing to the cardinalate both those who were French by birth and those who had been educated or made their religious profession in France.[65]

The pontificate of Hadrian IV, like those of Calixtus II and Honorius II, was the prelude to a papal schism: the schism of 1159, which, like that of 1130, was preceded by the formation of rival factions in the college. One faction originally consisted of perhaps nine cardinals, led by the Roman cardinal, Octavian of S. Cecilia (later the antipope Victor IV) and was dedicated to the preservation of the papal alliance with the emperor, inaugurated in the 1120s. The other was a faction of thirteen cardinals, called by its enemies the 'Sicilian party', led by the Sienese cardinal and papal chancellor, Roland of S. Marco (later Alexander III): it favoured an alliance with the emperor's enemies, the king of Sicily and the Lombard cities.[66] Hadrian IV's biographer, Cardinal Boso of SS. Cosma e Damiano, the papal chamberlain and a member of the 'Sicilian party', claimed that Hadrian's own policy was that of the anti-imperial faction in the college. The 'Sicilian party' came into existence in order to implement the alliance with the king of Sicily which the pope had desired since 1155.[67] Boso's claim suggests the possibility that Hadrian may have attempted to change the character of the college by appointing cardinals favouring his own political strategy: a reconstruction of the college similar to that which Klewitz and Schmale detected in the pontificates of Calixtus II and Honorius II. The crucial question is that of the identity of the 'Sicilian party': did Hadrian create this faction by a systematic policy of recruitment? The names of the 'Sicilian party' are known to us from two papal diplomas of 28 June and 30 July 1159, which between them contain the subscriptions of thirteen cardinals who were with the pope in Anagni when he negotiated his controversial alliance with the Lombard cities which were currently resisting the decrees of

[64] See below pp. 219–20.
[65] P. Classen, 'La curia romana et le scuole di Francia nel secolo XII' in *Le istituzioni ecclesiastiche della 'societas christiana' dei secoli XI–XII* 1 (Miscellanea del Centro di Studi Medioevali 7: Milan, 1974), 432–6.
[66] See below pp. 78–9, 389, 470–2.
[67] Boso, *Vita Hadriani IV* (n. 45) pp. 394–5. See below pp. 470–1.

Emperor Frederick I. It was on this occasion that the 'Sicilian party' was alleged by its enemies to have conspired to elect one of themselves as Hadrian's successor.[68] Of these thirteen cardinals, Odo of S. Giorgio in Velabro had been appointed by Innocent II, Hubald of S. Croce by Lucius II and Roland of S. Marco and Odo of S. Nicola in carcere Tulliano by Eugenius III. Hubald Allucingoli had been recruited to the college by Innocent II, but was promoted to the cardinal bishopric of Ostia by Hadrian IV; Gregory of Sabina, also originally recruited by Innocent II, likewise owed his cardinal bishopric to Hadrian; Hildebrand of SS. Apostoli and John of S. Anastasia had both been recruited as cardinal deacons by Eugenius III, but promoted to cardinal priests by Hadrian; Bernard of Porto, originally recruited by Eugenius III, received his cardinal bishopric from Hadrian. Walter of Albano, Ardicius of S. Teodoro, Boso of SS. Cosma e Damiano and Peter of S. Eustachio were all recruited to the college by Hadrian.[69] Hadrian had therefore recruited four members of the 'Sicilian party' and had advanced five others within the college. The party was clearly to some extent the pope's own creation. It would, however, be an exaggeration to speak of a systematic policy of recruitment in the late 1150s; since Hadrian can also be found promoting a cardinal hostile to the policy of the 'Sicilian party'. In 1158 he advanced the cardinal deacon Guido of Crema to the title of cardinal priest of S. Maria in Trastevere, although he was the kinsman and ally of Cardinal Octavian of S. Cecilia, leader of the pro-imperial faction. (In September 1159 Guido played a leading part in the election of Octavian as 'Victor IV' and in 1164 he himself became 'Paschal III'.)[70] Evidently even the most determined pope was sometimes obliged to placate the hostile elements in the college.

In the disputed papal election of September 1159 the candidate of the 'Sicilian party', Alexander III, gained the support of ten previously uncommitted cardinals, giving him a clear majority, while the support of his rival, 'Victor IV', is said to have dwindled from nine to five cardinals.[71] The fact that he enjoyed the support of approximately three-quarters of the college meant that Alexander III, unlike Innocent II in 1130, was not compelled to carry out a large-

[68] Hadrian IV, *JL* 10577, 10579, *MPL* 188, 1637AB, 1638D, 1639A. See W. Madertoner, *Die zwiespältige Papstwahl des Jahres 1159* (dissertation: Vienna, 1978) pp. 37–47. See below pp. 79–80.

[69] Zenker, *Mitglieder* (n. 40) pp. 159, 132, 86, 171; 23, 48–9, 108, 73–4, 30–1; 39, 157, 150, 176.

[70] *Ibid.*, pp. 56–9; Madertoner, *Papstwahl* (n. 68) pp. 111–14.

[71] See below p. 83.

scale recruitment of cardinals at the beginning of his pontificate. Indeed during his whole twenty-two-year pontificate he appointed only thirty-four cardinals. Among these were three Romans, one cardinal from the Patrimony of St Peter, eight northern Italians (five Lombards and three Tuscans, with one cardinal each from Pisa and Bologna), four Frenchmen and one German.[72] This German cardinal (the first to be appointed since 1134) was the illustrious opponent of the emperor, Conrad of Wittelsbach, archbishop of Mainz. His promotion – first as cardinal priest of S. Marcello in 1165, then as cardinal bishop of Sabina in 1166 – was an acknowledgement of his services to the Alexandrine cause in Germany.[73] The relatively numerous northern Italian and French appointments reflect the circumstances of the schism of 1159–77. During the eighteen-year conflict of papacy and empire Alexander was particularly dependent on the political support of the Lombard cities. The learned and saintly Galdin of Milan, whom Alexander appointed to the college in 1165 and consecrated as archbishop of Milan in the following year, served as papal legate in Lombardy. He became the principal link between the pope and his Lombard allies and an indispensable champion of the papal cause.[74] Alexander also relied during the schism on the political and material assistance of the French church and kingdom. He spent three years and five months in exile in France between 1162 and 1165.[75] His appointments of French cardinals (like those of Innocent II in the 1130s) were intended as a means of keeping the Alexandrine curia in close touch with the church on which he greatly depended, but also as a means of introducing distinguished reformers and intellectuals into the college.

The latter motive was particularly emphasised in Alexander III's request of 1178 to his legate in France, Cardinal Peter of S. Grisogono, to suggest suitable French candidates for the cardinalate. The legate's recommendations indicate the two categories to which the pope attached importance: monks well known for their sanctity and austerity (Simon, prior of Mont-Dieu, Henry of Marcy, abbot of Clairvaux, Abbot Peter of St Rémi of Rheims, Abbot Bernered of

---

[72] J. M. Brixius, *Die Mitglieder des Kardinalkollegiums von 1130 bis 1181* (Berlin, 1912) pp. 60–7; Pacaut, *Alexandre III* pp. 270–3.

[73] See below pp. 91, 170, 487–8.

[74] G. Dunken, *Die politische Wirksamkeit der päpstlichen Legaten in der Zeit des Kampfes zwischen Kaisertum und Papsttum in Oberitalien unter Friedrich I.* (Historische Studien 209: Berlin, 1913) pp. 79–80, 168–71; M. Pacaut, 'Les légats d'Alexandre III (1159–1181)', *RHE* 50 (1955), 834–5. See below p. 494.

[75] See below pp. 283, 286–7, 484.

St Crépin) and eminent scholars (Peter Comestor, Gerard Puella, Bernard of Pisa).[76] *Magistri* – graduates of the schools of northern Italy and France – had begun to appear in the college in the second quarter of the twelfth century. The curia early showed a preference for graduates in law rather than in theology: a preference that is especially evident in the pontificate of Alexander III, who appointed six eminent lawyers to the college.[77] This recruitment of legal experts was a necessary response to the rapid expansion of the legal business of the papal curia in the later twelfth century. The development of the curia into the 'omnicompetent court of first instance for the whole of Christendom' ensured that the lawyer cardinals would remain indispensable to the papacy.[78] The last four popes of the twelfth century had themselves been students of law: they inaugurated a series of lawyer popes which, with few exceptions, extended into the fourteenth century.

The emergence of the lawyers as an influential group was the first of the two major developments which altered the character of the college of cardinals in the late twelfth century: it was Alexander III's main contribution to the history of the college of cardinals. The second development was the work of Clement III, whose pontificate saw the last large-scale creation of cardinals of the twelfth century. As we have seen, Clement inherited a greatly diminished college, estimated at between eighteen and twenty cardinals, too small a number to carry out the regular duties of the college, notably the more important papal legations, which were now reserved for cardinals. Clement III therefore carried out three major series of promotions: in March 1188 (twelve cardinals), in May 1189 (an unspecified number) and in October 1190 (eleven cardinals). This creation of approximately thirty cardinals within a period of two-and-a-half years constitutes the most rapid transformation in the personnel of the college during the twelfth century. Clement's promotions also reversed the trend established in the 1120s and intermittently visible ever since. For the majority of the cardinals appointed by this Roman pope, connected with a number of the Roman aristocratic clans, were his compatriots. Clement III's pro-

---

[76] Peter of S. Grisogono, *Epistola* (n. 47) 1370D–1372A.
[77] Brixius, *Mitglieder* (n. 72) pp. 61, 63–4, 66–7; Pacaut, *Alexandre III* pp. 271, 275; B. Smalley, *The Becket conflict and the schools* (Oxford, 1973) p. 143. See below pp. 221, 483.
[78] F. W. Maitland, *Roman canon law in the Church of England* (London, 1898) p. 104. See below pp. 185–6.

motions reflected the fact that at the beginning of his pontificate the papacy had made peace with the city of Rome after forty-five years of conflict with the Roman commune which had frequently sent popes on their travels. The most important achievement of his pontificate was the papal treaty with the Roman senate (31 May 1188), which restored Rome to the lordship of the pope. Clement's appointments to the cardinalate were presumably intended to strengthen this papal accord with the Romans. For his new cardinals were members of the same great Roman families – the families of Malabranca, de Papa, Bobone–Orsini, Conti–Poli, Cenci, Pierleoni, Crescentii – who dominated the Roman senate.[79] At Clement's death there were eighteen Roman cardinals, comprising approximately three-fifths of the college. His successor, Celestine III, the Roman nobleman Hyacinth Bobo, recruited relatively few cardinals (perhaps only six or seven): of these, four were Romans, including two of the pope's nephews.[80] Celestine clearly had no intention of reducing the Roman aristocratic predominance established by his predecessor. The motive for creating this Roman predominance was political: the purpose was to make Rome a secure refuge for the papacy at a time of growing tension between papacy and empire.[81] For reasons of security the last two popes of the twelfth century gave the college a much less 'international' character. This did not, however, mean a deterioration in the spiritual and intellectual tone of the college. It still contained monks and regular canons, scholars and lawyers, men of saintly reputation and men of great practical ability – notably Cardinal Lothar of SS. Sergio e Baccho (soon to be Innocent III) and Cardinal Cencius of S. Lucia in Orthea, the papal chamberlain (later Honorius III). Even after the 'Romanization' of *ca.* 1190 the college of cardinals was still first and foremost an instrument of reform and the qualifications for membership were still those stipulated by Alexander III in 1178: 'morality, knowledge of letters and religion'.

---

[79] Pfaff, 'Clemens III.' (n. 40) pp. 269, 280; K. Wenck, 'Die römischen Päpste zwischen Alexander III. und Innocenz III. und der Designationsversuch Weihnachten 1197' in *Papsttum und Kaisertum. Forschungen zur politischen Geschichte und Geisteskultur des Mittelalters. Paul Kehr zum 65. Geburtstag dargebracht* ed. A. Brackmann (Munich, 1926) pp. 440–1 (estimating the number of promotions at 25).

[80] Wenck, 'Päpste' (n. 79) pp. 441, 454–6; Pfaff, 'Kardinäle' (n. 40) pp. 84–93.

[81] See below p. 509.

THE ELECTION OF THE POPE

In the eleventh and twelfth centuries an election – whether of pope, bishop, abbot or king – was regarded above all as a religious experience, both for the electors and for the elect. The electors met together so that the will of God might express itself through the unanimity of their election.[82] Hence an imperial chaplain in the early eleventh century could say of the election of a German king in 1024: 'I believe that the favour of heavenly grace was not lacking from this election'; and could add that those princes who left the assembly without acknowledging the king elect, did so 'at the instigation of the devil, the enemy of peace'.[83] Hence also a well-wisher of Gregory VII, Abbot Walo of Metz, could write on the occasion of the pope's election in 1073: 'where, I ask, could so great a unanimity, so great a harmony originate, except in the inspiration of the [Holy] Spirit?'[84] An election must culminate in a divinely inspired *unanimitas*, which was usually induced by following the electoral procedures prescribed in the case of royal elections by ancestral custom and in the case of ecclesiastical elections, by canon law. The procedures for electing a pope had, as we have already seen, been remodelled as recently as 1059. The Papal Election Decree of that year remained in force for a century and fifteen elections took place during this period, ostensibly according to the procedures which it prescribed. After the papal schism of 1159–77 had demonstrated the need for new legislation, the decree of 1059 was superseded in the Third Lateran Council of 1179 by a new decree regulating the election of the pope, *Licet de evitanda*, which still remained in force into the twentieth century. (The sixteenth-century ecclesiastical historian Onuphrius Panvinius claimed that after the earlier schism of the 1130s Innocent II had presented a papal election decree to the Second Lateran Council of 1139; but the decree which Panvinius cited is undoubtedly spurious.)[85]

The disputed elections of 1130 and 1159 revealed the dangers inherent in a papal election: the existence of factions among the electors might make *unanimitas* impossible. The elections of the late

[82] P. Schmid, *Der Begriff der kanonischen Wahl in den Anfängen des Investiturstreits* (Stuttgart, 1926) pp. 151–71; Krause, *Papstwahldekret* (n. 8) pp. 28–34.

[83] Wipo, *Gesta Chuonradi II imperatoris* c. 2, *MGH SS rer. Germ.*, 1915, p. 19.

[84] Walo of Metz, *Epistola* in J. M. Watterich, *Pontificum Romanorum Vitae* I (Leipzig, 1862), 741.

[85] O. Panvinius, *De cardinalium origine* ed. A. Mai, *Spicilegium Romanum* 9 (Rome, 1843), 502–6. See J. B. Sägmüller, 'Ein angebliches Papstwahldekret Innocenz' II. 1139', *Theologische Quartalschrift* 84 (1902), 364–87.

eleventh century indicated another danger, that of delay. On the death of Gregory VII (25 May 1085) a year elapsed before his successor, Victor III, was elected (24 May 1086) and almost another year passed by before the new pope was consecrated (9 May 1087). After Victor III's death (16 September 1087) there was a delay of six months before the election of Urban II (12 March 1088). These dangerous delays, readily exploited by Emperor Henry IV and his antipope, 'Clement III', indicate the paralysis of the Gregorian reform party in the years 1085–8, induced by political setbacks and internal disagreements. The successes of Urban II's pontificate ended this paralysis. Only a fortnight intervened between Urban's death (29 July 1099) and the election of Paschal II; and only three days between Paschal's death (21 January 1118) and the election of Gelasius II. On the latter's death (29 January 1119) only four days elapsed before the election of Calixtus II, despite the fact that Gelasius died far from Rome, in the abbey of Cluny. In the seven papal elections of the following four decades the electors never again allowed more than four days to pass after the death of the pope. On two occasions (1130 and 1154) they proceeded to elect on the day after the pope's death; and in the case of Eugenius III (15 February 1145) the election took place on the very day of his predecessor's death. The disputed election of 1159 was an exception: the election began on the third day after the death of Hadrian IV, but then took four days to complete (4–7 September), still without reaching *unanimitas*. Of the six elections which took place in the two decades after the issuing of the decree *Licet de evitanda*, none took place more than two days after the death of the pope and three of these elections – Urban III (25 November 1185), Celestine III (10 April 1191) and Innocent III (8 January 1198) – took place on the day on which the preceding pope had died.[86] This haste was quite contrary to the requirements of the *Ordines Romani*, the ancient rules of procedure regulating the ceremonial life of the pope. According to the *Ordines* (as edited from 'books of antiquities' by Cardinal Albinus *ca.* 1188 and by the papal chamberlain Cencius in 1192) the meeting of the electors should take place on the third day following the death of the pope, so as to allow time for the solemnities of the funeral: a regu-

---

[86] The data is found in P. Jaffé, *Regesta pontificum Romanorum* 1–2. But see V. Pfaff, 'Feststellungen zu den Urkunden und dem Itinerar Papst Coelestins III.', *HJb* 78 (1959), 132–4, with a correction of the date of the death of Clement III and the succession of Celestine III.

lation originating in the papal election decree of Boniface III of 606.[87] The electors were obliged to ignore this ancient regulation: they had learned to place speed and efficiency before customary solemnity in the sensitive matter of electing a pope.

According to the original version of the Papal Election Decree of 1059, 'on the death of the pontiff of this universal Roman church, firstly the cardinal bishops shall treat together with the greatest care, then they shall summon the cardinal clerks to them and then the rest of the clergy and the people shall approach to consent to the new election'.[88] As we have seen, the preeminent role of the cardinal bishops in the papal election was challenged in later versions of the decree of 1059 which substituted the word *cardinales* for 'cardinal bishops'. Whether the cardinal bishops in practice played the role which the original decree attributed to them is often difficult to decide from the surviving accounts of papal elections. To begin with the complex case of the election of Gregory VII on 22 April 1073: the official protocol (*Commentarius electionis*) survives; but it contains no reference to the cardinal bishops. 'Assembled in the basilica of S. Pietro in Vincoli, we – the cardinals, clerks, acolytes, subdeacons, deacons and priests of the holy Roman catholic and apostolic church, in the presence and with the consent of the venerable bishops and abbots, clerks and monks, and with the acclamation of very many crowds of both sexes and various orders – elected as our pastor and supreme pontiff . . . the archdeacon Hildebrand.'[89] These proceedings bear little resemblance either to the instructions of the decree of 1059 or to the account which Gregory VII himself gave of his election in six letters written on 26 and 28 April 1073.

> Suddenly, while our lord the pope [Alexander II] was being brought to the church of the Saviour for burial, there arose a great tumult and roaring of the people and they fell upon me like madmen, leaving no opportunity or time for speech or counsel, and forced me with violent hands into the place of apostolic rule.[90]

The narrative sources, both friendly and hostile, likewise speak of a tumultuous election and enthronement. When the German bishops, at the behest of King Henry IV, renounced their obedience to Gregory in January 1076, one of the reasons which they alleged was that his tumultuous election was against the terms of the decree of

---

[87] *Liber Censuum* 1, 311; 2, 123. Cf. *Liber pontificalis* 1, 316.
[88] Papal Election Decree of 1059, ed. Jasper, *Papstwahldekret* (n. 8) pp. 101–2.
[89] Gregory VII, *Registrum* I.1*, pp. 1–2.   [90] *Ibid.*, I.3, 4, pp. 5, 7.

1059, which required 'the election of the cardinals'.[91] However, most eleventh-century observers would have recognised in the turbulent election of 22 April 1073 an election 'by inspiration' (*per inspirationem*), in which mere human procedures were swept aside by the 'inspiration of God'.[92] The direct intervention of the Holy Spirit rendered the formalities of the Papal Election Decree superfluous.

Gregory VII's pontificate ended in defeat and exile: Henry IV installed his antipope 'Clement III' in Rome and Gregory had to be rescued from the city by his Norman vassal, the duke of Apulia and Calabria. As Gregory's entourage waited for his death in Salerno in May 1085, it was clear that the election of a successor at such a time of crisis would be extremely difficult. Therefore 'the bishops and cardinals' asked the dying pope whom he wished to succeed him and he named as suitable candidates Bishop Anselm II of Lucca (his legate in Lombardy and most trusted collaborator), Cardinal bishop Odo of Ostia and Archbishop Hugh of Lyons (his legate in France).[93] The decree of 1059 makes no reference to the right of the pope to designate his successor; but this procedure was recommended in an ancient text known to late eleventh-century canonists: the decree of the Roman synod of Pope Symmachus of 499. The electors of 1085 may have known it from the influential canon law handbook, the *Collection in 74 Titles*, or from the canonical collection of Anselm II of Lucca.[94] The death-bed consultation perhaps also bears witness to the prophetic reputation of a pope who had cast himself in the role of an Old Testament prophet.[95]

In the event it was Abbot Desiderius of Monte Cassino who after many delays succeeded Gregory as Victor III. According to the chronicle of Monte Cassino, on 23 May 1086 in the church of S. Lucia in Rome, Desiderius, who was organising the election

---

[91] Synod of Worms, 1076: *MGH Dt. Ma.* 1, 67–8. See A. Fliche, 'L'élection de Grégoire VII', *Le Moyen Age* ser. 2, 26 (1924), 71–90; I. S. Robinson, *Authority and resistance in the Investiture Contest* (Manchester, 1978) pp. 33–9.

[92] Schmid, *Begriff* (n. 82) pp. 151–5.

[93] *Hildesheimer Briefe* 35: *Briefsammlungen der Zeit Heinrichs IV.*, MGH *Briefe der deutschen Kaiserzeit* 5, 75–6. See H. E. J. Cowdrey, *The age of Abbot Desiderius of Monte Cassino* (Oxford, 1983) pp. 181–5.

[94] Symmachus, *Decretum synodale* c. 3, 4 ed. A. Thiel, *Epistolae Romanorum pontificum genuinae* 1 (Braunschweig, 1868), 641: *Diversorum patrum sententie sive Collectio in LXXIV titulos digesta* 174–6 ed. J. T. Gilchrist (Vatican City, 1973) pp. 110–11; Anselm of Lucca, *Collectio canonum* (n. 10) VI.1.

[95] C. Schneider, *Prophetisches Sacerdotium und heilsgeschichtliches Regnum im Dialog 1073–1077* (Münstersche Mittelalter-Schriften 9: Munich, 1972) pp. 19–22.

(perhaps in his capacity of senior cardinal priest), was himself compelled to accept the papal dignity. The chronicler described the electors on this occasion as 'both the bishops and the cardinals and the other Romans who remained faithful to St Peter, the prince of the apostles'. A few days later, however, Desiderius laid aside the papal insignia and he was only finally persuaded to resume them and to accept election on 21 March 1087 in Capua. His reluctance was overcome by 'the Roman bishops and cardinals', the Roman prefect Cencius 'with other noble Romans' and the Norman princes Jordan of Capua and Roger of Apulia.[96] In this, the most detailed account of the election of Victor III, there is no indication that the cardinal bishops played a preeminent role. Significantly, it was at approximately the same time as the election of 1086 that the canonist Deusdedit, cardinal priest of S. Pietro in Vincoli, compiled the discussion of papal elections in his *Collectio canonum* (dedicated to Victor III), a discussion which excludes the cardinal bishops from the election. The electors of the pope are the *cardinales*, meaning the cardinal priests and deacons: the rest of the Roman clergy must consent to their election. An election dominated by the emperor was automatically invalid, as was a tumultuous election precipitated by a crowd of laymen.[97] Deusdedit's opinions may well have been those of his fellow cardinal priests and they may indeed have influenced the election of 1086. There is at least one parallel between the Monte Cassino account of the election and Deusdedit's discussion. According to the chronicler, during the election of 23 May 1086 Abbot Desiderius tried to promote the candidature of Cardinal Odo of Ostia; but 'one of the cardinals declared that this election was against the canons and that he would never consent to it'. The explanation of this objection is perhaps to be found in Deusdedit's statement that the electors should choose the best of the cardinal priests or deacons of the Roman church: only in an emergency might they elect a clerk from another church. It is tempting to guess, but impossible to prove, that the anonymous cardinal who turned the electors against Odo of Ostia in 1086 was Deusdedit of S. Pietro in Vincoli. However, the chronicle of Monte Cassino also records that on his deathbed in

---

[96] *Chronica monasterii Casinensis* III.66, 68, *MGH SS* 34, 448–9, 450. See Cowdrey, *Desiderius* (n. 93) pp. 187–206. See below p. 414.

[97] Deusdedit, *Collectio canonum* I.168–9, 256–7, 320; II.100, 113; III.280; IV.13, 18, 20: (n. 10) pp. 107, 146–7, 187, 228, 240–1, 385–9, 406, 409–10. See Cowdrey, *Desiderius* pp. 188–90.

September 1087 Victor III designated Odo as his successor.[98] It was
a measure which was intended – but which failed – to prevent a long
vacancy.

On 12 March 1088 Cardinal bishop Odo I of Ostia was elected to
the papacy as Urban II; and on this occasion the procedures of the
Papal Election Decree of 1059 were followed faithfully. The election, held at Terracina, in the south of the papal patrimony, consisted
of three sessions (8, 9 and 12 March). All six cardinal bishops were
present: Odo himself, John III of Porto, Peter of Albano, John III of
Tusculum, Bruno of Segni and Hubald of Sabina. (The see of
Palestrina was vacant.) The other two orders of cardinals participated in the election only through single representatives: Rainer of S.
Clemente (the future Paschal II) for the cardinal priests, Abbot
Oderisius of Monte Cassino for the cardinal deacons. The Roman
prefect Benedict was the representative 'of all the faithful laymen'
(that is, of Rome).[99] The proceedings at Terracina suggest a deliberate avoidance of the precedents of 1073 and 1086 – perhaps also a
conscious rejection of the opinions of Cardinal Deusdedit – and a
return to the authentic tradition of the decree of 1059. It is possible
that the election of Paschal II on 13 August 1099 likewise adhered to
the norms of the Papal Election Decree. The official papal biography
in the *Liber pontificalis* refers to the election only in vague terms: 'the
cardinals and bishops, the deacons and nobles of the city', together
with the lesser clergy, met in the church of S. Clemente, the titular
church of Cardinal Rainer, whom they 'suddenly' decided to elect.
But the biography then reveals that on the next day six of the cardinal
bishops – Odo II of Ostia, Maurice of Porto, Walter of Albano,
Bovo of Lavicum (Tusculum), Milo of Palestrina and Offo of Nepi
– were present at the consecration of the new pope: only Bruno of
Segni was absent.[100] The presence of six of the seven cardinal
bishops in Rome on 14 August suggests that they may have participated in the election of 13 August as the preeminent *ordo* of cardinals
and the foremost electors.

In 1088, therefore, and perhaps also in 1099, the cardinal bishops
actually exercised the right conferred on them by the Papal Election

---

[98] *Chronica monasterii Casinensis* III.66: (n. 96) p. 449; cf. Deusdedit, *Collectio canonum*
      I.111–12, 118, 233; II.161; IV.20: (n. 10) pp. 84, 86, 135–6, 268, 409–10. *Chronica
      monasterii Casinensis* III.73: pp. 455–6: see Cowdrey, *Desiderius* p. 216 n. 9.
[99] Urban II, *JL* 5348–9: (n. 16) 283A–285D. See Klewitz, *Reformpapsttum* (n. 1) pp. 39–
      40; Becker, *Urban II.* 1, 91–6.
[100] Petrus Pisanus, *Vita Paschalis II: Liber pontificalis* 2, 296–7. See Klewitz, *Reform-
      papsttum* p. 40; but see also Servatius, *Paschalis II.* pp. 33–5.

Decree of 1059. Of the next papal election, that of Gelasius II on 24 January 1118, there is a very detailed account in Cardinal Pandulf's biography of the pope, which claims that the cardinal bishops took no part in the election. According to Pandulf, four cardinal bishops, twenty-seven cardinal priests, eighteen cardinal deacons, the lesser Roman clergy and 'some of the [Roman] senators and consuls' met in the church of S. Maria in Pallara 'to carry out the election according to the decrees of the canons'. The chancellor, John of Gaeta, cardinal deacon of S. Maria in Cosmedin, was elected and 'was approved by all, including the bishops, who have no authority in the election of a Roman bishop except that of expressing approval or disapproval'.[101] However, Pandulf's account of the election of Gelasius II, written between 1133 and 1138, contains many inaccuracies. It includes details of twenty-seven cardinal priests and eighteen cardinal deacons who participated in the election, although there were only eighteen cardinal priests and twelve cardinal deacons in existence in January 1118, two at least of whom were not in Rome at the time of the election. Moreover Pandulf's biography had a polemical purpose, arising not out of the pontificate of Gelasius II, but out of the schism of 1130. Pandulf owed his promotion to the cardinalate (as cardinal deacon of SS. Cosma e Damiano) to the antipope Anacletus II; and he used his account of the election of Gelasius II as a means of defending the legality of the election of Anacletus. A significant weakness in Anacletus' position was that, although a majority of the cardinal priests and deacons had concurred in his election, only two of the cardinal bishops had supported him; while his rival, Innocent II, could boast the support of five cardinal bishops. Hence Pandulf's determination to prove in his account of Gelasius II's election that the cardinal bishops 'have no authority in the election of a Roman bishop'.[102] Pandulf deliberately misrepresented the election of 1118; and the reader is bound to suspect that, in denying the cardinal bishops any role in the election, he was attempting to conceal the fact that they were able to play a major role.

The evidence suggests that Gelasius II, like Gregory VII and Victor III, participated in the selection of his successor. In 1119, as in 1085 and 1087, this measure was presumably adopted because of the current state of emergency: Gelasius II had been driven into exile in France and Emperor Henry V had established his antipope 'Gregory

---

[101] Pandulf, *Vita Gelasii II: Liber pontificalis* 2, 312–13.
[102] Fürst, 'Wähler Gelasius' II.' (n. 40) pp. 71–6.

VIII' (Maurice of Braga) in Rome. One version of the designation story was recorded by the chronicler Falco of Benevento. On his deathbed in the abbey of Cluny (January 1119) Gelasius sent for the formidable Cardinal bishop Cuno of Palestrina and 'strove to impose on him the highest honour of the Roman see'. But Cuno, declining the honour, suggested that Archbishop Guido of Vienne should be elected 'and the speech pleased the sick Pope Gelasius and the rest of the cardinals and all the other bishops'. On his arrival in Cluny, Guido 'was prevailed on to accept the papal office, since Gelasius was sick and willed this'.[103] Falco supposed that the new pope, Calixtus II, was elected before Gelasius' death; but it is clear from Calixtus' own account that he arrived at Cluny after the death of his predecessor. He was elected on 2 February, four days after Gelasius' death.[104] A different version of the designation story is found in the *History of Compostela*. 'Pope Gelasius, being on the brink of death, prophesied to the Roman clergy and people that either [Guido of Vienne] or Abbot Pontius of Cluny . . . would be elected Roman pontiff.' When Guido was elected, Pontius insisted that envoys be sent to Rome to seek the approval of the Roman clergy and people. The chronicler Geoffrey of Vigeois told a similar story, alleging that Pontius' disappointment at not being elected pope prompted him to insist on this ratification of Calixtus' election.[105] It is at least certain that the electors at Cluny sought the approval of their colleagues in Rome; for six letters of ratification are extant, addressed to 'our brothers, the cardinal bishops of St Peter who are beyond the mountains', 'the cardinals and other clerks and laymen who were with Pope Gelasius'. These letters were sent by Cardinal bishop Peter of Porto, whom Gelasius had left as his vicar in Rome, by the other cardinal bishops in Rome, by the cardinal priests and the cardinal deacons; and their message was: 'since we are prevented from making the election in the Roman manner, we consent with due charity to the election which you have made.'[106] These letters ratifying the election of Calixtus II serve to underline how small was the number of electors in Cluny on 2 February 1119. The leading figure in the election was undoubtedly Cardinal bishop Cuno of Palestrina.

[103] Falco of Benevento, *Chronicon* 1119 in *Cronisti e scrittori sincroni napoletani editi e inediti* ed. G. del Re 1 (Naples, 1845), 180. See below p. 230.
[104] Calixtus II, *JL* 6682, *MPL* 163, 1093AB. See G. Meyer von Knonau, *Jahrbücher des Deutschen Reiches unter Heinrich IV. und Heinrich V.* 7 (Leipzig, 1909), 108–9.
[105] *Historia Compostellana* II.9: (n. 33) 1043B; II.14: 1051A–1053A. Cf. Geoffrey of Vigeois, *Chronicon* c. 42, *MGH SS* 26, 200.
[106] *Codex Udalrici* nos. 192–7, ed. P. Jaffé, *Bibliotheca rerum Germanicarum* 5, 348–52.

The only other elector whose identity can be established with certainty was Cardinal bishop Lambert of Ostia.[107] It is clear that, although his electors were few in number, Calixtus had complete confidence in the legality of his election and did not wait to be informed of the ratification of the election before taking up his office. It was on 1 March that Peter of Porto secured the consent of the Romans to Calixtus' election; but he had already been crowned in the cathedral of Vienne on 9 February.[108]

The election of Calixtus' successor on 16 December 1124 almost led to a schism. After Theobald Boccapecus, cardinal priest of S. Anastasia, had been elected and was already being installed as 'Celestine II', the ceremony was interrupted and a new election held, in which Cardinal bishop Lambert of Ostia was elected as Honorius II. In the most detailed of the surviving narratives this turbulent election is presented in the context of the power struggle of the two great Roman noble clans, the Frangipani and the Pierleoni, and in particular of the attempt of the three Frangipani brothers, Cencius II, Leo II and Robert I, to gain control of the papacy.[109] During the pontificate of Paschal II the pope had been the close ally of the Pierleoni, who were his most reliable supporters in Rome. On Paschal's death, therefore, the Frangipani had been determined to control the election of his successor. On 24 January 1118, immediately after the election of Gelasius II, 'the enemy and disturber of the peace Cencius Frangipane, hissing like a monstrous dragon', had broken into the church of S. Maria in Pallara and 'dragged [Gelasius] by the hair and arms' into captivity.[110] The Frangipani regarded Gelasius with suspicion because he had been an ally of the Pierleoni since at least 1116.[111]

[107] Orderic Vitalis also identified 'Boso of Porto' (meaning Boso, cardinal priest of S. Anastasia?) and John of Crema, cardinal priest of S. Grisogono: *Historia ecclesiastica* XII.21 (n. 18) p. 254.

[108] Meyer von Knonau, *Jahrbücher* (n. 104) 7, 110–12.

[109] Pandulf, *Vita Honorii II: Liber pontificalis* 2, 327; biography of Honorius II in the Tortosa manuscript: J. M. March, *Liber pontificalis prout extat in codice manuscripto Dertusensi* (Barcelona, 1925) pp. 203–5. See F. Ehrle, 'Die Frangipani und der Untergang des Archivs und der Bibliothek der Päpste am Anfang des 13. Jahrhunderts' in *Mélanges offerts à M. Emile Chatelain par ses élèves et ses amis* (Paris, 1910) pp. 455–7.

[110] Pandulf, *Vita Gelasii II* (n. 101) p. 313. See P. F. Palumbo, *Lo scisma del MCXXX. I precedenti, la vicenda romana e le ripercussioni europee della lotta tra Anacleto e Innocenzo II* (Miscellanea della Deputazione romana di storia patria 13: Rome, 1942) pp. 114–27; Schmale, *Schisma* (n. 40) pp. 18–20.

[111] Ekkehard of Aura, *Chronica* III ed. F.-J. Schmale and I. Schmale-Ott (Ausgewählte Quellen zur deutschen Geschichte des Mittelalters 15: Darmstadt, 1972) p. 320. See Schmale, *Schisma* p. 19.

Petrus Leonis, the head of the Pierleone clan, together with his allies, had secured Gelasius' release; and the pope had subsequently taken refuge from the Frangipani and their ally, the emperor, in France. His successor, Calixtus II, had been elected out of reach of the Roman factions, in Cluny; but he had owed the ratification of his election in Rome to the efforts of Petrus Leonis.[112] It was obvious that the Frangipani would seize the opportunity of the election of December 1124 in Rome to impose their own papal candidate.

According to the account of Cardinal Pandulf, the candidate supported by Leo Frangipane was Cardinal bishop Lambert of Ostia (Honorius II). On the eve of the election, however, Leo pretended to support the candidate whom 'all the people asked for': Saxo, cardinal priest of S. Stefano in Celio monte, a member of the Conti family of Anagni. At first the electors feared to meet, 'remembering the fate of Pope Gelasius'; but eventually on 16 December (after observing the three-day delay required by the *Ordines Romani*) 'the bishops and cardinals' assembled in the monastery of St Pancratius. No more was heard of the candidature of Cardinal Saxo. After a short discussion Jonathan, cardinal deacon of SS. Cosma e Damiano (a close associate of the Pierleoni) proposed the election of Cardinal Theobald of S. Anastasia, of the noble Roman family of the Boccapecorini, 'with the approval of all, including Bishop Lambert [of Ostia]'. Theobald, taking the papal name 'Celestine', was ceremonially clad in the purple mantle of the papal office and the clergy began to sing the *Te Deum*; but these ceremonies were interrupted by the intrusion of Robert Frangipane. The military might of the Frangipani was sufficient to compel Petrus Leonis and the other Roman nobles to join in acclaiming Lambert of Ostia as Honorius II in the Lateran basilica (situated next-door to the monastery of St Pancratius). 'They were all compelled . . . to adore [Honorius], although he savoured of evil'. Theobald-Celestine resigned his office. On the following day, however, the lawful electors, under the leadership of the senior cardinal bishop, Peter of Porto, tried to regain control of the situation; but 'Honorius did not relinquish [the office] since, as a learned man, he remembered the profound avarice of the Romans'. During the following night Leo Frangipane and the papal chancellor Haimeric bribed Petrus Leonis with the promise of the city of Terracina and his ally, the Roman prefect Peter, with the fortress of Formello. These timely bribes brought about a unanimous acceptance of Honorius, who was crowned on Sunday, 21 December. The most detailed

[112] Meyer von Knonau, *Jahrbücher* (n. 104) 7, 113; Schmale, *Schisma* p. 20.

account of Honorius' election, therefore, presents it as a Frangipane plot; but this account was written after the outbreak of the schism of 1130 by an adherent of the Pierleone pope Anacletus II. The author's intention was to blacken the reputations of the Frangipani, because they had supported Anacletus' rival, Innocent II, in the early days of the schism.

Perhaps the most telling detail in the account is the revelation that one of the fellow conspirators of the Frangipani was Haimeric, cardinal deacon of S. Maria Nuova. Haimeric was appointed chancellor by Calixtus II in 1123 and held this office until his death in 1141, during which period he was the most influential politician in the papal curia. It is hard to believe that so astute a politician could be the dupe of the Frangipani; and equally hard to cast his candidate, Honorius – a Bolognese of humble birth, a regular canon of S. Maria in Rheno, austere and capable – as the puppet of an aristocratic Roman faction. When Haimeric cooperated with the Frangipani in December 1124 to secure the succession of Honorius II, was he pursuing his own private ambitions? H.-W. Klewitz (1939) and F.-J. Schmale (1961) have suggested that Haimeric was acting in 1124 (as he was to act again in 1130) as the leader of a faction in the college of cardinals, mainly composed of the 'new' cardinals created by Calixtus II between 1121 and 1124. Schmale has argued that the spiritual and political outlook of these 'new' cardinals differed in important respects from that of the 'old' cardinals, the survivors from the pontificate of Paschal II. The 'old' cardinals adhered to 'Gregorian' values and to the strategies of the Investiture Contest. The 'new' cardinals, often products of the new religious orders of *ca.* 1100, adopted the strategy of the concordat of Worms (1122), which had made peace between papacy and empire.[113] Haimeric's faction was very small in 1124. Klewitz calculated its size by assuming that those cardinals surviving from 1124 who supported Haimeric's candidate in 1130 must also have supported his candidate in 1124. This produces the figure of ten cardinals, less than a quarter of the college. (The faction was to be enlarged considerably by the promotions of Honorius II.)[114] It was this numerical inferiority in the college, Klewitz argued, which compelled Haimeric to use the dangerous weapon of the Frangipani in order to impose his candidate on the electors. The Frangipani had, of course, attempted before on

---

[113] Klewitz, *Reformpapsttum* (n. 1) pp. 243–7; Schmale, *Schisma* pp. 120–3. See above p. 49 and below pp. 70–3, 215–16, 381–2, 444.
[114] Klewitz, *Reformpapsttum* (n. 1) p. 243.

their own initiative to intervene in a papal election: on that occasion, in 1118, they had been defeated by the Pierleoni and the other noble clans. But in 1124 the Frangipani were able to overawe their rivals. This was because their power had been enhanced by Calixtus II, who had given them the command of the papal guards: an action inspired, Klewitz believed, by the papal adviser Haimeric. The chancellor had already begun his preparations before the death of Calixtus. When the papal vacancy occurred, he was able to mastermind the election, using the Frangipani as his instruments.[115]

The theory that Haimeric had laid his plans during Calixtus II's pontificate can only be conjectural; as also is the idea that the chancellor was acting as the leader of a faction of cardinals. What is certain about the events of 16–21 December 1124 is that the objectives of Haimeric and the Frangipani coincided. Both wished to prevent the election of a pope approved by the Pierleoni, not only because this would increase Pierleone influence in Rome but also for broader strategical reasons. Since the late eleventh century, the Pierleoni had been the allies of the Norman princes of Sicily, who as papal vassals had aided the papacy in the struggle against the emperor.[116] The Frangipani had become the allies of the emperor in 1116, hoping that the imperial presence would act as a counterweight to the Pierleoni in Rome.[117] Cardinal Haimeric feared the growing power of the Norman prince Roger II of Sicily and looked to the emperor for protection against this dangerous neighbour.[118] Both Haimeric and the Frangipani, therefore, desired a pope who was hostile towards Roger II and friendly towards the emperor. Cardinal Lambert of Ostia, as one of the negotiators of the concordat of Worms in 1122, evidently fulfilled their requirements. Tradition associates both Lambert-Honorius and Haimeric with the house of S. Maria in Rheno in Bologna.[119] If the two cardinals had indeed been brethren in religion, it is easy to understand why Lambert was the chancellor's preferred candidate. Cardinal Saxo of S. Stefano, the popular favourite on the eve of the election of 1124, had also participated in the negotiation of the concordat of Worms, but this does not seem to have recommended him to the conspirators. Since he figured in the election of 1130 as a prominent supporter of Anacletus II, it is poss-

[115] *Ibid.*, p. 245.
[116] J. Deér, *The dynastic porphyry tombs of the Norman period in Sicily* (Dumbarton Oak Studies 5: Cambridge, Mass., 1959) pp. 121–2. See above p. 49 and below p. 382.
[117] Palumbo, *Scisma* (n. 110) p. 114; Schmale, *Schisma* (n. 40) pp. 19–20.
[118] See below p. 444.   [119] See below p. 215.

ible that he was already a known supporter of the Pierleoni in 1124.[120] The candidature of Theobald-Celestine is at first sight the most puzzling aspect of the election of 1124. He was proposed by the pro-Pierleoni cardinal Jonathan of SS. Cosma e Damiano; but the candidate himself seems to have been more closely associated with the Frangipani than with the Pierleoni. (For twenty years, as cardinal deacon of S. Maria Nuova, he had served a church in the immediate neighbourhood of the Frangipane stronghold.)[121] Perhaps the advanced age of Theobald-Celestine provides the clue to his election: he was intended as a stop-gap who would be acceptable to the Frangipani. His candidature may indeed have been an attempt by Haimeric's opponents in the college to detach the Frangipani from their alliance with the chancellor – in which case they had clearly underestimated Haimeric's ruthless determination.

The disputed election of 14 February 1130, resulting in an eight-year papal schism, undoubtedly had many elements in common with that of 1124. One element was the Roman power struggle of the Pierleoni and the Frangipani. Another was the continuing determination of Cardinal Haimeric to secure the election of a pope after his own heart, another cardinal who had participated in the negotiation of the concordat of Worms, Gregory of S. Angelo in Pescheria (Innocent II). The rival factions in the college of cardinals which can only be conjectured in 1124, are clearly visible in 1130. The two groups of electors in the double election of 14 February stand revealed as the allies and the opponents of Haimeric, the electors respectively of Innocent II and Anacletus II. There are two significant ways in which the situation of 1130 differed from that of 1124. Firstly, the power of the Pierleoni was evidently greater in 1130 than it had been six years earlier. Cardinal Boso, the biographer of Innocent II, described how in 1130 the Pierleoni 'strove to buy the greater part of the venal city, corrupting the great and oppressing the small. The populace was so closely allied to [the antipope] that there was no protection for Pope Innocent in the city except for the fortifications of the Frangipani and the Corsi.'[122] When Innocent II went into exile in May 1130, Leo and Cencius Frangipani submitted to the Pierleone pope. It is likely that the Pierleone family had enhanced its power in Rome by supporting the demands for independence, characteristic of the Italian cities in this period, which eventually

[120] Schmale, *Schisma* (n. 40) pp. 63–5.
[121] Klewitz, *Reformpapsttum* (n. 1) pp. 244–5; Hüls, *Kardinäle* (n. 1) pp. 235–6.
[122] Boso, *Vita Innocentii II: Liber pontificalis* 2, 380.

resulted in the foundation of the Roman commune in 1143, with Jordan Pierleone (brother of Anacletus II) as its leading figure.[123] A second way in which the situation of 1130 differed from that of 1124 was that the number of cardinals who supported Haimeric had been increased by the promotions of Honorius II's pontificate. Of the twelve cardinals created by Honorius who survived to participate in the election of 1130, nine supported Innocent and only three supported Anacletus.[124] Honorius' promotions did not, however, give the 'Haimeric faction' a majority in the college. At the beginning of the schism Innocent was supported by nineteen or twenty cardinals and Anacletus by twenty-one.[125]

Anacletus II's most important supporter was the most senior cardinal in the college, Peter *Senex*, who had become cardinal bishop of Porto in 1102 and had already seen the pontificates of four popes. Early in the schism he wrote to the four cardinal bishops who had been among the original supporters of Innocent II – William of Palestrina, Matthew of Albano, Conrad of Sabina and John III of Ostia – denouncing Innocent's illicit election. Their conduct had been uncanonical because they were 'novices and very few in number' and they had acted 'without consulting the elder and more important brethren'.[126] Cardinal Peter's statement that Innocent's electors were 'novices' (*novitii*) seemed to Klewitz the essential clue to the division in the college which produced the double election of 1130. He showed that twelve of the cardinals who supported Anacletus (that is, over half of his supporters) had been appointed by Paschal II. Cardinals like Peter of Porto, Saxo of S. Stefano, Boniface of S. Marco, Gregory of S. Eustachio, Gregory of SS. Apostoli (Anacletus' successor as antipope 'Victor IV') and Oderisius of S. Agata (formerly abbot of Monte Cassino), who had been prominent figures in the college during Paschal's pontificate, formed the core of Anacletus' support in the college.[127] Of particular eminence was the jurist Peter Pisanus, cardinal priest of S. Susanna, Paschal II's closest adviser in legal matters: he 'had no equal (or scarcely any) in the curia', wrote John of Salisbury. Peter's erudition was so prized, even by his opponents, that although Innocent II deposed him for his sup-

[123] Palumbo, *Scisma* (n. 110) pp. 198, 291.

[124] Klewitz, *Reformpapsttum* (n. 1) p. 211; Schmale, *Schisma* (n. 40) p. 52.

[125] Klewitz, *Reformpapsttum* pp. 211–29; Schmale, *Schisma* pp. 32–3.

[126] Peter of Porto, *Epistola* in: William of Malmesbury, *Historia Novella* ed. K. R. Potter (London, 1955) p. 8. See Hüls, *Kardinäle* (n. 1) pp. 122–4.

[127] Klewitz, *Reformpapsttum* pp. 213–18; Schmale, *Schisma* pp. 57–64; Hüls, *Kardinäle* pp. 150–2, 186–7, 206–7, 221–2, 227.

port of the antipope, Innocent's learned successor, Celestine II restored Peter to the cardinalate.[128] Innocent himself had been appointed to the college by Paschal II; but among the cardinals who supported him, only two were of equal seniority: Cardinal bishop Conrad of Sabina (the future Anastasius IV) and John of Crema, cardinal priest of S. Grisogono. Of the other Innocentine cardinals, one owed his promotion to Gelasius II, seven were appointed by Calixtus II and nine by Honorius II. Of the Anacletan cardinals, only three were promoted by Calixtus and three by Honorius.[129] With few exceptions, therefore, the older cardinals supported Anacletus and the younger supported Innocent.

F.-J. Schmale's study of the schism of 1130 relates this division between the 'old' and 'new' cardinals to the impact on the college of the 'new spirituality' of *ca.* 1100: that is, the spirituality of the new orders of the Cistercians, the regular canons and Premonstratensians, with their emphasis on the apostolic life, the rejection of secular entanglements and respect for the role of the episcopate within the hierarchy of the Church. 'The Innocentine cardinals were representatives of all these aspirations. None of them belonged to the older Benedictine monasticism: the most important of them came from the regular canons or were closely connected with them.'[130] Innocent II himself was seen by contemporaries as closely associated with the regular canons.[131] Above all Cardinal Haimeric, the architect of Innocent's election, was intimately connected both with the canons (he was commemorated in the necrologies both of S. Maria in Rheno, Bologna and of St Victor in Paris) and with the central figure of the 'new spirituality', Bernard of Clairvaux, who regarded him as a model papal chancellor.[132] Schmale's study emphasises that the 'new' cardinals mainly originated – like their leader, the Burgundian Haimeric – in the areas most strongly influenced by the 'new spirituality': northern Italy and France. The 'old'

---

[128] John of Salisbury, *Policraticus* VIII.23 ed. C. C. A. Webb 2 (Oxford, 1909), 407. See Klewitz, *Reformpapsttum* pp. 214–15; Zenker, *Mitglieder* (n. 40) pp. 103–4; Hüls, *Kardinäle* pp. 210–11.

[129] Klewitz, *Reformpapsttum* pp. 211, 218–21; Schmale, *Schisma* pp. 34–79. See also the correction offered by Hüls, *Kardinäle* pp. 205, 231, in the case of Comes of S. Maria in Aquiro.

[130] F.-J. Schmale, 'Papsttum und Kurie zwischen Gregor VII. und Innocenz II.', *HZ* 193 (1961), 279, summarising his conclusions in *Schisma* pp. 43, 56–7. See below p. 215.

[131] Schmale, *Schisma* pp. 272–9.

[132] Bernard, *Epistola* 311: (n. 20) 513D–517C. See Schmale, *Schisma* pp. 124–44. See also below p. 95.

cardinals of the Anacletan party came mainly from Rome and southern Italy; their attitudes were rooted in the older Benedictine monasticism of the eleventh century and the ideals of the Gregorian papacy.[133] Schmale's analysis of these two factions in the college has been challenged on a number of points of detail by Gerd Tellenbach (1963), Peter Classen (1968), Helene Tillmann (1970, 1972, 1975) and Rudolf Hüls (1977). Most recently Werner Maleczek (1981) has subjected the analysis to full-scale criticism.[134] The effect of these revisions is to render far less clear-cut the contrasts which Schmale perceived between the Innocentine and the Anacletan factions. The presence of cardinals from France, Tuscany and Lombardy in the Innocentine faction is undeniable (two Frenchmen and six north Italians can be identified with certainty); although it is also possible to find a Frenchman (Giles of Tusculum) and a Tuscan (Peter Pisanus of S. Susanna) in the Anacletan faction.[135] Totally untenable is the theory that the faction of Anacletus was predominantly 'Roman', while that of Innocent was 'non-Roman'. Only one member of the Anacletan faction – the antipope himself, Peter Pierleone – is known to have belonged to a Roman family. Of the Innocentine faction, four cardinals seem to have been Romans: Innocent himself, (Gregory Papareschi), Conrad of Sabina, Gregory of SS. Sergio e Baccho and Rusticus of S. Ciriaco.[136] Similarly, the evidence does not fully sustain Schmale's contrast between an Anacletan faction rooted in the old Benedictine monasticism and an Innocentine faction closely allied with the new religious orders. Certainly two members of the Anacletan faction were former monks of Cluny (Anacletus himself and Giles of Tusculum) and two were former monks of Monte Cassino (Oderisius of S. Agata and Amicus of SS. Nereo e Achilleo); but information is lacking for their seventeen colleagues.[137] The evidence for linking the Innocentine faction with the regular canons is also very limited: only Gerard of S. Croce (later

---

[133] Schmale, *Schisma* pp. 56–7, 79–82. See below p. 215.

[134] G. Tellenbach, 'Der Sturz des Abtes Pontius von Cluny und seine geschichtliche Bedeutung', *QFIAB* 42/3 (1963), 13–55; P. Classen, 'Zur Geschichte Papst Anastasius' IV.', *ibid.*, 48 (1968), 36–63; Tillmann, 'Ricerche' (n. 49); Hüls, *Kardinäle* (n. 1) *passim*; Maleczek, 'Kardinalskollegium' (n. 56) pp. 27–78.

[135] Innocentine faction: Hüls, *Kardinäle* pp. 96–8, 108, 162–3, 164, 176–8, 193, 236, 239. Anacletan faction: Hüls pp. 142–3, 210–11. See Maleczek, 'Kardinals-kollegium' pp. 32–3.

[136] Hüls, *Kardinäle* pp. 128–9, 158, 223–4, 242; Maleczek, 'Kardinalskollegium' pp. 32–3.

[137] Hüls, *Kardinäle* pp. 142, 193, 221, 225.

Lucius II) can be identified with complete certainty as a regular canon. Peter Classen proved that the tradition connecting Conrad of Sabina (Anastasius IV) with the regular canons of St Rufus, Avignon, is inaccurate; and Werner Maleczek has cast doubt on the traditions identifying Innocent II and Haimeric as former regular canons.[138]

These criticisms demonstrate that the two rival groups of electors who can be identified on 14 February 1130 were not the homogeneous factions described in Schmale's study of 1961. They do not, however, affect the central thesis of Klewitz and Schmale, that the origins of the schism of 1130 are to be sought in the college of cardinals. The fact remains that the Anacletan cardinals were predominantly the older members of the college and the Innocentine cardinals were relative 'novices'. Too little reliable information is available about the cardinals' countries of origin to permit firm conclusions. However, it may well be significant that most of the north Italian and French cardinals recruited by Calixtus II and Honorius II supported Innocent. (We have already seen that their recruitment initiated a trend which continued into the middle of the century.) It may also be significant that of those Anacletan cardinals whose origins are identifiable, the majority came from the southern region of the papal patrimony and from southern Italy.[139] (We have seen that recruitment from these areas ceased in the pontificates of Innocent and his immediate successors.) Anacletus II's pontificate was devoted to furthering the interests of the papacy in southern Italy and to promoting the papal alliance with the Normans. It is possible that the crucial issue in 1130 was the attempt by Peter Pierleone and like-minded cardinals to save the Norman alliance, which Cardinal Haimeric was determined to destroy.[140]

As Anacletus pointed out to his correspondents, Innocent owed his election to Haimeric.[141] It was a central contention of the Anacletan party that the illegal tactics used by the chancellor invalidated the election of his candidate. All the extant accounts of the double election are polemics composed in defence of one or the other candidate; but they are agreed at least on the main outline of the events.[142] It is clear, firstly, that preparations for the succession had

---

[138] Hüls, *Kardinäle* p. 164; Classen, 'Anastasius IV.' (n. 134) pp. 36–63; Maleczek, 'Kardinalskollegium' (n. 56) p. 33.

[139] Hüls, *Kardinäle* pp. 150, 183, 206, 221, 40; Maleczek, 'Kardinalskollegium' p. 32.

[140] See below pp. 381–3.

[141] Anacletus II, *JL* 8376, 8379, *MPL* 179, 697B, 700C.

[142] See the reconstruction by Schmale, *Schisma* (n. 40) pp. 147–61.

already begun as Honorius II lay on his deathbed. The dying pope had been brought, probably on Haimeric's orders, to the monastery of S. Gregorio, in the immediate neighbourhood of the Frangipane fortifications. Haimeric may well have contemplated repeating his strategy of 1124 and using his alliance with the Frangipani to determine the election of 1130. Shortly before Honorius' death the cardinals, fearing that unrest in the city would inhibit the forthcoming election, decided to set up an electoral commission containing eight cardinals to choose a pope, whom the college agreed to recognise. (This commission is described both in an Anacletan polemic, a letter of the Romans to Archbishop Diego of Compostela, and in an Innocentine polemic, a letter of Bishop Hubert of Lucca to Innocent's distinguished supporter, Archbishop Norbert of Magdeburg.)[143] The commission, which was to meet in the church of S. Adriano, was to consist of two cardinal bishops, three cardinal priests and three cardinal deacons. The sources offer no clue to the origin of the electoral commission, but it is generally assumed to have been a device of Haimeric; for it contained an Innocentine majority, even though it was set up by a college in which Haimeric's supporters were in a minority.

This Innocentine majority was presumably a product of the method of voting used to create the commission: each of the three orders in the college elected its own representatives. The result was a commission containing five members of Haimeric's party – two cardinal bishops (Conrad of Sabina and William of Palestrina), one cardinal priest (Peter Rufus of SS. Martino e Silvestro) and two cardinal deacons (Gregory of S. Angelo and Haimeric) – and three opponents of Haimeric (the cardinal priests Peter Pierleone and Peter Pisanus of S. Susanna and the cardinal deacon Jonathan of SS. Cosma e Damiano). Cardinal Peter Pierleone and his ally, Cardinal Jonathan withdrew immediately from the commission. Realising that the commission would inevitably elect a supporter of Haimeric, they presumably withdrew in order to prevent the commission from functioning. The composition of the electoral commission suggests that, although there was a Haimeric faction in existence in the college before the death of Honorius II, there was not yet an opposition faction. The chancellor's opponents may well have banded together

---

[143] Letter of the Romans: *Historia Compostellana* III.23: (n. 33) 1185D–1188B. Hubert of Lucca, *Epistola: Codex Udalrici* 246: (n. 106) pp. 425–6. On the Innocentine polemics in the *Codex Udalrici* see F.-J. Schmale, 'Die Bemühungen Innozenz' II. um seine Anerkennung in Deutschland', *ZKG* 65 (1954), 240–69.

under the leadership of Cardinal Peter Pierleone only on 14 February
1130, some of them being prompted to do so by Haimeric's tactics
on that day. For when Honorius died during the night of 13–14
February, in the monastery of S. Gregorio, Haimeric arranged for
his hasty burial there and immediately held the papal election in the
monastery. The electors were the six remaining members of the electoral commission, Peter Pierleone and Jonathan not having returned.
Despite the protests of Peter Pisanus, Gregory of S. Angelo was
elected by the four other members of the commission, was invested
with the insignia of the deceased Honorius and enthroned in the
Lateran in the early hours of the morning of 14 February, as Innocent
II. When these events became known in Rome, the majority of the
cardinals assembled in the church of S. Marco and decided to proceed
to a new election. Cardinal Peter Pierleone proposed Cardinal
bishop Peter of Porto as pope; but on the latter's declining the
dignity, Peter Pierleone was elected and enthroned in St Peter's as
Anacletus II. The decree announcing his election states that
Anacletus was elected by a majority of the college, by the lesser
clergy of the Roman church and by the people of Rome.[144]

In the polemics of the ensuing schism each of the elections of 14
February was represented as the sole legal one; but the polemicists
were remarkably reticent about defining what they understood as
correct electoral procedures. There are only oblique references in the
polemics to the Papal Election Decree of 1059. Innocent's most
influential champion, Bernard of Clairvaux, in a possible allusion to
the terms of the decree of 1059, emphasised that the majority of the
cardinal bishops supported Innocent's candidature.[145] In the opinion
of the Anacletan party the support of the cardinal bishops invalidated
Innocent's election. Cardinal bishop Peter of Porto wrote to the
bishops of Palestrina, Albano, Sabina and Ostia: 'it was not for you
or for me to elect, but rather to reject or approve the man elected by
our brethren.' Anacletus' election was canonical because it was performed by 'your brethren the cardinals' – that is, the cardinal priests
and deacons – 'to whom the power of election especially belongs'.[146]
We have already seen that the Anacletan Cardinal Pandulf also
believed that the cardinal bishops 'have no authority in the election
of a Roman bishop except that of expressing approval or disapproval'.[147] The Anacletan party had evidently revived the views

---

[144] A. Chroust, 'Das Wahldekret Anaklets II.', *MIÖG* 28 (1907), 348–55.
[145] Bernard, *Epistola* 126: (n. 20) 280B.   [146] Peter of Porto, *Epistola* (n. 126) p. 8.
[147] Pandulf, *Vita Gelasii II* (n. 101) p. 313.

expressed on papal elections by Cardinal Deusdedit in his *Collectio canonum* of *ca*. 1086, in order to counter Innocent's claim to be the choice of the cardinal bishops.[148] The term which occurs most frequently in the polemics of both popes is the description of their own party of cardinals as the *sanior pars*, 'the sounder part' of the college. This term was not taken from any papal election decree, but from the monastic Rule of St Benedict, which prescribed that if 'the whole body of the congregation' could not agree on the election of an abbot, the brethren must accept the candidate elected by 'the part of the congregation, albeit small, with sounder counsel'.[149] The Anacletan party declared itself to be 'the sounder part' because it was both senior and more numerous. Innocent's election had taken place in the monasteryof S. Gregorio when 'the greater and sounder part dared not return to the monastery'; the electors' action was uncanonical because they were 'novices and very few in number'.[150] The Innocentine party, however, noted that the Benedictine Rule said nothing of a numerical majority: what counted was the personal 'soundness' of a candidate's supporters. Hence Bernard of Clairvaux emphasised 'the worthiness of the electors' of Innocent, which made them 'the sounder part'; while Innocent's biographer, Cardinal Boso, wrote that 'the bishops and cardinals divided into two parties, but the better and sounder part adhered to Innocent'.[151]

It is not clear why the Benedictine Rule was used by the rival parties in the papal schism: perhaps because it was the only available text which offered guidance in the case of a disputed election. It is natural to suspect that it was Innocent's champion, the Cistercian Bernard of Clairvaux, who introduced this monastic terminology into the polemics of the 1130s. But the evidence suggests that, on the contrary, it was the Anacletan party which first claimed to be the *sanior pars* of the electorate. In the event, of course, it was Bernard's definition of the term *sanior pars* which convinced most of western Christendom. According to Bernard, Innocent was the lawful pope because he was the worthier candidate, his electors were worthier, his election was 'earlier in time' and he had been consecrated by the cardinal bishop of Ostia, 'to whom [papal consecration] especially belongs'. Above all, he was the lawful pope because 'although he

---

[148] See above p. 61.

[149] *Benedicti Regula* c. 64.1, *Corpus Scriptorum Ecclesiasticorum Latinorum* 75 (Vienna, 1977), 163.

[150] Letter of the Romans: (n. 143) 1186C; Peter of Porto, *Epistola* (n. 126), 8.

[151] Bernard, *Epistola* 126 c. 13: (n. 20) 280B; Boso, *Vita Innocentii II* (n. 122) p. 380.

was expelled from the city, he is supported by the world'. 'Do not all the princes know that he is truly the elect of God?' wrote Bernard in 1131. 'The kings of the French, the English, the Spanish and finally the king of the Romans [Lothar III] accept Innocent as pope and recognise him as the unique bishop of their souls.' Soon afterwards Bernard proclaimed, more ambitiously: 'the kings of Germany, France, England, Scotland, Spain and Jerusalem, with all their clergy and people, favour and support the lord Innocent, as children obey their father and as the members support the head, anxious to preserve the unity of the spirit in the bond of peace'.[152] Although the college of cardinals had failed to achieve *unanimitas*, the Holy Spirit had produced unanimity throughout western Christendom; and this was the best guarantee of the validity of the title of Innocent II.

In Bernard's polemics in support of Innocent II, the rights of the cardinals as electors seem sometimes to be eclipsed by the idea of 'the world' as the arbiter in the case of a disputed election. This idea made no impression on the canon law of the mid-twelfth century. In the *Decretum* of Master Gratian of Bologna, compiled during Innocent's pontificate, the Papal Election Decree of 1059 is reinstated as the principal authority on this subject. Gratian included in his collection both the original version of the decree, with its emphasis on the special role of the cardinal bishops, and also the summary of the decree known to the Gregorian canonists, which identifies the *cardinales* in general as the electors of the pope.[153] Gratian's commentary on these texts ignores the special rights of the cardinal bishops in papal elections, stating simply that a pope must not be enthroned 'without a harmonious election of the cardinals'. Elsewhere Gratian interpreted the decree of 1059 as involving all the Roman clergy in the election of the pope: 'according to the authority of Pope Nicholas, the election of the supreme pontiff is to be made not only by the cardinals but also by the other religious clerks'.[154] The Papal Election Decree had limited the role of the lesser clergy to consenting to the election made by their superiors; but Gratian clearly regarded them as full participants in the electoral process. We have seen that the lesser clergy were mentioned as electors in the official protocol of Gregory VII; that they were present (their role unspecified) at the election of Paschal II and that they were mentioned in the election

---

[152] Bernard, *Epistolae* 126 c. 13: 124; 125: (n. 20) 280B; 268D–269A; 270B. See A. Grabois, 'Le schisme de 1130 et la France', *RHE* 76 (1981), 601.
[153] Gratian, *Decretum* D.23, I, c. I; D.79, I, c. I. See above pp. 36–7.
[154] Gratian, *Decretum* D.63 c. 34.

decree of Anacletus II as participants in his election. The records of
the papal elections of the 1140s, although sparse, suggest that the
lesser clergy of the Roman church also participated as electors on
these occasions. Celestine II announced on 6 November 1143 that he
had been elected by 'the cardinal priests and deacons, together with
our brethren the bishops and the subdeacons'.[155] Eugenius III on
2 March 1145 described how 'our brethren the cardinal priests and
deacons, together with the bishops and the subdeacons of the holy
Roman church met in the church of St Cesarius and elected me,
although unwilling and resisting . . . as Roman pontiff'.[156] However,
after the election of Eugenius III there are no further reports of the
lesser clergy as electors. It was in the middle of the twelfth century
that the cardinals established their right to be the exclusive electors of
the pope. The three orders in the college exercised this right as
equals. Henceforward there was no longer any question of the special right conferred on the cardinal bishops by the decree of 1059 nor
of the exclusive rights of election claimed for the cardinal priests and
deacons by Cardinal Deusdedit.

The papal elections of 1143 (Celestine II), 1144 (Lucius II), 1145
(Eugenius III), 1153 (Anastasius IV) and 1154 (Hadrian IV) took
place in the shadow of the communal revolution in Rome, which had
set up a regime hostile to the papacy. Nevertheless none of these elections was disputed. Cardinal Boso of SS. Cosma e Damiano, the
principal historian of the mid-twelfth-century papacy, commented
on the surprising unanimity of these elections which took place in the
midst of political turmoil in Rome. In 1145 Eugenius III 'was elected
by the bishops and cardinals in unexpected harmony in the monastery of St Cesarius, where all the brethren had gathered together for
fear of the senators and the Roman people, who were up in arms'.[157]
In the case of Hadrian IV in 1154, 'all the bishops and cardinals
assembled in the church of St Peter . . . and it happened – not without the direction of divine counsel – that they unanimously agreed on
[Hadrian]'.[158] Only five years later, on the death of Hadrian IV, tensions within the college of cardinals resulted in the double election of
Alexander III and 'Victor IV'. It is clear that the split within the
college which produced the disputed election of 7 September 1159

---

[155] Celestine II, *JL* 8435, *MPL* 179, 766c.
[156] Eugenius III, *JL* 8714, *MPL* 180, 1015a.
[157] Boso, *Vita Eugenii III: Liber pontificalis* 2, 386.
[158] Boso, *Vita Hadriani IV* (n. 45) p. 389. See W. Ullmann, 'The pontificate of
   Adrian IV', *Cambridge Historical Journal* 11 (1955), 237.

was of relatively recent date. It first becomes apparent to the historian in June 1156, when the treaty of Benevento was negotiated between Hadrian IV and King William I of Sicily. The cardinals who opposed this new accord between the papacy and the Sicilian king, preferring the traditional papal alliance with the emperor, regarded the treaty as the work of a 'Sicilian party' within the college. 'From the time when friendship was established at Benevento between the lord Pope Hadrian and William of Sicily, contrary to the honour of God's Church and of the empire, great division and discord have arisen (not without cause) among the cardinals.' The 'Sicilian party', led by the chancellor Cardinal Roland of S. Marco (the future Alexander III), 'blinded by money and many promises and firmly bound to the Sicilian, wickedly defended the treaty . . . and attracted very many others to share their error'.[159] The two factions whose rivalry caused the schism – the 'Sicilian party' and its pro-imperial opponents – came into being during the pontificate of Hadrian IV, inspired by the 'friendship . . . between the lord Pope Hadrian and William [I] of Sicily'. We have already seen evidence to suggest that the 'Sicilian party' was at least partly Hadrian's own creation. Of the thirteen cardinals of the 'party' who can be identified, Hadrian had recruited four and promoted five others within the college.[160] Hadrian may well have created a 'party' in the curia to enable him to replace the imperial alliance, in which he had lost confidence, by a Sicilian alliance. This crucial reversal of papal policy in 1156 was the principal cause of the double election of 1159.

During the last months of Hadrian IV's pontificate the cardinals were well aware of the serious risk of schism at the next election. There could be no doubt that the 'Sicilian party' and the pro-imperial party would put forward candidates who would be mutually unacceptable: respectively, the chancellor Roland of S. Marco and Octavian, cardinal priest of S. Cecilia, whose candidature was already being discussed. It is not surprising, therefore, to find rumours of various attempts to settle the succession before Hadrian's death. An imperial manifesto of 1160 declared that 'during the lifetime of Pope Hadrian, the chancellor Roland and certain cardinals . . . conspired with William the Sicilian (whom they had previously excommunicated) and with other enemies of the empire, the men of Milan, Brescia and Piacenza; and lest [their] evil faction should

---

[159] Letter of the cardinals of Victor IV: Rahewin, *Gesta Friderici imperatoris* IV.62, *MGH SS rer. Germ.*, 1884, p. 241. See below pp. 470–2.
[160] See above p. 53.

perhaps vanish because of the death of Pope Hadrian, they imposed an oath upon each other that on the death of the pope, no other should replace him except a member of their conspiracy'.[161] This seems to be a reference to a meeting of the envoys of the cities of Milan, Brescia and Piacenza with Hadrian and the thirteen cardinals of the 'Sicilian party' in Anagni in July 1159, which is known to us only from the accounts of hostile polemicists. It is impossible to discover what was the precise nature of this 'conspiracy'.[162] The 'Sicilian party' responded with the claim that Emperor Frederick I 'during [Hadrian's] lifetime planned, if the opportunity arose, to appoint Octavian as pope'.[163] In each of these cases the polemicist's purpose was to prove that his opponents' proceedings were invalidated by the involvement in their 'conspiracy' of an outsider who had no right to influence the sole lawful electorate, the college of cardinals.

Equally illicit was the attempt of outsiders or insiders to arrange the succession while the pope was still alive. As Peter of Porto had written in 1130, 'there must be no mention of the successor before the pope is buried'.[164] However, as we have seen in the cases of Gregory VII, Victor III and Gelasius II, it was lawful for the dying pope to designate a successor. Master Gratian of Bologna had recently restated this principle in his *Decretum*, when commenting on the synodal decree of Symmachus: 'the election of a Roman pontiff ought to be made with the counsel of his predecessor'.[165] Hadrian IV seems to have exercised this right. According to the reliable witness Bishop Eberhard II of Bamberg, one of the candidates considered at the beginning of the election of September 1159 was Cardinal bishop Bernard of Porto, 'whom the lord pope . . . is said to have designated by name'.[166] There is nothing improbable about this story of Bernard's designation. His probity and learning were generally acknowledged and his legation of 1153 (as cardinal priest of S. Clemente) had won him golden opinions in Germany. Hadrian had entrusted him and the chancellor Roland with the important mission to the imperial diet of Besançon in 1157 and had promoted Bernard to the cardinal bishopric of Porto in 1158. It seems quite possible

---

[161] Rahewin, *Gesta* IV.79: (n. 159) p. 263.

[162] Madertoner, *Papstwahl* (n. 68) pp. 33–42. See below p. 472.

[163] Alexander III, *JL* 10627–8: (n. 34) 89c, 91c. See below p. 473.

[164] Peter of Porto, *Epistola*: (n. 126) p. 8.

[165] Gratian, *Decretum* D.79, 5, ante c. 10. See above p. 60.

[166] Eberhard II of Bamberg, *Epistola* in Watterich, *Pontificum Romanorum Vitae* (n. 84) 2, 454–5.

that Hadrian regarded Bernard as a compromise candidate, acceptable to the pro-imperial party in the college and to the emperor himself in a way in which Roland of S. Marco clearly was not.[167] But
once the election of September 1159 began, Bernard's candidature
was forgotten: neither the pro-imperial party nor the 'Sicilian party'
was prepared to compromise.

The manifesto of the pro-imperial cardinals, issued immediately
after the election, gives details of a final attempt to avert a disputed
election by means of an electoral agreement (*pactum*) among the cardinals. The main points of their account are also found in a letter of
the canons of St Peter's in Rome to Emperor Frederick I. According
to these sources, the cardinals met in Anagni immediately after
Hadrian's death and reached the following agreement, which they
put into writing.

> The cardinal bishops, priests and deacons of the holy Roman church met
> together and gave their word that they would transact the election of the
> future pope according to the custom of that church: namely, that some of
> those brethren [the cardinals] should be deputed to listen to the opinions of
> individuals and should diligently investigate and record them accurately. If
> it was God's will that they could agree on any of the brethren, he should be
> elected with good will; if not, a man from outside [the college] should be
> considered and if they could agree on him, well and good; if not, no one
> should proceed without common consent. This should be observed without
> fraud or disingenuity.[168]

This agreement is not mentioned directly in the documents issued by
the 'Sicilian party'; but Willibald Madertoner (1978), who considers
that the 'existence [of the agreement] is indisputable', has detected an
indirect reference in the letters in which Alexander III announced his
election. Alexander's insistence that he was elected 'harmoniously
and unanimously' (*concorditer atque unanimiter*) seems to echo the
emphasis on unanimity in the agreement allegedly concluded after
Hadrian IV's death.[169] This agreement seems to envisage something
much less formal than the electoral commission of 1130: a committee
of cardinals whose task was to seek the agreement of all their colleagues – the 'Sicilian' and pro-imperial parties and the uncommitted
brethren – for a compromise candidate from inside or outside the
college. Although the creation of such a committee was an inno-

---

[167] Madertoner, *Papstwahl* (n. 68) pp. 55–60.
[168] Letter of the cardinals of Victor IV (n. 159) pp. 242–3. Cf. the letter of the canons
     of St Peter: Rahewin, *Gesta* IV.76 (n. 159) p. 255.
[169] Alexander III, *JL* 10584: (n. 34) 70B. See Madertoner, *Papstwahl* (n. 68) pp. 49–52.

vation, its purpose – the achievement of unanimity – could fairly be described as 'according to the custom of the [Roman] church'. The Papal Election Decree of 1059 assumed that an election must be unanimous to be valid.

The sources do not identify the membership of the informal committee nor do they confirm whether it actually performed its consultative function during the protracted election of 4–7 September in the basilica of St Peter. In their letter to the emperor the canons of St Peter's claimed that, when the college had failed to agree on any candidate, the pro-imperial party attempted to enforce unanimity by setting up an *ad hoc* electoral commission. The pro-imperial cardinals said to their opponents: 'give us the [right of] election and let us elect one of you or have [the right of] election yourselves and elect that one of us whom you wish'; but the 'Sicilian party' rejected this suggestion.[170] According to the manifesto of the pro-imperial party, the election was brought to an end by their opponents' breaking the electoral agreement and attempting to elect their own candidate, the chancellor Roland of S. Marco, contrary to their promise that the election would be unanimous. The election of Roland was consequently invalid.[171] Their opponents' reply to this charge is found in the manifesto of the electors of Alexander III. The Alexandrine cardinals claimed that by the end of the election the whole college was in favour of Roland-Alexander except for three cardinals: Octavian of S. Cecilia, Guido of S. Maria in Trastevere and John of SS. Martino e Silvestro. 'It seemed inappropriate that . . . the apostolic see . . . should remain any longer without a ruler because of the contentiousness of the aforesaid [three] men'.[172] According to the Alexandrine manifesto the principle of unanimity had been breached not by the precipitate election of the 'Sicilian party' but by the obstructive conduct of the pro-imperial party – a mere three cardinals – who stubbornly refused to recognise the candidate desired by the rest of the college. This became the official Alexandrine interpretation of the election, appearing, for example, in Cardinal Boso's biography of Alexander III.

All [the bishops and cardinals] who were present, except the cardinal priests Octavian of S. Cecilia, John of S. Martino and Guido [of S. Maria in Trastevere], by the Lord's will agreed unanimously on the person of the

---

[170] Rahewin, *Gesta* IV.76: (n. 159) p. 256.
[171] *Ibid.*, IV.62, p. 243.
[172] Letter of the cardinals of Alexander III: Watterich, *Pontificum Romanorum Vitae* (n. 84) 2, 494.

chancellor Roland and, invoking the grace of the Holy Spirit, with the assent of the clergy and people they named and elected him as the Roman pontiff, Pope Alexander III.[173]

The letter of the electors of Alexander III to the emperor is subscribed by twenty-two cardinals, while the Alexandrine accounts claim that the party of the antipope Octavian–Victor IV consisted of only three cardinals, including the candidate himself. The manifesto of the antipope's party claims that he was elected by nine cardinals, while the electors of Roland–Alexander numbered fourteen.[174] It is impossible to be certain about the numbers of the rival electors on 7 September, since it is not even clear how many of the thirty-one members of the college were present in Rome at this moment.[175] Evidently the 'Sicilian party' of thirteen cardinals eventually attracted the support of ten of their uncommitted brethren. If their opponents indeed numbered nine on 7 September, their numbers must soon have dwindled. The only aspect of the election which is not in doubt is the tumultuous last stage. The electors of Alexander III attempted to place upon him the purple mantle which symbolised the imposition of the papal office, but this 'immantation' was interrupted by Octavian, who snatched the mantle from Alexander's back. When a Roman senator seized the mantle from Octavian, the latter obtained another from his chaplain, 'who had come prepared for this', and put it on. At that moment an armed band of Octavian's supporters burst into the basilica. Alexander and his electors took refuge in the citadel of St Peter's, which was in the hands of the papal chamberlain, Cardinal Boso, a member of the 'Sicilian party' (and Alexander's future biographer). In their absence Octavian was enthroned as 'Victor IV'. His supporters subsequently defended their conduct on the grounds that Alexander's electors had broken the electoral agreement by attempting the 'immantation' of a candidate who had not been unanimously elected.[176] Alexander remained in the citadel of St Peter's for a week until he was rescued and escorted from Rome by Odo Frangipane. He finally assumed the papal mantle eleven days after the election.[177] This disputed election, like that of 1130, was destined not to be decided by the cardinals,

---

[173] Boso, *Vita Alexandri III: Liber pontificalis* 2, 397.
[174] Letter of the cardinals of Alexander III: Rahewin, *Gesta* IV.63: (n. 159) p. 244. Letter of the cardinals of Victor IV: *ibid.*, IV.62, p. 243.
[175] Madertoner, *Papstwahl* (n. 68) pp. 120–8.
[176] Rahewin, *Gesta* IV.62, p. 243.
[177] Boso, *Vita Alexandri III*: (n. 173) pp. 397–9. Cf. Rahewin, *Gesta* IV.62, 76, pp. 243–4, 256–7.

even though they were now generally acknowledged as the sole electors of the pope. The cardinals having once more failed to achieve *unanimitas*, the task of identifying the lawful pope again devolved upon 'the world'.

After the eighteen-year schism provoked by the election of 1159 the curia devised a means of electing a pope without the risk of a disputed election. This new measure appeared as the first canon of the Third Lateran Council of 1179, *Licet de evitanda*, in the form of an amendment to the Papal Election Decree of 1059. That decree had reserved the election of the pope to the cardinal bishops and cardinal clergy, in order to exclude the enemies of reform – especially the Roman nobility – from the electoral process. But the decree had foreseen the possibility neither of disagreement within the college nor of what the canon of 1179 called 'the audacity of wicked ambition' on the part of individual cardinals. The Third Lateran Council sought a remedy by abandoning the ideal of *unanimitas* and adopting in its stead the principle which the contending parties in the schism of 1130 had borrowed from the Rule of St Benedict, that of the *sanior pars*. The rival parties of cardinals in the schism of 1159 had likewise each claimed to be the 'sounder part' of the college. In the canon of 1179, however, *sanior pars* ceased to be the vague term of the polemicists of 1130 and 1159: it was defined as a two-thirds majority of the electors. 'We decree that if . . . it chances that there cannot be full agreement among the cardinals concerning the appointment of a pope and, while two-thirds agree, one-third refuses to agree or presumes to appoint another, in that case he is to be regarded as Roman pontiff who was elected and accepted by the two-thirds.' If the minority candidate assumed the papal title, he and his supporters would be punished with excommunication and deposition. 'Moreover if anyone is elected to the apostolic office by fewer than two-thirds, unless greater harmony prevails he should by no means assume [the office]; and he will fall under the aforesaid penalty if he will not humbly desist.'[178] To the authors of this canon, *Licet de evitanda*, belongs the credit for a major innovation in the history of ideas: from the vague expression *sanior pars*, as found in the Benedictine Rule and in the polemics of 1130 and 1159, they framed the principle of the majority decision. (The same principle was adopted in two other canons of the Third Lateran Council concerning ecclesiastical elections.)[179] Raymonde Foreville (1965) suggested that the idea of the two-thirds

---

[178] *Concilium Lateranense III* c. 1, *Conciliorum Oecumenicorum Decreta* p. 211.
[179] *Ibid.*, c. 16, 17: pp. 219–20.

majority derived from the principle that 'three make a college (*tres faciunt collegium*)'.[180] The authors of the canon must also have remembered the frustration of the 'Sicilian party' in 1159, when, having gained a clear majority of the college for Roland-Alexander, they found themselves obstructed by the obstinate insistence of the pro-imperial party on a unanimous election.

In the surviving accounts of the first five elections which followed the promulgation of *Licet de evitanda* – the elections of 1181 (Lucius III), 1185 (Urban III), 1187 (Gregory VIII and Clement III) and 1191 (Celestine III) – there is no specific reference to the canon of 1179. The letters in which the popes announced their accession in the 1180s, like those of the earlier twelfth century, emphasised the *unanimitas* of their election. Urban III wrote that after the burial of Lucius III 'a consultation was held by the brethren concerning the election of a successor, in which there was such unity and so great a harmony of individuals that they realised that God . . . by whom a diversity of opinions is united, was working in them'.[181] In his letter of congratulation to the newly elected Urban III Archbishop Baldwin of Canterbury likewise rejoiced that 'there was so great a unanimity on the part of those who elected you'.[182] Gregory VIII described in October 1187 how 'we bishops, priests and deacons' proceeded to the election of a new pope. 'When the opinions of the cardinals were sought, it pleased them all to place the burden of ecclesiastical care on us, insignificant though we are.'[183] The theme of these official announcements is *unanimitas* rather than election by the *sanior pars* of the electors. The principle stated in the canon of 1179 reappeared in the versions of the *Ordines Romani* drawn up by Cardinal Albinus *ca.* 1188 and by the papal chamberlain Cencius in 1192, but it was presented in much less precise language. Albinus stated that the pope must be elected by the 'major part' (*maior pars*) of the cardinals; Cencius that the lawful pope was he 'on whom the greater and better part (*maior et melior pars*) of the cardinals agreed'.[184]

---

[180] R. Foreville, *Latran I, II, III et Latran IV* (Histoire des Conciles Œcuméniques 6: Paris, 1965) p. 144.

[181] Urban III, *JL* 15518, *MPL* 202, 1352AB.

[182] Baldwin of Canterbury, *Epistola: ibid.*, 1533C–1534A.

[183] Gregory VIII, *JL* 16014, MPL 202, 1537BC. I have amended the reading *civium voluntates* in this edition to *cardinalium voluntates* in order to make sense of this letter. (S. Loewenfeld identified another major error in this edition: Jaffé, *Regesta pontificum Romanorum* 2, 529.) V. Pfaff, 'Sieben Jahre päpstlicher Politik', *ZSSRG KA* 67 (1981), 177, accepting the reading *civium*, supposes that Gregory's electors included the citizens of Ferrara.

[184] *Liber Censuum* 1, 311; 2, 123.

Careful scholars though they were and devoted to the interests of the papacy, Albinus and Cencius showed surprisingly little interest in the detailed arrangements of the canon of 1179. They were content to record the salient facts that the cardinals were the sole electors of the pope and that a numerical majority of the college was required for a valid election. The *senior pars* of the Benedictine Rule and of the polemicists of 1130 and 1159 had lost its ambiguity and become the *maior pars*, 'the majority'.

The *unanimitas* which allegedly characterised the elections of Alexander III's successors was the consequence of the threatening political situation: the outbreak of the last conflict between Emperor Frederick I and the papacy and subsequently the dangerous ambitions of his son, Emperor Henry VI. It is clear from the narrative sources that these elections took place in an atmosphere of extreme tension. The hasty election of Urban III, for example, took place at a moment when empire and papacy were engaged in a bitter dispute about the archbishopric of Trier and when the emperor was putting pressure on the pope to crown his son as co-emperor. Hubert Crivelli, cardinal priest of S. Lorenzo in Damaso and archbishop of Milan, was elected on 25 November 1185, the day of Lucius III's death. His electors seem to have numbered only eleven, the sole members of the college present at Lucius' deathbed in Verona. Eight of these cardinals were Urban's compatriots from northern Italy (the new pope was from a noble Milanese family). The Roman cardinals were absent, as was the papal chancellor, Albert of Morra, cardinal priest of S. Lorenzo in Lucina.[185] Two years later Cardinal Albert was elected to succeed Urban, as Gregory VIII, at a time of even greater tension, when Urban's implacable hostility towards the emperor had caused open conflict between them.

An unusually detailed account of this election on 21 October 1187 is found in a letter of Peter of Blois, the chancellor of the archbishop of Canterbury, who was visiting the papal curia in Ferrara at the time of the vacancy. According to this account three candidates were put forward by different groups of cardinals: Henry of Marcy, cardinal bishop of Albano, Paul Scolari, cardinal bishop of Palestrina and the papal chancellor, Cardinal Albert of S. Lorenzo in Lucina.

When the cardinals . . . had suggested these three and they were about to withdraw while [the others] considered whom they would elect, the lord of Albano at once replied, 'Why should we withdraw? I tell you truly that I shall

---

[185] Pfaff, 'Sieben Jahre' (n. 183) p. 177. See below pp. 502–3.

never accept this office. The lord of Palestrina is seriously ill and entirely unequal to such a burden. It only remains, therefore, to elect the chancellor; for no one among us is so suitable, no one knows the customs and rights of the Roman church as he does and is so pleasing to the princes of the earth'.[186]

Henry of Albano's renunciation of the papal office is also the subject of a semi-legendary account of the election in the chronicle of Alberic of Troisfontaines, written nearly half a century after the event. Alberic claimed that 'the sounder part' of the college desired Henry of Albano as pope, but Henry, fearing discord in the college, declined the office on the grounds that he was better fitted to serve as a crusading preacher. The cardinals therefore elected Gregory VIII, who appointed Cardinal Henry as his legate to preach the crusade in France and Germany.[187] The object of the Cistercian chronicler Alberic was clearly to draw attention to the exemplary conduct of the Cistercian cardinal Henry of Albano; but in the light of the contemporary report of Peter of Blois there is no reason to doubt that Cardinal Henry was largely responsible for the unanimous election of Gregory VIII. It is significant that Henry's intervention forestalled any attempt to apply the regulations of the canon of 1179: the cardinal of Albano preferred the traditional procedure of a unanimous election to the novel idea of a majority decision.

After a pontificate of only fifty-seven days Gregory VIII was succeeded by the candidate whose ill health had seemed to disqualify him in October, Paul Scolari, cardinal bishop of Palestrina. The health of the new pope, Clement III, continued to cause grave concern throughout his pontificate. For example, six months after his accession, in June 1188, it was rumoured that the cardinals, believing the pope's death to be imminent, planned to elect Cardinal bishop Theobald of Ostia to succeed him.[188] Clement's ill health was as much a disqualification as ever; but he was nevertheless elected on 19 December 1187. The explanation of this unexpected election is probably to be found in the small number of electors involved. Only eight cardinals seem to have been in Pisa, together with Paul Scolari, at the time of Gregory VIII's death. Of these eight, three are known to have been Romans – Hyacinth of S. Maria in Cosmedin, Octavian of SS. Sergio e Baccho and Peter of S. Nicola in carcere Tulliano –

[186] Peter of Blois, letter to Archbishop Baldwin of Canterbury: *Epistolae Cantuarienses* in *Chronicles and Memorials of the reign of Richard I* 2, RS 38/2 (1865), 107–8. See Wenck, 'Päpste' (n. 79) pp. 428–9.

[187] Alberic of Troisfontaines, *Chronica*, MGH SS 23, 860–1.

[188] *Epistolae Cantuarienses* 232: (n. 186) p. 218.

and therefore compatriots of the new pope.[189] It is possible that Clement III's electors were mainly members of that group of cardinals which had supported the candidature of Paul Scolari two months before. Thwarted by Cardinal Henry of Albano in October, they used the opportunity of his absence on legation to elect their candidate in December. (The accession of Clement III meant the eclipse of the influence of Henry of Albano, according to the representatives of the monastery of Christ Church, Canterbury at the curia. They noted with satisfaction that the pope was 'not well disposed towards the order of Cistercians and the lord of Albano'.)[190] The motive of the electors of Clement III was surely to appoint a pope who would negotiate the return of the curia to Rome. As we have already seen, Clement achieved this objective by his treaty of 31 May 1188 with the Roman senate. Simultaneously his numerous appointments of cardinals had the effect of creating a larger college of cardinals containing a majority of Romans.[191]

At the death of Clement III the college contained thirty-one members and was therefore larger than it had been at any time since the death of Hadrian IV in 1159. The situation in the curia in April 1191 was in some ways similar to that of September 1159. At a time of rapidly deteriorating relations between the empire and papacy, two rival factions were beginning to emerge in the college, one favouring a closer alliance with the king of Sicily, the other desiring reconciliation with the emperor. If these factions had been sufficiently organised to put forward rival candidates, the result might well have been a disputed election. Instead the college proved itself able to agree on a candidate associated with neither the 'Sicilians' nor the 'imperialists': namely, the senior member of the college, the 85-year-old Hyacinth, who for 47 years had been cardinal deacon of S. Maria in Cosmedin. The fact that he was elected as Celestine III on the day of Clement's death, 10 April 1191, suggests that his election was unanimous.[192] The English chronicler Ralph de Diceto was keenly aware of the danger that had been averted by the election of this compromise candidate: 'Hyacinth reluctantly consented to be

[189] Pfaff, 'Clemens III.' (n. 40) p. 263 n. 12; Tillmann, 'Ricerche' (1972) (n. 49) pp. 350–3; (1975) pp. 374–6, 376–8.
[190] *Epistolae Cantuarienses* 210: (n. 186) p. 195. Cf. no. 196, p. 180.
[191] See above pp. 55–6.
[192] The chronology has been established by Pfaff, 'Feststellungen' (n. 86) pp. 132–4. See also P. Zerbi, *Papato, impero e 'respublica christiana' dal 1187 al 1198* (Pubblicazioni dell' Università Cattolica del S. Cuore n.s. 55: Milan, 1955) pp. 83–4. See below p. 510.

made pope . . . lest a sudden schism arise in the church of God.'[193]
The possibility that the schism forestalled by Celestine's election
might actually break out on his death forms the background to a
story told by another English historian, Roger of Hoveden. About
two weeks before his death, according to Roger, Celestine, already
on his sickbed,

> summoned into his presence all the cardinals and commanded them to dis-
> cuss the election of his successor. He strove by every means that the lord
> John of St Paul, cardinal priest of S. Prisca should succeed him in the papacy
> . . . The pope offered moreover that he would depose himself from the
> papacy if the cardinals would consent to the election of the aforesaid John of
> St Paul. But all the cardinals replied with one voice that they would not elect
> him subject to conditions and said that it was unheard-of that the supreme
> pontiff should depose himself; and thus there was schism among them . . .
> Each of them sought with all his might to be made supreme pontiff.[194]

Roger of Hoveden's chronicle is the only source to refer to an
attempt by Celestine III to designate his successor; and since its
accounts of papal history contain strange inaccuracies, it is surely
wise to discount it. Roger's story is probably a conjecture based on
the predominance enjoyed by Cardinal John of St Paul in the curia
during the last months of the pontificate of Celestine III.

Certainly Roger's account of the papal election which followed a
fortnight after the alleged designation is inaccurate. Instead of the
wild scramble of the whole college to secure election, which Roger
described, there is every reason to suppose that only four candidates
were proposed, of whom Lothar of SS. Sergio e Baccho (Innocent
III) was elected without difficulty on the day of his predecessor's
death.[195] The papal election of 8 January 1198 seems to have been the
first in which the procedures of the canon *Licet de evitanda* were
rigorously followed. According to the anonymous early thirteenth-
century biography of Innocent III, the cardinals chose 'examiners'
(*examinatores*) from among themselves to scrutinise the written votes
of the college. After a first ballot the 'examiners' reported that 'very
many had agreed on [Lothar], even though three other [candidates]
had been nominated'. On a second ballot 'all agreed on him'.[196]

[193] Ralph of Diceto, *Ymagines historiarum* 1191, RS 68 (1876), 89.
[194] Roger of Hoveden, *Chronica*, RS 51/4 (1871), 32–3. See Wenck, 'Päpste' (n. 79)
pp. 456–74.
[195] Roger, *Chronica* pp. 33, 174–5. See H. Tillmann, *Pope Innocent III* (English translation: Amsterdam-New York-Oxford, 1980) p. 2.
[196] *Gesta Innocentii papae III* c. 5, MPL 214, xixB.

There is a marked contrast between this election of Innocent III and those elections of the past century and a quarter in which more than one candidate had been considered *papabile*. There was no longer any resort to improvisation or desperate expedients to avoid a disputed election. There was no reference to a designation by the deceased pope (*pace* Roger of Hoveden), as there had been after the deaths of Gregory VII, Victor III, Gelasius II and Hadrian IV. There was no electoral commission as in 1130, nor any electoral agreement as in 1159. There was no appeal to the vaguely defined *sanior pars* of the Benedictine Rule, 'the part of the congregation, albeit small, with sounder counsel', nor to the exclusive rights of the cardinal bishops or of the other orders of the college. The electors of 8 January 1198 accepted that the way to *unanimitas* was through the principle of the numerical majority.

THE CARDINALS AND THE PAPAL GOVERNMENT

Writing *ca.* 1065 Cardinal bishop Peter Damian of Ostia had accurately prophesied the future role of his order in the government of the Church.

The Roman church, which is the see of the apostles, ought to imitate the ancient court of the Romans. For just as that earthly senate imparted all its advice and devoted all its energy and skill to the end that the multitude of all the nations should be subjected to the Roman empire, so now the ministers of the apostolic see, who are the spiritual senators of the universal Church, ought to devote their skill to this endeavour: to subject the human race to the laws of the true emperor, Christ.[197]

By the early twelfth century the cardinals were recognised as the closest advisers and collaborators of the pope in the government of the Church and the foremost agents of papal reform. We have already noted Bernard of Clairvaux's conception of their preeminent role in the Church. They were the 'comrades and helpers' of the pope, 'the judges of the world', their task being 'to remove scandal from the kingdom of God, to cut down the thorns as they grow'. Exhorting them to act against unworthy clergy, Bernard apologised for his presumption in reminding them of their duty: 'it is not for me to instruct the teachers'.[198] Bernard's writings attributed an exalted status to the cardinalate, but did not attempt to define the precise

---

[197] Peter Damian, *Opusculum* 31 c. 7 (n. 7), 540B.
[198] Bernard, *De consideratione* IV.1.1 (n. 20), 772C; *Epistola* 230: 417C.

rank of the cardinals in the hierarchy of the Church. It was in the second half of the twelfth century that the papacy itself at last defined the cardinals' rank in the hierarchy.

This definition was made necessary by the relatively large number of cardinal priests and deacons who were promoted to bishoprics outside the diocese of Rome during the twelfth century. Such promotions presumably served the political objectives of the papacy. For example, the appointment of three cardinals as successive archbishops of Pisa – Hubert of S. Clemente in 1132, Baldwin of S. Maria in Trastevere in 1138 and Villanus of S. Stefano in 1146 – reflected the close alliance between Pisa and the curia in the pontificate of Innocent II and his immediate successors.[199] Klaus Ganzer's study of this phenomenon (1963) has shown that until the second half of the twelfth century, whenever a cardinal priest or deacon was appointed to an external bishopric, he automatically left the college of cardinals. It seems, therefore, that the rank of a cardinal of the Roman church and that of a bishop were regarded as incompatible and it also seems that the office of bishop was regarded as superior to that of cardinal: hence the renunciation of the cardinalate. In the pontificate of Alexander III, however, a change is apparent. There were still cases of cardinals leaving the college on accepting episcopal office (for example, Galdin of S. Sabina when he became archbishop of Milan); but there were now also cases of members of the college who were simultaneously cardinals and bishops. Conrad of Wittelsbach was both archbishop of Mainz and cardinal priest of S. Marcello (soon afterwards promoted to cardinal bishop of Sabina); William of Champagne was both archbishop of Rheims and cardinal priest of S. Sabina. Similarly in the pontificate of Lucius III Hubert Crivelli, cardinal priest of S. Lorenzo in Damaso (the future Urban III) retained his place in the college when he was elected archbishop of Milan. In the pontificate of Clement III a further development appeared. Cardinal priests and deacons who were elected to bishoprics renounced their titular churches without renouncing their membership of the college. For example, when Cardinal Adelhard became bishop of Verona in 1188, he ceased to be cardinal priest of S. Marcello but continued to use the cardinal's title, subscribing as 'bishop of Verona and cardinal of the holy Roman church'.[200] The office of cardinal priest or deacon and that of bishop were no longer seen as incompatible

---

[199] Zenker, *Mitglieder* (n. 40) p. 201. See above p. 51.
[200] Ganzer, *Entwicklung des auswärtigen Kardinalats* (n. 46) pp. 186–201; *idem*, 'Kardinalkollegium' (n. 1) pp. 179–80.

dignities, but had come to be regarded as of equivalent rank. Not only a cardinal bishop but also a cardinal priest or a cardinal deacon was held to be the equal of a bishop in the ecclesiastical hierarchy.[201]

Western Christendom experienced the rapidly growing authority of the cardinals as the pope's 'comrades and helpers' and 'judges of the world' when they appeared in the kingdoms of the west as the legates of the pope. They made impressive figures, 'clad in apostolic apparel and insignia, as if the pope himself had come'.[202] For cardinal legates were the vicars of the pope, enjoying his 'fullness of power', *plenitudo potestatis*. The expression *plenitudo potestatis* was used in the mid-twelfth century by Bernard of Clairvaux to express the supreme authority of the Roman Church over all the other churches of the world, a 'fullness of power' in which the pope allowed the bishops to participate. When, in the pontificate of Alexander III, the papal chancery adopted the expression *plenitudo potestatis* in papal letters, it was used to signify the authority which the pope conferred on the cardinal legates. (Only in the pontificate of Celestine III did *plenitudo potestatis* begin to be used by the pope in the sense in which Bernard of Clairvaux had used it.)[203] It was the reform papacy which had developed the legation into one of the most important instruments of papal government, precisely at the same period as the college of cardinals had emerged as 'the senate of the Roman church'. This was no coincidence: the readiness of the cardinals to serve as the agents of the papal reform movement was the factor which permitted the rapid increase in the use of legates.[204] From the early twelfth century onwards all the most important legations were entrusted to cardinals.[205] These cardinal legates were the principal link between the papacy and those regions which the curia never visited: Spain, England, Scandinavia, eastern Europe and Outremer. Their legatine synods permitted the enforcement of clerical discipline; their investigations improved the efficiency of papal justice in territories far from

[201] Sägmüller, *Tätigkeit* (n. 27) pp. 193–213.
[202] *Vita sancti Bernwardi episcopi Hildesheimensis* c. 22, *MGH SS* 4, 769.
[203] Alexander III, *JL* 10707: J. Pflugk-Harttung, *Iter Italicum* (Stuttgart, 1883) p. 264. Cf. Celestine III, *JL* 17203, *MPL* 206, 1075C. See G. B. Ladner, 'The concepts of "ecclesia" and "christianitas" and their relation to the idea of papal "plenitudo potestatis" from Gregory VII to Boniface VIII' in *Sacerdozio e Regno da Gregorio VII a Bonifacio VIII* (Miscellanea Historiae Pontificiae 18: Rome, 1954) pp. 61, 63–4; V. Pfaff, '"Pro posse nostro". Die Ausübung der Kirchengewalt durch Papst Coelestin III.', *ZSSRG KA* 43 (1957), 89–131.
[204] Klewitz, *Reformpapsttum* (n. 1) p. 107.
[205] See below p. 157.

Rome.[206] Above all the cardinal legates played a major role in the great crises of the later eleventh and twelfth centuries: the papal schisms and the conflicts between papacy and empire. The political and diplomatic skills of their legates made a significant contribution to the victory of Innocent II in the 1130s and of Alexander III in the schism of 1159–77.[207]

While these cardinals served as papal plenipotentiaries faraway from the papal curia, other members of the college served the pope in the curia itself. *Ca.* 1100 the curia emerged as the central organ of papal government, containing two rudimentary departments, both recently organised by Urban II: a financial office (the apostolic *camera*) and a secretariat (called from the 1180s onwards the *cancellaria*). The office of papal chamberlain (*camerarius*), director of the papal finances, was very occasionally given to a cardinal. The first cardinal to hold the office was Jordan of S. Susanna in the pontificate of Eugenius III. The two most influential chamberlains of the twelfth century were promoted to the cardinalate after they had begun to serve in the office of *camerarius*. Boso became cardinal deacon of SS. Cosma e Damiano after serving Hadrian IV as chamberlain for two years; Cencius Savelli became cardinal deacon of S. Lucia in Orthea after serving first Clement III then Celestine III for five years.[208] The office of chancellor (*cancellarius*), however, was invariably given to a cardinal priest or cardinal deacon during the twelfth century. (The only exception to this practice occurred when the antipope Calixtus III (1168–78) conferred the office on a cardinal bishop.)[209] The *cancellarius* directed the work of the group of notaries and *scriptores* who formed the papal secretariat.

There is no mistaking the preeminent position of the chancellor in the twelfth-century curia. The office proved to be a stepping-stone to the papacy for four of the chancellors of the twelfth century. John of Gaeta, cardinal deacon of S. Maria in Cosmedin, who served both Urban II and Paschal II as the first chancellor of the reorganised

[206] See below pp. 160–1.   [207] See below pp. 158–9, 166–7, 487–94.
[208] See below pp. 251–60.
[209] H. Bresslau, *Handbuch der Urkundenlehre für Deutschland und Italien* 1 (Leipzig, 1912), 200. See also P. Kehr, 'Scrinium und Palatium. Zur Geschichte des päpstlichen Kanzleiwesens im XI. Jahrhundert', *MIÖG* Ergänzungsband 6 (1901), 70–112; R. L. Poole, *Lectures on the papal chancery* (Cambridge, 1917) pp. 136–40; F. Claeys-Bouuaert, 'Chancelier', *Dictionnaire du Droit Canonique* 3 (Paris, 1942), 454–64; *idem*, 'Chancellerie', *ibid.*, pp. 464–71; P. Rabikauskas, *Die römische Kuriale in der päpstlichen Kanzlei* (Miscellanea Historiae Pontificiae 20: Rome, 1958).

chancery (1089–1118), became pope as Gelasius II.[210] Gerard, cardinal priest of S. Croce in Gerusalemme, served Innocent II and Celestine II as chancellor (1141–4) – using, however, the archaic title of 'librarian' (*bibliothecarius*) – until he succeeded to the papacy as Lucius II.[211] Roland, cardinal priest of S. Marco was appointed chancellor in the last weeks of Eugenius III's pontificate and served both Anastasius IV and Hadrian IV (1153–9) before succeeding the latter as Alexander III in the disputed election of 1159.[212] Albert of Morra, cardinal priest of S. Lorenzo in Lucina assumed the office of chancellor towards the end of Alexander's pontificate and after serving Lucius III and Urban III (1178–87) was elected pope as Gregory VIII.[213] Each of these chancellors was the most influential figure in the curia of his day. John of Gaeta was the principal adviser of Paschal II and 'the support of his old age in all things'.[214] Gerard of S. Croce was the curia's indispensable expert on German affairs, who had negotiated the alliance of the papacy with Emperor Lothar III.[215] Roland of S. Marco was the leader of the 'Sicilian party' in the college of cardinals, responsible for the reorientation of the papacy's political strategy in the later 1150s.[216] Albert of Morra enjoyed the special confidence of Alexander III; but in the pontificate of Urban III he became the principal opponent of the pope's aggressive policy towards the emperor.[217] Probably the most powerful chancellor of the twelfth century was Haimeric, cardinal deacon of S. Maria Nuova, who held the office from 1123 until 1141. Haimeric did not himself become pope, but he was the pope-maker who contrived the election of two of the popes whom he served, Honorius II and Innocent II.[218]

It happens that the most detailed portrait of a chancellor at work which survives from the twelfth century is an account by a litigant, Abbot Hariulf of Oudenbourg, who visited the curia in 1141: that is, in the last year of the life of the chancellor Haimeric. Hariulf's

---

[210] Santifaller, 'Cancellaria Pontificia' (n. 15) pp. 208–10.

[211] Zenker, *Mitglieder* (n. 40) p. 131.

[212] *Ibid.*, p. 86.

[213] P. Kehr, 'Papst Gregor VIII. als Ordensgründer' in *Miscellanea Francesco Ehrle. Scritti di storia e paleografia* 2 (Studi e testi 38: Rome, 1924), 252.

[214] Pandulf, *Vita Gelasii II*: (n. 101) pp. 311–12. See below pp. 103, 431.

[215] See pp. 159, 454.

[216] See above pp. 52–3, 79 and below p. 470.

[217] Alexander III, *JL* 11361: (n. 34) 461CD; Gregory VIII, *JL* 16075: (n. 183) 1560AB. See below p. 505.

[218] See above pp. 67–75.

account emphasises the importance of the chancellor's role in the judicial proceedings of the curia. Hariulf had been warned beforehand by his friend the bishop of Noyon to engage the sympathy of the chancellor, whose 'industry puts everything in order, deciding the lesser cases and directing the greater'. When the pope heard Hariulf's case in the presence of the cardinals, the chancellor sat on the pope's foot-stool and it was he who, on the second day of the hearing, pronounced the judgement reached by the pope in secret consultation with the cardinals.[219] It was likewise Cardinal Haimeric who was the recipient of the letter in which Bernard of Clairvaux presented his exalted view of the chancellor's office.

Scarcely any good thing is done in the world which does not in some measure have to pass through the hands of the Roman chancellor, so that a thing will hardly be judged good unless it has first been examined by his judgement, regulated by his counsel, strengthened by his zeal and confirmed by his help.

Bernard subsequently wrote in similar terms about the office to Eugenius III. 'To have a chancellor who is good, just and of good repute is no small part of the apostolic dignity, no small support of the apostolic ministry, no small protection of the apostolic conscience.'[220] For most of the period during which the influence of Bernard of Clairvaux was felt in the curia, the office was held by a series of chancellors whose correspondence with the abbot reveals them to be members of Bernard's friendship circle: Haimeric himself (1123–41), Gerard of S. Croce (1141–4), the Englishman Robert Pullen, cardinal priest of SS. Martino e Silvestro (1145–6) and Guido, cardinal deacon of SS. Cosma e Damiano (1146–9).[221] This sequence was broken when, between 1149 and 1152, the duties, although not the title, of chancellor were entrusted to Boso, who seems to have had no connection with Bernard. Boso became a member of the college only in 1156 (as cardinal deacon of SS. Cosma e Damiano): perhaps he was not given the title of chancellor in 1149–52 because he was not a cardinal. (Instead he subscribed documents

[219] E. Müller, 'Der Bericht des Abtes Hariulf von Oudenburg über seine Prozessverhandlungen an der römischen Kurie im Jahre 1141', *NA* 48 (1930), 101–11. See below pp. 189–90, 193.

[220] Bernard, *Epistolae* 311, 280: (n. 20) 517A, 487B.

[221] Schmale, *Schisma* (n. 40) pp. 123–34; Zenker, *Mitglieder* (n. 40) pp. 90–9, 131, 146–8.

with the title of a lesser functionary of the chancery, *scriptor*.)[222] In 1153 the title of *cancellarius* was given to Cardinal Roland of S. Marco and soon afterwards Boso obtained the office of chamberlain, which he transformed into an office almost as powerful as that of the chancellor.

The main function of the chancellor, according to Bernard of Clairvaux, was to act as the pope's principal adviser (the 'protection of the apostolic conscience'). Abbot Hariulf of Oudenbourg, writing from the point of view of a litigant, saw the chancellor primarily as a judge, second in importance only to the pope himself. No complete account of the chancellor's duties survives from the twelfth century. The earliest such account extant is in the regulations given to the chancery by Nicholas III in 1278. By that date the *cancellaria* had become completely independent of the other departments of the papal government and was presided over by a vice-chancellor, the office of *cancellarius* having lapsed. But it is not unlikely that the regulations of 1278 convey an accurate impression of the main duties of a twelfth-century chancellor. These regulations required the head of the chancery to maintain a careful supervision both of all the documents issued by the curia and of the registers which preserved an authentic copy of these documents. In particular he was required to examine those documents which confirmed existing privileges and which conferred privileges of exemption. No solemn act could be issued by the chancery unless he had subscribed it: if illness prevented his carrying out his duties, the operations of the chancery were suspended. Finally, the head of the chancery must always accompany the pope if he undertook a journey.[223] The chancellor's constant access to the pope was presumably one of the factors which made his office so influential.

Of equal importance was the fact that the chancellor, once appointed, seems to have retained his office for life – unless, as in the cases of John of Gaeta, Gerard of S. Croce, Roland of S. Marco and Albert of Morra, he happened to be elected pope. All the other chancellors of the twelfth century retained their office until their death. There is no instance of a chancellor's tenure of office ceasing with the end of the pontificate of the pope who appointed him, as seems increasingly to have been the case with the office of chamberlain. (It

---

[222] F. Geisthardt, *Der Kämmerer Boso* (Historische Studien 293: Berlin, 1936) pp. 80–2; Zenker, *Mitglieder* pp. 149–52.

[223] Claeys-Bouuaert, 'Chancelier' (n. 209) pp. 455–6.

is true that Boso was removed from the chancery to the *camera*; but, as we have seen, he was never given the title of *cancellarius*: he was a lesser functionary of the chancery temporarily carrying out the chancellor's duties during a vacancy.) It was this life tenure of office which enabled a chancellor like Cardinal Haimeric to achieve such an extraordinary accumulation of power in the curia. Towards the end of the century the office of chancellor may even have begun to seem a threat to the authority of the pope. Hence the suspension of the office by Alexander III (the former chancellor Roland) between 1159 and 1178 and the renewed suspension by Gregory VIII (the former chancellor Albert of Morra) in 1187. At the end of the twelfth century the chancery was manned by a less powerful, more accountable officer, a vice-chancellor who was not a member of the college. In the latter years of the pontificate of Celestine III (1194–8) the functions of the chancellor, without the title, were undertaken by the chamberlain, Cencius Savelli (the future Honorius III); but this expedient died with Celestine.[224]

On the general theme of the participation of the cardinals in the papal government, the most extensive body of evidence consists of the subscriptions of cardinals in papal diplomas. From the mid-eleventh century onwards papal privileges began to be subscribed by individual cardinals in their own hand: a measure presumably intended to establish the authenticity of the more important documents issued by the curia.[225] In the privileges of Paschal II there is a noticeable increase in the number of cardinals' signatures (except for the period from the end of 1107 until May 1112, for which there survive no papal diplomas subscribed by cardinals).[226] In the privileges of the first quarter of the twelfth century the formulas used by the cardinals in their subscriptions indicate that these were not merely routine signatures. In a privilege of Gelasius II of April 1118 appear the subscriptions: 'I, Bishop Peter of Porto, have consented and subscribed in my own hand. I, Hugh, cardinal priest of SS. Apostoli, have consented of my own free will and have subscribed.' In a privilege of Calixtus II of September 1120 appears the formula: 'I, Bishop Peter of Porto, have consented and subscribed'; and in a privilege of April 1124 the formula: 'I, Boniface, cardinal priest of S.

---

[224] *Ibid.*, p. 455. See below p. 260.

[225] B. Katterbach and W. M. Peitz, 'Die Unterschriften der Päpste und Kardinäle in den "Bullae maiores' vom 11. bis 14. Jahrhundert' in *Miscellanea Francesco Ehrle* 4 (Studi e testi 40: Rome, 1924), 177–274.

[226] *Ibid.*, pp. 185–6; Klewitz, *Reformpapsttum* (n. 1) p. 108.

Marco, was present, consented and subscribed.'[227] This emphasis on consent suggests active participation in the transaction recorded in these privileges. But the papal privileges of these years were also subscribed by prelates who were not cardinals: churchmen visiting the curia who had evidently taken part in the discussions leading to the issuing of the privileges. The papal diplomas of the early twelfth century reveal the informality of the papal government. The cardinals' subscriptions cannot necessarily be taken at this date as evidence of the cardinals' right to participate in the conferring of papal privileges. The presence of the cardinals' signatures in the privileges of the 1120s could well reflect the wish of the recipients of papal privileges to secure as many witnesses as possible to the authenticity of the grant.

It is in the diplomas of the pontificate of Innocent II that the importance of the cardinals' role in papal government suddenly becomes unmistakable. From the third year of Innocent's pontificate (that is, from the time of his return from France to Italy in April 1132) cardinals' subscriptions became an indispensable part of a wide range of papal diplomas: those privileges confirming existing rights and possessions and those extending rights or creating new rights, as well as papal diplomas announcing judicial decisions. From 1132 onwards the chancery proclaimed the active participation of the cardinals in the papal dispensing of favours and handling of litigation. This development was doubtless connected with the politics of the schism of the 1130s: a propaganda device intended to present a Roman church unified in support of Innocent II's claims to the papacy.[228] The practice continued after the end of the schism and became the normal chancery practice of the later twelfth century. It is possible that the cardinals were unwilling to relinquish their right to subscribe diplomas because it had become a lucrative right. A fifteenth-century archivist of the monastery of Walkenried recorded of his house's privilege from Alexander III (1168), that 'twelve cardinals subscribed [it], which cost the monastery much money'.[229]

The cardinals' subscriptions in papal diplomas reveal the development of the cardinals' role of principal advisers of the pope. During the twelfth century Peter Damian's idea of the cardinals as 'the

---

[227] Gelasius II, *JL* 6643; Calixtus II, *JL* 6861: *MPL* 163, 494AB, 1183C; Calixtus II, *JL* 7147: J. Pflugk-Harttung, *Acta pontificum Romanorum inedita* 2 (Tübingen-Stuttgart, 1880), 244. See Sägmüller, *Tätigkeit* (n. 27) p. 216.

[228] Maleczek, 'Kardinalskollegium' (n. 56) pp. 51–3.

[229] *Ibid.*, p. 52 n. 102.

spiritual senators of the universal Church' was realised in the shape
of the new institution of the consistory: a solemn assembly of the cardinals, presided over by the pope, to discuss and decide the graver
matters affecting the Roman church.[230] The term *consistorium* meant
originally the place in which the imperial counsellors met to advise
the emperor and it was still occasionally used in this sense in the
twelfth century.[231] When *consistorium* first appears in the letters of the
reforming popes it likewise signifies a place of counsel, specifically
the Lateran palace: its earliest occurrence is in the phrase 'the synod
held in the Lateran *consistorium*'.[232] Only in the pontificate of
Innocent II was the expression 'in the consistory of the holy Roman
church' finally applied to the consultation rather than to the place in
which it occurred.[233] However, the institution seems to have come
into existence nearly half a century before the name 'consistory'
became attached to it. 'It is possible to speak of a consistory when the
pope, together with the cardinals, considers and decides matters
which were usually reserved to the synod.'[234] In the pre-reform
period the local problems of the Roman church were settled in the
papal synod by the pope and the bishops of the ecclesiastical
province. At the end of the eleventh century, under the impact of the
programme of the reform papacy, this traditional institution was
displaced by two new institutions better fitted to cope with the
rapidly expanding jurisdiction and functions of the papacy. The first
was the 'general council', which formulated and publicised reforming legislation for the whole of western Christendom.[235] The other
was the consistory, which dealt with the growing volume of business – no longer solely from the ecclesiastical province of Rome but
from most regions of the west – inspired by the reformers' conception of the papal primacy. The consistory absorbed the judicial
functions of the papal synod[236] and in addition offered advice on all

---

[230] Sydow, '"Concistorium"' (n. 45) pp. 165–76; *idem*, 'Verwaltungsgeschichte'
(n. 13) pp. 52–5; Ganzer, 'Kardinalkollegium' (n. 1) pp. 167–71.

[231] *Thesaurus linguae latinae* 4 (Leipzig, 1906–9), 473. For twelfth-century examples
see *Chronica monasterii Casinensis* IV.108, 113–15, 125: (n. 96) pp. 572, 583, 587,
590, 600 (Emperor Lothar III); Otto of Freising, *Gesta Friderici* II.43: (n. 159) p. 151
(Emperor Frederick I).

[232] Alexander II, *JL* 4500, *MPL* 146, 1380A; Paschal II, *JL* 5908, *MPL* 163, 91B.

[233] *Vita sancti Berardi: prologus*, *Acta Sanctorum Novembri* 2 (Brussels, 1891), 128. See
Sydow, '"Concistorium"' (n. 45) p. 167.

[234] Sydow, 'Verwaltungsgeschichte' (n. 13) p. 52.

[235] See below pp. 121–45.   [236] See below pp. 188–92.

matters concerning the welfare of the papacy and the government of the universal Church.

There is no sign of the new institution of the consistory in the pontificate of Gregory VII. Gregory's governmental and judicial decisions were made in his Lenten synods (which were enlarged versions of the traditional papal synods) rather than in an assembly resembling the *consistorium* of the mid-twelfth century.[237] The only assembly of cardinals mentioned in the records of the pontificate is the *conventus* of 'bishops, cardinals, abbots and archpriests' in Rome on 4 May 1082, which unanimously agreed that the property of the Roman church could not be mortgaged in order to pay for the defence of the city. This was evidently a rejection by the Roman clergy of Gregory VII's plans for resisting King Henry IV of Germany.[238] The well-known polemic of the renegade Cardinal Beno of SS. Martino e Silvestro accused Gregory of having 'removed the cardinals from the counsel of the holy see'.[239] In fact Gregory found some of his closest collaborators among the cardinal bishops – Gerald of Ostia and his successor, Odo, Hubert of Palestrina and Peter of Albano – although it is as legates rather than advisers that they figure in the sources for his pontificate. With the other two orders of cardinals Gregory's relations were far less harmonious: eight cardinal priests (including Beno) and three cardinal deacons deserted him in the crisis of 1084.[240] The short pontificate of his successor, Victor III, suggests a contrast: Victor seems to have relied on the counsel of all the cardinals. For example, when he appointed Oderisius as his successor as abbot of Monte Cassino, 'the bishops and cardinals . . . sitting in the chapter confirmed' his appointment.[241]

The practice of seeking the advice of the cardinals – which may have been forced on Victor III by his ill health and the general weakness of his position as pope – continued in the more prosperous pontificate of Urban II. Urban's excommunication of Emperor Henry IV and his antipope in 1089 was pronounced, as he himself explained, 'on the advice of our brethren' the cardinals.[242] Urban's conduct differed sharply from that of Gregory VII, who allegedly

---

[237] See below pp. 123–4.
[238] Z. Zafarana, 'Sul "conventus" del clero romano nel maggio 1082', *Studi Medievali* ser. 3, 7 (1966), 399–403.
[239] Beno, *Gesta Romanae ecclesiae* I: (n. 12) p. 370.
[240] Hüls, *Kardinäle* (n. 1) pp. 90, 100–2, 110. See above p. 37.
[241] *Chronica monasterii Casinensis* III.73: (n. 96) p. 456.
[242] Urban II, *JL* 5393–4: (n. 16) 297B, 299B.

had 'excommunicated the emperor precipitately . . . contrary to the will and counsel of the cardinals'.[243] When Urban excommunicated King Philip I of France in 1095 (because of his matrimonial offences), the measure was likewise taken on the advice of the cardinals.[244] Urban II's letters reveal that numerous problems of ecclesiastical government, which in Gregory VII's pontificate would have been decided in a papal synod – disputed episcopal elections, disputes concerning the jurisdiction of metropolitans – were now settled 'in our presence and that of our colleagues, the bishops and cardinals'.[245] For most of his pontificate Urban was unable to establish himself in Rome and therefore unable to use the traditional institution of the papal synod; but it was nevertheless important that his decisions should be seen to have the support of the Roman church. It was for this reason that the cardinals became in the 1090s the indispensable colleagues of the pope, as judges and counsellors. Hence the portrayal of the curia of Urban II in the *Treatise of Garsias, canon of Toledo* of 1099, the earliest of the medieval satires against Roman avarice: the pope is 'surrounded by very stout cardinals', his inseparable boon-companions.[246]

The sources for the pontificate of Paschal II assume that the pope would consult the cardinals before reaching an important decision. Pope and cardinals shared the government of the Church, in the opinion of the two cardinal priests John of S. Anastasia and Benedict of S. Pudenziana, Paschal's legates in France, who wrote to the pope in 1100: 'it is the business of our government to provide for all the churches, to stretch out our hands in answer to the prayers of the needy'.[247] The assumption that the pope could not act without first receiving the advice of the cardinals appears in a letter of Prince Bohemund of Antioch, sent to Paschal in September 1106. Bohemund, desiring the pope to sanction his plan of attacking the Byzantine emperor Alexius I, wrote: 'it is our will . . . that you take counsel with the bishops and cardinals and Roman clergy or in a council convoked in the near future'.[248] The events of the crisis of 1111–12 compelled the pope himself to admit that a major papal

---

[243] Beno, *Gesta Romanae ecclesiae* I: (n. 12) p. 370.

[244] Urban II, *JL* 5774: 538C.

[245] See below p. 188.

[246] *Tractatus Garsiae Tholetani canonici de Albino et Rufino*, MGH *Libelli* 2, 427.

[247] Letter of Cardinals John and Benedict in Stephen of Cîteaux, *Exordium coenobii et ordinis Cisterciensis* c. 11, *MPL* 166, 1506AB. See Hüls, *Kardinäle* (n. 1) pp. 146, 200.

[248] Letter of Bohemund in: W. Holtzmann, 'Zur Geschichte des Investiturstreites (Englische Analekten II)', *NA* 50 (1935), 280.

decision could be made only with the cardinals' advice. The crisis arose from the attempt of King Henry V of Germany to force on Paschal II a solution to the question of investitures. After the failure of negotiations Henry took the pope prisoner, releasing him only after Paschal had conceded the privilege of Ponte Mammolo (11 April 1111). This privilege gave Henry the right to invest prelates with ring and staff, so legalising the practice which the reform papacy had been anathematising for over thirty years.[249] This 'evil privilege' (*pravilegium*) caused an outcry among reformers and prompted the summoning of the Lateran council of March 1112. It is possible that the council was summoned not by the pope but by hostile cardinals like John of Tusculum and Leo of Ostia, whom Paschal believed to be the leaders of a party of cardinals determined to revoke the *pravilegium*.[250] The council appointed a committee of three cardinals and three bishops to recommend corrective measures; and on this committee's advice the council revoked the privilege of Ponte Mammolo. Paschal II's role in the council was limited to making a confession of his orthodoxy and of his adherence to the reform programme of Gregory VII and Urban II. The pope confessed that the privilege which he had granted 'without the counsel or the subscriptions of the brethren' was 'an evil deed' and he entrusted 'the means of correcting this to the counsel and judgement of the assembled brethren'.[251]

The crisis in the curia between April 1111 and March 1112 cannot, however, be interpreted as a struggle between pope and cardinals for control of decision-making in the curia, in which the pope was compelled to admit defeat in the council of 1112. For it was not only Paschal II who had acquiesced in the settlement of Ponte Mammolo: sixteen cardinals held captive with him had also confirmed the *pravilegium* on oath and they continued to support the pope.[252] The conflict was between two parties in the curia with sharply differing

---

[249] See below pp. 128–30, 428–9.
[250] Paschal II, *JL* 6301: (n. 232) 290D–291A. See Servatius, *Paschalis II*. pp. 297, 309. See also below p. 129.
[251] Boso, *Vita Paschalis II: Liber pontificalis* 2, 370. See Servatius, *Paschalis II*. pp. 309–18; L. Pellegrini, 'Orientamenti di politica ecclesiastica e tensioni all'interno del collegio cardinalizio nella prima metà del secolo XII' in *Le istituzioni ecclesiastiche della 'societas christiana' dei secoli XI–XII* I (Milan, 1974), 465–73; U.-R. Blumenthal, 'Opposition to Pope Paschal II: some comments on the Lateran council of 1112', *Annuarium Historiae Conciliorum* 10 (1978), 82–98.
[252] Treaty of Ponte Mammolo: *MGH Constitutiones* I, 144–5; Bruno of Segni, *Epistola* I: *MGH Libelli* 2, 563.

attitudes towards Henry V and investiture. The cardinal bishops Leo of Ostia, Cuno of Palestrina and Bruno of Segni and the cardinal priests Robert of S. Eusebio and Gregory of SS. Apostoli opposed any compromise with the emperor; while the pope's closest advisers – the chancellor John of Gaeta, Cardinal bishop Peter of Porto and Peter Pierleone, cardinal deacon of SS. Cosma e Damiano – sought to avoid a breach.[253] This party hostility survived the death of Paschal II. When in 1118 the news reached Germany of Paschal's death and the accession of his trusted adviser, the chancellor John, as Gelasius II, Archbishop Conrad of Salzburg remarked to his ally, Cuno of Palestrina: 'hm! none of them was more worthless than John: could there perhaps be any good in Gelasius?'[254] Soon after his election in February 1119 Calixtus II received a letter of congratulation from the former cardinals Gregory of SS. Apostoli and Robert of S. Eusebio, who had been deposed by Paschal II because of the ferocity of their opposition in 1112. Calixtus – who as Archbishop Guido of Vienne had supported the opposition party of cardinals in 1112 – reinstated Gregory and Robert as cardinals.[255]

The papal letters and privileges of the 1120s show an impressive range of business being decided 'by the counsel of our brethren': the foundation of bishoprics or their elevation to archbishoprics, the defining of ecclesiastical boundaries, disputes between churches.[256] Archbishop Diego Gelmírez of Compostela obtained the metropolitan dignity for his church from Calixtus II in 1124 'after the pope had taken counsel with the cardinals and with the chief men of the Roman curia'. Similarly, twenty years earlier Diego had received the pallium 'through the intervention of all the cardinals'. Diego secured these privileges with the help of well-timed gifts (*benedictiones*) which he expected the pope to share with the cardinals.[257] When in 1123 William of Corbeil came to Rome, seeking confirmation of his election as archbishop of Canterbury, 'the cardinals and the curia conferred for several days and disputed among themselves', finally

[253] Klewitz, *Reformpapsttum* (n. 1) pp. 43–4, 109, 126–7; Schmale, 'Papsttum' (n. 130) pp. 275, 277; Hüls, *Kardinäle* (n. 1) pp. 105, 113, 122, 225, 232, 271.
[254] *Vita Theogeri abbatis sancti Georgii et episcopi Mettensis*, MGH SS 12, 470.
[255] E. Martène and U. Durand, *Veterum scriptorum . . . collectio* 1 (Paris, 1724), 649. See Klewitz, *Reformpapsttum* (n. 1) pp. 109, 126–7; Hüls, *Kardinäle* (n. 1) pp. 152, 165, 204.
[256] Sydow, 'Verwaltungsgeschichte' (n. 13) p. 65; Pellegrini, 'Callisto II' (n. 52) pp. 532–3.
[257] *Historia Compostellana* I.17, II.64: (n. 33) 913B, 1116BC. See above p. 42 and below pp. 263–5.

deciding that the election was not canonical. Calixtus II, however, wished to gratify King Henry I of England and his son-in-law, Emperor Henry V, both of whom had asked him to confirm William's election. The cardinals, therefore, 'thinking it hard not to grant the requests of their father and lord, agreed with the lord pope'. On this same occasion William's advisers produced a collection of papal privileges, by virtue of which they claimed for Canterbury a primacy over the English church. 'The cardinals and the curia' examined the privileges and proved them to be forgeries.[258] The intervention of Honorius II in support of the claims of Bishop Urban of Glamorgan in 1128 against his neighbours, the churches of Hereford and St Davids, was made 'according to the deliberations of our brethren, the bishops and cardinals'.[259] (According to the characteristic usage of the early twelfth century, the term 'bishops and cardinals' signified the three orders of the college.) When Archbishop Anselm V of Milan defended the customs of the Ambrosian church in Rome (1127/8), it was in the course of a conference 'with Pope Honorius and his cardinals'.[260] The most controversial issue of the decade was handled in the same manner. At each stage of the negotiation of the problem of investitures with Emperor Henry V, Calixtus II 'took counsel with the bishops and cardinals'. When in December 1122, after concluding the concordat of Worms with Henry V, Calixtus could welcome the emperor back into the fold, he wrote to Henry: 'our brethren the bishops, the cardinals and all the Roman clergy join us in greeting you and your princes and barons.'[261]

The effect of the schism of the 1130s was to enhance the importance of the consistory as an instrument of papal government. The diplomas of both Innocent II and Anacletus II frequently proclaim that papal decisions have been reached 'by the counsel of our brethren the bishops and cardinals'.[262] Each of the rival popes owed

---

[258] Hugh the Cantor, *The history of the Church of York 1066–1127* ed. C. Johnson (London, 1961) pp. 111–17. See K. J. Leyser, 'England and the Empire in the early twelfth century', *TRHS* 5th ser., 10 (1960), 79–83; D. Nicholl, *Thurstan, archbishop of York (1114–1140)* (York, 1964) pp. 86–90; D. Bethell, 'William of Corbeil and the Canterbury-York dispute', *JEH* 19 (1968), 155. See also below pp. 189, 263.

[259] Honorius II, *JL* 7305, *MPL* 166, 1291C. See M. Brett, *The English church under Henry I* (Oxford, 1975) pp. 52–4, 243–6.

[260] Landulf de S. Paulo, *Historia Mediolanensis* c. 52, *MGH SS* 20, 43–4.

[261] Hesso, *Relatio de concilio Remensi*, *MGH Libelli* 3, 23, 24, 25; Calixtus II, *JL* 6995: *MGH Constitutiones* 1, 163. See below pp. 437–8.

[262] Maleczek, 'Kardinalskollegium' (n. 56) pp. 49–50, 76–8.

his election to the fact that he was the representative of a faction of cardinals. Until such time as one or the other pope gained general recognition in Christendom, both depended for their legitimacy on the continued support of their electors. Innocent II in particular owed the rapid expansion of his obedience north of the Alps to the diplomatic skills of his cardinal legates.[263] Hence the tendency of northern observers to represent pope and cardinals as the inseparable components of a single institution. The chronicler of Morigny, for example, described how his abbot 'begged the pope and curia to consecrate the altar which was before the crucifix' and carefully identified the eleven cardinals who were present at this consecration in January 1131.[264] Innocent II himself underlined his reliance on the cardinals in the letter in which he summoned the faithful to the council of Rheims in October 1131. 'In order to preserve the unity of the Church and to check the schism which has recently sprung up in the holy Church of God, we have thought it useful – on the advice of our brethren, the bishops and cardinals – to celebrate a council . . . '[265] When the council met, the cardinals had a central part in its deliberations: they presided jointly with the pope over the public sessions and were entrusted with the investigation and judgement of several cases referred to the council. Equally significant as evidence of the growing consciousness of the importance of the cardinalate is the action of the council of Rheims in excommunicating and deposing not only the antipope but also his cardinals.[266] A comparison of the proceedings of the council of Rheims with those of Innocent II's Second Lateran Council of 1139 shows that the judicial functions of the cardinals had increased in the course of the pontificate. During the Second Lateran Council the case of the disputed election of the patriarch of Antioch was examined 'in the consistory'; the pope 'in discussion with the cardinals' judged the dispute between the abbey of St Bertin and Cluny; the dispute between the bishop and chapter of Cremona was 'carefully investigated by our brethren the cardinals'; and the disputed episcopal election in Constance was resolved 'by the counsel communicated by our brethren'.[267] In the final years

[263] See below pp. 158–9.

[264] *Historia Mauriniacensis monasterii* II, *MGH SS* 26, 40.

[265] Innocent II, *JL* 7475, *MPL* 179, 96B.

[266] Council of Rheims (1131): Mansi, *Sacra Concilia* 21, 466. See Maleczek, 'Kardinalskollegium' (n. 56) p. 46.

[267] William of Tyre, *Historia rerum in partibus transmarinis gestarum* XV. 13, *RHC Occ.* 1, 679; Simon, *Gesta abbatum Bertini Sithiensium* III. 5–6, *MGH SS* 13, 662; Innocent II, *JL* 8032: J. Pflugk-Harttung, *Acta pontificum Romanorum inedita* 2 (Tübingen-Stuttgart, 1880), 303; *JL* 7982: *NA* 4 (1878), 199.

of Innocent's pontificate the cases referred to the curia were regularly judged 'by the counsel of the cardinals'. It is from these years that we can date the regular use of what was to become the standard judicial practice of the late twelfth and early thirteenth-century curia: the referral of cases to one or more cardinals (from the early thirteenth century called *auditores*) who then recommended a verdict to the pope.[268]

The records of Innocent II's pontificate reveal a sustained attempt to expand the judicial business referred to the papal curia. The result was that great increase in the number of cases reaching the curia in mid-century, which is commemorated in the well-known tirade of Bernard of Clairvaux. 'Every day the palace is full of the noise of law, but it is the law of Justinian, not of the Lord . . . not law but litigation and sophistry intended to undermine judgement.'[269] The curia was able to cope with this expansion of its judicial functions only because of the availability of the cardinals as a team of investigators and judges. Of particular importance were those cardinals who had been trained in the law, the *magistri* who began to appear in the college in the second quarter of the twelfth century. The first *magister* to be promoted to the college seems to have been Guido of Castello, appointed cardinal deacon of S. Maria in Via Lata in 1128 (later cardinal priest of S. Marco and Pope Celestine II). He was one of the most learned men of his generation and possessed a library of over fifty volumes, including numerous books of canon law and Roman law.[270] In July 1137 he was a member of the delegation sent by Innocent II to Monte Cassino to investigate the legality of the election of Abbot Rainald; and in the final years of the pontificate he was a close collaborator of the chancellor Gerard of S. Croce in the business of the curia.[271] Innocent II appointed to the college four more *magistri* distinguished for their knowledge of the law: Master Boetius, Master Ivo of Chartres, Master Thomas of Milan and

---

[268] Maleczek, 'Kardinalskollegium' (n. 56) pp. 63, 68–9. This practice occurs sporadically in the pontificate of Paschal II: see below p. 190.

[269] Bernard, *De consideratione* II.4.5: (n. 20) 733A.

[270] Zenker, *Mitglieder* (n. 40) pp. 83–4; A. Wilmart, 'Les livres légués par Célestin II à Città di Castello', *Revue Bénédictine* 35 (1923), 98–102; D. Luscombe, *The school of Peter Abelard* (Cambridge, 1969) pp. 20–2.

[271] *Chronica monasterii Casinensis* IV.109: (n. 96) p. 574; Gerhoch of Reichersberg, *Libellus de ordine donorum sancti Spiritus* ed. D. van den Eynde and A. Rijmersdael, *Gerhohi praepositi Reichersbergensis Opera inedita* I (Spicilegium Pontificii Athenaei Antoniani 8: Rome, 1955), 66.

Master Hubald.[272] Eugenius III promoted five such *magistri*, four of whom became figures of great influence in the college: Master Bernard (later cardinal bishop of Porto), Master Guido Puella, Master Hildebrand and Master Odo of Brescia.[273] Hadrian IV promoted Master Albert of Morra (later chancellor and Pope Gregory VIII) and Master Raimundus of Nîmes.[274] The *magistri* Bernard, Hildebrand, Odo, Albert and Raimundus survived to serve Alexander III, whose pontificate – like that of Innocent II – witnessed a marked increase in the volume of judicial business referred to the curia. Alexander III recruited six more cardinals with legal training: Lombardus of Piacenza, the Spaniard Petrus de Cardona, the Parisian master Matthew, Gratian (nephew of Eugenius III), Master Vivian and, the most distinguished of these recruits, Laborans.[275] By the end of the twelfth century legal expertise had become an important qualification for promotion to the cardinalate and lawyer cardinals had begun to be elected to the papacy.

The intensification of the judicial functions of the curia increased the pope's dependence on the collaboration of the cardinals and gave particular prominence to the *magistri* in the college. Simultaneously the cardinals became involved in the resolution of questions concerning the catholic faith. The conduct of the reform papacy in such questions is evident from the controversial career of the 'heresiarch' Berengar of Tours. Leo IX, Nicholas II and Gregory VII referred Berengar's teachings on the Eucharist to the papal synod. The final examination of Berengar's doctrine took place in the Lenten synod of 11 February 1079 in Rome.

When all were assembled in the church of the Saviour, there was a debate concerning the body and blood of our lord Jesus Christ and at first many were of one opinion, but some thought differently. The largest party declared that the bread and wine are converted by the words of the holy prayer and the consecration of the priest, through the invisible agency of the Holy Spirit, substantially into the Lord's body . . . and blood . . . Before the synod assembled on the third day the other party ceased to strive against the truth.

This decision was reached by 'the archbishops, bishops and religious persons, both those near at hand and those from different provinces',

---

[272] Zenker, *Mitglieder* (n. 40) pp. 116, 77–9, 114, 136.
[273] *Ibid.*, pp. 29–32, 112–13, 107–9, 171–4. The fifth promotion was that of the obscure Master Grecus: *ibid.*, p. 156.
[274] *Ibid.*, pp. 125–9, 179–80.
[275] Brixius, *Mitglieder* (n. 72) pp. 61, 63–4, 66. See below p. 483.

after two days of debate in the synod.[276] When *ca.* 1100 the papal synod disappeared, to be replaced by the new institutions of the 'general council' and the consistory, both these new institutions inherited the synod's function of defining the catholic faith. A series of general councils promulgated decrees against heretics and their protectors in the south of France: the council of Toulouse (1119), the Second Lateran Council (1139), the councils of Rheims (1148), Montpellier (1162) and Tours (1163) and the Third Lateran Council (1179).[277] Meanwhile the consistory had begun to specialise in investigating the teachings of suspect theologians.

The first such case is recorded in a letter of Innocent II of July 1141 to Archbishops Henry of Sens and Samson of Rheims and to Bernard of Clairvaux.

We, who, although unworthy, are seen to sit on the seat of St Peter – to whom the Lord said, 'and when you have turned again, strengthen your brethren' [Luke 22. 32] – having received the counsel of our brethren, the bishops and cardinals, have condemned . . . all the teachings of Peter [Abelard] . . . together with their author.[278]

Innocent's announcement of the condemnation of Peter Abelard combines the two distinct ideas of the papal duty of defending the faith and the cardinals' duty of advising the pope. In this case the cardinals' role was not simply that of investigators and judges in a judicial matter: they were called upon to share the papal duty of defending the faith. Their exalted role was emphasised by Bernard of Clairvaux in the polemics against Peter Abelard with which he bombarded the curia after the council of Sens had condemned Abelard's teaching (June 1140). Bernard summoned the cardinals to condemn the 'heretic' 'by virtue of the office which you hold, by virtue of the dignity which you enjoy, by virtue of the power which you have received'.[279]

---

[276] Gregory VII, *Registrum* VI.17a, pp. 425–7. See M. Gibson, 'The case of Berengar of Tours', *Studies in Church History* 7 (Cambridge, 1971) pp. 61–8.

[277] Mansi, *Sacra Concilia* 21, 226–7, 532, 718, 1159, 1177–8; 22, 331. See H. Grundmann, *Religiöse Bewegungen im Mittelalter* (2nd edition: Hildesheim, 1961) pp. 52–4.

[278] Innocent II, *JL* 8148: (n. 265) 517A.

[279] Bernard, *Epistola* 188: (n. 20) 351A–353D. See E. Little, 'Bernard and Abelard at the Council of Sens' in *Bernard of Clairvaux. Studies presented to Dom Jean Leclercq* (Cistercian Studies 23: Washington, 1973) pp. 55–71; P. Zerbi, 'San Bernardo di Chiaravalle e il concilio di Sens' in *Studi su S. Bernardo di Chiaravalle nell' ottavo centenario della canonizzazione* (Bibliotheca Cisterciensis 6: Rome, 1975) pp. 115–80.

An analogous case was the examination of Bishop Gilbert of Poitiers' doctrine of the Trinity in the papal curia in 1147–8. Once again the demand for papal intervention came from Bernard of Clairvaux. His pupil, Eugenius III responded with an investigation, held while the curia was in Paris in April 1147, in the presence of between fourteen and seventeen cardinals and an unknown number of archbishops, bishops, abbots and theologians. The inquiry proved inconclusive partly because Gilbert's opponents disagreed about their objections to his teaching and partly because no copy was available of his suspect commentary on Boethius.[280] The investigation was resumed in Rheims, not in the general council which Eugenius held there in March 1148, but, according to the historian John of Salisbury, *in consistorio*: a consistory held a fortnight after the council 'with the archbishops and bishops of various provinces who had remained behind to decide this case'.[281] Before the public meeting of this consistory Bernard of Clairvaux had a private meeting with the leading churchmen, in which he pressed them to support the condemnation of Gilbert's teaching. This attempt to prejudge the case so infuriated the cardinals that, when the consistory met, they insisted on their exclusive right to judge the case. According to Bernard's disciple, Geoffrey of Auxerre, the cardinals declared to the pope: 'lo! we have heard what has been said: now we shall judge how the case ought to be settled'.[282] The historian Otto of Freising recorded a more grandiose version of the cardinals' statement to the pope. 'You ought to know that it was by us, the hinges around whom the universal Church revolves, that you were promoted to the government of the whole Church and changed from a private person to the father of the universal Church.' Eugenius should therefore seek the advice of the cardinals, not of Bernard ('your abbot') and the French church. Questions of the catholic faith can be decided only by the Roman see: that is, by the pope and 'the sacred senate of

---

[280] N. M. Häring, 'Das Pariser Konsistorium Eugens III. vom April 1147', *Studia Gratiana* 11 (Collectanea Stephan Kuttner 1, 1967), 93–117.

[281] John of Salisbury, *Historia pontificalis* c. 8–11: (n. 44) pp. 15–25. See N. M. Häring, 'Notes on the council and consistory of Rheims (1148)', *Medieval Studies* 28 (1966), 39–59; *idem*, 'Das sogenannte Glaubensbekenntnis des Reimser Konsistoriums von 1148', *Scholastik* 40 (1965), 55–90.

[282] Geoffrey of Auxerre, *Epistola ad Albinum* 7.34 ed. N. M. Häring, 'The writings against Gilbert of Poitiers by Geoffrey of Auxerre', *Analecta Cisterciensia* 22 (1966), 75.

the cardinals'.[283] A case similar to that of Gilbert of Poitiers was that of the theologian Peter Lombard, who was defended by a group of cardinals in the Third Lateran Council of 1179, when Alexander III had accepted the recommendation of an adviser that Peter Lombard's Christology should be condemned.[284] In the second half of the twelfth century the cardinals' role in the defence of the faith was widely recognised. When in 1163 Gerhoch of Reichersberg warned the papal curia of an outbreak of the Adoptionist heresy in Germany, he sent letters simultaneously to the pope and the cardinals; and it was a cardinal who communicated the results of their deliberations to Gerhoch.[285]

At the same time as the cardinals assumed their role of guardians of the faith, they also began to participate in the procedure of the canonisation of saints. The practice of the reform papacy was evidently to examine the cases of candidates for canonisation in the papal synod. In the Lenten synod of 1078, for example, Gregory VII announced the miracles which had occurred at the tombs of Erlembald of Milan and of the Roman prefect Cencius, two Gregorian allies recently murdered by the enemies of reform, these miracles being the evidence necessary for canonisation.[286] An undated letter of Urban II to Bishop Otto of Strassburg states that the pope has approved the canonisation of Adelaide, the empress of Otto I, 'relying on the help of our brethren the bishops and others in a Roman synod'; and a further letter, also undated, emphasises that canonisation depends on 'the common consent of a plenary synod'.[287] In the first three decades of the twelfth century papal letters announcing the canonisation of saints are more numerous, but most of them fail to specify how this decision was reached. Only in three cases is it evident that the canonisation was approved in a

---

[283] Otto of Freising, *Gesta Friderici* 1.60: (n. 159) pp. 68–9. See S. Gammersbach, *Gilbert von Poitiers und seine Prozesse im Urteil der Zeitgenossen* (Cologne-Graz, 1959) pp. 76–9; Alberigo, *Cardinalato* (n. 7) pp. 56–63.

[284] J. de Ghellinck, *Le mouvement théologique au XIIe siècle* (2nd edition: Bruges, 1948) pp. 260–1. See below pp. 140, 142.

[285] Gerhoch of Reichersberg, *Epistola* 19 (to Cardinal Hyacinth), *Epistola* 21 (to the college of cardinals), *Epistola* 21* (Cardinal C. to Gerhoch), *MPL* 193, 573B–574A, 576CD, 585D–586A.

[286] Berthold of Reichenau, *Annales* 1077, *MGH SS* 5, 305. See C. Erdmann, *Die Entstehung des Kreuzzugsgedankens* (Stuttgart, 1935) p. 198.

[287] Urban II, *JL* 5762: S. Loewenfeld, *Epistolae pontificum Romanorum ineditae* (Leipzig, 1885) p. 65; *Cartulaire de l'Abbaye de sainte Croix de Quimperlé* ed. L. Maître and P. de Berthou (Paris, 1903) p. 285. See E. W. Kemp, *Canonization and authority in the Western Church* (Oxford, 1948) pp. 67–9.

general council: that of Conrad of Constance in the First Lateran Council of 1123, that of Godehard of Hildesheim in the council of Rheims of 1131 and that of Sturmi of Fulda in the Second Lateran Council of 1139.[288] Other canonisations during these years seem to have involved less formal procedures. In 1120, for example, Calixtus II canonised Hugh of Cluny in the chapter of Cluny 'with the consent of the bishops and cardinals'.[289] In a letter of 1134–6 announcing the canonisation of Hugh of Grenoble, Innocent II referred to a similarly informal procedure: the pope decided to canonise Hugh 'on the advice of the archbishops, bishops and cardinals and of the others who were with us'.[290] This letter forms an interesting contrast with a letter from the latter part of Innocent's pontificate, concerning a request from the abbot and monks of St Peter's, Westminster, to canonise King Edward the Confessor (1140–2). In this case the pope's decision to postpone the canonisation was taken 'after consulting our brethren the bishops and cardinals': that is, solely on the advice of the three orders of cardinals in a consistory.[291]

Henceforward popes regularly decided cases of canonisation as part of the routine business of the curia, while continuing to state in their letters the principle that such decisions should more properly be taken in a general council. Thus Eugenius III, when approached by the bishop of Bamberg with a request to canonise Emperor Henry II, replied that 'a petition of this kind is customarily admitted only in general councils'. He nevertheless did not refer the matter to a council but authorised the canonisation 'on receiving the counsel of our brethren, the archbishops and bishops who were present', on the grounds that the Roman church 'is the chief support of all councils'.[292] Alexander III responded similarly in 1161 to a renewed request to canonise Edward the Confessor. Replying that 'so lofty

---

[288] Calixtus II, *JL* 7028: (n. 104) 1273D–1274B; Innocent II, *JL* 7496, 8007: (n. 265) 110BC, 450D–451A. See Kemp, *Canonization* pp. 71, 74–5, 76; S. Kuttner, 'La réserve papale du droit de canonisation', *Revue historique du droit français et étranger* 4. sér., 17 (1938), 184.

[289] Hugh, monk of Cluny, letter to Abbot Pontius, ed. H. E. J. Cowdrey, 'Two studies in Cluniac history 1049–1126', *SG* 11 (1978), 115–16.

[290] Innocent II, *JL* 7742: (n. 265) 256A. Kemp, *Canonization* p. 76, wishes to connect this canonisation with the council of Pisa of 1135; but since the dating clause of the letter, albeit incomplete, reads '22 April', it cannot refer to the council, which took place on 30 May.

[291] Innocent II, *JL* 8182: 568B. See Kemp, *Canonization* pp. 76–7.

[292] Eugenius III, *JL* 8882: (n. 156) 1119AB. See Kuttner, 'La réserve' (n. 288) p. 184; R. Klauser, 'Zur Entwicklung des Heiligsprechungsverfahrens bis zum 13. Jahrhundert', *ZSSRG KA* 40 (1954), 85–101.

and exalted an undertaking is permitted only infrequently except in solemn councils', he nevertheless authorised the canonisation 'on the common counsel of our brethren'. (Alexander III's English correspondent, Bishop Gilbert Foliot of Hereford had intimated to the pope that King Henry II of England regarded this canonisation as a suitable reward for the support which he was giving Alexander in the papal schism.)[293] None of the canonisations completed during Alexander's pontificate was in fact referred to a council: numerous requests for canonisation were presented to the council of Tours in 1163, but the pope postponed all these cases.[294] The four extant letters of Alexander III announcing the canonisation of a saint – Edward the Confessor (1161), King Canute Laward of Denmark (1169), Archbishop Thomas Becket of Canterbury (1173), Bernard of Clairvaux (1174) – record decisions made 'on the advice of our brethren': that is, of the cardinals.[295] Like Innocent II at the end of his pontificate, Alexander III decided such cases in a consistory. This practice continued in the last two decades of the twelfth century. In the pontificate of Lucius III the petition of the monks of Siegburg for the canonisation of their founder, Archbishop Anno of Cologne, was investigated by the cardinals. (One of them revealed a strong anti-German prejudice: 'your land usually produces fighters; it is remarkable that there can be saints there'.)[296] In 1189 Clement III entrusted the documents relating to the canonisation of Bishop Otto of Bamberg to a single cardinal, the distinguished canon lawyer Laborans. (He read the dossier overnight and made a positive recommendation in a consistory next morning.)[297] During the pontificate of Celestine III five saints – Peter of Tarentaise (1191), Ubald of Gub-

293 Alexander III, *JL* 10653: (n. 34) 106D–107C; Gilbert Foliot, *Letter* 133 ed. Z. N. Brooke, A. Morey and C. N. L. Brooke, *The letters and charters of Gilbert Foliot* (Cambridge, 1967) p. 177; Alexander III, *JL* 10837: *ibid.* pp. 183–4. See Kemp, *Canonization* (n. 287) pp. 82–3.

294 Alexander III, *JL* 12330, *MPL* 185, 622D; *JL* 10886: (n. 34) 235D–236B. See R. Somerville, *Pope Alexander III and the Council of Tours (1163)* (Berkeley-Los Angeles, 1977) pp. 59–60.

295 Alexander III, *JL* 10653, 11646, 12201: (n. 34) 106D–107C, 608D–609C, 900D–901C; *JL* 12329, *MPL* 185, 623AC. See Kuttner, 'La réserve' (n. 288) pp. 184 n. 3, 194; Kemp, *Canonization* (n. 287) pp. 82–3, 86–9, 90; M. Schwarz, 'Heiligsprechungen im 12. Jahrhundert und die Beweggründe ihrer Urheber', *Archiv für Kulturgeschichte* 39 (1957), 54–8.

296 *Translatio sancti Annonis*, *MGH SS* 11, 516. See Schwarz, 'Heiligsprechungen' pp. 45–8.

297 *Miracula et elevatio sancti Ottonis auctore incerto*, *MGH SS* 12, 914; Clement III, *JL* 16411, *MPL* 204, 1438BC. See Klauser, 'Entwicklung' (n. 292) pp. 94–6.

bio (1192), Bernward of Hildesheim (1193), John Gualbert (1193), Gerald of Sauve-majeure (1197) – were canonised on the advice of the cardinals.[298]

From the mid-twelfth century onwards visitors to the curia regularly remarked that the cardinals had become the pope's principal advisers on all major issues. In the early 1140s important cases might still be discussed in the presence not only of the cardinals but also of visiting ecclesiastical dignitaries and members of the Roman nobility. When in 1141 Hariulf of Oudenbourg presented his case to the curia, the chancellor Haimeric 'led him to the consistory of the palace, where the lord pope sat on the judgement-seat with the cardinals at his right hand, while the greater Roman noblemen, with curled hair and clad in silk, stood or sat at his feet'.[299] When in 1144 Lucius II confirmed the decision of Urban II to subordinate the church of Dôle to the archbishopric of Tours, his decision was taken in the presence not only of the cardinals but also of distinguished visitors including Archbishop Raymond of Toledo, the bishops Henry of Winchester and Nigel of Ely and Peter the Venerable, abbot of Cluny, together with 'the noble Romans' Cencius Frangipane and Leo Pierleone 'and many others, both clerks and laymen'.[300] However, there is also evidence from the 1140s of decisions taken by pope and cardinals in secret. In 1142 when the curia had heard the accusations of Abbot Herman of St Martin in Tournai against Bishop Simon of Noyon, Innocent II 'exhorted the cardinals who were sitting round him to assist him and, rising from his seat, withdrew with them into secret session (*in secretarium*)'.[301] Similarly in 1147 when a delegation from the abbey of Stablo appeared before the pope and cardinals seeking confirmation of the election of Wibald as their abbot, Eugenius III 'said that he would take counsel with the brethren and answer us according to their advice'. The secret deliberations of pope and cardinals lasted for ten days.[302]

Two contrasting views of Eugenius III's conduct in consistory are presented in the *Papal history* of John of Salisbury (who was the first

---

[298] Celestine III, *JL* 16690, 16830, 16943, 17039, 17527, *MPL* 206, 869D–871B, 918D–919D, 970BD, 1018B–1019C, 1211D–1212C. See Kemp, *Canonization* (n. 287) pp. 94, 96–7; Pfaff, 'Kardinäle' (n. 40) p. 72.

[299] Müller, 'Bericht' (n. 219) p. 102. See above pp. 94–5 and below pp. 189–90, 193.

[300] Lucius II, *JL* 8609, MPL 179, 876AB. Cf. Eugenius III, *JL* 8991: (n. 156) 1184A.

[301] *Liber de restauratione sancti Martini Tornacensis. Continuatio* c. 23, *MGH SS* 14, 326.

[302] Henry of Stablo, letter to Abbot Wibald: P. Jaffé, *Bibliotheca rerum germanicarum* 1 (Berlin, 1864), 123–4.

historian to make regular use of the term, *consistorium*). The *Papal history* contains an eyewitness account of the attempt of Count Hugh II of Molise to obtain a divorce (perhaps in 1150). During the discussion of this case in consistory 'there were not two present who opposed the divorce'; nevertheless when the pope came to give judgement, he refused the count a divorce, offering him instead remission of his sins in return for a reconciliation with the countess.[303] A similar case recorded by John of Salisbury was that of the bishop elect of Tripoli, suspended for disobedience by the papal legate Guido of Florence, who was examined *in consistorio* in 1149. 'All present considered the elect as good as deposed'; but Eugenius confirmed him in his office.[304] In both these cases Eugenius allegedly gave a judgement directly contrary to the unanimous opinion of the consistory; but in two other instances mentioned by John of Salisbury the pope seems to have been compelled to accept the cardinals' judgement. The first case was that of Gilbert of Poitiers in 1148 when, as we have already seen, the cardinals defied the attempt of Bernard of Clairvaux to secure the condemnation of Gilbert's teaching.[305] The second case was that of Archbishop Philip of Tours, who had been deposed and degraded from the priesthood by Innocent II because he had received ordination and consecration from the antipope Anacletus II. Bernard of Clairvaux and the whole Cistercian order requested Eugenius in 1148 to restore Philip to the priesthood. The pope, as a former Cistercian, 'was willing to listen to them; nevertheless he referred the matter to the cardinals and they said that it was impossible': in the Second Lateran Council Innocent II had decreed the perpetual condemnation of the antipope's ordinations and Eugenius III himself had recently confirmed this decree in the council of Rheims.[306]

This portrait of Eugenius obliged to accept the ruling of the cardinals is certainly corroborated by other contemporary observers. John of Salisbury's report of the case of Gilbert of Poitiers, for example, corresponds to the accounts of Geoffrey of Auxerre and Otto of Freising, who recorded an even more outspoken opposition than that presented in John's *Papal history*. Two members of

---

[303] John of Salisbury, *Historia pontificalis* c. 41 (n. 44) p. 81: see also pp. 99–100. See R. W. Southern, *Western society and the Church in the Middle Ages* (Harmondsworth, 1970) pp. 136–7.

[304] John of Salisbury, *Historia pontificalis* c. 37: pp. 73–4. See below pp. 357–8.

[305] See above p. 109.

[306] John of Salisbury, *Historia pontificalis* c. 16: p. 43.

Eugenius' curia also left impressions of a pope who depended on the advice of the cardinals. His legate in Poland and Germany, Guido, cardinal deacon of S. Maria in Porticu (the future antipope Paschal III) described an excommunication pronounced by Eugenius as the joint pronouncement of 'the lord pope and the Roman church'.[307] Eugenius' biographer, Boso (who served in his chancery) recorded an instance of the pope's seeking the cardinals' approval before appointing a new member of the college: Eugenius promoted Nicholas Breakspear cardinal bishop of Albano 'on the advice of his brethren'.[308] It is not necessary to take literally Otto of Freising's version of the cardinals' declaration in the consistory of 1148: 'you ought to know that it was by us, the hinges around whom the universal Church revolves, that you were promoted to the government of the whole Church'. There is, however, no doubt that by 1150 it was generally accepted that the pope must seek the advice of the cardinals before reaching a decision. The theory that the pope is bound by the cardinals' advice first appears in a privilege of Hadrian IV, dated 9 February 1156. 'Having taken counsel with our brethren', Hadrian confirmed the primacy enjoyed by the archbishopric of Toledo and cancelled a privilege which Archbishop Pelagius of Compostela had obtained from Anastasius IV, freeing his church from the jurisdiction of Toledo. This privilege of Anastasius was to be regarded as invalid 'especially because it was elicited with the advice neither of the brethren in general nor of the sounder part of the brethren'.[309]

Above all political decisions in the middle and later twelfth century were taken with the cardinals *in consistorio*. This practice had already been established in the pontificates of Paschal II and Calixtus II during the final stages of the Investiture Contest.[310] Innocent II's strategy during the schism of the 1130s was decided 'by taking counsel with his brethren, the cardinals and bishops'.[311] A French observer described an occasion, perhaps in 1135, on which Innocent received the envoys of the Byzantine emperor in a consistory.[312] The negotiations of Lucius II with King Roger II of Sicily at Ceprano in 1144 were referred to a consistory, in which the hope of reaching an

---

[307] Guido of S. Maria in Porticu, letter to King Conrad III: (n. 302) p. 344.
[308] Boso, *Vita Hadriani IV*: (n. 45) p. 388. See above p. 46.
[309] Hadrian IV, *JL* 10141: (n. 68) 1448A.
[310] See above pp. 101–3, 104.
[311] *Historia Compostellana* III.27: (n. 33) 1191D, paraphrasing Innocent II, *JL* 7475: (n. 265) 96B.
[312] Abbot Odo of St-Rémy, Rheims, *Epistola ad Thomam comitem*, MPL 172, 1331C.

agreement was abandoned 'because of the resistance of the cardinals'.[313] John of Salisbury recorded that when in 1148 Count Geoffrey of Anjou denounced King Stephen of England to the pope as a usurper, Eugenius III examined the case *in consistorio*.[314] The fullest account of the role of the consistory in deciding papal political strategy is provided by Cardinal Boso's biographies of Hadrian IV and Alexander III, which in many cases report discussions in which the author himself participated. The pope's dependence on the counsel of the cardinals is a central theme of Boso's biographies. When King Frederick I of Germany laid siege to Tortona in February 1155 and when he approached Rome, wishing to be crowned emperor; when in September 1155 the Apulian barons rebelled against King William I of Sicily and offered their fealty to the pope and when William I, threatened both by this rebellion and by a Byzantine invasion, promised to submit to the pope, Hadrian IV's responses were invariably determined 'by the advice of the brethren'.[315]

Boso's biography contains a striking instance of the political advice of the cardinals prevailing over the pope's own wishes. Hadrian IV wished to accept the generous terms of submission offered by William I of Sicily at the end of 1155.

> It seemed good to the pope that so useful an agreement and a settlement which brought great honour to the Church should be accepted. But because the greater part of the brethren, thinking it too dangerous and uncertain, would not consent to it, all that had been offered was frustrated and entirely rejected.

The result was a disastrous reversal for the papal curia: William I unexpectedly overcame his enemies and found himself in a position to impose a settlement on terms much less advantageous for the papacy. Hadrian 'sent the greater part of his brethren into the Campagna' and saw to it that the agreement with William I (the concordat of Benevento, 18 June 1156) was negotiated by the minority of the cardinals who shared his idea of the desirability of a Sicilian alliance.[316] By the end of Hadrian's pontificate a 'Sicilian party' of cardinals supporting the pope's new political strategy had appeared in the curia: in the summer of 1159 it numbered thirteen cardinals, the most prominent being the chancellor Roland, cardinal priest of S. Marco. We have already seen evidence to suggest that this

---

[313] Romuald of Salerno, *Annales* 1143, *MGH SS* 19, 424. See below p. 388.
[314] John of Salisbury, *Historia pontificalis* c. 18: (n. 44) p. 45.
[315] Boso, *Vita Hadriani IV*: (n. 45) pp. 390, 393, 394. See below pp. 463–5.
[316] *Ibid.*, p. 395. See below pp. 389–90.

'Sicilian party' was the deliberate creation of the pope: a response to the rebuff which his new political strategy had received from the cardinals in 1155.[317] The problems experienced by Hadrian IV in introducing his 'Sicilian party' indicate that by the 1150s the pope was bound by 'the advice of the brethren in general or of the sounder part of the brethren' on a major political issue. If he could not obtain the support of the college for a new political strategy, he was obliged to create a party of supporters in the college by judicious recruitment and promotion.

Alexander III inherited Hadrian IV's 'Sicilian party' as the core of his college of cardinals. According to Boso's biography, the pope referred all the major political issues of his turbulent pontificate to these brethren: in particular, papal relations with Emperor Frederick I, from the excommunication pronounced 'with the bishops and cardinals' in March 1160 until the peace terms negotiated in 1176–7 by the pope 'alone with his brethren in a secret council'. The proposals of Emperor Manuel Comnenus for a Byzantine-papal alliance in 1167–8 and the reconciliation of King Henry II of England to the Church after the murder of Archbishop Thomas Becket of Canterbury were also referred to the advice of the cardinals. Boso's descriptions of these discussions distinguish carefully between the *consistorium*, which he defined as a public hearing, and the secret council in which the pope heard the cardinals' opinions. The distinction is apparent, for example, in his report of the arrival in the curia of Henry II's envoys, who sought to avert their lord's excommunication after Thomas Becket's murder (25 March 1171). 'When the pope had taken counsel with his brethren, he went out into the *consistorium*' to give his reply to the envoys.[318] Similarly in Boso's account of the negotiation of the peace of Anagni (November 1176): 'when the pope was seated in the consistory in the presence of a multitude of clergy and nobles', the envoys of Emperor Frederick I delivered their lord's message in public. 'When they had been heard, the whole assembly withdrew and the pope, alone with his brethren, entered into a secret council with the envoys.'[319] Boso's account of the years 1159–77 contains thirteen references to important political decisions reached on the advice of the cardinals.[320] Especially notable is his report of the crisis of summer 1167 when Frederick I was

[317] See above p. 53.
[318] Boso, *Vita Alexandri III*: (n. 173) p. 425. See below p. 191.
[319] *Ibid.*, p. 434. See below p. 494.
[320] *Ibid.*, pp. 400, 403, 415–17, 420–1, 425, 430, 434, 440, 443.

besieging Rome and the papal curia was compelled to flee from the
Lateran palace: 'because of the threat of the emperor's malice a meeting of the bishops and cardinals was held every day; cases were discussed and answers given'.[321] According to Boso, Frederick was well
aware of Alexander's dependence on the cardinals and, 'like a cunning fox', tried to deprive him of his advisers. In 1167 he sent 'words
of peace' to the cardinals, intended to involve them in a plan to
secure the simultaneous abdication of Alexander and the antipope.
The cardinals vigorously resisted this suggestion: 'they adhered to
their head like limbs to their body'.[322] Frederick I was to try a similar
tactic nearly two decades later, when negotiating with Lucius III
about papal territorial claims in central Italy (1184). The emperor
offered the pope one-tenth and the cardinals one-ninth of his Italian
revenues in return for the renunciation of the papal claims: presumably an attempt to drive a wedge between pope and cardinals on this
issue. The cardinals would not be tempted, however, and they
strengthened Lucius III's resolve to refuse the emperor's other
request, the conferring of the imperial crown on his son.[323]

For the last two decades of the twelfth century no source is available that is as forthcoming and as determined to accentuate the role
of the cardinals as Boso's biographies of the popes whom he served.
The cardinals' advisory role is mentioned only sporadically in papal
letters and privileges. It is evident that the large-scale promotion of
cardinals in the pontificate of Clement III – the appointment of
approximately thirty cardinals between March 1188 and October
1190 – rapidly changed the character of the college. The
homogeneous college which Boso represented as cooperating
enthusiastically with Alexander III was transformed into the divided
college of the 1190s, containing supporters both of Emperor Henry
VI and of his rival for the Sicilian crown, Tancred of Lecce. During
the pontificate of Celestine III the hostile factions of cardinals para-
lysed political decision-making: decisions could only be made when
the members of one of the factions were absent from the curia.
Hence, for example, the papal decision to recognise Tancred (the
illegitimate cousin of the late king, William II) as king of Sicily was
taken in the spring of 1192, when nearly half the cardinals were
absent from Rome – including the most prominent supporter of

---

[321] *Ibid.*, p. 416. See below pp. 484, 486.
[322] *Ibid.*, p. 417.
[323] Frederick I, letter to Lucius III: *MGH Constitutiones* 1, 420–1. See above p. 42 and
below p. 502.

Henry VI, Cardinal Peter of S. Cecilia.[324] The decisions to give papal support to the emperor's opponents in Germany may well have been made in similar circumstances.[325] In the spring of 1193, however, the presence of almost all the cardinals in the curia prevented the pope from taking a firm stand against the emperor. Henry VI was currently holding to ransom King Richard I of England, whose status as a crusader placed him under the special protection of the pope; but Celestine was unable to take the strong measures which would compel the emperor to release his prisoner. Only a minority of the cardinals favoured excommunication: the rest were either imperial supporters or moderates who were afraid of strengthening the alliance between the emperor and Richard's enemy, King Philip II of France.[326] This paralysis of the curia came to an end only with the death of Henry VI (28 September 1197), which deprived the pro-imperial cardinals of their influence. The vigorous measures demanded by the emperor's opponents enjoyed the support of the majority of the college during the last three months of the pontificate.[327]

Like the frustration of Hadrian IV's Sicilian policy in 1155, the indecisive character of papal policy in the pontificate of Celestine III is evidence of the cardinals' crucial role as papal advisers. The pope could take no major political initiative without the agreement of a majority of the cardinals. Celestine's letters and privileges reveal that the cardinals' consent was required in every aspect of Church government. The condemnation of the divorce of King Philip II of France from Ingeborg of Denmark (May 1195); the commissioning of Bishop Meinard of Livonia as a missionary to the heathen (April 1193); the conferring of the office of papal legate on Archbishop Hubert Walter of Canterbury (March 1195) and the sending of the pallium to Archbishop Alan of Nicosia (January 1197); the measures to end the conflicts within the order of Grandmont: all were decided 'on the advice of the brethren'.[328] A privilege of 25 August 1196 contains the earliest extant reference to the confirmation of a new religious order in a consistory: namely, the order founded by Joachim of Fiore in southern Italy after he left the Cistercian order.

---

[324] V. Pfaff, 'Die Kardinäle unter Papst Coelestin III. (2. Teil)', *ZSSRG KA* 52 (1966), 342–4.
[325] See below pp. 513–14.
[326] Pfaff, 'Kardinäle (2. Teil)' pp. 347 50. See below p. 515.
[327] See below pp. 521–2.
[328] Celestine III, *JL* 17241, 16991, 17203, 17479, *MPL* 206, 1098A, 996A, 1075D–1076A, 1195A. See Pfaff, 'Kardinäle' (n. 40) p. 71.

(This procedure seems to have served Innocent III as a precedent when Francis of Assisi was received by the pope and the cardinals in a consistory.)[329] The range of ecclesiastical business transacted in the consistory in the last decade of the twelfth century reveals the extraordinary success of the papacy in establishing its claims to a universal jurisdiction throughout Christendom. Celestine III described to his correspondents the 'fullness of power' (*plenitudo potestatis*) possessed by the pope as head and teacher of all the churches. (He was the first pope to use this term, so familiar in the pronouncements of the thirteenth-century papacy.) It was by virtue of this 'fullness of power' that he claimed to confirm all the legal proceedings of the churches, to preserve the unity of the Church and to ensure 'the uniformity of faith and doctrine'.[330] However, in exercising this unique office the pope was dependent on the assistance and the agreement of his brethren. The cardinals had become his indispensable collaborators in the government of the Church, as judges, guardians of the faith and political advisers.

---

[329] Celestine III, *JL* 17425: D. Taccone-Gallucci, *Regesti dei romani pontefici per le chiese della Calabria con annotazioni storiche* (Rome, 1902) p. 82. See M. Maccarrone, 'Primato romano e monasteri dal principio del secolo XII ad Innocenzo III' in *Istituzione monastiche e istituzioni canonicali in Occidente* (Miscellanea del Centro di Studi Medioevali 9: Milan, 1977) pp. 77–8.

[330] Pfaff, '"Pro posse nostro"' (n. 203) pp. 91–2. See above p. 92.

3

PAPAL COUNCILS

•

The century which opened with the pontificate of Gregory VII and closed with that of Alexander III was a momentous period in the history of the councils of the western Church. At no other period in the history of the Church did popes preside so frequently over councils of bishops from all the provinces of the Latin Church, as in the later eleventh century and the twelfth century. Some of these councils played a notable role in shaping events: Urban II's council of Clermont (1095), at which the First Crusade was launched; Calixtus II's council of Rheims (1119), which attempted to solve the problem of investitures; Eugenius III's council of Rheims (1148), concerned both with the defence of orthodoxy and with the affairs of the English church and kingdom; Alexander III's council of Tours (1163), held in the midst of schism and likewise concerned to defend orthodoxy. Most imposing of all, by virtue of the number of their participants and of the definitive character of their legislation, were the three Lateran councils of 1123, 1139 and 1179, called 'ecumenical' in the tradition of the Latin Church.

The 'general' and 'ecumenical' councils of this period[1] developed

---

[1] On the terminology of the councils see H. Fuhrmann, 'Das Ökumenische Konzil und seine historische Grundlagen', *Geschichte in Wissenschaft und Unterricht* 12 (1961), 672–95; R. Foreville, 'Procédure et débats dans les conciles médiévaux du Latran (1123–1215)', *Rivista di storia della Chiesa in Italia* 19 (1965), 21, 37; *eadem, Latran I, II, III et Latran IV* (Histoire des Conciles Œcuméniques 6: Paris, 1965); G. Fransen, 'Papes, conciles généraux et œcuméniques' in *Le istituzioni ecclesiastiche della 'societas christiana' dei secoli XI–XII* 1 (Milan, 1974), 203–28 (esp. 203–7);

out of two very different kinds of assembly. The first of these antecedents was the papal synod of the pre-reform period. This was a synod attended mainly by the suburbican bishops, sometimes also by the other bishops of the Roman ecclesiastical province and very occasionally by bishops from those regions of Italy not under Byzantine control. It was the provincial synod of the bishop of Rome, concerned with the local problems of the Roman church: the traditional episcopal *synodus* by means of which each province of the Church had been accustomed to exercise ecclesiastical discipline. The second and more imposing antecedent was the imperial council, which the emperor summoned and over which he presided, in order to regulate ecclesiastical affairs throughout the Empire.[2] In the imperial councils of the Ottonians and Salians the pope himself might be present (as, for example, in 1022 and 1027), presiding jointly with the emperor. Indeed papal participation in imperial councils continued into the early years of the reform papacy: the last such occasion was the council of Florence in 1055, which issued its reforming decrees under the joint presidency of the German pope Victor II and Emperor Henry III. Meanwhile, however, in the pontificate of Leo IX (1049–54) the crucial innovation had occurred which produced one of the most important institutions of the reform papacy: an assembly attended by bishops from outside the Roman ecclesiastical province and from outside the imperial territories, an assembly under the sole presidency of the pope, the decrees of which were regarded as binding on the whole of Latin Christendom. Leo IX's pontificate was a period of transition in conciliar history, as in many other aspects of Church history. Leo took part in one of the last joint papal-imperial councils, in Mainz in October 1049; but a fortnight earlier he had held an assembly of a very different character in Rheims. It was a new kind of papal synod, to which for the first time the pope summoned non-Italian and non-imperial bishops and exercised the authority of supreme ecclesiastical judge outside the province of Rome and outside the Empire.[3] Leo IX's new form of papal synod was the model for the reforming synods of the late eleventh-century papacy, which functioned both as the highest

F.-J. Schmale, 'Systematisches zu den Konzilien des Reformpapsttums im 12. Jahrhundert', *Annuarium Historiae Conciliorum* 6 (1974), 36–8; *idem*, 'Synodus – synodale concilium – concilium', ibid., 8 (1976), 80–102.

[2] M. Boyle, 'Synoden Deutschlands und Reichsitaliens von 922 bis 1059', *ZSSRG KA* 18 (1929), 131–284; Schmale, 'Synodus' (n. 1) pp. 81–4.

[3] Hauck, *Kirchengeschichte Deutschlands* 3, 600; Schmale, 'Synodus' pp. 95–7.

tribunal of the Church and as a legislative assembly promulgating reforming decrees. For the next forty years these synods were usually held in the basilica and palace of St John Lateran in Rome, at first at Eastertide and subsequently at the beginning of Lent.

'As has been the custom in the apostolic see for some years, we have determined, with God's help, to hold a synod in the first week of Lent.' So wrote Gregory VII to the archbishop of Ravenna, summoning him to the second great reforming synod of his pontificate in 1075.[4] A synod was held almost every Lent during Gregory's pontificate and in 1078 an additional synod was held in November: all took place in Rome except his last synod, which had to be held in exile in Salerno (1084). The official records of these synods, and more particularly the papal letters summoning bishops to attend them and informing other bishops of their proceedings, all bear witness to the importance which Gregory VII attached to the papal synod as an instrument of reform. The synod provided the 'solace and remedy' necessary to avert 'the irreparable ruin and destruction of the Church in our time':[5] its function was to correct abuses, above all simony and clerical marriage, and to punish evildoers. The papal synod in Gregory VII's pontificate – no less than in the pontificates of his reforming and pre-reform predecessors – was a court of justice; and the extant papal summonses and synodal protocols suggest that the punishment of evildoers was the most time-consuming part of the business of Gregory's synods. For example, the earliest extant protocol, that of the Lenten synod of 1075, records sentences of excommunication against five advisers of King Henry IV of Germany, against King Philip I of France, against the Norman prince Robert Guiscard and his nephew and against seven imperial bishops; while the protocol of Lent 1076 records sentences against numerous French and imperial bishops, as well as the spectacular sentence against the German king.[6] All the subsequent papal synods of the pontificate were dominated by the case of Henry IV.

The terminology used in Gregory's letters to describe these judgements is instructive: 'we have decreed according to the immutable sentence of the holy synod and with the irrevocable consent of all the brethren in session there . . .'; 'the synodal assembly has decreed . . .'[7] These are *synodal* decrees as well as papal decrees: the bishops in the synod, acting as legal assessors and co-judges, are bound by their 'irrevocable consent' to the judgement of the synod.

---

[4] Gregory VII, *Registrum* II.42, p. 179.   [5] *Ibid.*, 1.42, p. 65.
[6] *Ibid.*, II.52a, p. 196; III.10a, p. 268.   [7] *Ibid.*, II.54, pp. 198–9; VII. 17, pp. 491–2.

Hence Gregory's insistence on the attendance of bishops whenever the synod was due to discuss the business of their locality. 'Not only the necessity and tribulation of the [French] church but also many other affairs relating to your kingdom demand that Your Fraternity should be present at the Roman council': so Gregory wrote to the archbishop of Sens in 1076, when the synod was due to consider the excommunication of the French king and of many French bishops.[8] The archbishop was wanted as an expert witness as well as a judge. 'The more fully and more closely we are surrounded by the counsels of Your Prudence and by frequent and careful consultation with other colleagues, the more securely and firmly we are armed for the defence of ecclesiastical liberty and religion.'[9] When, therefore, in 1083 'the treachery of the tyrant Henry [IV]' prevented the attendance of the bishops on whose counsels the pope most relied, the synod could not function effectively.[10] There is no suggestion in the sources that the bishops in the synod played a secondary role, merely ratifying decisions already made by the pope. On the contrary, decisions seem to have been reached by means of debate in the synod. On one occasion at least, in the Lenten synod of 1079, the debate on the Eucharistic heresy of Berengar of Tours was protracted by a vociferous minority faction who defended Berengar's thesis. The handling of the case of Henry IV in the same synod offers a useful illustration of the role of the pope in these debates. When the bishops heard the accusations of Henry's enemies, 'very many of the council decreed that the apostolic sword [of excommunication] should be unsheathed against his tyranny; but apostolic mildness prevented this'.[11] A majority in the synod formulated a decree of excommunication; but the pope vetoed their sentence. The papal veto made him effectively lord of the synod; but there is little indication that Gregory VII habitually played this role.

The eleven papal synods of the eleven-year pontificate of Urban II were very different in character from those of Gregory VII. Firstly, only three synods – those of the opening and closing years of the pontificate (1089, 1098–9) – were held in Rome (where the imperial antipope retained a stronghold throughout Urban's pontificate). The remainder were held outside the Roman ecclesiastical province and – with the important exception of the synod of Piacenza (1095)

[8] *Ibid.*, IV.9, pp. 307–8.
[9] *Ibid.*, I.42, p. 65 (to Patriarch Sigehard of Aquileia).
[10] *Ibid.*, IX.35a, pp. 627–8; Bernold of St Blasien, *Chronica* 1083, *MGH SS* 5, 438.
[11] *Registrum* VI.17a, pp. 425–7.

– outside the imperial territories. The other synods were held in southern Italy, where Urban enjoyed the protection of his Norman vassals – Melfi (1089), Benevento (1091), Troia (1093) and Bari (1097) – and in France: Clermont (1095), Tours (1096) and Nîmes (1096).[12] Secondly, there is reason to believe that a much greater number of churchmen attended Urban II's synods than had been present at those of Gregory VII. The synodal protocol of Piacenza in March 1095 reports that on the first and third days the synod met in a field: 'for so many people had assembled that no church could hold them; so they followed the example of Moses when he expounded the Law (Deuteronomy 1. 1) and our Lord Jesus Christ when he taught in the fields'. These biblical analogies serve to emphasise the unprecedented scale of the synod.[13] The various accounts of Clermont similarly emphasise the unusually large number of participants.[14] While Gregory VII's synods were attended mainly by persons concerned specifically with the judicial business of the synods, Urban II cast his net much more widely. So, for example, the synod of Piacenza was attended by 'bishops and abbots both from Germany and from Lombardy and Tuscany'.[15] The papal synods of Urban II's wandering pontificate brought the churchmen of Latin Christendom in direct contact with the supreme judicial authority of the pope on a scale hitherto unknown.

More important, however, than this increase in the number of participants were the developments in procedure in the synods of Urban II. The protocols sometimes suggest proceedings like those in the synods of Gregory VII, as in this formula from the protocol of Benevento (1091). 'Judgement was made in the presence of the whole council when the case had been very carefully investigated by our venerable bishops . . . We approve and have confirmed their sentence.' The synod judged the case and the pope acquiesced in their judgement. But increasingly more frequent in the synodal protocols of Urban II is the quite different formula found in canon 2 of Benevento: '[the decree] was acclaimed by all [with the words], *fiat,*

---

[12] R. Somerville, 'The French councils of Pope Urban II. Some basic considerations', *Annuarium Historiae Conciliorum* 2 (1970), 59–60, disproves the existence of a fourth French council at Limoges in December 1095.

[13] *Concilium Placentinum*, *MGH Constitutiones* 1, 561. Bernold, *Chronica* 1095 (n. 10) pp. 461–2, used these biblical analogies to defend the unorthodox proceeding of meeting outside a church.

[14] R. Crozet, 'Le voyage d'Urbain II et ses arrangements avec le clergé de France (1095–1096)', *Revue historique* 179 (1937), 271–2.

[15] *Concilium Placentinum* (n. 13) p. 561.

fiat![16] Similar formulas occur in the protocol of Troia (1093): canon 1 was decreed 'with the consent of all' and when canon 2 was announced, 'all replied: *fiat, fiat!*'[17] In these instances the function of the bishops is no longer that of formulating judgements and decrees: their work is now limited to the acclamation of decrees announced to the synod by the pope. In the synod of Piacenza, as in that of Benevento, some cases were judged by the bishops and confirmed by the pope 'according to the judgement of our brethren'; but the many reforming decrees were 'presented on the seventh day . . . and approved by the consent of the whole council'.[18] Similarly in Clermont, while the case of the primacy claimed by the archbishop of Lyons was decided by the synod, other cases were judged by the pope 'with the consent of the council' and once more the reforming decrees were promulgated by the pope and acclaimed by the synod.[19] In Nîmes (1096), according to the testimony of Bishop Ivo of Chartres, the pope alone judged the various cases before the synod.[20] In the case of the synod of Rome (1099), the most illustrious participant, Archbishop Anselm of Canterbury, described his own role and that of his colleagues with the single word *audivi*, 'I heard'.[21] In the synods of Urban II's pontificate, therefore, the pope assumed many of the functions which had previously belonged to the synod as a whole. The traditional procedure – debate and formulation of decrees by the bishops, followed (usually) by papal ratification – was in many instances, and especially in the issuing of reforming decrees, replaced by the procedure of promulgation of decrees by the pope and acclamation by the bishops. This new procedure was, if not caused, at least assisted by Urban's practice of repeating at a new synod the canons already decreed elsewhere in his own synods and those of his predecessors. So the chronicler Bernold of St Blasien recorded that at his first 'general synod' in Rome (1089) Urban 'confirmed by apostolic authority the ecclesiastical decrees of his pre-

---

[16]   Urban II, *JL* 5446, *MPL* 151, 328C–329C.
[17]   Synod of Troia: Mansi, *Sacra Concilia* 20, 789. See Schmale, 'Synodus' (n. 1) pp. 93–4.
[18]   Urban II, *JL* 5561: (n. 16) 416AD; *Concilium Placentinum* (n. 13) p. 561.
[19]   Urban II, *JL* 5600: 438D; R. Somerville, *The councils of Urban II* 1: *Decreta Claromontensia* (Amsterdam, 1972) pp. 25–32. See Schmale, 'Synodus' (n. 1) p. 99.
[20]   Synod of Nîmes: Mansi, *Sacra Concilia* 20, 937–40.
[21]   Anselm of Canterbury, *Epistola* 280 ed. F. S. Schmitt, *Sancti Anselmi Opera Omnia* 4 (Edinburgh, 1949), 195. Cf. the account of the synod of Bari (1097) by his biographer: 'we heard *fiat, fiat!* acclaimed by all': Eadmer, *Historia Novorum* II, *RS* 81 (1884), 114.

decessors'. The decrees of Clermont included canons of the southern Italian synods of 1089–93 and of Piacenza; the decrees of the other French councils repeated those of Clermont.[22] 'In the city of Tours', wrote Bernold, '[the pope] again corroborated the decrees of his past councils with the consent of the general synod.'[23] The re-promulgation of virtually the same decrees at each synod of the pontificate tended to transform the synod into a papal instrument for publicising the reform programme.

The evidence for the papal synods of Paschal II, especially those of the early years of the pontificate, is full of gaps and difficult to interpret.[24] Superficially the conciliar history of the pontificate somewhat resembles that of Urban II. Firstly, more than half of Paschal's synods were held outside Rome. Of the twelve identifiable synods of Paschal II, four were held in Norman Italy (Melfi in 1100 and three synods in Benevento in 1108, 1113 and 1117), two in imperial Italy (Guastalla and Florence in 1106), one in France (Troyes in 1107) and five in the Lateran (1102, 1105, 1110, 1112 and 1116). Secondly, as in the synods of Urban II, the same basic reform pro-gramme was promulgated in successive synods, the decrees empha-sising that they were in conformity with 'the regulations of our fathers' or that they had already been issued by Paschal in an earlier synod: 'that [decree] concerning the investiture of churches, promulgated in the council of Troyes, was repeated and con-firmed'.[25] Nevertheless the similarity to his predecessor's synods is deceptive; for the sources indicate that Paschal II did not play the same dominant role in his synods which Urban II had enjoyed in his later years. A rare exception is reported in an eyewitness account of the synod of Benevento of 1113. When envoys from the patriarch of Antioch complained of the encroachments of the patriarch of Jerusalem on their lord's jurisdiction, the pope judged their case him-self. However, Paschal explained that it was not his usual practice to judge important cases in haste: he did so now because a judgement

[22] Bernold, *Chronica* 1089 (n. 10) pp. 449–50. Somerville, 'French councils' (n. 12) pp. 62–3; Schmale, 'Synodus' (n. 1) p. 99.

[23] Bernold, *Chronica* 1096: p. 464.

[24] U.-R. Blumenthal, *The early councils of Pope Paschal II, 1100–1110* (Pontifical Institute of Mediaeval Studies: Studies and Texts 43: Toronto, 1978); F.-J. Schmale, 'Zu den Konzilien Paschals II.', *Annuarium Historiae Conciliorum* 10 (1978), 279–89.

[25] Synod of Guastalla (1106) c. 5: *MGH Constitutiones* 1, 566; Blumenthal, *Early councils* pp. 64–5. Lateran synod (1110) c. 5: *MGH Constitutiones* 1, 569; Blumenthal, *Early councils* pp. 119–20.

was readily available in a decision of Urban II's council of Clermont 'and we dare not rescind the decree of that most discreet father'.[26] Where the case was less clear-cut, however – as, for example, in the claim of Daimbert of Pisa to be restored to the patriarchate of Jerusalem, or in the claims of the church of Brindisi – it was decided by 'synodal judgement'.[27] On at least one occasion the formulation of an important reforming decree was entrusted to the synod: namely, the canon of the synod of Guastalla (October 1106) concerning the status of clerks ordained by schismatics. In 1105–6 Paschal was prompted by political developments in Germany – the readiness of the young King Henry V to embrace reform in return for an alliance with the papacy against his father, the old Emperor Henry IV – to soften the rigour of Urban II's decree (Piacenza, 1095) against the validity of schismatic ordinations. The papal letter of summons to the synod of Guastalla placed the issue on the agenda and the synod (well attended by German prelates) decided to recognise the validity of schismatic ordinations.[28] Paschal would not reverse his predecessor's decree by the exercise of his own authority: the decision was made by a synod including (as was emphasised by the papal summons) the churchmen directly affected by the issue.[29]

The Lateran synod of March 1112 is without parallel in the history of the papal synods of the late eleventh and twelfth centuries; for it was here that the pope was compelled by the synod to 'make a profession of the catholic faith in the presence of all, so that no one might doubt his faith'.[30] The main business of the synod was to revoke 'the evil privilege' (*pravilegium*) 'extorted from Pope Paschal by the violence of King Henry [V]' at Ponte Mammolo in April 1111. The German king had taken prisoner the pope and almost all the cardinals, after failing to negotiate a settlement of the problem of investi-

---

[26] Synod of Benevento (1113): J. von Pflugk-Harttung, *Acta pontificum Romanorum inedita* 2 (Tübingen-Stuttgart, 1884), 205.

[27] Paschal II, *JL* 6175, *MPL* 163, 230A (see below p. 355); *JL* 5879: Pflugk-Harttung, *Acta* (n. 26) 2, 188. On the dates of these cases see Schmale, 'Konzilien' (n. 24) p. 281.

[28] Paschal II, *JL* 6076: (n. 27) 188D–189A; Synod of Guastalla c. 3, 4: (n. 25) p. 565. See Servatius, *Paschalis II.* pp. 187–9, 200–1; Blumenthal, *Early councils* (n. 24) pp. 36–73.

[29] Paschal II, *JL* 6076: 188D. See Servatius, *Paschalis II.* p. 201 n. 12.

[30] Lateran synod (1112): *MGH Constitutiones* 1, 571. See Servatius, *Paschalis II.* pp. 309–20; P. R. McKeon, 'The Lateran council of 1112, the "heresy" of lay investiture and the excommunication of Henry V', *Medievalia et Humanistica* 17 (1966), 3–12; U.-R. Blumenthal, 'Opposition to Pope Paschal II: some comments on the Lateran council of 1112', *Annuarium Historiae Conciliorum* 10 (1978), 82–98.

tures in February 1111. In return for their freedom Henry obtained a papal privilege permitting him to 'confer the investiture of staff and ring' on the bishops and abbots elect of his kingdom – in direct violation of the synodal decrees of Gregory VII and Urban II.[31] It is clear from the sources that, just as the grant of *pravilegium* was extorted from Paschal by Henry V, so its revocation was forced on the pope by the synod of March 1112. It is possible that the Lateran synod was not convoked by Paschal himself, but was summoned in his name by the cardinals, in response to the outcry which the *pravilegium* caused among reformers.[32] 'The lord pope had to suffer great injury from the Roman church at this time', wrote the chronicler Ekkehard of Aura.[33] Henry V was informed by a north Italian correspondent that 'a synod is to be held in Rome, in which they say that Pope Paschal is to be deposed and another elected, who will cancel the peace-treaty which you made with Lord Paschal'.[34] In the event, however, the pope surrendered to the demands of the synod: he confessed that the granting of the *pravilegium* was 'a wicked deed' and he made a profession of faith, embracing 'especially the decrees of my lord Pope Gregory and Pope Urban of blessed memory'.[35] The business of the synod seems to have been managed throughout by the cardinals and bishops. The synod entrusted the drawing up of the revocation of the *pravilegium* to a committee of three cardinals and three bishops; and the resultant document was issued not on the authority of the pope but by 'all of us gathered in this holy council with the lord pope, according to canonical judgement and ecclesiastical authority'.[36]

The Lateran synod of 1112 appears strikingly different in character from the other synods of the reform period, even if we discount the rumour of the intended deposition of the pope. This rumour seems plausible in the light of the polemical literature generated by the *pravilegium*. In the works condemning Paschal's privilege – for example, the letters of Archbishop Josceran of Lyons, Archbishop Guido of Vienne and Cardinal bishop Bruno of Segni – the emphasis is on lay investiture as a heresy (according to the definition of

---

[31] *Pravilegium*: *MGH Constitutiones* 1, 144–5. See below pp. 428–9.
[32] McKeon, 'Lateran council' (n. 30) pp. 8, 10; Servatius, *Paschalis II.* p. 309.
[33] Ekkehard, *Chronica* III (Ausgewählte Quellen zur deutschen Geschichte des Mittelalters 15: Darmstadt, 1972) p. 306.
[34] Bishop Azo of Acqui: *Codex Udalrici* 161, ed. P. Jaffé, *Bibliotheca rerum germanicarum* 5 (Berlin, 1869), 288.
[35] *Vita Paschalis II: Liber pontificalis* 2, 370; Lateran synod (1112): (n. 30) p. 571.
[36] *Vita Paschalis II* p. 370; Lateran synod (1112): p. 572.

Gregory VII and Urban II).[37] In granting Henry V the right of
investiture, Paschal had become a heretic and the synod of 1112
might have considered deposing him on these grounds.[38] Against the
theory that the synod contemplated deposition is the attitude of
Bruno of Segni, sternest of the critics of Paschal II and convinced that
lay investiture was a heresy. Cardinal Bruno assured the pope at the
time of the synod: 'I wish to have no one else as pope while you are
alive'.[39] Three of the French sources which mention the synod claim
that the pope was prepared to abdicate: if so, perhaps this was the
basis of the rumour of a deposition.[40] The evidence of the synodal
protocol suggests that the majority of the members of the synod of
1112 desired neither deposition nor abdication. Their object was to
preserve the integrity of the papal reform programme of the late
eleventh century. Hence the elaborate reference to Gregory VII and
Urban II in Paschal's profession of faith: 'what they approved, I
approve; what they maintained, I maintain; what they confirmed, I
confirm; what they condemned, I condemn . . . ' The cardinals and
bishops seized control of the synod and imposed their will on Paschal
II; but they did so in order to protect the papal reform programme
from an apparently untrustworthy pope. The proceedings of the
synod of 1112 were far less radical than the theories presented in the
polemics of 1111–12. The most elaborate of these, the treatise of
Placidus of Nonantola, in its language and its ideas sometimes seems
to anticipate the 'conciliarism' of the later Middle Ages. The treatise
defines the Church as 'the congregation, or rather convocation, of
the faithful' and asserts that 'when the Church is thrown into confusion' by a question of faith, 'there must be a conference of priests'.
Placidus ignored the claim of the pope to be sole judge in questions
concerning the faith.[41] Placidus' 'conciliarism' – like the unprecedented conduct of the synod of 1112 – was a response to the threat
which a vacillating pope presented to 'the honour of the Church'.
Neither the theory of Placidus nor the practice of the Lateran synod
seems to have had any influence on the conciliar history of the

---

[37] Josceran of Lyons, *Epistola, MGH Libelli* 2, 656; Bruno of Segni, *Epistolae* 1, 4:
    ibid., pp. 563, 565; Guido of Vienne, *Epistola synodica concilii Viennensis, MPL* 163,
    465C–466C.
[38] This is argued by Blumenthal, 'Opposition' (n. 30) pp. 82–98.
[39] Bruno of Segni, *Epistola* 2: (n. 37) p. 564.
[40] *Epistola de Paschali papa, MGH Libelli* 2, 671; *Gesta episcoporum et comitum
    Engolismensium* c. 35, *MGH SS* 26, 823; Suger, *Vita Ludovici grossi regis* c. 10 (Les
    classiques de l'histoire de France au moyen âge: Paris, 1929) p. 66.
[41] Placidus of Nonantola, *Liber de honore ecclesiae* c. 2, 136, *MGH Libelli* 2, 575, 629.

twelfth century.[42] After the crisis of 1111–12 the pope reassumed the lordship of the council.

The term *concilium*, which is sometimes used to describe the synods of the reform papacy both in official documents and in chronicles, becomes the sole usage for the three councils of the pontificate of Calixtus II (Toulouse and Rheims in 1119, the First Lateran Council in 1123) and for all the subsequent papal councils of the twelfth century. Seven of these twelfth-century councils were given the title 'general council' (*concilium generale*) by the popes who summoned them.[43] These papal councils were 'general' because the participants came from every part of Latin Christendom, because their decrees were binding on the whole Church and because they guaranteed the orthodoxy of the Catholic Church. (In patristic usage 'general' and 'catholic' were synonymous terms. '[The Church] is called "catholic" because it is established throughout the whole world and because its doctrine is catholic: that is, general.')[44] The papal synod, which in the pontificate of Gregory VII still bore traces of the traditional Roman provincial synod, was now definitively transformed into the general council, dispensing laws to the Latin Church. This development, which began during the triumphal progresses of Urban II in southern Italy, Lombardy and France, was completed in the councils of Calixtus II. In Calixtus' first council, in Toulouse in July 1119, the canons, formulated as papal decrees, were read out to the bishops and then issued 'with the assent of the council'.[45] In the council of Rheims, at the end of the fifth session, on 29 October 1119, Calixtus followed the same procedure: 'wishing to end the council that day, he caused the synodal decrees to be brought and read'. However, when canon 2, the prohibition of lay investiture, was read, there was 'so great a murmuring from some of the clergy and many of the laity' that the pope was obliged to have the canon revised and presented to an extra session of the council the next day. The objection was to the very general terms in which the decree was cast: the words 'ecclesiastical possessions' in the prohib-

---

[42] Although Placidus' treatise contributed texts to Gratian's *Decretum*: S. Kuttner, 'Urbano II, Placido da Nonantula e Graziano', *Annali della facoltà di Giurisprudenza* 9 (1970).

[43] The councils of Rheims (1119), First Lateran (1123), Rheims (1131), Pisa (1135), Second Lateran (1139), Rheims (1148) and Third Lateran (1179). See Schmale, 'Systematisches' (n. 1) pp. 37–8.

[44] Isidore of Seville, *De ecclesiasticis officiis* 1.3, *MPL* 83, 740. See Fuhrmann, 'Ökumenische Konzil' (n. 1) pp. 682–3.

[45] Council of Toulouse: Mansi, *Sacra Concilia* 21, 225–6.

ition seemed to include the tithes and ecclesiastical patronage held by the laity. Before the revised canon was read to the bishops on 30 October, the pope addressed them on the subject of the role of the pope and that of the other members of the council.

We know that when the Lord Jesus said to his disciples, 'unless you eat the flesh of the Son of man and drink his blood, you have no life in you' [John 6. 53], many were offended and turned back and no longer followed him. Likewise when yesterday we made proposals for the sake of the liberty of the Church, certain unfaithful men were offended. Therefore we say with apostolic authority: whoever is unfaithful, let him depart and go and make room for the faithful to study what is necessary for the freedom of the Church. But to you who have the place and office of the apostles in the Church of God we say what the Lord said to the twelve: 'do you also wish to go away [John 6. 67]?'

After this address 'no one presumed to speak against the synodal decrees, which were then read out'.[46] According to Calixtus II, therefore, the role of the council was simply to acclaim the canons promulgated by the pope. Whoever failed to say *placet* when a canon was announced, was *infidelis*: no longer a member of the Church, he must be excluded from participation in her affairs. Thus, seven-and-a-half years after the Lateran synod had imposed its will on Paschal II, Calixtus II prohibited conciliar opposition to papal decisions.

The only early twelfth-century council for which we have a detailed account of proceedings is that of Rheims in 1119, our informants being the master of the cathedral school of Strassburg, Hesso, an eyewitness, and the English historian Orderic Vitalis. The scene which they described suggests a microcosm of the ecclesiastical hierarchy and above all a demonstration of the papal primacy. The papal throne, raised above the level of the rest of the assembly, was placed before the west door of Rheims cathedral, opposite the main altar. The place next in dignity belonged to the cardinal bishops, seated in a row in front of the pope. At the pope's side stood Cardinal deacon Chrysogonus, the librarian of the Roman church, who 'held *canones* in his hand, ready to read out the authentic judgements of the fathers as the business demanded'. Six other cardinal priests and deacons surrounded the papal throne and imposed silence when the discussion became too heated, as happened often during the council of Rheims (as also during the First Lateran Council of 1123). In the nave sat the prelates summoned to the council, the foremost places

---

[46] Hesso scholasticus, *Relatio de concilio Remensi, MGH Libelli* 3, 28.

belonging to the metropolitans in the order of precedence 'established from ancient times by the Roman pontiff': Rheims, Bourges, Lyons, Rouen, York (consecrated by the pope on the eve of the council), Sens, Tours, Dôle and eight other archbishops. In all 427 bishops and abbots were present, French prelates being the most numerous.[47] The council opened on 20 October 1119 with litany and prayers, after which the pope assumed his throne and delivered his opening discourse on a Gospel text relevant to the condition of the Church: Christ walking on the sea 'when the ship of holy Church is threatened by the waves of this world' [Mark 6. 48].[48] The council ended on 30 October with the anathemas pronounced by the pope against the enemies of the Church.

427 candles were brought, lit and given to all those who bore the pastoral staff, bishops and abbots [of exempt houses] . . . While they stood there, the names were read out of the many whom the lord pope intended to excommunicate, the foremost of whom were King Henry [V] and the intruder in the Roman church, Burdinus [antipope 'Gregory VIII']; and together with many others, they were solemnly excommunicated.[49]

The council was a religious celebration, governed by its own liturgical *ordo*, in which the chief celebrant was the pope.

Of the traditional function of the pre-reform papal synod – the judging by all the participants in the synod of cases brought before the pope – there was no longer any trace in the councils of Calixtus II. Two of the cases decided in the council of Toulouse illustrate this development. In the case of the dispute between the abbey of Aniane and that of Chaise-Dieu concerning the priory of Goudargues, the pope appointed a committee to judge the case, comprising the cardinal bishops of Palestrina and Ostia, three cardinal priests, three cardinal deacons, the archbishops of Tarragona and Auch, together with four bishops and two abbots. When their judgement was announced, the council gave its acclamation.[50] In the second case, that of the claim of the church of St Peter in Toulouse to the church of St Saturnin, the pope alone investigated the case and postponed his judgement until after the end of the council.[51] Not only, therefore,

---

[47] *Ibid.*, pp. 22–8; Orderic Vitalis, *Historia ecclesiastica* XII.21 ed. M. Chibnall 6 (Oxford, 1978), 252. See Foreville, 'Procédure' (n. 1) p. 22; Foreville, *Latran* (n. 1) pp. 35–6.

[48] Orderic, *Historia ecclesiastica* XII.21: pp. 255–7.

[49] Hesso, *Relatio* (n. 46) p. 28.

[50] Calixtus II, *JL* 6714, *MPL* 163, 1110D–1113C.

[51] Council of Toulouse: (n. 45) pp. 230–2. See Schmale, 'Synodus' (n. 1) p. 101.

did the council not judge the case: it did not even have the opportunity of assenting to the judgement. The most detailed illustration of the judicial proceedings of a twelfth-century papal council is provided by a case before the First Lateran Council in Lent 1123: the dispute between the archbishops of Pisa and Genoa concerning metropolitan rights in Corsica, recorded by a member of the Genoese delegation, the consul and historian Caffaro. According to his account, after 'the cardinals, bishops and archbishops' had debated the case 'for several days' without reaching any agreement, the pope

appointed as the judges of this conflict . . . twelve archbishops and twelve bishops . . . They separated from the others and sat apart elsewhere in the palace . . . and, causing an ancient register of the Roman church to be read, they found there that the retention of archiepiscopal rights in Corsica by the Pisans was unjust. All 24 were unanimous and came before the pope in the basilica of the palace, in the presence of 300 bishops, abbots and archbishops; and there Archbishop Walter of Ravenna pronounced in this manner the judgement which the others had agreed on: 'Lord, we dare not give a judgement in your presence, but we shall give you counsel which is effectively a judgement. My counsel and that of my colleagues is that the archbishop of Pisa should henceforward cease to consecrate in Corsica . . . ' Having heard this counsel, the pope rose and said, 'archbishops, bishops, abbots, cardinals, does this counsel please you all?' They rose and said three times, *placet, placet, placet.* The pope then said, 'on behalf of God and of St Peter and on my own behalf I approve and confirm it and tomorrow morning in a full session of the council, together with you all, I shall again approve and confirm it.'[52]

The commission appointed to examine this longstanding dispute regarded themselves not as judges but as advisers of the pope, the supreme judge; and the commission's decision accorded with the terms of a privilege issued by Calixtus earlier in the dispute.[53]

The fathers in the First Lateran Council 'assisted in the making of the peace treaty at the end of the Investiture Contest' by their solemn ratification of the concordat of Worms of September 1122.[54] The conciliar canons of the First Lateran Council likewise reflect the preoccupations of the papal reform movement and the struggles of the past fifty years, in particular echoing the decrees of Urban II's synods. The themes of the council were simony (canon 1), avoidance

---

[52] *Cafari Annales Ianuenses, MGH SS* 18, 16. See Foreville, 'Procédure' (n. 1) pp. 29–30.
[53] Calixtus II, *JL* 6886: (n. 50) 1192A–1194C.
[54] Suger, *Vita Ludovici* c. 27: (n. 40) p. 214.

of excommunicates (2), canonical election (3), clerical celibacy (7), alienation of church property by laymen (8), consanguineous marriages (9), the crusading indulgence (10), the peace and truce of God (15).[55] The council of 1123 was the last occasion when the characteristic Gregorian reform programme dominated conciliar legislation. The canon prohibiting lay investiture, a regular feature of papal synods since 1078, disappeared after 1123, as also did the decree concerning the canonical election of bishops. Among the decrees of Eugenius III's council of Rheims in 1148 was a prohibition of marriages contracted by bishops, clergy or religious; but when it was promulgated in the council, 'it seemed to some to be a futile and ludicrous decree. For who does not know that this is unlawful?' To some members of the council (whose opinion was recorded by John of Salisbury) this piece of Gregorian legislation seemed too much of a cliché to be included in the conciliar decrees.[56] For the five councils of Innocent II – Clermont (1130), Rheims (1131), Piacenza (1132), Pisa (1135) and the Second Lateran Council (1139) – introduced a new programme of legislation, which was subsequently adopted by Eugenius III and in part by Alexander III in their councils. It was a programme of ecclesiastical discipline which was in some respects more demanding than that developed between 1074 and 1123 and which pursued new objectives.

The programme inaugurated at Innocent II's council of Clermont in 1130 was concerned, firstly, with the dignity of the clerical estate. It prohibited 'the wicked and detestable custom' of the study of 'secular law and medicine for the sake of worldly lucre' by monks, regular canons and clerks. They were condemned not for their intellectual curiosity but because they 'neglect the cure of souls, not attending to the function of their order'.[57] Only properly qualified candidates, 'wise and religious persons' of mature age, should be received into holy orders. 'Ecclesiastical honours belong not to blood but to merit and the Church of God does not order succession

---

[55] *Concilium Lateranense I: Conciliorum Oecumenicorum Decreta* pp. 190–3.

[56] John of Salisbury, *Historia pontificalis* c. 3 ed. M. Chibnall (London, 1956) p. 8.

[57] Council of Clermont (1130) c. 5; Rheims (1131) c. 6: Mansi, *Sacra Concilia* 21, 438–9, 459; *Concilium Lateranense II* c. 9: *Conciliorum Oecumenicorum Decreta* pp. 198–9. See Schmale, 'Systematisches' (n. 1) p. 32; W. Maleczek, 'Das Kardinalskollegium unter Innocenz II. und Anaklet II.', *AHP* 19 (1981), 38–42; S. Kuttner, 'Dat Galienus opes et sanctio Justiniana' in *Linguistic and literary studies in honour of Helmut A. Hatzfeld* (Washington, 1964) pp. 237–46; R. Somerville, 'Pope Innocent II and the study of Roman Law', *Revue des Etudes Islamiques* 44 (1976), 105–44.

according to hereditary right.'[58] The possession of proprietary churches by laymen was forbidden.[59] Bishops and clerks must not give offence 'by the superfluity, cut or colour of their clothes nor by their tonsure'.[60] (In line with this canon, the council of Rheims in 1148 specifically prohibited 'cloaks made of various furs', arousing the indignation of Rainald of Dassel and other German members of the council.)[61] The persons and property of churchmen were sacrosanct. The anathema imposed on one 'who incurs the sacrilege of laying violent hands on a clerk or a monk' could be lifted only by the pope himself.[62] The 'right of spoil' was rejected. 'We command that the decree made in the sacred council of Chalcedon be observed without question, namely that the goods of deceased bishops should be seized by no man but should remain in the possession of the steward and the clergy for the use of their churches and their successors.' The decree of Chalcedon referred only to the property of bishops; but Innocent II's decrees extended the same protection to all 'priests or clerks'.[63] The most notable innovations in Innocent II's councils were the decrees imposing Christian and humane standards on secular society. Usury was condemned and usurers denied 'all ecclesiastical comfort'.[64] Tournaments, 'in which knights . . . gather to demonstrate their strength and rash audacity, from which the death of body and soul often results', were prohibited and their victims denied Christian burial. (The Church's campaign against tournaments intensified in the course of the century, as it appeared that 'those detestable festivities' interfered with recruiting for the crusade.)[65] The use of catapults and archery in wars against

---

[58] Clermont (1130) c. 11; Rheims (1131) c. 8, 15; Pisa (1135) c. 9: Mansi, *Sacra Concilia* 21, 439, 459–60, 461, 489–90; *Concilium Lateranense II* c. 10, 16: pp. 199, 201.

[59] Clermont (1130) c. 6; Rheims (1131) c. 7: Mansi, *Sacra Concilia* 21, 439, 459; *Concilium Lateranense II* c. 10: p. 199.

[60] Clermont (1130) c. 2; Rheims (1131) c. 2: Mansi, *Sacra Concilia* 21, 438, 458; *Concilium Lateranense II* c. 4: p. 197.

[61] John of Salisbury, *Historia pontificalis* c. 3: (n. 56) p. 8.

[62] Rheims (1131) c. 13; Pisa (1135) c. 12: Mansi, *Sacra Concilia* 21, 461, 490; *Concilium Lateranense II* c. 15: p. 200.

[63] Clermont (1130) c. 3; Rheims (1131) c. 3: Mansi, *Sacra Concilia* 21, 438, 458; *Concilium Lateranense II* c. 5: p. 197. (Cf. Council of Chalcedon c. 22).

[64] *Concilium Lateranense II* c. 13: p. 200.

[65] Clermont (1130) c. 9; Rheims (1131) c. 12: Mansi, *Sacra Concilia* 21, 439, 460–1; *Concilium Lateranense II* c. 14: p. 200. See N. Denholm-Young, 'The tournament in the thirteenth century' in *Studies in medieval history presented to F. M. Powicke* ed. R. W. Hunt, W. A. Pantin and R. W. Southern (Oxford, 1948), p. 243.

Christians was anathematised.[66] Anathema was also pronounced on 'the most evil, destructive and horrendous crime of arson', which was forbidden to kings and princes as a means of punishing their enemies. Incendiaries were given the penance of a year's service in the holy war in Jerusalem or in Spain. (It is worth noting that one of the motives attributed to King Louis VII of France for going on the Second Crusade was his desire to expiate the guilt of the burning of the town of Vitry by vassals under his command in 1144. The king may therefore have been responding to the conciliar decrees against arson.)[67] The conciliar programme of Innocent II differed most obviously from that of the Gregorian reform in its treatment of the role of the laity in Christian society. The older reform movement was preoccupied with protecting the *sacerdotium* from the encroachment of the secular power, especially in the sphere of ecclesiastical appointments. The new programme of the 1130s assumed that this battle had been won. The problem of the demarcation of the spiritual and the secular appears only in the form of warnings to churchmen not to imitate the way of life of the laity, but to behave like a separate, privileged caste. Laymen meanwhile must carry out their divinely ordained functions in conformity with the values of a Christian society.

This new conciliar programme was first announced during a schism in the Church, when Innocent II was exiled from Rome by his rival, Anacletus II. Innocent II's councils of 1130–5, like those of Urban II, served both to publicise the new reform programme and to demonstrate the growing strength of Innocent's party. The council of Clermont (18 November 1130), attended by churchmen from the provinces of Lyons, Bourges, Vienne, Arles, Tarentaise, Narbonne, Auch and Tarragona, took place soon after Innocent had been assured of the obedience of King Louis VI and of the French kingdom. During the council he received King Lothar III and the German kingdom among his adherents. The council of Rheims (18–26 October 1131) was equally a triumph for the pope. It was attended by a large number of French, German, English and Spanish bishops and it was the scene of the papal coronation of the future King Louis VII of France. During the council Innocent received an embassy from Lothar III, promising to enter Italy and to drive the

---

[66] *Concilium Lateranense II* c. 29: p. 203.
[67] Clermont (1130) c. 31; Rheims (1131) c. 17: Mansi, *Sacra Concilia* 21, 440, 461–2; *Concilium Lateranense II* c. 18–20: pp. 201–2. On Louis VII see *Sigeberti Chronici Continuatio Praemonstratensis*, MGH SS 6, 453; E. Vacandard, *Vie de St Bernard, abbé de Clairvaux* 2 (Paris, 1910), 273.

antipope and his allies out of Rome. The council of Pisa (May 1135) was of a similar character, attended by 126 archbishops and bishops and many abbots from the kingdoms of Italy, Germany, France, England, Spain and Hungary. On this occasion the promulgation of the new reform programme was accompanied by the excommunication of the antipope and his adherents, notably Roger II of Sicily, and by the deposition of seven prelates – the archbishop of Milan and the bishops of Halberstadt, Liège, Valence, Arezzo, Acera and Modena – on the grounds of simony, unchastity or support of the antipope.[68] This dramatic demonstration of papal authority was repeated in Innocent II's Lateran Council. The Second Lateran Council in Lent 1139 was, like the council of 1123, a triumphant celebration of the end of a schism. The sermon preached by Innocent II, probably on the opening day, 3 April, announced the theme of the council: that the unity of the Church was guaranteed solely by the primacy of the pope, to whom all churchmen owed obedience. 'You recognise that Rome is the head of the world and that the high honour of an ecclesiastical office is received by the permission of the Roman pontiff, as it were by feudal law and custom: without his permission it is unlawful to hold office. You also know that it belongs to him to pacify those who are in contention and to arrange and order according to his wisdom whatever is in confusion.'[69] Under the influence of this sermon the council unanimously declared null and void the ordinations and decrees of Anacletus II and his fellow schismatics. The session ended with the deposition of all those bishops present who had been in any way implicated in the schism of Anacletus, even though their presence in the council showed that they were by no means impenitent schismatics. The rigour of Innocent's proceedings is illustrated by the famous case of Peter Pisanus, cardinal priest of S. Susanna. Originally a member of Anacletus' party, he had been won over in 1137 by the efforts of Bernard of Clairvaux and had become a member of Innocent's curia; but in the Second Lateran Council the pope deposed him, despite Bernard's protests.[70]

---

[68] Mansi, *Sacra Concilia* 21, 437–40, 453–72, 485–92; *MGH Constitutiones* 1, 577–9. See R. Somerville, 'The canons of Reims (1131)', *Bulletin of Medieval Canon Law* 5 (1975), 122–30; *idem*, 'The council of Pisa, 1135: a re-examination of the evidence of the canons', *Speculum* 45 (1970), 105–8.

[69] *Historia Mauriniacensis monasterii*, *MGH SS* 26, 44.

[70] F.-J. Schmale, *Studien zum Schisma des Jahres 1130* (Cologne-Graz, 1961) p. 267; B. Zenker, *Die Mitglieder des Kardinalkollegiums von 1130 bis 1159* (dissertation: Würzburg, 1964) pp. 104, 250–1.

The chief concerns of the Second Lateran Council were the condemnation of schismatics and heretics and the promulgation of the definitive version of the programme of Clermont, Rheims and Pisa. The judicial business which had been the principal preoccupation of the eleventh-century papal synod was now relegated to a minor role in the council and some cases were not dealt with until after the final session. This was the fate of the complaint which Abbot Peter of Mons Coelius made against the Roman nobleman Odo Frangipane, who had attacked his abbey. 'The lord pope, hindered by the amount and importance of the business of the strangers then gathered in Rome, deferred the examination of our case until after the end of the council.' The case was eventually examined by the pope in the presence of the cardinals and members of the Roman nobility.[71] The dispute between the abbot of Nonantola and the bishop of Modena was decided by the pope during the council but not in an actual session of the council.[72] Likewise the case which Abbot Leo of Saint-Bertin brought before the council, seeking to end the subjection of his abbey to Cluny, was not judged in the council, but was decided by the pope in the presence of the cardinals.[73] Innocent II denied the council the opportunity of examining these cases or even of acclaiming his judgements; and by doing so, he demonstrated the supreme judicial authority of the pope. The transformation of the papal synod from a court of justice into a *concilium generale* was completed in the pontificate of Innocent II. By the time of the Second Lateran Council the judicial functions of the traditional papal synod had become the routine business of the new institution of the consistory: the cases which had once been examined and judged by the synod were now decided by the pope 'according to the advice of [his] brethren', the cardinals, in their formal consultations.[74]

The papal councils of the middle and later twelfth century followed closely the pattern of Innocent II's councils. The reform programme of 1130–9 formed the basis of the decrees of Eugenius III's council of Rheims (1148) and Alexander III's council of Tours (1163) and to a lesser extent of the Third Lateran Council (1179).[75]

---

[71] Mansi, *Sacra Concilia* 21, 451–6.

[72] Innocent II, *JL* 8002, *MPL* 179, 446D–448A.

[73] Innocent II, *JL* 8016–18: 459B–462A. Cf. Simon, *Gesta abbatum sancti Bertini Sithiensium* III.5, *MGH SS* 13, 662.

[74] See above pp. 99, 105–6.

[75] Foreville, *Latran* (n. 1) pp. 102, 119, 153–7.

The defence of the unity of the Church against schismatics and heretics was as much the theme of these later councils as it had been of the councils of the 1130s. Eugenius III's council of Rheims repeated the decree of 1139 against the schismatics of the Anacletan party.[76] The subject of the opening discourse of the council of Tours, given by Bishop Arnulf of Lisieux on 19 May 1163, was the unity and liberty of the Church; and it was followed by the excommunication of the leader of the new schism, the antipope 'Victor IV'.[77] The Third Lateran Council of 1179, like its two predecessors, marked the end of a schism and its first business was to annul the ordinations and decrees of the defeated schismatics. The problem of heresy continued to be as urgent as that of schism. Two of Innocent II's councils were concerned with suspected heretics: the wandering preacher Henry of Lausanne was condemned by the council of Pisa and the case of the reformer Arnold of Brescia was examined by the pope during the Second Lateran Council.[78] Similarly a number of sessions of Eugenius III's council of Rheims were devoted to the investigation of suspect doctrines. The council sentenced to imprisonment the millennarian preacher Eon de l'Etoile. A lengthy examination of the writings of the distinguished Paris master Gilbert de la Porrée was undertaken during the council, without reaching any conclusion.[79] Alexander III's council of Tours was the first to address itself to the problem of the Albigensian heretics in southern France. The council outlawed the heretics and called upon secular princes to punish them with imprisonment and the confiscation of their property. The same council witnessed a long but inconclusive debate about the christological opinions expressed in the *Sentences* of Peter Lombard.[80] Both the heresy of the Albigensians and the christology of Peter Lombard recurred sixteen years later in the Third Lateran Council, together with the new problem of the Waldensians.[81] Of the many who had urged Alexander III to

[76] Rheims (1148) c. 17: Mansi, *Sacra Concilia* 21, 717–18.

[77] Arnulf of Lisieux, *Sermo: ibid.*, 1167–75. Tours (1163): *ibid.*, 1179. See R. Somerville, *Pope Alexander III and the Council of Tours (1163)* (Berkeley-Los Angeles, 1977) pp. 14–18.

[78] H. Grundmann, *Religiöse Bewegungen im Mittelalter* (2nd edition: Hildesheim, 1961) p. 45; Foreville, *Latran* (n. 1) pp. 86–7.

[79] *Continuatio Gemblacensis* 1146, 1148, *MGH SS* 6, 389–90; John of Salisbury, *Historia pontificalis* c. 8–11: (n. 56) pp. 15–25. See above p. 109.

[80] Tours (1163) c. 4: Mansi, *Sacra Concilia* 21, 1177–8. See Somerville, *Tours* (n. 77) pp. 56, 60–1, 98.

[81] *Concilium Lateranense III* c. 27: *Conciliorum Oecumenicorum Decreta* pp. 224–5. See Foreville, 'Procédure' (n. 1) p. 28.

summon this council, the most illustrious was Henry of Marcy, abbot of Clairvaux. His letter emphasised that the principal task of the papal council was the extirpation of heresy. 'Arius has come to life again in the west; . . . heretics dispute publicly against the faith.' The pope must 'brandish the sword of the priest Phineas' against those Israelites who have embraced the false gods of the Moabites [Numbers 25. 1–8].[82] Henry of Marcy, and presumably most of his contemporaries, considered that the function of a *concilium generale* was to devise measures for the defence of the catholic faith.

Henry of Marcy's appeal to Alexander III envisaged the council as an assembly in which the pope, the only active participant, made laws for Christendom. 'Lo, in your day, with God's help, the schism has ceased. Well done, good shepherd: now lay the heretics to rest likewise.' A similar conception appears in the opening discourse of the Third Lateran Council, pronounced by the learned canon lawyer, Bishop Rufinus of Assisi, on 5 March 1179.

The holy Roman church, since she is the apex of all episcopal thrones and since she is the mother of all churches and the mistress of all, has most worthily deserved to obtain a unique monarchy of all churches . . . This church, the head of the world, . . . is never subject to any other see; through her the keys of power of judgement are dispensed to all sees and it belongs to her will and power alone to assemble a universal council, to make new canons and to obliterate old ones.[83]

The image of the monarch issuing his laws in a council is suggested also by the account of the Third Lateran Council in Roger of Hoveden's chronicle.

The lord pope celebrated the third day of his council on the Monday preceding Palm Sunday, which was 19 March. On that day he ordained that these decrees must be observed by all . . . When these decrees had been promulgated and had been received by all those present, clergy and people, the bishops and other churchmen who had assembled there, received the blessing and permission to return home.[84]

The conciliar decrees were formulated by canon lawyers and may in many cases have been prepared before the council assembled, since

---

[82] Henry of Clairvaux, *Epistola* 11, *MPL* 204, 223C–224A.

[83] Rufinus of Assisi, *Sermo habitus in Lateranensi concilio* ed. G. Morin, 'Le discours d'ouverture du concile général de Latran (1179)', *Atti della Pontificia Accademia Romana di Archeologia*, serie III, Memorie 2 (1928), 118–19

[84] Roger of Hoveden, *Chronica*, *RS* 51/2 (1869), 171, 189. Roger reworked the equivalent passage in the chronicle of Benedict of Peterborough, *RS* 49/1 (1867), 222, 238.

they were based either on conciliar canons of the 1130s and of 1148 or, more frequently, on papal decretals already issued by Alexander III.[85] The council is mentioned only once in these decrees. In canon 1 – 'that he who is elected and received by two-thirds [of the cardinals] is to be regarded as the Roman pontiff' – appears the formula: 'we have decreed on the advice of our brethren and with the approval of the sacred council . . . '[86] In the case of the most important innovation of the Third Lateran Council, the new papal election decree, therefore, the procedure was that the cardinals advised, the council approved and the pope decreed. All the other canons, however, were formulated in the name of the pope, who alone commanded, forbade, ordained and decreed.

The council as a whole was excluded from much of the detailed examination of the issues before it. The pope seems to have submitted some of these issues to experts for a preliminary investigation. The christology of Peter Lombard was examined by John of Cornwall: the preface of John's *Eulogium* on this subject, addressed to Alexander III, explains that the treatise was hastily composed for the purposes of the council.[87] It is possible that the theologian Hugh Etherian was similarly commissioned to examine the question of the reunion of the Greek and Latin churches. (Hugh lived for many years in Constantinople as the adviser of Emperor Manuel I Comnenus on Latin theology. A letter of Alexander III to Hugh Etherian is extant, dated 13 November 1177, suggesting that he urge the Byzantine emperor to be reunited with the Roman church.)[88] Perhaps Hugh's treatise on the heresies of the Greeks, like the *Eulogium* of John of Cornwall, was used in the Third Lateran Council. A third instance of preliminary investigation is the dossier on the Albigensians prepared by the papal legates in southern France, Cardinal Peter of S. Grisogono and Henry of Marcy, abbot of Clairvaux.[89] Those cases which had not been the subject of preliminary examination were entrusted, after the council assembled, to commissions appointed by

[85] Foreville, *Latran* (n. 1) p. 152.

[86] *Concilium Lateranense III* c. 1: (n. 81) p. 211.

[87] F. Pelzer, 'Eine bisher ungedruckte Einleitung zu einer zweiten Auflage des Eulogium ad Alexandrum III Johannis Cornubriensis', *HJb* 54 (1934), 226.

[88] Hugo Etherianus, *De haeresibus quas Graeci in Latinos devolvunt, MPL* 202, 227A–396D. Cf. Alexander III, *JL* 12957, *MPL* 200, 1154AC. See Foreville, *Latran* (n. 1) p. 150.

[89] Y. M-J. Congar, 'Henri de Marcy, abbé de Clairvaux, cardinal-évêque d'Albano et légat pontifical', *Analecta Monastica* (Studi Anselmiana 43: Rome, 1958) pp. 20, 26–7.

the pope. For example, the case of the double election in the archbishopric of Hamburg-Bremen was examined by two cardinals, Rainer of Pavia and John of Naples. On their recommendation Alexander deposed the candidate Berthold, who had come to the council as archbishop elect, expecting to be consecrated by the pope.[90] The commission which investigated the beliefs of the Waldensians was much larger, consisting of 'a great bishop' as president and 'a numerous assembly of jurists and wise men'. The best-known member of the commission wrote an account of its proceedings, in which he claimed to have played the foremost part: he was Walter Map, satirist, courtier and servant of King Henry II of England. Ordered by the president of the commission to interrogate two Waldensian witnesses, he had no difficulty in exposing their ignorance of theology.[91]

The papal letter convoking the Third Lateran Council speaks in conventional terms of summoning 'churchmen from the various regions, whose presence and counsel will permit the taking of sound decisions'.[92] But the growing sophistication of conciliar procedures – the preliminary investigations and conciliar commissions – meant that the council as a whole had little to do with decision-making, except for those individual fathers whom the pope appointed to commissions. Almost all cases were examined and decided by the pope's 'experts', his *viri periti*.[93] Only in two cases is there evidence of opposition in the council to the decisions taken by the experts. In the first of these cases – that of the christology of Peter Lombard – the opposition was successful. The expert entrusted with the examination, John of Cornwall, recommended the condemnation of the 'christological nihilism' of the Lombard and the pope agreed with him. However, the condemnation was opposed by a number of cardinals and by bishops in the council. The theologian Adam du Petit-Pont, formerly a colleague of the Lombard in the Paris schools and now bishop of Saint-Asaph, defended the opinions of 'the Master of the Sentences'. As a protest against the expert's recommendation, several of the fathers walked out of the assembly, saying that the council's time would be better spent in condemning the heresies

---

[90] Arnold of Lübeck, *Chronica Slavorum* II.9, *MGH SS* 21, 132. See Hauck, *Kirchengeschichte Deutschlands* 4, 308–9.

[91] Walter Map, *De nugis curialium* I.31 ed. M. R. James (Anecdota Oxoniensia 14: Oxford, 1914) pp. 60–1.

[92] Alexander III, *JL* 13097: (n. 88) 1184D.

[93] Schmale, 'Systematisches' (n. 1) p. 29.

which were attacking parts of Christendom.[94] The combined opposition of the two sets of adherents of Peter Lombard's teaching – the
cardinals and the fathers of the council – defeated the efforts of the
papal expert. The second case of opposition, recorded by the Paris
theologian, Peter the Chanter, was unsuccessful. 'In the Lateran
council, when the fathers were in session for the purpose of making
new decrees, John of Chartres said: "heaven forbid that new decrees
should be made or large numbers of old ones revised . . . It would be
better to command and compel men to observe the Gospel; for few
obey it nowadays."' Increasing the number of decrees merely
increased the number of transgressors and therefore also increased
the need for legal proceedings or for dispensations.[95] This critic of
the Third Lateran Council, 'John of Chartres', cannot be identified
with complete certainty; but it is possible that he was the author John
of Salisbury, who had become bishop of Chartres in 1176. This historian of the council of Rheims of 1148 and admirer of the austere
simplicity of the regime of Eugenius III may have been the critic who
found himself out of sympathy with the reform programme elaborated by Alexander III's legal experts. The opposition encountered by
the pope in the Third Lateran Council, therefore, came in one
instance from an individual and in the other from a pressure group:
just as in the First Lateran Council Calixtus II faced opposition from
the intransigent Gregorians on the question of investiture and in the
council of Rheims in 1148 Eugenius III was opposed by Rainald of
Dassel on the matter of clerical dress. In none of these assemblies was
the papal lordship over the council in any doubt. The same treatise of
Peter the Chanter which records the opposition of 'John of Chartres'
in the council of 1179 also contains the Chanter's remarks on canon
law.

It is clear that the decrees can be changed, since they are in the heart of the
lord pope and he may interpret them as he pleases. If he judges according to
[the decrees], he judges justly, if he judges contrary to them, he is likewise
said to have judged justly. For the making, interpreting and abrogating of
the canons is in his power.[96]

Canon law, therefore, was papal law.

When in the opening discourse of the Third Lateran Council the
canonist Rufinus of Assisi spoke of the unique power of the Roman

---

[94] J. de Ghellinck, *Le mouvement théologique au XIIe siècle* (2nd edition: Bruges, 1948)
       pp. 260–1; Somerville, *Tours* (n. 77) pp. 60–2.
[95] Peter the Chanter, *Verbum abbreviatum* c. 79, MPL 205, 235C–236A.
[96] *Ibid.*, c. 53, 164BC.

church 'to assemble a universal council, to make new canons and to obliterate old ones', he had in mind a statement of Master Gratian of Bologna in the *Decretum* (*ca.* 1140). This statement concerned the canonical tradition, found in Pelagius II, Nicholas I and Pseudo-Isidore, that no general council can be convoked without the permission of the apostolic see.[97] Master Gratian explained that the right to summon a general council 'belongs to the apostolic see', since the pope alone has the authority to make new laws. The pope has no need of a council to validate the laws which he pronounces: his 'decretal letters are equivalent to conciliar canons'. Even the canons of the eight councils of the ancient Church derived their legal authority only from papal approval.[98] It is instructive to compare Gratian's interpretation of this theme with that of the eleventh-century papal reform. 'A universal council must not be celebrated nor bishops condemned and deposed except by the will of the Roman pontiff . . . because it is not permitted to pass a definitive sentence without consulting the Roman pontiff.'[99] The eleventh-century interpretation assumes that the main function of a council is judicial: the twelfth-century interpretation assumes that its main function is legislative. By the time that Gratian composed his definition of *concilium generale*, judicial business was no longer the concern of the council. 'When the council was over, the more important persons remained behind to settle certain matters', wrote John of Salisbury of the council of Rheims in 1148. (These 'certain matters' included the cases of the English bishops and abbots suspended for disobedience.)[100] From the pontificate of Innocent II onwards 'the more important persons' who dealt with the judicial business were usually the members of the consistory. It was this separation of functions which allowed the 'general council' to develop as a legislative assembly in the period 1130–79.

[97] Schmale, 'Synodus' (n. 1) pp. 84–7.
[98] Gratian, *Decretum* D.17 c. 1–6; D.20 *dictum ante* c. 1: D.16 *dictum post* c. 4. See S. Chodorow, *Christian political theory and Church politics in the mid-twelfth century. The ecclesiology of Gratian's Decretum* (Berkeley–Los Angeles, 1972) pp. 135–41.
[99] Leo IX, *JL* 4304; *MPL* 143, 728C. Cf. Gregory VII, *Registrum* II. 55a (*Dictatus pape* 16), p. 205.
[100] John of Salisbury, *Historia pontificalis* c. 4: (n. 56) pp. 10–11.

4

PAPAL LEGATES

—— • ——

The years 1073–1198 witnessed the development of the papal legation as one of the most important instruments of papal government – the connecting link between the papal curia and the churches and secular rulers of western Christendom. This was an innovation of the reform papacy. The early medieval papacy had retained envoys (*apocrisiarii*) in Constantinople and subsequently at the Carolingian court to represent the interests of the Roman church. But the reform papacy began to use envoys on an unprecedented scale to implement its decrees and to promote its conception of the papal primacy throughout Christendom. This abrupt transformation of the Roman envoy into an instrument of reform occurred early in the career of Pope Gregory VII, who during the 1050s, as subdeacon (later archdeacon) Hildebrand, was one of the first to exercise the enhanced authority of a legate of the reform papacy. On his second legation in France (1056) he held a council in Chalon in which he deposed several bishops guilty of simony. His legatine duties also brought him to the German court and to Milan, soon to be the main focus of the curia's efforts to inculcate respect for the Roman primacy.[1] The pattern of Hildebrand's early career – successful legations strengthening a cardinal's influence in the curia – was repeated in the careers of most of his successors.

[1] T. Schieffer, *Die päpstlichen Legaten in Frankreich vom Vertrage von Meersen (870) bis zum Schisma von 1130* (Historische Studien 263: Berlin, 1935) p. 57; T. Schmidt, 'Hildebrand, Kaiserin Agnes und Gandersheim', *Niedersächsisches Jahrbuch für Landesgeschichte* 46/7 (1974–5), 299–309.

Of the nineteen popes of the period 1073–1198, all except four had been active as legates. Urban II had conducted a dangerous legation in Germany; Paschal II had specialised in Spanish legations; Calixtus II had been a legate in France, Burgundy and England. Both Honorius II and Innocent II had participated in the legation of 1122 which negotiated the concordat of Worms with the emperor; and Innocent had also conducted two legations in France. Celestine II had undertaken the forlorn task of persuading King Roger II of Sicily to change sides in the papal schism of the 1130s; Lucius II had for two decades been the curia's expert on German affairs; Anastasius IV had been papal vicar in Rome while the curia of Innocent II was exiled in France. Hadrian IV had been the legate who in 1152–3 had created the new ecclesiastical organisation of Scandinavia. Alexander III had participated in three momentous legations: that which concluded the treaty of Constance with Emperor Frederick I (1153), that which concluded the treaty of Benevento with King William I of Sicily (1156) and that to the imperial diet of Besançon (1157), which resulted in Frederick's first dispute with the papacy. Lucius III had been a negotiator both of the treaty of Benevento and of the peace of Venice, which ended the papal schism of 1159–77; Urban III had held a permanent legation in Lombardy (where he was archbishop of Milan). The two aged popes of the end of the twelfth century, Gregory VIII and Celestine III, had been extraordinarily active legates. Gregory VIII had travelled to Germany, Dalmatia, Hungary, Spain and Portugal and had negotiated the reconciliation of Henry II of England after the murder of Archbishop Thomas Becket of Canterbury (1171–3). Celestine III, during his sixty-five years in the service of the curia, had carried out two long legations to Spain (1154–6, 1172–4), two legations to the emperor (1158, 1177) and a legation to King Louis VII of France. Most of the popes of our period gained their first practical experience of government and had their first taste of power far from the curia, as papal legates. It is significant that half of them had represented the curia in the imperial territories and negotiated with the imperial court. Some of them owed their election to the papacy to their expertise in papal–imperial relations.

The first systematic study of the legatine office, that compiled by the canon lawyers of the thirteenth century, the 'Decretalists', identified three different categories of papal legate: the *legatus a latere*, 'legate from [the pope's] side', sent from the curia on an important mission as papal plenipotentiary; the *legatus missus* or *nuncius apostolicus*, an envoy with lesser powers, often a mere messenger without the authority to conduct negotiations; and the *legatus natus*, 'native legate', an honorific title attached to a particular archbishopric, whose holder however had none of the wide-ranging powers and functions of a Roman legate.[2] This neat thirteenth-century classification does not correspond exactly to what is known of the legates of 1073–1198. The papal documents of this earlier period use a terminology unknown to the Decretalists and use it in a manner which often seems vague and inconsistent. In the papal letters of the later eleventh century the most frequent expressions are 'Roman legate', 'legate of the apostolic see' or simply 'our legate', with no reference to different categories of envoy.[3] In the early twelfth century the phrase *a latere* begins to appear, sometimes accompanying the term *legatus*, but often accompanying a term unknown to the Decretalists in this context: *vicarius*. A clause in a famous letter of Paschal II (1117) reads: 'when a legate is sent [to Sicily] from our side, whom we in fact regard as a *vicarius* . . . ' Similarly Calixtus II in 1123 commended to King Louis VI of France his legate, Peter Pierleone, cardinal deacon of SS. Cosma e Damiano, with the words: 'According to the ancient custom of the apostolic see we have sent him from our side to the land under your jurisdiction to correct and confirm whatever is in need of correction and confirmation. We therefore ask Your Excellency . . . to receive him reverently as our *vicarius*.'[4] The term *vicarius* was used both for cardinals sent *a latere* and for archbishops and bishops to whom the pope granted a permanent legation in their own provinces.[5] After the mid-twelfth century, however, there was a tendency to differentiate between these two types of papal representative. From the pontificate of Alexander III the title *legatus a latere* was the almost exclusive title for cardinal legates (although as late as 1191 Cardinal bishop Albinus of Albano could still be called *vicarius* by King Tancred of Sicily). Those papal representatives who combined a permanent

[2] P. Hinschius, *Das System des katholischen Kirchenrechts mit besonderer Rücksicht auf Deutschland* I (Berlin, 1869), 511–17; K. Ruess, *Die rechtliche Stellung der päpstlichen Legaten bis Bonifaz VIII.* (Paderborn, 1912) pp. 103–15.

[3] Gregory VII, *Registrum* p. 694 (index). See Ruess, *Legaten* pp. 103–4.

[4] Paschal II, *JL* 6562: *Liber Censuum* 2, 125: see E. Caspar, 'Die Legatengewalt der normannisch-sicilischen Herrscher im 12. Jahrhundert', *QFIAB* 7 (1904), 201. Calixtus II, *JL* 7077, *MPL* 163, 1297CD. See H. Tillmann, *Die päpstlichen Legaten in England bis zur Beendigung der Legation Gualas (1218)* (dissertation: Bonn, 1926) pp. 122–3.

[5] Ruess, *Legaten* p. 104; Tillmann, *England* pp. 121–7.

legation with the office of archbishop began to attach to their archiepiscopal title the words 'and legate of the apostolic see'.[6]

Despite the confusing terminology it is clear that two of the categories of legate recognised by the thirteenth-century Decretalists were already known in the years 1073–1198. The papal plenipotentiary sent from the curia, usually a cardinal, was the most frequent and important type of legate in this period. He had already acquired in the course of the twelfth century his definitive title, *legatus a latere*. The second category of the less important envoy – not a cardinal – with limited powers and duties, was also well known in the late eleventh and twelfth centuries, although not yet under his thirteenth-century title of *legatus missus* or *nuncius apostolicus*. This office was most frequently performed by papal chaplains and subdeacons, although it could also be entrusted to a churchman returning to his native land after a visit to the curia. The third category of the Decretalists, the *legatus natus*, was missing from the eleventh and twelfth-century scene. Certainly we can identify numerous legates who were 'natives' in their legatine provinces and who combined a permanent papal legation with the office of bishop or archbishop; and historians have often regarded these as the forerunners of the thirteenth-century *legati nati*. But these earlier legates differed in many important respects from the *legati nati*: they were more numerous, more active, more powerful; their legatine title was far from being honorific.[7] They were in fact legates of a type unknown to the later Middle Ages, created by the needs of the reform papacy and transformed by the changing circumstances of the twelfth century into less powerful but still influential papal representatives. Never as numerous as the omnipresent cardinal legates or the lesser envoys of the papal curia, the 'native' legates of the central Middle Ages are nevertheless equally significant in the study of the curia's attitude towards the western Church and her clergy.

The letters of Gregory VII contain many statements of the importance of the legates' functions in a Church urgently in need of reform. He wrote of the duties of Bishop Amatus of Oloron as permanent legate in Aquitaine:

---

[6] Ruess, *Legaten* p. 110; I. Friedländer, *Die päpstlichen Legaten in Deutschland und Italien am Ende des 12. Jahrhunderts (1181–1198)* (Historische Studien 177: Berlin, 1928) pp. 112–17, 123 n. 3.

[7] W. Janssen, *Die päpstlichen Legaten in Frankreich vom Schisma Anaklets II. bis zum Tode Coelestins III. (1130–1198)* (Kölner Historische Abhandlungen 6: Cologne-Graz, 1961) pp. 170–3.

The Roman church had this custom from the earliest days of her foundation, that she sent her legates to all the lands known to be Christian and conferred her authority on the legates to do whatever the governor and ruler of the Roman church could not perform in person, to preach salvation and moral probity to all the churches throughout the world and diligently teach them apostolic doctrine in all things relating to holy religion.

The Gregorian legate was given a province in which he was vice-pontiff, possessing the *vicis* of the pope. The inhabitants of his province were commanded by the pope 'to receive him as if he were our self, or rather St Peter, in person' and 'to hear and obey him in all things as if he were our self and [spoke] the oracles of our own voice'.[8] The legate shared the pope's authority and his principal duty, the instruction of the faithful. For Gregory VII the Roman church was the *magistra*, the schoolmistress, of Christendom: the teaching office was – as Pope Innocent I had declared – her raison d'être.[9] The instrument by means of which the legate instructed the faithful was the synod. The legatine synod is the subject of the fourth sentence in Gregory VII's memorandum concerning papal authority, *Dictatus pape*: '[The pope's] legate presides over all bishops in a council, even if he is inferior in rank, and he can pronounce sentence of deposition against them.' In the preceding sentence of this memorandum Gregory reserved the deposition of bishops to the pope; but there was no contradiction here, since the legate was simply an extension of the pope himself, the vicar of the vicar of St Peter.[10] Gregory's letters make no distinction between the cardinal legates and the 'native' bishops on whom he conferred permanent legations. In 1078, for example, Archbishop Manasses of Rheims refused to recognise the authority of the 'ultramontane' Bishop Hugh of Die, Gregory's permanent legate in France, but promised instead to obey a 'Roman legate'. Gregory rejected this distinction between 'Roman' and 'ultramontane': 'Roman legates' were 'those, of whatever nation, on whom the Roman pontiff imposes any legation or – what is of greater importance – confers his own authority'.[11] All legates must equally be obeyed by the faithful; but

---

[8] Gregory VII, *Epistolae Vagantes* 21, ed. H. E. J. Cowdrey (Oxford, 1972) pp. 56, 58.

[9] Gregory VII, *Registrum* 1.64 (citing Innocent I, *JK* 311); 1.15, pp. 93–4; p. 24. See I. S. Robinson, *Authority and resistance in the Investiture Contest* (Manchester, 1978) pp. 17–24.

[10] Gregory VII, *Registrum* II.55a (*Dictatus pape* c. 4, 3) pp. 204, 203.

[11] *Registrum* VI.2, p. 392. Tillmann, *England* (n. 4) p. 125 interprets this clause as referring to two distinct classes of legate, the ordinary *legatus* and the *vicarius*. For

Gregory nevertheless behaved as though some of his legates possessed more authority than others. He rebuked his legate, the subdeacon Hubert, for presuming to negotiate with Bishop Hugh of Langres 'when we have committed our responsibilities and authority in all things in that land [Flanders] especially to the bishop of Die'. Evidently Hubert and his colleague, the monk Teuzo, were envoys of lesser competence than the permanent legate, Hugh of Die (although Hubert was the papal expert on Norman affairs, to whom was entrusted the delicate mission of 1080 to William the Conqueror, requesting him to swear fealty to the pope). Gregory's letters throw no light on this distinction, referring to Hugh, Hubert and Teuzo alike as 'our legate'.[12]

The legate was accountable only to the pope; and Gregory called his legates to account with characteristic vigour. Immediately on his accession as pope he wrote to remind Cardinal bishop Gerald of Ostia, the papal legate in Spain, that 'it has always been customary and extremely necessary that whenever a legate of the apostolic see has celebrated a council in a distant land, he should return without delay [to Rome] to announce all that he has done'. Gregory's emphasis on the legate's duty of reporting back to the curia (a 'custom' now appearing for the first time in legatine history) shows that already at the beginning of his pontificate he had realised how much the implementation of his reform programme would depend on legates.[13] The starting-point of many legations was the papal reforming synod in Rome, the decrees of which the legates disseminated in their provinces. Reforming decrees were promulgated throughout the world, Gregory claimed, 'by letters and legates'.[14] The first Gregorian legation to Germany, that of the cardinal bishops Gerald of Ostia and Hubert of Palestrina, set out in March 1074 after attending Gregory's first reforming synod. Their mission was to win the support of King Henry IV and the German episcopate for the vigorous campaign against simony and clerical marriage launched at the Roman synod.[15] The legations to the German kingdom in the mid-1070s were intended to implement this reform programme and

---

the opposite view, that Gregory here equated *legatus* and *vicarius*, see Ruess, *Legaten* (n. 2) p. 116 n. 1; Schieffer, *Frankreich* (n. 1) p. 240.

[12] Gregory VII, *Registrum* VII.1, pp. 459–60. Cf. *Registrum* IV.17, V. 22, VII.1, pp. 322–3, 385–6, 458–60. See Schieffer, *Frankreich* (n. 1) pp. 109–10.

[13] *Registrum* I.16, p. 25. See Schieffer, *Frankreich* p. 83.

[14] *Registrum* II.66, p. 221.

[15] C. Erdmann, *Studien zur Briefliteratur Deutschlands im. 11. Jahrhundert* (Schriften der MGH 1, 1938) pp. 227–31.

to inculcate respect for the Roman primacy. (Legates in 1076 introduced into Germany the influential 'Collection in 74 Titles', a canon law manual defining the authority of the pope). The legations of the later 1070s had a mainly political function: after the outbreak of the civil war in Germany the pope used his legates to negotiate with the rival parties of Henry IV and the anti-king Rudolf.[16] Almost all the legations of the 1070s consisted of members of the curia and all were of short duration. There is an obvious contrast between the German and French legations of this period. In France Gregory relied mainly not on short-term legates from the curia but on permanent 'native' legates who enjoyed his special confidence, Bishop Hugh of Die, later archbishop of Lyons, and Bishop Amatus of Oloron, later archbishop of Bordeaux. This arrangement was evidently not considered suitable for Germany in the 1070s. Gregory had come to the papal throne with grave doubts about the quality of the German episcopate (inspired by revelations of Henry IV's simoniacal practices *ca.* 1070). He was uncertain whether any German bishop could be entrusted with a permanent legation; and his detailed instructions to his legates reveal his determination to retain in his own hands the conduct of papal relations with Germany.[17] The intensification of the conflict of empire and papacy in the early 1080s, making communication between Rome and the imperial territories increasingly difficult, at last compelled Gregory to appoint a permanent legate in Germany, the loyal Gregorian Bishop Altmann of Passau. Another trusted supporter, Bishop Anselm II of Lucca, was appointed permanent legate in Lombardy. Such permanent legations were characteristic of the whole period of the Investiture Contest.

The Gregorian institution of the permanent legation originated, therefore, in Gregory's special relationship with his French legates and the problems presented by the Investiture Contest necessitated its use in the imperial territories. It was in France, however, that the permanent legation was used to most dramatic effect; for here the legates' reforming activities were unimpeded by civil war or by a powerful monarchy enjoying the support of the episcopate. (The duchy of Normandy was an important exception: the legates could not hope to diminish William the Conqueror's control over the ducal

---

[16] *Diversorum patrum sententie sive Collectio in LXXIV titulos digesta* ed. J. T. Gilchrist (Monumenta Iuris Canonici series B: Corpus Collectionum 1: Vatican City, 1973) pp. xxi–xxxi. See below pp. 406–8.

[17] *Registrum* IV.23, pp. 334–6; *Epistolae Vagantes* 31 (n. 8) pp. 80–4. Cf. *Registrum* VII. 3, pp. 462–3.

church. When they attempted to intervene in Norman affairs in 1081, they were warned off by Gregory himself, anxious to safeguard the interests of the only reform-minded prince in Christendom.)[18] The most impressive demonstration of the authority of a Gregorian permanent legate was Hugh of Die's council of Autun in 1077, where the legate consecrated an archbishop and suspended from their offices a considerable number of bishops and archbishops.[19] The most illustrious victim of his zeal was Archbishop Manasses of Rheims, whose long struggle against Hugh of Die culminated in the archbishop's deposition for simony in 1080. The legatine activity of Hugh of Die prompted Theodor Schieffer in his study of papal legations in France (1935) to conclude that the Gregorian legation was an instrument of aggression. In the interests of reform legates must compete for power with hostile or reluctant ecclesiastical authorities and any legatine victory meant 'a weakening of the power of bishop and metropolitan'.[20] Contemporary opponents of the Gregorian legates certainly identified them as an aggressive weapon of the curia. Archbishop Liemar of Bremen complained in 1075 of the conduct of the cardinal legates in Germany towards himself and his colleague, Archbishop Siegfried of Mainz: 'Like reckless madmen they adjured us by our obedience to the apostolic see either to do their bidding and summon a synod or to come to Rome and explain ourselves.' When Liemar did neither, the pope, influenced by 'the madness of those legates,' suspended him from his office. Liemar concluded that the pope intended to degrade all bishops and treat them 'like bailiffs on his estates'.[21] Gregory's critics often complained in similar terms that his 'unheard-of innovations' were undermining the ancient privileges of the churches. Gregory claimed on the contrary that his reforming measures followed 'the ancient footsteps of the holy Fathers'. Doubtless he sincerely believed that he was restoring the authentic institutions of the Church as described in the decrees of the early popes. In fact his most important intervention in French ecclesiastical affairs had the effect of exalting rather than diminishing the authority of an archbishop. He conferred on the archbishop of Lyons the primacy over

---

[18] H. E. J. Cowdrey, 'Pope Gregory VII and the Anglo-Norman church and kingdom', *SG* 9 (1972), 106–7.

[19] Schieffer, *Frankreich* (n. 1) pp. 100–1.

[20] *Ibid.*, p. 237.

[21] *Hildesheimer Briefe* 15 in *Briefsammlungen der Zeit Heinrichs IV.*, *MGH Die Briefe der deutschen Kaiserzeit* 5, 33–5.

the provinces of Sens, Tours and Rouen (1079), his purpose evidently being to implement 'the statutes of the Fathers', as found in the Pseudo-Isidorean Decretals.[22] No doubt Gregorian legatine institutions seemed to Gregory to be equally authentic, 'a custom', as he said of the permanent legation of Amatus of Oloron, 'from the earliest days of the foundation' of the Roman church. Gregory regarded his legates as an instrument of restoration; but opponents like Manasses of Rheims and Liemar of Bremen found that in practice the Gregorian legation could easily turn into an instrument of aggression against those who upheld the traditions of the pre-Gregorian church. By the end of the pontificate Gregorian legates in Germany had assumed responsibility both for coordinating the rebellion against Henry IV and for deposing the bishops who remained loyal to the excommunicate emperor. A decisive role was played by Cardinal bishop Odo of Ostia, who in December 1084 deposed Bishop Otto of Constance and consecrated Gebhard of Zähringen in his place. The legate's controversial action initiated the creation of two rival hierarchies within the German church, one loyal to the emperor, the other obedient to the reform papacy.[23]

When Odo of Ostia became Pope Urban II, Bishop Gebhard III of Constance became his permanent legate in the German kingdom (1089). Gebhard was responsible for the reform papacy's most important diplomatic coup in Germany. He bound the two leading rebel princes, Berthold II of Zähringen (his own brother) and Duke Welf IV of Bavaria, to the Roman church by the bond of vassalage, receiving homage from them as vassals of St Peter (1093). Gebhard remained the leader of the papal party in Germany until his death in 1110 and played a prominent part in the rebellion which finally toppled Henry IV from his throne (1105).[24] In France Urban retained Gregory VII's permanent legates Amatus of Bordeaux and Archbishop Hugh of Lyons (reinstated in 1094 after his excommunication by Urban's predecessor, Victor III, whose election to the papacy Hugh had vigorously opposed).[25] Urban II was forced to rely on 'native' legates to an even greater extent than Gregory VII. For most of his pontificate he was exiled from Rome and his wanderings

[22] Gregory VII, *Registrum* VI.34–5, pp. 447–52. See H. Fuhrmann, 'Studien zur Geschichte mittelalterlicher Patriarchate (II)', *ZSSRG KA* 40 (1954), 61–84.
[23] Becker, *Urban II.* 1, 64–5. See below p. 415.
[24] Becker, 'Urban II. und die deutsche Kirche' in *Investiturstreit und Reichsverfassung* ed. J. Fleckenstein (Sigmaringen, 1973) pp. 245, 267–8. See below p. 415.
[25] Becker, *Urban II.* 1, 195, 210–11.

– in the Norman territories of southern Italy, in the Patrimony of St Peter, in Lombardy and France – increased the difficulties of communication between the curia and the western churches. Hence it was during Urban's pontificate that the Gregorian permanent legation was most widely disseminated. Urban introduced the institution to Spain and also adapted it to the needs of his most important innovation, the crusade. The task of bringing the ritual and organisation of the Spanish churches into conformity with the Roman norm was at first entrusted by the reform papacy to cardinal legates (notably Hugh Candidus and Rainer, cardinal priest of S. Clemente, the future Paschal II). Gregory VII in addition employed the distinguished southern French reforming abbots, Frotard of Thomières and Richard of St Victor in Marseilles, to implement papal policy in Spain.[26] In 1096 Urban conferred a permanent legation on Archbishop Bernard of Toledo, on whom he had already conferred the office of 'primate of all the bishops who are in Spain'. The combination of the primacy and the legation created a papal vicariate like that enjoyed in France by Bernard's contemporary, Hugh of Lyons, as primate and legate. Like the permanent legates of Gregory VII, Bernard owed his office to his close relationship with the pope: he was Urban's compatriot and had been his contemporary in the abbey of Cluny.[27] (In his monastic profession Bernard resembled Urban's permanent legate in Germany, Gebhard of Constance, former monk of Hirsau, a Swabian monastery which had adopted the customs of Cluny.) A papal vicariate was also conferred on Bishop Adhémar of Le Puy, the legate who was appointed to accompany the crusade launched in November 1095. The nature of Adhémar's office is clarified by evidence which suggests that his legation was attached specifically to the southern French army of Count Raymond of St Gilles and that other legates were assigned to the armies led by other crusading princes, so as not to compromise their dignity.[28] If this was indeed the case, Adhémar and his colleagues were true 'native' legates, who by virtue of their vicariate provided their compatriots with immediate access to the papacy.

At first sight the Gregorian permanent legation seems to have continued unchanged during the early twelfth century. Paschal II

---

[26] G. Säbekow, *Die päpstlichen Legationen nach Spanien und Portugal bis zum Ausgang des 12. Jahrhunderts* (dissertation: Berlin, 1931) pp. 12–34, 62–9. Servatius, *Paschalis II.* pp. 18–32.

[27] Urban II, *JL* 5465, *MPL* 151, 346CD; *JL* 5643: *NA* 6 (1880), 299. See Säbekow, *Spanien* pp. 28–32, 71–2.

[28] H. E. Mayer, 'Zur Beurteilung Adhémars von Le Puy', *DA* 16 (1960), 547–52.

retained Gebhard III of Constance and Bernard of Toledo as his legates and he also created new legations. He appointed Archbishop Guido of Vienne as his legate in eastern France and Burgundy (*ca.* 1112–18) and when Guido became Pope Calixtus II, he created a similar legation for his successor in Vienne, Archbishop Peter (1120).[29] In 1108 Paschal created a permanent legation in Aquitaine to be held by Bishop Gerard of Angoulême, who was confirmed in this appointment by Calixtus II (1120) and Honorius II (1125). Paschal's letter of 1108, informing the archbishops of Bordeaux, Bourges, Tours, Auch and Dôle of Gerard's appointment, provides a useful summary of the functions of a Gregorian permanent legate:

To lighten your task, so that you have someone near you to whom you can bring requests and difficulties – someone who by his counsels and his encouragement assists you in accomplishing the work of salvation – we delegate our own authority for the duration of our pontificate to our dearly beloved brother, Gerard of Angoulême, who will share our responsibilities among you. For the honour of God and the salvation of your souls, faithfully obey him who will be our vicar and the vicar of the apostles in your lands . . . Do not disdain, beloved brothers, to hold synods with him when they are needed for the good of the Church. For this purpose we grant him the power to convoke [synods] in our place.[30]

Paschal's letter suggests that Gerard of Angoulême was to enjoy a vicariate in Aquitaine like that which Amatus of Oloron and Bordeaux had exercised for two decades. In fact his authority was from the outset more restricted than that of Amatus. His jurisdiction did not extend, like that of Amatus, to Narbonne nor to Gascony and the Spanish March; and his proceedings were supervised far more closely than those of his predecessor. Both Paschal and Calixtus II sent cardinal legates to confirm or overturn his decisions. In 1123 Calixtus summoned Gerard to Rome after the archbishop of Bordeaux had complained to the pope about the legate's decision to free the monastery of Saint-Macaire from its obedience to the abbey of Sainte-Croix. After hearing Gerard's explanation of his decision, Calixtus renewed his legation and commanded the metropolitan of his legatine province 'to receive him . . . as our vicar'; but he added: 'We recommend him to conduct himself with more condescension

[29] Schieffer, *Frankreich* (n. 1) pp. 195–8; Ruess, *Legaten* (n. 2) p. 216.
[30] Paschal II, *JL* 6262, *MPL* 163, 240D–241C. See H. Claude, 'Gérard d'Angoulême, ses pouvoirs de légat en Aquitaine au nom des papes Pascal II, Calixte II et Honorius II', *Mémoires de la Société Archéologique et Historique de la Charente* 1968, pp. 171–82.

towards you and the other brethren and in short to examine cases with more care and courtesy'.[31] Like the legatine province of Aquitaine, the neighbouring Spanish legation created for Archbishop Bernard of Toledo did not survive the first quarter of the twelfth century intact. In 1114 Paschal II freed the province of Braga from the authority of the legate and raised Bishop Maurice of Braga to the rank of archbishop and metropolitan, directly subject to the apostolic see. In 1120 Calixtus II conferred a legation in the provinces of Mérida and Braga on Diego Gelmírez, whom he likewise raised to the rank of archbishop and metropolitan.[32]

Evidently the early twelfth-century curia no longer felt the need which the papacy of the 1080s and 1090s had felt for permanent 'native' legates acting as papal vicars in their provinces. Perhaps indeed the curia had begun to distrust such concentrations of power in provinces too distant to be easily supervised. From the beginning of the twelfth century the most important legations were entrusted to cardinals: a development which reflected the growing importance of the cardinals during the pontificate of Paschal II. In eastern France, for example, Guido of Vienne possessed a permanent legation; but he was less active and influential than the formidable Cardinal bishop Cuno of Palestrina. During the crisis of 1111 the cardinal legate Cuno attempted to dictate policy to a beleaguered pope and a divided curia. When he heard the news that Emperor Henry V had extorted an investiture privilege from the pope, Cuno was on a legation in the crusader kingdom of Jerusalem. He at once excommunicated the emperor without consulting the pope. Sent on a legation to France in 1114–15, Cuno held three legatine synods (in Beauvais, Rheims and Chalon) in which he again excommunicated the emperor, even though the pope refused to do so. In the spring of 1115 Cuno entered the German kingdom in order to foment rebellion against Henry V. Finally, in the Lateran synod of 1116 Cuno confronted Paschal with the demand either to repudiate or to confirm his actions. The pope would do neither.[33] The career of Cuno of Palestrina provides an extreme example of the importance of the cardinal legate in the early

---

[31] Calixtus II, *JL* 7034: (n. 4) 1276C–1277B. See Claude, 'Gérard d'Angoulême' pp. 179–81.

[32] C. Erdmann, 'Mauritius Burdinus (Gregor VIII.)', *QFIAB* 19 (1927), 212–17; P. Kehr, *Das Papsttum und die Königreiche Navarra und Aragon bis zur Mitte des 12. Jahrhunderts, Abhandlungen der preussischen Akademie der Wissenschaften 1928, phil.-hist. Klasse* 4, 43; Säbekow, *Spanien* (n. 26) p. 72.

[33] Schieffer, *Frankreich* (n. 1) pp. 195–204; R. Hiestand, 'Legat, Kaiser und Basileus. Bischof Kuno von Praeneste und die Krise des Papsttums von 1111/1112' in *Aus*

twelfth century. Less dramatic but equally significant were the interventions of cardinal legates in Aquitaine during the permanent legation of Gerard of Angoulême. Cardinal bishop Richard of Albano was sent by Paschal II in 1110 to investigate Gerard's conduct towards the bishop of Clermont. (He confirmed Gerard's actions.) Calixtus II overturned Gerard's decision to annul the marriage of William Clito, son of Duke Robert II of Normandy, to the daughter of the count of Anjou and sent three cardinal legates – Peter Pierleone (the future antipope Anacletus II), Gregory of S. Angelo (the future Innocent II) and John of Crema – to deal with the case. (They confirmed the annulment.)[34]

The curtailing of the authority of the permanent legates was probably part of the reaction in the curia against Gregorian ideas and methods, which was accelerated by the formation of the party of the chancellor Haimeric in the early 1120s and which culminated in the schism of 1130. It is significant that Gerard of Angoulême – the last surviving permanent legate of the type created by Gregory VII – supported the 'conservative' candidate in the schism of 1130, the 'Gregorian' Anacletus II. Gerard's legatine province of Aquitaine was almost the only territory and its overlord, Count William X of Poitou, one of the few princes north of the Alps who recognised Anacletus, rather than Cardinal Haimeric's candidate, Innocent II, as pope.[35] From 1132 until Gerard's death in 1136 two rival permanent legates fought for the allegiance of Aquitaine; for Innocent II conferred on Bishop Geoffrey of Chartres a legation similar to that which Gerard had enjoyed since 1108 and which Anacletus II renewed in 1130.[36] Innocent was driven to this expedient by the obdurate resistance of Aquitaine and William X of Poitou. The Aquitanian legation was an exceptional measure, rendered palatable to Innocent by the close friendship of Geoffrey of Chartres with the pope's staunchest supporters in France, Bernard of Clairvaux and Bishop Stephen of Paris. Outside Aquitaine the Innocentine cause was mainly promoted by cardinal legates. In the other French territories Cardinal bishop Matthew of Albano was the most illustrious of the five cardinal legates sent to keep church and kingdom loyal and

---

Reichsgeschichte und Nordischer Geschichte. Karl Jordan zum 65. Geburtstag ed. H. Fuhrmann, H.-E. Mayer, K. Wriedt (Kieler Historische Studien 16: Stuttgart, 1972) pp. 141–52. See below p. 430.

[34] Claude, 'Gérard d'Angoulême' (n. 30) pp. 175, 181.

[35] Janssen, *Frankreich* (n. 7) pp. 5–14.

[36] *Ibid.*, pp. 18–30; F.-J. Schmale, *Studien zum Schisma des Jahres 1130* (Cologne-Graz, 1961) pp. 223–4.

well informed about the papal reform programme. Peter the Venerable, abbot of Cluny, believed that the success of the Innocentine cause was largely the result of Matthew's 'immense and unremitting labours and his comings and goings throughout almost the whole world'. Peter reminded the pope of his indebtedness to his legate, recalling 'what [Matthew] has done for you, what he has suffered, what sacrifices he has made, how faithful he has been in increasing your authority in the kingdom of the Church over which you preside'.[37] In Germany an equally energetic role was played by Gerard, cardinal priest of S. Croce in Gerusalemme (subsequently Lucius II). Gerard had already served Honorius II on two legations in Germany (1125 and 1126–7), during which he had negotiated the alliance between King Lothar III and the papacy. His four legations on behalf of Innocent II (1130, 1130–1, 1133 and 1135–6) helped to bring the kingdom into the Innocentine obedience and to remind Lothar III that it was his imperial duty to reinstate the legitimate pope in Rome. A quarter of a century after Gerard's last legation, the German theologian Gerhoch of Reichersberg remembered him as a model legate. Gerard and his colleague Martin, cardinal priest of S. Stefano in Celio monte (Innocent's legate in Scandinavia and perhaps also in Bohemia) 'like true citizens of the heavenly city and servants of God bearing peace and illuminating the land, brought joy to the cities and the monasteries when they arrived and left behind a blessing when they departed'.[38] Gerard was succeeded as the curia's expert in German affairs by Cardinal bishop Theodwin of S. Rufina, whose earliest legations (1135 and 1136) were devoted to the pacification of the kingdom, so as to enable Lothar III to march to the pope's aid.[39] In the later years of Innocent's pontificate Guido, cardinal priest of S. Grisogono, appeared in northern Italy using the title 'legate for Lombardy' (1139), while in Spain the interests of the papal curia were protected by Guido, cardinal deacon of SS. Cosma e Damiano (1134, 1135–7 and 1143).[40]

---

[37] Peter the Venerable, *Letter* 39 ed. G. Constable, *The Letters of Peter the Venerable* 1 (Cambridge, Mass., 1967), 132. See U. Berlière, 'Le cardinal Matthieu d'Albano', *Revue Bénédictine* 18 (1901), 113–40, 280–303; Janssen, *Frankreich* (n. 7) pp. 15–18, 30–4.

[38] Gerhoch of Reichersberg, *De investigatione Antichristi* c. 51, *MGH Libelli* 3, 358. See J. Bachmann, *Die päpstlichen Legaten in Deutschland und Skandinavien (1125–1159)* (Historische Studien: Berlin, 1913) pp. 6–46.

[39] Bachmann, *Deutschland* pp. 48–9.

[40] B. Zenker, *Die Mitglieder des Kardinalkollegiums von 1130 bis 1159* (dissertation: Würzburg, 1964) pp. 62–3, 147; Säbekow, *Spanien* (n. 26) pp. 43–6.

The period between the schism of 1130 and the outbreak of the schism of 1159 witnessed a notable expansion in the numbers and functions of the cardinal legates. It was during this period that the term 'legate *a latere*' acquired its definitive meaning in papal documents. In the pontificate of Innocent II the term was still not used exclusively for cardinal legates: for example, the pope in 1135 informed the French episcopate that he was sending the archbishop of Rouen to them *de latere suo*. But in a privilege issued by Hadrian IV between 1156 and 1158 the transformation in the meaning of the term is complete. The privilege announces that the abbey of St Gilles is to be exempt from the authority of Archbishop Berengar of Narbonne, who has been appointed legate in Provence, and from any other legate – except a *legatus a latere*.[41] By the later 1150s, therefore, a legate *a latere* was distinct from, and superior to, a native legate. The sources for 1130–59 record 109 legations, undertaken by fifty-one cardinals, comprising one-third of the membership of the college of cardinals during these three decades.[42] The legatine duties entrusted to the cardinal priests and deacons seem often to have been of a routine character: sometimes their function was merely to summon the clergy of a particular region to a papal council. To the cardinal bishops, however, were entrusted the most difficult and complex problems of ecclesiastical politics. (The curia may have felt that cardinal legates of lesser rank would prove unable to establish their precedence over the native episcopate – as was evidently the experience of John of Crema, cardinal priest of S. Grisogono in his legatine synod of London in 1125.)[43] Hence Cardinal bishop Matthew of Albano was appointed to the strenuous and crucially important legation in France on behalf of Innocent II. Matthew's former pupil (in the monastery of St Martin-des-Champs, Paris), Cardinal bishop Imar of Tusculum was entrusted by Pope Lucius II with the controversial English legation of 1144–5. Imar was sent to England at a time when the two most illustrious native prelates, Archbishop Theobald of Canterbury and Bishop Henry of Winchester, had gone to the papal curia to contest the office of permanent legate in England. Imar's principal tasks were to investi-

---

[41] Innocent II, *JL* 7726: S. Loewenfeld, *Epistolae pontificum Romanorum ineditae* (Leipzig, 1885) p. 90. Hadrian IV, *JL* 10354: E. Goiffon, *Bullaire de l'Abbaye de Saint-Gilles* (Nîmes, 1882) p. 77. See Janssen, *Frankreich* (n. 7) pp. 171–2.

[42] Zenker, *Mitglieder* (n. 40) p. 229.

[43] Gervaise of Canterbury, *Actus pontificum*, RS 71/2 (1879), 381–2. See Zenker, *Mitglieder* pp. 61 n. 49, 229–30; Tillmann, *England* (n. 4) pp. 28–9.

gate the claim of the bishopric of St David's to metropolitan rights over Wales and to confer the pallium on Archbishop William of York, nephew of the English king Stephen and of the bishop of Winchester. (William's appointment to York was opposed by Archbishop Theobald and by other notable reformers, including Bernard of Clairvaux.)[44] Of equal complexity was the legation of Nicholas Breakspear, cardinal bishop of Albano, in Scandinavia on behalf of Eugenius III (1152–3). Nicholas seized the opportunity of internal political conflict in Norway to introduce church reforms and to create the archbishopric of Trondheim, freeing the Norwegian church from the metropolitan authority of Lund.[45] Perhaps the most-travelled of the cardinal legates of the mid–twelfth century was Cardinal bishop Alberic of Ostia (like Matthew of Albano and Imar of Tusculum, a product of St Martin-des-Champs, Paris). Alberic acted as legate in England and Scotland (1138–9), in the crusader principality of Antioch (1139–41) and in France (1144). In England he deposed three abbots at his synod of Westminster and consecrated Theobald of Bec as archbishop of Canterbury; he worked for a rapprochement between England and Scotland and he reconciled to Innocent II the Scottish church and kingdom, which had supported the antipope Anacletus II during the schism of the 1130s. In Antioch he deposed the patriarch Ralph and attempted to settle the ecclesiastical quarrels of the crusader states in the interests of the more efficient prosecution of the holy war against the Moslems. In France he reformed the old Benedictine abbey of St Benoit-sur-Loire and secured the appointment of his nephew, Macarius of Morigny, as abbot.[46]

Alberic of Ostia, like Gerard of S. Croce in Gerusalemme, impressed contemporaries as a model of correct legatine conduct. He was 'distinguished for divine and secular learning, extremely experienced in the affairs of the Church, famous for his eloquence, farsighted in his counsel and, more important than all this, in his conduct and countenance, in all his relationships and actions, he showed evidence of great gentleness and religion'.[47] An encomium like this

---

[44] Zenker, *Mitglieder* pp. 44–5; Tillmann, *England* pp. 50–1.

[45] W. Seegrün, *Das Papsttum und Skandinavien bis zur Vollendung der nordischen Kirchenorganisation (1164)* (Quellen und Forschungen zur Geschichte Schleswig-Holsteins 51: Neumünster, 1967) pp. 146–70.

[46] Zenker, *Mitglieder* (n. 40) pp. 17–18; Tillmann, *England* (n. 4) pp. 38–40; Janssen, *Frankreich* (n. 7) pp. 39–40.

[47] Richard of Hexham, *De gestis regis Stephani* in *Chronicles of the reign of Stephen, Henry II and Richard I*, RS 82/3 (1886), 167.

– or like Gerhoch of Reichersberg's description of Gerard of S. Croce and Martin of S. Stefano – is infrequent in the twelfth-century literature concerning cardinal legates. For the growth in their numbers and responsibilities provoked sharp criticism of the Roman legates. Indeed Gerhoch's praise of Gerard and Martin is found in the middle of a denunciation of 'the pride of legates in modern times'. Those 'servants of God' had only nine or ten horses in their entourages. 'How many [legates] resembled them in their time or today [1161–2]? How many do we expect to find in the multitude of those who seek what is their own, not what is of Jesus Christ!'[48] The cardinal legates of the eleventh and twelfth centuries were granted the right to be 'clad in apostolic apparel and insignia, as if the pope himself had come'.[49] This privilege was intended to enhance their authority. Twelfth-century moralists rebuked the legates for their pomp and splendour; but a more serious grievance was the size of the retinues which accompanied them, for these must be fed and housed. Cardinal legates surrounded themselves with so many servants that their retinues were swelled to 'forty or more horses, so that the wealthiest monasteries (to say nothing of the poorer or middling houses) and even bishops and princes cannot afford to supply the wants of such a crowd'.[50] Gerhoch illustrated his complaint with a story of Gregory, cardinal deacon of S. Angelo, who was legate in Germany in 1153. 'Because a dinner prepared for him and his servants in the monastery of St Alban [in Mainz] was less sumptuous than he desired, [Gregory] kept the abbot under a cruel interdict until he redeemed for a great sum of money the office and honour which had been denied him.'[51] The reality behind this piece of monastic gossip was the duty of every church not specifically exempted by a papal privilege to provide food and accommodation for a visiting cardinal legate: that obligation which thirteenth-century canon lawyers would call *procuratio canonica*.[52] Hence the praise which Bernard of Clairvaux bestowed on Cardinal Martin of S. Stefano, who was 'so poor' during his legation to Denmark 'that

---

[48] Gerhoch, *De investigatione* c. 51 (n. 38) p. 358.
[49] *Vita sancti Bernwardi episcopi Hildesheimensis* c. 22, *MGH SS* 4, 769; William of Tyre, *Historia rerum in partibus transmarinis gestarum* XVIII.29, *RHC Occ.* 1, 870–1 (see below p. 363). See Ruess, *Legaten* (n. 2) p. 204.
[50] Gerhoch, *De investigatione* c. 50 (n. 38) p. 357.
[51] Gerhoch, *De quarta vigilia noctis* c. 12, *MGH Libelli* 3, 513.
[52] Ruess, *Legaten* (n. 2) p. 188. See below p. 267.

for lack of money and horses he could scarcely reach Florence'.[53] The moralists' criticism of the size of legates' retinues was not without result; for the legislation of the Third Lateran Council of 1179 finally set a limit of twenty-five horses to the retinue of a cardinal.[54]

Closely linked with the complaints about the expenses of entertaining legates were allegations of extortion and corruption. 'Is it not a phenomenon of another age, for a legate to return without gold from a land of gold?' asked Bernard of Clairvaux. It was indeed 'contrary to custom', said John of Salisbury, for legates to return poor from their legations. 'They love gifts, they pursue debts, they search and ransack provinces, they empty the pockets of others so as to fill their own.' According to a Lotharingian chronicler, 'we see not preachers but predators, not bringers of peace but stealers of money, not men who fortify the world but utterly insatiable devourers of money'.[55] A legate who left a particularly evil reputation behind him was the papal chamberlain Jordan, cardinal priest of S. Susanna, who (according to John of Salisbury) 'hid his avarice under the cloak of the Carthusian order'. In 1151 Eugenius III sent Jordan as his legate to Germany, accompanied by Octavian, cardinal priest of S. Cecilia. Both were 'greedy and avaricious in their own way', wrote John of Salisbury, mindful of Octavian's later career as the antipope Victor IV.[56] In the following year Jordan began a legation in France, where his alleged rapacity provoked the anger of the prior of his former Carthusian house, Le Mont-Dieu (near Rheims). When Jordan offered money to Le Mont-Dieu, Prior Hugh rebuked him in the words which St Peter had used to Simon Magus: 'Thy money perish with thee!' (Acts 8. 20). Prior Hugh denounced the legate to Bernard of Clairvaux, who in turn wrote to Cardinal bishop Hugh of Ostia that Jordan had left 'filthy and horrible traces everywhere among us'.[57] What neither Bernard's angry letter nor John of Salisbury's

---

[53] Bernard of Clairvaux, *De consideratione* IV.5.13, MPL 182, 782B. Cf. John of Salisbury, *Policraticus* V.15, ed. C. J. Webb 1 (Oxford, 1909), 348.

[54] *Concilium Lateranense III* c. 4: *Conciliorum Oecumenicorum Decreta* p. 213.

[55] Bernard, *De consideratione* IV.5.13, 783A; John of Salisbury, *Policraticus* VIII.7: (n. 53) 2, 355; *Continuatio Aquicinctina Sigeberti Chronici* 1157, MGH SS 6, 408. See J. Sydow, 'Bernhard von Clairvaux und die römische Kurie', *Cîteaux in de Nederlanden* 6 (1955), 5–11; G. Miczka, *Das Bild der Kirche bei Johannes von Salisbury* (Bonner Historische Forschungen 34: Bonn, 1970) pp. 157–9.

[56] John of Salisbury, *Historia pontificalis* c. 38 ed. M. Chibnall (London, 1956) p. 75. See Bachmann, *Deutschland* (n. 38) pp. 91–9.

[57] Bernard, *Epistola* 290, MPL 182, 496B; John of Salisbury, *Historia pontificalis* c. 39, p. 77. See Sydow, 'Bernhard' (n. 55) pp. 9–10; Janssen, *Frankreich* (n. 7) p. 53. See also below p. 254.

scathing anecdote makes clear is that Cardinal Jordan was not pursuing a private career of extortion, but performing one of his legatine duties: namely, the collection of the revenues of the Roman church. An important part of the income of the papacy came from the *census* paid by churches and territories – the exempt monasteries and the vassal kingdoms and principalities – which enjoyed a special relationship with St Peter and his vicar, the pope. Arrangements for the transmission of this *census* to the curia were haphazard and it often fell to legates to collect the arrears. Legates were sent to England to collect the arrears of Peter's pence: the subdeacon Hubert in 1080, Cardinal bishop John of Tusculum in 1101, Abbot Anselm of St Saba (in Rome) in 1116–19, Abbot Henry of St Jean d'Angely in 1123.[58] The cardinal legate Nicholas of Albano was probably responsible for introducing the payment of Peter's pence into Norway and Sweden in 1152–3.[59] The sole function of some of the legates sent to Spain – for example, Master Peter in 1168 and the subdeacon Nicholas in 1183 – was the collection of the extensive revenues owed to the curia.[60] The severe criticism of Cardinal Jordan of S. Susanna, on a similar mission in France in 1152, suggests simply that he had performed his duties too efficiently. The mid-twelfth-century denunciations of avaricious legates are in fact convincing evidence of the effectiveness of the cardinal legates as an instrument of papal government.

By the middle of the twelfth century the cardinal legates had displaced the Gregorian native legates with full powers to act as papal vicars. The title *vicarius papae* was now used to describe cardinals entrusted with long-term legations. Such *vicarii* were to be found throughout the second half of the twelfth century in northern Italy (where the power of the cities had become a central factor in the political calculations of the curia). In the pontificates of Anastasius IV and Hadrian IV Aribert, cardinal priest of S. Anastasia, was described as 'legate of all Lombardy' and 'vicar of the pope in Lombardy'. At the beginning of the pontificate of Alexander III Hildebrand, cardinal priest of SS. Apostoli, was for several years papal vicar in Venice and subsequently he was 'legate in all Lombardy' between 1166 and 1177 (except in 1175). In the late 1160s and early 1170s Lombardy also possessed a permanent legate who was a 'native' prelate, in the person of Archbishop Galdin of Milan; but Galdin was formerly cardinal priest of S. Sabina. He owed his

[58] Tillmann, *England* (n. 4) pp. 16–17, 22, 25, 27.
[59] Seegrün, *Skandinavien* (n. 45) p. 169.   [60] Säbekow, *Spanien* (n. 26) pp. 53, 55.

promotion to the archbishopric to his faithful service in the curia of Alexander III and conformed to the pattern of the cardinal legate rather than to that of the Gregorian 'native' legate.[61] Cardinal legates with similar functions were now also to be found in France, the territory where the Gregorian permanent legates had always been most influential and had lasted longest. This substitution of legates *a latere* for permanent native legates from the 1130s onwards reveals the determination of the curia to keep a firm control over legations. It also reflects a significant development inside the college of cardinals in the second quarter of the twelfth century: the recruitment of north Italian and French cardinals – apparently as a deliberate papal policy of countering the influence of the Roman and south Italian cardinals in the college.[62] One consequence of this policy was that the curia could now send to Lombardy and France legates *a latere* who were also 'natives', with special expertise in local affairs and who perhaps were more acceptable to local prelates and princes because they were natives. Alexander III's vicars in Lombardy were all north Italians: Hildebrand of SS. Apostoli was from Bologna, Galdin was Milanese. Their successors, the cardinal deacons Manfred of S. Giorgio in Velabro and Ardicius of S. Teodoro were respectively from Lavagna and Rivoltela.[63]

Like the Lombards, the French constituted a significant minority of the college of cardinals in the period 1130–98. Seven of these French cardinals were active as legates in this period: Cardinal bishop Giles of Tusculum (1131), Cardinal bishop Matthew of Albano (1128–9, 1131, 1135), Cardinal Ivo of S. Lorenzo in Damaso (1142), Cardinal bishop Alberic of Ostia (1144), Cardinal bishop Imar of Tusculum (1144), Cardinal bishop Henry of Albano (1180–2, 1188) and Cardinal Melior of SS. Giovanni e Paolo (1193–5).[64] French

[61] G. Dunken, *Die politische Wirksamkeit der päpstlichen Legaten in der Zeit des Kampfes zwischen Kaisertum und Papsttum in Oberitalien unter Friedrich I.* (Historische Studien 209: Berlin, 1931) pp. 21–3, 70–1, 79–80, 83–4, 110–11; M. Pacaut, 'Les légats d'Alexandre III (1159–1181)', *Revue d'histoire ecclésiastique* 50 (1955), 833–5. See below p. 494.

[62] See above pp. 48–9.

[63] Zenker, *Mitglieder* (n. 40) pp. 107, 157; J. M. Brixius, *Die Mitglieder des Kardinalkollegiums von 1130 bis 1181* (dissertation: Berlin, 1912) pp. 60, 64. The origins of their predecessor, Aribert of S. Anastasia, are not known.

[64] Janssen, *Frankreich* (n. 7) pp. 9–10, 17, 35, 39; Schieffer, *Frankreich* (n. 1) p. 229; Y. M.-J. Congar, 'Henri de Marcy, abbé de Clairvaux, cardinal-évêque d'Albano et légat pontifical' in *Analecta Monastica. Textes et Etudes sur la vie des moines au moyen âge* 5e série (Studia Anselmiana 43: Rome, 1958) pp. 30–40, 45–54; V. Pfaff, 'Die Kardinäle unter Papst Coelestin III. (1191–1198)', *ZSSRG KA* 41 (1955), 64, 77.

legations of equal importance were entrusted to three other cardinals who, though Italian by birth, had made their early careers in France. The Pisan Henry, cardinal priest of SS. Nereo ed Achilleo, had been a monk in Clairvaux. Alexander III exploited Henry's knowledge of France and his Cistercian connections when he chose him in 1160 as one of the legates commissioned to secure the recognition of the French church and king for Alexander as the rightful pope. Cardinal deacon Hyacinth of S. Maria in Cosmedin, who served Alexander on two French legations (1162 and 1165), was a Roman who had been educated in France. (He seems to have been a pupil of Peter Abelard.) Hyacinth's close friendship with King Louis VII fitted him for the role of intermediary between the curia and the French court and he frequently assumed responsibility for the papal correspondence with the Capetian king. The Pavian Peter, cardinal priest of S. Grisogono (later cardinal bishop of Tusculum) had been bishop of Meaux before becoming a cardinal (1173) and he was elected archbishop of Bourges shortly before his death. He became Alexander III's expert on French affairs and during his long legation of 1174–8 he succeeded in reconciling King Henry II of England and his rebellious sons and in negotiating a peace between the French and English kings.[65] The influence of French monastic reform and of the French schools was felt in the college of cardinals, as in the rest of western Christendom, creating in the curia a fund of expertise about the concerns of the French church and kingdom.

The responsibilities entrusted to Alexander III's vicars in Lombardy and his legates *a latere* in France illustrate the importance of the role of the legates during the schism of 1159–77. At the beginning of the pontificate their task was to win support for Alexander against the antipope Victor IV, who was supported by Emperor Frederick I. This was the purpose of the arduous, but ultimately successful legation of the cardinal priests Henry of SS. Nereo ed Achilleo and William of S. Pietro in Vincoli and the cardinal deacon Odo of S. Nicola in Carcere in 1160. They were commissioned to overcome the neutral attitude of Louis VII of France and Henry II of England and to draw north-western Europe into the Alexandrine obedience, a task greatly complicated by the rivalry of the two kings.[66] Throughout the eighteen-year schism Alexander was

[65] Janssen, *Frankreich* pp. 61–9, 92–3; Zenker, *Mitglieder* (n. 40) pp. 162, 165–6; Pacaut, 'Légats' (n. 61) pp. 835–7.
[66] W. Ohnsorge, *Die Legaten Alexanders III. im ersten Jahrzehnt seines Pontifikats (1159–1169)* (Historische Studien 175: Berlin, 1928) pp. 15–44; Janssen, *Frankreich* pp. 61–9.

threatened by the attempts of the emperor to win over the French and English kings to the support of the antipope; and he relied on his legates to counter these manoeuvres. Equally he relied on his legates to act as political advisers to his allies, to disseminate information among them and to coordinate their measures against the emperor. This was especially the function of the legates in northern Italy, who negotiated with the pope's most important allies, the cities of the Lombard League. The League was formed in 1167 with the purpose not of defending the claims of Alexander III but of destroying the system of government which Emperor Frederick I was attempting to introduce into Italy. The task of Alexander's legates was to ensure that the rebellion of the League served the interests of the Alexandrine cause.[67] Other legates sought financial aid for the impoverished Alexandrine curia, cut off from the revenues of the Patrimony of St Peter. In 1161–2, for example, Master Theodin and the chaplain Leo were sent to Spain to seek funds; while in 1162–4 John, cardinal priest of SS. Giovanni e Paolo collected a large sum of money in the crusader kingdom of Jerusalem.[68]

Throughout the schism the political and diplomatic duties of the legates were no doubt less numerous than their routine ecclesiastical functions: the confirmation of ecclesiastical possessions and rights, of episcopal elections and synodal judgements, the settlement of disputes between churches. Nevertheless the political functions far outweighed the ecclesiastical in importance. Legates were compelled to be diplomats and statesmen not only by the needs of the Alexandrine cause but also by the serious conflict which coincided with the schism, the Becket dispute in England. Nine legates were entrusted at different times with the duty of resolving the dispute between Henry II of England and Archbishop Thomas Becket of Canterbury: Cardinals William of S. Pietro in Vincoli and Odo of S. Nicola in Carcere (1167–8), the Carthusian priors Simon of Le Mont-Dieu and Engelbert of Le Val-St-Pierre and Bernard de Corilo of the order of Grandmont (1168–9); two officials of the papal curia, Gratian and Vivian (1169); and Archbishop Rotrod of Rouen and Bishop Bernard of Nevers (1170). The selection of these legates illustrates the political calculations of the curia in the late 1160s. The cardinals William and Odo were sent to Normandy in 1167 at the king's request (William being a declared enemy of Becket). The legate of 1168, Bernard de Corilo, the former general of the order of Grandmont, was under a heavy obligation to the king; and the two legates of 1170 were regarded as king's friends, Rotrod of Rouen being one of the leading prelates of the Angevin empire. The choice of these legates reveals the curia's anxiety not to alienate Henry II and drive him into the camp of the emperor and the antipope. The English king must be handled carefully, not least because he was the guarantor of the pope's only significant regular income, Peter's pence. (Henry was quite prepared to threaten to withhold payment.)[69] The murder of Becket (29 December 1170) shocked western Christendom and evoked from Louis VII and the French church in particular the demand that the pope should punish Henry severely. In fact Alexander's reaction was remarkably mild and the legates whom he sent to Henry II negotiated a compromise settlement on the crucial issue of the king's rights over the personnel and property of the English church. This difficult legation was entrusted to Theodin, cardinal priest of S. Vitale, whose earlier legation (in 1162 or 1163) had given him some experience of the English church, and Albert of S. Lorenzo in Lucina, the distinguished and long-serving cardinal who was to become chancellor and pope, as Gregory VIII.[70]

Even after the end of the Alexandrine schism the most important duties of the cardinal legates continued to be political and diplomatic in character. This was particularly the case in northern Italy, which continued to be a region of crucial strategic importance for both pope and emperor. The compromise peace reached with Emperor Frederick I in Venice in 1177 did not remove the tension from the relations of papacy and empire, so that it continued to be necessary for the cardinal legates in Lombardy to create alliances to defend papal interests. By the end of the century the term *generales in provincia legati* was being used to describe such cardinal legates in Italy. A 'general legate in a province' was a legate *a latere* who was given general (and often long-term) powers of supervision in his legatine province. The cardinal legates Hubert of S. Lorenzo in Damaso (1184), Peter of S. Cecilia (1188–93) and Fidantius of S. Marcello (1193–4) held such general legations in Lombardy, as did Pandulf of SS. Apostoli (1197) in Tuscany. (Two of the legates in Lombardy resembled their predecessors, the Alexandrine legates, in being natives of their legatine provinces: Cardinal Hubert was a

---

[69] Tillmann, *England* (n. 4) pp. 56–68; Janssen, *Frankreich* (n. 7) pp. 84–5; K. Jordan, 'Zur päpstlichen Finanzgeschichte im 11. und 12. Jahrhundert', *QFIAB* 25 (1933–4), 78. See below pp. 278–81.
[70] Tillmann, *England* pp. 68–72; Janssen, *Frankreich* pp. 85–8.

Milanese; Cardinal Peter was from Piacenza and continued as legate to show a keen interest in the affairs of his native city.)[71]

Elsewhere in western Christendom the political and diplomatic functions of legates *a latere* were probably increased by the central preoccupation of papal policy in the last quarter of the twelfth century: the launching of a crusade and, as a necessary preliminary, the pacification of Europe. The curia began to develop crusading plans in the mid-1170s and these culminated in the crusading encyclical of the short-lived Gregory VIII (1187) and the preaching of the Third Crusade (1187-9). The principal obstacle to the launching of a crusade in the 1180s was the hostility between the English king Henry II (succeeded in 1189 by his son, Richard I) and the new Capetian king of France, Philip II Augustus. A series of cardinal legates attempted to pacify the French and English kings. Peter of S. Grisogono (1177), Bobo of S. Angelo and Soffred of S. Maria in Via Lata (1187), Henry of Albano (1188) and Melior of SS. Giovanni e Paolo (1194) successfully negotiated truces; while the legations of Octavian of Ostia (1187) and John of Anagni (1189) were totally unsuccessful and provoked sharp criticism of the curia.[72] The legate commissioned by Gregory VIII and Clement III to preach the crusade north of the Alps was the eminent Cistercian Henry of Marcy, cardinal bishop of Albano. Between December 1187 and his death on 1 January 1189 Henry recruited Emperor Frederick I to the crusade, reconciled him to his opponent, the archbishop of Cologne, and held at Mainz a 'diet of Christ' (*curia Christi*) to preach the crusade to the German princes. He twice made peace between the kings of France and England (war broke out again between them after the first reconciliation) and recruited them to the crusade.[73] Cardinal Henry's first experience of secular politics had been acquired in 1181, when he had been entrusted with a legation to suppress heresy in the Languedoc. During this mission he became the first papal legate to raise an army and lead a military expedition in a Christian land: he captured the castle of Lavaur, the fortress of a prominent protector of heretics, Count Roger II of Béziers (July 1181).[74] Equally warlike were the activities of legates *a latere* in Spain, where the holy war against the Moslems raged as fiercely as in Outremer. The curia's expert on Spanish affairs, Hyacinth of S. Maria in Cosmedin on two occasions (1154-5 and 1172-5) organised

---

[71] Friedländer, *Deutschland* (n. 6) pp. 113-14.

[72] Janssen, *Frankreich* pp. 92, 128, 130, 134, 139, 177, 180.

[73] Congar, 'Henri de Marcy' (n. 64) pp. 45-54.   [74] *Ibid.*, pp. 30-8.

the holy war in the peninsula. His successor, Gregory of S. Angelo worked throughout 1191–4 to unite the Christian kings of Spain in a crusade and resumed his efforts in 1196–7.[75]

Throughout the west cardinal legates became in the course of the twelfth century the foremost executors of papal policy. They had absorbed the functions of the permanent 'native' legates of the Gregorian period and assumed the political and diplomatic duties necessitated by papal policy in the second half of the twelfth century. However, although the Gregorian legates had disappeared, 'native' legates continued to exist in the western Church in the twelfth century. In Germany a series of eminent prelates with strong pro-papal sympathies received the legatine office. Archbishop Adalbert of Mainz was 'legate of the apostolic see' throughout Germany from 1118 until his death in 1137. In that year Innocent II conferred on Archbishop Albero of Trier the legatine office in the provinces of Trier, Mainz, Cologne, Salzburg, Bremen and Magdeburg. Hadrian IV in 1155 conferred on Archbishop Hillin of Trier a legation throughout the German kingdom, although a year later he exempted the province of Mainz from the legate's authority. Archbishop Eberhard of Salzburg in 1163 received from Alexander III the office of legate throughout Germany with the special duty of defending the Alexandrine cause during the schism. A similar legation was given to Conrad of Wittelsbach, whose turbulent career brought him to the archbishopric of Mainz in the years 1161–77 and again in 1183–1200 and also to the archbishopric of Salzburg between 1173 and 1183. Conrad was simultaneously a 'native' legate and *legatus a latere*; for Alexander appointed him cardinal priest of S. Marcello in 1165 and cardinal bishop of Sabina a year later. In France, as in Germany, the legatine office was granted to archbishops who had deserved well of the papacy. Innocent II rewarded Arnold of Narbonne and Bernard of Arles with the office for supporting his cause during the Anacletan schism. Alexander III similarly gave the office of 'legate of the Roman see' to Bertrand of Bordeaux and William of Sens and Urban III conferred it on Henry of Bourges. Three archbishops of Vienne (Guido, Peter and Robert) and three archbishops of Lyons (Humbald, Peter and Wichard) appear as legates in the course of the twelfth century, perhaps owing their office as much to the traditions of their sees as to their personal services to the papacy.[76] These local

[75] Säbekow, *Spanien* (n. 26) pp. 48–51, 53, 55–6, 60.
[76] Ruess, *Legaten* (n. 2) pp. 215–24; H. Bastgen, 'Die Praerogativen der Salzburger Metropole', *HJb* 33 (1912), 570; Janssen, *Frankreich* (n. 7) pp. 157, 159, 171–5. On Conrad of Wittelsbach see below pp. 487–8, 497.

prelates who enjoyed the legatine office were less powerful than the Gregorian 'native' legates, but considerably more powerful than the *legati nati* of the thirteenth century. To distinguish them from these earlier and later functionaries, historians have called the 'native' legates of *ca.* 1130–98 the 'archbishop-legates'. Their legations were a reward for past loyalty and a guarantee of future service. This point is made most clearly in the letter of Urban III granting a legation to Archbishop Henry of Bourges (1186/7):

The proven devotion of our venerable brother Henry . . . inclines us to show the grace of the apostolic see more abundantly to [the church of Bourges]; for we know him to be a prudent and discreet man, noble in his conduct and his birth, showing such devotion to us and the Roman church that his merits demand that he be loved the more readily and honoured the more attentively by the apostolic see. Hence . . . we have committed to him the office of the apostolic legation so that in our place (*vice nostra*) he may correct what must be corrected, plant what he knows should be planted, root out vices and strive to sow the seeds of virtues.[77]

The authority of an 'archbishop-legate' was less than that of a legate *a latere*. When, for example, Innocent II made Archbishop Albero of Trier 'vicar of the apostolic see' in Germany, he was careful to give cardinal legates precedence over the native legate: 'We decree that whenever a priest, deacon or subdeacon or any customary legate is sent from our principal and apostolic see for the sake of ecclesiastical utility or to hold a synod . . . [Albero] shall obtain the primacy among the other bishops *after* that same apostolic legate.' Nevertheless in the absence of a cardinal legate, the clergy and people of the provinces of Trier, Mainz, Cologne, Salzburg, Bremen and Magdeburg must show 'obedience and reverence' to Albero and must attend his synods when summoned. Hadrian IV made the same distinction in his privilege for the abbey of St Gilles (1156–8), which exempted the abbey from the jurisdiction of the archbishop-legate, Berengar of Narbonne, but subordinated it to the authority of a legate *a latere*.[78] Although ranking lower than a legate *a latere*, the authority of an archbishop-legate was greater than the purely honorific dignity of the later *legatus natus*. He carried out visitations, presided over synods and settled ecclesiastical disputes 'by episcopal

---

[77] Urban III, *JL* 15834, *MPL* 202, 1475CD.
[78] Innocent II, *JL* 7851–2, *MPL* 179, 332AB, 333C; Hadrian IV, *JL* 10354: *Bullaire* (n. 41) p. 77.

and apostolic power': his archiepiscopal authority was enhanced by *apostolica potestas*.[79]

The authority of an archbishop-legate was likely to be greatest in regions less frequently visited by legates *a latere*; as for example in England. The twelfth-century English kings favoured the appointment of archbishop-legates as a means of discouraging the sending of cardinal legates. Henry I 'persuaded and commanded the archbishop of Canterbury to seek a legation so as not to have to receive a Roman legate in his kingdom again'.[80] (His grandson, Henry II, claimed – according to the hostile John of Salisbury – that Henry I 'was king, apostolic legate, patriarch, emperor and everything he wished to be, in his own land'.)[81] Twelfth-century archbishops of Canterbury shared the royal enthusiasm for native legations: not because they shared the kings' wish to limit papal interference in England, but because the legation gave weight to their claim that Canterbury possessed the primacy over the English church. Anselm of Canterbury had explained to Urban II in 1097 that the native legation was an immemorial custom.

Concerning the Roman legation over the kingdom of England, I told the lord pope that the men of this kingdom declared that the church of Canterbury had held it from ancient times until our own time; and I showed him how necessary this was and that to do otherwise was contrary to the interests of the Roman and the English church . . . The lord pope did not take away from me the legation which the church had held until our time.

However, Urban's successor, Paschal II, sent Archbishop Guido of Vienne (the future Calixtus II) on a legation to England in 1100. Anselm protested at this diminution of his dignity. He obtained from Paschal not a permanent legation but a promise that henceforward he would 'not be subject to the judgement of any legate but only of ourself'.[82] Historians of the Anglo-Norman church have

---

[79] Janssen, *Frankreich* (n. 7) pp. 156–69, 172.

[80] Hugh the Cantor, *The History of the Church of York* ed. C. Johnston (London, 1961) p. 123. See Tillmann, *England* (n. 4) pp. 22–38; M. Brett, *The English church under Henry I* (Oxford, 1975) pp. 34–50.

[81] John of Salisbury, *Letter* 275 ed. W. J. Millor and C. N. L. Brooke 2 (Oxford, 1979) p. 580. See J. Deér, 'Der Anspruch der Herrscher des 12. Jahrhunderts auf die apostolische Legation', *AHP* 2 (1964), 168–81.

[82] Anselm of Canterbury, *Epistola* 214 ed. F. S. Schmitt, *Sancti Anselmi Cantuariensis archiepiscopi Opera Omnia* 4 (Edinburgh, 1949), 112. Paschal II, *JL* 5908: *Anselmi Epistola* 222, *ibid.*, p. 125. See Tillmann, *England* (n. 4) p. 22; R. W. Southern, *Saint Anselm and his biographer* (Cambridge, 1963) pp. 130–2; Brett, *Henry I* (n. 80) pp. 35–6.

long been aware of 'the barrier interposed [by the Conqueror and his sons] to prevent papal interference'. Archbishop Anselm's devotion to the papal reform programme has been interpreted as the first breach of this 'barrier'.[83] Nevertheless in the years 1095–1101 Anselm was more vociferous than the king in keeping foreign legates out of England. For Anselm was the champion of the cause of Canterbury as well as that of Rome; and he could only reconcile his loyalties to the two churches by tolerating no Roman legate in England except himself.

Since the papacy was anxious to retain the friendship of the English king, a series of native prelates were invested with the coveted honour of the native legation. Until the pontificate of Alexander III the curia also refrained from sending legates *a latere* to whom the native legates must be subordinate. Honorius II conferred on William of Corbeil, archbishop of Canterbury, a legation in both England and Scotland (1126). Innocent II gave the legation to Henry of Blois, bishop of Winchester, brother of King Stephen (1139). Archbishop Theobald of Canterbury enjoyed a legation in England and probably also in Scotland under four successive popes from *ca.* 1150 to 1161 (although not uninterruptedly).[84] However, while willing to confer the legation, the curia was unsympathetic towards the ambition of Canterbury to subordinate the archbishopric of York to her authority. In the later twelfth century the legatine authority of the archbishops was explicitly restricted to the province of Canterbury. In 1162 Alexander III granted Archbishop Roger of York a privilege exempting him from the jurisdiction of the new archbishop-legate of Canterbury, Thomas Becket. The legations of Archbishops Richard (1174) and Baldwin (1185) were likewise confined to the southern province. Hubert Walter, alone of the later twelfth-century archbishops, regained the legation throughout England (1195); but only because Archbishop Geoffrey of York was regarded with great disfavour by Celestine III.[85] The authority of the archbishop-legates was further restricted towards the end of the century by the more frequent sending of legates *a latere*. When, for example, Hugh Pierleone, cardinal deacon of S. Angelo, arrived in England in 1175 to deal with jurisdictional questions left unsettled

---

[83] Z. N. Brooke, *The English church and the papacy from the Conquest to the reign of John* (Cambridge, 1931) pp. 138, 163; C. Duggan, 'From the Conquest to the reign of John' in *The English church and the papacy* ed. C. H. Lawrence (London, 1965) pp. 79, 81.

[84] Tillmann, *England* (n. 4) pp. 30–3, 36–8, 41–50.   [85] *Ibid.*, pp. 33–4.

after the Becket dispute, Archbishop Richard of Canterbury ceased
to exercise his legatine authority: indeed his legation may have been
suspended.[86] By the end of the century, therefore, the authority of
the English archbishop-legates had been brought into line with that
of other native legates.

The most important function of the archbishop-legates, in the
eyes of the curia, evidently lay in the judicial sphere. The number of
archbishop-legates increased during the second half of the century,
coinciding with the increase in the number of judicial appeals
addressed to the papacy; and it is likely that the appointment of more
native legates was the curia's response to the expansion of its judicial
business. The archbishop-legates were permitted to share in the
pope's authority as supreme judge in Christendom so as to relieve
the curia of the chore of judging large numbers of trivial cases.
Already in the pontificate of Innocent II the archbishop-legates
Bernard and William of Arles are found settling local disputes to
which the pope had drawn their attention. Eugenius III similarly
referred a complaint of the congregation of St Rufus to the
archbishop-legate Amadeus of Lyons.[87] Alexander III expanded
both the numbers of the archbishop-legates and their judicial duties.
Historians have long been aware of the importance of Alexander's
pontificate in the history of the appellate and first-instance jurisdiction of the Roman church. It was Alexander 'more than any other
single person, who established the papal curia as not only a court of
appeal for all Christendom, but also a court of first instance'.[88] An
unexpected view of this judicial activity is provided by the chronicle
of Andres, describing the church in Flanders at the end of
Alexander's pontificate. 'It was rare that a man in that region had
visited the threshold of the apostles and hardly anyone appealed to
the lord pope because of the legates whom almost every metropolitan church possessed.'[89] In short, much of the judicial business which
came to the curia during Alexander's pontificate was referred to the
archbishop-legates. This practice continued in the last two decades
of the century. Archbishop Milo of Milan is found assisting a cardinal legate to settle a quarrel between the bishop and chapter of
Tortona and Archbishop Conrad of Mainz helping to decide a juris-

---

[86] Tillmann, *England* pp. 73–7, 130.
[87] Janssen, *Frankreich* (n. 7) pp. 159–60, 161.
[88] *Papal Decretals relating to the diocese of Lincoln in the twelfth century* ed. W. Holtzmann
      and E. W. Kemp (Lincoln Record Society 47, 1954) p. xviii.
[89] William of Andres, *Chronica Andrensis* c. 83, MGH SS 24, 715.

dictional dispute between the abbot of Helmarshausen and the bishop of Paderborn.[90] Archbishop Hubert Walter of Canterbury is found hearing ecclesiastical lawsuits in York. It was during Hubert Walter's legation that the practice became established of the appellant seeking the 'protection' (*tuitio*) of the archbishop-legate when making an appeal to Rome. The archbishop protected the person and property of the appellant during litigation.[91]

In the sphere of judicial activity the duties of the archbishop-legates seem to shade into those of the 'judges delegate' (*iudices delegati*). The twelfth-century papacy developed the practice of appointing judges delegate to investigate cases of particular complexity. The *iudex delegatus* was a churchman of the country in which the case had arisen, whose local knowledge would be useful in establishing the facts of the case; his appointment ended with the termination of the particular case. As with the other judicial practices of the curia, delegation increased rapidly in the 1160s and 1170s, under Alexander III. The particularly abundant documentation of the English church reveals that Bishop Gilbert Foliot of Hereford (and subsequently of London), Bartholomew of Exeter and Roger of Worcester each served as judge delegate sixty or seventy times during these two decades.[92] As we have seen, archbishop-legates were also commissioned to investigate particular cases. Cardinal legates could also be given this limited mission of judging a specific case. This was the task of Cencius, cardinal deacon of S. Lucia in Orthea (the papal chamberlain and future Pope Honorius III) in the bishopric of Viterbo and of Peter, cardinal priest of S. Cecilia, in Tortona.[93] An 'atmosphere of informality and improvisation'[94] still surrounded both the papal judicial system and the legatine system in the later twelfth century. Celestine III was the first to offer a definition of the different roles of judges delegate and legates. He ruled that a papal legate could not alter a sentence made by a judge delegate, but might confirm and implement that sentence.[95] Of the two papal representatives, the legate was superior in rank; but the judge delegate took

[90] Friedländer, *Deutschland* (n. 6) pp. 64, 94, 131–2.
[91] C. R. Cheney, *Hubert Walter* (London, 1967) p. 120; J. E. Sayers, *Papal Judges Delegate in the province of Canterbury, 1198–1254* (Oxford, 1971) p. 97.
[92] See below p. 194.
[93] Friedländer, *Deutschland* (n. 6) pp. 77, 64.
[94] C. N. L. Brooke in *The Letters of John of Salisbury* I (London, 1955), xxxiv, referring to the activities of Archbishop Theobald of Canterbury as a representative of the papacy.
[95] Celestine III, *JL* 17667: *Decretales Gregorii IX* 1.30.2.

precedence in the judgement of the particular case to which he was assigned. The specialisation which characterised the thirteenth-century legatine system was already being developed between the pontificate of Alexander III and that of Celestine III.

One region of western Christendom strongly resisted the attentions of the papal legates, both cardinals and natives, throughout the twelfth century. The secular rulers of the island of Sicily claimed the right granted by Urban II to the Norman prince, Count Roger I of Sicily and to his heir (July 1098) to act 'in the place of a legate' (*legati vice*) in Sicily.[96] Both Roger I and his formidable successor, Roger II, made extensive use of this privilege, exercising the right of visitation and imposing ecclesiastical discipline. Paschal II in 1117 rebuked Roger II for presuming to judge churchmen and to summon bishops to synods. The pope insisted, in vain, that Roger receive any *legatus ex latere* or *vicarius* whom he sent to Sicily.[97] Towards the end of Roger II's reign Eugenius III was accused of having renewed the Sicilian privilege of 1098. The Romans, currently rebelling against the pope, tried in 1149 to discredit Eugenius with the story that he had conferred pontifical insignia on Roger II and granted 'that he would send no legate into his land unless the Sicilian asked for one'. The story was untrue: the insignia were conferred not on Roger but on the abbot of his recent foundation, the abbey of S. Giovanni degli Eremiti in Palermo.[98] The legatine question was in fact not raised again until 1156, in the reign of Roger's son, King William I, and in the pontificate of Hadrian IV. In 1156 William I took advantage of his victory over the pope's allies to extort from Hadrian a concession resembling the imaginary grant of 1149. The concordat of Benevento (18 June 1156) ruled that while papal legates might enter William's mainland territories of Apulia and Calabria, they should only be admitted into Sicily at the king's own request.[99] It was only after the death of William I's successor, King William II, in 1189, that the curia had the opportunity to renegotiate the terms of the concordat. On William II's death, his illegitimate cousin, Count

---

[96] Urban II, *JL* 5706: Geoffrey Malaterra, *De rebus gestis Rogerii Calabriae et Siciliae comitis* IV.29, *MRIS* 5/I (1925–8), 108. See Caspar, 'Legatengewalt' (n. 4) pp. 218–19. See also below p. 375.

[97] Paschal II, *JL* 6562: (n. 4) p. 201. See G. A. Loud, 'Royal control of the church in the twelfth-century kingdom of Sicily', *Studies in Church History* 18 (Oxford, 1982), 147–8.

[98] Wibald of Stablo, *Epistola* 214, ed. P. Jaffé, *Bibliotheca rerum germanicarum* 2 (Berlin, 1864), 332–4. See Deér, 'Anspruch' (n. 81) pp. 117–52.

[99] Concordat of Benevento c. 8, 9: *MGH Constitutiones* I, 589. See below p. 390.

Tancred of Lecce seized the throne from the designated heiress, his aunt Constance, wife of King Henry VI of Germany. Tancred's urgent need for papal recognition compelled him to make concessions. The concordat of Gravina which he concluded with Celestine III (June 1192) at last permitted the free entry of papal legates into Sicily.[100] But this success was shortlived; for after Tancred's premature death (1194) Henry VI conquered the Sicilian kingdom and repudiated the usurper's concordat.

Sicily was an exceptional case. Elsewhere in western Christendom the papal legation had become a familiar and generally respected institution. The legate's role had changed in the course of the twelfth century. By the end of the century he was undoubtedly a less powerful figure than he had been in the pontificate of Gregory VII. A Gregorian legate could 'preside over all bishops in a council, even if he [was] inferior in rank, and pronounce sentence of deposition against them'. The last occasion on which a legate was permitted to exercise this power of deposition was in 1143, when the archbishop-legate Amadeus of Lyons deposed Archbishop Stephen of Vienne.[101] The *Chronicle of Clairvaux* claims in the annal for 1181: 'Bishop Henry of Albano was sent to Burgundy as a legate and deposed the two archbishops of Lyons and Narbonne.' This report is not corroborated by any other source and it seems incredible.[102] By the end of Alexander III's pontificate the curia had ceased to give even cardinal legates a free hand in matters of such importance. When a late twelfth-century legate tried to behave in the manner of a Gregorian legate – as, for example, the controversial archbishop-legate Folmar of Trier – he was soon relieved of his office.[103] Legatine activity had become more and more specialised. The function of a cardinal legate was increasingly that of a diplomat; the task of an archbishop-legate was increasingly that of reducing the volume of judicial business attracted to the curia. The more powerful legates of the late eleventh and early twelfth centuries, with their general commission – 'to do whatever the governor and ruler of the Roman church could not perform in person, to preach salvation and moral probity to all the churches throughout the world' – were no longer necessary because they had achieved their purpose. The principal function of the Gregorian legates and their early twelfth-century suc-

---

[100] Concordat of Gravina c. 4; *ibid.*, p. 593. See below pp. 395–6.
[101] Janssen, *Frankreich* (n. 7) p. 161.
[102] *Chronicon Clarevallense* 1181, MPL 185, 1250A. See Janssen, *Frankreich* pp. 113–14.
[103] Friedländer, *Deutschland* (n. 6) p. 117.

cessors was to assert the rights of the Roman primacy against prelates claiming independence and against the opponents of reform. By the middle of the twelfth century the campaign for the primacy had been won. For the new duties of the second half of the century – the duties necessitated by the Alexandrine schism and the new papal policies of the 1180s and 1190s – the wide-ranging powers of the earlier legates were no longer needed. Nevertheless one crucial aspect of the legate's role remained unchanged throughout the period 1073–1198. The legate remained the all-important link between the Roman church and the western churches: the agent who enforced papal decrees and transmitted to the curia the local information on which papal policy-making was based.

5

PAPAL JUSTICE
AND PAPAL LEGISLATION

———— • ————

The whole Church throughout the world knows that the holy Roman church has the right of judging every church and that no one is permitted to dispute her judgement. Appeals are to be made to her from any part of the world but no one is allowed to appeal from her judgement. Nor do we omit the fact that the apostolic see has the power to absolve (without any synod taking place) those whom an unjust synod has condemned and to condemn (without a synod) those who should be condemned. This derives indisputably from her preeminence (*principatus*) which St Peter the apostle held and will always hold, according to the Lord's word.

This definition of the jurisdictional primacy of the Roman church is composed of sentences from a letter of Pope Gelasius I of 496. It first appeared in this edited form in the earliest canon law manual of the Gregorian reform, the *Collection in 74 Titles*, and was subsequently quoted by the influential canonists Bishop Anselm II of Lucca (1083) and Bishop Ivo of Chartres (1094/5), before being absorbed into the most important collection of our period, the *Decretum* of Master Gratian of Bologna (*ca.* 1140).[1] The Gelasian text elaborated the ruling of the council of Sardica (343), the earliest statement of the

---

[1] Gelasius I, *JK* 664: *Collectio Avellana* ed. O. Günther, *Corpus Scriptorum Ecclesiasticorum Latinorum* 35 (1895), 779–80 (Appendix 1): see W. Ullmann, *Gelasius I. (492–496)* (Päpste und Papsttum 18: Stuttgart, 1981) pp. 180–5. Cf. *Collectio in LXXIV titulos digesta* c. 10, ed. J. T. Gilchrist (Monumenta Iuris Canonici, series B: Corpus Collectionum 1: Vatican City, 1973) p. 24; Anselm of Lucca, *Collectio canonum* II.16; Ivo of Chartres, *Panormia* IV.9 (partial quotation); Gratian, *Decretum* C.9 q.3 c.17.

Roman claim to appellate jurisdiction over the other churches: the Roman see was the court of appeal for all bishops and the pope's decision was final.[2] The reform papacy derived its conception of the judicial supremacy of the Roman church partly from this authentic tradition of the fourth and fifth centuries and partly from the inauthentic tradition of the 'Pseudo-Isidorean Decretals'. The ninth-century forger of these decretals regarded the pope's principal function as the defence of the rights of the episcopate. He exalted the authority of the Roman church in the interests of improving the protection which Rome offered to bishops. 'Appeals are to be made to the Roman church by all, but especially by the oppressed. They should flock to her as to their mother, to be nourished by her breasts, defended by her authority and relieved of their oppressions.'[3]

The Gregorian conception of the pope's judicial authority, drawn from these two traditions, is sketched out in Gregory VII's memorandum, labelled *Dictatus pape*, found among the letters for 1075 in the papal register. Here the principle stated by the council of Sardica and by Gelasius I – 'that [the pope's] sentence must be retracted by no one' – is reinforced by a principle stated by Pope Nicholas I (865) and by Pseudo-Isidore: 'that [the pope] himself must be judged by no one'.[4] Having established the supremacy of the tribunal, the memorandum draws the consequences: 'that no one may dare to condemn someone appealing to the apostolic see' (an idea found in Pseudo-Isidore) and 'that the greater causes (*maiores causae*) of any church must be referred to [the apostolic see]' (an opinion stated by Pope Innocent I [404] and by Pseudo-Isidore).[5] Elsewhere in the memorandum the *maiores causae* are identified as the exclusive judicial business of the papacy. The pope 'alone can depose or reconcile bishops', can 'make an abbey out of a house of canons or vice versa, divide a rich bishopric and unite poor ones' and can 'translate bishops from see to see'.[6] Gregory VII's claims were vigorously defended by his successors. An unusually detailed defence of the

[2] H. Hess, *The canons of the council of Sardica A.D. 343* (Oxford, 1958) pp. 109–27. See Anselm of Lucca, *Collectio* II.77; Gratian, *Decretum* C.6 q.4 c.7.

[3] Ps.-Zephyrinus, *Epistola* 1.6, ed. P. Hinschius, *Decretales Pseudo-Isidorianae et Capitula Angilramni* (Leipzig, 1863) p. 132. See *Collectio in LXXIV titulos* c. 3, p. 20. Cf. Anselm of Lucca, *Collectio* II.6; Gratian, *Decretum* C.2 q.6 c.8.

[4] Gregory VII, *Registrum* II.55a, c. 18, 19, p. 206. Cf. Nicholas I, *JL* 2796, 2879; *MGH Epistolae* 6, 466, 600; *Decretales Pseudo-Isidorianae* (n. 3) p. 449.

[5] *Registrum* II.55a, c. 20, 21, p. 206. Cf. Innocent I, *JK* 286, *MPL* 20, 473A; *Decretales Pseudo-Isidorianae* pp. 228, 712.

[6] *Registrum* II.55a, c. 3, 7, 13, pp. 202–4.

judicial supremacy of Rome is found in a letter of Paschal II to King Henry I of England in 1115. The letter quotes the scriptural basis of the Roman primacy, together with Pseudo-Isidore on Rome as the final court of appeal, in order to counter the 'customs' of the Anglo-Norman kingdom, by means of which Henry I (like his father, William the Conqueror) tried to exclude papal influence from his dominions. The king was reminded that 'the more serious business of the churches throughout the provinces is handled and reviewed' by the pope:

but you settle the affairs of bishops without consulting us . . . You take away from the oppressed [the right of] appeal to the holy see, although it is ordained by the councils and decrees of the holy fathers that all the oppressed are to appeal to the Roman church . . . You presume, without our authority, to translate bishops; and this we know to be entirely forbidden without the authority and permission of the holy Roman see.

If the king did not mend his ways, he faced a severe punishment: 'we shall follow the apostles' example and cast you off like the dust on our feet [Matthew 10. 14] and hand you over to divine judgement, as one who has withdrawn from the catholic Church.'[7] Equally emphatic was the reminder which Innocent II issued to the arch-bishops and bishops of Germany in 1135.

St Peter, prince of the apostles, was placed by the Lord at the head of the Church so that he and his successors might strengthen their brethren [Luke 22. 32], correct errors and give to each his rights. Hence it was proclaimed as a general law of the Church that the *maiores causae* should be referred to the apostolic see for investigation and that the oppressed should fearlessly appeal to her. For the holy Roman church has reserved to herself this privilege [of receiving] appeals. Everyone knows how necessary is the practice of appeals, for it corrects the wickedness and ignorance of judges.

Innocent's reminder to the German prelates was accompanied by an impressive demonstration of his judicial authority: the deposition of a simoniacal bishop of Liège on the evidence of a canon of Liège who had denounced him to the pope.[8]

Of particular interest is the defence of this privilege of the Roman church in Hadrian IV's letter of 1155 to Archbishop Basil of Thessa-

---

[7] Paschal II, *JL* 6453: Eadmer, *Historia Novorum in Anglia* v, *RS* 81 (1884), 232–2. Cf. *JL* 6450: *ibid.*, pp. 228–9. See M. Brett, *The English church under Henry I* (Oxford, 1975) pp. 36–7.

[8] Innocent II, *JL* 7696, *MPL* 179, 226C. See W. Maleczek, 'Das Kardinalskollegium unter Innocenz II. und Anaklet II.', *AHP* 19 (1981), 59–61. See also below p. 459.

lonica, a letter written in the context of negotiations to reconcile the churches of Constantinople and Rome. The crucial issue, as in all papal negotiations with the Greek church, was the Roman primacy. Hadrian significantly chose to define that primacy in terms of its judicial functions. 'The holy fathers commanded that the holy Roman church should obtain unconditionally the primacy of all the churches and they ordered that the judgement of all things should be referred to her decision.'[9] Submission to Rome on these terms proved totally unacceptable to the Greek church in the twelfth century. How the Roman primacy was regarded by a twelfth-century Byzantine churchman is known to us from the *Dialogues* of Bishop Anselm of Havelberg. Anselm's work (addressed to Eugenius III) contains an account of his mission to Constantinople in 1136 to negotiate an alliance of the eastern and western empires against the kingdom of Sicily. The *Dialogues* also record a debate between Anselm and Archbishop Nicetas of Nicomedia on the claims of Rome, in which the Byzantine spokesman denounced the Roman church for having 'assumed a monarchy which does not belong to her office'. Nicetas expressed his distaste for the idea of Roman judicial supremacy by portraying the pope as Olympian Zeus, hurling thunderbolts at mankind.

If the Roman pontiff, seated on the lofty throne of his glory, wishes to thunder against us and, as it were, to hurl his commands from on high and if he wishes to judge – nay, rule – us and our churches, not according to our advice but according to his own will and pleasure, what kind of brother or what kind of father can he be? . . . Then indeed we could truly be called the slaves, not the sons of the Church.[10]

Nicetas considered that the role of supreme judge enabled the pope to rule the Church like an autocrat. The same conclusion was being drawn at this same moment by a western churchman; but for him this development seemed highly satisfactory. 'The fullness of power (*plenitudo potestatis*) over all the churches of the world has been given as a unique privilege to the apostolic see,' wrote Bernard of Clairvaux in 1135.

---

[9] Hadrian IV, *JL* 10437, *MPL* 188, 1581A. For the date of this letter see S. Runciman, *The Eastern Schism. A study of the papacy and the eastern churches during the eleventh and twelfth centuries* (Oxford, 1955) p. 119.

[10] Anselm of Havelberg, *Dialogi* III.8, *MPL* 188, 1219BC. See Runciman, *Schism* pp. 114–17; Y. M-J. Congar, *L'ecclésiologie du haut moyen âge* (Paris, 1968) pp. 384–6.

Therefore he who resists this power, resists the ordinance of God [Romans 13. 2] . . . She can degrade some [bishops] and exalt others, as her judgement dictates . . . She can summon the most eminent churchmen from the ends of the earth and compel them to her presence not once or twice, but as often as she sees fit. Moreover she is quick to avenge every act of disobedience [II Corinthians 10. 6] if anyone tries to resist.[11]

In the course of the twelfth century western churchmen became increasingly anxious to enlist the support of this formidable power.

In ecclesiastical cases the court of first instance was that of the bishop or archdeacon. The plaintiff could appeal from the judgement of this court to that of the metropolitan and finally from the judgement of the metropolitan's court to that of the pope. In the pontificate of Gregory VII only the most serious cases seem to have reached the final court of appeal: the cases of bishops deposed for simony or disobedience and the case (which Gregory regarded as analogous) of King Henry IV of Germany, deposed by the princes for misgovernment.[12] The potential for expansion of papal judicial activity was first revealed during Urban II's sojourn in France in 1095–6. Local chronicles and cartularies record a large number of papal judgements in ecclesiastical suits ranging from disputed episcopal elections to the most trivial quarrels between religious houses. (Urban's decision in a case concerning the contention between the monks of Montierneuf and the canons of St Hilary in Poitiers is accompanied by an expression of papal impatience at being drawn into such tedious disputes.)[13] The sudden availability of the papal curia in 1095–6 stimulated the enthusiasm of French churchmen for papal justice. By the middle of the twelfth century that enthusiasm had spread throughout the western Church and was strong enough even to overcome the obstacle of the weary and expensive journey to Rome. 'Appeals come to you from all the world,' wrote Bernard of Clairvaux to Eugenius III *ca.* 1150; 'and this bears witness to your unique primacy.'[14]

The growing attraction of papal justice can be illustrated most easily by the case of the English church, which is the best documented case. A well-known passage from the chronicle of Henry of Huntingdon states that 'in England appeals were not in use until Bishop Henry of Winchester in his wickedness cruelly intruded them

---

[11] Bernard of Clairvaux, *Epistola* 131, MPL 182, 286C–287A.
[12] Gregory VII, *Registrum* IV.23, p. 335.
[13] Urban II, *JL* 5642: Becker, *Urban II.* 1, 219.
[14] Bernard of Clairvaux, *De consideratione* III.2.6, MPL 182, 761A.

while he was a legate' – that is, between 1139 and 1143, when Henry
of Winchester (brother of King Stephen of England) was permanent
papal legate in the kingdom.[15] The chronicler's hostility towards the
bishop of Winchester caused him to exaggerate his part in encouraging appeals. For appeals had gone to Rome from the English church
even in the reign of King Henry I (1100–35), who had the reputation
of being 'king, apostolic legate, patriarch, emperor and everything
he wished to be, in his own land'.[16] During his reign four *maiores*
causae had brought English churchmen to the curia: the investiture
dispute, in which Archbishop Anselm of Canterbury (1093–1109)
strove to uphold the papal decree prohibiting lay investiture and
homage, in the face of the king's opposition; the claim of the archbishop of Canterbury to be 'primate of the whole of Britain' and his
demand for a profession of obedience from the archbishop of York
(which was referred to Rome in 1102–3, 1117, 1119–20, 1123 and
1125–6); the claim of the archbishop of York, as metropolitan, to the
obedience of the Scottish bishops; and the appeal of the bishop of
Llandaff against the encroachments of his neighbours, the bishops of
Hereford and St Davids (1119–34). There is also evidence from
Henry I's reign that the lesser clergy were beginning to feel the
attraction of Roman justice: the case of an anonymous clerk appealing against his eviction from his benefice.[17] Appeal to Rome was
undoubtedly a recognised procedure in England even before the
permanent legation of Henry of Winchester. By the middle of the
century it had become a frequent procedure. The principal evidence
comes from the letters written by John of Salisbury between 1153
and 1161, as secretary of Archbishop Theobald of Canterbury: they
record fifty appeals, mainly directed to Hadrian IV.[18]

The volume of business increased during the pontificate of
Alexander III: 359 decretals of Alexander have been discovered,
answering questions or giving rulings on cases directed to the curia
from England. The preamble of one such decretal, addressed to
Abbot Simon of St Albans, contains a characteristic reminder of the
judicial supremacy of Rome. 'We are compelled by the servant's

[15] Henry of Huntingdon, *Historia Anglorum* 1151, RS 74 (1879), 282. See L. Voss,
       Heinrich von Blois Bischof von Winchester (1129–71) (Historische Studien 210: Berlin,
       1932) pp. 41–53.
[16] John of Salisbury, *Letter* 275, ed. W. J. Millor and C. N. L. Brooke 2 (Oxford,
       1979) p. 580.
[17] Brett, *Henry I* (n. 7) pp. 50–7.
[18] C. N. L. Brooke in: *The Letters of John of Salisbury* ed. W. J. Millor, H. E. Butler
       and C. N. L. Brooke 1 (London, 1955), xxxii.

office which we have assumed, to answer the enquiries of individuals so that any doubt or question that arises in anyone's mind may be resolved by the Roman church, which has deserved to obtain among other things the *principatus*.'[19] Alexander III recognised that the procedure of appeal was the basis of the pope's judicial primacy. In the *cause célèbre* of his pontificate, the case of Archbishop Thomas Becket of Canterbury, Alexander was called upon to champion the right of appeal to the papacy, together with other rights of the English clergy which King Henry II sought to curtail. Of the sixteen 'ancestral customs', the Constitutions of Clarendon, to which the king demanded the bishops' agreement in January 1164, Alexander condemned ten as being offensive to the freedom of the Church. The constitution next in importance to the famous and crucial clause 3 (which placed the trial of criminous clerks in the royal, rather than the ecclesiastical court) was clause 8, on appeals. The constitution forbade appeals to proceed from any church court to the papal curia without the king's consent. This 'custom' can have done nothing to restrict contact between England and the papacy, since the dispute caused by Becket's defence of the freedom of the English church soon took the form of a series of rival appeals to the pope by the archbishop, the king, their supporters and many of the bishops. In the final settlement of the Becket dispute, the 'compromise' of Avranches (May 1172), negotiated after Becket's six-year exile and his tragic death, Henry II agreed to 'renounce all the customs introduced against the churches of his kingdom in his time'. Significantly, the only such 'custom' to be specified in the settlement was the eighth constitution of Clarendon: '[the king] will allow appeals of ecclesiastical cases to be made freely to the lord pope and will allow the cases to be tried and concluded by him'.[20]

Before the end of the twelfth century the papal curia was acting not only as the final court of appeal but also as a court of first instance. The growing conviction of the Roman *principatus* prompted litigants

---

[19] Alexander III, *JL* 12636: *Gregorii IX Decretales* 1.29.10. See W. Holtzmann, 'Über eine Ausgabe der päpstlichen Dekretalen des 12. Jahrhunderts', *Nachrichten der Akademie der Wissenschaften in Göttingen, phil.-hist. Klasse* 1945, p. 34.

[20] Constitutions of Clarendon: *Councils and Synods with other documents relating to the English Church* 1.2 ed. D. Whitelock, M. Brett and C. N. L. Brooke (Oxford, 1981), 852–93; W. L. Warren, *Henry II* (London, 1973) pp. 473–84; F. Barlow, *Thomas Becket* (London, 1986) pp. 98–105. 'Compromise of Avranches': *Councils and Synods* 1.2, 942–56; M. G. Cheney, 'The compromise of Avranches of 1172 and the spread of canon law in England', *EHR* 56 (1941), 177–97; Warren, *Henry II* pp. 518–34; Barlow, *Becket* pp. 260–2.

to bring their cases directly to the curia without first having recourse to a lower court. The canonists of the late twelfth century justified this practice by claiming for the pope the title of 'universal ordinary', *iudex ordinarius omnium*. Master Huguccio of Pisa, for example, wrote *ca.* 1190: 'the Roman church is the common and general court of all clerks and of all churches and the lord pope is the universal ordinary, as though no intermediary existed; and indeed appeals can be made to him ignoring any intermediary'.[21] The development of the papal curia into the 'omnicompetent court of first instance for the whole of Christendom' was first studied by F. W. Maitland (1898). He concluded that the canonists' conception of the pope as 'universal ordinary' became a reality because of 'the settled practical habit of looking to Rome for declarations of the common law of the Church'.[22] This process is already evident in the papal decretals of the late twelfth century – especially those of Alexander III, of which 700 have so far been discovered – which offer to local judges and litigants these 'declarations of the common law of the Church'.

The twelfth-century papacy contributed directly to the development of first-instance jurisdiction in two ways: by granting privileges of exemption to monasteries and by reserving certain categories of cases to the judgement of the pope. The papacy had begun in the eleventh century to confer privileges on monasteries which placed them under the protection of St Peter and in some cases exempted them from all jurisdiction save that of the pope. During the pontificate of Alexander III the special status of these exempt houses was made clear by including in monastic privileges the formula *nullo mediante*: 'who are known to belong especially to St Peter's and our jurisdiction *with no intermediary*'.[23] If these privileged monasteries went to law, the papal curia was necessarily the court of first instance. The reservation of certain types of case to papal judgement is already apparent in the *Dictatus pape* of Gregory VII. We have already seen that Gregory claimed the deposition and reconciliation of bishops as an exclusive papal right (so dispensing with the provincial synods, which had formerly had this function). Bernard of Clairvaux reminded Eugenius III of this aspect of his 'fullness of power'. 'Surely, if you have cause, you can close heaven against a

---

[21] J. A. Watt, *The theory of papal monarchy in the thirteenth century* (New York, 1965) p. 94.

[22] F. W. Maitland, *Roman canon law in the Church of England* (London, 1898) pp. 104, 129.

[23] D. Knowles, *The monastic order in England* (Cambridge, 1963) pp. 583–6. See below pp. 234–5.

bishop, you can also depose him from his bishopric and deliver him to Satan?'[24] Eugenius exercised this right in 1153 when he sent two legates to Germany to depose Archbishop Henry of Mainz 'because of the discord in his church' and the aged Bishop Burchard of Eichstädt 'because of his uselessness'. King Frederick I of Germany wished to be rid of both prelates, but he recognised that he could do so only by means of a papal judgement.[25] Gregory VII had also referred in the *Dictatus pape* to the pope's right to translate bishops. Gregory did not identify this as an exclusively papal right, but his twelfth-century successors claimed that the translation of bishops could only be performed with papal permission. Paschal II rebuked King Henry I of England in 1115 for presuming to translate Ralph d'Escures from Rochester to Canterbury: 'this we know to be entirely forbidden without the authority and permission of the holy Roman see'.[26] The canonists of the Gregorian reform had secured this right to the pope by interpolating the phrase 'not without the authority and permission of the holy Roman see' into the Pseudo-Isidorean text describing the procedure of translation; and the interpolated text passed into the *Decretum* of Master Gratian of Bologna. Here it was found by Huguccio of Pisa (*ca.* 1190), whose commentary on the text extended the pope's jurisdiction to the bishopric left vacant by the translation. 'Some say that . . . the metropolitan can immediately ordain another bishop without consulting the pope; but I do not believe it. An episcopal abdication, condemnation or any translation must not be received or made without the pope's permission.'[27] Episcopal translations became more frequent in the second half of the twelfth century (more than sixty are recorded), but the procedures adopted in most cases are not known. The surviving papal letters show that the popes did not keep pace in their claims with the canonists, but they nevertheless assumed that their approval was needed for the translation of a bishop.[28]

We have already seen that in the pontificate of Gregory VII the

---

[24] Bernard, *De consideratione* II.8.16 (n. 14), 752B.

[25] Otto of Freising, *Gesta Friderici I imperatoris* II.9, *MGH SS rer. Germ.*, 1884, p. 89.

[26] Paschal II, *JL* 6453 (n. 7), pp. 232–3.

[27] *Collectio in LXXIV titulos* c. 188 (n. 1) p. 118; Anselm of Lucca, *Collectio canonum* VI.90; Ivo of Chartres, *Panormia* III.69; Gratian, *Decretum* C.7 q.1 c.34. See K. Pennington, *Pope and bishops. The papal monarchy in the twelfth and thirteenth centuries* (Pennsylvania, 1984); pp. 86–8.

[28] E.g. Alexander III, *JL* 10837: *The Letters and Charters of Gilbert Foliot* ed. Z. N. Brooke, A. Morey and C. N. L. Brooke (Cambridge, 1967) pp. 183–4 (no. 141). See Pennington, *Pope and bishops* pp. 92–5.

judicial business of the papacy was dealt with in the papal synod, which still resembled the traditional synod of the pre-reform period: the provincial synod of the bishop of Rome, in which the suburbican bishops assembled to judge cases arising in the Roman ecclesiastical province. However, in the late eleventh century the papal synod became an instrument of reform: it developed into a 'general council', legislating for the whole of western Christendom. The scale and complexity of the general council prevented its meeting with the frequency and regularity of the old papal synod, so that another institution was needed to deal with the routine business of the synod: the institution which eventually took the name of *consistorium*.[29] It was the consistory which *ca.* 1100 assumed the synodal role of reaching judicial decisions. Already in the pontificate of Urban II the *maiores causae* were being settled 'in [the pope's] presence and that of our colleagues, the bishops and cardinals': the disputed elections in the bishoprics of Halberstadt and Arras (1094), the attempt of Dôle to escape the metropolitan jurisdiction of Tours (1094), the conflict between the rival metropolitans Lyons and Sens (1099).[30] From the year 1100, in the pontificate of Paschal II, comes perhaps the earliest reference to an attempt to secure a favourable decision from the pope by bribing his counsellors to give the appropriate advice. The canonist Bishop Ivo of Chartres warned the pope's legates in France that Stephen, the intruder in the bishopric of Beauvais, intended to go to Rome, win over members of the curia 'by gifts or promises and deceive the lord pope by whatever tricks he can'.[31] A graphic description of the cardinals acting as legal assessors is found in Abbot Seher's account of his defence of the interests of his abbey of Chaumouzey in February 1107 in Rome. On the day on which his case was to be heard, the pope could not hear it himself because he had just been bled by his physician. The cardinals, therefore, at the pope's command, examined the case *in consistorio*, which was an unfortunate development for Seher, because his opponents possessed 'the favour of the whole curia'. However, in the middle of the examination 'the universal pastor, mindful of his poor, came in

---

[29] See above pp. 99–100, 103–7.
[30] Urban II, *JL* 5505, *MPL* 151, 376A (Halberstadt); *Gesta quibus Atrebatensium civitas . . . in antiquam reformatur dignitatem*, *MPL* 162, 636C–638C (Arras); Urban II, *JL* 5519: 385C–387A (Dôle); *JL* 5788: 544C (Lyons and Sens). See J. Sydow, 'Untersuchungen zur kurialen Verwaltungsgeschichte im Zeitalter des Reformpapsttums', *DA* 11 (1954–5), 54.
[31] Ivo of Chartres, *Epistola* 87, *MPL* 162, 108B.

like another Daniel, raised up by the Lord to save us'.[32] When the dispute between Canterbury and York concerning the primacy of the English church was referred to Calixtus II in 1123, it was 'the cardinals and the curia' who examined the privileges produced by the delegations of the two churches and who demonstrated that the Canterbury privileges were forgeries. The Canterbury delegation was questioned about the absence of bulls from the nine privileges which they produced, 'because privileges or charters are not to be trusted unless they have bulls attached or bear signatures'. After some hesitation the delegates 'said that the bulls had wasted away or were lost. When they said this, some [cardinals] smiled, some wrinkled their noses and some roared with laughter, ridiculing them and saying how miraculous it was that lead should waste away or be lost and parchment should survive'.[33] Another *cause célèbre* of the 1120s, the deposition of Abbot Pontius of Cluny and the confirmation of Peter the Venerable as his successor (1126), was decided by Honorius II 'after receiving the advice and the general agreement of our brethren, the bishops and cardinals'. Peter the Venerable's account of these proceedings contains an early example of the practice of dealing with the more important cases in a 'secret', as opposed to a 'public', consistory. 'Having heard [both] parties, the pope immediately arose and withdrew, taking the whole Roman curia with him.'[34]

The most detailed report of a judicial hearing in the papal curia during the twelfth century comes from the pontificate of Innocent II, who was indeed noticeably more active than his predecessors in encouraging the judicial business of the curia. The report in question was written by Abbot Hariulf of Oudenbourg about his litigation against the abbot of St Médard of Soissons in 1141. The eighty-year-old Hariulf came to Rome to protect the independence of his abbey against the claim of the abbot of St Médard that Oudenbourg was a priory of his house. On the day after his arrival in Rome, following the shrewd advice of the bishop of Noyon, Hariulf sought an interview in the Lateran palace with the papal chancellor, Haimeric, cardinal deacon of S. Maria Nuova. For, as Hariulf said to the

[32] Seher, *Primordia Calmosiacensia* I, *MGH SS* 12, 337–8.
[33] Hugh the Cantor, *The history of the church of York* ed. C. Johnson (London, 1961) pp. 114–17. See above p. 104.
[34] Honorius II, *JL* 7268, *MPL* 166, 1267D; Peter the Venerable, *De miraculis* II.13, *MPL* 189, 925BC: see G. Tellenbach, 'Der Sturz des Abtes Pontius von Cluny', *QFIAB* 42–3 (1963), 15. See below p. 230.

chancellor, 'although the examination of every case is in the care of the lord pope, the chariot of Israel and its horseman have rightly been given to you [IV Kings 2. 12], since your industry puts everything in order, deciding the lesser cases and directing the greater'. Haimeric warned Hariulf not to attempt bribery in the curia ('if I learn that you have [offered bribes], you will lose my counsel and the help of the lord pope'). The chancellor then conducted him to the *consistorium palacii* (evidently the public audience chamber), 'where the lord pope sat on the judgement-seat (*in tribunali*) with the cardinals at his right hand, while the greater Roman noblemen, with curled hair and clad in silk, stood or sat at his feet'. Welcoming Hariulf, the pope said, 'Come to us tomorrow or the next day and we shall hear you.' The abbot came every day to the palace, but no opportunity occurred for the pope to hear his case. Whenever the pope saw Hariulf, he said with a smile, 'It is not the custom of our curia to dismiss a venerable visitor in a hurry: let him linger and wander among us, let him improve his mind and learn to bear the dominion of the Romans with equanimity.' Hariulf eventually prevailed on the chancellor and the more influential cardinals to persuade the pope to fix a day for the hearing, which he did on the ninth day after Hariulf's arrival in Rome. The hearing took place in the pope's bedchamber in the presence of the cardinals. Hariulf 'was ordered to sit on the pope's footstool, where the chancellor also sat'. The pope himself directed the proceedings, which consisted of the abbot's statement of his grievances and of the reading of several diplomas, and then retired with the cardinals to reach a judgement in secret. On the following day Hariulf was summoned to hear the judgement, which was in his favour, pronounced by the chancellor.[35]

Despite the informality of the conduct of Hariulf's case, it is evident that the judicial proceedings of the curia were becoming increasingly specialised. The most significant information is that the chancellor, the formidable Cardinal Haimeric, decided the lesser cases. The papal practice of delegating cases to members of the curia can be traced back to the pontificate of Paschal II, when the chancellor John of Gaeta (the future Gelasius II) and the cardinals Maurice of Porto and Albert of Sabina were all commissioned to hear cases and to advise the pope and the rest of the cardinals on the appropriate judgement.[36] As the pressure of judicial business grew in the pontifi-

---

[35] E. Müller, 'Der Bericht des Abtes Hariulf von Oudenburg über seine Prozess-verhandlungen an der römischen Kurie im Jahre 1141', *NA* 48 (1930), 101–11.

[36] P. Kehr, *Italia Pontificia* 1, 72; Servatius, *Paschalis II*. p. 68.

cate of Innocent II (this process is already apparent in Hariulf's account of his nine-day wait in 1141), the delegation of cases to officials of the curia increased. By the thirteenth century this specialisation had resulted in the creation of a body of *auditores generales sacri palatii*, papal chaplains commissioned by the pope to hear (but not to decide) cases in a special court, the *audientia causarum* (which later developed into the *Sacra Romana Rota*). There is no firm evidence that the *auditores* and their court were in existence before the end of the twelfth century. It has been suggested that the intense judicial activity of Alexander III's pontificate was responsible for the creation of the court of *auditores*.[37] The only evidence for this suggestion, however, is the appearance of the term *audientia* in Cardinal Boso's biography of Alexander III, written *ca.* 1177. Boso described how the envoys of King Henry II of England came to the curia after the murder of Archbishop Thomas Becket of Canterbury to intercede with the pope on the king's behalf and prevent his excommunication by taking an oath that Henry would submit to papal judgement (25 March 1171). 'When the pope had taken counsel with his brethren, he went out into the consistory and in the general *audientia* he received the oath, as it had been devised and worded by the cardinals, from the envoys and granted a truce to the king.'[38] It is very unlikely, however, that the phrase used here, *in communi audientia*, denoted a specialised court of justice. If *audientia* is being used here as a concrete noun, it is simply a synonym for *consistorium*, intended to contrast the public hearing with the secret council of the pope and cardinals which had preceded it. But the phrase *in communi audientia* is probably used here in its abstract sense (as Boso used it, for example, in his account of the negotiations between Alexander's cardinals and Emperor Frederick I in Pavia in 1175), meaning 'in the hearing of all'.[39] Less ambiguous is the use of the term *auditorium* in a decretal of Celestine III of 1193: the pope referred to a case concerning clergy of Tortona which 'was presented in our *auditorium*'. Celestine's letters of May 1195 concerning the divorce of King Philip II of France and Ingeborg of Denmark ruled that 'so difficult a case . . . must, according to the statutes of the fathers, be reserved to the

---

[37] V. Martin, *Les cardinaux et la Curie; tribunaux et offices, la vacance du Siège apostolique* (Paris, 1930) pp. 75–8. But see Pacaut, *Alexandre III* p. 276.

[38] Boso, *Vita Alexandri III: Liber pontificalis* 2, 425. See Barlow, *Becket* (n. 20) pp. 255–6.

[39] Boso, *Vita* p. 430; see below p. 493. G. M. Ellis in *Boso's Life of Alexander III* (Oxford, 1973) p. 85 translates *in communi audientia* as 'in the hearing of all' in the passage referring to 25 March 1171.

auditorium of the Roman church'. This *auditorium* was evidently a judicial tribunal: the term continued to be used in this sense in the pontificate of Innocent III. It is impossible to determine, however, whether Celestine III's *auditorium* resembled the later court of auditors.[40] The term *auditores* began to appear only in Innocent III's pontificate and even then it did not yet denote a body of permanent officials. Papal chaplains, cardinals and even prelates visiting Rome were pressed into service to hear individual cases.[41]

More important than the delegation of cases to members of the curia in the twelfth century was the appointment by the pope of local 'judges delegate' (*iudices delegati*). Judges delegate were not permanent officials: they were prelates appointed to hear individual cases which had originated in their localities and their appointment lapsed with the completion of the case. No doubt the rapid expansion of judicial business promoted this delegation of cases to local judges; but the curia's ignorance of local conditions must have been the decisive factor. For example, one of the earliest cases involving delegation was the appeal of Bishop Urban of Llandaff against encroachments on his diocese by the bishops of Hereford and St Davids, which Innocent II referred to local judges in 1132. Until the pope decided to delegate the case, Bishop Urban had profited greatly from the curia's ignorance. (He had managed for some time to conceal the fact that the bishopric of Hereford was vacant: a fact which, if known, would have prevented him from pursuing his case against the bishopric.)[42] The pontificate of Innocent II provides the earliest detailed evidence of the employment of judges delegate (although they were not yet given this title). Innocent's letter to five imperial prelates concerning the case of Bishop Altman of Trent (preserved in the *Decretum* of Gratian of Bologna) is the earliest extant commission to local churchmen to settle a case on behalf of the pope. The charge

---

[40] Celestine III, *JL* 17055: *Decretales Gregorii IX* II.30.3 (Tortona); *JL* 17241–3: *MPL* 206, 1096D (divorce of Philip II of France). See V. Pfaff, 'Die Kardinäle unter Papst Coelestin III. (1191–1198)', *ZSSRG KA* 41 (1955), 73; *idem*, 'Pro posse nostro. Die Ausübung der Kirchengewalt durch Papst Coelestin III.', *ibid.*, 43 (1957), 130–1. See also N. Iung, 'Auditeurs', *Dictionnaire de Droit Canonique* I (Paris, 1935), 1399–1411; R. Naz, 'Auditoire', *ibid.*, 1411–12. However, Boso used *auditorium* in the same abstract sense in which he used *audientia*: e.g. *Vita Alexandri III* p. 440 (*in communi auditorio*).

[41] E.g. *Decretales Gregorii IX* II.27.10. See J. E. Sayers, *Papal judges delegate in the province of Canterbury, 1198–1254* (Oxford, 1971) pp. 14–16.

[42] Cheney, 'Compromise of Avranches' (n. 20) pp. 178–80; Brett, *Henry I* (n. 7) pp. 52–5.

of simony had been brought against Altman in consistory but 'neither the witnesses nor the accusers could proceed in that case according to the form of the canons of the holy fathers'. Therefore pope and cardinals decided that Altman must 'purge himself of simony in your presence'.[43] When Abbot Hariulf of Oudenbourg came to the curia in 1141, the institution of the judges delegate was invoked to protect his abbey against the encroachment of the abbot of St Médard of Soissons. Hariulf was invited to choose 'three religious persons from the land of the French to whom the lord pope may entrust your business' and to whom Hariulf was to appeal if the abbot of St Médard continued to oppress the abbey of Oudenbourg. It proved difficult, however, to find three suitable judges, since the papal chancellor Cardinal Haimeric vetoed all Hariulf's suggestions. 'The lord pope does not permit the abbot of Clairvaux [Bernard] to be troubled because he is sick, nor the abbot of Cîteaux [Rainald] because he is too far-off.' Bishop Geoffrey of Chartres was 'both too remote from [Oudenbourg] and too busy with Roman affairs'; Bishop Bartholomew of Laon had obtained from the pope the favour 'that he should be burdened with no case except his own'.[44] This last detail shows that the institution of the judge delegate was sufficiently developed by 1141 for a prelate to have gained exemption from the office.

By the end of the century such exemptions were evidently much sought after by bishops and abbots groaning under the demands of this time-consuming and expensive duty. The biographer of Hugh of Avalon, bishop of Lincoln (1186–1200) recorded that the saintly bishop was so burdened by judicial business that on two or three occasions he sought the pope's permission to resign his see; but he was too useful to the curia to be allowed to abdicate. 'Each of the popes who presided over the Roman church in his time delegated to the bishop of Lincoln the settlement of the more difficult of all the cases which occurred throughout England.' The controversial cases which were delegated to Hugh included the suits of the archbishops of Canterbury, Baldwin and Hubert Walter, concerning the foundation of a collegiate church at Hackington; the suits between Geoffrey Plantagenet, archbishop of York and his chapter; and between Geoffrey of York and Bishop Hugh du Puiset of Durham.[45]

---

[43] Innocent II, *JL* 8289: (n. 8) 626C–627A = Gratian, *Decretum* C.2 q.5 c.17.
[44] Müller, 'Bericht' (n. 35) pp. 112–13.
[45] *Magna vita Sancti Hugonis* v.13 ed. D. L. Douie and D. H. Farmer 2 (Oxford, 1985), 149–50. See *ibid.*, 1, xxx–xxxii; C. R. Cheney, *Pope Innocent III und England* (Päpste und Papsttum 9: Stuttgart, 1976) pp. 28, 29, 78, 216.

The unusually rich documentation which survives for the English church shows that delegation on this scale had begun in the 1160s and 1170s. The expansion of business begins to be apparent in the evidence for the episcopate of Hilary of Chichester (1147–69), who was judge delegate in fifteen cases, and culminates in the records of Bishops Bartholomew of Exeter (1161–84) and Roger of Worcester (1164–79), who each judged between sixty and seventy cases.[46] Gilbert Foliot, bishop of Hereford (1148–63) and London (1163–87) was at least as burdened with judicial duties as Hugh of Lincoln. Sixty cases have been traced in which he acted as judge delegate and twenty extant decretals of Alexander III are concerned with the delegation of cases to Gilbert.[47] Alexander III's decretals formed the basis of the definition of the status and functions of the judge delegate in canon law. In the *Decretales*, the official collection which Pope Gregory IX published in 1234, Alexander appears as the principal legislator on the subject of delegation. Of the forty-three chapters under the title 'Concerning the office and power of the judge delegate' eighteen are Alexandrine decretals (compared with fifteen of Innocent III, the next most frequently cited legislator). Alexander ruled that in the conduct of the cases delegated to them, the jurisdiction of the *iudices delegati* was superior to that both of the ordinary (usually the bishop or archdeacon) and of the metropolitan. He also gave them authority over any persons who (although not involved in the original case) might try to impede their investigation.[48] It remained for Celestine III at the end of the century to complete this work of definition by commenting on the jurisdiction of the judge delegate compared with that of the papal legate. The legate was superior in status; nevertheless he could not alter a judgement pronounced by a judge delegate.[49]

Not only on the subject of delegation but in all other matters touching the pope's judicial supremacy Alexander III was the

---

[46] H. Mayr-Harting, 'Hilary, Bishop of Chichester (1147–69) and Henry II', *EHR* 78 (1963), 211 and n. 5; A. Morey, *Bartholomew of Exeter* (Cambridge, 1937) pp. 44–78; M. G. Cheney, 'Compromise of Avranches' (n. 20) pp. 180–1; *eadem*, 'Pope Alexander III and Roger, Bishop of Worcester, 1164–1179: the exchange of ideas' in *Proceedings of the Fourth International Congress of Medieval Canon Law, 1972* ed. S. Kuttner (Monumenta Iuris Canonici, series C; Subsidia 5: Vatican City, 1976) p. 226.

[47] A. Morey and C. N. L. Brooke, *Gilbert Foliot and his Letters* (Cambridge, 1965) p. 243.

[48] *Decretales Gregorii IX* 1.29.1–18. See Pacaut, *Alexandre III* p. 265.

[49] Celestine III, *JL* 17667; *Decretales* 1.30.2. See above pp. 175–6.

foremost legislator of the twelfth century. The most striking evidence of his influence occurs in the section of the *Decretales* of Gregory IX 'concerning appeals'. Of the seventy-three chapters under this title, thirty-five are decretals of Alexander III (compared with nineteen of Innocent III).[50] In the Becket dispute Alexander III had been the champion of the right of the oppressed to appeal to the papacy. His clarification of the law concerning appeals, as it survives in the *Decretales* and in the sixth decree of the Third Lateran Council, reveals a quite different preoccupation: to reform procedures so as to combat the practice of fraudulent or frivolous appeals. As early as 1096 Urban II had grumbled at the burden of dealing with trivial cases.[51] By the mid-twelfth century Bernard of Clairvaux was warning Eugenius III that appeals 'could become a great plague if they are not used with the greatest moderation': 'those who are too well disposed towards appellants encourage appeals'.[52] The papal correspondence of the later twelfth century contains many illustrations of the abuse of the right of appeal. A clerk facing disciplinary action from his bishop could easily escape from episcopal jurisdiction for at least a year by initiating an appeal to Rome; or he could harass his superior by making false accusations at the curia. For example, Bishop William Turbe of Norwich suffered greatly in 1155–6 at the hands of Archdeacon Walkelin of Suffolk, 'who persecute[d] the holy bishop merely because the bishop oppose[d] his crimes' and made a fraudulent appeal to Hadrian IV. (Walkelin added to his offences by giving the name Hadrian to a bastard born to his concubine during his first visit to the papal curia. The concubine being pregnant again at the time of the archdeacon's second visit to the curia, he left instructions that if the baby was a girl, she should be called Hadriana.)[53] The appeal could also be used by litigants as a device to forestall defeat when their case was going badly in the local court. This was the tactic used by the English litigant William of Sturminster in his dispute with Robert Winegot concerning tithes (between 1153/4 and 1161). William appealed the case from the court of the archdeacon of Dorset to that of the archbishop of Canterbury, who sent the case back to the diocesan, the bishop of Salisbury. When the latter was about to pronounce judgement, William appealed the case again to the archbishop's court. Likewise, when

[50] *Decretales* II.28.1–35. See Pacaut, *Alexandre III* p. 264.
[51] See above p. 183.
[52] Bernard, *De consideratione* III.2.6, 8 (n. 14), 761A, 762C.
[53] John of Salisbury, *Letters* 14, 15 (n. 18) pp. 22–5.

Archbishop Theobald of Canterbury was on the point of pronouncing judgement, William 'without the excuse of any hardship
and against the forms of law' appealed the case to the pope.[54]

This problem of 'frustratory appeals' was the subject of a letter of
Alexander III of 1171/2 to Archbishop Henry of Rheims, who had
sought a ruling from the pope on such delaying tactics. The papal
remedy was to set a time-limit of one year (or two years 'if there is
an urgent and evident necessity') within which the appeal must be
prosecuted. The practice of appealing before the pronouncing of
judgement was prohibited: the appellant was 'to be forced to submit
to the judgement of him from whom he is known to have
appealed'.[55] Alexander's predecessors in the 1140s and 1150s had
already tried to prevent the nuisance of second appeals to the curia by
inserting in the commissions of judges delegate a clause forbidding
further appeals: *appellatione remota* became the standard formula. The
evident failure of this measure compelled Alexander to devise rules
to determine when the clause *appellatione remota* was binding on
appellants and when not.[56] Alexander's principal reforms of appeal
procedures are summarised in the sixth canon of the Third Lateran
Council (1179). The canon identified two sets of offenders who were
responsible for the increasing number of unnecessary appeals: firstly,
prelates who resorted to the sentence of suspension or excommunication without giving the accused the due 'canonical warning'; and
secondly, clerks who, in fear of 'the judgement of their superior and
canonical discipline', exploited the right of appeal and 'usurp for the
defence of iniquity what is known to have been created for the protection of the innocent'. In order to restrain both tyrannical prelates
and guilty clerks 'a suitable time-limit is to be fixed for proceeding
with an appeal; and if [the accused] fails to appeal within it, the
bishop may then freely use his authority'. Fraudulent appeals were
discouraged by compelling an appellant who failed to appear at his
hearing, to pay his rival's expenses. Finally, the conciliar decree tried
to eliminate one category of appeal: that of monks and canons against
their superiors. 'Monks or other religious . . . are not to presume to
appeal against the regular discipline of their prelate and chapter, but
are to accept it humbly and devoutly, because it has been enjoined
upon them as useful for their salvation.'[57]

[54] John of Salisbury, *Letter* 84, pp. 131–2.
[55] Alexander III, *JL* 12020: *Decretales Gregorii IX* II.28.5–7.
[56] C. N. L. Brooke in *Letters of John of Salisbury* (n. 18) p. xxxv; C. R. Cheney, *From
Becket to Langton* (Manchester, 1956) pp. 63–4.
[57] *Concilium Lateranense III* c. 6 in *Conciliorum Oecumenicorum Decreta* p. 214.

Alexander III's reforms seem, however, to have done little to diminish the judicial business of the curia. Eight-and-a-half years after the Third Lateran Council Gregory VIII complained that he was oppressed by a daily volume of business with which it was beyond his strength to deal efficiently. Gregory VIII's analysis of the problem concentrated not so much on the problem of fraudulent appeals as on the mass of trivial cases and 'complaints of opposing petitioners' which distracted the pope from more important cases. The reform which he proposed in his letter of 18 November 1187 to all archbishops and bishops was to prohibit tactical appeals from the local court to the curia in lawsuits 'concerning trifling matters, beneath the sum of twenty marks'. Such cases must be tried by trustworthy judges appointed by the ordinary and any appeal must be directed to the archbishop or primate. The pope decreed that after next Candlemas (2 February 1188) the curia would issue no more commissions to judges delegate for litigants who ignored this ruling.[58] The effect of the decree is not known; but its impact must have been reduced by the death of Gregory VIII a month-and-a-half before it was due to come into effect. His successor, Clement III, was preoccupied with another problem which multiplied appeals. His letter of 9 March 1189 to all archbishops and bishops condemned the practice of malicious persons who obtained papal letters initiating judicial proceedings and used them to blackmail the persons named in these letters. These persons were compelled to pay dearly to have the letters destroyed and so avoid litigation. The pope ruled that after Easter the curia would only accept petitions which had been sealed by a prelate and which identified the petitioner. Clement's letter contains a significant admission. 'Because we cannot remember everything, cases already committed to one set of judges are soon afterwards committed, at the request of new petitioners, to other judges. One commission frustrates the other and so the Roman curia earns the reproach of levity.'[59] Clement III's explanation of the ease with which the curia could be deceived reminds us that the papal government of the late twelfth century was still in a rudimentary state. The papal chancery had been accustomed for centuries to keep registers of papal letters (although the unique survival from our period – the Register of Gregory VII – reveals that registration was

---

[58] Gregory VIII, *JL* 16056, *MPL* 202, 1552C–1553C. See W. Holtzmann, 'Die Dekretalen Gregors VIII.', *MIÖG* 58 (1950), 114; Cheney, *From Becket to Langton* pp. 70–1.
[59] Clement III, *JL* –: Holtzmann, 'Dekretalen' (n. 58) pp. 122–3.

by no means consistent).[60] Clement III's letter of March 1189 indicates that it was not yet the practice to keep a register of papal instructions to judges delegate. Clement's attempted reform corroborates that evidence of the over-straining of the system which survives from the pontificate of Alexander III – who had once been obliged to write to Archbishop Richard of Canterbury concerning a petition of two clerks to the curia: 'we do not believe that we wrote so positively; and if we did so, it was because we were overworked'.[61]

The effects of 'the mischief of appeals' were the subject of a famous analysis by William Stubbs (1865). Examining the English evidence, he concluded that the right of appeal had caused 'the paralysis of judicial power in the English church' by the end of the twelfth century.

It was practically in the power of any contumacious priest to lodge an appeal to Rome, which at once removed him from the authority of his diocesan and placed him, whatever his merits might be, under the protection of the holy see . . . All-powerful money could purchase, or wearisome pertinacity extort a mandate; pains and penalties would follow the refusal of the bishop to obey; from that moment he ceased to be a judge and became a defendant; and that under a charge on which the Italian lawyers never acquitted a bishop.[62]

Similar complaints were made in the protest literature inspired by the papal judicial system, which began to appear as soon as Gregory VII first championed the right of appeal. Already in 1075 prelates complained that the right of appeal undermined the episcopal dignity. The effect of the assertion of papal judicial supremacy was 'to arm sons against fathers and to destroy reverence and piety'.[63] The satirical literature attacking the venality of papal justice and the devotion of the curia to 'the relics of the precious martyrs Albinus and Rufinus' (silver and gold) originated in the pontificate of Urban II.[64] The rapid growth of judicial business in the twelfth century inspired protests as different in character as the *De consideratione* of Bernard of Clairvaux and the anonymous satire *The Gospel according*

---

[60] A. Murray, 'Pope Gregory VII and his letters', *Traditio* 22 (1966), 149–202.

[61] Alexander III, *JL* 14317: *Decretales Gregorii IX* 1.3.2. See Cheney, *From Becket to Langton* p. 65.

[62] W. Stubbs in: *Chronicles and memorials of the reign of Richard I* 2, RS 38/2 (1865), cxvii–cxviii.

[63] Archbishop Udo of Trier to Gregory VII in: *Briefsammlungen der Zeit Heinrichs IV., MGH Die Briefe der deutschen Kaiserzeit* 5, 39. See I. S. Robinson, '*Periculosus homo*: Pope Gregory VII and episcopal authority', *Viator* 9 (1978), 128–9.

[64] *Tractatus Garsiae Tholetani canonici de Albino et Rufino*, *MGH Libelli* 2, 423–35.

to the Mark of Silver ('blessed are the wealthy, for theirs is the Roman curia').[65] The best known theme of this protest literature is the castigation of the avarice of 'the scribes and pharisees' of the curia, who 'stir up lawsuits, bring clergy and people into strife, . . . sell justice'.[66] Critics of papal justice considered that the venality of papal officials, like the prevalence of fraudulent appeals, was an inevitable concomitant of the system. Rather than suffer any diminution of her judicial supremacy, the Roman church was prepared to live with corruption and fraud. That the popes were aware of such criticism and had their own misgivings on the subject is clear enough from the reforms decreed by Alexander III, Gregory VIII and Clement III. The delegation of cases to local judges offered a sensible compromise between the demands of papal supremacy and the practical limitations of the papal judicial system. The papacy was willing enough to reform the system; but what it could never contemplate was the dismantling of the system. For it was the right of appeal which kept the papal monarch directly in touch with all his subjects and which gave substance to his *primatus* and *magisterium*. As the canonist Stephen of Tournai reminded Clement III, 'it is in the common refuge of appeal that the dignity of the Roman church consists and all the oppressed find refuge'.[67]

The statement of Stephen of Tournai (1135–1203) most frequently quoted by historians is the famous diatribe which he addressed to the pope *ca.* 1200 against 'the multitude of decretals'.

When a dispute occurs which is to be tried according to canon law, either committed to you or to be handled by the ordinary judges, an impenetrable forest of decretals (*decretales epistolae*) is produced by the corrupt, supposedly under the name of Pope Alexander [III] of holy memory, and the more ancient holy canons are rejected, held in contempt and ignored.[68]

The learned Stephen defended the appellate jurisdiction of the Roman church because it was based on 'the more ancient holy canons'; but he distrusted the innovation of the later twelfth century that preferred the authority of papal decretals – among which Stephen suspected the existence of forgeries, or at least of documents

---

[65] P. Lehmann, *Die Parodie im Mittelalter* (Munich, 1922) pp. 43–69; R. W. Southern, *The making of the Middle Ages* (London, 1953) p. 153.
[66] John of Salisbury, *Policraticus* ed. C. C. J. Webb 2 (Oxford, 1909), 67–8.
[67] Stephen of Tournai, *Epistola* 143, *MPL* 211, 429A.
[68] *Idem, Epistola* 251: 517C. See Cheney, 'Compromise of Avranches' (n. 20) pp. 182–3; S. Kuttner, *Harmony from dissonance. An interpretation of medieval canon law* (Latrobe, Pennsylvania, 1960).

fraudulently extorted from the curia – to that of the ancient law of the Church. His complaint reminds us of the importance of papal decretals not only in the administration of papal justice but also in the development of canon law. The term *decretales epistolae* (according to the bull with which Gregory IX introduced the edition of his own and his predecessors' decretals in 1234) signified papal writings concerned with legal matters, collected and published for use in judicial proceedings and in the schools. In the words of Stephen of Tournai's polemic, 'a new volume composed of [decretals] is solemnly read in the schools and corruptly expounded in court, to applause from the ranks of the lawyers'. This process of compiling collections of papal decretals to be used both for settling ecclesiastical cases and for teaching in the schools of canon law seems to have begun in earnest in the 1170s. It was a response to the startling proliferation of the papal practice of issuing judicial instructions in the form of *decretales epistolae* during the pontificate of Alexander III. The evidence of the decretal collections underlines the suddenness of this proliferation. According to the findings of Walther Holtzmann (1945) the collections have preserved twenty decretals from the fourteen years preceding the election of Alexander III (that is, from the pontificates of Eugenius III and Hadrian IV) and over 700 from Alexander's twenty-two-year pontificate.[69]

Alexander III's decretals were of two distinct types: firstly, answers to the enquiries (*consultationes*) of judges delegate covering a wide range of disparate legal problems arising from the cases under investigation; secondly, papal *mandata* referring to specific cases, conveying papal decisions or seeking information concerning cases of first instance or of appeals. The decretals of Alexander III were not, therefore, generalised legal statements, but invariably related to particular cases. It was the shortlived Gregory VIII – the lawyer-pope whose 57-day pontificate furnished the collections with eight decretals – who began the practice of issuing general statements of law in decretal form. These papal *constitutiones* (usually known by historians as 'encyclicals') were addressed 'to all archbishops and bishops whom this letter reaches'.[70] (Such generalised statements of

[69] Holtzmann, 'Ausgabe' (n. 19) pp. 15–21, 34. Holtzmann's estimate of between 713 and 731 Alexandrine decretals has been swelled by further discoveries. See K. W. Nörr, 'Päpstliche Dekretalen und römisch-kanonischer Zivilprozess' in *Studien zur europäischen Rechtsgeschichte. Helmut Coing zum 28. Februar 1972* ed. W. Wilhelm (Frankfurt/M., 1972) pp. 53–4.

[70] Holtzmann, 'Dekretalen' (n. 58) pp. 113–23.

principle, analogous to the reforming decrees of the 'general councils' of the twelfth century, were to be characteristic of the decretals
of Innocent III.) In the decretal collections of the late twelfth century
constitutiones appear side-by-side with decretals concerning specific
cases, the different types of *decretales epistolae* being accorded the
same weight as authoritative statements of canon law. The Alexandrine decretals often appear in these collections shorn of their particular details and provided by the compilers with inscriptions and
commentary which give them the character of abstract legal statements. In this way papal statements originally intended as clarification of judicial procedures in specific cases were converted into
papal legislation.

The twelfth-century popes increasingly acquired the role of legis-
lators. We have already seen how the 'general councils' of the twelfth
century developed into legislative assemblies. In 1179 the canonist
Rufinus of Assisi explained the relationship of the pope and the council in the words, 'it belongs to [the Roman church's] will and power
alone to assemble a universal council, to make new canons and
to obliterate old ones'. The basis of this claim was the authentic
canonical tradition that 'a universal council must not be celebrated
. . . except by the will of the Roman pontiff'. Rufinus and his fellow
canonists transformed this tradition into the idea of the pope as a
monarch who summoned his council in order to issue his legislation.[71] The compilers of decretal collections similarly transformed
the papal *mandata* and the pope's replies to the enquiries of judges
delegate into legislative enactments. It is important to notice that the
decretal collections of the later twelfth century were not official pub-
lications of the papacy, but were the private compilations of enter-
prising canonists. The first collection to acquire 'official' status was
the so-called *Compilatio prima* of Bernardus Papiensis of *ca.* 1190,
which rapidly acquired the status of a canon law book equalling in
authority the *Decretum* of Master Gratian of Bologna. The earliest
compilers were English canonists: of the surviving 'primitive'
decretal collections, fifteen were of English origin; Italy, France and
Spain together produced only twelve. (The awakening of the collecting enthusiasm of English canonists in the 1170s, in advance of their
continental colleagues, probably explains why so large a proportion
of the extant decretals of Alexander III – approximately one half –

[71] See above p. 141.

were addressed to English recipients.)[72] The motive of the compilers, according to the hostile Stephen of Tournai, was to add to
the profits of their profession: the lawyers 'rejoice that their labour is
diminished and their reward increased'.[73] A more likely explanation
is that the practitioners in the ecclesiastical courts and the teachers in
the schools, seeking a guide to the perplexities of canon law,
followed the direction of their master, Gratian, who had taught that
the pope's 'decretal letters are equivalent to conciliar canons'.[74]

'The holy Roman church confers right and authority on the sacred
canons.'[75] This *dictum* of Master Gratian ultimately derived from two
canonical traditions which had greatly influenced the Gregorian
canonists of the later eleventh century: the tradition that no council
was valid unless summoned or approved by the pope and the text
known as 'The Gelasian decree concerning the reception and non-
reception of books' (*Decretum Gelasianum de recipiendis et non
recipiendis libris*). This ancient document, a catalogue of the writings
regarded by the Roman church as canonical, conveyed to its late
eleventh-century commentators the idea that papal approval alone
could confer authority on any text. On these two traditions was
based the central theory of the canonists who wrote in defence of the
Gregorian papacy, namely the theory of 'harmony' (*consonantia*):
whatever conformed to the decrees of the popes was to be regarded
as canon law.[76] The principle of 'harmony' provided the Gregorian
canonists with a method of interpretation when dealing with conflicting canons. In such cases, wrote Bernold of Constance during
the 1080s, the canon 'which seems more acceptable to the apostolic
see' should be regarded as authoritative. Bernold was the first author
to write in defence of Gregory VII's reforming decrees (his earliest
polemic was composed in 1075); he was the most distinguished

---

[72] Holtzmann, 'Ausgabe' (n. 19) pp. 16, 34; C. Duggan, *Twelfth-century decretal
collections and their importance in English history* (University of London Historical
Studies 12: London, 1963). See also the pioneering work on the English decretal
collections by Z. N. Brooke, 'The effect of Becket's murder on papal authority in
England', *Cambridge Historical Journal* 2 (1926–8), 213–88 and in his *The English
church and the papacy from the Conquest to the reign of John* (Cambridge, 1931).

[73] Stephen of Tournai, *Epistola* 251: (n. 67) 517C.

[74] Gratian, *Decretum* D.20 *dictum ante* c. 1.

[75] *Ibid.*, C.25 q.1 *dictum post* c. 16.

[76] The tradition that papal approval validated a council was best known to the
canonists from various Pseudo-Isidorean versions of it: *Decretales Pseudo-
Isidorianae* (n. 3) pp. 19, 224, 228, 459, 471, 479, 503, 721. E. von Dobschütz, *Das
Decretum Gelasianum* (Leipzig, 1912). See S. Kuttner, '*Liber canonicus*. A note on
Dictatus papae c. 17', *SG* 2 (1947), 387–401.

canonist among the polemicists of the Investiture Contest and the author of a scholarly treatise 'on the sources of ecclesiastical law' which explains the theory of 'harmony'. According to Bernold, the popes were 'the authors of the canons'. 'The apostolic see . . . has always held and will hold the primacy, so as to order the churches of the whole world in accordance not only with the ancient statutes but also with new ones, as necessity demands at different times.' Bernold attributed to the pope the power both to make new laws and to suspend the operation of the old laws. 'It is certainly the privilege of the apostolic see to be the judge of the canons or the decrees and sometimes to enforce them and sometimes to relax them, as may seem most useful to the Church at the time.'[77] Bernold's contemporary, the canonist Bishop Bonizo of Sutri wrote in similar terms of the legislative and dispensing power of the pope. 'It has been and it always will be lawful for Roman pontiffs to make new canons and to change old ones, according to the needs of the times.' 'The Roman pontiffs are not bound by the canons which they themselves have made.'[78]

These Gregorian canonists who represented the pope as 'above the canons' were responding to Gregory VII's own claims for the papal office. In Gregory's memorandum *Dictatus pape* appears the well-known statement: 'that [the pope] alone has the right to make new laws according to the needs of the times.'[79] In particular Gregory claimed the right to emend or cancel the privileges issued by his predecessors: 'certain things can be conceded in privileges with respect to a particular case, person, time and place, which, if considerations of necessity or utility demand it, may lawfully be changed.'[80] These claims represented a complete departure from early medieval tradition, which had imposed on the newly elected pope the obligation 'to diminish or change nothing of the tradition of [his] most

---

[77] Bernold of Constance, *De excommunicatis vitandis, de reconciliatione lapsorum et de fontibus iuris ecclesiastici* c. 43, 58, *MGH Libelli* 2, 131; *Apologeticus* c. 21, ibid., p. 86; *De statutis ecclesiasticis sobrie legendis, ibid.*, p. 157. On Bernold see most recently I. S. Robinson, 'Bernold von Konstanz und der gregorianische Reformkreis um Bischof Gebhard III.', *Freiburger Diözesan-Archiv* 109 (1989), forthcoming.

[78] Bonizo of Sutri, *Liber de vita christiana* I.44, v.6, ed. E. Perels (Texte zur Geschichte des römischen und kanonischen Rechts im Mittelalter 1: Berlin, 1930) pp. 33, 177.

[79] Gregory VII, *Registrum* II.55a, c. 7, p. 203. For the extensive literature on this subject see H. Fuhrmann, 'Das Reformpapsttum und die Rechtswissenschaft' in *Investiturstreit und Reichsverfassung* ed. J. Fleckenstein (Vorträge und Forschungen 17: Sigmaringen, 1973) pp. 175–203.

[80] *Registrum* VI.2, p. 393. On Gregory VII's cancellation of his predecessors' privileges see below p. 238.

virtuous predecessors nor to admit any novelty'.[81] Gregory VII's
challenge to this tradition, together with the scholarly justification of
this challenge presented by the Gregorian canonists, have been seen
by historians as a major development in the legal history of the
medieval west. The Gregorian reform was the moment at which
'law shifted from the divine sphere into that of human control'.[82]
Hans Martin Klinkenberg (1969) argued that this Gregorian claim
was inspired by the legal theory of the later Roman empire: it was a
papal borrowing of the Roman Law principle, 'what pleases the
prince has the force of law'.[83] It is indeed tempting to interpret
Gregory VII's claim as part of the 'imitation of empire' (imitatio
imperii) which was an undeniable feature of the reform papacy
(especially when we find Gregory boasting in 1075 that 'the law of
the Roman pontiffs has taken possession of more lands than that of
the Roman emperors').[84] However, the limitations which Gregory
VII imposed on the papal right 'to make new laws' suggest a different
interpretation. Firstly, Gregory's statements emphasised that the
pope made new laws only when compelled to do so by necessitas,
'according to the needs of the times'. When new evils appeared in the
Church, it was necessary to counter them with new laws. 'It has been
and always will be lawful for this holy Roman church to provide new
decrees and remedies against the new abuses which spring up.'[85]
Secondly, he insisted that the purpose of the new laws was 'to snatch
[the Church] from servile oppression, or rather tyrannical slavery,
and restore her to her ancient freedom': that is, not to introduce
innovations into the Church but to return 'to the ancient pattern and
state of religion'.[86] The pope's new laws were therefore necessarily in
harmony with the truth of the Gospel and of the Fathers. Hence

[81] Formula 83 of the mid–seventh–century Liber Diurnus. But Nicholas I (858–67) had
claimed the power of dispensation for the Roman church. See H. M. Klinkenberg,
'Die Theorie der Veränderbarkeit des Rechtes im frühen und hohen Mittelalter' in
Lex et Sacramentum im Mittelalter ed. P. Wilpert (Miscellanea Mediaevalia.
Veröffentlichungen des Thomas-Instituts der Universität zu Köln 6: Berlin, 1969)
p. 167.

[82] Ibid., p. 157.

[83] Ibid., p. 174. So also K. Ganzer, 'Päpstliche Gesetzgebungsgewalt und kirchlicher
Konsens: zur Verwendung eines Dictum Gratians in der Concordantia Catholica
des Nikolaus von Kues' in Von Konstanz nach Trient. Beiträge zur Geschichte der
Kirche von den Reformkonzilien bis zum Tridentinum. Festgabe für August Franzen ed.
R. Bäumer (Munich-Paderborn-Vienna, 1972) p. 176.

[84] Gregory VII, Registrum II.75, p. 237. On the 'imitation of empire' see above
p. 23.

[85] Registrum II.67, p. 224.   [86] Registrum VIII.12, pp. 531–2.

Gregory's famous juxtaposition of truth and custom. 'Perhaps you will point out to me that this is the custom; in which case it must be observed that the Lord said, I am the truth and the life. He did not say, I am the custom, but the truth.'[87] It was to uproot pernicious customs which threatened the purity of the Church that the pope exercised his right to make laws. According to Gregory VII, therefore, papal legislation had the strictly limited purpose of restoring the primitive purity and freedom of the Church. It was in fact a conception far removed from the dictum that 'what pleases the prince has the force of law'.

Gregory VII's idea of the pope's law-making as a carefully limited instrument of reform recurs in the writings of the Gregorian canonists. Bernold of Constance, for example, first encountered Gregory's conception of legislation in a papal letter of 1075 proposing new measures against simoniacs and married clergy: 'for it seems to us far better to reestablish the righteousness of God by means of new counsels, than to allow the souls of men to perish along with the laws which they have neglected'.[88] In his own exposition of the relationship of the pope and ecclesiastical law, Bernold described the popes as 'the authors of the canons', but he was careful to add: 'it must be noted that Roman pontiffs have always been accustomed to observe and implement the ancient laws rather than to create new ones, unless some reasonable cause compels them to do so'.[89] Bonizo of Sutri likewise emphasised that the popes made new laws only in cases of *necessitas* and cited the saying of Pope Innocent I that when the necessity ceased, the law which it had provoked must also cease.[90] The canonist Bishop Ivo of Chartres wrote on the subject of legislation that 'a change in the law is made out of necessity' and on the subject of dispensation that 'some dispensations are permitted after sound deliberation, but when the state of necessity ceases, [the dispensations] must also cease'.[91] It was in the second

---

[87] Gregory VII, *JL* 5277: *The Epistolae Vagantes of Pope Gregory VII* ed. H. E. J. Cowdrey (Oxford, 1972) p. 151. See G. Ladner, 'Two Gregorian letters. On the sources and nature of Gregory VII's reform ideology', *SG* 5 (1956), 225–42; K. F. Morrison, *Tradition and authority in the western Church 300–1140* (Princeton, 1969) pp. 273–4.

[88] *Registrum* II.45, p. 184. On Bernold's knowledge of this letter see I. S. Robinson, 'Zur Arbeitsweise Bernolds von Konstanz und seines Kreises. Untersuchungen zum Schlettstädter Codex 13', *DA* 34 (1978), 65–82.

[89] Bernold, *De excommunicatis vitandis* (n. 77) pp. 140–1.

[90] Bonizo, *Liber de vita christiana* 1.44 (n. 78) p. 33. See H. Krause, 'Cessante causa cessat lex', *ZSSRG KA* 46 (1960), 81–111.

[91] Ivo of Chartres, *Decretum, prologus, MPL* 161, 57A, 58B.

quarter of the twelfth century that these qualifications tended to disappear from pronouncements on the legislative and dispensing power of the pope. Many examples can be found in the letters and privileges of Innocent II, who, as we have already seen, vigorously promoted the judicial business of the curia. Innocent II's chancery developed the practice of beginning papal privileges with a 'primacy arenga', an opening protocol celebrating the papal primacy, especially the judicial authority of the papacy. A privilege of 1139 for Bamberg connects the pope's right to make laws with the scriptural text John 21. 16–17, 'Feed my sheep'. 'The holy Roman church, who . . . judges not only earthly but also heavenly things, is accustomed, like an affectionate mother, to fill her sons with the food of divine law and to adorn them with various prerogatives.' Innocent claimed the right to make the most sweeping innovations in Christian society – 'to divide bishoprics or join them up, to transform the jurisdictions of kingdoms, to create new metropolitan sees and to confer metropolitan rights on primates' – not on the grounds of *necessitas* but 'according to [the pope's] will'. Innocent was similarly confident about the papal dispensing power. 'Although we ought, according to the decrees of the holy fathers, to punish them for this', he wrote in 1136 concerning churchmen who had not obeyed a summons to attend a papal council, 'nevertheless, imitating the gentleness of the apostolic see, we have been induced . . . to show them mercy.'[92] In the second half of the twelfth century, beginning in the pontificate of Innocent II's successor, Celestine II, the pope's right to change the law was proclaimed in every papal privilege issued by the chancery, by including the formula 'saving the authority of the apostolic see' (*salva sedis apostolicae auctoritate*). This formula had sometimes been used in earlier papal privileges to protect particular papal rights. After 1143 it was used in all privileges as a general reservation clause, protecting the right of future popes to alter or cancel their predecessors' privilege.[93]

The period in which these confident claims were made for the legislative and dispensing power of the pope was, as we have seen, one of expanding judicial activity in the papal curia. These two themes were commemorated, for example, in the writings of

---

[92] Innocent II, *JL* 8048, 7908, 7763: (n. 8) 483AB, 372B, 272A. On the 'primacy arenga' see below p. 232.

[93] On this formula see most recently S. Chodorow, *Christian political theory and church politics in the mid-twelfth century* (Berkeley–Los Angeles, 1972) pp. 152–3; Fuhrmann, 'Rechtswissenschaft' (n. 79) pp. 191–2. See also below p. 238.

Bernard of Clairvaux, who was both a severe critic of the expansion of papal justice and an exuberant defender of the papal power to make and unmake law. He addressed his pupil, Eugenius III, as the 'moderator of the laws, the dispenser of the canons' and referred to the corpus of ecclesiastical law as 'your canons' (*ca.* 1150).[94] A decade earlier, but in the same context of the expansion of papal justice, Master Gratian of Bologna had composed the definitive twelfth-century statement concerning the relationship of the pope and the canons. 'The holy Roman church confers right and authority on the sacred canons, but she herself is not bound by them, because she has the right of making the canons.' The pope 'gives authority to the canons: he does not subject himself to them'. 'Sometimes [the popes] show by means of their mandate, decision, judgement or by some other means that they are the lords and makers of the laws.' Gratian had a similarly broad conception of the papal dispensing power: 'it is lawful for [the pope] to grant special privileges contrary to the general decrees and as a special favour to concede what is forbidden by general decree'. 'It is to be noted above all that [the pope] can make new laws wherever the evangelists have made no pronouncement.' According to Master Gratian, the principal function of papal legislation was to fill the gaps in Christian tradition: to provide laws for those circumstances which were not specifically foreseen by 'the Lord and his apostles and the holy fathers following them'.[95] Historians have long debated whether Gratian had any direct influence on the twelfth-century papacy's attitude to its legislative authority. In particular the introduction of the reservation clause 'saving the authority of the apostolic see' in papal privileges from 1143 onwards has been attributed to the influence of Gratian's *Decretum*.[96] All that is known for certain is that in the 1190s the *Decretum* became the canon law book of the papal curia, regularly cited by the pope when pronouncing judgement. Before the pontificate of Clement III there is no unambiguous evidence that the *Decretum* was consulted in the curia.[97] Master Gratian's great work was not an official papal

---

[94] Bernard of Clairvaux, *De consideratione* II.8.16, IV.7.23: (n. 14) 752B, 788B.

[95] Gratian, *Decretum* c.25 q.1 c.16, c.6, c.1.

[96] F. Thaner, 'Über Entstehung und Bedeutung der Formel: "Salva sedis apostolicae auctoritate" in den päpstlichen Privilegien', *SB der Kaiserlichen Akademie der Wissenschaften in Wien, phil.-hist. Klasse* 71 (1872), 807–49; Chodorow, *Christian political theory* (n. 93) pp. 152–3. On the influence of Gratian see also S. Kuttner, *Gratian and the schools of law, 1140–1234* (London, 1983), with full bibliography.

[97] W. Holtzmann, 'Die Benutzung Gratians in der päpstlichen Kanzlei im 12. Jahrhundert', *Studia Gratiana* I (1953), 323–49.

canonical collection but, like all the other canon law collections of our period, a piece of private enterprise.

None of the numerous collections of the later eleventh century inspired by the reform programme of Gregory VII claims to be an official collection commissioned by the pope: not even the *Collection in 74 Titles*, which was used by Gregory VII's legates in Germany; not the *Collectio canonum* of Bishop Anselm II of Lucca, Gregory's faithful disciple and legate in Lombardy; not the collections of the canonists closely associated with the Roman church, Cardinal Atto of S. Marco, Cardinal Deusdedit, Bonizo of Sutri and Cardinal Gregory of S. Grisogono.[98] Likewise, as we have already seen, the compilers of the decretal collections of the later twelfth century were entirely self-appointed. Only in the thirteenth century did the papacy assume the responsibility for the codification of papal law. The authors who developed so exalted a view of the pope's legislative authority were not commissioned by a papacy anxious to vindicate its right to make and unmake law. They were scholars attempting to transform the heterogeneous materials of Christian tradition into a coherent body of law, a 'Common law of the Church'.[99] (It was an enterprise characteristic of the 'Twelfth-century Renaissance' in western Europe.) To construct this 'Common law' the canonists needed a legitimating source of authority; and this they found in the principle best known in Master Gratian's formulation: 'the holy Roman church confers right and authority on the sacred canons'. This principle, originally formulated in order to defend the Gregorian reform programme against its critics, was given a new relevance by the expansion of papal judicial activity in the course of the twelfth century. Elaborated in the twelfth-century schools as an instrument for the interpretation of canon law, the doctrine of the pope as 'the moderator of the laws, the dispenser of the canons' was to provide the intellectual basis of the papal monarchy of the later Middle Ages.

[98] Fuhrmann, 'Rechtswissenschaft' (n. 79) pp. 199–201, taking issue with P. Fournier, 'Un tournant de l'histoire du droit (1060–1140)', *Nouvelle Revue historique du droit français et étranger* 41 (1917), 129–80. See also H. Mordek, 'Kanonistik und gregorianische Reform. Marginalien zu einem nichtmarginalen Thema' in *Reich und Kirche vor dem Investiturstreit. Vorträge beim wissenschaftlichen Kolloquium aus Anlass des 80. Geburtstags von Gerd Tellenbach* ed. K. Schmid (Sigmaringen, 1985) pp. 65–82.

[99] Kuttner, '*Liber canonicus*' (n. 76) p. 391.

6

THE PAPACY, THE RELIGIOUS ORDERS AND THE EPISCOPATE

•

In a letter of 1081 Gregory VII informed the faithful that the founders of the Poitevin monastery of St Peter in *Maskarans* had surrendered the monastery to the pope and that consequently he had 'received it into the jurisdiction and defence of the apostolic see'. 'Therefore we command by apostolic authority that no one shall presume henceforward to trouble the aforesaid place, fortified by apostolic defence, but that it shall remain in peace and free from any disturbance under the protection of St Peter, to whose jurisdiction it belongs.'[1] During the late eleventh and twelfth centuries religious houses sought St Peter's protection – called variously *protectio, defensio, tutela, tuitio, munimen, patrocinium* – on a scale unsurpassed during the rest of the Middle Ages. In the early Middle Ages monasteries had generally looked to kings for protection; but the disintegration of the Carolingian empire in the ninth century compelled them to find stronger protectors. 'For the dwindling protection of Charles the Bald and Charles the Fat was substituted the *defensio* or *tuitio* of the saints, but especially that of St Peter, that is, of the Roman see.'[2] This development began in 863, when Count Gerald of Roussillon commended to St Peter the two monasteries which he had founded on his allodial lands of Vézelay and Pothières. The most famous case of such a commendation occurred in 910, when Duke William 'the Pious' of Aquitaine secured for his monastery of Cluny 'the protec-

---

[1] Gregory VII, *Registrum* IX.7, p. 584.
[2] Y. M.-J. Congar, *L'ecclésiologie du haut Moyen-Age* (Paris, 1968) pp. 203–4.

tion of the apostles [Peter and Paul] and the defence of the Roman pontiff. Once invested with this apostolic protection, the house ceased to be a 'proprietary monastery', subject to the will of the founding family, and obtained freedom from all secular authority. One of its early privileges describes Cluny as 'entirely free from disturbance or domination both of kings and of all princes and of kinsmen of [the founder, Duke] William and indeed of all men'. A series of papal privileges in the later tenth and eleventh centuries confirmed and extended Cluny's freedom, so that the abbey was freed from all secular and spiritual authority save that of the pope. Cluny was transformed into a model of what, from the mid-eleventh century onwards, was known as 'Roman liberty' (*Romana libertas*).[3] Few monasteries ever enjoyed Cluny's intimacy with the Roman church, but hundreds sought, if not 'Roman liberty', at least Roman protection. During the eleventh century 270 religious houses obtained papal letters guaranteeing them the protection of St Peter and his vicar, the pope. During the twelfth century the number rose to approximately 2,000.[4] This statistic offers convincing evidence of growing confidence on the part of religious communities and their founders and patrons in the power of St Peter and his vicar to protect the interests of the faithful and to avenge their injuries. Confidence in the protection of St Peter in turn contributed to the extension of papal authority in western Christendom. The obedience owed by a monastery to the Roman church in return for St Peter's protection was valuable propaganda for the primacy claimed by the papacy: a working model of the obedience which the whole Church theoretically owed to Rome.

The late eleventh and twelfth centuries were a crucial period in the development of monasticism and of the life of regular canons. The religious orders – the *ordo monasticus* and the *ordo canonicus* – expanded as a result both of numerous new foundations and of new interpretations of the ancient Rules of the religious life. In pursuing their reforming aspirations and their desire for freedom from all external controls, religious houses often encountered opposition from the local ecclesiastical hierarchy. The papacy was a much-needed ally in

---

[3] *Recueil des chartes de l'abbaye de Cluny*, ed. A. Bernard and A. Bruel 1 (Collection de documents inédits sur l'histoire de France, série 1: Paris, 1876), 125–6, 281. See H. E. J. Cowdrey, *The Cluniacs and the Gregorian reform* (Oxford, 1970) pp. 4–57; B. Szabó-Bechstein, *Libertas Ecclesiae. Ein Schlüsselbegriff des Investiturstreits und seine Vorgeschichte* = SG 12 (1985), 91–101.

[4] A. Blumenstock, *Der päpstliche Schutz im Mittelalter* (Innsbruck, 1890) p. 44.

the struggle for reform and monastic liberty. Historians have often commented on the 'synchronism' between the development of the religious orders and the growth of papal authority in the central Middle Ages.[5] The Gregorian papacy initiated, and the twelfth-century popes continued, the practice of employing monks and canons as papal agents in the work of reforming the Church. Monks and canons assisted in the reform not only of religious communities but also of the secular Church by acting as reform propagandists and by advising the papal curia about local conditions. Their dependence on the religious as agents of reform explains the popes' willingness to intervene in the affairs of the religious orders and to ensure the protection and liberty of individual houses.

The most striking evidence of the close alliance between the papacy and the religious orders is the fact that of the nineteen popes of the period 1073–1198, eleven were former monks or canons. Five of the six popes of the 'Investiture Contest' were formerly monks. Firstly, 'the false monk Hildebrand' – as his enemies called him – took the pontifical name 'Gregory', which commemorated the great monk-pope Gregory I. The claim that Gregory VII had made his monastic profession at Cluny (first made by his earliest biographer, Bonizo of Sutri, *ca*. 1085) is probably erroneous. It is more likely that he had been a monk in St Mary's-on-the-Aventine, a Roman monastery closely associated with Cluny.[6] Gregory's two immediate successors were both figures of great eminence in the monastic world: Victor III, formerly Abbot Desiderius of Monte Cassino, and Urban II, formerly the grand-prior Odo of Cluny.[7] Paschal II was also a monk. His monastery is unknown (although he has been identified, on very slender evidence, as a Cluniac).[8] Gelasius II was formerly a monk of Monte Cassino. These five monk-popes were succeeded firstly by Archbishop Guido of Vienne, as Calixtus II, and then by a series of popes who were former regular canons. Honorius II was a

---

[5] J. Hourlier, *L'âge classique 1140–1378. Les religieux* (Histoire du Droit et des Institutions de l'Eglise en Occident 10: Paris, 1974) p. 425. Cf. Cowdrey, *Cluniacs* (n. 3) pp. 120–56; M. Maccarrone, 'Primato romano e monasteri dal principio dal secolo XII ad Innocenzo III' in *Istituzione monastiche e istituzioni canonicali in Occidente* (Miscellanea del Centro di Studi Medioevali 9: Milan, 1977) p. 50.

[6] Cowdrey, *Cluniacs* (n. 3) p. 148 n. 4; C. N. L. Brooke, *Europe in the Central Middle Ages* (London, 1964) p. 250 n. 1. See also the works mentioned in I. S. Robinson, 'Pope Gregory VII (1073–1085)', *Journal of Ecclesiastical History* 36 (1985), 448.

[7] H. E. J. Cowdrey, *The age of Abbot Desiderius of Monte Cassino* (Oxford, 1983); Becker, *Urban II.* 1, 41–51.

[8] Servatius, *Paschalis II.* pp. 10–14.

former canon of S. Maria in Rheno in Bologna.[9] Innocent II may have been a former canon of St John Lateran in Rome; while his rival in the schism of 1130, Anacletus II, was formerly a monk of Cluny.[10] Two other popes of the mid-twelfth century were former regular canons: Lucius II had been a canon of S. Frediano in Lucca and Hadrian IV, a canon of St Rufus in Avignon.[11] Eugenius III was a former Cistercian: a monk of Clairvaux and a pupil of St Bernard and subsequently abbot of Trefontane in Rome.[12] The popes of the period 1124–59 were, therefore, all representatives of the new religious orders of *ca.* 1100, with the two shortlived exceptions of the former secular clerks, Celestine II and Anastasius IV.[13] The second half of the twelfth century, however, presents a completely different picture. Of the six popes of the years 1159–98, all were secular clerks except for Gregory VIII, a former canon of St Martin in Laon (which was subsequently a principal centre of the Premonstratensian order).[14] Lucius III has been claimed as a Cistercian; but although he undoubtedly had close links with the order, he seems never to have become a monk.[15] The cardinals actually attempted in October 1187 to elect a Cistercian – Henry of Marcy, abbot of Clairvaux and cardinal bishop of Albano – but he declined the papal dignity.[16] There was, therefore, no animus in the later twelfth-century college of car-

9 F.-J. Schmale, *Studien zum Schisma des Jahres 1130* (Cologne-Graz, 1961) p. 140. Cf. R. Hüls, *Kardinäle, Klerus und Kirchen Roms 1049–1130* (Tübingen, 1977) p. 106.

10 Schmale, *Schisma* pp. 39–40. But see W. Maleczek, 'Das Kardinalskollegium unter Innocenz II. und Anaklet II.', *AHP* 19 (1981), 33.

11 B. Zenker, *Die Mitglieder des Kardinalkollegiums von 1130 bis 1159* (dissertation: Würzburg, 1964) pp. 129, 36.

12 *Ibid.*, pp. 185–6.

13 P. Classen, 'Zur Geschichte Papst Anastasius' IV.', *QFIAB* 48 (1968), 36–63, refutes the claim that Anastasius was formerly a canon of St Rufus in Avignon.

14 P. Kehr, 'Papst Gregor VIII. als Ordensgründer' in *Miscellanea Francesco Ehrle. Scritti di storia e paleografia* 2 (Studi e testi 38: Rome, 1924), 250. Alexander III has been claimed as a canon by Zenker, *Mitglieder* (n. 11) pp. 86, 210n. But see J. T. Noonan, 'Who was Rolandus?' in *Law, church and society. Essays in honor of Stephan Kuttner* ed. K. Pennington and R. Somerville (Pennsylvania, 1977) pp. 21–48, on the difficulty of establishing the details of Alexander III's early career.

15 For Lucius III as a Cistercian see J. M. Brixius, *Die Mitglieder des Kardinalkollegiums von 1130 bis 1181* (dissertation: Berlin, 1912) p. 43; V. Pfaff, 'Sieben Jahre päpstlicher Politik', *ZSSRG KA* 67 (1981), 173. For the contrary opinion see K. Wenck, 'Die römischen Päpste zwischen Alexander III. und Innocenz III. und der Designationsversuch Weihnachten 1197' in *Papsttum und Kaisertum. Forschungen zur politischen Geschichte und Geisteskultur des Mittelalters. Paul Kehr zum 65. Geburtstag dargebracht* ed. A. Brackmann (Munich, 1926) pp. 421–2; Zenker, *Mitglieder* (n. 11) p. 23.,

16 See above pp. 86–7 and below pp. 242, 505.

dinals against the election of a religious as pope. (Indeed in 1198 they elected a former regular canon of St John Lateran as Innocent III.)

Throughout the period 1073–1198 the papal curia and the college of cardinals contained many men whose careers had begun in religious communities: some of the most important papal advisers and servants of the papal government were former monks or canons. In the last quarter of the eleventh century all the cardinal bishops whose origins are known were former monks.[17] Prominent among the advisers of Gregory VII, for example, was the former monk, Cardinal bishop Peter 'Igneus' of Albano. He obtained his nickname, 'fiery Peter' when, as a monk of the Tuscan house of Vallombrosa, he successfully underwent the ordeal by fire in order to prove that the bishop of Florence was guilty of simony.[18] The Cluniac contribution to papal government in the late eleventh century is particularly well documented. According to a Tournai chronicler, 'when Pope Gregory VII commissioned Hugh [abbot of Cluny] to send him some wise men from among his monks, suitable for him to appoint as bishops, [Hugh] sent among others Odo'. Odo, grand-prior of Cluny was appointed in 1080 to the senior bishopric in the college of cardinals, that of Ostia. His predecessor in this office was Gerald, also a former grand-prior of Cluny. When Odo became pope, as Urban II, he appointed as his successor in the bishopric of Ostia, Odo II, a monk and probably a Cluniac (and perhaps Urban's nephew).[19] It was during Urban II's pontificate that the administration of the papal finances was reorganised under the direction of a papal chamberlain (*camerarius*). This office of chamberlain was imitated from the practice of Cluny and the first papal *camerarius* was the monk Peter of Cluny.[20] Even more important than the influence of Cluny was that of the abbey of Monte Cassino on the Gregorian papacy. Hans-Walther Klewitz (1936) described Monte Cassino as 'the spiritual armoury of the reform papacy'.[21] During the period 1073–1118 Monte Cassino gave the Roman church eleven cardinals, two of whom subsequently became pope: Abbot Desiderius, cardi-

---

[17] H.-W. Klewitz, *Reformpapsttum und Kardinalkolleg* (Darmstadt, 1957) pp. 115–18; Hüls, *Kardinäle* (n. 9) pp. 90–2, 100–5, 110–12, 118–19, 125–7, 129–30, 134–7, 139–40.

[18] G. Miccoli, *Pietro Igneo. Studi sull'età gregoriana* (Rome, 1960).

[19] *Historia Tornacensis* IV. 11, *MGH SS* 14, 340–1. See Klewitz, *Reformpapsttum* (n. 17) p. 115; Becker, *Urban II.* 1, 51–62, 213; Cowdrey, *Cluniacs* (n. 3) pp. 169–71; Hüls, *Kardinäle* (n. 9) pp. 100–5.

[20] See below p. 251.

[21] Klewitz, *Reformpapsttum* (n. 17) p. 103.

nal priest of S. Cecilia and John of Gaeta, cardinal deacon of S. Maria in Cosmedin. John of Gaeta, a pupil of the eminent rhetorician Alberic of Monte Cassino, served both Urban II and Paschal II as chancellor and librarian. On Paschal's death in January 1118 John was elected pope, as Gelasius II, in the monastery of S. Maria in Pallara, Monte Cassino's dependent house in Rome.[22] John's predecessor as chancellor and librarian, Cardinal Peter II of S. Grisogono, was probably also a monk of Monte Cassino: he served as the chancellor of Alexander II, Gregory VII and the antipope 'Clement III'.[23] Leo, cardinal deacon of SS. Vito e Modesto was another Monte Cassino monk who worked in the papal chancery: he was responsible for transcribing the register of Urban II.[24] In the last years of the eleventh century Monte Cassino's dependency, S. Maria in Pallara served as 'a branch of the papal archive'.[25] Monte Cassino also provided the college of cardinals with its two most distinguished intellectuals during the Investiture Contest. Leo Marsicanus, historian of Monte Cassino, became cardinal bishop of Ostia in succession to the three Cluniacs, Gerald, Odo I and Odo II.[26] Bishop Bruno of Segni, biblical exegete and polemicist, trusted adviser of Urban II and critic of Paschal II, was both cardinal and abbot of Monte Cassino.[27] The abbey was most strongly represented in the college of cardinals during the pontificate of Paschal II, who appointed seven monks of Monte Cassino to the cardinalate. These appointments were prompted by the current preoccupation with extending papal control over the Church in southern Italy, a process in which the alliance with Monte Cassino was of particular importance to the reform papacy.[28]

Paschal II's pontificate was the apogee of the influence of the older Benedictine monasticism in the college of cardinals: of the sixty-six cardinals whom he created, one-third were monks.[29] His successor, Gelasius II, was the last of the Gregorian monk-popes: from the 1120s onwards the new religious orders began to appear in the papal

---

[22] Cowdrey, *Desiderius* (n. 7) pp. 177–213; Hüls, *Kardinäle* (n. 9) pp. 231–2.

[23] Klewitz, *Reformpapsttum* (n. 17) p. 66; Hüls, *Kardinäle* pp. 170–2.

[24] Klewitz, *Reformpapsttum* p. 134; Hüls, *Kardinäle* pp. 243–4.

[25] H.-W. Klewitz, 'Montecassino in Rom', *QFIAB* 28 (1937/8), 45.

[26] Hüls, *Kardinäle* pp. 105–6; H. Hoffmann in *Chronica monasterii Casinensis, MGH SS* 34, VII–IX.

[27] Klewitz, *Reformpapsttum* (n. 17) pp. 37–9; Hüls, *Kardinäle* pp. 129–30.

[28] Klewitz, *Reformpapsttum* pp. 103, 119, 126–7, 132–4.

[29] *Ibid.*, p. 106.

curia. The dominant figure in the curia was now Haimeric, cardinal deacon of S. Maria Nuova, a former regular canon of S. Maria in Rheno in Bologna, who served as papal chancellor from 1123 until his death in 1141. He was the leader of the party in the curia responsible for the election of Honorius II (a regular canon from S. Maria in Rheno) and of Innocent II (a canon of St John Lateran). At both elections Haimeric was opposed by the Cluniac Cardinal Peter Pierleone, who became Anacletus II, the ultimately unsuccessful candidate in the disputed election of 1130.[30] Franz-Josef Schmale's study (1961) of the schism of 1130, following a suggestion of Hans-Walther Klewitz (1939), emphasises the importance of rival allegiances to the ideals of the old and the new religious orders as an issue in the schism. The electors of Anacletus were cardinals of the older generation, who, like Anacletus himself, were under the influence of the older Benedictine monasticism. Innocent's electors were the younger cardinals, influenced by the new spirituality associated with the regular canons and the new monastic orders, especially the Cistercians. The factor which determined Innocent's victory in the schism was the support which he received from the representatives of the new spirituality: Bernard of Clairvaux, Norbert of Magdeburg, Peter the Venerable, Walter of Ravenna and Gerhoch of Reichersberg.[31] However, Klewitz's and Schmale's interpretation of this aspect of the schism has been challenged by Gerd Tellenbach (1963). In a study concerned primarily with the internal changes in Cluny in the 1120s, Tellenbach incidentally cast doubt on the theory that Cardinal Haimeric and his party were influenced by a 'new spirituality' which superseded the ideals of the older Benedictine monasticism. Tellenbach's study questions whether the reforming ideas of the Innocentine party reveal any sign of a new spiritual influence and asks how the 'new spirituality' could manifest itself in the politics of the curia. 'How precisely was Bernardine mysticism connected with Bernard [of Clairvaux]'s important role in the schism?' Schmale's portrait of the 'Innocentine party' has also been challenged by Peter Classen (1968) and Werner Maleczek (1981). Classen showed that Innocent's elector, Cardinal bishop Conrad of Sabina was not, as Schmale thought, a regular canon; while Maleczek

---

[30] Schmale, *Schisma* (n. 9) pp. 93–191.
[31] Klewitz, *Reformpapsttum* (n. 17) pp. 210–11, 254–5; Schmale, *Schisma* pp. 56–7, 77–80, 253–79: F.-J. Schmale, 'Papsttum und Kurie zwischen Gregor VII. und Innocenz II.', *HZ* 193 (1961), 265–85.

doubted whether Haimeric and Innocent himself were regular canons.[32]

The tensions inside the college of cardinals which produced the schism of 1130 are difficult to investigate because of the limitations of the evidence. However, on the question of the promotion of brethren from religious orders to the college, it is clear that during the second quarter of the twelfth century regular canons and to a lesser extent members of the new monastic orders outnumbered the older Benedictines. Nevertheless representatives of the older Benedictine monasticism did not disappear from the twelfth-century college of cardinals. For example, Innocent II (allegedly the candidate of those cardinals influenced by the 'new spirituality') promoted to the cardinalate seven members of the older Benedictine orders and only four regular canons. The two cardinal bishops of Ostia appointed by Innocent (Drogo and Alberic) were, like those of the Gregorian papacy, old Benedictines. During most of Innocent's pontificate four of the seven cardinal bishoprics (Ostia, Porto, Albano and Tusculum) were in old Benedictine hands.[33] Of the older Benedictine houses, Monte Cassino in particular continued to be represented in the college of cardinals throughout the twelfth century. Innocent II promoted the monk Rainald of Monte Cassino to the college; Hadrian IV, the monk Simon; Alexander III, the monk Roger; Clement III, the monk John; Celestine III promoted Abbot Roffred of Monte Cassino.[34] These appointments were presumably prompted by the same consideration which brought so many brethren of Monte Cassino into the Gregorian college of cardinals: the papal alliance with Monte Cassino was still necessary for maintaining papal influence in southern Italy.

The first representatives of the new orders to appear in the college of cardinals were the regular canons promoted by Paschal II: Cuno, cardinal bishop of Palestrina (one of the founders of the order of Arrouaise) ca. 1108, Gregory, cardinal deacon of S. Angelo (the future Innocent II) in 1116 and Lambert, cardinal bishop of Ostia (the future Honorius II) likewise in 1116.[35] Their numbers were swelled

[32] G. Tellenbach, 'Der Sturz des Abtes Pontius von Cluny', QFIAB 42/3 (1963), 40–4, 54–5; Classen, 'Anastasius IV.' (n. 13) pp. 36–63; Maleczek, 'Kardinalskollegium' (n. 10) p. 33.

[33] Zenker, Mitglieder (n. 11) pp. 13–20, 26–8, 32–5, 44–6, 160–1, 191–2, 208.

[34] Ibid., pp. 191–2; 140–1; Brixius, Mitglieder (n. 15) p. 66; V. Pfaff, 'Die Kardinäle unter Papst Coelestin III. (1191–1198)', ZSSRG KA 41 (1955), 87, 90.

[35] Klewitz, Reformpapsttum (n. 17) pp. 119, 120, 133; Hüls, Kardinäle (n. 9) pp. 113–16, 223–4, 106–7; Schmale, Schisma (n. 9) pp. 38–40. Schmale claims Conrad,

by the appointments made by Calixtus II in 1123: four regular canons were promoted to the college, including Cardinal Haimeric and Gerard, cardinal priest of S. Croce in Gerusalemme (the future Lucius II).[36] The first representative of the new monastic orders to enter the college was John, prior of Camaldoli, whom Honorius II appointed cardinal bishop of Ostia.[37] The first Cistercians appeared in the college in the pontificate of Innocent II, who promoted four monks of Clairvaux, including Bernard of Pisa (the future Eugenius III).[38] Innocent promoted only four regular canons, compared with eleven monks; but his successors in the years 1143–59 preferred to appoint canons rather than monks to the cardinalate. Celestine II seems to have promoted only one religious, a regular canon; Lucius II promoted two canons and a Carthusian (Jordan, cardinal priest of S. Susanna, the papal chamberlain).[39] Eugenius III promoted three fellow-Cistercians (all former monks of Clairvaux), but he also appointed at least five canons to the college, including Cardinal bishop Nicholas of Albano (the future Hadrian IV). In mid-century the regular canons constituted approximately a quarter of the membership of the college: eight out of thirty-five cardinals on the death of Eugenius III; seven out of twenty-seven on the death of Anastasius IV.[40] Hadrian IV's appointments were in the same proportion: of his thirteen promotions, three were canons, including Albert, cardinal priest of S. Lorenzo in Lucina (the future Gregory VIII) and the papal chamberlain Boso.[41] For the thirty-four cardinals of Alexander III's pontificate biographical information is in relatively short supply. It is possible to identify three monks, including one Cistercian (Henry of Marcy, abbot of Clairvaux and cardinal bishop of Albano) and one regular canon. (Another canon whom Alexander brought into the curia, Soffred of Pistoia, was sub-

cardinal priest of S. Pudenziana, later cardinal bishop of Sabina (Anastasius IV), appointed 1114, as a regular canon; but see Classen, 'Anastasius IV.' (n. 13) pp. 36–63.

[36] Schmale, *Schisma* pp. 48–51, 98–100; Zenker, *Mitglieder* (n. 11) pp. 51–2, 115–16, 129–31, 142–4; Hüls, *Kardinäle* pp. 138, 162, 164, 236. But on Haimeric see also Maleczek, 'Kardinalskollegium' (n. 10) p. 33.

[37] Schmale, *Schisma* pp. 53–4; Zenker, *Mitglieder* pp. 11–12; Hüls, *Kardinäle* p. 108.

[38] Zenker, *Mitglieder* pp. 40–1, 55–6, 133–4, 184–7.

[39] *Ibid.*, pp. 71–2, 77, 114; 144; 41, 132, 104. On Jordan see below p. 254.

[40] Zenker, *Mitglieder* pp. 21, 96, 148; 29, 36, 107, 112, 179, 210. Zenker also wishes to place Roland, cardinal priest of S. Marco (Alexander III) among the canons promoted by Eugenius III: see above n. 14.

[41] Zenker, *Mitglieder* pp. 125–6, 149, 180.

sequently promoted to the cardinalate by his successor.)[42] Lucius III promoted four canons and one monk (the papal chamberlain Melior, cardinal priest of SS. Giovanni e Paolo); Urban III promoted one canon and one monk. Clement III promoted the regular canon Lothar, cardinal deacon of SS. Sergio e Baccho (the future Innocent III), whom Gregory VIII had brought into the curia. Celestine III promoted two 'old Benedictines' but seems to have promoted no brethren of the newer religious orders.[43] Representatives of the new orders, therefore, continued to be present in the college of cardinals in the second half of the twelfth century, although they no longer constituted as large a proportion of the college as they had done in the middle of the century.

Certain houses of the newer religious orders evidently enjoyed a special prestige in the curia, analogous to that of Monte Cassino and Cluny. The most obvious case is that of Clairvaux, where all eight of the Cistercian cardinals of the twelfth century had once been monks.[44] Five of these cardinals from Clairvaux became particularly influential in the curia. Bernard of Pisa became pope, as Eugenius III. Hugh of Châlons became cardinal bishop of Ostia and a zealous promoter of Cistercian interests in the curia. Martin, cardinal priest of S. Stefano in Celio monte completed a successful legation in Denmark and Sweden in 1133. Henry, cardinal priest of SS. Nereo e Achilleo played a major part in the attempt to make peace between empire and papacy in 1158. After the outbreak of schism in 1159 he was one of the legates who negotiated French support for Alexander III. Henry of Marcy, cardinal bishop of Albano was active as a legate in France and as a crusading preacher. In 1187 his colleagues wished to elect him to the papacy, but he declined the office.[45] The prestige which Clairvaux enjoyed in the curia was derived from the reputation of the great abbot Bernard. The involvement of Bernard of

---

[42] Brixius, *Mitglieder* (n. 15) pp. 60–2, 66; 65–6; Pacaut, *Alexandre III* p. 272; Pfaff, 'Kardinäle' (n. 34) p. 88; Y. M.-J. Congar, 'Henri de Marcy, abbé de Clairvaux, cardinal-évêque d'Albano et légat pontifical' in *Analecta Monastica. Textes et Etudes sur la vie des moines au moyen âge* 5e série (Studia Anselmiana 43: Rome, 1958) p. 30.

[43] Pfaff, 'Kardinäle' (n. 34) pp. 84–5, 87–8, 90; 88, 89; 92; 85, 87.

[44] B. Jacqueline, 'Saint-Bernard de Clairvaux et la curie romaine', *Rivista di storia della Chiesa in Italia* 7 (1953), 29 counts only four monks of Clairvaux in the second quarter of the twelfth century; but see Zenker, *Mitglieder* (n. 11) pp. 21, 40, 55, 96, 133, 148, 184. Cardinal bishop Drogo of Ostia had spent some years in the Cistercian abbey of Pontigny, but subsequently returned to his old Benedictine allegiance: Zenker p. 13.

[45] Zenker, *Mitglieder* pp. 21–2, 96–7, 133–4, 184–7; Congar, 'Henri de Marcy' (n. 42) pp. 30–40, 45–54. See above pp. 86–7 and below p. 505.

Clairvaux in the business of the papal curia is well-known: the influential support which he gave to the cause of Innocent II during the schism of the 1130s; his interventions in the controversial episcopal elections of Tours, Langres, Châlons, Paris and York; his efforts to secure the condemnation of the teachings of Peter Abelard and Gilbert de la Porrée; his preaching of the Second Crusade; above all, the advice which he gave to his former pupil, Eugenius III. One of Bernard's most frequent correspondents was the all-powerful papal chancellor Cardinal Haimeric, whom Bernard described as 'like a mother to me'.[46] Among his many other correspondents in the curia were Haimeric's successors in the chancellor's office, Cardinal Gerard of S. Croce (Lucius II), Robert Pullen, cardinal priest of SS. Martino e Silvestro and Guido, cardinal deacon of SS. Cosma e Damiano; together with the cardinal bishops Matthew of Albano, Imar of Tusculum and Alberic of Ostia.[47] Bernard naturally called upon his own former pupils in the college – especially Stephen, cardinal bishop of Palestrina – to promote the causes which he favoured.[48] The links between Clairvaux and the curia were strengthened when in 1140 Innocent II gave the Roman monastery of Trefontane to the Cistercians. During its early years Trefontane was ruled by a series of pupils of Bernard of Clairvaux, two of whom – Bernard of Pisa and Henry – were rapidly promoted to the college of cardinals.[49]

In the case of the regular canons, two houses in particular were well represented in the twelfth-century curia: S. Frediano in Lucca and S. Maria in Rheno in Bologna. The influence of S. Frediano in Rome stemmed from the fact that Calixtus II entrusted the reform of the canons of St John Lateran to that congregation. Gregory VII's reform of the Lateran canons had proved shortlived; a lasting reform was achieved only with the introduction of regular canons from S. Frediano. Gerard Cacciaminici, whom Calixtus II appointed cardinal priest of S. Croce in Gerusalemme (1123) was perhaps one of the canons brought from Lucca to the Lateran. Both as cardinal

---

[46] Bernard of Clairvaux, *Epistola* 144, *MPL* 182, 302A. Letters to Haimeric: *Epistolae* 15, 20, 48, 51–4, 157, 160, 162, 181, 311, 316, 338; *ibid.*, 118B–119A, 123AB, 154B–157B, 158C–160D, 315A, 320AB, 321AB, 344AC, 513D–517C, 522BD, 542D–544A.

[47] Bernard, *Epistolae* 219 (Gerard), 362 (Robert Pullen), 367 (Guido), 21 (Matthew), 219, 230–2 (Imar and Alberic): *ibid.*, 382D–385A, 563A–564B, 572C–573A, 123B–124B, 382D–385A, 417A–420A.

[48] Bernard, *Epistolae* 219, 224, 230–2, 331: *ibid.*, 382D–385A, 391B–394B, 417A–420A, 536C–537B.

[49] Jacqueline, 'Saint-Bernard' (n. 44) p. 29; Zenker, *Mitglieder* (n. 11) pp. 97, 186.

and as pope (Lucius II) he was devoted to the interests of S. Frediano: he gave the church of S. Croce to the congregation.[50] Four other canons of S. Frediano became cardinals during the twelfth century (including the longlived Hubald, kinsman of Lucius II, who appointed him his successor as cardinal priest of S. Croce).[51] The Lateran canons who entered the college (including the future popes Innocent II and Innocent III) may also be regarded as representatives of the S. Frediano interest. The house of S. Maria in Rheno in Bologna was one of the most important religious centres of northern Italy – and indeed of western Christendom – in the twelfth century. The Bolognese congregation produced a pope – Honorius II – and at least five cardinals. These included some of the most influential members of the twelfth-century college: the great chancellor Haimeric; the saintly Guarinus, cardinal bishop of Palestrina (canonised by Alexander III); Guido, cardinal priest of S. Pudenziana, Eugenius III's legate in Italy and Germany and the energetic agent of Hadrian IV's reconquest of the papal patrimony; Hildebrand, cardinal priest of SS. Apostoli, Alexander III's permanent legate in Lombardy during the papal schism. It is possible that the papal chamberlain Boso, cardinal deacon of SS. Cosma e Damiano, had also been a canon in Bologna.[52]

The papacy in the 1150s, according to Classen (1968), was 'already on the threshold of the period in which the lawyers . . . overtook the religious in the curia'.[53] As early as the pontificate of Urban II the curia had acquired legal advisers: the canonist John, cardinal priest of S. Anastasia, one of Urban's most trusted agents, and the monk Peter of Monte Cassino, skilled in both civil and canon law. Peter was appointed cardinal priest of S. Susanna by Paschal II, who also appointed the canonist Gregory (author of the canonical collection *Polycarpus*) to the college as cardinal priest of S. Grisogono.[54] In the second quarter of the twelfth century cardinals with the title *magister* began to appear in the college, their title denoting men distinguished for their learning, especially in law. The earliest of these *magistri* to

---

[50] Zenker, *Mitglieder* pp. 129–31; T. Schmidt, 'Die Kanonikerreform in Rom und Papst Alexander II. (1061–1073)', *SG* 9 (1972), 199–221.

[51] Zenker, *Mitglieder* pp. 41, 129, 132, 144; Pfaff, 'Kardinäle' (n. 34) p. 89.

[52] Zenker, *Mitglieder* pp. 142, 41, 112, 107, 149. (Guarinus was a canon both in S. Maria in Rheno and in S. Frediano.) See also Brixius, *Mitglieder* (n. 15) pp. 65–6.

[53] Classen, 'Anastasius IV.' (n. 13) pp. 38–9.

[54] John: Klewitz, *Reformpapsttum* (n. 17) p. 123; Hüls, *Kardinäle* (n. 9) pp. 146–7; Peter: Zenker, *Mitglieder* (n. 11) p. 103; Brixius, *Mitglieder* pp. 38–9; Gregory: Klewitz, *Reformpapsttum* p. 122; Hüls, *Kardinäle* p. 175.

enter the college seems to have been Guido of Castello in 1128, as cardinal deacon of S. Maria in Via Lata (subsequently cardinal priest of S. Marco and Pope Celestine II). He was the pupil of Peter Abelard and one of the most learned men of the age.[55] Innocent II promoted to the cardinalate four lawyers with the title of *magister*, Eugenius III promoted five and Hadrian IV, two.[56] Alexander III, who promoted six lawyers to the college, has often been claimed as the first of the 'lawyer popes'; but J. J. Noonan (1977) has questioned the traditional view of Alexander III as a former professor of canon law in Bologna.[57] Even if Alexander III was not a 'lawyer pope', there is no doubt that the late twelfth century saw the beginning of a long and impressive series of 'lawyer popes' and of a period in which lawyers outnumbered religious in the college of cardinals.

It is tempting to emphasise the contrast between the papal curia of the late eleventh and earlier twelfth century and that of the later twelfth century: the former under the influence of the religious (firstly of old Benedictines and subsequently of the new orders), the latter under the influence of the lawyers. But it is important not to overlook the fact that some of the religious in the twelfth-century curia were also lawyers. The most famous example is the 'lawyer pope' Gregory VIII. He was a *magister* with a distinguished reputation as a canon lawyer ('no one knows the customs and rights of the Roman church as he does,' said Cardinal Henry of Albano in 1187); but Gregory VIII was also a former regular canon of S. Martin in Laon and the founder of a new order of regular canons in Benevento.[58] Of the ten lawyers with the title *magister* who can be identified in the college of cardinals before the schism of 1159, six were also regular canons: Bernard of Porto, Ivo of S. Lorenzo in Damaso, Hildebrand of SS. Apostoli, Guido of S. Pudenziana, Thomas of S. Vitale and Albert of S. Lorenzo in Lucina (Gregory VIII).[59] Two of these cardinals, Hildebrand and Guido, were former

---

[55] Zenker, *Mitglieder* pp. 83–4; Brixius, *Mitglieder* pp. 34–5; D. Luscombe, *The School of Peter Abelard* (Cambridge, 1969) pp. 20–2.

[56] Innocent II: Zenker, *Mitglieder* pp. 77–9, 114, 116, 136. Eugenius III: *ibid.*, pp. 29–32, 107–9, 112–13, 156, 171–4. Hadrian IV: *ibid.*, pp. 125–9, 179–80. See above pp. 106–7.

[57] Brixius, *Mitglieder* (n. 15) pp. 61, 63–4, 66–7. For Alexander's early career see Noonan, 'Rolandus' (n. 14) pp. 21–48. See below pp. 482–3.

[58] Peter of Blois, letter to Archbishop Baldwin of Canterbury: *Epistolae Cantuarienses* in *Chronicles and Memorials of the reign of Richard I 2*, RS 38/2 (1865), 108. See Kehr, 'Gregor VIII.' (n. 14) pp. 248–75.

[59] Zenker, *Mitglieder* (n. 11) pp. 29–30, 77–8, 107, 112, 114, 125–6.

canons of S. Maria in Rheno in Bologna, the city which was already the principal centre of legal studies in western Christendom. We have already seen that in the opinion of Schmale (1961) the regular canons in the college of cardinals were the most important promoters of the 'new spirituality' of the early twelfth century. But these six 'lawyer-canons' may well have been more important to the curia as legal advisers than as promoters of the spiritual ideals of the regular canons. These six cardinals, constituting approximately a quarter of all the canons promoted to the college before 1159, may indeed have been appointed because of their legal qualifications, not because they were regular canons. If that is so, historians may have misinterpreted the apparent preference of the popes of the first half of the twelfth century for promoting regular canons to the college of cardinals.

The evidence for the influence exercised by members of the religious orders in the papal curia is both sparse and difficult to interpret. However, some impression of the papacy's preoccupation with the interests of the religious orders in the period 1073–1198 is given by the surviving papal letters of protection granted to religious houses during these years. Gregory VII issued 54 letters of protection during his pontificate of twelve years. Urban II issued 101 such letters during his eleven-year pontificate, Paschal II issued 141 in an eighteen-and-a-half-year pontificate and Calixtus II, 122 in a pontificate of nearly six years. Honorius II in a pontificate of five years granted 54 letters of protection; Innocent II in thirteen-and-a-half years granted 288 letters; Celestine II granted 44 in a pontificate of five months and Lucius II granted 44 in a pontificate of eleven months. In mid-century the issuing of letters of protection reached its highest level: Eugenius III in a pontificate of eight-and-a-half years issued 397 letters and Anastasius IV in a pontificate of one-and-a-half years issued 74. For the rest of the century the level remained high: Hadrian IV granted 207 letters in a pontificate of four-and-three-quarter years; Alexander III granted 635 in a twenty-two-year pontificate; Lucius III granted 222 in four years. But after the end of the twelfth century fewer letters of protection were issued: Innocent III granted only 394 in eighteen-and-a-half years and the popes of the later thirteenth century issued such letters at the rate of thirty in each pontificate.[60] These statistics certainly suggest that the close alliance

---

[60] Blumenstock, *Schutz* (n. 4) p. 44, using the data provided by P. Jaffé, *Regesta pontificum Romanorum* 1–2. The figure for Gregory VII's pontificate is based on the data in L. Santifaller, *Quellen und Forschungen zum Urkunden- und Kanzleiwesen*

with the religious which was a feature of the Gregorian papacy, continued throughout the twelfth century, doubtless encouraged by the continued presence of the religious in the curia, and began to flag only at the end of the century.

The religious houses most closely linked to the papacy were those which had been surrendered by their founders or patrons to the Roman church as the property of St Peter. Until the middle of the eleventh century it seems to have been customary for monasteries receiving the protection of St Peter to become the property of the papacy. After *ca.* 1050 St Peter's protection no longer automatically involved papal proprietorship: protection became widely diffused but the number of religious houses belonging directly to the papacy remained a small proportion of those enjoying the saint's protection.[61] At the end of the twelfth century these papal proprietary houses were listed in the *Liber Censuum*, the description of papal properties and revenues compiled by the papal chamberlain Cencius (1192). Under the heading, 'These are the names of the abbeys and houses of regular canons of St Peter', Cencius listed 279 houses.[62] In the privileges of Gregory VII such houses are described as 'offered to St Peter and his apostolic see' and 'delivered into the jurisdiction of the holy Roman church'; while Paschal II spoke of a monastery being received 'into the bosom of the Roman church'. Innocent II spoke of a monastery being 'offered to St Peter and his holy Roman church as their own allod'; and Eugenius III described the monastery of Vézelay as 'the allod and patrimony of St Peter'. Hadrian IV used the expression 'monasteries belonging to the Roman church' and in the *Liber Censuum* Cencius referred to 'the monasteries of the lord pope'.[63] All these expressions were chosen to emphasise that full proprietorship was vested in the Roman church. The religious communities residing in these houses were granted the unrestricted use of the houses and their possessions: but these properties remained

---

Papst Gregors VII. 1 (Studi e Testi 190: Vatican City, 1957), including privileges no longer extant but mentioned in other documents.

[61] F. Pfurtscheller, *Die Privilegierung des Zisterzienserordens im Rahmen der allgemeinen Schutz- und Exemtionsgeschichte vom Anfang bis zur Bulle 'Parvus Fons' (1265)* (Europäische Hochschulschriften, Reihe 23, 13: Bern, 1972) pp. 10–13.

[62] *Liber Censuum* 1, 243–7. See V. Pfaff, 'Sankt Peters Abteien im 12. Jahrhundert', *ZSSRG KA* 57 (1971), 150–95. See also below p. 269.

[63] P. Fabre, *Etude sur le Liber Censuum de l'Eglise romaine* (Bibliothèque des Ecoles françaises d'Athènes et de Rome 72: Paris, 1892) p. 69; G. Schreiber, *Kurie und Kloster im 12. Jahrhundert* 1 (Kirchenrechtliche Abhandlungen 65–8: Stuttgart, 1910), 31, 51; Maccarrone, 'Primato romano' (n. 5) pp. 50–1.

entirely at the disposal of the papacy. In the late eleventh century the papacy exercised this right of disposal in order to contribute to the building of the monastic empire of Cluny. Papal proprietary monasteries in France – Vézelay, Sauxillanges, Saint-Gilles, Montierneuf, Gigny, Saint-Germain in Auxerre, La Charité-sur-Loire – were commended to the care of the abbot of Cluny.[64] The Gregorian conception of the papal proprietary monastery is expressed in Gregory VII's privilege entrusting a papal monastery to Abbot Hugh of Cluny. The privilege speaks of the pope's special duty of promoting 'sacred learning and the religious life' in those houses 'which belong to the Roman church's own jurisdiction'. In order to fulfil this duty, 'the government and guardianship' of the monastery was committed in perpetuity to Abbot Hugh and his successors 'on our behalf' (*in nostra vice*).[65] The papal proprietary rights remained undisturbed: the abbots of Cluny were to act as the pope's vicars. The point was made more emphatically by Eugenius III when he entrusted to Cluny the task of reforming the abbey of Saint-Benoit sur Loire, Fleury: 'although . . . we have ordered the religious observance to be reformed by the brethren of Cluny, the monastery itself is to be subject to no one except the Roman pontiff'.[66]

The abbey of Cluny was intensely aware of its special status as an abbey of St Peter. Two of the twelfth-century biographies record the story of St Peter appearing to one of the abbey's peasants to give warning of Abbot Hugh's imminent death (1109). Asked by the saint whose field he was ploughing, the peasant answered: 'that of St Peter and the lord abbot of Cluny'. 'It is my field,' said the saint, 'and the abbot is my servant (*famulus*).'[67] Gregory VII likewise emphasised the closeness of Cluny's relationship with St Peter. When he confirmed the privileges of Cluny in the Roman synod of March 1080, Gregory pronounced a eulogy on the abbey which focussed on this special relationship. Cluny was 'attached to St Peter and to this [Roman] church by a special right as a personal possession'. Her abbots and monks had 'never bowed down to any foreign or worldly

---

[64] Cowdrey, *Cluniacs* (n. 3) pp. 82–3, 85–7, 95–7; Pfaff, 'Abteien' (n. 62) pp. 166–8, 171–2.

[65] Santifaller, *Quellen und Forschungen* (n. 60) pp. 125–6 (no. 126).

[66] Eugenius III, *JL* 9632: S. Loewenfeld, *Epistolae pontificum Romanorum ineditae* (Leipzig, 1885) p. 110.

[67] Gilo, *Vita sancti Hugonis abbatis* II.7; Hugh, *Vita sancti Hugonis abbatis* c. 28 ed. H. E. J. Cowdrey, 'Memorials of Abbot Hugh of Cluny (1049–1109)', *SG* 11 (1978), 97, 136.

power, remaining subject to, and under the protection of St Peter and this church alone'.[68] This eulogy marked the end of a crisis in the affairs of Cluny, in which the abbey's special status, its 'Roman liberty', had encountered opposition, but had been vindicated by the papacy. The crisis of 1079–80 began with complaints by the diocesan of Cluny, Bishop Landeric of Mâcon, supported by the metropolitan, Archbishop Gebuin of Lyons, concerning Cluny's alleged violation of certain local rights of the church of Mâcon. The dispute soon developed into an episcopal attack on the most controversial aspect of Cluny's liberty: exemption from the bishop's spiritual jurisdiction. Abbot Hugh of Cluny appealed to the pope, who sent the legate Cardinal bishop Peter of Albano to Cluny to uphold the papal privileges against the bishop's aggression. Gregory VII's championing of Cluny's liberty culminated in the declaration in the Roman synod of 1080 that Cluny was 'to possess fully and perpetually the immunity and liberty which have been granted to her by the Roman see'.[69]

The hostility of the diocesan and the metropolitan towards the privileged status of Cluny reemerged a generation later in Calixtus II's council of Rheims (October 1119). Archbishop Humbald of Lyons, Bishop Berard of Mâcon and other suffragans denounced Cluny for having usurped diocesan rights over churches, tithes and ordinations. Abbot Pontius of Cluny replied that 'the church of Cluny is subject to the Roman church alone' and that it was for the pope himself to defend his church. Cluny's privileges were successfully defended before the council by John of Crema, cardinal priest of S. Grisogono, one of the pope's closest advisers. Cardinal John represented the papal protection of Cluny's privileges as an expression of the 'Roman authority' by which the whole Church was governed.

Since the abbey of Cluny is subject only to the pope and he, who by God's command is over all men on earth, protects it, Roman authority strengthens the privileges of the Cluniacs and on God's behalf forbids all the sons of the Church rashly to deprive them of their former liberty, to despoil them of their possessions or to burden them with unaccustomed exactions.[70]

[68] Cowdrey, *Cluniacs* (n. 3) pp. 272–3.
[69] H. E. J. Cowdrey, 'Cardinal Peter of Albano's legatine journey to Cluny', *Journal of Theological Studies* n.s., 24 (1973), 481–91; *idem, Cluniacs* (n. 3) pp. 51–7.
[70] Orderic Vitalis, *Historia ecclesiastica* XII.21 ed. M. Chibnall 6 (Oxford, 1978), 268–72. See Maccarrone, 'Primato romano' (n. 5) p. 55.

To the bishop of Mâcon and the archbishop of Lyons Cluny's special status represented an affront to episcopal authority. Cluny's exemption was contrary to canon law, since the council of Chalcedon (451) had stated that 'monks are to be subject to the bishop'.[71] To the adherents of the new monastic ideals of *ca*. 1100 Cluny's special relationship with Rome seemed to have tempted her from the path of true monasticism. The collaboration of Abbot Hugh of Cluny and the Gregorian papacy had led Cluniacs into activities more appropriate for secular clerks than for monks, whose duty was to renounce the world. Both these two distinct criticisms appeared in the famous polemic of Bernard of Clairvaux against the monastic ideal of Cluny (1124–5). In reply to Bernard's criticisms Abbot Peter the Venerable defended Cluny's privileges – in language similar to that of Gregory VII in 1080 and Cardinal John of Crema in 1119 – as an expression of the supremacy of the Roman church. Answering Bernard's charge that the Cluniacs refused to be subject to 'their own bishop' (that is, the bishop of Mâcon), Peter wrote:

we reply that this is the exact opposite of the truth, since it is clear that we have our own bishop. For who is to be found more appropriate, more fitting, worthier than the Roman bishop? . . . It is our boast that we have only one bishop, the greatest of bishops; we are bound in special obedience to him alone; if (which God forbid) it becomes necessary, we can be placed under interdict, suspended and excommunicated by him alone. The indisputable authority of the [Roman] see itself has sanctioned this.[72]

The spiritual exemption of the monasteries subject to the Roman church was one of the gravest points of contention between the episcopate and the reform papacy in the late eleventh and early twelfth century. Gregory VII conceived of spiritual exemption as a defensive weapon, intended to protect reformed monasteries from the malice or incompetence of their diocesan. He explained to Bishop Cunibert of Turin in 1075 that 'the holy fathers have often freed monasteries from their diocesan bishop and bishops from their metropolitan in order to deliver them from the tyranny of their superiors; they have decreed that they should be permanently free and be attached to the apostolic see as members to their head'.[73]

[71] Council of Chalcedon c. 4, 8: Mansi, *Sacra Concilia* 7, 374, 375. Cf. Gratian, *Decretum* C.16 q.1 c.12; C.18 q.2 c.10. See Cowdrey, *Cluniacs* (n. 3) p. 24.

[72] Peter the Venerable, *Letter* 28 ed. G. Constable, *The Letters of Peter the Venerable* I (Cambridge, Mass., 1967), 79. See A. H. Bredero, 'Cluny et Cîteaux au XIIe siècle. Les origines de la controverse', *Studi Medievali* ser. 3, 12 (1971), 135–75.

[73] Gregory VII, *Registrum* II.69, p. 228.

However, in the hands of a pope hostile to the episcopate, spiritual exemption might become an offensive weapon, capable of undermining a bishop's authority in his diocese. In January 1075 Gregory VII confided to Abbot Hugh of Cluny his growing conviction that bishops were incapable of assisting the papacy in reforming the Church, since they were either simoniac or disobedient. Secular rulers were equally unsatisfactory, being consumed by their love of wealth and of their own honour. The papacy could rely only on the reformed monks and on 'those who love St Peter' among the feudal aristocracy.[74] During the Investiture Contest in Germany this alliance of papacy, monks and princes became a reality. The reformed monasteries of Hirsau, Schaffhausen and St Blasien became the refuges of the papal party and 'wandering monks' from reformed houses 'sowed the greatest discord everywhere' by propagating the doctrines of the Gregorian papacy.[75] A further effect of Gregory VII's concern for the protection of reformed monasteries was the acquisition of spiritual exemption by monasteries which were not among the favoured few with papal privileges guaranteeing their special relationship with St Peter and the Roman church. This proliferation of spiritual exemption was not the deliberate policy of the reform papacy: it arose accidentally from the circumstances of the Investiture Contest. The great majority of the privileges which Gregory VII issued to monasteries, while conferring papal protection, did not exempt the monks from the spiritual jurisdiction of their diocesan: protection was granted 'saving the canonical reverence' (or 'canonical jurisdiction') 'of the diocesan bishop'. But after the outbreak of the Investiture Contest, when many imperial bishops fell under papal excommunication because of their disobedience, this clause in favour of the rights of the diocesan necessarily became conditional. Papal privileges began to require subjection to the diocesan 'if he is a catholic and in communion with the holy see'.[76] Gregory VII's privilege for the south German monastery of Schaffhausen (1080) is quite explicit: in order to ensure that the monastery enjoys the gift of 'Roman liberty', 'if ever the bishop of Constance [Schaffhausen's diocesan] is not in accord with the holy

---

[74] *Registrum* II.49, pp. 188–90.
[75] Bernold of St Blasien, *Chronicon* 1083, 1091, *MGH SS* 5, 439, 452–3; *Annales Augustani* 1075, ibid., 3, 128. See Hauck, *Kirchengeschichte Deutschlands* 3, 872–6; E. Werner, *Pauperes Christi. Studien zu sozial-religiösen Bewegungen im Zeitalter des Reformpapsttums* (Leipzig, 1956) pp. 89–100; H. Jakobs, *Die Hirsauer* (Cologne, 1961) pp. 204–15; Cowdrey, *Cluniacs* (n. 3) pp. 207–10.
[76] Fabre, *Etude* (n. 63) p. 93.

see and is disobedient, . . . the abbot has full permission to request any catholic bishop to fulfil all the episcopal functions, such as ordinations and consecrations, or to have recourse to the holy see'.[77] The excommunication of a bishop created a temporary spiritual exemption, which monasteries might well attempt to render permanent.

The proliferation of spiritual exemption seems also to have been accidentally assisted by an attempt on the part of the curia to clarify the significance of the monastic *census*. The *census* was the regular payment which since the eighth century had been made to the Roman church by the monasteries which enjoyed the protection of St Peter.[78] At the beginning of the eleventh century papal privileges began to contain the idea that the monastic *census* was paid 'in respect of the liberty conceded [to the monastery] and as evidence of it': that is, as a sign of the freedom from secular control which St Peter's protection conferred.[79] This idea of the payment of *census* as proof of a monastery's freedom was made explicit in the privileges of Urban II, in a formula which was henceforward used regularly in papal privileges that confirmed or introduced the payment of *census*. The formula appears for the first time in a privilege of 19 May 1089 for the canons regular of St John of Ripoll. 'As proof of this liberty received from the Roman church (*ad indicium perceptae huius a Romana ecclesia libertatis*) it is fitting that Your Honour should pay three *mancusi* of the mint of Valencia to the Lateran palace every year.'[80] The 'liberty' conferred by this privilege is freedom from secular control: nothing is said about spiritual exemption. The monastery is to be subject to the diocesan (although there is a characteristic late eleventh-century reservation: obedience is due 'as long as [the bishop] treats the aforesaid abbey kindly'). The formula *ad indicium huius perceptae libertatis* is also used in Urban II's privileges for Saint-Pierre de Blesle, Notre-Dame de Saintes and Sainte-Croix de Quimperlé, which likewise confer only secular freedom.[81] However, the same formula appears in Urban II's privilege confirming the rights of La Trinité de Vendôme, which had enjoyed spiritual exemption since the early eleventh century; and his privilege conferring on Aurillac the right to

---

[77] Gregory VII, *Registrum* VII.24, pp. 504–5.
[78] See below pp. 269–73.
[79] E.g. Sylvester II, *JL* 3900, *MPL* 139, 271C. See Fabre, *Etude*, pp. 74–85; A. Dumas, 'Protection apostolique', *Dictionnaire de droit canonique* 7 (Paris, 1965), 383.
[80] Urban II, *JL* 5395, *MPL* 151, 300D. See Fabre, *Etude* pp. 94–5.
[81] Urban II, *JL* 5572: 423B; *JL* 5590, 5732: *Analecta iuris pontificii* 10 (Rome, 1855), 539, 514.

'summon whatever bishop it preferred' to perform ordinations and consecrations in the monastery.[82] In these latter two cases the 'liberty' of which the payment of *census* was a proof, was exemption from both spiritual and secular authority. The *census* formula which came into general use after 1089 confusingly used the term *libertas* to describe both complete exemption and partial exemption; and this inevitably had the effect of blurring the distinction between these two different types of freedom. The process continued during the early twelfth century as the papal chancery, in renewing the privileges of monastic houses, omitted the detailed clauses of the original privileges which recounted the circumstances in which the *census* had been imposed and replaced them with the statement that the *census* was the 'proof of this liberty received from the Roman church'.[83] The curia had no conscious intention of proliferating spiritual exemption by deliberately effacing the distinction between temporal and spiritual liberty. The main concern of the curial officials responsible for these privileges was to emphasise that *libertas*, of whatever kind, depended on the regular payment of *census*. Hence the most important record of the monasteries enjoying papal protection, the *Liber Censuum* of 1192, does not differentiate between those houses enjoying spiritual and those enjoying temporal liberty, but is concerned solely with the amount of *census* paid.[84]

Episcopal objections to monastic claims of spiritual exemption became especially voluble in the pontificate of Calixtus II. We have already seen how the liberty of Cluny came under attack in Calixtus' council of Rheims (1119). In the First Lateran Council (Lent 1123) an even noisier debate was provoked by the pope's renewal of the privileges of Monte Cassino. There was a general attack on insubordinate monks. 'They hunger insatiably for the rights of bishops . . . they strive by fair means and foul to destroy what belongs to bishops.'[85] The outcome of the debate was canon 16 of the First Lateran Council, which restated the principle of the fourth canon of Chalcedon (451). 'Following in the footsteps of the holy fathers, we confirm that monks are to be subject to their own bishops with all humility and are to show due obedience and devout subjection in all

---

[82] Urban II, *JL* 5511: *Analecta iuris pontificii* 10, 534; *JL* 5563: J. Pflugk-Harttung, *Acta pontificum Romanorum inedita* 1 (Tübingen-Stuttgart, 1880), 59. See Fabre, *Etude* (n. 63) pp. 93, 94, 96.

[83] Fabre, *Etude* pp. 96-7.

[84] See below pp. 269-70.   [85] *Chronica monasterii Casinensis* IV.78: (n. 26) p. 542.

things to them, as to the masters and pastors of the Church of God.'[86]
This canon did not in fact diminish the rights of Monte Cassino,
Cluny and other 'monasteries of St Peter'; but it inhibited the
ambitions of less privileged houses. In the pontificate of Calixtus II
the episcopal reaction against monastic privileges, after being held in
check for the past fifty years by the reform papacy, was at last permitted to influence the legislation of a papal council. There were two
main reasons for this development. Firstly, the restoration of peace
in the Church by means of the concordat of Worms (1122) rendered
unnecessary the Gregorian alliance of papacy and monks against disobedient bishops (just as it ended the temporary spiritual exemption
enjoyed by monasteries situated in the dioceses of excommunicate
bishops). Secondly, Calixtus II himself was the first non-monastic
pope since 1073. According to gossip recorded by a Spanish and a
French chronicler, Calixtus' predecessor, Gelasius II, on his deathbed
in Cluny named as his two possible successors, Abbot Pontius of
Cluny and Archbishop Guido of Vienne. The latter – the non-
monastic candidate – was elected.[87] Whatever truth there may be in
this anecdote, it reveals that in some quarters at least the election of
Calixtus II was regarded as a conscious departure from the monastic
papacy of the immediate past. Two famous cases of the 1120s,
involving the two most illustrious of the 'monasteries of St Peter',
Cluny and Monte Cassino, seem to provide striking evidence of a
break with the monastic past. The rule of Abbot Pontius of Cluny
provoked bitter dissension in the abbey: he came to Rome and
Calixtus II declared that he had abdicated. When in 1126, denying the
intention of abdicating, Pontius tried to regain the office of abbot, he
was deposed by Honorius II and died in a Roman prison. Likewise in
1126 Honorius II deposed Abbot Oderisius of Monte Cassino after
he disobeyed repeated summonses to Rome to answer charges
brought by local enemies of Monte Cassino.[88] The fates of the two

---

[86] *Concilium Lateranense I* c. 16: *Conciliorum Oecumenicorum Decreta* p. 195.

[87] *Historia Compostellana* II.9, *MPL* 170, 1043B; Geoffrey of Vigeois, *Chronicon*
c. 42, *MGH SS* 26, 200. See H. E. J. Cowdrey, 'Abbot Pontius of Cluny (1109–22/
6)', *SG* 11 (1978), 219–21. See also above p. 64.

[88] Tellenbach, 'Pontius' (n. 32) pp. 13–55; H. Hoffmann, 'Petrus Diaconus, die
Herren von Tusculum und der Sturz Oderisius' II. von Montecassino', *DA* 27
(1971), 1–109; P. Zerbi, 'Intorno allo scisma di Ponzio, abate di Cluny (1122–26)'
in *Studi Storici in onore di Ottorino Bertolini* 2 (Pisa, 1972), 835–91; J. Leclercq, A. H.
Bredero and P. Zerbi, 'Encore sur Pons de Cluny et Pierre le Vénérable', *Aevum.
Rassegna di scienze storiche, linguistiche e filologiche* 48 (1974), 134–49; Cowdrey,
'Pontius' (n. 87) pp. 181–268.

abbots were essentially dissimilar in character. Oderisius was probably the victim of a personal vendetta on the part of Honorius II, while Pontius was the victim of faction-fighting in his abbey. However, in both cases among the factors which precipitated the fall of the abbot was the attack on monastic spiritual exemption which also manifested itself in the councils of Calixtus II.

Historians have long regarded the pontificate of Calixtus II as 'a cesura in the history of the papacy': a reaction against the Gregorian past, which showed itself in papal relations both with the secular powers and with the episcopate and the monasteries.[89] As far as the monastic 'policy' of the papacy is concerned, there was certainly a change in direction, although it was by no means a violent change. Calixtus II defended and confirmed the privileges of Cluny and Monte Cassino when they were attacked in the councils of 1119 and 1123. Certainly canon 16 of the First Lateran Council stated that 'monks are to be subject to their own bishops'. But the Gregorian papacy had also respected this principle, so long as bishops were 'catholic and in communion with the holy see'. It was the schism of the late eleventh century which had compelled the papacy to sanction monastic disobedience. Canon 16 of the First Lateran Council was an attempt to restore the principle of the council of Chalcedon, now that the Investiture Contest was over. Indeed the dominant theme of Calixtus II's pontificate was the restoration of order in the aftermath of the Investiture Contest: especially the restoration of the role of the episcopate in the government of the Church, a role which had inevitably been undermined by Gregorian emergency measures against excommunicate bishops. Calixtus' anxiety to restore episcopal authority must have encouraged the bishops' complaints about the spiritual exemption of the monasteries. Calixtus, while no doubt sympathetic to these complaints in cases of illicit claims of monastic exemption, refused to disturb the rights of those 'monasteries of St Peter' to which his predecessors had granted 'Roman liberty'. He did not need to be reminded by the monks of Monte Cassino in 1123 that chaos would ensue 'if the concessions of the Roman pontiff are violated'.[90] The papal privileges of the exempt houses and the spiritual relationship with the Roman church which they created, were an important expression of the papal primacy and must therefore be respected by the episcopate.

Throughout the twelfth century these privileges continued to be

---

[89] See above p. 49 and below pp. 382–3, 444.
[90] *Chronica monasterii Casinensis* IV.78: (n. 26) p. 543.

reissued and each reissue gave the papal chancery an opportunity for the inclusion of a 'primacy arenga'. This, the opening protocol of the papal privilege, was an elaborate reminder that 'the holy Roman church, who holds from God a principate over all the churches, like a diligent mother provides for the individual churches with constant vigilance: all must have recourse to her, as to their head and origin, to be defended by her authority'.[91] The special relationship of exempt houses with the papacy continued to flourish as in the Gregorian period; but from the 1120s onwards it was no longer regarded as a weapon to be used against the authority of a disaffected episcopate. Increasingly this special relationship was regarded by the curia, not as a means of conferring independence on the 'monasteries of St Peter', but rather as a means of subjecting them to the *correctio* of the pope. This emphasis on the exclusive right of the pope to 'correct' the exempt houses is apparent in the papal proceedings against Pontius of Cluny and Oderisius of Monte Cassino. The papal desire for closer control over its own proprietary houses is evident in the attempt of Innocent II in 1137 to exact an oath of fealty from the abbey of Monte Cassino. The monks protested that the papal protection which they enjoyed did not entail a relationship of dependence; but the papal legate, Cardinal Gerard of S. Croce (the future Lucius II) insisted that the rights which derived from the papal primacy included that of demanding an oath from the abbot of Monte Cassino, by virtue of the privilege which reserved his consecration of the pope alone.[92] The clearest statement of the pope's rights over exempt houses appears in a letter of Alexander III, which rebukes the monastery of All Saints, Bari, for refusing to receive the archbishop of Bari, whom the pope had sent to reform the house. 'Since the aforesaid monastery has no bishop and master except the Roman pontiff, not only the correction of your persons but also the care and disposal of the whole monastery are our concern.'[93]

This insistence that the special relationship between the exempt monasteries and the papacy existed essentially for the purposes of reform was partly a response to continued criticisms of spiritual

---

[91] Hadrian IV, *JL* – : W. Holtzmann, *Papsturkunden in England* 3 (*Abhandlungen der Gesellschaft der Wissenschaften in Göttingen, phil.-hist. Klasse* 3. Folge 33, 1952, 234–5 (no. 100). See H. Fichtenau, *Arenga. Spätantike und Mittelalter im Spiegel von Urkundenformen* (Cologne–Graz, 1957) pp. 101–12.

[92] *Chronica monasterii Casinensis* IV.108: (n. 26) p. 572. See Schmale, *Schisma* (n. 9) p. 172.

[93] Alexander III, *JL* 12631: Pflugk-Harttung, *Acta* (n. 82) 3, 242. See Maccarrone, 'Primato romano' (n. 5) pp. 59–60.

exemption. These criticisms were more formidable than those of the bishops in the councils of Calixtus II. They came from the influential representatives of the new religious orders, who sought to restore the way of life of the primitive, apostolic Church. According to their standards, spiritual exemption was a human innovation which disturbed the good order which God had ordained for the Church. The theologian Gerhoch of Reichersberg, for example, in 1161/2 attacked 'the innovations (*novae ordinationes*) by which certain monasteries are placed by their founders under the special obedience of the Roman pontiff'. 'I do not approve of this and regard it as a sign of disorder, as if the hand were attached to the ear without the arm between them or the foot were attached to the thigh with no leg in-between.'[94] The most serious grievance was the large number of spurious claims to exemption, which the legislation of the First Lateran Council seemed to have done nothing to abate. This is one of the themes of the treatise *De consideratione*, which Bernard of Clairvaux addressed to Eugenius III *ca.* 1150. 'There is a very great difference between those monasteries which are placed by their founders in the power of the holy see and those which strive, by attaching themselves to Rome, to withdraw from the obedience which they owe to their bishops and which they refuse to give them.' For the papacy to recognise the claims of houses in this second category was intolerable. 'There is no fruit, except that it makes bishops more insolent and monks more dissolute.'[95] There is no reason to believe that the twelfth-century papacy actively encouraged these spurious claims: the papal attitude remained that expressed in canon 16 of the First Lateran Council of 1123. The grievances originated in the *census* formula of 1089, still used by the papal chancery in privileges for religious houses – *ad indicium huius perceptae libertatis* – which failed to differentiate between temporal and spiritual freedom. Monasteries which enjoyed only temporal liberty could exploit the ambiguity of this formula and claim that the *census* which they paid to the Roman church exempted them from the spiritual jurisdiction of their diocesan.

Two letters of Alexander III concerning the diocese of Novara reveal the curia's attempts to deal with such cases of deception. The first (of unknown date) is directed to the brethren of San Silvano di Romagnano, about whom Bishop Boniface of Novara had complained to the pope. 'You disdain to show the obedience and rever-

---

[94] Gerhoch of Reichersberg, *De investigatione Antichristi* I.72, MGH Libelli 3, 391.
[95] Bernard of Clairvaux, *De consideratione* III.4.18, III.4.15, MPL 182, 769B, 767C.

ence which the other churches of the bishopric of Novara pay to [the bishop], in the belief that your church is freed from subjection to him because of the *census* which you pay annually to St Peter and to us.' However, the *census* due from San Silvano was payment in return for temporal protection, not for spiritual exemption. 'Just as not all the churches which belong especially to the Roman church are subject to *census*, so not all the churches subject to *census* are exempt from the subjection and obedience due to bishops.'[96] Here is an attempt to eliminate the ambiguity in the conventional formula describing *census* 'as proof of the liberty received from the Roman church': payment of *census* cannot be regarded as evidence of spiritual exemption. The second letter – addressed *ca.* 1177 to the papal legate, the subdeacon Albert, and concerned with the claims of the monastery of San Pietro di Carpignano – makes this point even more forcibly.

The privileges of churches must be examined and their content very carefully noted so that if it is evident that the church which owes *census* belongs especially to the jurisdiction of St Peter and that the annual *census* is paid as a proof of the receipt of liberty, [the church] may deservedly enjoy the special prerogative. But if the *census* is paid as proof of the receipt of protection, [the church] is evidently not withdrawn from the jurisdiction of the diocesan bishop.[97]

This decretal removes all ambiguity from the *census* formula, *ad indicium perceptae libertatis*. Henceforward the term *libertas* in this formula is to be understood as meaning exclusively spiritual exemption. The lesser privilege of the monasteries which enjoyed the temporal protection of St Peter is given a separate formula: *ad indicium perceptae protectionis*. The words *libertas* and *protectio*, which in the vague terminology of the Gregorian period seem to be synonymous terms, are now sharply juxtaposed as quite distinct in meaning.

This greater precision in terminology is characteristic of Alexander III's privileges for religious houses: with relatively few exceptions they distinguish carefully between *libertas* and *protectio*.[98] Alexander's privileges were also the first to make regular use of the formula which in the late twelfth century became the standard means of defining the relationship of an exempt house with the papacy: the formula *nullo mediante*, 'with no intermediary'. This formula appears

[96] Alexander III, *JL* 14237: *Collectio Lipsiensis* 34.4 ed. E. Friedberg, *Quinque compilationes antiquae nec non collectio canonum Lipsiensis* (Leipzig, 1882) p. 198.
[97] Alexander III, *JL* 14037: *Decretales Gregorii IX* v.33.8.
[98] Fabre, *Etude* (n. 63) p. 102.

sporadically in the privileges of Innocent II: in two privileges for St Peter's, Westminster (1133 and 1139) – which are, however, of doubtful authenticity – and in a privilege for S. Croce di Sassovivo (1138).[99] The privileges of Alexander III consistently use the *nullo mediante* formula: an exempt house is 'a special daughter belonging to the Roman church with no intermediary'.[100] The formula was applied not only to monasteries and houses of regular canons but also to bishoprics: to Glasgow by Alexander III; to all the Scottish bishoprics by Celestine III (in the bull *Filia specialis* of 1192).[101] 'We know that the Roman pontiffs granted most of these exemptions for the sake of the peace of the monasteries and because of the tyranny of the bishops.' So a critic of exemptions, Archbishop Richard of Canterbury wrote to the pope in 1178, in a fierce denunciation of the exemption granted to the abbey of Malmesbury. The archbishop's argument was that the days of episcopal tyranny were now past: nowadays the bishops could be trusted to safeguard the *quies* of religious houses.[102] The papacy of the later twelfth century was indeed committed to alliance with the bishops in the interests of reform; but it never lost the conviction that the best guarantee of monastic peace was the protection of St Peter.

The papacy's purpose in conferring the protection of St Peter and 'Roman liberty' was first and foremost to achieve the reform of the religious life. Hence the clause which appeared in papal privileges with increasing frequency from the late eleventh century: a warning that the favours which they conferred would cease, if the recipients failed to observe the Rule of their order. To cite an early example: Urban II's privilege for the canons regular of St John of Ripoll (1089) granted protection 'as long as they and their successors keep to the path of religion according to apostolic discipline'.[103] The earliest papal privilege for the abbey of Cîteaux, that of Paschal II in 1100, places abbot and monks under the 'special' protection of the apos-

---

[99] Holtzmann, *Papsturkunden in England* (n. 91) 1, 241, 244 (nos. 17, 20). Innocent II, *JL* 7898: V. de Donato, *Le carte dell'abbazia di S. Croce di Sassovivo* 2 (Florence, 1975), 117–19 (no. 97).

[100] Schreiber, *Kurie und Kloster* (n. 63) 1, 47–55.

[101] R. K. Hannay, 'The date of the "Filia specialis" bull', *Scottish Historical Review* 23 (1926), 171–7; R. Foreville, *L'Eglise et la royauté en Angleterre sous Henri II Plantagenet* (Paris, 1943) p. 514.

[102] Richard of Canterbury, *Epistola*, MPL 200, 1459A.

[103] Urban II, *JL* 5395: (n. 80) 300B. See M. Maccarrone, 'I papi del secolo XII e la vita comune e regolare del clero' in *La vita comune del clero nei secoli XI e XII* 1 (Miscellanea del Centro di Studi Medioevali 3: Milan, 1962) p. 356.

tolic see 'as long as you and your successors remain in that discipline
and observance of frugality which you observe today'.[104] When
Calixtus II conferred the protection of St Peter on the Cistercian
monastery of Bonneval (1120), the privilege was granted 'so that
henceforth, with the Lord's protection, the discipline of monastic
religion may be preserved there'.[105] The clause making papal protection dependent on *regularitas*, the continued observance of the
Rule, appears in the privileges which Honorius II granted to the
Camaldolese and the Premonstratensians. In the pontificate of
Innocent II the *regularitas* clause appears in all papal privileges for
monasteries and houses of regular canons. 'First and foremost,' says
Innocent's privilege for the canons regular of Auxerre (1131), 'we
command that the canonical order according to the Rule of St
Augustine shall be preserved in perpetuity in that church.'[106] The
primary objective of the papacy in intervening to protect the
religious was to ensure the perpetual observance of the Rule. If,
therefore, the religious relaxed their observance or failed in some
other way to fulfil the requirements of their papal privilege, their
misconduct would provoke immediate papal intervention. Eugenius
III, as befitted a monastic pope, was particularly vigilant on the subject of regular observance. In the case of the abbey of Saint-Benoit
sur Loire, Fleury, he 'ordered the religious observance to be
reformed by the brethren of Cluny'. He quashed the election of an
abbot of Fulda in 1148 and his legate deposed an abbot of Corvey in
the same year, in order to ensure the observance of the Rule in these
houses.[107] Disobedience towards the Roman church was of course
the most heinous offence which a religious house could commit. In
1147 Eugenius III punished the abbey of Baumes-Les-Messiers for its
failure to obey a papal legate: he deprived it of its status as an abbey
and reduced it to a priory, under the jurisdiction of the abbot of
Cluny. (In 1155 Hadrian IV confirmed the punishment of 'the over-
weening rebels' and made this deprivation permanent.)[108] When

---

[104] Paschal II, *JL* 5842, MPL 163, 47D. See Pfurtscheller, *Privilegierung* (n. 61) pp. 24,
60, 67.

[105] Calixtus II, *JL* 6812, MPL 163, 1157D–1158A.

[106] Innocent II, *JL* 7486, MPL 179, 101C. See J. Dubois, 'Les ordres religieux au XIIe
siècle selon la Curie romaine', *Revue Bénédictine* 78 (1968), 285–7.

[107] Eugenius III, *JL* 9632: (n. 66) p. 110; *JL* 9232, 9226, MPL 180, 1335AB, 1332BC.

[108] Eugenius III, *JL* 9061: *ibid.*, 1227BC; Hadrian IV, *JL* 10053, MPL 188, 1415C–
1417C. See R. Sejourné, 'Baume-Les-Messiers', *Dictionnaire d'histoire et de
géographie ecclésiastique* 6 (Paris, 1932), 1464–8.

after the outbreak of the schism of 1159 Abbot Hugh III of Cluny declared for Emperor Frederick I and the antipope Victor IV, Alexander III deposed Hugh and ordered the election of a new abbot (1161). On this occasion the pope suspended one of Cluny's most important privileges, the right of free election. Alexander ordered the bishop of Beauvais 'not to hesitate in putting another in [Hugh's] place, even though the privilege which is said to have been bestowed on the church of Cluny by the Roman pontiffs . . . is cited as an impediment and obstacle'.[109] The clearest papal statement that privileges can be lost through misconduct appears in the decree *Ad abolendam* of the synod of Verona, Lucius III's decree of November 1184 for the suppression of heresy. The decree states that religious who fall into heresy automatically lose their 'privileges of liberty'.[110]

The papal privileges conferred on religious houses were not, therefore, necessarily perpetual and immutable: they could be withdrawn, suspended, diminished or enhanced, according to the conduct of the recipients. Master Gratian of Bologna stated this important principle in the section of his *Decretum* devoted to privileges. 'The privileges of churches are to be preserved undisturbed at all times and it is forbidden to any to contravene them – except with the authority of him by whom they were granted.' The Roman church 'may out of motives of piety or necessity alter either wholly or partially what she has previously conceded'.[111] Gratian's statement was elaborated *ca.* 1150 in a gloss by the canonist Master Roland. 'It appears that the Roman pontiff can alter ancient privileges. On this subject it must be noted that the Roman church . . . confers right and authority on the sacred canons; that she never binds herself to them, but freely judges them and reserves to herself the right to change them.'[112] The papal privileges for religious houses are indeed an important source for the study of the development of that vital aspect of the Roman primacy, the idea of the pope as legislator. Students of this development have inevitably paid close attention to the statement of Gregory VII in his memorandum

---

[109] Alexander III, *JL* 10660, 10661, *MPL* 200, 112AD, 113A–114C. See Maccarrone, 'Primato romano' (n. 5) pp. 85–6.

[110] Lucius III, *JL* 15109, *MPL* 201, 1299D–1300A.

[111] Gratian, *Decretum* C.25 q.2 c.21, 25.

[112] Rolandus, Glossa a C.25 q.2 in F. Thaner, *Die Summa magistri Rolandi* (Innsbruck, 1874) p. 108. 'Master Roland' has often been identified with Cardinal Roland Bandinelli (Alexander III); but see Noonan, 'Rolandus' (n. 14) pp. 21–48.

Dictatus pape, that the pope has 'the right to make new laws'.[113]
Equally significant as evidence of Gregory's conception of the pope's
legislative authority is his cancellation of three of the privileges of his
predecessor, Alexander II. He annulled a privilege for S. Maria di
Butrio (Tortona) because he regarded it as suspect, a privilege for
Schaffhausen because it was 'against the statutes of the holy fathers'
and a privilege for Chaise-Dieu (Clermont) because it contravened
'righteousness'.[114] Gregory declared in 1078 that 'certain things can
be conceded in privileges with respect to a particular case, person,
time and place, which, if considerations of necessity or utility
demand it, may lawfully be changed'.[115] This idea became enshrined
in the reservation clause – 'saving the authority of the apostolic see'
(*salva sedis apostolicae auctoritate*) – which begins to appear in the papal
privileges of Celestine II. From the pontificate of Alexander III
onwards, in those privileges which conferred protection but not
spiritual exemption, this reservation clause was amalgamated with
that which protected the rights of the diocesan bishop: 'saving the
authority of the apostolic see and the canonical jurisdiction of the
diocesan'.[116]

Privileges for religious houses provided the papacy with its earliest
opportunities of exercising its controversial power of changing the
law. Of similar importance in the development of the concept of the
papal primacy was the relationship of the papacy with the new
religious orders which sprang up in the last quarter of the eleventh
and the first quarter of the twelfth century. These 'new orders' – the
monks of Chartreuse, Cîteaux, Fontevrault, Savigny, the Knights of
the Temple and of the Hospital; the canons of St Rufus in Avignon,
Prémontré, Arrouaise and Saint-Victor in Paris – claimed to have
restored the ancient forms of the religious life. The recognition given
by the pope to these claims – expressed by conferring the protection
of St Peter on the monks and canons – was an impressive demonstration of the papal power of legitimation. The 'new orders' were

---

[113] Gregory VII, *Registrum* II.55a (*Dictatus pape* 7), p. 203. See H. Fuhrmann, '"Quod
catholicus non habeatur, qui non concordat Romanae ecclesiae." Randnotizen
zum Dictatus Papae' in *Festschrift für Helmut Beumann zum 65. Geburtstag* ed. K.-U.
Jäschke and R. Wenskus (Sigmaringen, 1977) pp. 263–87. Gregory VII, *Registrum*
II.55a (*Dictatus pape* 7), p. 203. See above p. 203.

[114] Gregory VII, *Registrum* I.33, VIII.24, IX.19, pp. 54, 504, 599–600. See T. Schmidt,
Alexander II. (1061–1073) und die römische Reformgruppe seiner Zeit (Päpste und
Papsttum 11: Stuttgart, 1977) pp. 215–16.

[115] Gregory VII, *Registrum* VI.2, p. 393.

[116] Schreiber, *Kurie und Kloster* (n. 63) I, 56–63.

founded as a result of local initiative and private enterprise: papal recognition transformed them into authentic expressions of the Rule of St Benedict and the Rule of St Augustine. Once an order had been placed under the protection of St Peter, it became subject to papal interventions which might fundamentally change its character in the interests of the current *necessitas* of the Church. An early example is provided by Camaldoli. During the eleventh century under the inspiration of Romuald (d. 1012) the Camaldolese had followed the way of life of hermits; but in the early twelfth century they had also begun to found monasteries. Paschal II in 1113 declared that both the hermit colonies and the monasteries should be subject to the prior of Camaldoli, united 'as a single body under a single head'. Clement III reiterated this formula when in 1187 he introduced measures to safeguard the unity of the Camaldolese monks and hermits.[117] Papal intervention successfully incorporated the Camaldolese experiments in the religious life into a single religious order.

The constitution of the Carthusian order originated in a similar papal intervention. The individual Carthusian houses remained autonomous until the papacy converted them into an order, subject to the authority of the prior of la Grande Chartreuse. Unity was imposed by the introduction of a Carthusian chapter general (on the model of that of the Cistercian order), which in 1163 finally accepted the new constitution. The transformation was completed by Alexander III's privilege of 17 April 1164.[118] A similar development occurred in the case of the Premonstratensian order. A privilege of Hadrian IV (1155) recognised the chapter general as the central institution of the order; and a privilege of Alexander III (1177) recognised Prémontré as the head of the order and guarantor of its unity.[119] The successive interventions of Lucius III, Urban III, Clement III and Celestine III in the affairs of the order of Grandmont were occasioned by the prolonged crisis in the order between 1185 and 1188. The crisis was provoked by the lay brothers (who were numerous and had an unusually important role in the order): they caused a schism by compelling the clerks to abandon the houses of the order and electing a lay prior whom the clerks refused to recog-

---

[117] Paschal II, *JL* 6357: (n. 104) 330D–332B; Clement III, *JL* 16095, *MPL* 204, 1275A–1278B. See A. des Mazis, 'Camaldules', *Dictionnaire d'histoire et de géographie ecclésiastique* 11 (Paris, 1949), 515–17.

[118] Alexander III, *JL* 11019: (n. 109) 293C–294A.

[119] Hadrian IV, *JL* 9970: (n. 108) 1373D–1375A; Alexander III, *JL* 12813: (n. 109) 1105A–1108D.

nise. The papal curia was not content with the deposition of the lay prior, the holding of a free election and the restoration of the status quo. In 1188 Clement III imposed major changes: a diminished role for the lay brethren, spiritual exemption and the payment of an annual *census* of two ounces of gold. This settlement of the affairs of Grandmont provides a good example of the papal power of legitimation: the new Rule of the order received papal recognition and at once became as authentic an expression of the religious life as the Rule of Augustine and that of Benedict.[120]

The history of the most successful of the new orders, that of Cîteaux, best illustrates the vigilant concern of the papacy with the religious life during the twelfth century. The earliest papal privileges for Cîteaux particularly emphasise the papal duty of enforcing the regular observance in the monasteries under St Peter's protection. The pope offered his protection to the new monastery because 'we must increase religion and must establish by the authority of our office whatever is right and whatever is done for the salvation of souls'.[121] The papal privileges of the early and mid-twelfth century make no reference to spiritual exemption: they are concerned principally with temporal protection and the confirmation of the Cistercian statutes. Paschal II's privilege of 1100 grants the 'special protection' (*specialis tutela*) of the Roman church. The privilege of Calixtus II of 1119 confirms 'certain chapters concerning the observation of the Rule of St Benedict and other matters which seem necessary in your order': namely the basic Cistercian constitution, *Carta Caritatis*, the historical explanation of the order's origin and aims, *Exordium Cistercii* and the earliest statutes guaranteeing the uniformity of the order.[122] A further series of statutes was confirmed by Eugenius III's privilege for his old order, *Sacrosancta* (1152): 'everything which is contained in your charter which is called "the Charter of Charity" and whatever you have decreed among yourselves for the sake of religion and according to the Rule'.[123] Meanwhile in 1132 Cîteaux and the other abbeys of the order had obtained from Innocent II the valuable privilege of exemption from the pay-

---

[120] Clement III, *JL* 16294, 16298: (n. 117) 1375AD, 1376D–1377B. See R. Foreville and J. Rousset de Pina, *Du premier Concile du Latran à l'avènement d'Innocent III* (Histoire de l'Eglise 9/2: Paris, 1953) pp. 303–4.

[121] Calixtus II, *JL* 6795: (n. 105) 1147B. Cf. Paschal II, *JL* 5842: (n. 104) 47D.

[122] J. A. Lefèvre, 'La véritable constitution cistercienne de 1119', *Collectanea Ordinis Cisterciensium Reformatorium* 16 (1954), 97–104.

[123] Eugenius III, *JL* 9600: (n. 107) 1541D–1543B. See Maccarrone, 'Primato romano' (n. 5) pp. 75–6.

ment of tithes.[124] Exemption from tithes was commonly granted to monasteries enjoying papal protection during the period of the reform papacy and in the first half of the twelfth century. It was a privilege strongly resented by the episcopate; and this resentment finally succeeded in influencing papal policy during the pontificate of Hadrian IV. In a radical break with the practice of his predecessors Hadrian IV in 1156 restored the jurisdiction of the diocesan by restricting the tithes exemption of religious houses to *novalia*, newly cultivated land.[125] This restriction was, however, partially reversed by his successor, Alexander III, who granted (in July 1169) a complete tithes exemption to the Cistercians in return for their valuable service to the papacy during the schism. He made the same grant to the Knights of the orders of the Temple and the Hospital, on whose financial services the Alexandrine curia was so dependent.[126]

The Cistercian order enjoyed the particular favour of Alexander III because of the tireless support which the order gave him in the dangerous years 1159–77. Emperor Frederick I had hoped that his close connections with the order would win them to his party; but the Cistercian Archbishop Peter of Tarentaise brought his order into the Alexandrine party. In September 1161 the Cistercian chapter declared for Alexander. The persecution which the order subsequently suffered in the imperial territories, as well as the Cistercian efforts to secure French and English recognition for Alexander, stimulated papal generosity.[127] Alexander's two privileges of July 1169 reserved to the chapter general the sole right of disciplining the Cistercian order, depriving abbots deposed by the chapter general of the right of appeal to the apostolic see.[128] His privileges of 1160 and

---

[124] Innocent II, *JL* 7537, 7544: (n. 106) 123BC, 126AC. See Pfurtscheller, *Privilegierung* (n. 61) pp. 26–7.

[125] Hadrian IV, *JL* 10189a: G. Schmidt, *Urkundenbuch des Hochstifts Halberstadt und seiner Bischöfe* 1 (Leipzig, 1883), 215. See Schreiber, *Kurie und Kloster* (n. 63) 1, 259–65.

[126] Alexander III, *JL* 11632, 11633: (n. 109) 592D–594A, 594A–595B. See J. B. Mahn, *L'ordre cistercien et son gouvernement des origines au milieu du XIIIe siècle* (Paris, 1945) pp. 102–8.

[127] M. Preiss, *Die politische Tätigkeit der Cisterzienser im Schisma von 1159–1177* (Historische Studien 248: Berlin, 1934) pp. 28–36; Mahn, *L'ordre cistercien* pp. 142–7; T. Reuter, 'Das Edikt Friedrich Barbarossas gegen die Zisterzienser', *MIÖG* 84 (1976), 328–36.

[128] Alexander III, *JL* 11632, 11633: (n. 109) 592D–594A, 594B–595B. See J. Leclercq, 'Passage supprimé dans une épître d'Alexandre III', *Revue Bénédictine* 62 (1952), 149–51; *idem*, 'Epîtres d'Alexandre III sur les cisterciens I', *ibid.*, 64 (1954), 68–70; Maccarrone, 'Primato romano' (n. 5) pp. 91, 93–4.

1169 virtually freed Cistercian houses from the jurisdiction of the diocesan. All that remained to the bishop was 'due reverence' (*debita reverentia*), which Alexander glossed with a warning against any episcopal involvement in the internal affairs of the order 'against the liberty of the order granted by us and our predecessors'.[129] Alexander's successor, Lucius III, was similarly well-disposed towards the Cistercians. (He has indeed occasionally been claimed as a Cistercian pope.)[130] His privilege of November 1184 prohibited bishops from exercising their power of correction over Cistercian houses and forbade the passing of sentence of excommunication, suspension or interdict against the Cistercians.[131] The historical context of this papal privilege offers a striking illustration of the order's influence in the later twelfth century and of the importance to the papacy of an alliance with the Cistercians. Lucius' privilege was issued at the end of the synod of Verona, in the aftermath of unsuccessful negotiations with Emperor Frederick I. The failure to reach a peaceful settlement in October 1184 seemed to threaten the renewal of the conflict of empire and papacy; in which event Lucius III was anxious to benefit (as his predecessor had benefited) from the support of the Cistercian order.[132]

The central figure in the papal–Cistercian alliance of the last quarter of the twelfth century was Henry of Marcy, abbot firstly of Hautecombe and later of Clairvaux, subsequently cardinal bishop of Albano: the illustrious Cistercian who in 1187 declined the offer of the papal dignity.[133] To Henry of Marcy belonged the principal responsibility for three vital areas of papal policy: the suppression of heresy, the negotiation of peace between the French and English kings, and the crusade. In 1178 and again in 1181 he was in the Languedoc, organising the preaching against the Albigensian heretics. From 1187 until his death in 1189 his energies were divided between reconciling the Capetian king Philip II and the Plantagenet king Henry II and preaching the Third Crusade.[134] Other members

---

[129] Alexander III, JL 10635, 11632: (n. 109) 95BC, 593BC–594A. See Pfurtscheller, *Privilegierung* (n. 61) pp. 47–8, 53–4, 107–8.

[130] See above p. 212 and n. 15.

[131] Lucius III, JL 15118, MPL 201, 1301B–1302B. On the interpretation of this privilege see G. Schreiber, 'Studien zur Exemtionsgeschichte der Zisterzienser. Zugleich ein Beitrag zur Veroneser Synode vom Jahre 1184', *ZSSRG KA* 4 (1914), 74–112; Pfurtscheller, *Privilegierung* pp. 108–16.

[132] Schreiber, 'Exemtionsgeschichte' pp. 74–112. See below p. 502.

[133] Congar, 'Henri de Marcy' (n. 42) 1–55.

[134] *Ibid.*, pp. 45–55. See above p. 169.

of Henry's order, less eminent but equally devoted to the Roman church, dedicated themselves to diplomatic missions and to the conversion of the heretics.[135] The Cistercian alliance demonstrates that at the end of our period, as at the beginning, the papacy depended on the help of the religious orders to carry out its demanding reform programme.

The Gregorian papacy had allied itself with the monasteries under St Peter's protection because of a growing dissatisfaction with the conduct of the episcopate. After the Investiture Contest papacy and episcopate were reconciled and became allies in the work of reforming the Church. From the 1120s onwards, therefore, the papacy must safeguard the 'canonical jurisdiction' of the bishops over the religious houses as zealously as he preserved the 'liberty' of the religious houses themselves. Papal diplomacy must balance the rival claims of the religious houses and the episcopate. There could be no question of sacrificing the interests of the religious, since in an emergency their loyalty and the diversity of their skills were indispensable. The financial support of the Templars and Hospitallers proved invaluable to the curia during the schism of 1159–77, as did the diplomatic efforts of the Cistercians. (The services of these orders provided a parallel to those of the Cluniacs during the Investiture Contest.) In the great enterprises of the twelfth century to defend or to propagate the faith – the preaching of the crusade, the mission to the heathen Slavs and to the heretical Albigensians – the religious orders were prominent. Throughout the century religious continued to be recruited to the curia as papal servants and advisers. The role of the religious in the service of the papacy, their special relationship with St Peter, was completely at odds with the norms of ancient canon law, as expressed in the council of Chalcedon. There could be no more striking demonstration of the pope's power 'to make new laws' – to adapt existing institutions to the changing needs of the Church – than the papal alliance with the religious orders in the period 1073–1198.

---

[135] Foreville and Rousset de Pina, *Du premier Concile du Latran* (n. 120) p. 301.

7

PAPAL FINANCE

—— • ——

In a century and a quarter which witnessed three papal schisms and two bitter conflicts between pope and emperor, the papacy inevitably experienced prolonged periods of financial crisis. The first such period began in the last years of the pontificate of Gregory VII and continued into the early twelfth century. Until he was driven into exile in July 1084, Gregory's pontificate was comparatively sedentary by the standards of the central Middle Ages. The dating clauses of his letters and privileges show that for at least seven years and two months of his fifteen-year pontificate the papal government was stationed in the Lateran palace in Rome.[1] For most of his pontificate, therefore, the pope had access to the revenues due to St Peter as landlord of the papal patrimony – the various rents, services and other dues claimed by all secular princes from their territories. But after the outbreak of hostilities between Gregory VII and Henry IV of Germany, these revenues were insufficient to pay for the defence of Rome against the emperor. The breakdown in the papal finances first became evident in May 1082, when the pope proposed to mortgage the property of the Roman church to pay for the war against the emperor. His proposal was vetoed by a meeting of the Roman clergy.[2] Thereafter the sources reveal the pope's increasing depen-

---

[1] Jaffé, *Regesta pontificum Romanorum* 1, 598–649.
[2] Z. Zafarana, 'Sul "conventus" del clero romano nel maggio 1082', *Studi medievali* ser. 3, 7 (1966), 399–403.

dence on the emergency supplies of his secular allies. In 1082 Countess Matilda of Tuscany melted down the treasure of the monastery of S. Apollonio di Canossa and sent 700 pounds of silver and 9 pounds of gold to the pope; and in 1083 the pope's Norman vassal, Duke Robert Guiscard of Apulia 'sent more than 30,000 *solidi* to the Romans, so as to reconcile them to the pope'.[3] Such emergency supplies became the principal source of papal revenue when, from 1084 to 1100, the emperor installed his antipope 'Clement III' (Wibert of Ravenna) in Rome and denied the reform papacy access to the resources of the Patrimony of St Peter. The letters of Urban II (notably those addressed to French churchmen) appeal for financial help for 'the Roman church labouring in many dangers and the greatest need'.[4] Urban spent much of his wandering pontificate in the Norman territories of southern Italy and one year in France. His attempt to gain a foothold in Rome in 1094 – by bribing the antipope's garrison to surrender the Lateran palace – had to be financed by the generosity of a visiting well-wisher, Abbot Godfrey of Vendôme.[5] The eagerness of the papal curia to extort such gifts from visitors inspired the composition of the earliest known satire on Roman avarice during Urban's pontificate.[6]

The reconquest of the Patrimony of St Peter and the recovery of its revenues began tentatively in 1109, in the pontificate of Paschal II, and gained momentum in the 1120s, during the pontificates of Calixtus II and Honorius II. In the papal schism of 1130 the beneficiary of this recovery was the antipope Anacletus II, whose family, the powerful clan of the Pierleoni, dominated Rome and the patrimony in the early 1130s. Anacletus' rival, Innocent II, spent most of the first seven years of his pontificate in exile in France and Burgundy, in Lombardy and Tuscany: he finally established his curia in Pisa between November 1133 and February 1137. During his exile 'by visiting the churches of Gaul [Innocent] repaired his poverty by means of their riches'.[7] Bernard of Clairvaux appealed in his letters for financial help for the exile and Emperor Lothar III responded to

---

[3] Memorandum in the Canossa manuscript of Donizo's *Vita Mathildis, MGH SS* 12, 385; Lupus Protospatarius, *Chronicon* 1083, *ibid.*, 5, 61.

[4] E.g. Urban II, *JL* 5351, 5494–5, *MPL* 151, 286D, 369A, 369D; J. Ramackers, 'Analekten zur Geschichte des Reformpapsttums', *QFIAB* 23 (1931–2), 42.

[5] Godfrey of Vendôme, *Epistolae* 1.8, *MPL* 157, 48AB.

[6] *Tractatus Garsiae Tholetani canonici de Albino et Rufino, MGH Libelli* 2, 423–35.

[7] Suger of St Denis, *Vita Ludovici grossi regis* c. 32, ed. H. Waquet (Paris, 1929) p. 264.

his appeal, 'not sparing his own money for the service of St Peter'.[8] But in the midst of the hardships of the schism the pope obtained a new source of income which seemed likely to free the Roman church from future financial difficulties: the income from the Matildine lands. Countess Matilda of Tuscany (*ca.* 1050–1115), the most reliable secular ally of the reform papacy, had willed all her extensive allodial lands in Tuscany and Lotharingia to the Roman church. Her original will had been made during the pontificate of Gregory VII (probably between 1077 and 1080) and it was confirmed in a document dated 17 November 1102. In the last years of her life, however, Matilda reached a rapprochement with her kinsman, Emperor Henry V. On her death the emperor claimed her allodial lands as her heir and the papacy was unable to gain possession of the Matildine inheritance.[9] The alliance between Innocent II and Henry V's successor, Lothar III, produced a settlement of the rival claims. On 8 June 1133 (two days after the imperial coronation of Lothar) Innocent invested the emperor with the Matildine lands in return for the payment of an annual census of 100 pounds of silver, with the condition that on the emperor's death the lands should revert to the Roman church.[10]

This settlement contributed significantly to the stability of papal finances in the mid-twelfth century,[11] when the papacy also began once more to enjoy the revenues of the Patrimony of St Peter. The reconquest of the patrimony was interrupted by the 'Roman revolution' of 1143–5, when the Romans rebelled against papal lordship and restored the senate; but the reconquest was resumed in the pontificates of Eugenius III and Hadrian IV.[12] The papal acquisitions of the mid-twelfth century offered critics further evidence of papal avarice. Hadrian's confidant, John of Salisbury, reported to the pope

---

[8] Bernard of Clairvaux, *Epistolae* 138–9, *MPL* 182, 292B–295A; Innocent II, *JL* 7633: *MGH Constitutiones* I, 169.

[9] *Mathildis comitissae donatio*, *MGH Constitutiones* I, 654–5: see A. Overmann, *Gräfin Matilde von Tuscien. Ihre Besitzungen* (Innsbrück, 1895) pp. 143–4. See also D. B. Zema, 'The houses of Tuscany and of Pierleone in the crisis of Rome in the eleventh century', *Traditio* 2 (1944), 157–69; L. Simeoni, 'Il contributo della contessa Matilde al Papato nella lotta per le investiture', *SG* I (1947), 353–72; Servatius, *Paschalis II.* pp. 100–4.

[10] Innocent II, *JL* 7633: (n. 8) 169–70. See below p. 449.

[11] Overmann, *Mathilde* (n. 9) p. 51; V. Pfaff, *Kaiser Heinrichs VI. höchstes Angebot an die römische Kirche (1196)* (Heidelberger Abhandlungen zur mittleren und neueren Geschichte 55: Heidelberg, 1927) pp. 4–5; K. Jordan, 'Zur päpstlichen Finanzgeschichte im 11. und 12. Jahrhundert', *QFIAB* 25 (1933–4), 70.

[12] See above pp. 30–1.

'what men thought of him and of the Roman church'. 'The Roman pontiff is oppressive to all and almost impossible to bear and all complain that while the churches built by the piety of our ancestors go to ruin and their altars are abandoned, he builds palaces and goes about not only in purple but even in gold.' Hadrian replied with the old fable of the limbs who conspired against the belly, only to find that this supposedly useless member was indispensable to the health of the body. The papal revenues were not used to enrich the pope, but to pay the personnel of the papal government: 'no soldier can serve without wages and when the wages are not forthcoming, the soldier is weakened and broken'.[13]

During the papal schism of 1159–77 and the conflict between Alexander III and Emperor Frederick I the achievements of Eugenius III and Hadrian IV were largely undone. When Alexander III fled to France in 1162 (where he established his curia until the end of summer 1165), much of the papal patrimony fell into the hands of the schismatics. Alexander attempted to return to Rome in November 1165, but was forced to flee again by the imperial attack on Rome in July–August 1167. For the remaining years of the schism the pope stayed either in the kingdom of William II of Sicily or in the region of the papal patrimony bordering on the Sicilian kingdom.[14] Throughout the eighteen-year schism Alexander III could rarely draw on the regular income of the Roman church to finance his wandering curia. Numerous begging letters to French churchmen (notably to Archbishop Henry of Rheims) describe the financial straits of the Alexandrine curia. In February 1161 Frederick I, 'the tyrant and violent persecutor of the Church . . . has laid ambushes and so obstructed the approach-roads with the accomplices of his barbaric ferocity that those from whom the Roman church is accustomed to receive timely relief in her hour of need cannot now reach us'. In January 1166 'the voracity of the usurers devours whatever alms are offered to us'.[15] After the defeat of the emperor by the Lombard cities at the battle of Legnano (29 May 1176) the peace negotiations seemed at first to offer the restoration of the prosperity which the papacy had enjoyed in the middle of the century. In the preliminary negotiations at Anagni the pope was assured the resti-

[13] John of Salisbury, *Policraticus* VI.24, ed. C. C. J. Webb 2 (Oxford, 1909), 67–73. See R. W. Southern, *Medieval humanism and other studies* (Oxford, 1970) pp. 244–5.
[14] Pacaut, *Alexandre III* p. 214; P. Partner, *The lands of St Peter* (London, 1972) pp. 203–15.
[15] Alexander III, *JL* 10655, 11256, *MPL* 200, 107D, 405D.

tution both of the papal patrimony ('all the *regalia* and other possessions of St Peter . . . which the Roman church had from the time of Innocent [II]') and of the Matildine lands ('the possession of the land of Countess Matilda [which] the Roman church had in the time of Emperor Lothar and the lord King Conrad and also in the time of the present lord Emperor Frederick'). But in the further negotiations which produced the Peace of Venice (July 1177) Frederick exploited the war-weariness of the pope and his allies so skilfully that he was eventually able to concede far less than had been promised by his representatives at Anagni. The Peace of Venice restored the papal patrimony with the conditional phrase, 'saving every right of the empire', and made no mention of the Matildine lands.[16] When Lucius III attempted to renegotiate the question of the Matildine inheritance with Frederick I in 1184, the emperor was still unwilling to recognise the papal claim. Frederick proposed that the pope should renounce all claim to the inheritance and in return the emperor would give the pope one-tenth and the cardinals one-ninth of his Italian revenues.[17] Only in the will of Frederick's son and successor, Henry VI, in 1197 was promise made of restitution of the greater part of the Matildine lands and of those parts of the Patrimony of St Peter still under Staufen military occupation.[18] By the end of the century the papacy, finally restored to Rome by Clement III's treaty with the Roman senate (1188), was regaining the lordship of the papal patrimony and recovering the prosperity of the mid-twelfth century.

For long periods during the late eleventh and twelfth centuries, therefore, the papacy was deprived of the ordinary revenues of the patrimony and simultaneously forced into extraordinary expenditure by the demands of schism and warfare. These prolonged periods of emergency compelled the papacy to find new sources of income and to administer the papal finances more efficiently. The crises of the central Middle Ages eventually produced the new papal financial office of the *camera apostolica* and its most important functionary, the *camerarius* or papal chamberlain. When this new office and new official first appeared is difficult to decide, because the papal financial administration of the eleventh century is so sparsely documented. The term *camera* occurs only four times in papal documents between

---

[16] Pact of Anagni c. 3, 6, *MGH Constitutiones* 1, 350. Peace of Venice c. 3, *ibid.*, p. 362. See below pp. 494–7.

[17] Frederick I, letter to Lucius III: *ibid.*, pp. 420–1. See below pp. 501–2.

[18] Henry VI, testament: *ibid.*, pp. 530–1. See below p. 521.

921 and 1062 and these documents, although authentic, do not resemble the usual productions of the papal chancery in this period, reflecting instead the influence of the imperial chancery.[19] The term *camerarius*, 'chamberlain of the lord pope', first appears in a papal document of 1123. Its first appearance in a document from outside the papal curia occurs in 1099.[20] Some historians have assumed that the reform of the papal finances was a consequence of the papal reform movement of the eleventh century and that the central figure in the reform movement was also prominent in the administrative reform. Paul Fabre, the pioneer of the study of the papal finances (1892), detected here 'the initiative of archdeacon Hildebrand': 'it is quite certain that he fulfilled the functions which would later belong to the *camerarius*'.[21] The evidence for this opinion is the title '*economus* of the holy Roman church', which is attributed to Gregory VII before his accession to the papacy. There are, however, no grounds for supposing that there was in the mid-eleventh century a fixed office of *economus*, equivalent to that of the twelfth-century papal chamberlain. The term *economus* was attributed to Hildebrand-Gregory both because as archdeacon of the Roman church (1059–73) he was responsible for the administration of the property of the Church and because he was simultaneously responsible for the administration of the Roman abbey of S. Paolo fuori le Mura during a vacancy in the abbatiate.[22] On his accession to the papacy Gregory VII was succeeded as archdeacon by Theodinus, who was presumably responsible for financial administration during Gregory's pontificate. In 1084 Archdeacon Theodinus was one of the many members of the Roman clergy who deserted Gregory for his rival,

[19] John X, *JL* 3565, *MPL* 132, 806A; Benedict VIII, *JL* 4021, *MPL* 139, 1617B; Victor II, *JL* 4348: *Italia pontificia* 4, 312; Alexander II, *JL* 4490, *MPL* 146, 1284C. See Jordan, 'Finanzgeschichte' (n. 11) pp. 91–3.

[20] Calixtus II, *JL* 7056, *MPL* 163, 1290A (see Jordan, 'Finanzgeschichte' pp. 99–104); Archbishop Hugh of Lyons, *Epistola* 23, *MPL* 157, 524D. See M. Michaud, 'Chambre apostolique', *Dictionnaire de Droit Canonique* 3 (Paris, 1942), 398; J. Sydow, 'Cluny und die Anfänge der Apostolischen Kammer', *SMGBO* 63 (1951), 56.

[21] P. Fabre, *Etude sur le Liber Censuum de l'Eglise Romaine* (Bibliothèque des Ecoles françaises d'Athènes et de Rome 72: Paris, 1892) pp. 151–2, 155.

[22] Decree of the synod of Brixen (1080) in *Die Briefe Heinrichs IV.*, *MGH Dt. Ma* 1, 70; Bonizo, *Liber ad amicum* v, *MGH Libelli* 1, 588. See Jordan, 'Finanzgeschichte' (n. 11) pp. 65–6; J. Sydow, 'Untersuchungen zur kurialen Verwaltungsgeschichte im Zeitalter des Reformpapsttums', *DA* 11 (1954–5), 27; T. Schmidt, *Alexander II. (1061–1073) und die römische Reformgruppe seiner Zeit* (Päpste und Papsttum 11: Stuttgart, 1977) pp. 199–200.

the antipope 'Clement III' (Wibert of Ravenna).[23] Thereafter the office of archdeacon lost its connection with the papal finances. In the pontificates of Urban II and Paschal II the archidiaconate seems to have become fused with the office of chancellor, in the person of John of Gaeta, cardinal deacon of S. Maria in Cosmedin. After John of Gaeta became pope as Gelasius II (1118), the archidiaconate retained only liturgical functions.[24]

It was evidently during the pontificate of Urban II that the new office of *camerarius* was created to administer the papal finances. The earliest known appearance of this office is in a reference to the presence of 'Peter, chamberlain of the lord pope' at a legatine council in Lyons in 1099. Scattered references to the same officer – always as *camerarius* of the pope, rather than of the Roman church – appear in diplomas and letters of the first decade of the twelfth century; but the fullest information is provided by the Anglo-Norman historian, Eadmer of Canterbury, writing between 1109 and 1125: 'Peter, a monk of Cluny and a man of great authority in his day, who was the chamberlain of the lord Pope Urban and Paschal'.[25] The first known papal *camerarius* was, therefore, like his first master, Urban II, a monk from the great Burgundian abbey of Cluny. This information lends particular interest to two references to Cluny in letters of Urban II concerning papal finances. The first begs Abbot Hugh of Cluny for 'relief and solace' in Rome's hour of greatest need. The second requests Archbishop Lanfranc of Canterbury to 'send to Cluny as quickly as possible' the 'Peter's pence' customarily paid to the Roman church by the English kingdom.[26] In this instance (April 1088) Cluny was evidently playing a direct role in the administration of papal finances. Similar evidence survives from the pontificate of the Burgundian pope Calixtus II, in the *History of Compostela*, which describes how Archbishop Diego Gelmírez of Compostela persuaded Calixtus to confer metropolitan status on his church by

[23] Beno, *Gesta Romanae ecclesiae contra Hildebrandum* I, *MGH Libelli* 2, 369. See Sydow, 'Untersuchungen' (n. 22) pp. 36, 42; R. Hüls, *Kardinäle, Klerus und Kirchen Roms 1049–1130* (Bibliothek des Deutschen Historischen Instituts in Rom 48: Tübingen, 1977) p. 254.

[24] Hüls, *Kardinäle* pp. 43–4, 232.

[25] Hugh of Lyons, *Epistola* 23 (n. 20): 524D; Eadmer, *Vita sancti Anselmi* II.55 ed. R. W. Southern (Oxford, 1972) p. 134. See Jordan, 'Finanzgeschichte' (n. 11) pp. 94–7; Michaud, 'Chambre apostolique' (n. 20) 398; Sydow, 'Cluny' (n. 20) pp. 56–8; Servatius, *Paschalis II*. pp. 63–4.

[26] Ramackers, 'Analekten' (n. 4) p. 42; Urban II, *JL* 5351: (n. 4) 287D. See Jordan, 'Finanzgeschichte' p. 97.

means of well-timed gifts to the papal curia. In 1119 Diego's envoys conveyed to France 'the money necessary for this business' with the help of 'Stephen, the chamberlain of Cluny': part of the treasure was sent to the pope in Toulouse, the rest was 'commended for safe keeping to Abbot [Pontius] of Cluny'. In 1120 a further gift (*benedictio*) was received at Cluny by 'Stephen of Besançon, the chamberlain of Pope Calixtus' (who seems, however, not to be identical with Stephen, *camerarius* of Cluny). According to the historian of Compostela, Cluny was 'most dear to the heart of Pope Calixtus' because the abbey served him 'as *camera* and base (*asseda*)' during the period in which he was excluded from Rome by the imperial antipope Burdinus.[27] This papal reliance on Cluny is not surprising, given both the financial importance of the abbey in this period – as expressed, for example, in the right to mint coins – and the consequent sophistication of Cluny's financial administration. Hence Karl Jordan's suggestion (1933–4) that the papal financial reform of the end of the eleventh century was inspired by the example of the *camera* of Cluny. The Cluniac pope Urban II, compelled to reorganise the administration of the papal finances because of the defections at the end of Gregory VII's pontificate, imitated the practice of his former abbey (where the *camerarius* was an official second in importance only to the prior) and recruited the Cluniac monk Peter as the first papal chamberlain.[28] The office of papal *camerarius* was, therefore, monastic in inspiration; but Cluniac influence was evidently limited to financial administration. Other offices in the twelfth-century papal curia had no monastic equivalents and were presumably drawn from secular models – the imperial court or that of Capetian France or Norman Sicily. For example, the office of *dapifer* (steward) appears already in documents of the pontificate of Urban II and Paschal II (to be renamed *senescalcus* in the pontificate of Alexander III) and the offices of *marescalcus* (marshal) and *pincerna* (cupbearer) appear before the end of the twelfth century.[29]

The office of *camerarius* absorbed the financial functions of the archdeacon and of two lesser officers of the early medieval papacy, the *arcarius* (who received the alms given to St Peter) and the

---

[27] *Historia Compostellana* II.10–11, 16, 14, *MPL* 170, 1045D, 1047C, 1056C, 1052D–1053A. See Jordan, 'Finanzgeschichte' pp. 98–9.

[28] Jordan, 'Finanzgeschichte' pp. 97–8. See also G. de Valous, *Le monachisme clunisien des origines au XVe siècle* I (Paris, 1935), 124–9; Sydow, 'Cluny' (n. 20) pp. 54–5.

[29] Sydow, 'Cluny' p. 58; F. Geisthardt, *Der Kämmerer Boso* (Historische Studien 293: Berlin, 1936) p. 41 and n. 5.

sacellarius (the papal paymaster). From the beginning of the twelfth century the *camerarius* figures with increasing frequency in papal diplomas and occasional references in the narrative sources also bear witness to the importance of the office. It is characteristic of the attitude of outsiders to the papal financial system that the chroniclers' references to the papal chamberlain are often negative in tone. The historian Abbot Guibert of Nogent described the chamberlain Peter of Cluny as 'a poisoned cup' and his advice as 'illicit honey'. When Guibert was sent to Paschal II as a member of a legation to secure papal approval for the bishop elect of Laon, Peter secretly advised him that his mission would be assured of success if the bishop elect promised future obedience and material support to the pope. Guibert regarded this advice as tantamount to simony: 'what is worse than to pay a price to men so as to obtain the grace of God?'[30] Similarly, the chronicle of Morigny describes Stephen of Besançon, the chamberlain of Calixtus II in 1119–20, as 'a most cruel and most avaricious man'.[31] An unnamed *camerarius* of Calixtus II figures in the account of the English legation to Rome in 1123 written by Hugh the Cantor, historian of the church of York. The legation of 1123 was the moment in the long English primacy dispute between the churches of Canterbury and York (1072–1128) when Canterbury suffered her most serious defeat. The papal privileges on which Canterbury based her claim to the primacy of the English church were rejected by the papal curia as forgeries. The response of the Canterbury delegation was to secure the help of 'a certain chamberlain, treacherous and worthless, a familiar of the lord pope and influential with him'. The York delegation complained to their many supporters among the cardinals: 'we are not afraid of the curia, but we fear the *camera*'. But the cardinals reassured them that the *camera* would not dare to oppose the will of the curia.[32]

This evidence is difficult to interpret because it is coloured by Hugh's hostility towards his opponents in the Canterbury delegation. It is clear, however, that in 1123 the influence of the office of *camerarius* (or at least of one particular *camerarius*) was such that it seemed to outsiders to challenge the role of the cardinals as papal advisers. A possible explanation of this tension is suggested by Karl

---

[30] Guibert of Nogent, *Histoire de sa vie* III.4 ed. G. Bourgin (Paris, 1907) p. 143.
[31] *La Chronique de Morigny* ed. L. Mirot (Paris, 1909) p. 32.
[32] Hugh the Cantor, *The history of the church of York 1066–1127* ed. C. Johnson (London, 1961) p. 116. See Jordan, 'Finanzgeschichte' (n. 11) p. 101.

Jordan's identification of two *camerarii* functioning simultaneously in 1123. An inscription on the high altar of the church of S. Maria in Cosmedin, dated May 1123, commemorates the consecration of the altar by Calixtus II and the rich gifts made to the church on this occasion by his *camerarius* Alfanus; while a papal diploma of April 1123 mentions Guido, 'chamberlain of the Roman curia'. Since the title *Romanae curiae camerarius* does not recur in the papal documents of the twelfth century, it would be rash to place too much emphasis on the contrasting titles of Alfanus and Guido. But it is clear that the contrast 'papal chamberlain' and 'chamberlain of the Roman curia' corresponds to Hugh the Cantor's account of the tension between *curia* and *camera* in 1123. We know that at the end of the twelfth century the college of cardinals possessed its own chamberlain, whose functions were independent of the papal *camera*: Cencius Savelli, who was the chamberlain of Clement III and Celestine III, subsequently became chamberlain of the college of cardinals in the pontificate of Innocent III.[33] Did the chamberlain Guido hold a similar office three-quarters of a century before Cencius' time? Or was it the case that in the early years of the papal *camera* the duties of the *camerarius* were sometimes shared by two officials? There is, for example, evidence of a 'Tiberius, *camerarius* of Pope Paschal' at a date (1101) when Peter of Cluny is known to have held the chamberlain's office.[34] Similarly, papal diplomas of 1151 identify two *camerarii*: Franchus (3 April) and Rainerius (23 November).[35] Whether these two officers shared the same duties or had distinct functions, as papal chamberlain and chamberlain of the cardinals, is impossible to decide.

The workings of the papal *camera* in the first half-century of its existence cannot, therefore, be studied in detail; but there are signs that by the mid-twelfth century the office of *camerarius* had acquired some at least of the features characteristic of the better documented age of Cencius Savelli. Firstly, the chamberlain was already entrusted with the responsibility for the territorial possessions of the papacy. For example, in 1127 John, the *camerarius* of Honorius II, is

---

[33] *Italia pontificia* 1, 114 (no. 1); 6/2, 324 (no. 10). See Jordan, 'Finanzgeschichte' pp. 99–101; Geisthardt, *Boso* (n. 29) p. 82; Michaud, 'Chambre apostolique' (n. 20) 397–8; Sydow, 'Cluny' (n. 20) pp. 60–3.

[34] In a diploma of King Henry I of England (to whom Tiberius was sent as papal legate): see K. Jordan, 'Die Entstehung des römischen Kurie. Ein Versuch', *ZSSRG KA* 28 (1939), 107 n. 1; Sydow, 'Cluny' p. 58.

[35] Geisthardt, *Boso* (n. 29) p. 44.

found purchasing land in Benevento on behalf of the curia.[36] This aspect of the chamberlain's duties was to grow greatly during the pontificates of Eugenius III and Hadrian IV as a consequence of the conquest and reorganisation of the Patrimony of St Peter during the late 1140s and 1150s. Secondly, the chamberlain's office began in mid-century to be given to a member of the college of cardinals. The first cardinal who is known to have held the office appears in Eugenius III's pontificate: Jordan, a Carthusian from Le Mont-Dieu, whom Eugenius made cardinal priest of S. Susanna in December 1145 and who is first mentioned as *camerarius* in March 1147.[37] Like his Cluniac predecessor, Peter, and other early *camerarii*, Jordan acquired an evil reputation. The historian John of Salisbury claimed that Jordan 'made the Carthusian order infamous by his custom, while he was chamberlain, of adding a mark which was heavier than normal when weighing out the gifts of the supreme pontiff'. This is the earliest extant reference to the fact that the *camerarius* had assumed the duties of the *sacellarius*, the paymaster who, before the financial reorganisation of the late eleventh century, had been responsible for papal almsgiving and for the customary distribution of money at papal ceremonies. We also owe to John of Salisbury the information that Cardinal Jordan ceased to be chamberlain at the latest in 1151, when he participated in a legation to Germany. In 1152 Jordan was papal legate in France, where his activities as collector of the papal revenues added to his reputation for extortion. 'He cloaked his avarice with the habit of the Carthusian order, wearing poor garments, being severe in speech and manner and sparing expense.'[38] The bitterness of the author's invective can be taken as a measure of Cardinal Jordan's success in promoting the financial interests of the papacy.

The first chamberlain whose career is known in detail is Boso, cardinal deacon of SS. Cosma e Damiano, *camerarius* of Hadrian IV and also the biographer both of Hadrian and his successor, Alexander III. Hadrian seems to have appointed Boso to the chamberlain's office shortly after his accession to the papacy (December 1154) and raised him to the cardinalate two years later. This promotion and the English pope's obvious reliance on him inspired the tradition that

---

[36] O. Vehse, 'Benevent als Territorium des Kirchenstaates', *QFIAB* 22 (1930–1), 85 n. 5.

[37] *Italia pontificia* 6/2, 119 (no. 6). See Geisthardt, *Boso* (n. 29) pp. 42–3.

[38] John of Salisbury, *Historia pontificalis* c. 38–9, ed. M. Chibnall (London, 1956) pp. 75–8. See above pp. 163–4.

Boso was Hadrian IV's compatriot. Archbishop Thomas Becket of Canterbury claimed Boso as a friend of his youth and as a friend also of his predecessor, Archbishop Theobald: indeed during the 1160s Boso was one of the principal defenders of Becket's cause in the papal curia. However, Boso's Canterbury friendships do not necessarily prove his English origin: they may well have stemmed from the Canterbury legations to Rome of 1143–5 – in which Becket participated – intended to secure for the archbishop a permanent papal legation in England. It is worth noting that in the curia of the 1150s and 1160s Boso often figured as an expert in Tuscan affairs and a defender of Tuscan interests, which certainly suggests a Tuscan rather than an English origin.[39] The main evidence for Boso's activity as chamberlain is a collection of twenty-three diplomas from the years 1157–9 concerning the papal lordship in the Patrimony of St Peter, found in the *Liber Censuum*, the register of payments due to the Roman church, compiled in 1192 by Cencius Savelli. These diplomas present Boso as enjoying far greater authority in the patrimony than any previous papal official. He was clearly the principal figure in the reorganisation of the patrimony during Hadrian IV's pontificate. 'As the representative of the lord pope and of the Roman church' Boso took possession of estates and fortresses acquired for the papacy by purchase or mortgage and received the oaths of fealty of the nobility of the papal patrimony. The chamberlain appears for the first time in the diplomas of 1157–9 at the head of a staff of 'officials of the chamberlain's *camera*' (*officiales camerae camerarii*), drawn from the servants in the papal palace, including Alexius 'the cupbearer (*pincerna*) of the lord pope'. He also appears in command of a military following to assist him in asserting his lord's rights in the patrimony.[40]

No less impressive was Boso's authority in Rome itself. It was to him, 'on behalf of the lord pope', that the *hostiarii*, the 'doorkeepers' who guarded the Lateran palace, took their oath of loyalty (December 1157). The other papal residence in Rome, the palace adjacent to the basilica of St Peter, built by Eugenius III, was protected by a fortification, the garrison of which also swore fidelity to Boso.[41] In the period 1157–9, therefore, the *camerarius* was effectively

---

[39] Thomas Becket, *Epistola* 250: *Materials for the history of Thomas Becket, Archbishop of Canterbury* 6, *RS* 67/6 (1882), 57–9; John of Salisbury, *Letter* 315, ed. W. J. Millor and C. N. L. Brooke 2 (Oxford, 1979), 774. Geisthardt, *Boso* (n. 29) pp. 26–40 suggests that Boso was a native either of Lucca or of Pisa.

[40] *Liber Censuum* 1, 385–400 (nos. 98–120). See Geisthardt, *Boso* pp. 44–55.

[41] Geisthardt, *Boso* pp. 55–6, 60.

head of the papal household and all the pope's secular power, both in the city and in the patrimony, was entrusted to him. Hence the important role which Boso played in the disputed papal election which followed the death of Hadrian IV (September 1159). Boso's conduct is known principally from the hostile account of the canons of St Peter's, who regarded the chamberlain as 'the instigator of the crimes' of the schism of 1159 and 'the firstborn of Satan'. Immediately after Hadrian's death in Anagni Boso assumed command of the garrison of the palace of St Peter's in order to control the place where the election of a successor was to be held. He invited the cardinals to join him, but some of them 'replied that they would never enter the citadel, for they feared Boso and had been told that they would be taken prisoner by those who had sworn fidelity to Boso'. After the election of September 1159 had produced two rival popes, Alexander III and the antipope 'Victor IV', Boso placed the citadel and garrison of St Peter's at the disposal of Alexander, the candidate of those cardinals who wished to continue the policies of Hadrian IV ('the Sicilian party', as their opponents called them).[42] The extensive power which Boso enjoyed between 1157 and 1159 had doubtless been entrusted to him because he could be relied on to support Hadrian against his opponents in the college of cardinals and among the Roman nobility. Boso remained faithful to his lord even after Hadrian's death, using his authority as *camerarius* to forestall an attempt by Hadrian's opponents to control the election of his successor.

The collapse of the papal lordship in the Patrimony of St Peter in the early 1160s and the extension of imperial authority in central Italy during the Alexandrine schism deprived the office of papal chamberlain of the authority revealed in the diplomas of 1157–9. The political setbacks of Alexander III's pontificate combined with the withdrawal of the dominant figure of Boso to change the character of the office. Boso ceased to be *camerarius* after the accession of Alexander III. In the years 1159–61 he was probably in Tuscany, raising money for the poverty-stricken Alexandrine curia. In 1162 he joined Alexander in France and the papal diplomas show that he remained in the papal entourage (promoted in 1165/6 to the dignity of cardinal

---

[42] Letter of the canons of St Peter's to Emperor Frederick I: Rahewin, *Gesta Friderici imperatoris* IV.76, *MGH SS rer. Germ.*, 1884, pp. 255–6; Boso, *Vita Alexandri III: Liber pontificalis* 2, 398. See Geisthardt, *Boso* pp. 60–3; W. Madertoner, *Die zwiespältige Papstwahl des Jahres 1159* (dissertation: Vienna, 1978) pp. 74–6. For the 'Sicilian party' see above pp. 52–3, 79–81 and below pp. 389, 391, 470–2.

priest of S. Pudenziana) until the end of the schism. The detailed knowledge of events revealed in his biography of Alexander III suggests that Boso may have played an important role as a papal adviser during these years; but there is no evidence that he continued to exercise influence over the financial affairs of the papacy.[43] During Alexander III's pontificate the *camerarius* was altogether a lesser figure than in the pontificate of Hadrian IV. In the papal diplomas of the 1160s and 1170s *camerarii* make infrequent appearances as the receivers of papal revenues – no longer as the administrators of the landed property of the papacy. This duty now belonged to the papal vicars to whom Alexander entrusted the affairs of Rome and the patrimony: Cardinal Julius of Palestrina and his able successor, John, cardinal priest of SS. Giovanni e Paolo (who in 1165 temporarily won over the Romans and achieved the submission of Sabina).[44] The earliest extant reference to the office of *camerarius* in Alexander's pontificate is in a receipt for papal revenues from Spain, dated August 1163: 'Master Theodin and Bernard the Templar, chamberlains of the lord pope'.[45] Once again, as in 1101, 1123 and 1151, two officials appear simultaneously with the title *camerarius*; but in 1163 there is no question of one being the papal chamberlain and the other the chamberlain of the cardinals, for both are described unambiguously as 'chamberlains of the lord pope'. Neither was at this time a cardinal. The subdeacon Theodin became cardinal priest of S. Vitale in 1166. He had served in 1161–2 on a fundraising legation in Spain and soon afterwards appeared in England to summon English prelates to the council of Tours (1163).[46] Presumably, therefore, in August 1163 he had only recently begun his duties as chamberlain. His colleague Bernard, however, was perhaps the immediate successor of Boso.[47]

Bernard belonged to the order of the Knights Templars and his appearance as *camerarius* is the earliest surviving evidence of the role of the Knights Templars in papal financial administration in the pontificate of Alexander III. The Templars' role in the 1160s and

---

[43] Geisthardt, *Boso* pp. 63–76.

[44] *Ibid.*, p. 69; J. M. Brixius, *Die Mitglieder des Kardinalkollegiums von 1130 bis 1181* (dissertation: Berlin, 1912) pp. 52, 104–5; 55, 109.

[45] C. Erdmann, *Papsturkunden in Portugal, Abhandlungen der Gesellschaft der Wissenschaften zu Göttingen, phil.-hist. Klasse*, N.F. 20/3 (Berlin, 1927) p. 380 (no. 159/3).

[46] G. Säbekow, *Die päpstlichen Legationen nach Spanien und Portugal bis zum Ausgang des 12. Jahrhunderts* (dissertation: Berlin, 1931) p. 52; H. Tillmann, *Die päpstlichen Legaten in England bis zur Beendigung der Legation Gualas (1218)* (dissertation: Bonn, 1926) p. 55. See above p. 167.

[47] Geisthardt, *Boso* (n. 29) p. 78.

1170s was at least as important as that of the Cluniacs in the pontificates of Urban II, Paschal II and Calixtus II. Not only the chamberlain, Bernard, but also his successor, Franco, belonged to the order of the Temple. Franco first appears as *camerarius* in a letter of 1175 – 'the Templars brother Franco, chamberlain of the lord pope and brother Peter, his almoner' – and thereafter he appears in papal diplomas and receipts for papal revenue until 1181.[48] The Templar Franco may already have been in the papal service more than a decade before his first appearance as chamberlain: a 'brother Franco' was a member of the Alexandrine curia during its exile in Sens in 1164; and in 1171 he was involved in the reconciliation of King Henry II of England to the pope after the murder of Thomas Becket.[49] While the Templars Bernard and Franco served in the *camera*, their order assisted Alexander in the same way that Cluny had assisted the reform papacy, by arranging the transmission of money. Two papal letters to Archbishop Henry of Rheims reveal the curia's reliance on the Templars. A letter of June 1165 seeks information about the sum of 158 pounds which 'we commended to be assigned to our beloved son Eustace, master of the brethren of the order of the Temple'. A letter of January 1166, bemoaning 'the burden of our debts and the insistence of our creditors', begged the archbishop to send what money he could spare 'to our beloved sons, the master and brethren of the order of the Temple in Paris'.[50] The Templars placed at the disposal of the curia the resources of the sophisticated financial organisation which they had developed in the west, with its headquarters in Paris. In addition to solving problems of depositing and transporting cash, they arranged loans for the impoverished curia. Compelled at the beginning of his pontificate to resort to Italian and Jewish bankers and thereafter haunted by 'the voracity of the usurers', Alexander III found the Templars indispensable as moneylenders. Alexander's relations with the Templars reveal the greatly altered state of the papal finances after the prosperity of the late 1150s. Cut off from the regular sources of income which Hadrian IV had enjoyed, Alexander needed financial advisers and administrators whose services were very different in character from those which

[48] Gaufridus Fulchier, letter to Alexander III: *Recueil des historiens des Gaules et de la France* 15 (Paris, 1808), 967. See also Geisthardt, *Boso* pp. 78–9; Michaud, 'Chambre apostolique' (n. 20) p. 396.
[49] Letters to Thomas Becket no. 61: *Materials* (n. 39) 5, 117; Richardus de Wallace, letter to Henry II: *Recueil* (n. 48) 16, 478.
[50] Alexander III, *JL* 11204, 11256: (n. 15) 373C, 406C.

Boso had performed. Hence the appearance of one of the leaders of the Jewish community in Rome as an important official in the curia between 1159 and 1167.[51] Hence also the importance of the role of Bernard and Franco as *camerarii*. They placed the curia immediately in touch with the financial operations of their order and they offered advice, notably about credit facilities, which the circumstances of the schism made urgently necessary.

The end of the schism (1177) left the papacy in a state of financial exhaustion which continued throughout the 1180s because of the curia's inability to regain full control of Rome and the Patrimony of St Peter. Although Alexander III was restored to the city in March 1178 with the help of the imperial commander Archbishop Christian of Mainz, the turbulence of the citizens forced him to spend the last two years of his pontificate outside Rome. His successor Lucius III was able to spend only five months in Rome and his successors, Urban III and Gregory VIII, did not set foot in the city during their pontificates. The consequence of this exile was, in the words of the contemporary Welsh author, Giraldus Cambrensis, an 'extreme penury and lack even of the necessities of life'.[52] The English Cistercian Ralph Niger, looking back on the relations of the papacy with the Staufen emperors Frederick I and Henry VI, commented that 'from the pontificate of Alexander III until our own times the condition of the Church deteriorated gravely and uninterruptedly'.[53] Yet although hardpressed by the emperor during the last decade of the century, the papacy was striving to recover some of the prosperity of the mid-century. The turning-point in the fortunes of the late twelfth-century papacy was the treaty between the pope and the Roman senate (31 May 1188), which permitted Clement III to establish the curia in Rome and permitted his successor Celestine III to begin the reconquest of the papal patrimony. The return to Rome and the gradual recovery of the landed revenues of the papacy was accompanied by the reappearance of a *camerarius* whose power and

---

[51] F. Schneider, 'Zur älteren päpstlichen Finanzgeschichte', *QFIAB* 9 (1906), 2–5, 8–12; V. Pfaff, 'Aufgaben und Probleme der päpstlichen Finanzverwaltung am Ende des 12. Jahrhunderts', *MIÖG* 64 (1956), 22.

[52] Giraldus Cambrensis, *Speculum Ecclesiae* IV.19, *RS* 21/4 (1873), 302. See K. Wenck, 'Die römischen Päpste zwischen Alexander III. und Innozenz III. und der Designationsversuch Weihnachten 1197' in *Papsttum und Kaisertum. Forschungen zur politischen Geschichte und Geisteskultur des Mittelalters. Paul Kehr zum 65. Geburtstag dargebracht* ed. A. Brackmann (Munich, 1926) pp. 417–20; V. Pfaff, 'Zur Geschichte des Papsttums von 1181 bis 1198', *ZSSRG KA* 69 (1983), 250–1.

[53] Ralph Niger, *Chronicon universale*, *MGH SS* 27, 337.

influence both in the curia and in the patrimony equalled that of Cardinal Boso. The subdeacon Cencius Savelli (later canon of the church of S. Maria Maggiore and cardinal deacon of S. Lucia in Orthea) was a member of a noble Roman family, like the two popes whom he served as *camerarius*, Clement III and Celestine III. Cencius' first appearance as *camerarius* is in a document of 22 January 1188 (in the second month of Clement III's pontificate): the chamberlain received the oath of fidelity from the *hostiarii* of the Lateran palace, using the same formula that Boso had used thirty years before.[54] Cencius' career resembles that of Boso at certain points. He was raised to the cardinalate in March 1193, after he had already served as chamberlain for five years. Like Boso, he acted as the pope's representative in the patrimony and directed the recovery and reorganisation of the papal lands. By 1194 Cencius had also become the most important official in the curia: for in that year the offices of chancellor and vice-chancellor had both become vacant and Cencius seems to have assumed the functions without assuming the title of chancellor. Again like Boso, Cencius lost his office and his dominant role in curia and patrimony on the death of the pope who was the architect of his power (8 January 1198).[55]

Cencius' most important achievement as chamberlain was the compilation in 1192 of the *Liber Censuum*, the register of the financial rights of the papacy throughout western Christendom. The author described it as a definitive list of 'those monasteries, hospitals . . . cities, castles, manors . . . or those kings or princes belonging to the jurisdiction and property of St Peter and the holy Roman church and owing *census* and how much they ought to pay'. In the original manuscript of this register (now Vaticanus latinus 8486) Cencius caused his assistant William Rofio, clerk of the papal *camera*, to leave large blank spaces so that future *camerarii* could add future financial rights 'until the end of the world'.[56] These spaces are now filled with

---

[54] *Liber Censuum* 1, 419–20 (no. 158).

[55] Fabre, *Etude* (n. 21) pp. 2–3; Geisthardt, *Boso* (n. 29) pp. 80–2; Michaud, 'Chambre apostolique' (n. 20) 393–6; V. Pfaff, 'Die Kardinäle unter Papst Coelestin III. (1191–1198)', *ZSSRG KA* 41 (1955), 93; idem, 'Papst Coelestin III.', ibid., 47 (1961), 115–18; Partner, *Lands* (n. 14) pp. 224–6.

[56] *Liber Censuum* 1, 2, 4. Description of the manuscript: Fabre, *Etude* pp. 171–5. See M. Michaud, 'Censuum (Liber)', *Dictionnaire de Droit Canonique* 3 (Paris, 1942), 233–53; V. Pfaff, 'Der Liber Censuum von 1192 (Die im Jahre 1192/93 der Kurie Zinspflichtigen)', *Vierteljahrschrift für Sozial- und Wirtschaftsgeschichte* 44 (1957), 78–96, 105–20, 220–42, 325–51; idem, 'Die Einnahmen der römischen Kurie am Ende des 12. Jahrhunderts', ibid., 40 (1953), 97–118; idem, 'Aufgaben' (n. 51) pp. 1–24.

thirteenth-century additions; but the modern editors of the *Liber Censuum*, Paul Fabre and Louis Duchesne (1910) have reconstructed the original compilation of Cencius. The *Liber Censuum* was the latest and most authoritative of a series of attempts, starting in the late eleventh century, to keep an accurate record of the financial claims of the Roman church. The Gregorian canonist Cardinal Deusdedit included a description of the proprietary rights of the Roman church in the canonical collection which he completed in 1087 and dedicated to Victor III. In the early 1140s the canon Benedict dedicated to Cardinal Guido of S. Maria in Via Lata, the future Celestine II, a *polypticus* containing further information about papal financial rights. Cencius found in the papal archives collections of papal diplomas concerning the patrimony, commissioned by 'Eugenius [III] of happy memory and Pope Hadrian [IV], his successor': the collection of Hadrian IV's diplomas was probably the work of the chamberlain Boso.[57] The most ambitious of these earlier collections was completed only three years before the *Liber Censuum*. Albinus, cardinal bishop of Albano completed in 1189 a volume containing 'whatever I knew or found in books of antiquities or what I myself heard and saw concerning the rights of St Peter'. Albinus' work absorbed the material in the earlier collections and this compilation of 1189 became in turn the principal source of the *Liber Censuum*.[58]

The earliest surviving reference to the use of such a register of papal rights in the papal *camera* occurs in a letter of Alexander III of 1163/4. The pope requested from the abbot of Lagny-sur-Marne the annual payment of one ounce of gold which his abbey owed to the Roman church, according to 'a certain work among the books of the apostolic see'. The curia was at this time based in Sens, but the staff of the *camera* had evidently brought with them from the Lateran palace a register containing information about the *census* owed by those monasteries that enjoyed papal protection. The abbey of Lagny-sur-Marne rejected the claim of the *camera* in 1163/4 and the pope pressed the matter no further. However, the papal claim was perfectly valid: it dated from the pontificate of Urban II.[59] It was in order to avoid such mischances that the *Liber Censuum* was com-

57 Fabre, *Etude* pp. 13–19, 20–4; Michaud, 'Censuum' (n. 56), 237–9.

58 Fabre, *Etude* pp. 10–13.

59 Alexander III, *JL* 10967: *Epistolae pontificum Romanorum ineditae* ed. S. Loewenfeld (Leipzig, 1885) p. 134; *JL* 11121: (n. 15) 333D–334A. Cf. Urban II, *JL* 5728: (n. 4) 524B. See Fabre, *Etude* p. 158 and n. 6.

piled. In the preface Cencius complained of the limitations of the earlier compilations, 'incomplete and neither written nor arranged authentically': from their inadequacies 'the Roman church incurred no little damage and loss'.[60] The *Liber Censuum* has been described as 'the most effective instrument and . . . the most significant document of ecclesiastical centralisation' in the central Middle Ages.[61] It is important to add that the *Liber Censuum* was not conceived as an innovatory work, but was entirely defensive in character. The chamberlain Cencius was preoccupied with the double threat to the rights of the Roman church in 1192. The papal patrimony was threatened by the Staufen emperor and the other financial resources of the papacy – the payments due from the monasteries, cities, principalities and kingdoms 'belonging to the jurisdiction and property of St Peter and the holy Roman church' – were threatened both by the evasions of the payers of *census* and by the inefficiency of the *camera*. The *camerarius* was in a much better position than the English chronicler to observe how 'the condition of the Church deteriorated gravely and uninterruptedly' in the late twelfth century. The *Liber Censuum* was an attempt to arrest this deterioration.

'The Roman church has never been accustomed to make demands, but has rather to be requested to impose on other churches the duty of paying a *census* to her.' Thus Alexander III explained to Bishop Maurice of Paris his action in allowing the abbey of Lagny-sur-Marne to evade payment of the *census* due to the apostolic see.[62] In theory this was the curia's attitude to all the papal revenues from sources outside the patrimony (a theory which had been emphasised particularly by Pope Gregory I). Such revenues were voluntary offerings, spontaneous expressions of gratitude to the Roman church for her protection or favour, like the gifts made by pilgrims to the tomb of St Peter.[63] In practice, however, from the eleventh century onwards these gifts were regarded by the papal curia as obligatory charges: the custom of making voluntary offerings hardened into a system of fixed payments. The classic example is the offering made when the pope conferred on a new archbishop the

[60] *Liber Censuum* I, 2.
[61] J. Rousset de Pina in R. Foreville and J. Rousset de Pina, *Du premier Concile du Latran à l'avènement d'Innocent III (1123–1198)* (Histoire de l'Eglise 9: Paris, 1953) p. 246.
[62] Alexander III, *JL* 11121: (n. 15) 334A.
[63] Gregory I, *Registrum* v.57a, *MGH Epistolae* I, 364–5. See Jordan, 'Finanzgeschichte' (n. 11) pp. 80–1.

ceremonial garment of his office, the pallium. From the middle of the eleventh century and the inauguration of the reform papacy the pope began to insist that archbishops should come to Rome to receive the pallium in person.[64] This requirement was primarily intended to provide an opportunity of investigating the suitability of the new archbishop; but a number of twelfth-century witnesses suggest that it was also an occasion for imposing charges which contemporaries regarded as exorbitant. In 1108, for example, Archbishop Thomas II of York complained to Anselm of Canterbury that because of his predecessor's extravagance, his diocese was too poor to raise the sum necessary to make the customary offering for the receipt of the pallium.[65] The German annals of Disibodenberg contain a curious anecdote describing how Archbishop Marculf of Mainz paid for his pallium in 1141/2. The monastery of St Martin in Mainz possessed a golden crucifix, donated by Archbishop Willigis during the reign of Emperor Otto III and bearing the inscription, 'This golden cross contains 600 pounds of gold.' According to the annalist, 'Bishop Marculf took one of the feet of the image and sent it to Rome [as payment] for the pallium.'[66]

Other special marks of papal favour must, like the pallium, be paid for. When, for example, in 1123 William of Corbeil, archbishop elect of Canterbury came to Rome with a delegation from his church to seek papal confirmation of his election, the delegation seized the opportunity to secure papal recognition of Canterbury's claim to primacy over the English church. The Canterbury delegation came armed with nine forged papal privileges and a large sum of money; but neither the forgeries nor the gold could prevail against the authority of the canons, which clearly repudiated Canterbury's claim.[67] The efforts of the Canterbury delegation in 1123 were recorded by a hostile witness, Hugh the Cantor (probably a member of the rival York delegation in Rome). For a less tendentious account of a similar enterprise it is necessary to turn to the *History of Compostela*, a narrative of the successful ambitions of Diego Gelmírez, bishop of Santiago de Compostela (1100–40). No other twelfth-century source describes in such detail the expenditure

---

[64] C. B. von Hacke, *Die Palliumverleihungen bis 1143. Eine diplomatische-historische Untersuchung* (Marburg, 1898) p. 131.
[65] Eadmer, *Historia novorum in Anglia* IV, RS 81 (1884), 200.
[66] *Annales sancti Disibodi* 1160, MGH SS 17, 29.
[67] Hugh the Cantor, *History* (n. 32) pp. 114–17. See above pp. 104, 189.

required to obtain a papal privilege.[68] In 1104 Diego Gelmírez attained the pallium; in 1120 he received the dignity of metropolitan until such time as the traditional metropolitan church, Mérida, was reconquered from the Moslems; in 1124 the metropolitan dignity was rendered permanent and Diego also received the title of archbishop. These successes followed long negotiations and the sending to the curia of splendid gifts, which the *History* describes by the conventional twelfth-century expression, 'blessings' (*benedictiones*). For example, when Diego first broached the question of the metropolitan dignity to Gelasius II (1117/18), the pope in reply admonished him to remember the current troubles of the Roman church and to 'come to her aid and ours with due charity'. Diego's response was to send a *benedictio* of 120 ounces (*unciae*) of gold to Rome. Unfortunately his gift was seized by 'Aragonese bandits', servants of Diego's enemy, King Alfonso I of Aragon; but Diego was soon able to send a second *benedictio* of 100 ounces of gold.[69] Calixtus II on his accession received from Compostela a *benedictio* of 20 ounces of gold, part of a large consignment of treasure entrusted to Abbot Pontius of Cluny, who was assisting Diego in his negotiations with the curia. When Calixtus made a conditional grant of the metropolitan dignity in a privilege of 1120, Diego raided the treasury of St James to send to the pope a *benedictio* of 260 marks of silver. (It was smuggled past the hostile Aragonese in small sums carried by pilgrims.) The diminution of Compostela's new jurisdiction was averted in 1121 by the sending of a golden reliquary worth 3,000 shillings and a golden crucifix and censer; and averted again in 1123 by a *benedictio* of 400 gold pieces. The appointment of Diego as permanent papal legate for the provinces of Mérida and Braga, the new privilege granting the metropolitan dignity in perpetuity and the conferring of the title of archbishop followed two further gifts: another *benedictio* of 400 gold pieces and a *benedictio* of 300 ounces of gold (part of which was lost in transit and had to be replaced).[70] These considerable sums of

[68] C. Erdmann, *Das Papsttum und Portugal im ersten Jahrhundert der portugiesischen Geschichte*, Abhandlungen der preussischen Akademie der Wissenschaften 1928, phil.-hist. Klasse no. 5, pp. 14–23; Jordan, 'Finanzgeschichte' (n. 11) pp. 82–8; R. A. Fletcher, *The episcopate in the kingdom of León in the twelfth century* (Oxford, 1978) pp. 186–8; idem, *Saint James's Catapult. The life and times of Diego Gelmírez of Santiago de Compostela* (Oxford, 1984) pp. 196–221.

[69] *Historia Compostellana* II.4, 6: (n. 27) 1036C–1038C, 1039B–1041A. Cf. Gelasius II, JL 6645, *MPL* 163, 494C. See Erdmann, *Papsttum und Portugal* (n. 68) pp. 20–1.

[70] *Historia Compostellana* II.10: 1045A–1046D; II.16, 57, 63, 64: 1055A–1056C, 1105A–1106A, 1114A–1119A. See Jordan, 'Finanzgeschichte' (n. 11) pp. 83–6.

money were obviously of great importance to a papal curia impoverished by a protracted struggle with the emperor and with a series of antipopes and now attempting to reestablish itself in Rome. Likewise, during the schism of the 1130s Innocent II had great need of the 40 marks of silver which Diego sent to him in exile in Genoa in 1130 and the 300 gold pieces which Innocent's legate, Cardinal deacon Guido of SS. Cosma e Damiano, begged from Diego in 1136. The papal response was a series of letters safeguarding the rights of the church of Compostela.[71]

Papal privileges of a more modest character than those conferred on Compostela also had to be paid for. It was 'the custom of the Roman church' that 'neither pen nor paper is to be had free of charge', wrote Bishop Ivo of Chartres to Cardinal bishop Richard of Albano (1105). He attributed the heavy charges made for papal privileges to the fact that not only the pope but also the officials of the curia required payment. 'The servants of the sacred palace make many demands from consecrated bishops and abbots, which are disguised by the name of "offering" or "blessing".'[72] At the end of the eleventh century, as a consequence of the Gregorian reform programme, the papal curia was extending the range of its duties and perhaps also increasing the number of its personnel: the growth of papal government had to be paid for. We have already noted the mid-twelfth-century criticisms of Roman avarice and Hadrian IV's explanation that papal demands were large because the costs of papal government were so great: 'no soldier can serve without wages'.[73] During the twelfth century the wages of curial officials were mainly derived from the 'offerings' of the faithful who petitioned for papal favours. Once more the principal source of information is the *History of Compostela*, unusual among twelfth-century narrative sources in the richness of its financial details. The historian specifies that the *benedictio* of 300 gold pieces of 1124 was intended to be shared by the pope with the cardinals and principal officials of the curia, the pope receiving the lion's share. Similarly, when in 1126 Diego Gelmírez sent to Rome a *benedictio* of 300 *marabotini* (the Arabic gold coins of Spain), 220 coins were given to Honorius II and 80 to the curia.[74] This method of remunerating the personnel of the curia encouraged

---

[71] Innocent II, *JL* 7415–19, *MPL* 179, 58C–60B. Cf. *Historia Compostellana* III.25, 49: 1190B–1191A, 1225CD. See Fletcher, *León* (n. 68) p. 215.

[72] Ivo of Chartres, *Epistola* 133, *MPL* 162, 142C.

[73] See above p. 247.

[74] *Historia Compostellana* II.64, III.10: (n. 27), 1117D, 1173B.

abuses which provoked the famous twelfth-century satires against Roman avarice and which inspired demands for reform. The most distinguished critic of the curia in the twelfth century was Bernard of Clairvaux in his treatise on the papal office, *De consideratione*, addressed to his disciple, Eugenius III. Bernard's treatise denounced the financial preoccupations of the curia: did not Christ have Judas Iscariot as his steward; did not the apostle say, 'gold and silver have I none'?[75] Bernard had only one wish – so he wrote to Eugenius III in 1145 – and that was to hear the pope say what his predecessor, St Peter, had said to Simon Magus: 'your money go with you to perdition!'[76] The necessary reform of the curia could only be achieved by the recruitment of suitable personnel. Like Moses, Eugenius must choose not young, but old men – men, that is, not necessarily of advanced years, but whose morals conformed to the pattern of the apostolic age.[77] Bernard's criticisms of the curia can hardly have taken Eugenius by surprise. Before his accession to the papacy, as abbot of the Cistercian house of S. Anastasio in Rome, he had spoken of the need to prohibit members of the curia from receiving 'unlawful gifts', but as pope he proved unable to enforce this reform.[78] Thirty years later Gregory VIII was able to exploit the shock of the fall of Jerusalem and enthusiasm for the Third Crusade to obtain from the cardinals a promise that until Jerusalem was recovered they would take no gifts from petitioners, except what was intended 'for their needs and sustenance'.[79]

A similar reform was imposed in the late twelfth century on papal legates, who were of all the agents of the papacy the most frequently criticised for avarice and corruption. During his pontificate Gregory VII had required individual prelates to swear an oath to provide for legates visiting their dioceses. The earliest extant oath is that of Patriarch Henry of Aquileia in 1079: 'I shall treat [any] Roman legate honourably . . . and shall assist him with his needs.'[80] In the course of the following century it came to be assumed that all churches (un-

[75] Bernard of Clairvaux, *De consideratione* IV.6.19–20, II.6.10, MPL 182, 785D–786C, 748A.
[76] Bernard, *Epistola* 238: (n. 8) 340B. See B. Jacqueline, 'Saint-Bernard de Clairvaux et la curie romaine', *Rivista di storia della Chiesa in Italia* 7 (1953), 38–42.
[77] Bernard, *De consideratione* IV.4.9: 778C.
[78] Gerhoch of Reichersberg, letter to Bernard of Clairvaux: G. Hüffer, *Der heilige Bernhard von Clairvaux* I (Münster, 1886), 222. See Jordan, 'Finanzgeschichte' (n. 11) p. 82.
[79] Peter of Blois, *Epistola* 219, MPL 207, 508D.
[80] Gregory VII, *Registrum* VI.17a, c. 4, p. 429.

less they were specifically exempted by a papal privilege) were obliged to provide accommodation and food for a visiting papal legate and his entourage. This was the obligation which canon lawyers would later call *procuratio canonica*.[81] The obligation was included, for example, in the oath exacted from an archbishop before the pope conferred the pallium on him: 'I shall treat honourably a legate of the apostolic see whom I know for certain to be [the pope's] legate . . . and shall assist him with his needs.'[82] The rapid expansion of legatine activity inaugurated by the Gregorian reform meant that many churches were forced to pay considerable sums for the maintenance of legates. A particular grievance was the size of the entourages which accompanied some of the cardinal legates. In a characteristic polemic against the financial demands of the curia, written in 1161/2, the theologian Gerhoch of Reichersberg described how cardinals allowed a legatine appointment to go to their heads.

As long as they remain at home, they behave with moderation and are content with a few servants, but as soon as one of them is given a legation to a foreign land, he immediately collects together a retinue from wherever he can, appointing some of them stewards, others cupbearers, chamberlains and marshals, and these in turn provide themselves with followers and servants. This considerable entourage then requires forty or more horses, so that the wealthiest monasteries (to say nothing of the poorer or middling houses) and even bishops and princes cannot afford to supply the wants of such a crowd.[83]

In an attempt to reduce the financial burden of the *procuratio canonica* the Third Lateran Council of 1179 decreed that the entourage of a cardinal legate should not exceed twenty-five persons.[84]

'The sacred hunger for gold and silver in the [papal] curia has grown so great that the whole world cannot satisfy it, even though

---

[81] K. Ruess, *Die rechtliche Stellung der päpstlichen Legaten bis Bonifaz VIII.* (Paderborn, 1912) p. 188; C. Brühl, 'Zur Geschichte der procuratio canonica vornehmlich im 11. und 12. Jahrhundert' in *Le istituzioni ecclesiastiche della 'societas christiana' dei secoli XI–XII* 1 (Miscellanea del Centro di Studi Medioevali 7: Milan, 1974), 427–9.

[82] Archbishop Hubert Walter of Canterbury, profession to Celestine III (1193): *Epistolae Cantuarienses* 409, *RS* 38/2 (1865), 368. Cf. *Liber Censuum* 1, 417. See M. Tangl, *Päpstliche Kanzleiordnungen von 1200 bis 1500* (Innsbruck, 1894) pp. 51–2 (no. 19).

[83] Gerhoch of Reichersberg, *De investigatione Antichristi* c. 50, *MGH Libelli* 3, 357. See above p. 162.

[84] Concilium Lateranense III c. 4, *Conciliorum Oecumenicorum Decreta* p. 213.

[the members of the curia] are prepared to drain it dry.'[85] Gerhoch of
Reichersberg, writing early in the Alexandrine schism (1161/2),
attributed this 'sacred hunger' to the *necessitas*, the state of emergency
in which the papacy had so often found itself since the days of
Gregory VII. Papal schism and conflict with secular princes often
compelled the curia to appeal to the faithful for emergency supplies.
For example, Urban II appealed to Abbot Hugh of Cluny for 'relief
and solace' and Bernard of Clairvaux appealed for money on behalf
of Innocent II to King Henry I of England and Emperor Lothar III.[86]
W. E. Lunt in his studies of papal finances (1934, 1939) called these
emergency supplies 'papal subsidies' and described them as
'analogous to the gracious aids levied by feudal lords'.[87] The term
subsidia is indeed used for these supplies during the pontificate of
Alexander III, but it is only one of a number of terms, of which
eleemosyna (alms) and *subventio* (help) are the most frequent. The
pope of course, like other feudal lords, received aids from his vassals:
such as, for example, the 40,000 marks sent by King William I of
Sicily on his deathbed in 1166.[88] However, in other cases the analogy
between the papal 'subsidies' of the twelfth century and the feudal
aid is perhaps a misleading one. The letters of Alexander III appealing for financial help do not use feudal terminology: the pope, faced
with an emergency (*necessitas*), asked for 'alms' from 'the sons of the
Church', 'so that we can vigorously resist the enemies of the
Church'.[89] Critics of the curia emphasised that such 'alms' or
'subsidies' were extraordinary payments, to which the papacy had
no legal claim. In particular, Gerhoch of Reichersberg in 1161/2 criticised the dependence of the Alexandrine curia on the emergency
supplies provided by the emperor's enemies. Although Gerhoch
eventually became a supporter of Alexander III, at the beginning of
the schism he took a neutral stance and paid heed to the imperial
propaganda which represented Alexander as the stooge of the king of

[85] Gerhoch, *De investigatione* c. 19, p. 329.
[86] Urban II: Ramackers, 'Analekten' (n. 4) p. 42 (see above p. 250); Bernard of
    Clairvaux, *Epistolae* 138–9:(n. 8) 292B–295A.
[87] W. E. Lunt, *Papal revenues in the Middle Ages* I (Columbia Records of Civilization
    19: Columbia, 1934), 77; *idem, Financial relations of the papacy with England to 1327*
    (Medieval Academy of America Publications 33: Cambridge, Mass., 1939)
    p. 175.
[88] John of Salisbury, *Letter* 168: (n. 39) p. 116; Boso, *Vita Alexandri III* (n. 42)
    pp. 416–17. See below p. 392.
[89] Alexander III, *JL* 10655–6, 10880, 11204, 11256, 11342–3: (n. 15) 107D–109C,
    233AB, 373CD, 405D–406D, 441B–442A, 446D–447D.

Sicily and the citizens of Milan: 'this present schism has sprung from the gold and silver of the Sicilian [king] and the Milanese'.[90] Anglo-Norman historians agreed that the Alexandrine curia was too fertile in devising means of raising extraordinary revenues: even Alexander's reforming councils were made to serve this purpose. Stephen of Rouen's satirical account of the council of Tours (May 1163) describes how 'the English nobility crossed the sea and came in haste, together with a great abundance of silver. The papal curia rejoiced to see the metal shine and the red [gold] was, quite rightly, more beloved there than the white [silver]'. 'The pope kept the silver and the gold: that, I think, was the secondary purpose of the council.'[91] The chronicler William of Newburgh likewise claimed that the Third Lateran Council (March 1179) was not summoned entirely from motives of reform. By an 'artifice of Roman avarice' those prelates who found the journey to Rome too difficult were excused from attending, once they had made an offering to the curia.[92]

The most important way in which the western churches and princes contributed to the income of the papacy was the regular payment of the traditional revenues of the *census*. The annual *census* paid by monasteries in return for the protection (*tuitio, tutela, defensio, protectio*) of St Peter was one of the oldest papal revenues, dating from the late eighth century. In the tenth century and with greater frequency from the later eleventh century onwards the papacy, in return for an annual *census*, began to confer on monasteries the valuable privilege of *Romana libertas*. 'Roman liberty' conferred exemption from the spiritual as well as the temporal authority of the bishop to whose diocese the monastery belonged: the monastery was subject to no one except the pope. Such a monastery was described in papal privileges of the late twelfth century (in what became the standard formula of the thirteenth-century papal chancery) as 'belonging to the Roman church with no intermediary' (*nullo medio* or *nullo mediante*). In the *Liber Censuum* Cencius Savelli described such monasteries as 'belonging to the jurisdiction and property of St Peter and the holy Roman church'.[93] The *Liber Censuum* makes no distinction between those monasteries enjoying the temporal protection of St Peter and those enjoying 'Roman liberty': the payment

---

[90] Gerhoch, *De investigatione* c. 58 (n. 83) p. 373. Cf. c. 68, pp. 384–5.
[91] Stephen of Rouen, *Draco Normannicus* III.13, 15, *RS* 82/2 (1885), 743, 752.
[92] William of Newburgh, *Historia rerum Anglicarum* III.2, *RS* 82/1 (1884), 206.
[93] *Liber Censuum* 1, 2. See Fabre, *Etude* (n. 21) pp. 26–115; Lunt, *Financial relations* (n. 87) pp. 85–123. For *Romana libertas* see above pp. 226–9.

of *census* is assumed to be evidence of the proprietorship of the Roman church. What interested the *camerarius* Cencius was not legal distinctions and historical origins, but the amount of *census* to be paid. The amount varied widely, from the two silver *solidi* owed by Cluny to the pint of almonds owed by Romans (near Arles). Reichenau owed an annual *census* of two white horses, a sacramentary and a Gospel book; the monastery of Woffenheim must provide the golden rose which the pope carried on the fourth Sunday of Lent. For the great majority of monasteries and churches which paid in gold or silver coins, the average payment, according to the *Liber Censuum*, was 2 golden *marabotini* or 5 silver *solidi*. A few paid less than 1 *solidus* and a few paid as much as 2 ounces (*unciae*) of gold (1 *uncia* being generally regarded as equivalent to 7 *marabotini*).[94]

The number of churches and monasteries owing *census* which Cencius was able to identify in 1192 was approximately 530. (Volkert Pfaff's examination of the extant papal privileges for religious houses [1956] has produced another 129 institutions owing *census* which Cencius missed, although a thirteenth-century successor added 59 of them to the *Liber Censuum*.)[95] Of the 493 churches and monasteries which paid their *census* in cash rather than kind, approximately 42 per cent were situated in northern or central Italy, 20 per cent in Germany, 19 per cent in the French-speaking territories, 8 per cent in the kingdom of Sicily and 6 per cent in Spain. However, although the kingdom of Italy contained so large a proportion of the institutions owing *census* – 207 in all – the great majority of these churches paid only very small sums: only forty-nine paid 2 *marabotini* or more and only twelve paid 1 ounce of gold or more. The small sums paid by northern and central Italian *census*-payers contrast with the large sums derived from the kingdom of Sicily: of the thirty-eight Sicilian churches owing *census*, thirty-three paid 2 *marabotini* or more and twenty-five paid 1 ounce of gold or more. There is a similar contrast between the sums paid by the monasteries of the old-established 'inner kingdoms' of western Christendom and the *census* emanating from the 'peripheral kingdoms' of Spain. Of the ninety-four German churches paying *census*, thirteen paid 2 *marabotini* or more; of the ninety-two houses in France, forty-eight paid 2 *marabotini* or more. In the case of Spain, thirty churches owed *census*, twenty-one paid 2 *marabotini* or more

---

94 G. Schreiber, *Kurie und Kloster im 12. Jahrhundert* 1 (Stuttgart, 1910), 34; Jordan, 'Finanzgeschichte' (n. 11) p. 72; Pfaff, 'Aufgaben' (n. 51) p. 7.
95 Pfaff, 'Aufgaben' p. 2.

and thirteen paid 1 ounce of gold or more. (The Spanish house of S. Servandus in Toledo and Valladolid were among the very few monasteries which paid more than 2 ounces of gold as a *census*.)[96] As for the monasteries of the English kingdom, which comprise approximately 2 per cent of the houses recorded in the *Liber Censuum*, Chertsey, Malmesbury and St Albans, together with St John's abbey, Dublin, paid a *census* of 1 ounce of gold or more.[97] This discrepancy between the amount of *census* paid by the monasteries and churches of the 'inner kingdoms' of Italy, Germany and France and those of the 'peripheral kingdoms' of Sicily, Spain and England is closely related to the chronology of the spread of papal protection and 'Roman liberty' in the 'inner' and 'outer' regions of western Christendom. In northern and central Italy, Germany and France, many monasteries had secured their papal privileges before 1100: the monasteries of Sicily, Spain and England in most cases obtained their privileges after 1100. Before 1100 the amount of *census* to be paid by a monastery seems often to have been fixed arbitrarily without reference to its relative wealth (evidently by the benefactor who gave the monastery to the Roman church). The principal purpose of the *census* was not to provide the Roman church with revenue but to symbolise a monastery's special relationship with the papacy. After 1100, however, the amount of the *census* bore a closer relationship to the wealth of the monastery receiving papal exemption. Perhaps this was a side-effect of the financial reorganisation of the papal curia in the late eleventh century: a realisation that monastic exemption, like other papal favours, could become a useful source of revenue (combined with the knowledge that the monasteries of the 'peripheral kingdoms' were extremely wealthy). But there was no attempt to rationalise the *census*: there is very little evidence of the raising or lowering of the amount of *census* during the twelfth century.[98] The monasteries of the 'peripheral kingdoms', therefore, contributed to the papal revenues far more, relatively speaking, than the monasteries of the 'inner kingdoms'.

The monastic *census*, whether from the 'inner' or from the 'peripheral' kingdoms, presented the curia with the practical problem of collection. Cencius Savelli defined the current practice in his introduction to the *Liber Censuum*.

---

[96] *Ibid.*, pp. 5–8: see in particular the table on p. 7.
[97] Lunt, *Financial relations* (n. 87) pp. 91–123; Pfaff, 'Aufgaben' p. 7.
[98] Jordan, 'Finanzgeschichte' (n. 11) pp. 73–6; Pfaff, 'Aufgaben' pp. 8–12.

Whenever the *census* is not sent to the apostolic see by those who owe it,
using their own envoys (which often happens), the pontiff who is then presiding over the Roman church, being informed by his chamberlain (who
receives the *census*) that he has received *census* from some but not from
others, . . . should not hesitate to seek the *census* from those who have not
paid it, either through his own legate or envoy or through someone else sent
especially for this purpose; for certain [payers of *census*] are so remote from
the holy Roman church that they cannot visit her every year.[99]

The collection of overdue *census* is a regular theme of papal letters
both to legates and to prelates whom the pope particularly trusted.
The earliest extant letter on this subject is that of Gregory VII to the
French abbots in 1075, informing them that his permanent legate in
France, Bishop Hugh of Die, was responsible for the collection of the
census.[100] Two letters of 1093 show Urban II entrusting the collection
of the *census* in southern France to the abbots of two monasteries in
Poitiers, Rainald of St Cyprien and Gervasius of St Savin. Urban,
appealing to the prelates of Aquitaine for financial help, added: 'but
even if you neglect to pour out the bowels of your charity, at least do
not fail to send what you know that you owe the Lateran palace as an
annual *census*'. A careful distinction is made here between a voluntary
gift, a 'papal subsidy', which the recipients of his letter might be
moved to send to the pope, and the obligatory payment of *census*.[101]
This reliance on local churchmen (which is not mentioned by
Cencius in his account of the collection of the *census*) continued
during the twelfth century. Eugenius III in 1150 gave the duty of
collecting the *census* in the ecclesiastical province of Tarragona to the
bishop of Pamplona.[102] Alexander III in 1168/70 requested
Archbishop Henry of Rheims to assist the papal envoy 'brother
Rostaim' in collecting the *census* of the province of Rheims, which
had long fallen into arrears.[103] During the 1170s the *census* owed by
German monasteries was collected by the permanent papal legate in
southern Germany, Conrad of Wittelsbach (former archbishop of
Mainz and future archbishop of Salzburg).[104] The other ways in
which the *census* might reach the curia in the later twelfth century are
illustrated by the cartulary of the Portuguese monastery in S. Cruz
in Coimbra. Carl Erdmann (1927) discovered here a list of seven

---

[99] *Liber Censuum* 1, 4–5.
[100] Gregory VII, *Epistolae Vagantes* 12, ed. H. E. J. Cowdrey (Oxford, 1972) p. 28.
[101] Urban II, *JL* 5494–5: (n. 4) 368C–370A.
[102] Erdmann, *Papsturkunden* (n. 45) p. 214 (no. 49).
[103] Alexander III, *JL* 11697: (n. 15) 630BC.
[104] Jordan, 'Finanzgeschichte' (n. 11) p. 77. See below p. 488.

payments of *census* covering the years 1156–86. In 1156 the amount of *census* due for the past six years was brought to the curia by a monk of S. Cruz and in 1163 likewise the annual payment was delivered by a member of the convent. But on the other five occasions the *census* was received by a member of the papal curia in Coimbra: by a sub-deacon of the Roman church in 1162 and 1183 and by a papal legate in 1168, 1173 and 1186 (in 1173 the legate was the illustrious Cardinal Hyacinth Bobo, the future Celestine III).[105] By the end of the twelfth century the collection of the *census* had become a characteristic duty of legates and lesser papal envoys visiting the 'peripheral kingdoms' of western Christendom.[106]

The *Liber Censuum* records the details not only of the *census* paid by monasteries enjoying papal protection but also of three quite distinct types of payment: the feudal dues paid by princes who were papal vassals, the *census* paid by princes who were not vassals, but who had been granted papal protection, and the payment of Peter's pence by the 'peripheral kingdoms' of northern Europe. Of the feudal payments the earliest in date were those paid by the Norman princes of the Hauteville dynasty for their fiefs of southern Italy and Sicily. Cencius recorded these important revenues in unusual detail.

When Robert Guiscard from beyond the mountains conquered the kingdom of Sicily, he swore on the holy Gospels, both for himself and for his heirs, to give to Pope Nicholas [II] and his successors twelve *denarii* of the mint of Pavia for each yoke of oxen. Subsequently, when Pope Innocent [II] went to Galluccio, Roger [II], then king of Sicily, agreed to give him 600 *squifati* annually for Apulia and Calabria. But afterwards his son, King W[illiam I], added a further 400 *squifati* in the days of Pope Hadrian [IV] for Marsia (which he had seized in the days of Pope Innocent), when he performed homage and fealty at Benevento.

According to the terms of the treaty of Benevento (18 June 1156), therefore, the Norman king of Sicily owed a feudal payment of 1,000 *squifati* to the Roman church.[107] (The *squifatus* was the most valuable gold coin in circulation, reckoned by the papal curia to be worth 2 *marabotini*.)[108] During the late eleventh century a few other princes imitated the Norman example and became vassals of the papacy. The duke of Dalmatia and Croatia, raised to the kingship by Gregory

[105] Erdmann, *Papsturkunden* (n. 45) pp. 379–80 (no. 159).
[106] See above p. 164.
[107] *Liber Censuum* I, 15–16. Cf. Treaty of Benevento c. 13, *MGH Constitutiones* I, 590. See below p. 390.
[108] Pfaff, 'Einnahmen' (n. 56) p. 109.

VII, was perhaps of their number. Certainly he paid an annual tribute of 200 *bizantii* (equivalent to 200 *marabotini*).[109] Count Peter of Substancion-Melgueil surrendered his lands to the Roman church in 1085 and became a papal vassal, paying an annual *census* of 1 ounce of gold.[110] Count Berengar Raimund II of Barcelona surrendered his city of Tarragona in 1090 and likewise became a papal vassal, owing a *census* of 25 marks of silver every five years.[111] A number of other princes from the Iberian peninsula – King Sancho Ramirez of Navarre and Aragon, Count Bernard II of Besalú and Duke (later King) Alfonso I of Portugal – entered into a special relationship with the papacy which was not, however, a conventional feudal relationship. Their lands did not become fiefs of the Roman church but they were permitted to enjoy the protection (*protectio, defensio, tuitio, tutela, patrocinium*) of St Peter.[112] Like the monasteries which enjoyed a similar privilege, these secular princes paid an annual *census*. The king of Aragon paid a *tributum* of 500 *mancusi* and each of his vassals paid a further *mancusus*; the count of Besalú paid 100 *mancusi*. (The *mancusus* was an Arab gold coin older than, but regarded as equal in value to the *marabotinus*.)[113] Alfonso I as duke of Portugal paid a *census* of 4 ounces of gold; but when Alexander III recognised him as king in 1179, Alfonso increased his *census* fourfold to 2 marks of gold and in addition sent a gift of 1,000 gold pieces to the pope.[114]

These secular princes from the peripheral lands of western Christendom were among the principal contributors to the papal revenues. Their payments far exceeded the *census* paid by all the monasteries and churches enjoying protection or spiritual exemption. The payment of 'St Peter's pence' by the peripheral kingdoms of northern Europe provides a similar case-study. This payment was different in character both from the feudal dues of papal vassals and from the *census* paid by princes in return for St Peter's protection. It originated in England, perhaps in the late ninth century, as a pious

[109] *Liber Censuum* 1, 356. See Fabre, *Etude* (n. 21) p. 125; Jordan, 'Finanzgeschichte' (n. 11) p. 79.
[110] Jordan, 'Finanzgeschichte' p. 79; J. Fried, *Der päpstliche Schutz für Laienfürsten. Die politische Geschichte des päpstlichen Schutzprivilegs für Laien (11.–13. Jh.)*, *Abhandlungen der Heidelberger Akademie der Wissenschaften, phil.-hist. Klasse* 1980/1, pp. 72–3.
[111] Jordan, 'Finanzgeschichte' p. 79; Fried, *Schutz* pp. 87–101.
[112] Fried, *Schutz* pp. 49–53, 56–87, 140–2. See below p. 304.
[113] Jordan, 'Finanzgeschichte' p. 79; Fried, *Schutz* pp. 59, 71, 74; Pfaff, 'Einnahmen' (n. 56) pp. 108–9.
[114] Erdmann, *Papsttum und Portugal* (n. 68) p. 49; Jordan, 'Finanzgeschichte' p. 80.

offering by the Anglo-Saxon kings (*Romfeoh*), the joint recipients being the English school in Rome and the papacy. By the later eleventh century this royal almsgiving had come to be regarded by the papal curia as a fixed annual payment to the Roman church.[115] Alexander II described the payment as 'an annual tribute (*pensio*) in respect of pious devotion and religious obligation'; Gregory VII as 'the property of St Peter which is collected in England'; Urban II as 'the money which, according to custom, St Peter used to receive from the [English] kingdom'; Paschal II as 'the *census* of St Peter' and 'the alms of St Peter'.[116] In the *Liber Censuum* the payment is described as 'the *denarius* of St Peter'. The money was collected from the churches in each diocese (every church possessing an income of at least 30 *denarii* contributing 1 *denarius*) and forwarded to the archbishop of Canterbury; but the responsibility for sending St Peter's pence to Rome belonged to the king. Cencius Savelli calculated the total annual payment as 'one mark short of 300 marks [of silver]'.[117]

Peter's pence played a decisive role in Anglo-papal relations in the period 1073–1198. During the pontificate of Gregory VII the papacy developed an interpretation of the payment which differed sharply from that of the English king, William the Conqueror (1066–87) and his adviser, Archbishop Lanfranc of Canterbury (1070–89). In the summer of 1080 Gregory linked a demand for the payment of arrears of Peter's pence with a demand that the king perform fealty to the pope. The linking of these two demands suggests that Gregory regarded Peter's pence either as a feudal payment or as 'tribute' (*pensio*) paid in acknowledgement of papal jurisdiction over the kingdom. William I accepted the obligation to pay but rejected the Gregorian interpretation of the payment. Peter's pence was an imposition on the English churches levied by the king and sent as alms to Rome: it was not a 'tribute' imposed by the pope and had no feudal implications.[118] The demand for fealty was not repeated:

---

[115] Fabre, *Etude* (n. 21) pp. 129–38; Z. N. Brooke, *The English church and the papacy from the Conquest to the reign of John* (Cambridge, 1931) pp. 141–3; Jordan, 'Finanzgeschichte' pp. 77–8; Lunt, *Financial relations* (n. 87) pp. 3–34; F. Barlow, *The English church 1000–1066* (London, 1963) pp. 295–7.

[116] Alexander II, *JL* 4757: (n. 19) 1413D; Gregory VII, *Registrum* 1.70, p. 102; Urban II, *JL* 5351: (n. 4) 287D; Paschal II, *JL* 5883, 6450: *MPL* 163, 81A, 377C.

[117] *Liber Censuum* 1, 226.

[118] Z. N. Brooke, 'Pope Gregory VII's demand for fealty from William the Conqueror', *EHR* 26 (1911), 225–38; *idem*, *English church* (n. 115) pp. 140–3; Lunt, *Financial relations* (n. 87) pp. 5, 31–3, 45–7; H. E. J. Cowdrey, 'Pope Gregory VII and the Anglo-Norman church and kingdom', *SG* 9 (1972), 89–94; M. Gibson, *Lanfranc of Bec* (Oxford, 1978) pp. 135–6. See below pp. 307–8.

Gregory would not risk conflict with the English king. 'It must not be considered unworthy that his power is treated fairly leniently,' Gregory warned his legates in France. 'For it seems to us that he can be won for God and drawn to a constant love of St Peter much more easily by mildness and a show of reason than by the severity and rigour of righteousness.'[119] This advice became the basis of papal policy towards the English kingdom throughout the Investiture Contest. How much the need for Peter's pence was bound up with the willingness to conciliate the English king is suggested both by the numerous papal letters urging payment and the number of papal envoys sent to collect the money: one by Gregory VII, at least three by Urban II and at least four by Paschal II.[120] In the first month of his pontificate Urban II wrote to Lanfranc of Canterbury to ask for payment of Peter's pence, promising that he would be 'ever prompt and ready to increase and exalt [William II's] kingship'.[121] But the new king, William II (1087–1100) preferred to remain neutral in the contest between Urban and his rival, the imperial antipope 'Clement III'. For seven years the pope went unrecognised and Peter's pence went unpaid. According to the Lotharingian chronicler Hugh of Flavigny, Urban finally secured payment in 1096 as a reward for withdrawing a papal legate whose commission was to obtain more freedom from royal control for the English church.[122] King Henry I (1100–35) soon after his accession made a voluntary payment of Peter's pence to the new pope, Paschal II. This gesture was intended to persuade the pope to exempt the English king from the papal decrees against lay investiture. When it failed in its effect, the king threatened Paschal with the loss of the obedience of the English kingdom and 'the payment which he was accustomed to have from there every year'.[123]

The English kings' use of Peter's pence as a bargaining counter must have had some influence on the situation of Archbishop Anselm of Canterbury (1093–1109) in his lonely campaign against the 'customs' of the Anglo-Norman kings. Anselm twice suffered

---

[119] Gregory VII, *Registrum* IX.5, p. 580. See Cowdrey, 'Anglo-Norman church' pp. 102–3, 106–7.

[120] Tillmann, *Legaten* (n. 46) pp. 16–17, 18, 20, 22, 23, 25.

[121] Urban II, *JL* 5351: (n. 4) 286D–288A. See Becker, *Urban II*. 1, 169–71.

[122] Hugh of Flavigny, *Chronicon* II, *MGH SS* 8, 474–5. See Tillmann, *Legaten* (n. 46) p. 21; N. F. Cantor, *Church, kingship and lay investiture in England, 1089–1135* (Princeton, 1958) pp. 103–4.

[123] Eadmer, *Historia novorum* (n. 65) pp. 128–32, 152–4. See Lunt, *Financial relations* (n. 87) pp. 36–7, 47.

exile for opposing abuses to which the reform papacy was also strongly opposed: William II's exclusion of papal influence from his kingdom and Henry I's violation of the papal decrees against lay investiture. But when Anselm incurred the royal displeasure by taking a stand on these issues, he found both Urban II and Paschal II anxious to reach a compromise with the king. When Urban secured recognition of his title from William II in 1095, both found it expedient to exclude Anselm from their negotiations. Likewise, throughout the English investiture dispute of 1100–6 Paschal II showed himself much more willing to negotiate with Henry I than with Anselm.[124] It is instructive to compare the papal attitude towards Anselm with that towards Archbishop Thurstan of York (1114–40) a decade later. Like Anselm, Thurstan suffered exile because of his opposition to the king: he resisted Henry I's attempt to diminish the dignity of the church of York. However, the papacy was far less cautious in its support for Thurstan than it had been in its dealings with Anselm: Calixtus II in 1119 was willing to defy Henry I in defence of Thurstan's rights.[125] In the pontificate of Calixtus II the curia could be more confident in its dealings with England. English churchmen had begun to feel the centripetal attraction of Rome: the pope no longer depended on the king as his principal means of exercising influence over the English church.[126] This development, together with the gradual improvement in the financial position of the papacy, made Calixtus II less vulnerable than his predecessors to the royal manipulation of Peter's pence.

From the 1120s until the early 1160s papal agents in England seem to have collected Peter's pence without difficulty: the papal legate Abbot Henry of Saint-Jean d'Angely (a kinsman of Henry I) in the pontificates of Calixtus II and Honorius II, and subsequently the permanent papal legates in England, Bishop Henry of Winchester (legate, 1139–43) and Archbishop Theobald of Canterbury (*ca.* 1150–61).[127] No papal letter of this period complains of the non-payment of Peter's pence or accuses the king, as did Paschal II in 1115, of collecting 'the alms of St Peter . . . falsely and deceitfully'.[128] Henry I did not use the opportunity of the schism of the 1130s, as William II had used the late eleventh-century schism, to

[124] R. W. Southern, *Saint Anselm and his biographer* (Cambridge, 1963) pp. 151–63, 165–79; Cantor, *Church* (n. 122) pp. 87–108, 149–67, 197–201, 253–73.
[125] D. Nicholl, *Thurstan, archbishop of York (1114–40)* (York, 1964) pp. 64–70.
[126] M. Brett, *The English church under Henry I* (Oxford, 1975) pp. 34–62, 234–46.
[127] Tillmann, *Legaten* (n. 46) p. 27; Lunt, *Financial relations* (n. 87) pp. 41–2, 47–8.
[128] Paschal II, *JL* 6450: (n. 116) 377C.

avoid payment of St Peter's pence. Henry recognised Innocent II as pope when he met him in Chartres in 1131. There was no question of a policy of neutrality like that of 1087–95: too many English churchmen took too keen an interest in papal affairs for such a tactic to be feasible in the 1130s.[129] During Innocent II's pontificate the English kingship became distinctly less formidable in appearance. Henry I's successor, Stephen (1135–54), was a usurper who initially needed the support of the English church and the sanction of the papacy. During his reign royal control over the church was seriously undermined, notably by the ambitions of the king's brother, Henry of Blois, bishop of Winchester and papal legate. Far from being able to manipulate the payment of Peter's pence so as to exert pressure on the papacy, Stephen seems to have lost control of its collection. The single extant document referring to Peter's pence in his reign is a letter written by Henry of Winchester in his capacity of papal legate, complaining of the delay in the sending of the contribution of the diocese of Worcester. The legate commanded, by apostolic authority and under pain of interdict, that the money be brought to Winchester within fifteen days.[130] In this instance the papal agent had assumed direct control of the collection of Peter's pence: the king seems to have lost his responsibility for transmitting the royal alms to Rome.

Stephen's successor, Henry II (1154–89) was determined to restore royal control over the English church. Henry intended to govern like his grandfather, Henry I, who (the grandson boasted) had been 'king, apostolic legate, patriarch, emperor and everything he wished to be, in his own land'.[131] The outbreak of the papal schism in the fifth year of his reign seemed likely to favour his designs. Henry followed the advice of his clergy in recognising Alexander III as pope: Archbishop Theobald of Canterbury urged the king to 'decide nothing to the prejudice [of the Church] without the advice of your clergy'. But a pope as vulnerable and as anxious for English support as Alexander might well prove amenable to royal pressure.[132] It became particularly necessary for Henry II to influence Alexander

[129] F.-J. Schmale, *Studien zum Schisma des Jahres 1130* (Cologne–Graz, 1961) pp. 233–4; Brett, *Henry I* (n. 126) pp. 34–62.

[130] L. Voss, *Heinrich von Blois Bischof von Winchester (1129–71)* (Historische Studien 210: Berlin, 1932) p. 49; Lunt, *Financial relations* (n. 87) pp. 41–2.

[131] John of Salisbury, *Letter* 275 (n. 39) p. 580. See above p. 172.

[132] John of Salisbury, *Letter* 122, ed. W. J. Millor, H. E. Butler, C. N. L. Brooke 1 (London, 1955), 202. See F. Barlow, 'The English, Norman and French councils called to deal with the papal schism of 1159', *EHR* 51 (1936), 264–8; M. G.

when in 1164 Archbishop Thomas Becket of Canterbury became the champion of ecclesiastical liberty and appealed to the pope against the 'ancestral customs' which the king wished to impose on the English church.[133] It was in the context of the Becket dispute that Henry II resumed Henry I's device of using Peter's pence as a bargaining counter in the king's relations with the papacy. The clearest reference to this tactic occurs in a story told by Becket's biographer, William Fitzstephen. When the archbishop went into exile in November 1164, the king tried to persuade the pope to depose Becket with a secret offer to increase the annual payment of Peter's pence by 1,000 pounds of silver; but Alexander III refused the bribe.[134] William's story, containing incorrect details and uncorroborated by any other author, cannot be regarded as an accurate account of the king's negotiations with the pope; but it indicates how much the king's opponents feared the influence of Peter's pence at the curia. More reliable information about Peter's pence in the mid-1160s is to be found in the correspondence of Gilbert Foliot, bishop of London, whom the pope commissioned to collect the sum due in 1165. The letter in which Foliot announced his appointment to Henry II contains a hint that the king was considering withholding payment in 1165; the letter urges the king not to give the pope occasion to oppose him in the matter of Becket's appeal. Foliot was subsequently able to inform the pope that the king had permitted him to collect Peter's pence: 'no one in the kingdom would have considered paying us for an instant if the king had not given his general command'.[135] In 1166 (according to Becket's biographer, Edward Grim) the king's council commanded that 'the offering of the faithful, which is called Peter's penny because it is owed particularly to Peter's successors', should be detained in the treasury with the royal revenue. A letter of Gilbert Foliot, written either in 1166 or in 1167, advises the king that it would be in his interests to release the money to the pope, so as not to 'offer just cause and matter for complaint against you or your kingdom'.[136] In the final phase of the

---

Cheney, 'The recognition of Pope Alexander III: some neglected evidence', *EHR* 84 (1969), 474–97.

[133] See above p. 185.

[134] William Fitzstephen, *Vita sancti Thomae: Materials* (n. 39) 3, 70–4.

[135] Gilbert Foliot, *Letter* 155 ed. Z. N. Brooke, A. Morey and C. N. L. Brooke, *The Letters and Charters of Gilbert Foliot* (Cambridge, 1967) p. 206. See Lunt, *Financial relations* (n. 87) pp. 49–50.

[136] Edward Grim, *Vita sancti Thomae* c. 56: *Materials* (n. 39) 2, 406. Cf. Gilbert Foliot, *Letter* 177: (n. 135) p. 250.

Becket dispute, when in the autumn of 1169 the kingdom was threatened with an interdict, Henry issued a series of constitutions intended to suspend communication between the English church and the papacy. The constitution relating to Peter's pence ordered that payment should no longer be made to the pope, but should be kept in the royal treasury and disbursed at the king's command.[137]

Henry II was clearly prepared to exploit Alexander III's poverty and his dependence on Peter's pence in order to secure a favourable settlement of the Becket dispute. Nevertheless there is some evidence that Peter's pence continued to be sent to the papal curia throughout the period 1166/7 to 1171/2: namely, the record of the regular payment of Peter's pence 'to the lord pope' during these years by the royal custodians of the vacant bishopric of Lincoln.[138] Although on three occasions the king delayed the sending of Peter's pence, ultimately he was persuaded by the advice which Gilbert Foliot gave in 1165 and 1166: to withhold payment would prompt the pope to reach an unfavourable judgement. The king and his advisers did not question the papal right to this money; but, like Henry's grandfather and great-grandfather, they emphasised its traditional character of royal alms. 'According to ancient custom it is collected at a fixed time by [the king's] command.'[139] Precisely how important was the English financial contribution to the papal finances appears from the statistics produced by Volkert Pfaff (1953). Pfaff's calculation of the ordinary annual income of the papacy in 1192, based principally on the *Liber Censuum*, shows that of all the western kingdoms, England made the largest single contribution, paying slightly more than the vassal kingdom of Sicily.[140] It is not surprising, therefore, that Alexander III felt obliged to heed the 'terrible threats' of Henry II and consequently (as he admitted to Becket in September 1170) might 'seem to have acted negligently in [Becket's] cause and that of the English church'.[141] Had Henry chosen to carry out his threat to renounce his obedience to Alexander

---

[137] M. D. Knowles, A. J. Duggan and C. N. L. Brooke, 'Henry II's supplement to the Constitutions of Clarendon', *EHR* 87 (1972), 757–71; *Councils and Synods with other documents relating to the English Church* 1.2 ed. D. Whitelock, M. Brett and C. N. L. Brooke (Oxford, 1981), 926–39.

[138] Lunt, *Financial relations* (n. 87) p. 53.

[139] Gilbert Foliot, *Letter* 155 (n. 135) p. 206.

[140] Pfaff, 'Einnahmen' (n. 56) p. 114.

[141] Alexander III, *JL* 11397, 11832: (n. 15) 483B, 699C. See F. Barlow, *Thomas Becket* (London, 1986) pp. 143–4, 177–8.

and to recognise the imperial antipope, his defection would have spelled financial disaster for the Alexandrine curia.

The Peter's pence paid by the English kingdom seems to have provided the model for the royal alms which the papacy received from the more distant peripheral lands. The best documented case is that of the Danish kingdom, where, according to tradition, the payment of alms had been introduced by Cnut the Great, king of Denmark and England (1016–35). Alexander II reminded the Danish king Swein Estrithson *ca.* 1070 of 'the *census* of your kingdom which your predecessors were accustomed to pay to the holy Roman church'.[142] The *Liber Censuum* contains an extract from a letter of Paschal II to the Danish bishops (1104) 'concerning the *census* which your predecessors provided every year for St Peter'. The bishops 'together with our brother, the archbishop of Lund' were given the responsibility for collecting the *census* 'so that the Roman church suffers no further fraud in this matter'.[143] The total amount raised by the Danish *census* is not known; nor is that raised in the other two Scandinavian kingdoms. The *Liber Censuum* merely records in the case of both Norway and Sweden: 'note that the individual households . . . each pay a *denarius* of the mint of that land'.[144] This *census* was probably introduced into Norway and Sweden by the legate Cardinal bishop Nicholas Breakspear of Albano during his reorganisation of the Scandinavian church in 1152–3. For at the end of his legation Pope Anastasius IV urged King Sverker and the Swedish magnates to continue to follow the commands of Bishop Nicholas of Albano, legate of the apostolic see, and to deliver to the bishops the annual *census* promised to St Peter.[145] A similar *census* may also have been paid during this period by the kingdom of Poland. There is a reference to the promise of the king of the Poles to pay *census* in 1013, but no further reference to the *census* during the eleventh and twelfth centuries. Only in the fourteenth century does the official record of the apostolic *camera* refer to the Polish payment of 'the *census* which is commonly called "St Peter's pence"'.[146]

[142] Alexander II, *JL* 4495: (n. 19) 1283B. See Fabre, *Etude* (n. 21) p. 123; Jordan, 'Finanzgeschichte' (n. 11) p. 78.
[143] Paschal II, *JL* 6335: *Liber Censuum* I, 227.
[144] *Ibid.*, I, 229.
[145] Anastasius IV, *JL* 9938: *MPL* 188, 1088AB; cf. *JL* 9937: 1086AB. See W. Seegrün, *Das Papsttum und Skandinavien bis zur Vollendung der nordischen Kirchenorganisation (1164)* (Quellen und Forschungen zur Geschichte Schleswig-Holstein 51: Neumünster, 1967) pp. 154–5, 167, 169–70.
[146] Fabre, *Etude* (n. 21) p. 120; Jordan, 'Finanzgeschichte' (n. 11) p. 79.

The papal revenues from secular sources – feudal dues, the *census* of princes enjoying papal protection and royal alms – provided the curia with an income four times as great as that from protected monasteries and churches. It was these secular princes from the 'outer' regions of western Christendom who were the principal contributors to the papal finances (just as the monasteries of the 'outer' regions contributed more, relatively speaking, than the more numerous houses of the 'inner' regions). According to Pfaff's calculation of the papal income at the end of the twelfth century, England contributed 366 gold *unciae*, Sicily 310 and Spain 105, the secular ruler being in each case the main contributor. Of the 'inner' kingdoms, Italy paid 160 gold *unciae*, Germany 72 and France 24, mainly from protected churches (together with feudal dues in the case of Italy).[147] The papal revenues from the 'outer' regions were therefore three times as great as those from the 'inner' regions of western Christendom. The most surprising of the statistics produced by Pfaff is that relating to France. The 'inner kingdom' with which the papacy became most intimately connected during the twelfth century contributed a smaller *census* payment than any other major western kingdom. The French contribution was composed of the *census* paid by seventy-seven monasteries and churches, the collection of which is, as we have seen, a recurrent theme of papal letters to the French clergy.[148] A single papal letter from our period lays claim to Peter's pence from France. Gregory VII in 1081 instructed his legates in France, Cardinal bishop Peter of Albano and Prince Gisulf of Salerno, to command 'that each household pay at least one *denarius* annually to St Peter, if they recognise him as their father and pastor in the ancient manner'. Charlemagne had instituted an annual payment 'for the service of the apostolic see' totalling 1,200 pounds of silver, 'as is read in his diploma which is kept in the archives of St Peter's church'. This forged diploma of Charlemagne had already been mentioned by Pope Leo IX.[149] Of Gregory VII's claim to royal alms from France nothing further is known, except that none of his successors saw fit to repeat it.

Although the *census* received from the kingdom was relatively small, it is certain that in the course of the twelfth century France

---

[147] Pfaff, 'Einnahmen' (n. 56) p. 114.,

[148] See the letters of Gregory VII, Urban II and Alexander III cited above, nn. 100, 101, 103.

[149] Gregory VII, *Registrum* VIII.23, pp. 566–7. Cf. *MGH Diplomata Karolingorum* I, 363–7; Leo IX, *JL* 4292, *MPL* 143, 705B. See Fabre, *Etude* (n. 21) p. 124.

contributed far more to the financial needs of the papal curia than appears in the *Liber Censuum*. This contribution originally took the form of providing for the maintenance of the curia during the numerous and often lengthy papal visits to France from the pontificate of Urban II to that of Alexander III. Between 1095 and 1165 seven popes took refuge in France after losing control of Rome: Urban II in 1095–6, Paschal II in 1106–7, Gelasius II in 1118–19, Calixtus II in 1119–20, Innocent II in 1130–2, Eugenius III in 1147–8, Alexander III in 1162–5.[150] Only after the end of the Alexandrine schism and the return to Rome negotiated by Clement III (1188) did the popes cease to rely on their refuge in France. (It was precisely at this period that the eruption of conflict between the Capetian king and the Plantagenet king of England made France a less secure refuge.) In their French exile the popes were deprived of the normal revenues of the Patrimony of St Peter and compelled to make demands on the hospitality of the French: demands which canonists would later call *procuratio canonica*. The historian Abbot Suger of St Denis noted this papal dependence on the French church on two occasions in his biography of King Louis VI. In 1120 Calixtus II was 'enriched by the votive offerings of the churches'.[151] In 1131 Innocent II settled in Compiègne after 'visiting the churches of Gaul and using their abundance to supply his needs'.[152] Similarly, John of Salisbury recorded the welcome given by the Roman magnates to Eugenius III on his return from France in 1148: 'they scented the gold and silver of Gaul'.[153]

The origins of *procuratio canonica* are unclear. Dom Ursmer Berlière (1919) suggested that papal procurations were originally offered 'in the form of a spontaneous gift or a charitable subsidy'.[154]

[150] Jaffé, *Regesta pontificum Romanorum* 1, 680–90, 727–32, 778–80, 781–94, 844–56; 2, 39–58, 156–95. See A. Graboïs, 'Les séjours des papes en France au XIIe siècle et leurs rapports avec le développement de la fiscalité pontificale', *Revue d'histoire de l'Eglise de France* 49 (1964), 5–18; C. Brühl, 'Zur Geschichte der *procuratio canonica* vornehmlich im 11. und 12. Jahrhundert' in *Le istituzioni ecclesiastiche della 'societas christiana' dei secoli XI–XII* 1 (Miscellanea del Centro di Studi Medioevali 7: Milan, 1974), 422–4.

[151] Suger, *Vita Ludovici grossi regis* c. 27, ed. H. Waquet (Les classiques de l'histoire de France au moyen âge 11: Paris, 1929) p. 204: *votivis beneficiis*. (Waquet translates *beneficia* as 'bienfaits'; but Graboïs, 'Séjours' (n. 150) p. 11 misleadingly uses 'bénéfices'.)

[152] *Ibid.*, c. 32, p. 264.

[153] John of Salisbury, *Historia pontificalis* (n. 38) c. 21, p. 51.

[154] U. Berlière, 'Le droit de procuration ou de gîte', *Bulletin de la classe des Lettres et des Sciences morales et politiques de l'Académie Royale de Belgique, 1919* pp. 510–11. But see Brühl, '*Procuratio canonica*' (n. 150) pp. 426–7.

But it seems more likely that the *procuratio* developed from two earlier institutions originally unconnected with the papacy: the right to food and shelter claimed by a secular ruler and those enjoying his protection and the right to hospitality claimed by a bishop on a visitation of his diocese. During the 'Byzantine period' of papal history which ended in the early eighth century, when the pope travelled on imperial business, he could demand the hospitality due to the emperor or his chief officials on their travels. During the Carolingian period a pope travelling in the Frankish empire could likewise demand the *servitia* due to his protector, the Frankish ruler. Similarly a bishop making a pastoral visitation of his diocese could demand 'accommodation and service' (*mansio et servitium*) from each church in his diocese.[155] The claim of the pope and his legates to *procuratio canonica* developed partly by analogy with the demands made by a bishop during a visitation, partly as a survival of the *servitia* due to an imperial protégé. The claim evidently originated in the reform programme of the late eleventh century. As early as 1079 Gregory VII imposed on a prelate an oath to provide for legates visiting his diocese.[156] Urban II, travelling in France in 1095–6, was the first pope to claim the same right for himself and his entourage. Urban seems, however, to have been cautious in making this novel demand for papal procurations. He sought accommodation mainly in monasteries which owed *census* to Rome or with bishops who were under the protection of St Peter (like those of Le Puy or Maguelonne): that is, in churches which already enjoyed a direct relationship with the papacy.[157] By the middle of the twelfth century such restraint had disappeared. When Eugenius III travelled through France and Germany in 1147–8, he had no hesitation in demanding 'the service of procuration of the lord pope' from all the churches on his route.[158]

Throughout the twelfth century the popes sought the aid of the Capetian kings of France, beginning with Paschal II's appeal to Philip I in an interview with the king in 1107. The pope 'begged [the king] to bring help to St Peter and to himself, his vicar, to maintain the Church and – as was the custom of his predecessors, the kings of the Franks, Charlemagne and others – to resist with boldness the

---

155 Brühl, '*Procuratio canonica*' pp. 419–26.
156 See above n. 80.
157 Becker, *Urban II.* 1, 219; Brühl, '*Procuratio canonica*' p. 426 n. 58.
158 H. Gleber, *Papst Eugen III. (1145–1153) unter besonderer Berücksichtigung seiner politischen Tätigkeit* (Beiträge zur mittelalterlichen und neueren Geschichte 6: Jena, 1936) pp. 191–206; Brühl, '*Procuratio canonica*' p. 426.

tyrants and enemies of the Church, especially Emperor Henry [V]'.[159] The help given by the Capetian kings during the twelfth century was, however, political and diplomatic rather than financial in character. (It is unusual to find a papal letter like that of Innocent II of February 1132, thanking Queen Adelaide, consort of Louis VI, for her gifts.)[160] The material resources of the Capetians were very limited. A well-known anecdote records how Louis VII, in conversation with a servant of Henry II, contrasted the wealth of the English king with his own poverty: 'we in France have nothing except bread and wine and joy'.[161] Living in straitened circumstances on the income produced by a small royal demesne, the Capetian king had often to make financial demands on the churches within his jurisdiction. In the twelfth century the churches which enjoyed royal protection (*tuitio*), and consequently came under the king's jurisdiction, were the metropolitan church of Sens and its suffragans, Auxerre, Chartres, Orléans, Paris and perhaps Meaux; the metropolitan church of Rheims and all its suffragans except the imperial bishopric of Cambrai; the metropolitan church of Bourges and its suffragans, Clermont, Le Puy and Mende (from 1161); and the metropolitan church of Tours (contested in the later twelfth century by the Plantagenet kings of England). In these twenty-six royal archbishoprics and bishoprics the Capetian king claimed from archbishops and bishops the right of *gistum* (food and accommodation for his wandering court); he exercised the right of *spolia* (the seizure of the personal property of a deceased prelate) and assumed the *regalia* (the governmental and financial rights of a bishopric) during an episcopal vacancy.[162] The best that such an impecunious king could offer the pope was to allow the refugee papal curia to join him in exploiting the wealth of the French church.

Hence during the papal sojourns in France in the twelfth century the curia was usually to be found in the royal archbishoprics and bishoprics. Paschal II spent nearly three months of his five-and-a-half-month visit to France in 1107 as the guest of royal churches.[163] The three-month stay of his successor, Gelasius II, was spent entirely

[159] Suger, *Vita Ludovici* c. 10: (n. 151) p. 54.
[160] Innocent II, *JL* 7531: (n. 71) 119D.
[161] Walter Map, *De nugis curialium* distinctio v, c. 5, ed. M. R. James (Anecdota Oxoniensia 14: Oxford, 1914) p. 225. See Southern, *Medieval humanism* (n. 13) p. 147.
[162] J. Gaudemet in: *Histoire des institutions françaises au moyen âge* 3 ed. F. Lot and R. Fawtier (Paris, 1962), 172–3.
[163] Jaffé, *Regesta pontificum Romanorum* 1, 728–32; Graboïs, 'Séjours' (n. 150) p. 7.

outside the royal sphere of jurisdiction; but Gelasius was on his way
to meet King Louis VI at Vézelay when he fell ill at Mâcon and was
taken to Cluny to die (January 1119).[164] Calixtus II was elected at
Cluny and remained in Burgundy and France for eleven months in
1119–20, spending nearly five months as the guest of royal prelates.
It was in the royal archbishopric of Rheims that he held his first
general council (October 1119).[165] Innocent II fled to France in the
seventh month of the papal schism of 1130. At this moment
(September 1130) King Louis VI's attitude towards Innocent's
claims was not yet known. However, as soon as the council of
Etampes, assembled by the king in October, had recognised him as
pope, Innocent moved into the Capetian sphere of influence. On
Christmas day 1130 he was crowned in Autun; in January 1131 he
joined Louis VI in Orléans; and in October 1131 he held a general
council in Rheims.[166] Innocent remained in France for seventeen
months, of which thirteen and a half were spent as the guest of the
royal churches.[167] In 1147–8 Eugenius III visited France for nine
months, the whole period in the Capetian jurisdiction except for a
fortnight spent in the dioceses of Meaux and Troyes, in the county
of Champagne. In March 1148 Eugenius presided over the third
general council of the twelfth century to be held in Rheims.[168] The
last and longest twelfth-century papal exile in France began on
8 April 1162, when Alexander III arrived at Montpellier, in the
county of Melgueil. This county had been since 1085 a vassal principality of the Roman church. The pope, as feudal overlord, could
establish his curia there and he evidently seized the opportunity to
demand feudal aids.[169] However, Alexander remained in Montpellier only for three months. He needed to be closer to his most
important allies, the kings of France and England, and the papal curia
needed rapid and regular access to information about events in the
empire, which was not available in Montpellier. Alexander moved

[164] Suger, *Vita Ludovici* c. 27: (n. 151) p. 202. See Jaffé, *Regesta* 1, 778–80; Graboïs,
'Séjours' p. 8.
[165] Jaffé, *Regesta* 1, 782–93; Graboïs, 'Séjours' p. 7.
[166] *Annales sancti Germani minores* 1131, *MGH SS* 4, 4; Boso, *Vita Innocentii II: Liber
pontificalis* 2, 381. See A. Graboïs, 'Le schisme de 1130 et la France', *Revue d'histoire
ecclésiastique* 76 (1981), 593–612.
[167] Jaffé, *Regesta pontificum Romanorum* 1, 844–54; Graboïs, 'Séjours' (n. 150) p. 7.
[168] Jaffé, *Regesta* 2, 40–57; Gleber, *Eugen III.* (n. 158) pp. 83–102; Graboïs, 'Séjours'
p. 8.
[169] M. Pacaut, 'Louis VII et Alexandre III (1159–80)', *Revue d'histoire de l'Eglise de
France* 39 (1953), 18; Graboïs, 'Séjours' p. 12; Fried, *Schutz* (n. 110) p. 130. See
above p. 274 and n. 110.

to Tours, on the Capetian-Plantagenet frontier (September 1162–January 1163, May–June 1163), where he held a general council in May 1163. Finally he moved into the heartland of the Capetian kingdom and after brief stays in Paris (February–April 1163), Chartres (April–May 1163), the monastery of Déols (June–July 1163) and Bourges (August–September 1163), he settled in Sens, where he remained from October 1163 until April 1165. Of Alexander's three years and five months in France, all except seven months were spent as the guest of the royal churches.[170]

The papal right of *procuratio canonica* could only be enjoyed on the spot and as soon as the host's hospitality had been exhausted, the papal curia must seek a new host. Until the mid-twelfth century the practice of the curia was to remain in episcopal cities for only a fortnight at a time and to make even shorter stays in abbeys (except for the great abbeys of St Denis and Cluny). Certain episcopal cities, however, were visited more frequently than others and seem to have been the preferred residences of the curia. The most obvious case is that of Rheims, chosen on three occasions during the early twelfth century as the scene of a papal council (1119, 1131, 1148). Rheims figured frequently in the papal itinerary, partly no doubt because the archbishop could afford the expense of accommodating the papal curia: the archbishop possessed the office and revenues of the count of Rheims. His episcopal city was also conveniently close to the German kingdom, so that information about imperial affairs was easily available there, while the city was readily accessible to German prelates wishing to visit the papal curia or to attend a papal council in Rheims.[171] The episcopal city of Clermont was likewise the scene of two important councils: that of November 1095, in which Urban II preached the crusade, and that of November 1130, in which French and imperial prelates rallied to the support of Innocent II against the antipope Anacletus II.[172] The choice of Clermont was probably determined by the city's convenient geographical position; as also in the case of Tours, where both Urban II and Alexander III held councils.[173] The most surprising aspect of the papal itinerary in France is the frequency with which the curia stayed in the episcopal city of Auxerre. Calixtus II remained in Auxerre for most of December

---

[170] Jaffé, *Regesta* 2, 157–95; Pacaut, 'Louis VII' pp. 18–23.

[171] Jaffé, *Regesta* 1, 787–90, 850–2; 2, 52–6; Graboïs, 'Séjours' p. 9.

[172] Jaffé, *Regesta* 1, 681–3 (Urban II), 782 (Calixtus II), 845 (Innocent II); 2, 160–1, 192–3 (Alexander III); Graboïs, 'Schisme' (n. 166) pp. 604–5.

[173] Jaffé, *Regesta* 1, 685–6 (Urban II), 786 (Calixtus II); 2, 161–5, 168–71 (Alexander III).

1119; Innocent II from July to September 1131 and again in December 1131; Eugenius III from mid-July to early September 1147, returning for a fortnight in late September.[174] The explanation of these long papal sojourns seems to be that the twelfth-century bishops of Auxerre – former Cluniac or Cistercian monks – were particularly devoted to the service of St Peter.[175] The expense of this hospitality, however, outran the bishop's means on at least one occasion. According to the chronicle of Morigny, during the papal visit to Auxerre in 1147 the abbot of Morigny 'paid twenty pounds [of silver] towards [the pope's] procuration at the suggestion of the archbishop of Sens'.[176] The bishop of Auxerre had evidently appealed for help to his metropolitan, the archbishop of Sens, who had shared the cost of accommodating the curia among the churches of his province. The bishop of Paris (according to a ruling of 1127) was permitted to collect the offerings of the faithful throughout his diocese in order to defray his expenses when 'he received the lord pope in his church'.[177] The popes themselves assisted their hosts in such fund-raising exercises by presiding over the impressive ceremonies in which churches and altars were consecrated. When Urban II consecrated altars in southern France in 1095–6, and when first Calixtus II (1119), then Innocent II (1131) consecrated the altars of the abbey of Morigny, these ceremonies were intended to benefit the churches by attracting the offerings of the faithful.[178] When Eugenius III consecrated the altar of the abbey of St Denis de Montmartre in 1147, he provided for the future prosperity of the abbey by granting 700 days' remission of penance to all pilgrims who visited the church on the anniversary of the consecration and gave alms to the nuns.[179]

During the exile of Alexander III the pattern of papal residence in France changed and with it the character of the papal financial demands on the French church. On his arrival in France Alexander stayed for three months in Montpellier, living on his feudal revenues

---

[174] Jaffé, *Regesta* 1, 790–1 (Calixtus II), 850, 852–3 (Innocent II); 2, 45–9 (Eugenius III).

[175] Graboïs, 'Séjours' (n. 150) pp. 11–12.

[176] *Chronique de Morigny* (n. 31) p. 87.

[177] *Cartulaire de l'église Notre-Dame de Paris* 1 ed. B. Guérard (Collection des cartulaires de France 4: Paris, 1840), 28. See Graboïs, 'Séjours' pp. 9–10.

[178] *Chronique de Morigny* (n. 31) pp. 32–3, 54–5. See R. Crozet, 'Le voyage d'Urbain II et ses négociations avec le clergé de France', *Revue historique* 179 (1937), 271–310; Graboïs, 'Séjours' p. 10.

[179] Eugenius III, *JL* 9078, *MPL* 180, 1242AC.

as suzerain of the county of Melgueil. For the next fourteen months the curia resided in a number of episcopal cities (notably Clermont, Tours, Paris and Bourges) and one abbey (Déols), living by the exaction of *procuratio canonica*. But in October 1163 the curia settled in Sens and remained there without interruption for nineteen months.[180] The papacy was compelled to give up the wandering way of life of earlier visits to France and to adopt a permanent residence. Presumably the expansion of the business of papal government in the second half of the twelfth century and the resultant increase in the number of curial staff made the curia too unwieldy for the nomadic life of the earlier twelfth century. The immediate consequence was that the pope could no longer exact the *procuratio canonica* except in Sens (where the archdeacon, William of Toucy, brother of Archbishop Henry of Sens, was responsible for lodging and feeding the curia).[181] The Alexandrine curia therefore attempted to extract financial contributions from those churches where the pope could no longer demand hospitality. One of the curia's measures has already been noted: the appeal for emergency supplies which Alexander's letters call *subsidia* or 'alms'.[182] The only appeals for 'subsidies' which have survived from the period of residence in Sens are addressed to Archbishop Henry of Rheims; but presumably similar appeals were sent to the other French metropolitans, who then decided what proportion of the subsidy was to be paid by each church in his province.[183]

A second measure by which the Alexandrine curia sought to pass on the expenses of papal government to the French church was that of papal provisions. The pope requested the king or a bishop to confer a benefice on a member of the papal curia. The revenues of the benefice served as the salary of the curial official: he continued to serve the pope in the curia, but the pope was relieved of the expense of his maintenance. The earliest extant papal provision comes from the pontificate of Innocent II and belongs to the history of papal–Spanish relations. Innocent requested Archbishop Diego Gelmírez of Compostela in 1137 to confer 'an ecclesiastical benefice with a prebend in the church of Compostela' to 'our son and clerk' Arias, who had been 'bred' in Diego's church and was now returning to Compostela.[184] Thirty years later Alexander III was seeking

---

[180] Jaffé, *Regesta pontificum Romanorum* 2, 157–74 (April 1162–September 1163), 174–90 (October 1163–April 1165).

[181] Graboïs, 'Séjours' (n. 150) p. 15.

[182] See above p. 268.   [183] Alexander III, *JL* 10880–1: (n. 15) 233AD.

[184] Innocent II, *JL* 7831: (n. 71) 323AB. See Fletcher, *León* (n. 68) pp. 215–16.

prebends in French churches for clerks who seem to have been complete strangers to those churches and who had no intention of leaving the service of the papal curia. An important motive in promoting papal provisions in the 1160s was the need to compensate members of the curia who had lost their property because of their adherence to the Alexandrine party. The pope wrote to King Louis VII about such a case on 25 April 1165. 'When we were talking together in Paris last Monday [19 April], we remember suggesting to Your Serenity that we should grant a certain archdeaconry in Chartres to a clerk of ours, a respectable and learned man, who has been despoiled of all his property because of his loyalty to us and his devotion to the Church.' The king had replied that he would seek advice about this case and now, six days later, Alexander was pressing him for an answer.[185]

These emergency measures continued after the end of the French exile and the return of the Alexandrine curia to Italy. In March 1167 Alexander, now residing in the Lateran palace, was still appealing to Archbishop Henry of Rheims for *subsidia* and simultaneously requesting Archbishop Thomas Becket of Canterbury to persuade the count of Flanders to send alms to the papal curia.[186] The increasing reliance of the curia on *subsidia* is illustrated by the papal appeals of 1173 and 1184 to the English church. The response of the English clergy to the appeal of 1184 is instructive. They informed King Henry II that if he chose to grant Lucius III financial aid from the royal treasury, they would reimburse him; but they resisted the sending of a papal legate to collect a 'subsidy', lest this become a precedent.[187] *Subsidia* were threatening to become a regular part of the papal revenues: an anticipation of the papal taxation of the Church in the later Middle Ages. Papal provisions likewise continued to be exploited as a means of rewarding the services of curial officials. The curia's concern to safeguard this source of income is evident in Alexander III's letter of 1170/2 to the dean and chapter of Paris. This papal letter approves the constitution adopted by the chapter punishing non-resident members with the loss of their prebends; but it insists on an exception to this rule: 'except for those who remain in our service or in that of the king of the French'.[188] In

---

[185] Alexander III, *JL* 11183: (n. 15) 354CD.

[186] Alexander III, *JL* 11342–3: (n. 15) 441B–442A, 446D–447D.

[187] Ralph de Diceto, *Ymagines historiarum* 1173, *RS* 68/1 (1876), 378–9; Roger of Hoveden, *Chronica* 1183, *RS* 51/2 (1869), 283. See Lunt, *Financial relations* (n. 87) pp. 175–7.

[188] Alexander III, *JL* 11959: (n. 15) 760C–761B.

this instance a local reforming initiative has to be modified in the interests of preserving the income of the papacy.

It is the first hint of a conflict of interests which would become an important theme of thirteenth- and fourteenth-century criticisms of papal provisions. The two apparent innovations of the papal exile of 1163–5 – provisions as a means of rewarding servants of the curia and the emergency supplies or *subsidia* – ultimately became the major grievances of anti-papal polemic in the later Middle Ages. As Aryeh Graboïs (1964) has pointed out, 'the experience accumulated in the course of the exiles of the popes in the twelfth century was the foundation of the fiscal organisation of the papacy, which reached its culmination during the residence of the popes in Avignon'.[189] These financial developments have to be reconstructed from occasional references in papal letters. They do not figure in the *Liber Censuum* of 1192: the chamberlain Cencius Savelli was interested in the traditional annual revenues which seemed likely to survive long after the emergency measures of Alexander III's pontificate had been forgotten. In the event, however, the financial expedients of the Alexandrine exile in France became the principal ordinary revenues of the later medieval papacy.

[189] Graboïs, 'Séjours' (n. 150) p. 17.

PART II
THE PAPACÝ
AND THE SECULAR POWERS

8

THE POLITICAL IDEAS OF THE PAPACY

Who is not aware of the voice of our Lord and Saviour Jesus Christ saying in the Gospel, 'you are Peter, and on this rock I shall build my Church and the gates of hell will not prevail against it; and I shall give you the keys of the kingdom of heaven, and whatever you bind on earth will be bound in heaven and whatever you loose on earth will be loosed in heaven' [Matthew 16. 18–19]? Surely kings are not excepted here: or do they not belong to the sheep which the Son of God committed to St Peter? . . . Is he to whom the power of opening and closing heaven has been given, not permitted to judge the earth? Far from it![1]

The political authority of the papacy was emphasised for the first time in the polemical writings of the papal reform movement. The reformers realised that they could not enforce their programme without the support of secular rulers. Only kings had the power to 'restore the health of the whole ecclesiastical order, which is failing even to extinction, and reforge this age of iron into gold with the hammer of righteous rule': that is, to eradicate simony and clerical marriage from the Church.[2] It was the failure of kings to discharge this duty which prompted Gregory VII to claim an active role in the politics of western Christendom: 'since there is no prince who troubles himself about such things, *we* must protect the lives of

---

[1] Gregory VII, *Registrum* VIII.21, pp. 548, 550.
[2] Abbot William of Hirsau, letter to anti-king Herman of Salm: *Hildesheimer Briefe* 18, *Briefsammlungen der Zeit Heinrichs IV.*, *MGH Briefe der deutschen Kaiserzeit* 5, 41–3.

religious men.'[3] When Henry IV of Germany first resisted the Gregorian reform programme and then attempted to depose the pope, Gregory invoked against him the power of St Peter 'to withdraw and to concede to anyone whomsoever, according to his merits, empires, kingdoms, principalities, duchies, marches, counties and the property of all men'.[4] Critics of Gregory VII regarded his claims as unprecedented and sacrilegious. 'Although Christ . . . alone transmutes time and transfers kingdoms . . . we read that Pope Hildebrand taught that he himself had power over kings and kingdoms and that he could do what can be done only by God, as the Psalmist says: "He humbleth one and exalteth another" (Psalm 74, 8).'[5]

Gregory VII's critics considered that his involvement in secular politics violated the divinely ordained separation of spiritual and secular government. 'See how Hildebrand and his bishops . . . resisting God's ordination, uproot and bring to nothing these two principal powers by which the world is ruled, desiring all other bishops to be like themselves, who are not truly bishops, and desiring to have kings whom they themselves can command with royal licence.'[6] Gregory's conduct, therefore, seemed to contravene that 'authority' which dominated medieval political thinking, the letter of Pope Gelasius I to Emperor Anastasius I of 494: 'the world is chiefly governed by these two, the sacred authority of bishops and the royal power'. Gelasius I had acknowledged that the emperor's function was to 'rule over the human race', but had reminded the emperor that 'in what concerns the receiving and correct administering of the heavenly sacraments you must be subject rather than in command'.[7] Gelasius' statement seemed to eleventh-century scholars to be a commentary on the New Testament text Luke 22. 38, 'Lord, here are two swords.' Interpreted allegorically, the two swords which the disciples offered to Christ signified the coercive power of secular government (the material sword) and the ecclesiastical power of

---

[3] *Registrum* II.49, p. 190.
[4] *Ibid.*, VII.14a, p. 487.
[5] *Liber de unitate ecclesiae conservanda* II.1, *MGH Libelli* 2, 211–12. See I. S. Robinson, *Authority and resistance in the Investiture Contest* (Manchester, 1978) pp. 95–8.
[6] *Liber de unitate* II.15, p. 231.
[7] Gelasius I, *Epistola* 12 (*JK* 632) ed. A. Thiel, *Epistolae Romanorum pontificum genuinae* I (Braunsberg, 1868), 350. On the influence of this text see W. Ullmann, *Gelasius I.* (Päpste und Papsttum 18: Stuttgart, 1981) pp. 198–212; L. Knabe, *Die gelasianische Zweigewaltentheorie bis zum Ende des Investiturstreits* (Historische Studien 292: Berlin, 1936).

excommunication (the spiritual sword).[8] Henry IV's denunciation of Gregory VII in 1076 concentrated on the pope's alleged violation of the Lucan and Gelasian doctrine of the two powers. Gregory had

usurped the royal power (*regnum*) and the priestly power (*sacerdotium*) and thereby shown contempt for the ordination of God, who wished government to consist principally not in one but in two . . . as the Saviour himself . . . made clear through the allegory of the two swords. When they said to him, 'Lord, here are two swords', he replied, 'it is enough'; signifying by this sufficient duality that the spiritual and the carnal sword should be wielded in the Church . . . the priestly sword to enforce obedience to the king after God, the royal sword to attack the enemies of Christ without and enforce obedience to the teaching of the priesthood within.[9]

Gregory VII and his supporters, on the contrary, considered that the papal claim 'to judge the earth' conformed entirely to the teaching of Luke's Gospel and of Gelasius I. Gregory's doctrinal letter of 15 March 1081, defending the excommunication and deposition of Henry IV, cited the Gelasian 'authority' to justify the view 'that the priests of Christ are to be considered the fathers and masters of kings and princes and of all the faithful'. What Gregory cited, however, was a tendentious version of Gelasius. His quotation omits both the description of the emperor as ruling over the human race and the statement that the emperor is subject to the priesthood only in matters concerning the sacraments – and hence implies an unlimited subjection to the priesthood on the part of the emperor. It was this interpretation of the Gelasian doctrine which entered the canon law collections of the Gregorian papacy.[10]

The allegory of the two swords was likewise used in defence of Gregory VII's political interventions by the Gregorian scholar John of Mantua. 'The place of the sword is the righteous power which is not divided from the authority of St Peter. Peter by his divine power delivers the sword when his vicar praises and strengthens the secular

---

[8] J. Lecler, 'L'argument des deux glaives (Lc 22, 38) dans les controverses politiques du moyen âge: ses origines et son développement', *Recherches de Science religieuse* 21 (1931), 299–339; 22 (1932), 151–77, 280–303; H.-X. Arquillière, 'Origines de la théorie des deux glaives', *SG* 1 (1947), 501–21; W. Levison, 'Die mittelalterliche Lehre von den beiden Schwerten', *DA* 9 (1951), 14–42; H. Hoffmann, 'Die beiden Schwerter im hohen Mittelalter', *DA* 20 (1964), 78–114.

[9] Henry IV, *Epistola* 13, *MGH Dt. Ma.* 1, 19.

[10] Gregory VII, *Registrum* VIII.21, p. 553. At the beginning of his pontificate Gregory had used this Gelasian 'authority' in a more traditional sense: see below p. 398. See Robinson, *Authority* (n. 5) pp. 137–8.

powers.[11] According to John of Mantua, therefore, the material sword must be used by the legitimate secular ruler: the secular ruler, that is, who enjoys the approval of the pope, the vicar of St Peter. The spiritual sword is wielded directly by the pope, the secular sword is wielded by his permission. In the 1080s this interpretation of Luke 22. 38 seemed to be a dangerous innovation. By the mid-twelfth century such an interpretation had become a commonplace of political thought. John of Salisbury explained in his *Policraticus* of 1159 that

the prince receives this [material] sword from the hand of the Church, since she herself does not hold the sword of blood . . . She uses [the secular sword] by means of the hand of the prince, on whom she conferred the power of coercing men's bodies, having reserved for herself the authority of spiritual coercion in [the persons of] the bishops. The prince is therefore indeed the servant of the priestly power (*sacerdotium*) and performs that part of the sacred duties which seems unworthy of the hands of the priesthood.

John of Salisbury characteristically attributed authority over the two swords to 'the Church', not to the pope: a 'sacerdotalist' rather than a papalist, he was wary of exalting the authority of the papacy at the expense of the *sacerdotium* as a whole.[12] John's colleague in the household of Archbishop Thomas Becket of Canterbury, Master Herbert of Bosham, similarly wrote that the clergy 'are not subject, but are superior to earthly kings, since they appoint kings and it is from them that the king receives the belt of knighthood and the power of the material sword'.[13] The most influential twelfth-century exposition of Luke 22. 38 also attributed the two swords to 'the Church'. Bernard of Clairvaux wrote in his treatise *De consideratione* of *ca.* 1150 that 'both the spiritual and the material sword belong to the Church'; but elsewhere he made it clear that this signified that the two swords

---

[11] John of Mantua, *In Cantica Canticorum et de Sancta Maria Tractatus ad Comitissam Matildam* ed. B. Bischoff and B. Taeger (Spicilegium Friburgense 19: Freiburg, 1973) p. 52.

[12] John of Salisbury, *Policraticus* IV.3 ed. C. C. J. Webb I (Oxford, 1909), 239. On John's attitude to the Roman church see G. Miczka, *Das Bild der Kirche bei Johannes von Salisbury* (Bonner Historische Forschungen 34: Bonn, 1970) pp. 145–60; J. P. McLoughlin, *John of Salisbury (c. 1120–1180): the career and attitude of a schoolman in church politics* (doctoral dissertation: Trinity College, Dublin, 1988). For a different view see Ullmann, *The growth of papal government in the Middle Ages* (3rd edition: London, 1970) pp. 420–6.

[13] Herbert of Bosham, *Vita sancti Thomae* c. 24 in *Materials for the history of Archbishop Thomas Becket* 3, RS 67/3 (1877), 268. But see B. Smalley, *The Becket conflict and the schools* (Oxford, 1973) p. 68.

belonged to the pope. Summoning Eugenius III to launch a new crusade in 1150, Bernard wrote: 'put forth both swords, now that Christ is suffering again where he suffered before. Who except you should do so? Both are Peter's, the one to be unsheathed at his nod, the other by his hand, whenever necessary.'[14]

The mid-twelfth-century authors who were to prove most influential were those who elaborated the Gregorian idea of the political supremacy of the papacy. Above all it was Bernard of Clairvaux who was to furnish 'authorities' to later medieval papalists who claimed dominion over secular affairs for the pope. He wrote that St Peter had 'received the whole world to govern'; his vicar's task was 'to direct princes, to command bishops, to set kingdoms and empires in order' and he bore 'a sword to execute vengeance upon the nations and to rebuke the peoples, to bind their kings with chains and their nobles with fetters of iron (Psalm 149. 8)'.[15] It was presumably under Bernard's influence that his pupil, Eugenius III, wrote that Christ 'gave to St Peter the keys of the kingdom of heaven, the power of both the earthly and the heavenly empire'.[16] The fundamental canon law manual of the twelfth century, the *Decretum* of Master Gratian of Bologna of *ca.* 1140, contains material both for and against this Gregorian theory. The only personal opinion expressed in the *Decretum* on the theme of *regnum* and *sacerdotium* adopted the strict Gelasian view of two independent powers with separate functions: 'just as kings are preeminent in the affairs of the world, so priests are preeminent in the affairs of God'. But he also included in his *Decretum* Gregorian material borrowed directly from Gregory VII's doctrinal letter of 1081. Under the rubric, 'Priests are considered the fathers and masters of kings and princes', Gratian presented two extracts from this letter, the second of which was Gregory VII's tendentious version of Gelasius I's letter to Emperor Anastasius concerning the two powers.[17]

The canon lawyers of the later twelfth century – the 'Decretists'

[14] Bernard of Clairvaux, *De consideratione* IV.3.7, *MPL* 182, 776C; *idem, Epistola* 256, *ibid.*, 463D–464A. See Ullmann, *Papal government* (n. 12) pp. 430–7; A. M. Stickler, 'Il "gladius" negli atti dei concili e dei RR. Pontefici sino a Graziano e Bernardo di Clairvaux', *Salesianum* 13 (1951), 414–45; Y. M.-J. Congar, 'L'ecclésiologie de S. Bernard', *Analecta Sacri Ordinis Cisterciensis* 9 (1953), 168–71.

[15] Bernard, *De consideratione* II.8.16: 752BC; *Epistola* 237: 426C. See E. Kennan, 'The *De consideratione* of St Bernard of Clairvaux and the papacy in the mid-twelfth century: a review of scholarship', *Traditio* 23 (1967), 73–115.

[16] Eugenius III, *JL* 9149, *MPL* 180, 1285A.

[17] Gratian, *Decretum* D.96 c 9–10; C.2 q.7 *dictum post* c. 41.

who composed commentaries on Gratian's *Decretum* – found in their master's work, therefore, two alternative approaches to the question of the relations of *regnum* and *sacerdotium*. Some favoured a 'Gregorian' and some a 'Gelasian' solution. The Decretist Rufinus (later bishop of Assisi and archbishop of Sorrento) claimed in the mid-1150s that 'the supreme pontiff, who is the vicar of St Peter, possesses the rights of the earthly kingdom'. 'It must be noticed', Rufinus added, 'that the right of authority is one thing and the right of administration another.' The former right belongs to the pope, the latter to the emperor. The pope

possesses the right of the earthly empire in the sense of the right of authority, in the first instance because by his authority he confirms the emperor in the earthly kingdom through consecration and furthermore because by his sole authority he punishes the emperor and other secular rulers if they abuse their secular power and when they repent, he absolves them.[18]

Rufinus' distinction between the right of *auctoritas* and that of *administratio* expressed in more precise terms the theory of Bernard of Clairvaux that the pope possessed the two swords, 'the one to be unsheathed at his nod, the other by his hand'. The same idea was expressed by the anonymous Decretist who composed the commentary *Imperatorie maiestatis* (1175–8). 'The lord pope possesses the material and the spiritual sword but . . . the spiritual is his by [right of] authority and use, the material sword only by authority.'[19] However, the Decretist Simon of Bisignano in his commentary, the *Summa* of 1177–9, rejected the Gregorian interpretation in favour of the Gelasian idea of two separate and independent powers. 'The emperor holds the power of the sword from God, not from the pope . . . Although the pope is inferior to the emperor in temporal matters, he can never be judged by the emperor: the pope can be judged by God alone.'[20] The same opinion is found in a gloss attributed to Albert of Morra, the future Pope Gregory VIII: 'the emperor does not hold the power of the sword from the pope'.[21] The most eminent of the Decretists, Master Huguccio (later bishop of Ferrara) likewise adopted a Gelasian view. In his *Summa decretorum* (1180–91) he claimed that 'both powers, namely the apostolic and the imperial power, were instituted by God; neither depends on the other and the emperor does not hold the sword from the pope. The emperor holds

---

[18] Rufinus, *Summa Decretorum* D.22 c.1 ed. H. Singer and F. Schöningh, *Die Summa Decretorum des Magister Rufinus* (Paderborn, 1902) p. 47.
[19] Cited by Pacaut, *Alexandre III* p. 358.
[20] *Ibid.*, p. 357.   [21] *Ibid.*, p. 356.

power in temporal affairs and the pope in spiritual affairs from God alone; and it is thus that authority is separated.'[22] The Decretists of the late twelfth century differed as much on the relations of pope and emperor as had the polemicists of the Investiture Contest. The doubts of Decretists like Simon of Bisignano and Master Huguccio were evidently shared in the papal curia. The papal letters of the second half of the twelfth century which referred to the political authority of the papacy always avoided the expression of 'Gregorian' opinions.[23]

There was no doubt, however, that according to tradition the primary duty of the emperor was the protection of the pope and the lands of St Peter. Alexander III expressed the general opinion of the eleventh- and twelfth-century intellectuals when he wrote: 'we recognise that the lord emperor, by virtue of the duty which belongs to his dignity, is the advocate and special defender of the holy Roman church.'[24] Of the emperors of our period, only one ever fulfilled this duty to the satisfaction of the papacy: 'the most Christian emperor Lothar [III], fired with zeal for God and the Christian faith, like a catholic advocate of the Church'.[25] Lothar's predecessors, Henry IV and Henry V, had been tyrants who had conspired against the freedom of the Church. His successor, Conrad III, was prevented from fulfilling the duty of the advocate of the Church by the political turmoil in Germany.[26] The Staufen emperors Frederick I and Henry VI proved to be formidable opponents of the Roman church. In 1160 Alexander III wrote to his supporters that although the emperor 'ought to be the special protector and defender' of St Peter's vicar and his property, Frederick I was instead the oppressor of the Roman church.[27] Urban III made a similar complaint to Frederick in 1186 about the conduct of his son, Henry VI, in Italy: 'your illustrious son seems to be bent not on the defence, but on the oppression of our land'.[28] The failure of the emperor to perform his duty compelled the pope to seek allies elsewhere. This consequence of the emperor's neglect or hostility is made most explicit in a letter of Alexander III

---

[22] *Ibid.*, p. 365. See J. A. Watt, *The theory of papal monarchy in the thirteenth century* (Fordham, 1965) pp. 15–20, 23.

[23] See below pp. 481–4.

[24] Alexander III, JL 10597: Boso, *Vita Alexandri III*: *Liber pontificalis* 2, 401.

[25] Boso, *Vita Innocentii II*: *ibid.*, p. 383. See below p. 451.

[26] See below pp. 403, 409, 418, 420–1, 428–9, 455–6.

[27] Alexander III, JL 10627–9, MPL 200, 88A–92D; NA 6 (1880), 369.

[28] Urban III, JL 15634, MPL 202, 1411B.

to King Louis VII of France in January 1161. This letter represents the king as the 'praiseworthy imitator of [his] forebears'.

Following their example you have very readily shown your love towards your singular and unique mother, the holy Roman church . . . you have faithfully assisted her in her affliction and her need and nothing could ever distract your royal mind from showing devotion and assistance to her. Frederick, whose office requires him to be the advocate and defender of the Church, rages cruelly against her; while you, as a most Christian prince, love and honour her and revere her with a sincere affection. In her every tribulation she has always found a haven of longed-for peace and a timely refuge with you, as she did with your predecessors.[29]

The reform papacy, lacking imperial support, had found its first allies in the Norman princes of southern Italy. The twelfth-century papacy sought military, diplomatic and financial help throughout western Christendom, finding its most dependable supporters in the kingdom of France and the cities of northern and central Italy.

The relationship of the papacy with the Norman princes of southern Italy was that of lord and vassal: the princes took an oath to be 'faithful to the holy Roman church and to the apostolic see and to my lord the pope'.[30] This particular relationship, unmistakably feudal in character, has prompted some historians to write of the 'feudal policy' adopted by the reform papacy as a protection against the hostility of the empire. Alois Dempf (1929), for example, argued that 'the double meaning of *fidelitas*, as both religious and feudal fidelity, as both spiritual and political loyalty in the Germanic world, prompted Gregory [VII] to the false design of the feudal suzerainty of the holy see over all Christian peoples'.[31] Walter Ullmann (1955) wrote of 'the harnessing of feudal principles to the hierocratic theme' by the reform papacy.[32] Karl Jordan (1958) likewise wrote of the reforming popes' plan 'to translate the *regimen universale* of the papal see in Christendom into practical reality in the most comprehensive way through the construction of a curial feudal system'.[33] However, this 'curial feudal system' has left relatively few traces in the records

---

[29] Alexander III, *JL* 10644: (n. 27) 100BC.

[30] Gregory VII, *Registrum* 1.21a, VIII.1a, pp. 36, 515. Oath of William II of Sicily: *MGH Constitutiones* 1, 592; oath of Tancred: *ibid.*, pp. 592–3.

[31] A. Dempf, *Sacrum Imperium. Geschichts- und Staatsphilosophie des Mittelalters und der politischen Renaissance* (Munich–Berlin, 1929) p. 187.

[32] Ullmann, *Papal government* (n. 12) pp. 331–2.

[33] K. Jordan, 'Das Reformpapsttum und die abendländische Staatenwelt', *Die Welt als Geschichte* 18 (1958), 130.

of the late eleventh and twelfth centuries. Apart from the vassals in the Patrimony of St Peter on whom the papacy succeeded in imposing its lordship in the mid-twelfth century, the Normans of southern Italy were the only vassals who gave the papacy effective military support in this period. Few other princes followed the example of the princes of Apulia and Capua and became papal vassals. King Demetrius-Zvonimir of Croatia and Dalmatia may have been of their number. He was 'invested with banner, sword, sceptre and crown and installed as king' by the papal legate Gebizo in 1076 and subsequently described himself as 'legally provided with the diadem and sceptre of the kingship by the vicar of Peter the key-bearer, namely the most blessed Pope Gregory [VII]'.[34] Two Spanish princes became vassals of the papacy in the late eleventh century. Count Peter of Substancion-Melgueil in 1085 donated to St Peter and the Roman church 'myself and all my honour, both the county . . . and the bishopric [of Maguelonne] . . . which I and the counts, my predecessors have hitherto possessed and held as an allod' and henceforward held his lands as a fief of the pope. Count Peter decreed that his heirs should be 'knights of the Roman pontiff and obtain the county from his hand' and that in the absence of a direct heir, the pope should determine the succession.[35] Similarly in 1090 Count Berengar Raimund II of Barcelona granted the city of Tarragona, being his share of the family *honor*, to God, St Peter and his vicar and received it back as a fief from the papal legate, Cardinal Rainer of S. Clemente (the future Paschal II).[36]

Three other Spanish princes entered into a special relationship with St Peter and his vicar, symbolised by the payment of an annual *census* to the Roman church. King Sancho Ramirez of Navarre and Aragon came on a pilgrimage to Rome in 1068 and 'delivered [his] kingdom into the power of God and [St Peter]'. A privilege of Urban II of 1089 confirmed the arrangement and this privilege was renewed

---

[34] Deusdedit, *Collectio canonum* III.278 ed. V. Wolf von Glanvell (Paderborn, 1905) pp. 383–5. Cf. *Codex diplomaticus regni Croatiae, Dalmatiae et Slavoniae* 1, ed. M. Kostrenčić (Zagreb, 1967), 180: cited by J. Deér, *Papsttum und Normannen* (Studien und Quellen zur Welt Kaiser Friedrichs II. 1: Cologne-Vienna, 1972) p. 14 n. 48.

[35] *Gallia Christiana* 6: *Instrumenta* 349–50 (no. 11). Cf. Urban II, *JL* 5375, *MPL* 151, 293B–294D. See J. Fried, *Der päpstliche Schutz für Laienfürsten. Die politische Geschichte des päpstlichen Schutzprivilegs für Laien (11.–13. Jh. (Abhandlungen der Heidelberger Akademie der Wissenschaften, phil.-hist. Klasse 1980/1)* pp. 72–3.

[36] *Liber Censuum* 1, 468–9. See Fried, *Päpstlicher Schutz* pp. 87–101; Servatius, *Paschalis II.* p. 25.

for King Peter I in 1095.[37] Count Bernard II of Besalú in 1077 agreed to pay an annual *census* to the Roman church 'so that St Peter may receive me as a special knight (*peculiaris miles*)'.[38] Duke (subsequently King) Alfonso I of Portugal in 1143 took an oath to the papal legate, Cardinal Guido of SS. Cosma e Damiano, and promised payment of an annual *census*. His assumption of the royal title was ignored by the papacy until 1179, when Alexander III recognised Alfonso as king in a privilege which stated 'that the aforesaid kingdom belongs to the jurisdiction of St Peter'.[39] The relationship of these three princes with the Roman church has usually been described as a feudal one;[40] but, as Johannes Fried (1980) points out, it was a relationship of a different character from that of the counts of Melgueil and Barcelona with the papacy. Aragon, Besalú and Portugal did not become fiefs of the Roman church: their rulers continued to hold their lands directly from God rather than from St Peter, as the vassals of the pope. Their relationship with the saint involved not feudal subordination but 'protection': *patrocinium, protectio, defensio, tuitio, tutela*. This *patrocinium* for secular princes developed by analogy with the protection which the vicar of St Peter had accorded since the midninth century to religious houses. The monastic analogy is most evident in the payment of an annual *census* in return for St Peter's protection. Gerd Tellenbach (1950) noted, in the context of Urban II's privileges conferring protection on Sancho Ramirez and Peter I of Navarre and Aragon, that 'the *census* formula corresponds exactly to those of the privileges of monasteries enjoying "Roman freedom"'.[41]

[37] P. Kehr, 'Wie and wann wurde das Reich Aragon ein Lehen der römischen Kirche?', *Sb. der Preussischen Akademie der Wissenschaften, 1928, phil.-hist. Klasse* p. 218; Fried, *Päpstlicher Schutz* pp. 63–87.

[38] Fried, *Päpstlicher Schutz* pp. 56–63.

[39] Lucius II, *JL* 8590, *MPL* 179, 860C–861A; Alexander III, *JL* 13420: (n. 27) 1237A–1238B. See C. Erdmann, *Das Papsttum und Portugal im ersten Jahrhundert der portugiesischen Geschichte* (*Abhandlungen der Preussischen Akademie der Wissenschaften 1928, phil.-hist. Klasse* 5, 29–32, 49–50; Fried, *Päpstlicher Schutz* pp. 141–2.

[40] K. Jordan, 'Das Eindringen des Lehnswesens in das Rechtsleben der römischen Kurie', *Archiv für Urkundenforschung* 12 (1932), 73, 77–8, 87–9; P. Kehr, *Das Papsttum und die Königreiche Navarra und Aragon bis zur Mitte des 12. Jahrhunderts* (*Abhandlungen der Preussischen Akademie der Wissenschaften 1928, phil.-hist. Klasse* 4, 28; C. Erdmann, *Die Entstehung des Kreuzzugsgedankens* (Stuttgart, 1935) pp. 347–62; idem, *Portugal* (n. 39) pp. 29–32.

[41] G. Tellenbach, 'Vom Zusammenleben der abendländischen Völker im Mittelalter' in *Festschrift für Gerhard Ritter zu seinem 60. Geburtstag* (Tübingen, 1950) p. 53; Fried, *Päpstlicher Schutz* (n. 35) pp. 38–53, 79–80. See above pp. 269, 274.

The first prominent recipients of this quasi-monastic protection were secular princes from the Iberian peninsula; and the institution of papal *patrocinium* stemmed from the same period which witnessed the beginning of the 'reconquest' of Spain from the Moslems. Johannes Fried's study of papal *patrocinium* underlines the connection between this protection and the holy war both in Spain and in Outremer.[42] Immediately after the launching of the First Crusade the papacy began to confer a special status on crusaders, an elaboration of the protection traditionally accorded by the Church to pilgrims. As the canonist Ivo of Chartres noted in 1106, this development was 'a new institution which extends ecclesiastical protection to the property of knights setting out for Jerusalem'. It was a *nova institutio* which permitted the pope to intervene in matters of secular jurisdiction.[43] The most impressive instances of this papal protection for crusaders come from the Second Crusade. When Louis VII of France and Conrad III of Germany took the cross in 1146, Eugenius III conferred the protection of the Roman church on both kingdoms. Eugenius declared that Louis VII had 'left his kingdom under our protection and that of holy Church'; while the papal biographer Cardinal Boso presented the event in even more imposing terms. 'Coming to St Denis, where the king, together with the bishops and barons, received him with due veneration, [Eugenius] placed on the king the sign of the cross, according to the Lord's will; and at [Louis'] request he received the kingdom into his hands and into his power.'[44] The regent appointed by Louis VII, Abbot Suger of St Denis, was simultaneously appointed by the pope as the guardian of the interests of the absent crusader (the officer subsequently known as the *conservator crucesignatorum*). Suger's biographer described the abbot's dual status: 'the new ruler was immediately equipped with twin swords, one of them material and royal and the other spiritual and ecclesiastical, but both from heaven and committed to him by the supreme pontiff'.[45] In the case of Germany the kingdom was entrusted to Conrad III's eldest son, the ten-year-old King Henry. Eugenius wrote: 'we do not wish [Henry's] honour to suffer any damage or diminution in his father's absence, while he is under the

[42] Fried, *Päpstlicher Schutz* pp. 105–22.
[43] Ivo of Chartres, *Epistola* 173, *MPL* 162, 177A. See below pp. 337–8.
[44] Eugenius III, *JL* 9345, *MPL* 180, 1394D; Boso, *Vita Eugenii III: Liber pontificalis* 2, 387.
[45] William, *Vita Sugerii* ed. A. Lecoy de La Marche, *Oeuvres complètes de Suger* (Paris, 1867) p. 394. See below pp. 338–9.

protection of St Peter'.[46] When Count Henry I of Champagne took the cross and departed for Outremer in 1179, he requested the same protection from Alexander III and obtained a papal letter of protection for his countess, Marie of Champagne, who was to act as regent. A letter which Henry of Marcy, abbot of Clairvaux, wrote to the pope on behalf of the absent crusader underlines the value of the papal *patrocinium*. Alexander III was requested to 'remember that the land which [the count] entrusted with great confidence to your *patrocinium* is to be fittingly surrounded by the apostolic protection, so that anyone who plots any harm to it in the prince's absence may be in no doubt of incurring your indignation'.[47] The importance which crusading princes attached to papal protection explains the anger aroused by the captivity of the crusader King Richard I of England in Germany (1192–4). Celestine III came under strong pressure to excommunicate Emperor Henry VI, the enemy who had imprisoned Richard.[48]

These papal interventions into secular affairs were clearly not the consequences of 'the construction of a curial feudal system': they stemmed from the duty of St Peter's vicar to confer his *patrocinium* on those who sought the saint's protection. Nevertheless the language used to describe the relationship of *patrocinium* has obvious feudal overtones. Eugenius III referred to Conrad III of Germany in 1146 as 'the special knight of St Peter'. Cardinal Boso described Eugenius receiving the French kingdom 'into his hands and into his power'.[49] The language used by the papal curia to describe its relations with the secular powers is often deceptive; and this is particularly the case in the letters of Gregory VII, which use feudal terminology to describe a variety of political relationships. For example, Gregory VII's claims concerning Spain and Hungary were expressed in unmistakably feudal language. He wrote to 'the kings, counts and other princes of Spain' that 'according to ancient decrees the kingdom of Spain was surrendered to the jurisdiction and proprietorship of St Peter and the holy Roman church'. He wrote to King Salomo of Hungary that 'the kingdom of Hungary is the property of the holy

---

[46] Eugenius III, *JL* 9214: 1321A.

[47] Henry of Marcy, abbot of Clairvaux, *Epistola* 1, *MPL* 204, 216AB. Cf. Alexander III, *JL* 13345: S. Loewenfeld, *Epistolae pontificum Romanorum ineditae* (Leipzig, 1885) p. 179. See Fried, *Päpstlicher Schutz* (n. 35) pp. 114–16.

[48] J. A. Brundage, 'The crusade of Richard I: two canonical *quaestiones*', *Speculum* 38 (1963), 448–52. See above p. 119 and below p. 515.

[49] Eugenius III, *JL* 8976: (n. 44) 1176A (see Fried, *Päpstlicher Schutz* p. 111); Boso, *Vita Eugenii III*: (n. 44) p. 387.

Roman church, having been offered and devoutly surrendered to St Peter by King Stephen with all his rights and his power'.[50] Gregory was not inventing these claims. He was referring to a relationship with the papacy which in the case of Spain dated back to John XIII (965–72) and in the case of Hungary, to Sylvester II (999–1003); but he construed their 'ancient decrees' in novel language. 'Gregory VII, who was dominated by feudal theory, interpreted these proceedings in feudal terms.'[51]

Gregory VII also used feudal language to describe his relationship with King William I of England. In the summer of 1080 Gregory sent the subdeacon Hubert as a legate to the English king with a message, the content of which is known only from the reply sent by the Conqueror to the pope.

Your legate Hubert . . . on your behalf urged me to perform fealty to you and your successors and to remember the money which my predecessors were accustomed to send to the Roman church. One [request] I have granted; the other I have not granted. I neither wished nor wish to perform fealty; for I made no such promise nor do I find that my predecessors ever performed it to yours.[52]

The papal message has been interpreted as a demand for fealty in respect of the English kingdom, which would thus have assumed the status of a papal fief like the principalities of the Norman conquerors of southern Italy.[53] How Gregory justified his demand is not clear. In a letter of 24 April 1080 the pope had called the king *'fidelis* of St Peter and of us' – the term *fidelis* generally signified 'vassal' in this period – and reminded William of his indebtedness to the saint. This might imply that Gregory's demand was based on the support which the papacy had given to William's invasion of England. However, the theory that the English kingdom became a papal fief as a result of papal support in 1066 – that Gregory's predecessor, Alexander II, had 'conferred a banner on William as a token of the kingship' – is

---

[50] Gregory VII, *Registrum* IV.28, pp. 345–6 (cf. *Registrum* I.7, p. 11); *Registrum* II.13, p. 145.

[51] Jordan, 'Eindringen' (n. 40) pp. 67–8.

[52] Lanfranc of Canterbury, *Letter* 39 ed. H. Clover and M. Gibson (Oxford, 1979) pp. 130–2.

[53] Z. N. Brooke, 'Pope Gregory VII's demand for fealty from William the Conqueror', *EHR* 26 (1911), 225–38; *idem, The English church and the papacy from the Conquest to the reign of John* (Cambridge, 1931) pp. 140–3; H. E. J. Cowdrey, 'Pope Gregory VII and the Anglo-Norman church and kingdom', *SG* 9 (1972), 89–94; M. Gibson, *Lanfranc of Bec* (Oxford, 1978) pp. 135–6.

explicitly stated only by twelfth-century authors.[54] An alternative explanation is suggested by Gregory's linking of the demand for fealty with the request for Peter's pence, 'the money which [William's] predecessors were accustomed to send to the Roman church'. Alexander II had described Peter's pence as 'an annual tribute (*pensio*) in respect of pious devotion and religious obligation'. Gregory may have deduced from this payment of 'tribute' a papal right of jurisdiction over the tributary kingdom. William rejected this view of Peter's pence: it was a tax imposed by the king and sent as alms to Rome, not a *pensio* owed to the papacy by a tributary kingdom.[55]

Gregory VII's request for fealty had larger implications than appear in the surviving correspondence of pope and king in the spring and summer of 1080. In these months Gregory was urgently seeking allies, having recently deposed and excommunicated Henry IV of Germany. In June he was reconciled with his rebellious vassal Robert Guiscard, duke of Apulia and Calabria. Looking farther afield, in March 1081 the pope instructed his legate in Germany to encourage Duke Welf IV of Bavaria 'to perform fealty to St Peter': 'we desire to place him wholly in the bosom of St Peter and to summon him especially to his service.' The legate was also requested to secure the performance of fealty from 'other powerful men' devoted to St Peter. (Welf IV, together with his ally, Berthold II of Zähringen, eventually performed homage to the legate of Urban II in 1093).[56] William the Conqueror was the most illustrious of the new *fideles* whom Gregory attempted to recruit in the aftermath of his second excommunication of Henry IV. The papal letter of April 1080 urged him to 'show all obedience' when the Roman church was in danger, 'that you may deserve to be the norm of righteousness and a model of obedience to all the princes of the earth; so that you will doubtless be the prince of princes in future glory and until the end of the world princes will be saved by the example of your obedience'. The king's duties were explained to him more specifically in a letter from Gregory's legate in Lombardy, Bishop Anselm II of Lucca. William was 'the hammer by which the nations are ground to

54 Gregory VII, *Registrum* VII.23, p. 500. Cf. William of Malmesbury, *Gesta regum Anglorum* III, *RS* 90/2 (1889), 299. See Cowdrey, 'Anglo-Norman church' pp. 91–2.

55 Alexander II, *JL* 4757, *MPL* 146, 1413D: see Brooke, *English Church* pp. 141–3. See also above p. 275.

56 Gregory VII, *Registrum* IX.3, p. 574. See below pp. 372, 415.

pieces', the instrument of God, 'who changes the nations and the kingdoms'. 'You ought', the letter concludes, 'to come to [the Roman church], as to your head and mother; to hasten and rescue her from the hands of strangers. For she has a special reliance on you: she has more confidence in you than in other princes because of your many donations and the probity of your conduct.'[57] Evidently William's duty was to be the hammer by which Henry IV was ground to pieces: he was intended to achieve in the Italian kingdom what he had previously achieved in England. In the crisis of the early 1080s Gregory needed the Conqueror primarily as a military ally rather than a vassal; but (as also in the case of Welf IV of Bavaria) he sought to strengthen the alliance by means of the strongest bond known to the secular ruling caste: the feudal oath.

Gregory VII used a single feudal vocabulary to describe the various different relationships of the papacy with secular princes. His twelfth-century successors were more cautious in their use of feudal terminology (perhaps under the influence of their legal advisers). However, all the popes of this period drew on the same ancient 'authorities' in making their political claims. The 'authority' which has attracted most attention from historians is the *Constitutum Constantini*, the forged 'Donation of Constantine'. The *Constitutum*, in granting to the papacy the Lateran palace, the city of Rome and 'the various imperial ornaments and every procession of the imperial majesty', inspired the 'imitation of the empire' characteristic of the reform papacy and strongly influenced the ceremonial life of the papacy.[58] The *Constitutum* also conferred on the pope in clause 17 'all the provinces, places and cities of Italy and of the western regions' and, in the vaguer language of clause 13, the imperial 'largesse in Judea, Greece, Asia, Thrace, Africa and Italy and in the various islands'.[59] The latter clause seems to have inspired the statement in Gregory VII's letter of 1077 to the people of Corsica that 'the island which you inhabit belongs to no mortal and to no power except the holy Roman church by due proprietary right'.[60] The same papal jurisdiction over 'the various islands' is claimed in Gregory's threatening letter of 1080 to the Sardinian prince Orzocor, claiming the right to dispose of the island.

[57] Anselm of Lucca, letter to William I in *Briefsammlungen* (n. 2) pp. 15–16.
[58] See above p. 23.
[59] *Constitutum Constantini* c. 17, 13, *MGH Fontes iuris germanici antiqui* 10, 93, 85–6.
[60] Gregory VII, *Registrum* v.4, p. 351.

We do not wish to hide from you the fact that your country has been sought from us by many peoples: we have been promised great tributes if we would allow it to be invaded; such that they wish to leave one half of the whole land for our own use and to hold the other half in fealty from us. Although this was repeatedly demanded of us – not only by Normans, Tuscans and Lombards, but also by certain people from beyond the Alps – we determined never to give our assent to anyone in this matter, until we had sent our legate to you and discovered your opinion . . . If you persevere in your fealty to St Peter, we promise that beyond doubt his help will not fail you now or in the future.[61]

Urban II was the first pope to make explicit reference to the *Constitutum Constantini* in support of a territorial claim. In 1091 Urban renewed Gregory VII's claim to Corsica, citing clause 13 of the *Constitutum*. 'Since all islands are held, according to the statutes, to belong to the public jurisdiction, it is certain that they were bestowed by the generosity and the privilege of the religious Emperor Constantine on St Peter and his vicars as their property.'[62] In the same year Urban laid claim to the Italian islands of Lipari in a letter which combined clauses 13 and 17 of the *Constitutum*: 'it is certain that by the privilege of the religious Emperor Constantine all western islands – especially those situated near the coast of Italy – were surrendered to the proprietorship of St Peter and his successors'.[63] Although Urban II claimed possession of islands 'situated near the coast of Italy' by virtue of the Donation of Constantine, there is no evidence that he or any of his twelfth-century successors used the *Constitutum* to claim the island of Sicily, even though it was regarded as part of 'the patrimony of the Roman church'. (As Paschal II observed in 1117, 'before the invasion of the Saracens the island of Sicily was so closely linked with the Roman church that the Roman pontiffs always had guardians of their patrimonies and representatives of their authority on [the island]'.)[64]

The only occasion on which the *Constitutum Constantini* was cited in support of the papal jurisdiction over islands during the twelfth century was the papal bestowal of Ireland on King Henry II of England. The historian John of Salisbury claimed in 1159 that this papal grant of Ireland was prompted by his own negotiating skills when he came to the papal curia as a royal envoy in 1156. 'At my

---

[61] *Ibid.*, VIII.10, pp. 529–30.
[62] Urban II, *JL* 5449: (n. 35) 330D–331A. See G. Laehr, *Die Konstantinische Schenkung in der abendländischen Literatur des Mittelalters bis zur Mitte des 14. Jahrhunderts* (Historische Studien 166: Berlin, 1926) p. 34.
[63] Urban II, *JL* 5448: 329C.   [64] Paschal II, *JL* 6562: *Liber Censuum* 2, 125.

request [Hadrian IV] conceded and gave Ireland as a hereditary possession to the illustrious king of the English, Henry II, as his letter still bears witness today. For all islands are said to belong to the Roman church by ancient right, according to the donation of Constantine, who richly endowed it.'[65] The historian Giraldus Cambrensis inserted into his narrative of Henry II's invasion of Ireland a document which he claimed to be the papal letter mentioned by John of Salisbury. This letter states that 'Ireland and all islands on which Christ the sun of justice shines belong to the dominion of St Peter and the holy Roman church'.[66] The authenticity of this famous letter, *Laudabiliter*, has long been a matter of dispute: English-speaking historians have generally regarded it as authentic, while continental scholars have regarded it with suspicion.[67] *Laudabiliter* is, to say the least, problematical. The historian must take account of the fact that in Giraldus' narrative *Laudabiliter* is accompanied by a forged letter of Alexander III, purporting to be a confirmation of Hadrian IV's letter; and that the three authentic letters of Alexander III of 20 September 1172 which greeted Henry II's successful invasion of Ireland contain no reference to *Laudabiliter*.[68] Equally suspicious is the fact that although *Laudabiliter* imposed a *census* on Ireland (Henry II was to pay 'an annual tribute [*pensio*] of one penny from every household to St Peter'), this payment does not appear in the *Liber Censuum*, the register of the financial rights of the papacy throughout western

---

[65] John of Salisbury, *Metalogicon* IV. 42 ed. C. C. J. Webb (Oxford, 1929) pp. 217–18.

[66] Hadrian IV, *JL* 10056: Giraldus Cambrensis, *Expugnatio Hibernica* II.5 ed. A. B. Scott and F. X. Martin (Dublin, 1978) pp. 144–6; cited also in his *De rebus a se gestis*, *RS* 21/5 (1867), 317–18 and his *De instructione principum*, *RS* 21/8 (1891), 196–7; and borrowed from Giraldus by Ralph de Diceto, Roger of Wendover and Matthew Paris: *RS* 68/1 (1876), 300–1; 84/1 (1886), 11–13; 57/2 (1874), 210–11.

[67] For the most recent discussions in English see M. P. Sheehy, 'The bull *Laudabiliter*: a problem in medieval diplomatique and history', *Journal of the Galway Archaeological and Historical Society* 29 (1961), 45–70; *idem*, *Pontificia Hibernica. Medieval Papal Chancery documents concerning Ireland 640–1261* (Dublin, 1965), 15–16 (edition); J. Watt, *The Church and the two nations in medieval Ireland* (Cambridge, 1970) pp. 35–40; W. L. Warren, *Henry II* (London, 1973) pp. 194–7. But these works do not take account of the criticisms of P. Scheffer-Boichorst, *Gesammelte Schriften* I (Berlin, 1903), 132–57. Cf. W. Holtzmann, *NA* 46 (1925), 338; C. Bémont, 'La bulle *Laudabiliter*' in *Mélanges d'histoire du moyen âge offerts à Ferdinand Lot* (Paris, 1925), 41–53.

[68] Alexander III, *JL* 12174: Giraldus, *Expugnatio Hibernica* II.5, p. 46; cf. Sheehy, *Pontificia Hibernica* p. 329. Alexander III, *JL* 12162 (to Henry II), 12163 (to the kings and princes of Ireland), 12164 (to Bishop Christian of Lismore): (n. 27) 883B–884C, 884D–885B, 885B–886B.

Christendom, compiled by the chamberlain Cencius in 1192.[69] The very appearance of *Laudabiliter* is suspicious: the opening and closing protocols closely resemble those of a letter of Hadrian IV to Louis VII of France (1159) concerning a Spanish crusade contemplated by Louis and Henry II of England.[70] This authentic letter to Louis VII may have been the model used by the forger of *Laudabiliter*. Leaving aside this problematical document, there remains a single papal letter of the twelfth century which claims a special jurisdiction over islands on the basis of the Donation of Constantine: namely, Alexander III's letter of September 1172, congratulating Henry II on his successes in Ireland.

The *Constitutum Constantini* had more impact on the ceremonial life of the papacy than on papal political claims in this period. More important in the political thought of the papacy was a papal claim based on an 'authority' first quoted by Gregory VII in defence of his deposition and excommunication of King Henry IV of Germany. 'A Roman pontiff deposed a king of the Franks from the kingship not so much for his iniquities as for the fact that he was not useful enough to hold such great power, and put Pippin, father of the Emperor Charlemagne in his place and absolved all the Franks from the oath of fealty which they had sworn to him.'[71] This example from the year 751 – when the legitimating authority of Pope Zacharias had been invoked to justify the deposition of the last Merovingian king, Childeric III, and the accession of the first Carolingian, Pippin III – inspired the central Gregorian political idea of 'suitability' (*idoneitas*). According to Gregory VII, a Christian kingdom must be ruled by 'a suitable king for the honour of holy Church'. As he explained to his supporters in Germany in March 1081, when they were contemplating the election of a new anti-king, 'unless he is obedient, humbly devoted and useful to holy Church – just as a Christian king ought to be . . . then beyond a doubt holy Church will not only not countenance him but will oppose him'.[72] The Gregorian concept of 'suitability', together with the 'authority' of the deposition of Childeric III, entered the *Decretum* of Master Gratian of Bologna, thus assuring its survival and dissemination throughout the twelfth century.[73]

The survival of the Gregorian theory of *idoneitas* in the papal curia

---

[69] See above p. 260.
[70] Hadrian IV, *JL* 10546, *MPL* 188, 1615B–1617B.
[71] Gregory VII, *Registrum* VIII.21, p. 554. Cf. IV.2, p. 294.
[72] *Ibid.*, IX.3, p. 575.   [73] Gratian, *Decretum* C.15 q.6 c.3, citing *Registrum* IV.2.

is most evident in the case of the popes' relations with their vassals, the Norman princes of southern Italy. In 1080 Gregory VII was forced by the outbreak of hostilities with Henry IV of Germany to make peace with his over-mighty vassal, Robert Guiscard, duke of Apulia and Calabria, whom he had excommunicated three times in six years for his annexation of lands claimed by the pope. Gregory received Guiscard's homage and recognised his title to the duchy; but he did so on condition 'that you will hereafter conduct yourself, for the honour of God and of St Peter, as is appropriate for you and acceptable to me'. Gregory took the opportunity to redraft the oath of fealty to be taken by Guiscard, so as to underline the idea of 'suitability': 'I shall observe this fealty to those of your successors . . . who confirm the investiture which you have conceded to me – if my fault does not remain.'[74] The idea of *idoneitas* regularly reappeared in papal letters written to or about the Norman princes. Urban II granted the request of Guiscard's son, Roger Borsa, for a privilege for the archbishopric of Salerno (1098) because Roger had 'always faithfully obeyed the apostolic see'.[75] Urban also granted to Guiscard's brother, Count Roger I of Sicily, a privilege permitting him to act 'in the place of a legate' in his territory on the grounds that he had 'greatly extended the Church of God in the territory of the Saracens and always shown himself devoted to the holy apostolic see in many ways'.[76] The elevation of Count Roger II of Sicily to the kingship was likewise an occasion for emphasising the idea of *idoneitas*. His ally, the antipope Anacletus II issued a privilege (1130) which stated that Roger II deserved the royal title because 'divine providence caused [him] to surpass the other princes of Italy in breadth of wisdom and preeminence of power'. Nine years later Anacletus' rival, Innocent II, was compelled to issue a similar privilege on the grounds that Roger was 'adorned with prudence, fortified with justice and suitable to rule the people'.[77]

In the case of the popes' relations with their Norman vassals, the

---

[74] Gregory VII, *Registrum* VIII.1a, 1b, pp. 515, 516. See below pp. 371–2.

[75] Urban II, *JL* 5707: (n. 35) 508A.

[76] Urban II, *JL* 5706: Geoffrey Malaterra, *De rebus gestis Rogerii Calabriae et Siciliae comitis* IV.29, *MRIS* 5/1 (1925–8), 108. See E. Caspar, 'Die Legatengewalt der normannisch-sicilischen Herrscher im 12. Jahrhundert', *QFIAB* 7 (1904), 218–19. See also above p. 176 and below p. 375.

[77] Anacletus II, *JL* 8411, *MPL* 179, 715D–717A = J. Deér, *Das Papsttum und die süditalienischen Normannenstaaten 1053–1212* (Historische Texte/Mittelalter 12: Göttingen, 1969) p. 62. Innocent II, *JL* 8043, *MPL* 179, 478C–479D = Deér, *Normannenstaaten* p. 74. See below pp. 384, 386–7.

concept of 'suitability' served to emphasise the vassals' dependence on the superior authority of their lord: they held their lands subject to papal approval and would lose them if they ceased to be 'suitable' in papal eyes. Gregory VII's favourite 'authority', the deposition of Childeric III and his replacement by Pippin III, suggested that the theory of *idoneitas* applied not only to papal vassals but to all secular rulers. Gregory put the theory into practice in 1076 in the case of Duke Demetrius-Zvonimir of Croatia and Dalmatia, 'whom the apostolic authority appointed king in Dalmatia'. Demetrius had no hereditary claim to the kingship; but as the champion of the Romans against the Slavonic liturgy he seemed to the pope to be eminently qualified for the royal office.[78] The classic example of the Gregorian principle of 'suitability' was the support which the reform papacy gave to King William I of England. William had seized the throne in 1066 from the perjured usurper Harold Godwineson; and Gregory VII subsequently attributed the success of this enterprise to the help which St Peter and he himself had given. 'I believe that it is known to you, most excellent son, with how great and sincere an affection I always loved you before I acceded to the papacy, how effective I showed myself in your affairs and with how much effort I laboured so that you might attain the dignity of the kingship.' William's qualification for kingship was his reputation for piety, which as king he fully justified. He 'showed himself to be more laudable and worthier of honour than other kings' by his zeal against simony, clerical marriage and non-payment of tithes.[79] However, Gregory VII's own reputation suffered as a result of his support for William the Conqueror. 'It was for this that I was branded with infamy by some of the brethren, who complained that by conferring such a favour, I had devoted my energies to perpetrating so many murders.' Gregory indeed never shook off the reputation which he acquired in 1066 for promoting bloody usurpations on the grounds that the usurper was 'more suitable' than the established ruler. The anti-Gregorian polemicist Wenrich of Trier satirised the papal principle of *idoneitas* in a letter of 1081. 'There is no lack of men who seized kingdoms by tyrannical violence, whose paths to the throne lay through blood, who set a gory diadem upon their heads. All these are called the friends of the lord pope; all are honoured by his blessings and saluted by him as victorious princes.'[80]

[78] Gregory VII, *Registrum* VII.4, p. 463. See Deér, *Papsttum* (n. 34) pp. 52–5.
[79] *Registrum* VII.23, pp. 499–500; cf. IX.5, p. 580. See Cowdrey, 'Anglo-Norman church' (n. 53) pp. 77–114.
[80] Wenrich of Trier, *Epistola* c. 6, *MGH Libelli* 1, 294.

Wenrich was thinking in particular of Gregory VII's interventions in the politics of the German kingdom in the years 1076–80. During these years both Henry IV and the faction of princes which opposed him, vied for papal support by publicly embracing the Gregorian principle of *idoneitas*: the princes by inviting the pope to come to a diet in Germany and judge between the king and his accusers; Henry by doing penance for his offences and receiving absolution from the pope.[81] In March 1080 Gregory finally decided against Henry IV and in favour of the candidate of the rebel princes, Rudolf of Rheinfelden, duke of Swabia. 'For just as Henry is justly degraded from the dignity of the kingship because of his pride, disobedience and falsehood, so the power and dignity of the kingship is conceded to Rudolf because of his humility, obedience and truth.'[82] After Rudolf's premature death Gregory urged his supporters in Germany to elect as a replacement 'a suitable king for the honour of holy Church' and devised an oath to be administered to the new anti-king. The king elect was to swear to 'be the vassal in good faith of the blessed apostle Peter and of his vicar, who now lives in the flesh, Pope Gregory' and to 'become St Peter's knight and his by an act of homage'. Gregory characteristically used feudal language to explain the meaning of *idoneitas* to the future king.[83] None of the papal anti-kings of the Investiture Contest ever took this oath; but the most formidable of them, King Conrad, the rebel son of Henry IV and ally of Urban II, certainly proved his suitability by promising to obey 'the apostolic decrees' and especially that concerning lay investiture.[84]

Of the German kings of the twelfth century only Lothar III – 'terrible to the enemies of God, the friend of justice, the enemy of injustice' – conformed fully to the papal concept of *idoneitas*. The chronicler of Monte Cassino applied to him the highest terms of praise in the Gregorian vocabulary: Lothar was 'useful and suitable for the honour of the empire'.[85] His election to the kingship was a practical application of the papal principle of 'suitability'. In the disputed election which followed the death of the childless Henry V (1125) Lothar was the candidate most closely associated with the papal party. He owed his election to the influence of Archbishop Adalbert of Mainz, the pope's permanent legate in Germany, who

[81] See below p. 405.   [82] Gregory VII, *Registrum* VII. 14a, pp. 486–7.
[83] *Ibid.*, IX.3, pp. 575–6. See below pp. 410–11.
[84] See below p. 417.
[85] *Chronica monasterii Casinensis* IV.87, MGH SS 34, 548. Cf. *Vita Norberti archiepiscopi Magdeburgensis* c. 21, *ibid.*, 12, 702.

saw in Lothar a guarantor of the freedom of the Church.[86] The election of Lothar III's successor in 1138 provided another demonstration of the principle by papal legates. The permanent legate, Archbishop Albero of Trier and his allies hastened to elect Conrad III eleven weeks before the date nominated by the princes for the election. Albero thereby stole a march on the supporters of the more powerful rival candidate, who might have proved a threat to the freedom of the Church. A second papal legate, Cardinal bishop Theodwin of S. Rufina, ensured the success of the conspiracy by crowning Conrad 'according to the will and command of Pope Innocent [II]'.[87] An analogous case was the usurpation of the English throne by King Stephen in December 1135. As in the case of Lothar III and Conrad III, the successful royal contender owed his election and coronation to a papal legate. The permanent papal legate in England, William of Corbeil, archbishop of Canterbury, was persuaded to support Stephen's claim after the latter had sworn an oath to restore and maintain the freedom of the Church. The new king repaid his debt to the Church in his 'Oxford' charter of liberties (April 1136). The opening clause both emphasised the legitimating authority of the pope and asserted the king's own suitability for office.

I, Stephen, by the grace of God elected king of England with the assent of the clergy and people and consecrated by William, archbishop of Canterbury and legate of the holy Roman church and afterwards confirmed by Innocent [II], pontiff of the holy Roman see, out of respect and love for God, grant that holy Church shall be free and confirm the reverence due to her.[88]

By the second quarter of the twelfth century, therefore, the principle of *idoneitas* was sufficiently widely disseminated to be invoked on the occasion of disputed royal elections. Such disputed elections might even be acknowledged as belonging to the *maiores causae* which could be judged only by the pope. Hence Stephen's rival for the English throne, his cousin Matilda, pursued her claim both on the battlefield and at the papal curia: her case against Stephen was eventually heard by Innocent II at the Second Lateran Council in 1139.[89]

---

[86] See below pp. 441–2.

[87] *Annales sancti Jacobi Leodensis* 1138, *MGH SS* 16, 640. See below pp. 454–5.

[88] *Councils and synods with other documents relating to the English church* I/2 ed. D. Whitelock, M. Brett and C. N. L. Brooke (Oxford, 1981), 764. See R. H. C. Davis, *King Stephen 1135–1154* (London, 1967) pp. 18–20.

[89] R. L. Poole in his edition of John of Salisbury, *Historia pontificalis* (Oxford, 1927) pp. 107–13; A. Morey and C. N. L. Brooke, *Gilbert Foliot and his letters*

An important twelfth-century development of the principle of *idoneitas* was anticipated by Gregory VII in a letter of 1075 addressed to King Swein II Estrithson of Denmark.

There is not far from us a certain very wealthy province by the sea, which is held by base and ignoble heretics, and we desire that one of your sons be made duke and prince and defender of Christianity in that province, if (as a bishop of your land has reported to be in your mind) you would give him to the apostolic court as a warrior, with a considerable following of knights in fealty to him.[90]

Gregory's proposal to use the army of a Viking prince to rid himself of unsuitable neighbours provides a striking illustration of his belief in the power of St Peter 'to withdraw and to concede to anyone whomsoever, according to his merits, empires, kingdoms, principalities, duchies, marches, counties and the property of all men'.[91] What is particularly interesting about this case, however, is the evidence of unsuitability alleged by Gregory VII against his neighbours: they were 'heretics'. Ecclesiastical law had long recognised the principle that heretics were automatically disqualified from holding office or property in Christian society. The canonists of the 1080s who compiled canon law manuals justifying the Gregorian reform programme, extracted from the writings of Augustine against the Donatists and of Pope Gregory I against the Lombards a theory of 'righteous persecution' of heretics and schismatics. The most influential Gregorian canonist, Bishop Anselm II of Lucca contended that 'heretics must be coerced by the secular powers' and 'that catholics may take possession of the property of excommunicates until they are converted'. Anselm's theory 'that the Church can practise persecution' was absorbed into the *Decretum* of Master Gratian of Bologna and so entered the mainstream of canon law.[92] In the case of

---

(Cambridge, 1965) pp. 105–23; *The Letters of Peter the Venerable* ed. G. Constable 2 (Harvard Historical Studies 78: Cambridge, Mass., 1967), 252–6.

[90] Gregory VII, *Registrum* II.51, p. 194. On the identity of the 'base and ignoble heretics' see most recently W. Seegrün, *Das Papsttum und Skandinavien bis zur Vollendung der nordischen Kirchenorganisation, 1164* (Quellen und Forschungen zur Geschichte Schleswig-Holsteins 51: Neumünster, 1967) p. 82, who argues that these 'heretics' were the Normans of southern Italy.

[91] *Registrum* VII.14a, p. 487.

[92] Anselm of Lucca, *Collectio canonum* XII.53 (= Gratian, *Decretum* C.23 q.4 c.39); XII.57 (C.23 q.7 c.3); XII.54, XIII.14–16 (C.23 q.7 c.3; C.23 q.4 c.42–3). Anselm's *Collectio* is cited here from Vaticanus latinus MS. 1363, since the edition of F. Thaner (Innsbruck, 1906–15) is incomplete. See Erdmann, *Entstehung* (n. 40) pp. 225–7.

secular rulers who were heretics or schismatics, the principle of
idoneitas (based on Gregory VII's favourite 'authority' of Pope
Zacharias) was reinforced by the traditional function of the pope as
the guardian of the faith. For this function the main 'authority' was
Luke 22. 32: Christ's assurance that Peter's faith would not fail and
his command that Peter should strengthen his brethren. Master
Gratian's *Decretum* emphasises both that the apostolic see will always
guard the purity of the catholic faith and that Christian princes must
assist the Roman church in performing this function. The secular
power is expected to suppress 'those who disturb the peace of the
Church': 'if they disdain to do so, they are to be excluded from
communion'.[93] Secular princes must be prepared to wage a holy war
against the enemies of the faith at the instigation of the Roman
church.

The theory of 'righteous persecution' developed by the Gregorian
canonists was the ancestor both of the idea of crusade and of the
coercive measures against heretics developed during the twelfth century.[94] As early as 1085 the Gregorian canonist and polemicist
Bonizo of Sutri defended the right of the papacy to summon the
faithful to persecute the enemies of reform. He commended the
example of Gregory VII's ally, Countess Matilda of Tuscany, who
'with all her strength and by every means attacks the heresy which
now rages in the Church'.[95] This heresy was simony, the principal
target of Gregorian reform legislation, and the chief disseminator of
the heresy was Emperor Henry IV. Similarly in 1102 Paschal II
summoned Count Robert II of Flanders to make war on Henry IV.
Robert had participated in the First Crusade and Paschal drew an
analogy between this expedition and the equally meritorious war
against the emperor.

> For it is just that those who separate themselves from the catholic Church
> should be separated by catholics from the benefits of the Church . . . You
> should persecute Henry, the chief of the heretics, and his supporters with all
> your might, wherever you can. You can offer no sacrifice more pleasing to
> God than that of attacking him who has set himself up against God.[96]

After the end of the Investiture Contest the growth of popular
heretical movements in western Christendom gave a new direction
to the 'righteous persecution' organised by the papacy. In July 1119

---

[93] Gratian, *Decretum* c.24 q.1 c.11, 14; c.23 q.5 c.18–45.
[94] Erdmann, *Entstehung* pp. 216–37, 247–9.
[95] Bonizo of Sutri, *Liber ad amicum*, *MGH Libelli* 1, 620.
[96] Paschal II, *JL* 5889, *MPL* 163, 108AC.

the council of Toulouse, under the presidency of Calixtus II, condemned those who, 'simulating the appearance of religion', rejected the sacraments of the Church, together with their 'defenders': 'we drive them from the Church and condemn them and command them to be coerced by foreign powers.'[97] This legislation was repeated by Innocent II's Second Lateran Council in 1139.[98] From 1148, the year of Eugenius III's council of Rheims, conciliar legislation began to specify southern France as the region most endangered by heresy.[99] Alexander III's council of Montpellier in May 1162 took the novel step of threatening excommunication to 'any secular prince who, on being admonished by ecclesiastical authority, failed to exercise his temporal jurisdiction against heretics'.[100] Alexander's council of Tours in May 1163 decreed that the heretics were to be dispossessed of their lands by the secular power.[101] The Third Lateran Council of 1179 conferred the status of crusaders on those of the faithful who made war on the heretics. 'We enjoin on all the faithful for the remission of their sins that they manfully resist such great dangers and take up arms to protect the Christian people against them. Let [the heretics'] property be confiscated and let princes be free to reduce such men to slavery.'[102] The definitive statement of the twelfth-century papacy on the subject of heresy is found in the decree *Ad abolendam* issued jointly by Lucius III and Emperor Frederick I on 4 November 1184. The decree was an acknowledgement of the need for the Church and the secular power to join forces 'to abolish the wickedness of the various heresies which have begun to increase in very many regions of the world in modern times'.[103]

By 1184 the papacy had devised a series of measures for dealing with heretics which anticipated Innocent III's famous code of practice, the decree *Excommunicamus* of the Fourth Lateran Council.[104]

---

[97] Council of Toulouse, c. 3: Mansi, *Sacra Concilia* 21, 226–7. See H. Grundmann, *Religiöse Bewegungen im Mittelalter* (2nd edition: Hildesheim, 1961) pp. 52–3.

[98] *Concilium Lateranense II* c. 23: *Conciliorum Oecumenicorum Decreta* p. 202.

[99] Council of Rheims c. 18: Mansi, *Sacra Concilia* 21, 718. See Grundmann, *Religiöse Bewegungen* (n. 97) pp. 53–4.

[100] Council of Montpellier c. 4: Mansi, *Sacra Concilia* 21, 1160. See R. Somerville, *Pope Alexander III and the Council of Tours* (Berkeley–Los Angeles, 1977) p. 54.

[101] Council of Tours c. 4: Mansi, *Sacra Concilia* 21, 1177–8. See Somerville, *Tours* pp. 50, 53.

[102] *Concilium Lateranense III* c. 27: *Conciliorum Oecumenicorum Decreta* p. 225.

[103] Lucius III, *JL* 15109, *MPL* 201, 1297C–1300A.

[104] H. G. Walther, 'Häresie und päpstliche Politik: Ketzerbegriff und Ketzergesetzgebung in der Übergangsphase von der Dekretistik zur Dekretalistik' in *The*

Indeed already in 1181 the papal legate Henry of Marcy, cardinal bishop of Albano had led an army which besieged the castle of Lavaur and captured the Albigensian heretics who had taken refuge there: the first occasion on which military force was applied to the problem of heresy in southern France.[105] However, such initiatives were few in number before the pontificate of Innocent III: the immediate importance of the twelfth-century papal decrees against heretics and their 'defenders' belongs to the sphere not of practical politics but of political theory. The writings of the Decretists of the later twelfth century reveal how the need to defend the Church against heresy influenced their conception of the relations of *regnum* and *sacerdotium*. Their starting-point was the judgement of Master Gratian of Bologna that 'the necessity of defending churches falls on the administrators of secular offices. If they disdain to do so, they are to be excluded from communion'. The Decretists concluded from this opinion of their mentor that where the defence of the Church was concerned, princes were obliged to act as the servants of the *sacerdotium*. Master Huguccio commented that 'secular rulers were established for this purpose: that whatever the Church is unable to achieve by her own means, should be performed by them, as if they were servants . . . If [the Church] wishes to use the secular arm, he from whom help is sought is bound to obey her and defend her.'[106] Huguccio was one of the first authors to use the term 'secular arm' (*seculare brachium*) to denote the secular authority in the context of its relations with the Church. We have already seen that Master Huguccio was no papalist. He rejected the Gregorian in favour of the Gelasian view of the relationship of pope and emperor when he wrote: 'neither depends on the other and the emperor does not hold the sword from the pope.'[107] Nevertheless he assumed that secular princes must act as the servants of the Church when called upon to defend her. He admitted the justice of the 'righteous persecution', the holy wars which must be waged against the enemies of the Church. Since in the twelfth century the papacy alone could legitimate such a holy war, Huguccio's conception of the secular power

---

concept of heresy in the Middle Ages ed. W. Lourdaux and D. Verhelst (Mediaevalia Lovaniensia ser. 1, Studia 6: Louvain, 1976) pp. 136–43.

[105] Y. M.-J. Congar, 'Henri de Marcy, abbé de Clairvaux, cardinal-évêque d'Albano et légat pontifical', *Analecta Monastica. Textes et Etudes sur la vie des moines au moyen âge* 5 (Studia Anselmiana fasc. 43: Rome, 1958) pp. 32–8.

[106] Huguccio, *Summa Decretorum*, quoted in A. Stickler, 'Der Schwerterbegriff bei Huguccio', *Ephemerides Iuris Canonici* 3 (1947), 217.

[107] See above pp. 300–1.

was not far removed from that of Bernard of Clairvaux in his exposition of the two swords of Luke 22. 38. In 1150 Bernard summoned Eugenius III to launch a new crusade with the words: 'put forth both swords, now that Christ is suffering again where he suffered before. Who except you should do so? Both are Peter's, the one to be unsheathed at his nod, the other by his hand, whenever necessary'.[108] When a holy war was to be waged either against heretics or against infidels, the pope took command. The fighting was done by secular princes and knights in their capacity of the 'secular arm' of the Church, being unleashed against the enemy 'at the nod' of the pope.

[108] Bernard, *Epistola* 256: (n. 14) 463D–464A. See above p. 299.

9

THE PAPACY AND THE CRUSADE

—— • ——

The crusade was a holy war which differed from earlier wars against the enemies of Christendom in that it was waged by command of the pope. The military leaders of the First Crusade acknowledged that it was Pope Urban II 'who started this expedition, who by your sermons caused us all to leave our lands . . . who commanded us to take up the cross and to follow Christ'. In September 1098 the crusading princes urged the pope as 'the father and head of the Christian religion' to 'bring to completion the war which is your own' and 'as the vicar of St Peter, take your seat in his church and receive us as your obedient sons in well doing'.[1] Even though the papal sermon at the council of Clermont in November 1095 may have spoken of Christ as the leader of the enterprise,[2] the papal letters of the following months assumed the leadership for Urban II himself: 'we have made our dearest son Bishop Adhémar of Le Puy leader of this expedition and this struggle in our place, so that those who may choose to undertake this journey should obey his commands as if they were our own.'[3] The earliest reference to the First Crusade in a

---

[1] Letter of the crusading princes to Urban II: Fulcher of Chartres, *Historia Hierosolymitana* 1.23, *RHC Occ.* 3 (1866), 351.

[2] Balderic of Dol, *Historia Ierosolimitana*, *RHC Occ.* 4, 15. This theme occurs in all the extant accounts of Urban's sermon: see D. C. Munro, 'The speech of Pope Urban II at Clermont, 1095', *American Historical Review* 11 (1906), 239–40. See also K. M. Setton (ed.), *A history of the Crusades* 1 (2nd edition: Madison, 1969), 221–2.

[3] Urban II, *JL* 5608 (to the faithful in Flanders): H. Hagenmeyer, *Epistulae et chartae ad historiam primi belli sacri spectantes* (Innsbruck, 1901) pp. 136–7.

narrative source – that of Bernold of St Blasien in his chronicle – states that 'the lord pope was the principal author of this expedition';[4] and this theme recurs in the crusading histories of the early twelfth century.[5] It was evidently through these historical writings that the tradition of the papal leadership of the crusade reached Pope Eugenius III. For Eugenius' encyclical of December 1145 proclaiming the Second Crusade, *Quantum praedecessores*, begins with the words: 'we have learned from the accounts of writers of former times and we have found written in their *gesta* how much our predecessors the Roman pontiffs laboured for the liberation of the eastern Church. Indeed our predecessor of happy memory Pope Urban cried out like a heavenly trumpet and exhorted the sons of the holy Roman church from the various regions of the world to consider this.'[6] In conscious imitation of Urban II, Eugenius III placed himself at the head of the crusade. Similarly, when Alexander III in 1165 and Gregory VIII in 1187 assumed the leadership of the crusading movement, they did so in encyclicals which were modelled on Eugenius' letter *Quantum praedecessores* of 1145.[7] By the end of the twelfth century it was generally accepted that the decision to launch a crusade belonged to 'the privilege of the apostle Peter and to the general authority of the Church'.[8] In the Roman curia indeed the launching of a crusade was felt to be not only a papal privilege but also a papal obligation: 'the apostolic see, *recognising its duty*', has proclaimed a crusade, wrote Celestine III in 1193.[9]

THE THEOLOGY OF THE CRUSADE

The crusade which Urban II initiated – and which his successors institutionalised – was a synthesis of various pious activities which the Church had long recommended to the laity. Since the publication of Carl Erdmann's magisterial study of the origins of the idea of crusade (1935), three of these pre-crusading movements have particularly preoccupied historians: the holy war, the 'peace of God' and

---

[4] Bernold, *Chronica* 1096, *MGH SS* 5, 464.
[5] E.g. Guibert of Nogent, *Historia quae dicitur Gesta Dei per Francos* II. 1–5, *RHC Occ.* 4, 135–40.
[6] Eugenius III, *JL* 8876: ed. P. Rassow in E. Caspar, 'Die Kreuzzugsbullen Eugens III.', *NA* 45 (1924), 302. See also Eugenius III, *JL* 8796, *MPL* 180, 1064AB.
[7] Alexander III, *JL* 11218, *MPL* 200, 384–6; Gregory VIII, *JL* 10678, *MPL* 202, 1561A.
[8] Peter of Blois, *De Hierosolymitana peregrinatione acceleranda*, *MPL* 207, 1061A.
[9] Celestine III, *JL* 16944, *MPL* 206, 971A.

the pilgrimage.[10] All three movements had attracted the attention of the reform papacy in the later eleventh century.

Among the 'proto-crusades' – the holy wars of the period immediately preceding the First Crusade – that against the Moslems in Spain in 1064, renewed in 1073, has seemed to historians to be the most significant.[11] The expedition qualifies as a 'proto-crusade' because of the participation of Aquitanian, Burgundian and Norman, as well as Catalan and Aragonese knights, and because of the intervention of the papacy. The 'proto-crusade' inspired the first recorded sending of papal legates to Spain (outside the province of Catalonia).[12] Their duties included the reorganisation of the Spanish church in the areas restored to Christian lordship by the 'Reconquest' and the defence of the rights of St Peter in the peninsula. Gregory VII defined these rights in his letter of April 1073 to the French 'princes wishing to set out for the land of Spain': 'since the kingdom of Spain was from ancient times the property of St Peter', all lands conquered by the French invaders must be held as fiefs from the saint.[13] A similar war waged against the Moslems in the name of St Peter was the Norman conquest of Sicily, begun in 1061 and completed in 1091. The Norman prince who began this conquest, Robert Guiscard, had obtained from the pope the title 'by the grace of God and St Peter duke of Apulia and Calabria and, with the help of both, future duke of Sicily'.[14] His brother, Count Roger I of Sicily, received from the pope the banner of St Peter (*vexillum sancti Petri*) as a protection in his wars against the Moslems.[15] A similar banner was granted to Duke William II 'the Conqueror' of Normandy in 1066 for his invasion of

---

[10] C. Erdmann, *Die Entstehung des Kreuzzugsgedankens* (Stuttgart, 1935) (see also the English translation: *The origin of the idea of crusade* (Princeton, 1977) with additional bibliography); M. Villey, *La croisade. Essai sur la formation d'une théorie juridique* (Paris, 1942); P. Rousset, *Les origines et les caractères de la première croisade* (Geneva, 1945); P. Alphandéry, *La Chrétienté et l'idée de croisade* ed. A. Dupront 1 (Paris, 1954); J. A. Brundage, *Medieval canon law and the crusader* (Madison, 1969); J. Riley-Smith, *What were the crusades?* (London, 1977).

[11] Erdmann, *Entstehung* pp. 124–7, 267–70; Rousset, *Origines* pp. 49–51; P. David, *Etudes historiques sur la Galice et le Portugal* (Lisbon-Paris, 1947) pp. 341–439; B. W. Wheeler, 'The reconquest of Spain before 1095', in Setton (ed.), *Crusades* (n. 2) 1, 31–9.

[12] G. Säbekow, *Die päpstlichen Legationen nach Spanien und Portugal bis zum Ausgang des 12. Jahrhunderts* (dissertation: Berlin, 1931) pp. 13–17; Erdmann, *Entstehung* (n. 10) pp. 126–7.

[13] Gregory VII, *Registrum* 1.7, pp. 9–10.

[14] *Liber Censuum* 1, 422. See below p. 372.

[15] Geoffrey Malaterra, *De rebus gestis Rogerii Calabriae et Siciliae comitis* II.33, MRIS 5/1 (1925–8), 45.

England and his war against the perjured English king.[16] Subsequently Gregory VII requested from the Conqueror, 'the most beloved son and vassal (*fidelis*) of St Peter and of us', the performance of fealty in respect of the conquered kingdom.[17] A more conventional 'proto-crusade' was the Pisan campaign of 1087 against the Moslems of Mahdia in Tunisia. According to the chronicles of Monte Cassino, Pope Victor III granted the participants the banner of St Peter and 'remission of all sins'.[18] However, the most obvious anticipation of the First Crusade was the 'proto-crusade' which never took place: Gregory VII's abortive campaign of 1074 to the aid of Constantinople. Gregory planned to lead an expedition as 'commander and pontiff' to defend the eastern Christians against the Seljuk Turks.[19] Hence the biography of Urban II in the *Liber pontificalis* credits Gregory VII with the invention of the crusading idea. Urban

had heard that his predecessor Pope Gregory had preached to the men beyond the mountains an expedition to Jerusalem for the defence of the Christian faith and the liberation of the Lord's Sepulchre from the hands of enemies, but he could not achieve this because King Henry's persecution beset him on all sides. However, what his predecessor had not the strength to do, this excellent pontiff, chosen by God, achieved, relying on the grace of God.[20]

Urban II's crusade doubtless owed something to the example of earlier holy wars which enjoyed the patronage of St Peter and his vicar. Equally the crusade was partly inspired by the tradition of the 'peace of God' (*pax Dei*) and 'truce of God' (*treuga Dei*). The 'peace of God' was initially the response of bishops in Aquitaine and Burgundy *ca.* 1000 to the private warfare of the aristocracy: the bishops held peace councils in which they anathematised those who attacked the clergy, robbed churches and molested 'poor men' (*pauperes*) and pilgrims. The 'truce of God' was a more far-reaching episcopal initiative of the years 1027–1054 which sought not only to

---

[16] Erdmann, *Entstehung* (n. 10) pp. 139–40, 172–3, 181–3.

[17] Gregory VII, *Registrum* VII.23, p. 500. See above p. 307.

[18] *Chronica monasterii Casinensis* III.71, *MGH SS* 34, 453. See Erdmann, *Entstehung* (n. 10) pp. 272–4; H. E. J. Cowdrey, 'The Mahdia campaign of 1087', *EHR* 92 (1977), 1–29.

[19] Gregory VII, *Registrum* II.31, pp. 165–8. See H. E. J. Cowdrey, 'Pope Gregory VII's "crusading" plans of 1074', *Outremer. Studies in the history of the crusading kingdom of Jerusalem presented to Joshua Prawer* (Jerusalem, 1982) pp. 27–40.

[20] *Vita Urbani II: Liber pontificalis* 2, 293.

protect the clergy and the poor from the *invasiones* and *depraedationes* of knights, but also to suspend warfare for limited periods so that the whole community might benefit from the truce. A summary of the legislation of the councils of the *treuga Dei* is found in the canon law collection of Bishop Ivo of Chartres, the *Panormia* of 1093/4:

We command that priests, clerks, monks, pilgrims, merchants coming and going, as well as peasants, their plough-animals, seed and sheep, shall always be in safety. And we command that the truce be strictly preserved by all from sunset on Wednesday until sunrise on Monday and from the Lord's Advent to the octave of Epiphany and from Septuagesima to the octave of Pentecost. If anyone tries to break the truce, let him be struck with excommunication and let no bishop dare to absolve him, unless he is in immediate danger of death.[21]

The spread of the peace and truce of God into northern Europe and into Italy coincided with the early years of the reform papacy and with the first signs of papal interest in the peace movement. Leo IX seems to have proclaimed the *pax Dei* in his synod of Rheims in October 1049;[22] and Nicholas II gave a general papal sanction to the peace and truce of God in the Lateran synod of 1059.[23] However, the active promotion of the peace movement by the papacy began in the pontificate of Urban II, in a series of papal councils in southern Italy and France: Melfi (1089), Troia (1093), Clermont (1095).[24] The council of Clermont enacted peace legislation more sweeping than that of earlier councils: it was binding on the whole of western Christendom and it was to last for three years.

The chroniclers of the First Crusade emphasised the close connection between the peace legislation of Clermont and the holy war in their versions of Urban II's sermon. 'Since, O sons of God, you have promised God to maintain peace among yourselves more energetically than has been customary and promised faithfully to uphold the rights of holy Church, there still remains work for you to do . . . For you must hasten to bring help to your brothers living in the

---

[21] Ivo of Chartres, *Panormia* VIII.147, *MPL* 161, 1343AC. See Erdmann, *Entstehung* (n. 10) pp. 53–60, 335–8; H. Hoffmann, *Gottesfriede und Treuga Dei* (Schriften der MGH 20, 1964); G. Duby, 'Les laïcs et la paix de Dieu' in *I laici nella 'societas christiana' dei secoli XI et XII* (Miscellanea del Centro di Studi Medioevali 5: Milan, 1968) pp. 448–69; H. E. J. Cowdrey, 'The peace and the truce of God in the eleventh century', *Past and Present* 46 (1970), 42–67.

[22] Hoffmann, *Gottesfriede* p. 218.

[23] Nicholas II, *JL* 4404: *MGH Constitutiones* 1, 549. See Hoffmann, *Gottesfriede* p. 219.

[24] Hoffmann, *Gottesfriede* pp. 220–3; Becker, *Urban II*. 2, 277–8.

east . . . '[25] 'You mangle your own brothers and cut each other in pieces. This is not the warfare of Christ . . . However, if you desire good counsel: abandon this kind of warfare; set off boldly as soldiers of Christ and hasten to defend the eastern Church.'[26] The crusade – 'the warfare of Christ' (*militia Christi*)[27] – was an 'anti-war', fought to attain peace: peace for the eastern Christians by defeating their Saracen persecutors and peace for western Christendom by encouraging the peacebreakers to fight overseas. Urban II's plan, wrote the chronicler Fulcher of Chartres, was to 'turn against the pagans the strength formerly used by the Christians in waging wars amongst themselves'.[28] It was a plan which had been recommended in the past by religious reformers, most forcefully by the monastic reformer Abbo of Fleury *ca.* 1000. 'Warriors . . . do not fight against each other in the womb of their mother, but wisely attack the enemies of the holy Church of God.'[29] This idea was first given practical expression when the bishops who proclaimed the truce of God began to administer oaths to knights committing them to make war on those who broke the truce. The first recorded case was that of the oath administered by Archbishop Haimo of Bourges in 1037.[30] A similar concept of 'righteous warfare' is found in the legislation of Gregory VII's Roman synod of November 1078. 'Any knight . . . or anyone committed to a profession which cannot be exercised without sin . . . is to recognise that he cannot perform true penance, through which he can attain to eternal life, unless he lays down his arms and bears them no more except on the advice of religious bishops for the defence of righteousness.'[31] The same preoccupation with the salvation of noble warriors and the same solution – warfare at the behest of the Church – lay behind the crusade proclaimed by Urban II.

'If any man sets out to free the church of God at Jerusalem out of pure devotion and not for love of glory or gain, the journey shall be accounted a complete penance on his part.'[32] This canon of the council of Clermont seems to echo the legislation of the eleventh-century

[25] Fulcher of Chartres, *Historia Hierosolymitana* I.3: (n. 1) p. 323.
[26] Balderic of Dol, *Historia Ierosolimitana* I.4: (n. 2) p. 14.
[27] Erdmann, *Entstehung* (n. 10) pp. 313–15.
[28] Fulcher, *Historia* I.3: (n. 1) p. 324.
[29] Abbo of Fleury, *Apologeticus*, MPL 139, 464B.
[30] Hoffmann, *Gottesfriede* (n. 21) pp. 104–8.
[31] Gregory VII, *Registrum* VI.5b, c. 6, p. 404.
[32] *Decreta Claromontensia* 2 [8] ed. R. Somerville, *The Councils of Urban II* I (Amsterdam, 1972), 74.

peace councils, which prescribed a pilgrimage to Jerusalem as a penance for a homicide committed during the truce of God.[33] There is no doubt that the penitential pilgrimage to Jerusalem was an important constituent of the First Crusade.[34] Precisely how important it was appears from a rather neglected account of the crusade: that of the Chronicle of Monte Cassino.

It is said that this enterprise was undertaken in Gaul at the behest of certain penitent princes. Because they could not perform a worthy penance for their innumerable offences in their own land – for being laymen, they were ashamed to dwell among their friends while renouncing warfare – they pledged themselves to make a journey beyond the seas, as a penance and for the remission of their sins, to wrest the Lord's Sepulchre from the Saracens . . . This they promised on the authority and on the advice of the wise Pope Urban of happy memory, a truly apostolic man, who was in the region at that time on the business of the Church.[35]

The importance of this passage is that, in the opinion of the most recent editor of the chronicle, it was composed by Leo Marsicanus, monk of Monte Cassino and subsequently cardinal bishop of Ostia and confidant of Urban II in the latter years of the pontificate.[36] It is possible, therefore, that this passage from the Chronicle of Monte Cassino records an authentic tradition of the papal entourage in the late 1090s: the First Crusade originated as a penitential exercise for the warrior nobility of 'Gaul'.

Certainly this is the interpretation of the First Crusade given by the contemporary French theologian Abbot Guibert of Nogent, in his crusading chronicle, *Gesta Dei per Francos*. 'In our own time God has instituted a holy war, so that the order of knights and the unstable multitude, who used to engage in mutual slaughter in the manner of ancient paganism, might find a new way of gaining salvation.' As a monastic theologian, Guibert was naturally struck by the novelty of an offer of salvation to 'the order of knights' (*ordo equestris*) without the traditional requirement of monastic conversion. 'No longer are they obliged to leave the world and choose a monastic way of life or some religious profession, as used to be the case, but in their accustomed liberty and habit, by performing their own office, they may in

---

[33] Hoffmann, *Gottesfriede* (n. 21) p. 84.

[34] Setton (ed.), *Crusades* (n. 2) I, 68–78; Brundage, *Canon law* (n. 10) pp. 3–18.

[35] *Chronica monasterii Casinensis* IV.11: (n. 18) p. 475.

[36] H. Hoffmann, *ibid.*, pp. vii–ix, xxviii–xxx.

some measure achieve the grace of God.'[37] This was also the view of the crusade elaborated and publicised by a much more influential monastic theologian, Bernard of Clairvaux, in his letters and sermons of 1146–7, preaching the Second Crusade. He depicted the crusade as 'the day of plentiful salvation', 'a time rich in indulgence', 'a year of jubilee' for the lay aristocracy. It was a 'great artifice' which God had invented for their salvation. 'What is it but an opportunity for salvation, carefully considered and such as God alone could devise, which the Almighty uses to summon from their servitude murderers, robbers, adulterers, oath-breakers and men guilty of other crimes?'[38] Similarly, in a crusading polemic composed in 1188/9 Peter of Blois described the crusade as a 'remedy', a 'medicine' for the sins of the laity.[39] In the course of the twelfth century this attitude was reinforced by the legislation of church councils, which imposed crusading as a penance for serious offences, notably in cases of arson.[40] The crusade gradually replaced pilgrimage as a normal part of the penitential system.

The two penitential activities of pilgrimage and crusade were inextricably linked together in the twelfth-century western mind by their identical terminology and their common legal status.[41] It was only in the mid-thirteenth century that a specific terminology for the crusade (*passagium generale, expeditio crucis*) began to be used. During the twelfth century the term *peregrinatio* signified both 'pilgrimage' and 'crusade', *peregrinus* signified both 'pilgrim' and 'crusader'. Crusaders thought of their army as *peregrinus exercitus*;[42] although they were aware that to non-westerners this was a contradiction in terms. The 'Greeks feared us very much, believing that we were not

---

[37] Guibert of Nogent, *Gesta Dei* I.1: (n. 5) p. 124. See C. Morris, '*Equestris ordo*: chivalry as a vocation in the twelfth century', *Studies in Church History* 15 (Oxford, 1978), 87–96.

[38] Bernard of Clairvaux, *Epistola* 363, *MPL* 182, 565A–566B. See G. Constable, 'The Second Crusade as seen by contemporaries', *Traditio* 9 (1953), 247.

[39] Peter of Blois, *De Hierosolymitana peregrinatione*: (n. 8) 1065.

[40] *Concilium Lateranense II* c. 18: *Conciliorum Oecumenicorum Decreta* p. 201 = Gratian, *Decretum* c.23 q.8 c.32; Council of Clermont (1130) c. 13: Mansi, *Sacra Concilia* 21, 440; Council of Rheims (1131) c. 17: *ibid.*, 461–2; Council of Rheims (1148) c. 15: *ibid.*, 717. See Villey, *Croisade* (n. 10) pp. 145–6. See also above p. 137.

[41] U. Schwerin, *Die Aufrufe der Päpste zur Befreiung des Heiligen Landes von den Anfängen bis zum Ausgang Innocenz IV.* (Berlin, 1937) p. 45; Brundage, *Canon law* (n. 10) pp. 30–1.

[42] Constable, 'Second Crusade' (n. 38) pp. 223, 225.

pilgrims but that we wished to plunder their land and to kill them'. [43]
The crusader was indeed an armed warrior; but the western Church
saw him first and foremost as a penitent who had vowed to make a
journey to a sacred shrine, that is, a *peregrinus*. He could therefore
expect the spiritual reward of the pilgrim, as well as his legal
privileges. These privileges – the protection of person and property
– had long been known to canon law, but they were redefined by the
reforming popes as part of the legislation for the peace and truce of
God, notably that of Nicholas II's Lateran synod of 1059. [44] Urban II
in 1095 conferred this same privileged status on those penitents who
undertook the journey to free the church of Jerusalem.

These traditional elements – *peregrinatio*, holy war and *pax Dei* –
provided the basis for a novel theology of crusade. The innovatory
character of Urban II's crusading theology needs to be emphasised:
the expedition envisaged by the pope in 1095 was different in kind
from any previous holy war. The difference lay in the spiritual and
temporal privileges which Urban conferred upon the crusaders and
also in the obligations which he imposed upon them. The crusading
vow, the crusade indulgence and the privileged legal status of the
crusader were the instruments by means of which impulsive noble
penitents were organised into an army and the momentary
enthusiasm inspired by the council of Clermont was converted into
a binding commitment. Urban II's conception of the obligations and
the privileges of the crusader made an important contribution to the
effectiveness of the First Crusade. Adapted and elaborated by his
successors, Urban's theory of the crusaders' status was to shape the
crusade into a dominant institution of medieval Latin Christendom.
The formulation of crusading theology remained firmly under papal
control during the twelfth century. It is to be studied in papal crusading bulls and in sermons and propaganda writings inspired by
papal crusading initiatives; and these offer valuable insights into the
popes' conception of their role in the government of Christian
society.

Of Urban II's innovations in 1095, that which attracted most
attention from contemporary chroniclers was the *votum crucis*, the
crusading vow. Canon law had long been familiar with religious
vows and their attendant obligations; nevertheless no systematic

---

[43] *Gesta Francorum et aliorum Hierosolymitanorum* 1.4 ed. R. M. T. Hill (London, 1962)
p. 8.

[44] Nicholas II, *JL* 4404: (n. 23) p. 549. Cf. Ivo of Chartres, *Panormia* v.114: (n. 21)
1238A; Gratian, *Decretum* c.24 q.3 c.25.

doctrine of the *votum* had been worked out before the end of the eleventh century.[45] Perhaps it was the formulation of the *votum crucis* of the First Crusade which prompted canonists and theologians to develop a coherent doctrine of the vow and its consequences.[46] It was generally understood that vows belonged solely to the sphere of private morality, as in the case of the vow to remain celibate, to fast, to enter a monastery or to observe the truce of God. The vow was a *votum voluntarium* by means of which the author of the vow placed himself under an *obligatio* which was not generally binding on all Christians.[47] It was a promise to God; and the author of the vow staked his salvation on the fulfilment of his promise. The vows sworn by the faithful as an immediate response to the papal sermon at the council of Clermont were precisely of this character: the chronicler Robert the Monk used the term *sponsio Deo*.[48] The penitent 'pledged themselves (*se spoponderunt*) to make a journey beyond the seas.'[49] However, a *votum voluntarium* made in the emotional aftermath of the council of Clermont scarcely provided a secure basis for a long-term enterprise. The first major organisational problem of the First Crusade, therefore, was that of translating momentary enthusiasm into firm commitment. This was achieved by attributing to the crusading vow an obligation not only in the private but also in the public sphere, so that the vow could be enforced, if necessary, by legal sanctions.[50] Presumably this was not a complete novelty, but rather an extension of the eleventh-century practice of taking a vow to observe the truce of God (the regulation of the *treuga Dei* was a major preoccupation of the council of Clermont and undoubtedly influenced the nascent crusade).[51]

Urban II's innovation lay in combining the vow with the potent symbol of the cross – the *votum crucis*. 'He instituted a sign well suited

---

[45] See, for example, the canonical collections of Ivo of Chartres, compiled in the mid-1090s: *Decretum, prologus*, VII.9, 19, 20, 32, 146; VIII.73, 136–7; XII.64: *MPL* 161, 49, 546, 549, 553, 580; 599, 614; 796; *Panormia* III.183, 192, 200: *ibid.*, 1173, 1175–6, 1177. See Villey, *Croisade* (n. 10) p. 124.

[46] Brundage, *Canon law* (n. 10) pp. 33–7; *idem*, 'The votive obligations of crusaders: the development of a canonistic doctrine', *Traditio* 24 (1968), 77–118; *idem*, 'The army of the First Crusade and the crusade vow', *Medieval Studies* 33 (1971), 334–43.

[47] Ivo of Chartres, *Decretum, prologus*: (n. 45) 49AB. See Hoffmann, *Gottesfriede* (n. 21) pp. 199–200.

[48] Robert the Monk, *Historia Iherosolymitana* I.2, *RHC Occ.* 3, 729.

[49] *Chronica monasterii Casinensis* IV.11: (n. 18) p. 475.

[50] Villey, *Croisade* (n. 10) pp. 119–20.

[51] Erdmann, *Entstehung* (n. 10) pp. 311–13; Hoffmann, *Gottesfriede* pp. 221–4.

to so honourable a profession, proposing to those who were about to make war on God's behalf, as a badge of their knighthood, the mark of the Lord's Passion; and he commanded that the shape of the cross, in whatever cloth was available, be sewn on to the tunics, mantles or cloaks of those who were to make the journey.'[52] Guibert of Nogent's account is corroborated by other chroniclers of the First Crusade, who also emphasised that these crosses were worn 'by command of the pope'.[53] The cross of cloth was the outward sign of the crusading vow; and some contemporaries evidently believed that this material sign imposed on the recipient the obligations of the *votum crucis*. For example, when in the summer of 1096 the crusader prince Bohemund of Tarento had overcome the reluctance of his Norman knights to undertake the expedition, he produced cloth crosses, saying (according to Robert the Monk): 'If you wish to join deeds to your words, let each take one of these crosses; and the acceptance of the cross becomes a promise to make the journey.'[54] In his account of the distribution of crosses at the council of Clermont, Guibert of Nogent claims that the pope on this occasion mentioned a legal sanction.

He commanded that if any one after accepting this badge or after making this vow openly should shrink from performing this good deed, either through perversity or for love of his friends, he should forever be regarded as an outlaw, unless he came to his senses and undertook to complete whatever of his obligation was left undone.[55]

The Anglo-Norman chronicler Orderic Vitalis claims more specifically that Urban II pronounced excommunication upon any crusader who failed to fulfil his vow.[56] Guibert wrote more than a decade after the event and Orderic later still: in the absence of any earlier evidence it is tempting to discard the story of Urban II's anathema. Indeed it has even been argued that Urban had not formulated the crusading vow at the time of the council of Clermont, that the distribution of the crosses had no legal significance and that the *votum crucis*

[52] Guibert of Nogent, *Gesta Dei* II.5: (n. 5) p. 140.
[53] Fulcher of Chartres, *Historia Hierosolymitana* I.4: (n. 1) p. 325. Cf. *Gesta Francorum* I.1: (n. 43) p. 2; Robert the Monk, *Historia Iherosolymitana* I.2: (n. 48) pp. 729–30; Ekkehard, *Chronica* (Ausgewählte Quellen zur deutschen Geschichte des Mittelalters 15: Darmstadt, 1972) pp. 136–8.
[54] Robert the Monk, *Historia* II.4: p. 741.
[55] Guibert of Nogent, *Gesta Dei* II.5: (n. 5) p. 140.
[56] Orderic Vitalis, *Historia ecclesiastica* X.12 ed. M. Chibnall 4 (Oxford 1975), 268.

developed out of the crusading experience of the late 1090s.[57] It is true that the only appearance of the term *votum* in Urban's letters concerning the crusade is imprecise and makes no mention of the consequences of the vow.[58] Nevertheless there is extant an unambiguous statement by the legate to whom Urban committed the leadership of the expedition, Adhémar of Le Puy. The legate wrote from Antioch in October 1097 that it was well known that 'those who have remained apostate in deed after having been signed with the cross, are in truth excommunicate'.[59] The same assumption is made in three other letters of 1098–9 sent from Outremer to the west by Simeon, patriarch of Jerusalem, Anselm of Ribemont, a vassal of the church of Rheims, and by Archbishop Manasses II of Rheims.[60] Manasses' letter commands his suffragans to 'constrain by threat all who vowed to go on the expedition and took the sign of the cross upon themselves'. There was, in short, a belief among crusaders, as well as among chroniclers of the crusade, that the *votum crucis* carried with it the sanction of excommunication.

The pronouncements of Urban II's successors show no ambiguity about the nature and consequences of the *votum crucis*. Shortly after Urban's death Pope Paschal II wrote to the French archbishops and bishops:

Compel those who have taken the sign of the cross as a vow to undertake this service (*militia*) to hasten thither, unless they are held back by the obstacle of poverty; otherwise we decree that they are to be regarded as infamous. The fainthearted men who, wavering in their faith, withdrew from the siege of Antioch, are to remain excommunicate, unless they confirm, with reliable guarantees, that they will return.[61]

It was perhaps in response to this letter that a provincial council in Anse excommunicated those crusaders who had not kept their vows.[62] The effectiveness of this sanction is demonstrated by the conduct of the most distinguished deserters from the First Crusade. Hugh, Count of Vermandois, brother of King Philip I of France, felt

---

[57] A. Noth, *Heiliger Krieg und heiliger Kampf in Islam und Christentum. Beiträge zur Vorgeschichte und Geschichte der Kreuzzüge* (Bonn, 1966) pp. 120–39. The opposite view is presented by Brundage, 'Army of the First Crusade' (n. 46) pp. 334–43.

[58] Urban II, *JL* 5608: (n. 3) p. 137.

[59] Letter of Patriarch Simeon of Jerusalem and Bishop Adhémar of Le Puy: Hagenmeyer, *Epistulae* (n. 3) p. 132.

[60] *Ibid.*, pp. 148–9, 160, 176.

[61] Paschal II, *JL* 5812, *MPL* 163, 45D–46B.

[62] Hugh of Flavigny, *Chronicon* II, *MGH SS* 8, 487.

compelled to fulfil the *votum crucis* by participating in the ill-fated crusade of 1101.[63] Likewise Stephen, count of Blois, son-in-law of William the Conqueror, who had deserted the siege of Antioch in 1098 'was forced to undertake the warfare of Christ again [in 1101] by fear as much as by shame'.[64] Another deserter from Antioch was Guy Troussel of Montlhéry, one of the notorious 'secret rope-dancers', who had escaped from the city by climbing over the wall. Guy's brother and uncle joined the crusade of 1101, evidently seeking to wipe out the infamy of their kinsman.[65]

The summary of reforming legislation promulgated at the First Lateran Council of 1123 contains a definitive statement of the sanctions supporting the *votum crucis*. The council decreed that 'those who are known to have placed crosses on their garments and afterwards to have abandoned them are to take up the crosses again and make the journey between this Easter and the next'. If they failed to do so, they would be forbidden to enter churches and their lands would be placed under an interdict.[66] Similar severity was shown in the decrees of Alexander III and Celestine III.[67] Simultaneous with this energetic papal insistence on the fulfilment of the crusading vow was the gradual formalisation of the rite for taking the cross. The earliest evidence comes from the preliminaries of the Second Crusade. The conduct of Bernard of Clairvaux at the council of Vézelay on 31 March 1146, in the presence of King Louis VII of France, when he distributed to the French nobility 'the sign of pilgrimage, as is the custom – that is, the cross',[68] was intended as an illustration of the crusading theory in his sermons and letters. For Bernard the crusader's cross was 'a heavenly sign', 'a token of life'

---

[63] Guibert of Nogent, *Gesta Dei* VII.23: (n. 5) p. 243.

[64] Orderic Vitalis, *Historia ecclesiastica* X.20: (n. 56) p. 324. See J. A. Brundage, 'An errant crusader: Stephen of Blois', *Traditio* 16 (1960), 380–95.

[65] Orderic Vitalis, *Historia ecclesiastica* IX.10: p. 98; Suger of St Denis, *Vita Ludovici grossi regis* c. 8 ed. H. Waquet (Paris, 1929) pp. 36, 38, 40; Albert of Aachen, *Historia Hierosolymitana* VIII.6, *RHC Occ.* 4, 563.

[66] *Concilium Lateranense I* c. 10: *Conciliorum Oecumenicorum Decreta* p. 192. Noth, *Heiliger Krieg* (n. 57) p. 138 argues that this was the first formal papal statement of the sanctions attached to the *votum crucis*. For the opposite view see Brundage, 'Army of the First Crusade' (n. 46) pp. 334–43.

[67] Alexander III, *JL* 14077: Mansi, *Sacra Concilia* 21, 1098; Celestine III, *JL* 17307: (n. 9) 1135BD.

[68] *Anonymi Chronicon ad annum 1160*, *Recueil des historiens des Gaules et de la France* 12, 120. Cf. Odo of Deuil, *De profectione Ludovici VII in orientem* 1 ed. V. G. Berry (New York, 1948) p. 9.

which miraculously freed the recipient from the servitude of sin.[69] However, the most explicit reference to taking the cross as a liturgical rite in the Second Crusade is found in the anonymous narrative *The storming of Lisbon*, which describes the capture of this Moslem city by an Anglo–Flemish–German naval expedition in 1147. Immediately before the final assault on Lisbon a priest exhorted them to make the vow to go to Jerusalem. According to the anonymous chronicler, the priest exclaimed (remembering the example of Emperor Constantine I), 'In this sign . . . you will conquer', and signed the crusaders with the cross.[70] Thirty years later, Henry of Marcy, abbot of Clairvaux and cardinal bishop of Albano, described in a letter to Pope Alexander III the ceremony in which Henry 'the Liberal', count of Champagne, made the crusading vow at Christmastide 1177, 'most devoutly receiving the sign of the life-giving cross from the hand of your legate', Peter of Pavia, cardinal priest of S. Grisogono.[71] Liturgical texts for the ceremony of taking the cross begin to appear in French and English pontificals of the later twelfth century, side-by-side with the models on which they were based, the texts of the vow of pilgrimage.[72]

Throughout the twelfth century crusading propaganda insisted on the binding nature of the *votum crucis*. However, papal legislation on the subject of the *votum crucis* in the latter half of the century was increasingly concerned with the dispensation of the vow. For the experience of the first fifty years of crusading had demonstrated that many who took the cross, though full of pious enthusiasm, were lacking in the necessary military ability and were merely an encumbrance to the army. Already in 1095 Urban II seems to have foreseen this danger – 'we do not command or persuade the old, the feeble or those unfit for bearing arms to undertake this journey . . . for such are more of a hindrance than a help' – but he was unable to prevent

---

[69] Bernard of Clairvaux, *Epistola* 363: (n. 38) 566B, 567A.

[70] *De expugnatione Lyxbonensi* ed. C. W. David (New York, 1936) p. 156. See V. Cramer, 'Kreuzpredigt und Kreuzzugsgedanke von Bernhard von Clairvaux bis Humbert von Romans' in *Das Heilige Land in Vergangenheit und Gegenwart* ed. V. Cramer and G. Meinertz (Cologne, 1939) pp. 60–2; Constable, 'Second Crusade' (n. 38) pp. 221–2, 234–5, 239.

[71] Henry of Clairvaux, *Epistola* 1, MPL 204, 215A–216B. See Y. M.-J. Congar, 'Henri de Marcy, abbé de Clairvaux, cardinal-évêque d'Albano et légat pontifical', *Analecta Monastica* 5e série (Studia Anselmiana 43: Rome, 1958) p. 8.

[72] J. A. Brundage, '*Cruce signari*: the rite for taking the cross in England', *Traditio* 22 (1966), 289–310.

thousands of non-combatants from joining the First Crusade.[73] The similar composition of the armies of the Second Crusade seemed to contemporaries to be a reason for the failure of the expedition.[74] Hence the tendency of papal legislation in the later twelfth century was to dissuade all except fully equipped, experienced warriors from participating in the crusade. The development of the papal theory of dispensation, redemption and commutation can be traced in letters of Alexander III and Clement III which survive in decretal collections of *ca.* 1200.[75] Two decretals of the 1160s explain how a vow of *peregrinatio* may be redeemed by almsgiving.[76] A further decretal of Alexander III, of uncertain date, states that the crusading vow must either be fulfilled in person or be commuted to another pious act.[77] Finally, a decretal of Clement III, dated 12 August 1190, specifies that an acceptable commutation of the *votum crucis* is the payment of a subsidy to enable other persons to make the journey to the Holy Sepulchre. Celestine III confirmed this opinion in a letter of 12 January 1196.[78] The vows of 'the old, the feeble or those unfit for bearing arms' could now be converted into financial support for the crusade; and the pious enthusiasm of non-combatants might be channelled in a direction which would not impair the efficiency of the army.

Like the crusading vow, the temporal privileges of the crusader owed much to the early medieval pilgrimage tradition and to the peace and truce of God. The Church had long been concerned to protect the traveller in a strange land where he had neither lord nor kindred, especially when he was a *peregrinus* making a penitential journey. The reform papacy had taken the persons and possessions of *peregrini* under papal protection in the Lateran synod of 1059.[79] Evidently the same protection was extended by Urban II to the

---

[73] Robert the Monk, *Historia Iherosolymitana* 1.2: (n. 48) p. 729. See W. Porges, 'The clergy, the poor and the non-combatants on the First Crusade', *Speculum* 21 (1946), 1–21.

[74] *Annales Herbipolenses* 1147, *MGH SS* 16, 3. See Constable, 'Second Crusade' (n. 38) pp. 266–76; Brundage, *Canon Law* (n. 10) pp. xiv, 69.

[75] *Compilatio prima* (1187–91) and *Compilatio secunda* (1210–12): Brundage, 'Votive obligations' (n. 46) pp. 77–118; *idem*, *Canon law* (n. 10) pp. 68–76.

[76] Alexander III, *JL* 13916, 11339: *Decretales Gregorii IX* III.34.1–2.

[77] Alexander III, *JL* 14077: (n. 67) 1098.

[78] Clement III, *JL* 16552, *MPL* 204, 1482C (1500D). Cf. Celestine III, *JL* 17307: (n. 9) 1135D.

[79] Nicholas II, *JL* 4404; (n. 23) p. 549.

peregrini of the First Crusade.[80] The legislation of the council of
Clermont on the temporal privileges of the crusader is not precisely
known. According to Fulcher of Chartres, the council pronounced
excommunication on those who attacked and despoiled *peregrini*;
and the chronicle of Guibert of Nogent adds that the pope
'anathematised all those who dared during the next three years to
molest the wives, children and possessions of those who were undertaking this journey for God'.[81] However, such a protection appears
only in two late versions of the conciliar decrees of Clermont: 'Whoever shall go [to Jerusalem] as a penance, both he and his property
shall be under the truce of the Lord.'[82] The firmest evidence that the
council of Clermont issued a decree of the type mentioned by
Guibert comes from a letter of Paschal II, probably of December
1099, addressed to the prelates of France. 'We command that all their
property be restored to the brethren who return after achieving this
victory, which, as you remember, was decreed by our predecessor of
blessed memory, Urban, in a synodal decision.'[83] Similarly, the First
Lateran Council in 1123 received 'the houses, households and all the
property [of crusaders] under the protection of St Peter and of the
Roman church, as was decided by our lord Pope Urban.'[84] The
earliest known invocation of this guarantee of protection for the
property of absent crusaders comes from the year 1106, when the
crusader Hugh II of le Puiset complained of a violation of his jurisdiction by Count Rotrou of Perche. The case was referred to the
diocesan, the distinguished canonist Bishop Ivo of Chartres; and he
was obliged to seek from Paschal II further information about this
'new institution which extends ecclesiastical protection to the
property of knights setting out for Jerusalem'.[85] The case of Hugh of
le Puiset demonstrates the readiness of bishop and pope to vindicate
the temporal privileges promised to crusaders a decade before. It also

---

[80] Villey, *Croisade* (n. 10) p. 151 emphasises the innovatory character of the protection granted by Urban II; but see Brundage, *Canon law* (n. 10) p. 161.

[81] Fulcher, *Historia Hierosolymitana* 1.2: (n. 1) p. 322; Guibert, *Gesta Dei* II.5: (n. 5)
p. 140.

[82] *Decreta Claromontensia* (n. 32) pp. 108, 124. See Hoffmann, *Gottesfriede* (n. 21)
pp. 221–3.

[83] Paschal II, *JL* 5812: (n. 61) 44B.

[84] *Concilium Lateranense I* c. 10: *Conciliorum Oecumenicorum Decreta* p. 167.

[85] Ivo of Chartres, *Epistolae* 168–70, 173, *MPL* 162, 170D–174A, 176B–177B. See
Hoffmann, *Gottesfriede* (n. 21) pp. 200–2; Brundage, *Canon Law* (n. 10) pp. 165–6;
J. Fried, *Der päpstliche Schutz für Laienfürsten. Die politische Geschichte des
päpstlichen Schutzprivilegs für Laien (11.–13. Jh.)* (*Abhandlungen der Heidelberger
Akademie der Wissenschaften, phil.-hist. Klasse* 1980/1) p. 106.

reveals that, despite the close analogy of the protection granted to pilgrims, these temporal privileges seemed to a learned canonist like Ivo of Chartres to be a *nova institutio* – an extension of ecclesiastical jurisdiction into the secular sphere.

The duty of the bishop to protect crusaders' property in his diocese, which Ivo of Chartres assumed in 1106, was made a binding episcopal responsibility in the first papal crusading bull, that of Eugenius III, *Quantum praedecessores*, in 1145: 'We decree that the wives and children [of crusaders] and also their property and possessions are to remain under the protection of holy Church and of us, of archbishops, bishops and other prelates of the Church of God.'[86] This sentence recurs, with slight variations, in the three crusading bulls of Alexander III in 1165, 1169 and 1181 and in the encyclical of Gregory VIII, *Audita tremendi* of 1187, launching the Third Crusade.[87] Prelates were reminded of their duties by the exhortations of Bernard of Clairvaux during the Second Crusade and by provincial councils during the Third Crusade;[88] and the pope himself demanded the intervention of churchmen in individual cases, 'prompted by the obligations of our office, according to which we are bound to defend with special care the persons and property of all who are in God's service'.[89] Particularly expressive of the direct involvement of the papacy in ensuring crusader privileges are the personal letters guaranteeing protection which were requested from the pope by prominent crusaders.[90] In the case of princes undertaking the crusade, the pope authorised the appointment of a special officer, the *conservator crucesignatorum* – usually a churchman – to protect the crusaders' interests. This was the office held (to cite the best-known example) by Abbot Suger of St Denis during the absence of King Louis VII of France on the Second Crusade. Suger performed the secular function of regent of the Capetian kingdom; but according to the papal theory of the temporal privileges of

---

[86] Eugenius III, *JL* 8876: (n. 6) p. 304.

[87] Alexander III, *JL* 11218 (*Quantum praedecessores*), *JL* 11637 (*Inter omnia*), *JL* 14360 (*Cor nostrum*): (n. 7) 385D, 601B, 1295D; Gregory VIII, *JL* 16019: (n. 7) 1542C.

[88] Bernard of Clairvaux, *Epistola* 457: (n. 38) 651B–652B. See Brundage, *Canon Law* (n. 10) p. 162.

[89] Alexander III, *JL* 12028 (to Abbot Peter of St. Rémi in Rheims), *JL* 11638 (to Archbishop Henry of Rheims): (n. 7) 807B, 602C.

[90] E.g. Hadrian IV, *JL* 10514, *MPL* 188, 1603AC; Alexander III, *JL* 12028: 807B; Lucius III, *JL* 14554: P. Jaffé, *Regesta pontificum Romanorum* 2, 435; Celestine III, *JL* 16765 (n. 9) 899B–900B.

crusaders, his role was that of papal vicar in the lands of the absent crusader.[91]

Eugenius III's crusading legislation not only confirmed the protection given by Urban II to the crusader and his property, but also gave him further financial and jurisdictional privileges. In order to help finance the crusader's expedition, the crusading bull *Quantum praedecessores* granted that 'those who are burdened with debt to others and begin the holy journey with a pure heart, are not to pay interest for time past'.[92] This formula was adopted in later twelfth-century crusading bulls;[93] and it prompted the suggestion of a hostile chronicler that some crusaders used 'the holy journey' as a pretext for evading their debts.[94] *Quantum praedecessores* also conceded to crusaders that 'if their kinsmen or the lords to whom their fiefs belong either will not or cannot lend them money, after due warning they may pledge their lands or other possessions, freely and without any appeal, to churches or churchmen or any other of the faithful'. This clause (which is also found in later twelfth-century crusading bulls)[95] is the first official statement of a privilege already available to participants in the First Crusade. The well-known case of the pledging of the duchy of Normandy by the crusader Duke Robert II to his brother King William II of England in 1096 marks the starting-point of the papal concern with the financing of the crusade. The negotiation of the loan of 10,000 silver marks for Robert, with his duchy as security, was the work of Urban II's legate, Abbot Jarento of St-Bénigne de Dijon,[96] adopting the procedure which was summarised half a century later in *Quantum praedecessores*. This procedure was undoubtedly a *nova constitutio* – an intrusion of papal legislation into a wholly new sphere, involving the cancellation of traditional rights. The kindred of the feudal lords who were unable or unwilling to lend money for the crusaders' expenses, automatically lost their customary rights over the crusaders' lands. The

---

91 William, *Vita Sugerii* ed. A. Lecoy de La Marche, *Oeuvres complètes de Suger* (Paris, 1867) p. 394. See A. Graboïs, 'Le privilège de croisade et la régence de Suger', *Revue historique de droit français et étranger* 4th ser., 42 (1964), 458–65. See above p. 305.
92 Eugenius III, *JL* 8876: (n. 6) p. 304.
93 Alexander III, *JL* 11218, 11637: (n. 7) 386AB, 601B; Gregory VIII, *JL* 16019: (n. 7) 1542D.
94 *Annales Herbipolenses* 1147: (n. 74) p. 3.
95 Eugenius III, *JL* 8876: (n. 6) p. 304; Alexander III, *JL* 11218, 11637, 14360: (n. 7) 386B, 601BC, 1295D–1296A.
96 Hugh of Flavigny, *Chronicon* (n. 62) pp. 474–5.

crusaders themselves obtained, by taking the cross, the novel power of mortgaging their fiefs or family lands.

Eugenius III's crusading bull demanded the delaying of all judicial proceedings which affected the interests of absent crusaders 'in respect of all those things of which they were in peaceful possession when they took the cross'. This became a standard formula in later crusading bulls; and Alexander III explained this privilege (without, however, setting a term for the delay in proceedings) in a letter to Abbot Simon of St Alban's between 1173 and 1176. The delay could be claimed by any person absent 'for the sake of studies, pilgrimages or any other cause', 'unless he absented himself out of obstinacy'.[97] This privilege appears under its technical name of *essoin* in the English treatise on secular law named after Henry II's great justiciar, Ranulf Glanvill. Here the crusaders' right to delay in proceedings (*essonium de esse in peregrinatione*) is limited to one year.[98] More controversial, however, than the *essoin* was the crusaders' claim to the *privilegium fori* – the right to trial in the ecclesiastical courts rather than in the secular courts in which, as laymen, they must answer charges. The claim to the *privilegium fori* is the most striking illustration of the change in legal status which resulted from taking the cross: not only was the crusader under the protection of the Church, he was also under her jurisdiction.[99] The earliest papal rulings on this privilege are found in two letters of Eugenius III. The first assumes that a crusader (Count William II of Ponthieu) should answer in the ecclesiastical court even in a case of title to property.[100] However, the second stipulates that a crusader may not claim the *privilegium fori* in a case which predates his taking the cross. (This second letter refers to the English barons who took the cross after losing their lands in the civil war of King Stephen's reign.)[101] Later twelfth-century papal legislation was concerned to limit rather than to extend this privilege. Most importantly, Alexander III ruled that a crusader could not be tried in an ecclesiastical court in a case concerning feudal

[97] Alexander III, *JL* 12636: (n. 7) 1054A.
[98] *Tractatus de legibus et consuetudinibus regni Anglie* II.29 ed. G. D. G. Hall (London, 1965) pp. 16–17.
[99] R. Génestal, *Le Privilegium fori en France du Décret de Gratien à la fin du XIVe siècle* I (Paris, 1921), 57–9.
[100] Eugenius III, *JL* 9166: S. Loewenfeld, 'Documents relatifs à la croisade de Guillaume comte de Ponthieu', *Archives de l'Orient latin* 2 (1884), 253.
[101] Eugenius III, *JL* 8959: S. Loewenfeld, *Epistolae pontificum Romanorum ineditae* (Leipzig, 1885) pp. 103–4.

tenure or other secular matters.[102] Of the temporal privileges instituted for crusaders by Urban II and Eugenius III, all except the
privilegium fori developed into a formidable system of protections
which created an élite, set apart from the rest of the laity. The single
exception of the *privilegium fori* is perhaps to be explained by the
development of effective systems of secular justice in the twelfth century, especially in territories like France and England where the pope
was anxious to preserve the friendship of the king.

The spiritual privilege accorded to the crusaders – the crusade
indulgence – has received more attention from historians than any
other aspect of the papal involvement in the crusades. The extensive
literature on this subject emphasises above all the difficulty of
deciding precisely what the popes promised the crusaders.[103] The
first problem is the vagueness of the language used by Urban II and
his twelfth-century successors in their statements of the crusaders'
privileges; and the second problem is the evident contradiction
between the papal concessions and the way in which they were
interpreted by contemporaries (including the chroniclers of the
crusades). The papal concessions were made at a time when scholastic theologians had not yet elaborated the doctrine of indulgences –
that work which began with Hugh of St Victor (*ca.* 1150) and was
developed by Hugh of St Cher (*ca.* 1230) and by Bonaventura and
Thomas Aquinas in the third quarter of the thirteenth century.[104]
When Urban II and the twelfth-century popes granted their crusading privileges, therefore, they had no access to a precise terminology
in which to frame their grant. Alexander III in his crusading bull of
1169 referred to his grant as 'this indulgence of [crusaders'] sins' and
in that of 1181 he spoke of 'the indulgence of the penance imposed
upon [the crusader]'.[105] Similarly Gregory VIII promised in his
crusading bull of 1187 'the full indulgence of all [the crusaders']
offences'.[106] Nevertheless the term *indulgentia* did not yet have the

---

[102] Alexander III, *JL* 14002: *Decretales Gregorii IX* IV.17.7. See Brundage, *Canon Law*
(n. 10) p. 171.
[103] E.g. Brundage, *Canon law* pp. 139–58; H. E. Mayer, *The crusades* (English translation: Oxford, 1972) pp. 25–40; Riley-Smith, *What were the crusades?* (n. 10)
pp. 57–62.
[104] P. Anciaux, *La théologie du sacrement de pénitence au XII siècle* (Louvain-Gembloux,
1949) pp. 295–302; A. Gottlob, *Kreuzablass und Almosenablass. Eine Studie über die
Frühzeit des Ablasswesens* (Kirchenrechtliche Abhandlungen 30–1: Stuttgart, 1906)
pp. 270–88.
[105] Alexander III, *JL* 11637, 14360: (n. 7) 601A, 1296B.
[106] Gregory VIII, *JL* 16019: (n. 7) 1542C.

technical meaning which it acquired in the course of the thirteenth century: that is, the remission by the Church of the temporal penalties imposed by God (in this world and the next) for men's sins – a remission guaranteed by the treasury of the spiritual merits of the Church. In the papal letters of the twelfth-century *indulgentia*, 'remission of punishment', has the non-technical meaning found also, for example, in the letter of Bernard of Clairvaux representing the Second Crusade as 'a time rich in *indulgentia*'. [107]

The indulgence has been seen as the most striking innovation of Urban II's crusade; although possible precedents for the grant of 1095 have been found in two earlier papal letters. The first is a fragmentary letter of Alexander II referring to the campaign against the Spanish Moslems of Barbastro in 1063. The letter contains this promise to the southern French knights engaged in the campaign: 'We release them from their penance and make remission of their sins.'[108] If this is an authentic letter of 1063,[109] the connection which it makes between *remissio peccatorum* and war against the Moslems is an obvious anticipation – albeit on a much smaller scale – of Urban II's conception of crusade. The terminology of Alexander II's letter is significant. What it seems to grant is a commutation of penance: the knights are invited to regard the Barbastro campaign as a substitute for a previous penance imposed upon them. The letter attaches to this commutation a remission of sins. A thirteenth-century theologian would have seen an important distinction between these two concepts: 'remission of sins', which he would have regarded as a crusading indulgence, was a different process from the commutation of penance, a more conventional exercise of the Church's penitential discipline. Apparently such a distinction was unknown to Alexander II.

Equally instructive is a second letter, also concerned with Spain, written in the name of Urban II six years before the council of Clermont. This letter of 1089 exhorts the nobility and clergy of Catalonia to assist in the rebuilding of the bishopric of Tarragona as a defence against the Moslems. The pope adds:

We advise those who are about to travel to Jerusalem or elsewhere in a spirit of penitence and piety, to devote all the labour and expense of the journey to the restoration of the church of Tarragona . . . and we promise them through

[107] Bernard of Clairvaux, *Epistola* 363: (n. 38) 566B.
[108] Alexander II, *JL* 4530: Loewenfeld (n. 101) p. 43.
[109] Its authenticity is doubted by Villey, *Croisade* (n. 10) pp. 143–4, and defended by Erdmann, *Entstehung* (n. 10) p. 125 and Brundage, *Canon law* (n. 10) pp. 145–6.

God's mercy the same indulgence which they would obtain if they under-took that journey.[110]

This equation of defensive measures against the Moslems with the pilgrimage to Jerusalem marks an important stage in the development of Urban II's idea of crusade (although the vital element of holy war is missing). The terminology of the letter of 1089 bears a significant resemblance to that of 1063. Its subject is again the commutation of penance – the rebuilding of Tarragona is substituted for pilgrimage – and the commuted penance produces *indulgentia*. Urban II referred again to this enterprise in a letter addressed to the counts of Besalú, Empurias, Roussillon and Cerdana and their knights after the beginning of the First Crusade. The letter draws an analogy between the defence of Tarragona and the crusaders' attempts to free 'the Church in Asia' and exhorts the Catalan nobility to abandon any intention of joining the First Crusade and instead to restore the city 'for the remission of [their] sins'. 'If anyone dies in that expedition for the love of God and of his brothers, let him not doubt that he will assuredly find indulgence of his sins and will participate in eternal life, through the most merciful compassion of our God.'[111] These two letters concerning Tarragona allow a comparison of the papal attitude to the enterprise both before and after the council of Clermont. In the letter of 1089 the restoration of Tarragona is sub-stituted for a pilgrimage to Jerusalem; in the letter of 1096–9 it is substituted for the crusade. In both cases it is judged worthy of *indulgentia*. In these letters the pilgrimage 'to Jerusalem or elsewhere', 'the expedition to Asia' and the rebuilding of Tarragona are all seen as equivalent penitential exercises. The obvious con-clusion is that Urban II had no conception of a specific crusading indulgence. What he offered to potential crusaders at the council of Clermont was what he offered Catalan nobles who were prepared to restore Tarragona: commutation of penance.

This conclusion is borne out by the text of the second canon of the council of Clermont: 'whoever sets out to free the church of God in Jerusalem purely out of devotion and not for the acquisition of honour or wealth, he may reckon that journey as a substitute for

---

[110] Urban II, *JL* 5401, *MPL* 151, 303B. See Erdmann, *Entstehung* (n. 10) pp. 292–3; Mayer, *Crusades* (n. 103) pp. 29–32.

[111] P. Kehr, *Papsturkunden in Spanien*, 1 (*Abhandlungen der Gesellschaft der Wissen-schaften zu Göttingen* N.F. 26) p. 287 (no. 23). For the date of this letter (1096–9) see Erdmann, *Entstehung* (n. 10) pp. 294–5; Becker, *Urban II.* 1, 228–9; Mayer, *Crusades* (n. 103) pp. 29–30.

every penance (*pro omni penitentia*).'[112] Urban II defined this concession more precisely in his letter to the faithful in Bologna in the autumn of 1096: 'we release them from all penance for those sins for which they make a true and perfect confession, through the mercy of almighty God and the prayers of the catholic Church, by our own authority and that of almost all the archbishops and bishops in *Galliae*'.[113] This is the only surviving document in which the pope specifies what was offered at Clermont; and what it describes is the commutation of penance. Only one of the narrative sources interprets the crusaders' spiritual privilege in language similar to that of the letter to the Bolognese: namely, the Chronicle of Monte Cassino, which, as we have seen, perhaps recorded an authentic tradition from Urban II's entourage. For this chronicler, the crusade was a penance suggested by the pope to 'certain penitent princes' who 'could not perform a worthy penance for their innumerable offences in their own land'.[114] No other chronicle of the First Crusade uses the term 'penance' to describe the spiritual privilege obtained by the crusaders: the preferred term is 'remission of sins'. The emphasis in the crusading chronicles is indeed on the reward of the crusaders who died during the expedition, with no precise reference to the reward of the survivors. Fulcher of Chartres, for example, attributed to Urban the promise: 'to all those who set out thither, if they should lose their lives on the way by land or in crossing the sea or in fighting the pagans, immediate remission of sins will be given';[115] and similar versions of the promise were given by Balderic of Dol and Guibert of Nogent.[116] The same emphasis is found in the earliest non-papal documents referring to the crusaders' spiritual privilege – the letters sent by the crusaders themselves from Outremer. The crusader princes wrote of their losses at the battle of Nicaea (21 May 1097), 'three thousand of us rest in peace, who doubtless glory in eternal life'; and Count Stephen of Blois wrote of the crusaders who perished in the struggle for Antioch (1097–8): 'Their souls have truly gone to the joys of Paradise.'[117]

While Urban II spoke of commutation of penance, the crusaders and the chroniclers spoke of 'remission of sins' and the rewards of

---

[112] *Decreta Claromontensia* (n. 32) p. 74.

[113] Urban II, *JL* 5670: Hagenmeyer, *Epistulae* (n. 3) p. 137.

[114] *Chronica monasterii Casinensis* IV.11: (n. 18) p. 475. See above p. 328.

[115] Fulcher, *Historia Hierosolymitana* I.3: (n. 1) p. 324.

[116] Balderic, *Historia Ierosolimitana* I.4: (n. 2) pp. 14–15; Guibert, *Gesta Dei* II.4: (n. 5) p. 138.

[117] Hagenmeyer, *Epistulae* (n. 3) pp. 150, 154.

martyrdom. Recent historians have suggested that the pope failed to communicate to the faithful precisely what he had promised the crusaders. 'Popular crusading propaganda at once went unhesitatingly far beyond the more limited formula used at the council [of Clermont].'[118] Consequently the papal curia was obliged to adopt the popular interpretation of the spiritual reward of the crusaders. The principal evidence for this theory is the changing language of papal letters. Urban II's letter to the Bolognese speaks of releasing the crusaders 'from all penance'; but his letter to the Flemings concerning the crusade speaks of 'remission of all sins'[119] – which is the language of the chroniclers and presumably also of popular crusading propaganda. Paschal II wrote in 1100 of 'the remission and pardon (*venia*) of their sins';[120] in 1118 Gelasius II promised to those participating in the war against the Spanish Moslems: 'we absolve them from the bonds of their sins';[121] and Calixtus II in a letter of 1121–4 referred to the 'remission of sins which we have made for the defenders of the eastern Church'.[122] The tenth canon of the First Lateran Council of 1123 uses similar language: 'To those who journey to Jerusalem and give effective help in defending the Christian people and in conquering the tyranny of the infidels, we grant remission of their sins.'[123] In these cases the term *remissio peccatorum* has replaced the earlier formulation of Urban II; and it is tempting to interpret this as the conscious policy of the papacy, keeping pace with popular crusading theory. However, it is also possible to find the papal curia in the first quarter of the twelfth century still using the imprecise terminology of the papal letters of the eleventh century – the promise of Alexander II to 'release [knights] from their penance and make remission of their sins' and Urban II's grant to the defenders of Tarragona of 'the same indulgence which they would obtain' if they made the pilgrimage to Jerusalem. For example, although Paschal II referred to 'remission of sins' in his letter of 1100 concerning the crusade, he used different language in his letter of March 1101 forbidding Castilians to journey to Jerusalem and neglect the war against the Spanish Moslems: 'There you may complete your penances through God's bounty; there you may obtain the remission and grace of the holy apostles Peter and

[118] Mayer, *Crusades* (n. 103) p. 33. [119] Urban II, *JL* 5608: (n. 3) p. 136.
[120] Paschal II, *JL* 5812: (n. 61) 45C. [121] Gelasius II, *JL* 6665, *MPL* 163, 508C.
[122] Calixtus II, *JL* 7116, *ibid.*, 1305C.
[123] *Concilium Lateranense I* c. 10: *Conciliorum Oecumenicorum Decreta* p. 167.

Paul and of their apostolic church.'[124] This is the language of the
second canon of the council of Clermont and of Urban II's letter to
the Bolognese – crusade as the commutation of penance. Similarly,
the letter of Gelasius II of December 1118 which contains the absolution of the crusaders 'from the bonds of their sins' also includes a
promise to those assisting in the siege of Saragossa of 'remission and
indulgence of their penances'.[125] *Remissio peccatorum* was the term
most frequently used in early twelfth-century papal documents concerning crusaders; but the drafters of papal letters occasionally
adopted formulas reminiscent of those of Urban II. Perhaps even a
quarter of a century after the council of Clermont the papal curia
made no distinction between 'remission of sins' and commutation of
penance.

'Remission of sins' is granted in Eugenius III's crusading bull of
1145, *Quantum praedecessores*, which many historians regard as the
first coherent statement of the crusading indulgence. 'The transcen-
dental efficacy of the indulgence was emphasised for the first time in
the Second Crusade', wrote Adolf Gottlob in 1906.[126] Subsequent
historians have agreed that Eugenius III's conception of *remissio
peccatorum* was not related to the penitential discipline of the Church,
but signified instead full remission of all the temporal penalties for
sin imposed by God.[127] Eugenius promised 'remission of sins and
absolution according to the ordinance of [Urban II], so that whoever
begins and completes such a holy journey in a spirit of devotion, or
dies during the journey, may obtain absolution from all the sins of
which he has made confession with a contrite and humble heart, and
may receive the fruit of eternal recompense from him who rewards
all goodness'.[128] Although this grant is made 'according to the ordinance' of Urban II, it does not resemble any of Urban's surviving
statements on the subject. Eugenius evidently did not know his
predecessor's letters of 1095–6: he claimed in *Quantum praedecessores*
to derive his knowledge of Urban's crusade from 'the accounts of
writers of former times' and the *gesta* of the popes.[129] The statement
of the crusaders' spiritual privilege in Eugenius' bull of 1145 was
derived, that is, from the crusading chronicles, which speak only of

---

[124] Paschal II, *JL* 5863: (n. 61) 65A.   [125] Gelasius II, *JL* 6665: (n. 121): 508D.
[126] Gottlob, *Kreuzablass* (n. 104) p. 105.
[127] N. Paulus, *Geschichte des Ablasses im Mittelalter* I (Paderborn, 1922), 199;
       B. Poschmann, *Die abendländische Kirchenbusse im frühen Mittelalter* (Breslau, 1930)
       pp. 225–7; Constable, 'Second Crusade' (n. 38) pp. 249–52; Riley-Smith, *What
       were the crusades?* (n. 10) p. 60.
[128] Eugenius III, *JL* 8876: (n. 6) pp. 304–5.   [129] See above p. 323.

remissio peccatorum. It was at this moment, therefore, that popular crusading theory, promising the full remission of the temporal penalties due to sin, was adopted by the papal curia.[130] The crusading letters of Bernard of Clairvaux, the official preacher of the Second Crusade, provide a commentary on *Quantum praedecessores.* In his earliest crusading appeal Bernard interpreted the papal promise thus: 'take the sign of the cross and simultaneously you will obtain indulgence for all those things which you have confessed with contrite heart.'[131] He subsequently revised this appeal so as to emphasise the extent of the grant and the authority by which it was made: 'take the sign of the cross and this full indulgence of all the offences which you have confessed with contrite heart is offered to you by the supreme pontiff, the vicar of him to whom it was said, "Whatever you loose upon earth will be loosed in heaven".'[132]

Urban II's idea of commutation of penance was discarded in Eugenius III's bull of 1145 and in Bernard's crusading propaganda in favour of more elaborate versions of the formula 'remission of sins'. *Quantum praedecessores* was the first crusading encyclical and was 'in a formal sense the model for all the later crusading appeals of the popes'.[133] Nevertheless Eugenius' formulation of the crusader's 'absolution from all sins' was not regarded as definitive by his successors. Alexander III's first crusading bull in 1165 was simply a reissue of *Quantum praedecessores,* in which Alexander granted 'that remission of sins which Pope Urban of pious memory and our predecessor Eugenius instituted'.[134] However, Alexander III's crusading bull of 29 July 1169, *Inter omnia,* while mentioning 'the remission of all sins', also referred to this same spiritual privilege in quite different language.

We make that remission of penance imposed by the priestly ministry which our predecessors, the Fathers of happy memory Urban and Eugenius are known to have instituted, so that . . . he who undertakes the penance and remains there for two years to defend the land . . . shall rejoice in the acquisition of remission of the penance imposed on him.[135]

In the covering letter sent with this bull to Archbishop Henry of Rheims Alexander referred to this grant as an 'indulgence of penances'.[136] In these two letters there was a reversion to the idea of

---

[130] So Mayer, *Crusades* (n. 103) pp. 36, 98.
[131] Bernard of Clairvaux, *Epistola* 363: (n. 38) 567A.
[132] Bernard, *Epistola* 458: 653C.
[133] Cramer, 'Kreuzpredigt' (n. 70) p. 48.   [134] Alexander III, *JL* 11218: (n. 7) 386BC.
[135] *Ibid.,* 11637: 600D–601A.   [136] *Ibid.,* 11638: 602C.

commutation of penance and it was assumed that Urban II and Eugenius III had granted no more than this. The subsequent letters of Alexander III concerning the crusaders' spiritual privilege combined the language of commutation of penance with that of 'remission of sins'. A letter of 1171/2 offered Scandinavian princes who made war on the pagan Esthonians remission of 'the sins for which they have made confession and received a penance . . . as we are accustomed to grant to those who go to the Lord's Sepulchre'.[137] Alexander's final crusading bull, *Cor nostrum* of 16 January 1181, distinguished different degrees of spiritual privilege according to the length of service: for two years' service 'absolution of all their offences for which they have made confession with contrite and humbled heart'; for one year's service 'indulgence of half the penance imposed on them and remission of sins'.[138] The reward for one year's service was commutation of half the crusader's penance; so presumably the reward for two years' service was the commutation of all his penance – even though the pope described it in another letter of 16 January 1181 as simply 'remission and indulgence of sins'.[139]

For the rest of the twelfth century papal crusading bulls described the spiritual privilege of the crusader in the language of Alexander III's bulls of 1169 and 1181. (Similar language appears in the crusading treatise of Peter of Blois *ca.* 1189.)[140] Gregory VIII's bull *Audita tremendi* of 29 October 1187, which launched the Third Crusade, contained a similar formulation.

To those who take up the labour of this expedition with contrite heart and humbled spirit and depart as a penance for their sins and in right faith, we promise full indulgence of their crimes and eternal life. Whether they survive or perish, they may know that they will obtain release from the satisfaction imposed for all their sins which they have rightly confessed.[141]

Clement III's bull *Quam gravis* of 27 May 1188 offered 'remission of all sins' to the 'truly penitent' crusaders and to those who, 'being truly penitent', contribute financially to the crusade.[142] The last

---

[137]   Alexander III, *JL* 12118: 861A.
[138]   *Ibid.*, 14360: 1296AB. A similar distinction is made, in less precise language, in *JL* 11637 (601A).
[139]   *Ibid.*, 14361: 1296D. Villey, *Croisade* (n. 10) p. 149 describes the reward for two years' service as 'l'indulgence plénière'.
[140]   Peter of Blois, *De Hierosolymitana peregrinatione* (n. 8) 1061A.
[141]   Gregory VIII, *JL* 16019: (n. 7) 1542C.
[142]   Clement III, *JL* 16252: Giraldus Cambrensis, *De instructione principum* III.4, *RS* 21/8 (1891), 238.

crusading bull of the twelfth century, Celestine III's bull *Misericors et miserator* of 25 July 1195, combined the formulas of Alexander III's *Inter omnia* and Gregory VIII's *Audita tremendi*.

We make that remission of penance imposed by the priestly ministry which our predecessors are known to have instituted in their day, so that those who take up the labour of this expedition with contrite heart and humbled spirit and depart as a penance for their sins and in right faith, shall have full indulgence of their crimes and eternal life. [143]

In the last three decades of the twelfth century, therefore, the papal curia abandoned the simple formulation of Eugenius III's bull *Quantum praedecessores*, 'absolution of all sins'. From 1169 onwards the curia adopted more complex and more cautious formulas with varying degrees of emphasis on the idea of 'indulgence of penances'. This caution – or uncertainty – was perhaps a response to current developments in the schools. Whereas Eugenius III's bull reflected the popular crusading theory of the chronicles of the First Crusade, the late twelfth-century bulls perhaps reflected the development of the scholastic doctrine of indulgence. That doctrine grew up side-by-side with the crusading theology of the twelfth century and they may well have influenced each other. Certainly neither was fully formulated at the time of the Third Crusade: for both, the definitive statement was to come in the thirteenth century.

POPES, LEGATES AND PATRIARCHS

The obvious conclusion to be drawn from this survey of papal crusading theory from 1095 to 1195 is that the pope was indeed 'the principal author of this expedition'. A survey based on papal crusading documents would of course inevitably produce this conclusion. A comparison of papal documents with chronicles and other material from outside the papal curia at once throws doubt on the effectiveness of papal direction of the crusade. We have already seen this in the case of the crusading 'indulgence', where the papal curia held one view of the crusader's spiritual privilege and the faithful held quite another, the two views converging only in Eugenius III's bull *Quantum praedecessores*. Hans Eberhard Mayer argues that 'right at the start of the crusading movement control had slipped out of the hands of the curia':[144] not only because popular preachers

---

[143] Celestine III, *JL* 17270: (n. 9) 1109C.
[144] Mayer, *Crusades* (n. 103) pp. 10–11, 35.

reinterpreted the commutation of penance offered by the council of Clermont, but also because the crusaders reinterpreted the main objective of their enterprise. In the letter sent to the Flemings in December 1095 Urban II stated the purpose of his crusade as 'the liberation of the eastern churches'; but in the letter sent to the Bolognese in September 1096 he spoke of 'going to Jerusalem . . . for the liberation of the Church'.[145] From these contrasting formulas Mayer deduces that Urban II was compelled to modify his original plan, in which Jerusalem had not figured prominently, because of the popular appeal of the Jerusalem pilgrimage. The evidence is too sparse to permit firm conclusions about this theory;[146] but it raises the important question of how much influence Urban II was able to exert over the crusade which he had preached at Clermont.

The crusaders were 'without a lord, without a prince, at the instigation of God alone', wrote Guibert of Nogent, to whom the First Crusade seemed to be the fulfilment of the prophecy of Proverbs 30. 27: 'The locusts have no king, yet all of them march in rank.' Guibert observed that God had punished the presumption of those princes – Stephen of Blois and Hugh of Vermandois – who claimed to command the expedition, since he wished his people to be solely under the direction of the Church.[147] The chronicler Raymond of Aguilers recorded the opinion of a priest accompanying the crusading army, that there was no secular lord in the army and that 'they place their trust in a bishop'.[148] This was Bishop Adhémar of Le Puy, whom the pope had appointed 'leader (dux) of this expedition and this struggle in our place' and whom the crusaders described as 'the father committed to us' and 'vicar' of the pope.[149] Adhémar himself wrote that he had 'received from Pope Urban the care (cura) of the Christian army'.[150] It is difficult to determine precisely what this cura involved: whether it was a purely spiritual office or whether it involved the political and military command of the First Crusade.[151] The earliest

---

[145] Urban II, *JL* 5608, 5670: (n. 3) pp. 136–7.
[146] H. E. J. Cowdrey, 'Pope Urban II's preaching of the First Crusade', *History* 55 (1970), 177–88, argues that Jerusalem was the objective of Urban's crusade from the outset. See also Erdmann, *Entstehung* (n. 10) pp. 363–77, distinguishing between the liberation of the eastern Church as the 'object of the war' (*Kampfziel*) and Jerusalem as the 'goal of the march' (*Marschziel*).
[147] Guibert of Nogent, *Gesta Dei* I.1, VII.31: (n. 5) pp. 123–4, 250.
[148] Raymond of Aguilers, *Historia Francorum qui ceperunt Iherusalem*, *RHC Occ.* 3, 256.
[149] Urban II, *JL* 5608: (n. 3) p. 137; letter of the crusading princes: (n. 1) p. 259.
[150] Letter of Simeon, patriarch of Jerusalem and Adhémar of Le Puy: (n. 59) p. 132.
[151] J. H. Hill and L. Hill, 'Contemporary accounts and the later representation of Adhémar, Bishop of Puy', *Medievalia et Humanistica* 8 (1955), 30–8, conclude that

official description of the duties of a crusading legate is found in a letter of Paschal II, announcing the appointment of Adhémar's successor, Cardinal bishop Maurice of Porto. This letter of 4 May 1100 assumes that the legate's duties are purely spiritual in character: 'to order the Church which God has liberated through your efforts', 'to correct whatever he finds to be not in keeping with canonical rules'.[152] However, the crusading princes in their letter to the pope reporting the death of Adhémar on 1 August 1098 spoke of his courageous role in the recent battle for Antioch; and there is also a suggestion in the narrative sources that Adhémar was responsible for the strategy of the battle of Dorylaeum (30 June 1097).[153] These references, together with the statements of the chroniclers that the legate kept the peace among the quarrelsome princes, constitute the evidence for Adhémar as statesman and military commander. Adhémar may have acted occasionally as the 'leader of this expedition': what makes it unlikely that he consistently dominated the crusade is the evidence that he was not the only papal legate on the expedition. The chronicle of St Pierre-le-Vif in Sens records that Urban II also gave legatine authority to Arnulf of Choques (future patriarch of Jerusalem) and to Alexander, the chaplains respectively of the crusading princes Robert II of Normandy and Stephen of Blois.[154] After writing to the Flemings in December 1095 that he had appointed Adhémar as his vicar and *dux* of the crusading army, Urban seems to have changed his original plan and to have appointed legates to the two new crusading armies. It is likely that the pope sacrificed his original plan under pressure from the northern French princes: the duke of Normandy and count of Blois probably refused to recognise the authority of Adhémar, whom they regarded as the legate only of the Provençal army of Raymond of Saint-Gilles. At the very outset of the crusade, therefore, Urban's conception of the

his 'recorded accomplishments fell far short of the encomiums heaped upon him'. Their conclusions are challenged in J. A. Brundage, 'Adhémar of Puy: the bishop and his critics', *Speculum* 34 (1959), 201–12. H. E. Mayer, 'Zur Beurteilung Adhémars von Le Puy', *DA* 16 (1960), 547–52, takes a minimising view of Adhémar's role in the crusade.

[152] Paschal II, *JL* 3835: (n. 61) 42c–43c.
[153] Letter of the crusading princes: (n. 1) p. 351. For Adhémar at Dorylaeum see *Chronique de Saint-Pierre du Puy* in: *Histoire générale de Languedoc* ed. C. de Vic 5 (Toulouse, 1875), 163; *Gesta Francorum* III: (n. 43), p. 20.
[154] J. Richard, 'Quelques textes sur les premiers temps de l'église latine de Jérusalem', *Recueil de travaux offert à M. Clovis Brunel 2* (Mémoires et documents publiés par la Société de l'Ecole des Chartes 12/2, 1955), 421; Mayer, 'Beurteilung' (n. 151) p. 550.

expedition – of a single army led by the pope's vicar – was discarded by the crusading princes.

Urban II's ultimate objective in launching the crusade was, in the opinion of some historians, the creation in the Holy Land of 'an ecclesiastical state under the patriarch' of Jerusalem, a second Patrimony of St Peter, subject to the pope.[155] According to this interpretation, Urban's objective was achieved – although only for a very short time – during the pontificate of his successor, Paschal II, through the zeal of his legate, Daimbert, archbishop of Pisa and subsequently patriarch of Jerusalem (1099–1102). The evidence for this interpretation comes from the events of the months immediately following the capture of Jerusalem: the insistence of the clergy that the election of the patriarch should precede that of a secular ruler; the fact that the secular ruler, Godfrey of Bouillon, took the title 'Advocate of the Holy Sepulchre' instead of that of king; above all, the Patriarch Daimbert's action of investing Godfrey with the lordship of Jerusalem.

The first of these events is recounted by Raymond of Aguilers: 'some of the clergy' urged the crusading princes to 'choose first a spiritual vicar; since eternal matters come before temporal . . . Otherwise, we shall consider whatever you do to be invalid.'[156] This Gregorian language certainly suggests a clerical attempt to establish a theocratic state in Jerusalem.[157] However, the chronicler Raymond himself reveals that 'the instigator and manager of this affair' was the northern Italian Bishop Arnulf of Marturano, whose motives had nothing to do with Gregorian ideas of theocracy. He had gained possession 'fraudulently' of the church of the Nativity in Bethlehem and now sought to protect his interests by hastening the election of his ally Arnulf of Choques as patriarch and so anticipating the election of a secular prince who would challenge his possession of the church of the Nativity.[158] The schemes of Arnulf of Marturano were

---

[155] S. Runciman, *A history of the crusades* 1 (Cambridge, 1951), 289, 305–7; 2 (1952), 310; M. Spinka, 'The Latin church of the early crusades', *Church History* 8 (1939), 113–31. The alleged attempt to create a theocratic state is discussed in detail by J. Hansen, *Das Problem eines Kirchenstaates in Jerusalem* (dissertation: Freiburg, 1928). This interpretation is refuted by J. G. Rowe, 'Paschal II and the relation between the spiritual and temporal powers in the kingdom of Jerusalem', *Speculum* 32 (1957), 470–501; H. E. Mayer, *Bistümer, Klöster und Stifte im Königreich Jerusalem* (Schriften der MGH 26, 1977) pp. 15–43; *idem*, *Crusades* (n. 103) pp. 61–2, 66–7.

[156] Raymond of Aguilers, *Historia Francorum* c. 20: (n. 148) p. 301.

[157] So Hansen, *Kirchenstaat* (n. 155) pp. 11–17.

[158] Raymond, *Historia Francorum* c. 20: (n. 148) pp. 301–2. See Rowe, 'Paschal II' (n. 155) pp. 472–3; Mayer, *Bistümer* (n. 155) pp. 44–5.

cut short when he 'was captured by the Saracens on the third or fourth day and was never seen again'.[159] Like the election of the patriarch in 1099, the title taken soon afterwards by Duke Godfrey, 'Advocate of the Holy Sepulchre', is difficult to interpret as evidence of an attempt to create an ecclesiastical state. Godfrey's religious sensibilities – apparently shared by some of his colleagues[160] – caused him to reject the title of king. Nevertheless the chroniclers regarded Godfrey as a *princeps* with full secular authority. He is represented by the anonymous *Gesta Francorum* as 'the prince of the city', elected 'to make war on the pagans and to protect the Christians';[161] and by Fulcher of Chartres as 'the prince of the kingdom' (*regni princeps*), who 'continued energetically to rule the territory of Jerusalem'.[162] It is not surprising that in the summer or autumn of 1099 'a true and joyful rumour' circulated in northern France that 'the army of Christ raised up [Godfrey] as king'.[163]

The crucial evidence is that of the relations of Godfrey with Daimbert of Pisa. Archbishop Daimbert came to the Holy Land as the leader of a Pisan naval expedition. On Christmas Day 1099 he was consecrated patriarch of Jerusalem, his ally Prince Bohemund I of Antioch having assisted him in replacing Arnulf of Choques. Immediately after his consecration Daimbert invested Godfrey with the lordship of Jerusalem and Bohemund with that of Antioch. This investiture was followed by a series of donations in which Godfrey ceded to the patriarch the property of the former Greek patriarchs in Jerusalem (25 December 1099), a quarter of the city of Jaffa (2 February 1100) and the city of Jerusalem, including the tower of David, and all his lands (Easter, 1 April 1100).[164] On Easter day 1100 the patriarch granted these possessions to Godfrey to be held for his lifetime or until he made fresh conquests, as 'the vassal (*homo*) of the Holy Sepulchre and of us'.[165] The evidence of the investiture and the

---

[159] Raymond's account (p. 301) is defended by Mayer, *Bistümer* p. 47.

[160] Notably Raymond of Saint-Gilles: Raymond, *Historia Francorum* c. 20: (n. 148) p. 301.

[161] *Gesta Francorum* x: (n. 43) pp. 92–3.

[162] Fulcher, *Historia Hierosolymitana* 1.30, 31, 33: (n. 1) pp. 307–8, 361, 364, 366. See J. Richard, *The Latin kingdom of Jerusalem* 1 (English translation: Amsterdam, 1979), 4.

[163] Archbishop Manasses II of Rheims, letter to Bishop Lambert of Arras: Hagenmeyer, *Epistulae* (n. 3) p. 175.

[164] William of Tyre, *Historia rerum in partibus transmarinis gestarum* ix.16, *RHC Occ.* 1, 388. See Mayer, *Bistümer* (n. 155) pp. 5–29.

[165] Daimbert, letter to Bohemund of Antioch in William of Tyre, *Historia* x.4, p. 405. On the authenticity of this letter see Mayer, *Bistümer* pp. 11–12.

donations seems unambiguous: Daimbert, the 'papal legate, with a prestige derived from his appointment by Pope Urban', 'a great prelate close to the pope', put into effect the intention of Urban II 'that the Holy Land should become an ecclesiastical patrimony'.[166] However, it is in fact very unlikely that Daimbert was a papal legate in 1099–1100. Although two chroniclers regarded him as a legate – either of Urban II (Bernold of St Blasien) or of Paschal II (Guibert of Nogent) – Daimbert is never identified as a papal legate in any official document.[167] In his letters the patriarch speaks not of Rome but of Jerusalem, 'the unique mother of all the churches and mistress of the nations'[168] and never claims to be a legate. Paschal II's letter of 4 May 1100 to 'the Christian army triumphing in Asia' commands the crusaders to obey the bearer of the letter, his new legate, Cardinal bishop Maurice of Porto. There is no mention of any other legate – nor indeed of the Holy Land as an ecclesiastical patrimony.[169]

Patriarch Daimbert was therefore acting on his own account and not on that of Rome when he received Godfrey as his vassal. A convincing reconstruction of Daimbert's attitude has been made by Rudolf Hiestand. He has pointed out that the patriarch's political assumptions must have been formed by his experience in Pisa, where as archbishop he had enjoyed both spiritual and secular dominion.[170] He had not recognised the superior authority of the emperor, because the latter was excommunicate; and his part in the settlement of the civil strife in Pisa in 1085 had given him a dominant position in the nascent city republic.[171] As patriarch of Jerusalem he continued to think like an archbishop of Pisa and therefore regarded the Advocate of the Holy Sepulchre as the equivalent of a Pisan

[166] Runciman, *Crusades* (n. 155) I, 305–6; Villey, *Croisade* (n. 10) pp. 171–2. Cf. Richard, *Latin Kingdom* (n. 162) I, 99.

[167] Bernold, *Chronica* 1098: (n. 4) p. 466; Guibert, *Gesta Dei* VII.15: (n. 5) p. 233. See Rowe, 'Paschal II' (n. 155) p. 476.

[168] Daimbert, letter to Bohemund (n. 165) p. 405. Cf. Daimbert's letter to the Germans: Hagenmeyer, *Epistulae* (n. 3) pp. 176–7.

[169] Paschal II, *JL* 5835: (n. 61) 42C–45C.

[170] R. Hiestand, *Die päpstlichen Legaten auf den Kreuzzügen und in den Kreuzfahrerstaaten vom Konzil von Clermont (1095) bis zum vierten Kreuzzug* (Habilitationsschrift [typescript]: Kiel, 1972) pp. 93–4, summarised by Mayer, *Bistümer* (n. 155) pp. 18–19.

[171] Hence Daimbert appears as *rector et ductor* of the Pisan expedition to the Holy Land in 1099: Bernardus Marangone, *Annales Pisani* 1099, MGH SS 19, 239. See C. Moeller, 'Godefroy de Bouillon et l'avouerie du saint-sépulchre' in *Mélanges Godefroid Kurth* (Liège-Paris, 1908) p. 79.

advocatus: not as a ruler but a secular official, an agent of the Church. In Jerusalem, as in Pisa, the lordship was to belong to Daimbert. His plans were frustrated, however, by the death of Godfrey and the succession of his brother, Baldwin I (1100–18). Baldwin rejected the title of advocate in favour of the unambiguous title of king. He was crowned by Daimbert on 25 December 1100 and was enabled soon afterwards to rid himself of the patriarch by the help of two successive papal legates. Cardinal bishop Maurice of Porto suspended Daimbert when the latter's enemies denounced him as unfit for his office; and the legate subsequently deposed the patriarch for misappropriating crusading funds. [172] On Maurice's death in the summer of 1102 Daimbert was restored by some of the higher clergy of Jerusalem, only to be deposed once more by a synod convoked by the new papal legate, Robert of Paris, cardinal priest of S. Eusebio. [173] The mid-twelfth-century chronicler Albert of Aachen, who offers the most detailed narrative of these events, represents the two depositions as the result of a close alliance between the legates and the king. His account suggests that the legates' main concern was to strengthen the secular power in Jerusalem in the interests of the holy war. Daimbert was deposed because his ambitions seemed to impede the progress of the crusade; and he was replaced by Ebremar, 'a faithful helper of King Baldwin against the Saracens and unbelievers'. [174] However, Daimbert was restored yet again, this time by the direct intervention of Paschal II, to whom the deposed patriarch appealed in person in the spring of 1105. A papal letter of 4 December 1107 explains the decision (and records that Daimbert did not survive to enjoy his triumph). The pope states that he restored the patriarch when he learned that he had been deposed 'because of fear of the king'. [175] The freedom of the church had been compromised by secular interference and this Paschal II could not overlook. There is no suggestion here that the pope approved of Daimbert's constitutional theory of Jerusalem as an ecclesiastical patrimony with the patriarch as its suzerain. Paschal II's attitude towards *regnum* and *sacerdotium* in Jerusalem was essentially that of his legates in 1101–2: the authority of the king must be reinforced even at the expense of the patriarch. Hence in 1108 he granted Baldwin's urgent request to

---

[172] Albert of Aachen, *Historia Hierosolymitana* VII.46–9, 58–63: (n. 65) pp. 538–40, 545–8; William of Tyre, *Historia* X.25:(n. 164) p. 439.
[173] Albert, *Historia* IX.16–17: pp. 599–600.
[174] *Ibid.*, IX.17: p. 600.   [175] Paschal II, *JL* 6175: (n. 61) 230B–231D.

transfer the episcopal dignity from Ascalon to Bethlehem and permitted the deposition of the patriarch who opposed this transfer.[176]

Paschal II's relations with Baldwin I are mentioned in a letter of Pope Honorius II of 29 May 1128 to the king's cousin and successor, Baldwin II (1118–31). The letter was a response to an embassy sent by Baldwin II to Rome, the theme being that 'the due honour of the kingdom of Jerusalem and the church should be preserved intact'. The pope adds: 'we concede to you the kingdom of Jerusalem together with the dignity conceded by our predecessor of happy memory, Pope Paschal, to your predecessor, King Baldwin.'[177] This has been interpreted as a declaration of papal suzerainty over the kingdom of Jerusalem.[178] If that is the correct interpretation, Honorius II's letter of 1128 provides the only extant papal statement of the vassal status of the king of Jerusalem: neither Honorius nor any of his successors repeated the claim. Likewise, as we have seen, no papal document from the pontificate of Paschal II makes such a statement, despite Honorius' claim to be following Paschal's precedent. The most convincing explanation of the papal letter of 1128 is that given by J. G. Rowe: that the issue was not papal suzerainty over Jerusalem, but the boundaries of the jurisdiction of the kingdom and patriarchate of Jerusalem. Honorius II was upholding the principle enunciated by Paschal II in 1111, that the territories ruled by the king of Jerusalem should be placed under the jurisdiction of the patriarch of Jerusalem: ecclesiastical should follow royal jurisdiction.[179] Like Paschal II and his legates, Honorius II seems to have been concerned primarily with strengthening the kingdom of Jerusalem, rather than with exercising papal authority over it.

Honorius' 'concession' of the kingdom almost coincided with the revival of the plan of Daimbert to establish the patriarch of Jerusalem as suzerain of the kingdom. Our sole source of information about this attempt – made by Patriarch Stephen (1128–30) – is the chronicle of William of Tyre. Stephen of La Ferté, abbot of Saint-Jean-en-Vallée, Chartres, was 'the kinsman of King Baldwin [II]' and 'a

[176] William of Tyre, *Historia* XI. 12: (n. 164) pp. 472–4. See Mayer, *Bistümer* (n. 155) pp. 44–61.

[177] Honorius II, *JL* 7314, *MPL* 166, 1279D–1280C.

[178] H. S. Fink in Setton (ed.), *Crusades* (n. 2) 1, 379 n. 15. Cf. M. W. Baldwin, 'The papacy and the Levant during the twelfth century', *Bulletin of the Polish Institute of Arts and Sciences in America* 3 (1945), 281–3.

[179] J. G. Rowe, 'The papacy and the ecclesiastical province of Tyre (1100–1187)', *Bulletin of the John Rylands Library* 43 (1960–1), 174–5, 166. For the attitude of Paschal II, see *JL* 6297–8: (n. 61) 289A–290A.

watchful *prosecutor* of his rights'. He incurred the hostility of the king by 'alleging that the city of Jaffa belonged to his own jurisdiction' and 'that after the capture of Ascalon the holy city itself should be surrendered to the Church'.[180] Like Daimbert, Stephen of La Ferté expected the secular ruler to make new conquests, relinquishing the secular lordship of Jerusalem to the patriarch. There is no evidence that Stephen sought the backing of the papacy in his contest with Baldwin II. William of Tyre's brief account suggests that Stephen (again like Daimbert) was an ambitious prelate, a *homo magnificus*, who acted on his own initiative when he sought to transform Jerusalem into a vassal state of the Church. His premature death brought an end to the conflict of *regnum* and *sacerdotium* in Jerusalem and the restoration of friendly relations between king and patriarch in the pontificate of William I (1130–45).[181]

During these first decades in the history of the crusading principalities there was continuous papal intervention in the Latin churches of the east. Legates had been sent to Outremer almost every year. Some had presided over councils which deposed patriarchs and elected their successors. The legate Maurice of Porto acted as head of the church of Jerusalem during the vacancy caused by his deposition of Daimbert; while the legate Archbishop Gibelin of Arles himself took the place of Patriarch Ebremar, whom he deposed in 1108.[182] The legate Bishop Berengar of Orange secured the deposition of Patriarch Arnulf in 1115 on the grounds of simony,[183] and the cardinal legate Alberic of Ostia that of Patriarch Ralph of Antioch in 1141 on the grounds of his uncanonical election.[184] The most active legate in Outremer in the twelfth century was Guido of Florence, cardinal priest of S. Grisogono. He accompanied the Second Crusade as papal legate in 1147 and, remaining in the east after the failure of the expedition, summoned a council in 1149. The patriarch of Antioch, Aimery of Limoges, failed to attend, alleging that the Saracens were about to attack Antioch; and the bishop elect of Tripoli (his identity is unknown) followed his example. The legatine council suspended

---

[180] William of Tyre, *Historia* XIII.25: (n. 164) pp. 594–5. See R. Hiestand, 'Chronologisches zur Geschichte des Königreiches Jerusalem um 1130', *DA* 26 (1970), 226–9.

[181] William of Tyre, *Historia* XIII.25, 26: (n. 164) pp. 594–5, 598.

[182] Albert of Aachen, *Historia Hierosolymitana* x.9: (n. 65) p. 659.

[183] R. Foreville, 'Un chef de la première croisade: Arnoul Malecouronne', *Bulletin du comité des travaux historiques* 1953–4 (1955) pp. 377–90.

[184] William of Tyre, *Historia* xv.16–17: (n. 164) pp. 683–6. See Hiestand, *Legaten* (n. 170) p. 199.

the bishop elect for his non-attendance; and the latter went to defend his cause in Rome. There 'in consistory was examined the case of him who obeyed a patriarch rather than a legate of the Roman church'. The case is recorded in the *Papal history* of John of Salisbury, generally unsympathetic to the claims of legates. 'The many and manifest privileges relating to the primacy of the apostolic see were read both from the histories of princes and from the decrees and acts of the council and were dinned in the ears of the bishop elect.' After this lecture, to the surprise of the cardinals, Pope Eugenius III confirmed the bishop elect of Tripoli in his office. The pope subsequently sent his legate a letter 'in which he criticised his want of discretion and moderation in presuming to harass with litigation a church already greatly harassed by the Saracens'.[185] John of Salisbury's anecdote pinpoints the dilemma which the papal curia faced when dealing with Outremer. On the one hand, the curia might well have wished to enforce respect for legatine – and therefore papal – authority in the churches of the Latin east as well as those of the west. Antioch in particular seems to have been regarded in the 1140s as dangerously independent. William of Tyre's *History* contains the instructive anecdote of Patriarch Ralph of Antioch coming to Rome and claiming that the church of Antioch was superior to that of Rome, because it was St Peter's first see. (Ralph subsequently made an abject recantation.)[186] Equally instructive is the assumption in the chronicle of Otto of Freising that the first duty of a papal legate in Outremer was to see to it that 'Antioch began to be fully subject to the Roman see'.[187] However, the curia was keenly aware of the Saracen threat to the churches of Outremer; and this frequently inhibited Rome from taking strong measures. Demonstrations of papal supremacy had often to take second place to considerations of defence and strategy.

The unwillingness of popes to intervene in Outremer, even to enforce their own decisions, is the theme of Archbishop William of Tyre's history of his own church. According to tradition, the archbishopric of Tyre and its suffragans belonged to the patriarchate of Antioch; but in the new political framework created by the crusade these territories came under the jurisdiction of the kingdom of

---

[185] John of Salisbury, *Historia pontificalis* c. 37 ed. M. Chibnall (London, 1956) pp. 74–5.

[186] William of Tyre, *Historia* XV.13: (n. 164) pp. 678–9.

[187] Otto of Freising, *Chronica sive historia de duabus civitatibus* VII.33, *MGH SS rer. Germ.*, 1912, pp. 363–4. See Rowe, 'Tyre' (n. 179) pp. 186–7.

Jerusalem. In 1111 the pope accepted the proposal of Baldwin I that all the lands which he conquered should be placed under the ecclesiastical jurisdiction of the kingdom of Jerusalem rather than of Antioch.[188] This decision provoked a long and bitter dispute between the two patriarchs, which in turn prompted both Honorius II in 1128 and Innocent II in 1138–9 to restate the principle.[189] Papal decisions concerning Tyre were expressed in increasingly grandiloquent terms. In 1111 Paschal II explained his decision to place Tyre in the patriarchate of Jerusalem as papal acquiescence in the will of God. 'The kingdoms of the earth are transformed with the changing times; and therefore it is expedient for the boundaries of ecclesiastical jurisdictions in most provinces to be transformed . . . We ought to support this divine mutation and to set in order whatever is in disarray, according to the needs of the times.'[190] By 1138, however, Innocent II was confidently claiming this *mutatio* not as an act of God but as the work of the pope.

> The regulation and the management of the whole Church of God on earth was conceded to St Peter, the bearer of the keys of heaven, and to his vicars. Hence it is, and always will be, lawful for him, according to circumstances, to divide bishoprics or join them up, to transform the jurisdictions of kingdoms, to create new metropolitan sees and to confer metropolitan rights on primates according to his will.[191]

This is an impressive statement of papal supremacy; but no real attempt was made to enforce it in the case of Tyre. The patriarch of Antioch consecrated bishops in the northern sees of the archbishopric of Tyre in defiance of the papal ruling; the suffragans of Tyre had divided loyalties; papal legates came and went but did nothing to safeguard either the rights of the patriarch of Jerusalem or the unity of the archbishopric of Tyre. The historian William of Tyre, who succeeded to the archbishopric in 1175, believed that the integrity of his church had been destroyed by their negligence. 'We justly attribute the cause of this great evil to the Roman church, which commanded us to obey Jerusalem, while allowing us to be mutilated by Antioch.'[192] The failure of the curia to carry out its own

---

[188] Paschal II, *JL* 6297–8: (n. 61) 289A–290A. See Rowe, 'Tyre' pp. 163–6.

[189] Honorius II, *JL* 7314: (n. 177) 1279D–1280C (see above p. 356). Innocent II, *JL* 7906, 7908, 7940–3, *MPL* 179, 370BC, 372BC, 399A–401C.

[190] Paschal II, *JL* 6298: (n. 61) 289D.

[191] Innocent II, *JL* 7908: (n. 189) 372B. There is an echo here of Gregory VII, *Registrum* II.55a (c. 7) p. 203.

[192] William of Tyre, *Historia* XIV.14: (n. 164) p. 626.

decisions in the case of Tyre illustrates the severe limitations on the exercise of papal authority in the Latin east. The curia was reluctant to antagonise the king of Jerusalem and the prince of Antioch, each of whom supported the claims of his own patriarch. The difficulty in obtaining regular and accurate information from Outremer must have added to papal hesitancy. Above all there was the fear of impeding the progress of the holy war.

The last serious attempt by the twelfth-century papacy to direct the course of the holy war occurred during the Second Crusade. To some observers the crusade of 1147 seemed, like the First Crusade, to be under the direction of papal legates. 'In that expedition the legates of the apostolic see, Bishop Theodwin of Santa Rufina and the Cardinal priest Guido, commanded the people of God.'[193] This was also how Pope Eugenius III saw the crusade:

> We have sent from our side the prudent and honest men Bishop Theodwin of Santa Rufina and Guido, cardinal priest of S. Grisogono, who are to keep [the armies] in harmony and love and are to make provision for their salvation both in spiritual and in temporal matters, with God's help.[194]

Neither legate, however, succeeded in playing the role in the Second Crusade which Adhémar of Le Puy had played in the First. The fullest account of their legation is found in the *Papal history* of John of Salisbury, who judged them 'good men indeed but scarcely suitable for so great an office'. The German Theodwin 'was regarded by the French as a barbarian'; the Florentine Guido 'had only slight knowledge of French': he was 'a lover of literature' who 'delighted in spiritual conversation but hated tumult'. Their incapacity played into the hands of other churchmen on the expedition, 'the Bishops Arnulf of Lisieux and Godfrey of Langres, who boasted that they held the office of legate of the apostolic see in the army, although they had not received this power'.[195] John of Salisbury may well have been mistaken in rejecting the claim of these two French bishops to be papal legates. For both were associated with Bernard of Clairvaux, the principal preacher of the Second Crusade – Arnulf as a protégé, Godfrey as a former prior of Clairvaux – and this may have qualified them, in the eyes of Eugenius III, for the legatine office. Moreover another observer assumed that their task was 'to journey with the king [Louis VII of France] to Jerusalem and act in

---

[193] *Annales Ratisponenses* (Prüfening codex) 1147, MGH SS 17, 586.
[194] Eugenius III, *JL* 9095, *MPL* 180, 1251D.
[195] John of Salisbury, *Historia pontificalis* c. 24: (n. 185) pp. 54–5.

[the pope's] place in the government of the Christian people'.[196] According to this witness, therefore, Arnulf of Lisieux and Godfrey of Langres were papal legates accredited to the French army. A further French legate is identified by the historian of the monastery of Anchin, although not confirmed elsewhere: Bishop Alvisus of Arras was appointed by the pope 'father and pastor of the whole army on the expedition to Jerusalem' but he died during the journey.[197] Finally, Eugenius III commanded Bishop Henry of Olmütz to accompany the German army of King Conrad III and to 'offer counsel and aid' to the legates Theodwin and Guido. (There is no indication, however, that he conferred legatine powers on Henry.)[198]

The presence of four, perhaps five, legates on the Second Crusade shows that Eugenius III closely followed the practice of Urban II in creating separate legations for the different crusading armies.[199] Giles Constable has suggested that Eugenius hoped to exercise greater control over the crusade 'through this plethora of legates'.[200] It is also possible that Eugenius felt that the dignity of the leading crusaders, the German and French kings, demanded separate legations. Whatever his motive, there is no doubt that this arrangement contributed to the confusion in the leadership of the crusade. The most able and energetic of the legates were Arnulf of Lisieux and Godfrey of Langres; and 'they were so discordant that they rarely or never agreed in any counsel'. In the opinion of John of Salisbury, 'few if any inflicted greater ruin on the army and the commonwealth of the Christians'.[201] Godfrey of Langres, consistently hostile towards the Greeks, urged King Louis VII of France to attack Constantinople. Overruled in this advice by a majority of the crusaders, Godfrey continued to do all in his power to block cooperation with the Byzantine

---

[196] *Anonymi vera narratio fundationis prioratus Sanctae Barbarae, Recueil des historiens des Gaules et de la France* 14, 502. See F. Barlow in *Arnulfi Lexoviensis episcopi Epistolae* (Camden Society 3rd ser., 61: London, 1939) pp. xxv–xxvii; Constable, 'Second Crusade' (n. 38) pp. 263–4.

[197] *Historia monasterii Aquicinctini, MGH SS* 14, 588. Cf. Odo of Deuil, *De profectione Ludovici VII* II: (n. 68) pp. 22, 24, 28, 44.

[198] Eugenius III, *JL* 9095: (n. 194) 1251D–1252A. V. G. Berry in Setton (ed.), *Crusades* (n. 2) 1, 480, identified Henry of Olmütz as a legate; but there is nothing in Eugenius' letters to suggest this. In the event Henry joined the Wendish crusade instead: Eugenius III, *JL* 9110: 1262BC.

[199] See above p. 351.

[200] Constable, 'Second Crusade' (n. 38) p. 264.

[201] John of Salisbury, *Historia pontificalis* c. 24: (n. 185) pp. 54–5.

emperor, Manuel Comnenus.[202] The attitude of this legate was clearly at odds with that of Eugenius III, for whom one of the objectives of the crusade was the peaceful reunion of the churches of Constantinople and Rome. The pope wished to use the opportunity offered by the marriage alliance between King Conrad III and Emperor Manuel; and accordingly his conception of the German king's role in the crusade was 'that he should strive by all means to promote the honour and exaltation of his mother, the holy Roman church, and to unite the church of Constantinople to her, just as she used to be'.[203] The counsels of the legate Godfrey of Langres ensured that this aspect of papal policy remained a dead letter.

The failure of the crusade – in the words of Eugenius, 'the severe damage to the Christian name which the Church of God has suffered in our time'[204] – prompted severe criticism both of Bernard of Clairvaux, the principal preacher of crusade, and of the papacy. Twelve years after the crusade, Pope Hadrian IV assessed the effect of the disaster in a letter to Louis VII. The French king was contemplating a crusade against the Moslems in Spain in 1159; but Hadrian advised caution and reminded him of the expedition to Jerusalem undertaken 'without caution' in 1147.

> Your Highness ought to remember . . . how great a disaster and what damage was inflicted on the Church of God and almost all the Christian people. Moreover, since the holy Roman church had given you counsel and support in this matter, she herself was not a little injured by it; and everyone cried out against her with much indignation, saying that she was the author of so great a peril.[205]

The sources for the history of papal intervention in Outremer are rather sparser for the later twelfth century than for the earlier period and it is difficult to discover whether papal interest and legatine activity were diminished after the disaster of 1147. Legatine activity on the scale of that of Adhémar of Le Puy, Maurice of Porto, Godfrey of Langres and Guido of Florence is not apparent in the later twelfth century; but two legates at least attracted the attention of the chroniclers. The first was John, cardinal priest of SS. Giovanni e Paolo, who arrived in Outremer in 1161, seeking support for Alexander III in his struggle against the antipope 'Victor IV'. King

[202] Odo of Deuil, *De profectione* IV: (n. 68) pp. 68–70, 78.
[203] Eugenius III, *JL* 9095: (n. 194) 1252A.
[204] *Ibid.*, 9385: 1414C.
[205] Hadrian IV, *JL* 10546: (n. 90) 1616C. See Constable, 'Second Crusade' (n. 38) p. 275.

Baldwin III of Jerusalem was anxious to avoid taking sides in the schism and therefore, on the advice of a council of prelates and barons, he informed John that 'if he wished to visit the Holy Places to pray as a pilgrim without the insignia of a legate, permission would be granted'. It was an attempt, not to free Outremer from papal influence, but to remain neutral in a difficult political situation. 'Many were pleased by [the legate's] arrival', commented William of Tyre, 'but afterwards they found him burdensome.' For the legate paid another visit to Outremer, this time gathering a large sum of money which he subsequently used to bribe the Romans to support Alexander III.[206] The second notable legate was Archbishop Ubaldo Lanfranchi of Pisa, papal legate on the Third Crusade. He arrived in Outremer in April 1189 in command of a Pisan fleet, just as his predecessor Daimbert of Pisa had done nearly a century before; but Ubaldo did not have Daimbert's ambitions or taste for power. Ubaldo's most important role in crusading politics was his participation in the annulment of the marriage of Isabella, heiress to the kingdom of Jerusalem. His action permitted the princess to bestow her hand and her claim to the throne on the most able commander among the princes of Outremer, Conrad of Montferrat.[207] The other glimpses of Ubaldo in the chronicles of the Third Crusade reveal him preoccupied with the spiritual duties of his office; as when, on 16 July 1191 he carried out the rite of purification of the churches of newly captured Acre.[208]

Turning from the narrative sources to the official papal documents of the later twelfth century, we find that the principal issue still seems to be the church of Tyre. The long dispute between the patriarchs of Jerusalem and Antioch concerning the ecclesiastical province of Tyre continued to generate appeals to Rome and papal privileges. Lucius II, Anastasius IV, Hadrian IV and Alexander III all supported the claims of Jerusalem.[209] In the latest of these privileges, dated

---

[206] William of Tyre, *Historia* XVIII.29: (n. 164) pp. 870–1; Boso, *Vita Alexandri III: Liber pontificalis* 2, 403, 412. See W. Ohnsorge, *Die Legaten Alexanders III. im ersten Jahrzehnt seines Pontifikats (1159–1169)* (Berlin, 1928) pp. 65–6; B. Zenker, *Die Mitglieder des Kardinalkollegiums von 1130 bis 1159* (dissertation: Würzburg, 1964) p. 137. On the attitude of the clergy of Outremer towards Alexander III, in contrast to that of the king, see their letter of 1160 recognising him as their 'temporal lord and spiritual father': *MPL* 200, 1362D–1363C.

[207] *L'Estoire de Eracles Empereur et la conqueste de la terre d'Outremer* XXV.11–12, *RHC Occ.* 2, 152–4. See S. Painter in Setton (ed.), *Crusades* (n. 2) 2, 66.

[208] *Gesta regis Ricardi*, RS 49/2 (1867), 181.

[209] Alexander III, *JL* 11379: (n. 7) 470A. See Mayer, *Bistümer* (n. 155) pp. 199–201.

8 February 1168, Alexander III restated the principle first stated by Paschal II and Innocent II: 'We have determined, O venerable brother in Christ, Patriarch Amalric . . . that all the cities and provinces which divine grace restored to Christendom in the times of the two Baldwins and of Fulk, kings of Jerusalem . . . are to remain firmly and inalienably in your, and your successors' hands.'[210]. It was Alexander's successor, Lucius III, who at last abandoned this principle and accepted the situation which his predecessor had ignored: in 1182 he acknowledged that the diocese of Tripoli, although part of the province of Tyre, was under the jurisdiction of the patriarch of Antioch.[211]

One of the two lines of papal policy formulated at the time of the First Crusade – the defence of the rights of the patriarchate of Jerusalem and the subjection of Antioch to the Roman church – was being quietly abandoned by the end of the century. The other – papal leadership of the holy war in the east, through encyclicals and legates – survived. The launching of the Third Crusade owed almost as much to the efforts of Pope Gregory VIII and his principal crusading preacher, Henry of Marcy, abbot of Clairvaux and cardinal bishop of Albano, as the launching of the Second Crusade owed to Eugenius III and Bernard of Clairvaux. Gregory VIII succeeded to the papacy in October 1187, three weeks after Saladin captured Jerusalem. His predecessor, Urban III, had allegedly died of grief at the news of the Christian defeat.[212] Gregory's two-month pontificate was devoted to energetic preparations for a crusade and to the reforms deemed necessary for its success. Gregory's letters, beginning with the crusading bull *Audita tremendi*, issued four days after his consecration, can be read as a summary of crusading theory and practice, as understood by the papal curia. There would be a thorough reform of Christian society, starting with the curia itself: there would be a fast every Friday for the next five years and abstinence from meat on Wednesdays and Saturdays; the pope's kindred and the cardinals would also fast on Mondays. All the princes of Christendom would observe a truce of seven years.[213] The crusading programme of

---

[210] Alexander III, *JL* 11379: 469D–470B.

[211] Lucius III, *JL* 14681: J. Pflugk-Harttung, *Acta pontificum Romanorum inedita* 3 (Tübingen–Stuttgart, 1886), 293–5. See Rowe, 'Tyre' (n. 179) p. 187.

[212] So *Gesta regis Henrici secundi*, RS 49/2 (1867), 14. Roger of Hoveden, *Chronica*, RS 51/2 (1869), 322, claimed that it was the news of the fall of Jerusalem which killed Urban III; which is 'almost impossible' (W. Stubbs, *ibid.*, p. 322 n. 3).

[213] Gregory VIII, *JL* 16019 (*Audita tremendi*), 16018, 16079: (n. 7) 1539D–1542D, 1539BC, 1561BC.

Gregory VIII and his legate, Henry of Marcy, with its emphasis on pilgrimage, penitence, *indulgentia*, the truce of God, echoes and elaborates the crusading ideas of Urban II, of Eugenius III and Bernard of Clairvaux.[214]

Gregory VIII's programme looked back to 1095 and 1145; and to some contemporary intellectuals it must have seemed old-fashioned and even irrelevant. The only author known to have argued against the holy war on the eve of the Third Crusade, the English Cistercian Ralph Niger, included among his practical objections to the crusade cautious doubts about the role of the pope.

I do not presume to dispute [the pope's] judgement; but one thing I believe: that the vicar [of God] is permitted to do only what equity and justice demands. For God does not grant forgiveness of sins before the sins have been cast away and before penance and suitable satisfaction have been performed; and perhaps shedding the blood of anything, let alone a human being, is not a suitable satisfaction and perhaps the crusade (*peregrinatio*) neither helps nor is appropriate to the satisfaction of any sin.[215]

No other writer of the twelfth century called into question the validity of the papal crusading absolution; but a very different treatise of *ca.* 1189, *On Speeding up the Crusade to Jerusalem* by Peter of Blois, servant of the English royal court, seems to question another aspect of Gregory VIII's crusading programme. A month after issuing the crusading bull *Audita tremendi* Gregory had appealed to Emperor Frederick I to participate in the crusade, since 'we recognise our own insufficiency and we know that we cannot bear the burden placed upon us nor remedy those evils which afflict the Christian people in these days, except with the help of the great'.[216] Gregory VIII, therefore, conceived of the crusade as an expedition of 'the great', like the Second Crusade and indeed the First Crusade, although the earlier crusade had involved no monarch (the foremost western kings in 1096 were either excommunicate or in danger of becoming so). Peter of Blois considered that this conception of the crusade had been found wanting. 'I leave aside the rich because they will not heed my message and I turn to the poor . . . Let the poor run [to Jerusalem], for theirs is the kingdom of heaven.'[217] Peter of Blois'

[214] Congar, 'Henri de Marcy' (n. 71) pp. 43–54, 77–90.
[215] Ralph Niger, *De re militari et triplici via peregrinationis Ierosolimitanae* c. 12, ed. G. B. Flahiff, '*Deus non vult*: a critic of the Third Crusade', *Medieval Studies* 9 (1947), 183.
[216] Gregory VIII, *JL* 16071: (n. 7) 1558AD.
[217] Peter of Blois, *De Hierosolymitana peregrinatione* (n. 8) 1067AB.

'crusade of the poor' was to become the dominant crusading idea of the early thirteenth century, doubtless encouraged by disappointment at the achievements of the Third Crusade. As expounded in the bulls of Innocent III, it was a conception alien to the twelfth-century crusading idea: a crusade with detailed ecclesiastical organisation, from which 'the great', especially kings, were excluded.[218]

[218] Innocent III, *Registrum* I.336, II.270–I, *MPL* 214, 308B–312D, 828B–835C.

10

THE PAPACY AND THE NORMANS

·

The building of the Norman principalities in southern Italy and Sicily and the papal reform movement – two of the most influential enterprises of eleventh-century western Christendom – were intimately connected. Similarly the creation of a single Norman kingdom of Sicily in the twelfth century and the strivings of the papacy for political independence and security were closely related developments. The connecting thread was the feudal relationship which bound the Norman princes to the pope as their secular lord. The constitutional history of the Norman principalities, and of the Norman kingdom into which they were absorbed, is recorded in a series of oaths of fealty sworn to the apostolic see and in a series of papal privileges outlining the vassal duties of the Norman rulers. Here was the only region, other than the Patrimony of St Peter, where the claims of the papacy to feudal overlordship could be of practical significance. The relations of the popes with their Norman neighbours and vassals offer a unique insight into the feudal theory of the papal curia.

The immediate impression is of the vast discrepancy between papal claims and political realities in southern Italy. Throughout the period of Norman domination in southern Italy the papacy experienced political reversals and territorial losses at the hands of its Norman vassals. On three occasions – in 1053, 1139 and 1156 – a pope led an army in person against the Normans and suffered the humiliation of defeat and capture. Every territorial dispute between the apostolic see and its vassals – the struggle for possession of

Salerno, Amalfi, Naples, Marsia, even the long contest for control of the papal territory of Benevento – was decided by the armed might of the Normans. Popes were compelled to legitimise territorial encroachments which they had fiercely resisted with great expenditure of men and treasure. The bitterest defeat was the union of all the Norman principalities in the hands of the most ambitious and most able of the princes, Roger II of Sicily (1105–54). Since the beginning of Norman state-building in the south, successive papal regimes had pursued a strategy of dividing and ruling the Norman princes. By 1139 the strategy of playing off each prince against his neighbour was in ruins: Roger II forced the pope to recognise him as 'king of Sicily, of the duchy of Apulia and of the principality of Capua'. After seventeen years of further expansion, in the treaty of Benevento (1156) the Norman king of Sicily was acknowledged by the pope as the independent ruler of the whole southern Italian mainland. The effect of the treaty of Benevento was that the pope was despoiled of considerable revenues and jurisdictional rights and that Rome was hemmed in, both to the south and to the north-east, by the power of the victorious Norman king.[1]

The full extent of this papal defeat can only be appreciated when papal–Norman relations are approached from the point of view of constitutional theory. An investigation of the texts of the Norman oaths of fealty and of the papal privileges of the period 1059–1156 reveals how the papacy was gradually forced to accept the Norman definition of their relationship. The papal curia and the Norman princes held fundamentally differing interpretations of the rights of a feudal lord; and the attempt of the papacy to impose its own interpretation was as unsuccessful as the attempt to curtail Norman territorial expansion. The theory of the feudal relationship which the popes sought to impose on their Norman vassals was strikingly anachronistic in character. It had more in common with Carolingian practice than with the feudal practice of the eleventh and twelfth centuries.[2] According to the papal theory, the south Italian fiefs were held by the Norman vassals solely through an act of grace on the part

---

[1] D. Clementi, 'The relations between the papacy, the western Roman empire and the emergent kingdom of Sicily and south Italy, 1050–1156', *BISI* 80 (1968), 192–7.

[2] P. Kehr, *Die Belehnungen der süditalienischen Normannenfürsten durch die Päpste (1059–1192), Abhandlungen der Preussischen Akademie der Wissenschaften 1934, phil.-hist. Klasse* 1, 9; J. Deér, *Papsttum und Normannen. Untersuchungen zu ihren lehnsrechtlichen und kirchenpolitischen Beziehungen* (Cologne-Vienna, 1972) pp. 31–6, 126–8, 197–9.

of their lord. Each pope on his accession renewed the investiture of the fiefs. The vassals had no automatic claim to their lands, nor had their heirs any right of hereditary succession. On the death of the vassal, the fief returned to the pope, who could make a free choice of successor. The counter-theory of the Normans accorded with the more conventional eleventh- and twelfth-century conception of feudal law. The vassal's land was an 'hereditary fief' (*hereditale feudum*). The papal act of investiture was *not* a constitutive act, without which the vassal's claims were invalid: rather, it was merely a ceremonial recognition of the vassal's rights. This difference concerning the significance of papal investiture played a major part in the turbulent events of 1059–1156. The papal theory that investiture alone gave legal title to a fief became the principal feudal weapon of the curia in its attempts to prevent the union of the Norman principalities.

The papal theory was first stated in the summer of 1059, when the Norman warlords Richard of Aversa and Robert Guiscard, founder of the Apulian branch of the dynasty of Hauteville (Altavilla), became vassals of the apostolic see. 1059 was a critical year in the history of the reform papacy, when the beleaguered reformers, bereft of their secular patron, Emperor Henry III, took radical measures to protect themselves against the Roman aristocracy. The alliance with the Norman princes (according to the historian Bonizo of Sutri) 'very quickly freed the city of Rome from the tyranny of the captains'.[3] Pope Nicholas II had been obliged in the opening months of his pontificate to fight for possession of Rome against a rival pope appointed by these local tyrants. It was to prevent the recurrence of such an outrage that half a year later Nicholas II invested Richard of Aversa with the principality of Capua and Robert Guiscard with the duchy of Apulia and Calabria. Nicholas II's action marked a sharp reversal in papal policy: his three predecessors, Leo IX, Victor II and Stephen IX, had regarded the Normans as enemies whose land-hunger endangered the Patrimony of St Peter. The oath administered to the Norman princes in 1059 sought to avert this danger by means of a personal oath of fealty to the apostolic see and the present pope, combined with an oath of security covering the life and liberty of the pope and the integrity of the '*regalia* of St Peter and his possessions'. In addition to these negative elements, the oath of 1059 promised aid and defence to the present pope and to his successors, provided that they were elected according to the terms of the papal

[3] Bonizo, *Liber ad amicum* VI, MGH Libelli I, 593.

election decree of 1059.[4] The oath contained the usual elements of the eleventh-century oath of fealty, as defined, for example, in the famous letter of Fulbert of Chartres of 1020 concerning *fidelitas*;[5] but it also contained traces of the peculiarly archaic feudal theory of the papal curia. The principal emphasis in the oath was on the rights of St Peter, from whom the vassal derived his title to the fief: 'Robert, by the grace of God and St Peter, duke of Apulia and Calabria and, with the help of both, future duke of Sicily'; 'Richard, by the grace of God and St Peter, prince of Capua'. The vassal promised to make an annual payment (*pensio*) to the Roman church 'for the land of St Peter which I hold or shall hold'. The meaning of 'the land of St Peter' in this clause is crucial for an understanding of the papal feudal theory. Josef Deér (1972) has argued convincingly that the clause does not mean that the Norman princes were permitted to retain control of parts of the Patrimony of St Peter which they had invaded before 1059. Instead the term refers to the south Italian principalities conferred by the pope in 1059: Apulia–Calabria, Capua and Sicily, still to be conquered, were regarded as 'lands of St Peter'.[6] (This terminology survived into the twelfth century: for example, in the writings of John of Salisbury, who understood 'all Sicily' – that is, all the territories of Roger II *ca.* 1150 – 'to belong to the patrimony of the Roman church'.)[7] The framers of the oath of 1059 used the term 'land of St Peter' to emphasise the superior right of the apostolic see over the southern Italian duchy and principality, which the vassals acknowledged by the payment of a *pensio*. This clause was intended to suggest the precariousness of the tenure of the Norman vassals; as likewise the final clause, which states that the vassals must seek confirmation of their original investiture from the successors of Nicholas II. When the oath was redrafted in 1073, on the occasion of the investiture of Richard I of Capua by Gregory VII, the idea of

---

[4] Oath of Robert Guiscard, 1059: *Liber Censuum* 1, 422. The oath of Richard of Aversa of 1059 is not extant; but see that of 1061, *ibid.*, 2, 93–4, and that of 1073: Gregory VII, *Registrum* 1.21a, pp. 35–6.

[5] Fulbert of Chartres, *Letter* 51 (to Duke William of Aquitaine), ed. F. Behrends, *The Letters and Poems of Fulbert of Chartres* (Oxford, 1976) pp. 90–2. See F. Behrends, 'Kingship and feudalism according to Fulbert of Chartres', *Medieval Studies* 25 (1963), 93–9.

[6] Deér, *Papsttum* (n. 2) pp. 70–8, arguing against the interpretation of Kehr, *Belehnungen* (n. 2) pp. 21–4, who argued that *terra sancti Petri* must be part of the papal patrimony.

[7] John of Salisbury, *Historia pontificalis* c. 34 ed. M. Chibnall (London, 1956) pp. 68–9.

precariousness was intensified: 'I shall observe this fealty to those of your successors . . . who *wish to confirm* the investiture which you have conceded to me.'[8]

The repetition of the investiture of the Norman princes by each new pope was the means by which the papal curia demonstrated the vassals' dependence on the superior authority of the papacy. 'I, Pope Gregory, invest you, Duke Robert, with the land which my predecessors of holy memory, Nicholas and Alexander, granted to you', pronounced Gregory VII to Robert Guiscard in 1080.[9] Forty years later Calixtus II declared to Duke William of Apulia: 'we give and concede to you the land and the whole honour which our predecessors Pope Nicholas and Alexander and Gregory once gave to Robert Guiscard, your grandfather, and then Pope Urban and Paschal, his successor, gave to Duke Roger your father, and afterwards the same Paschal and Pope Gelasius gave to you'.[10] This evocation of an uninterrupted series of papal investitures from 1059 to 1120 was a reminder that the continuity of Hauteville rule in Apulia depended on apostolic authority. Power had been transmitted through three generations of the Hauteville dynasty not by hereditary succession but 'by the grace of St Peter and of us'.[11] It was Gregory VII who made the most important contribution to papal feudal theory and his redrafting of the feudal oath dominated the relations of the papal curia with the Normans until 1156. The crucial revision is found in the final clause of the oath of fealty sworn to the pope by Robert Guiscard on 29 June 1080: 'I shall observe this fealty to those of your successors . . . who confirm the investiture which you have conceded to me – if my fault does not remain.'[12] The meaning of this conditional clause is made clear in Gregory's declaration on the occasion of Guiscard's investiture:

Concerning that land which you hold unjustly – such as Salerno, Amalfi and part of the march of Fermo – we bear with you patiently for the present, having confidence in almighty God and in your goodness, that you will hereafter conduct yourself, for the honour of God and of St Peter, as is appropriate for you and acceptable to me, without peril to your soul and mine.[13]

---

[8] Gregory VII, *Registrum* I.21a, p. 36.
[9] *Registrum* VIII.1b, p. 516.
[10] Romuald of Salerno, *Annales* 1120, MGH SS 19, 417.
[11] Paschal II, *JL* 6053, *MPL* 163, 178AD (privilege for S. Nicola in Bari).
[12] Gregory VII, *Registrum* VIII.12, p. 515. [13] *Registrum* VIII.1b, p. 516.

Robert Guiscard's seizure of these territories had earned him three papal excommunications since 1074.[14] In 1080, however, Gregory VII's desperate need for allies in his conflict with King Henry IV of Germany forced him to be reconciled with his powerful vassal. He was clearly in no position to dictate terms to Guiscard; but the indomitable pope contrived even in this situation of weakness to proclaim the theory that papal investiture alone conferred title to the duchy of Apulia. The implication of the oath of 1080 was that future popes might refuse Robert Guiscard investiture of his fief on the grounds of his 'fault'. Gregory VII had introduced into the Norman oath of fealty the concept which always dominated his attitude towards secular rulers: 'suitability' (*idoneitas*).[15] Princes derived their right to govern not from their ancestors but from their own *idoneitas*, judged in terms of moral worth and political effectiveness. The duke of Apulia held his lands subject to the approval of the pope, who would withhold investiture if the duke ceased to be worthy of it.

This interpretation of his relationship with the apostolic see was never accepted by Robert Guiscard himself. He did not accept the title conferred on him by the oath of fealty which he swore to the pope in 1059 and again in 1080: 'by the grace of God and St Peter, duke of Apulia and Calabria'. In his ducal diplomas he used the title 'Robert, by the favour of divine mercy, duke'.[16] The eleventh-century princes of Capua, Richard I and Jordan I and Richard II, similarly adopted in their diplomas the formula 'by the grace of God, prince of Capua',[17] rather than that of the oath of fealty of 1059. The Norman princes rejected the title formulated in the papal chancery because of its emphasis on the vassal's obligations to St Peter and hence to his vicar, the pope. The documents issued in the name of Robert Guiscard represent him as deriving his authority directly from God, in the manner of the traditional monarchs of western Christendom. Diplomas of 1079 and 1080, for example, refer to Salerno – annexed by Guiscard in the teeth of papal opposition – as 'the city of Salerno granted to us by God'.[18] The chroniclers of the Norman conquests in the south – Amatus of Monte Cassino, William of Apulia and Geoffrey Malaterra – assumed that the

[14] *Registrum* I.85a, II.52a, V.14a, pp. 123, 197, 371.
[15] See above pp. 312–14 and below pp. 386–7, 395, 411, 451.
[16] J. Deér, *Das Papsttum und die süditalienischen Normannenstaaten 1053–1212* (Historische Texte / Mittelalter 12: Göttingen, 1969) pp. 20, 31 (nos. V.7a, IX.17).
[17] *Ibid.*, p. 21 (no. VI.3).
[18] L. von Heinemann, *Normannische Herzogs- und Königsurkunden aus Unteritalien und Sicilien* (Tübingen, 1899) pp. 1–3 (nos. 1, 2).

Norman princes owed their territories to God's intervention and to their own physical courage (*virtus*). In their accounts the papal investiture of the Norman princes is presented not as the crucial factor in the creation of their principalities, but merely as a ceremonial recognition of a *fait accompli*. Both Robert Guiscard and Richard of Aversa are presented as established rulers of their principalities *before* their investiture by Nicholas II in 1059: Guiscard succeeding his brother Humphrey in 1057, Richard I receiving consecration as the heir of the defeated Lombard dynasty of Capua in 1058.[19] The chroniclers also assumed that Apulia and Capua were hereditary principalities. For example, William of Apulia described how in 1081, on the eve of his departure to make war on Byzantium, Robert Guiscard designated as his successor, his son Roger Borsa, 'a most worthy heir of so great a father, adorned with the morals of his uncle [Humphrey] and of his father'.[20] On Guiscard's death in 1085, Roger Borsa succeeded 'by hereditary right'.[21] By the end of the century the claim to hereditary succession was stated by the Norman princes themselves in their diplomas. Roger Borsa's title is given as 'Roger, by the favour of divine mercy, duke, heir and son of the magnificent Duke Robert' and that of his son is 'William, by the favour of divine mercy, duke, heir and son of the glorious Duke Roger'.[22] Prince Richard II of Capua likewise proclaimed his hereditary right in his diplomas.[23]

When, therefore, Gregory VII invested Robert Guiscard with his duchy in 1080, lord and vassal held completely opposite views of their relationship. However, this difference of attitude did not immediately lead to conflict. The reconciliation of 1080 in fact inaugurated half a century of peaceful relations between the papacy and the Normans, ending only with the extinction of the mainland branch of the Hauteville dynasty in 1127. Gregory VII's struggle

---

[19] Geoffrey Malaterra, *De rebus gestis Rogerii Calabriae et Siciliae comitis* I.18, *MRIS* 5/1 (1925–8), 18; Amatus of Monte Cassino, *Historia Normannorum* IV.11 ed. V. De Bartholomaeis (Rome, 1935) pp. 189–90. Cf. *Chronica monasterii Casinensis* III.15, *MGH SS* 34, 379. See Deér, *Papsttum* (n. 2) pp. 110–14: H. Hoffmann, 'Langobarden, Normannen, Päpste. Zum Legitimätsproblem in Unteritalien', *QFIAB* 58 (1978), 137–80.

[20] William of Apulia, *Gesta Roberti Wiscardi* IV.189–91 ed. M. Mathieu (Palermo, 1961) p. 214.

[21] Orderic Vitalis, *Historia ecclesiastica* VII.7 ed. M. Chibnall 4 (Oxford, 1973), 28–30. See Deér, *Papsttum* (n. 2) p. 124.

[22] Von Heinemann, *Herzogs- und Königsurkunden* (n. 18) pp. 11, 28 (nos. 5, 16).

[23] M. Inguanez, *Diplomi inediti dei principi normanni di Capua, Conti di Aversa* (Miscellanea Cassinese 3: Monte Cassino, 1926) pp. 9–10 (no. 3).

against Henry IV and the latter's attacks on Rome (1081–4) brought about an increasing dependence on the Normans. The pope had to be rescued from Rome by Robert Guiscard in the summer of 1084; and at the time of his death, a year later, Gregory was still in Guiscard's entourage in Salerno. Guiscard himself died two months after his lord, and a generation passed before another Norman prince emerged to threaten papal territorial interests in the way that he had done. Norman support – both that of Prince Jordan of Capua and that of Roger Borsa of Apulia – was vital for the security of the short-lived Victor III (May 1086–September 1087), the former Abbot Desiderius of Monte Cassino, the favourite churchman of the Normans in the south.[24] His successor, Urban II, was equally in need of military support and of a place of refuge which did not acknowledge his opponent, the imperial antipope 'Clement III'. Urban spent almost one third of his pontificate among the Normans (almost as much time as he spent in Rome). It was here in southern Italy that he held the first of the councils – Melfi (1089), Benevento (1091) and Troia (1093) – by means of which the reform papacy eventually regained the obedience of western Christendom.[25] Paschal II and Calixtus II likewise held councils in the Norman south and found there an important new source of revenue. In 1099, for example, Count Roger I of Sicily sent the newly elected Paschal II a thousand gold pieces to assist him in his struggle against the antipope.[26] It was during this period of peaceful relations from 1080 to 1127 that the papal curia learned to enjoy the benefits of the Norman conquest of southern Italy and Sicily. Not the least of these was the restoration of the churches of southern Italy to the obedience of the Roman church after the lapse of more than three centuries.[27] (The Byzantine emperor had transferred the province from the jurisdiction of the pope to that of the patriarch of Constantinople in order to punish Rome for her opposition to the imperial policy of iconoclasm.) The Norman oaths of fealty of 1059 provided for this restoration: 'I shall surrender into your power all the churches which are under my dominion, together with their possessions.' Accordingly, wherever Greek bishoprics survived in the newly conquered Norman terri-

---

[24] H. E. J. Cowdrey, *The age of Abbot Desiderius of Monte Cassino* (Oxford, 1983) pp. 185–213.

[25] Becker, *Urban II.* 1, 115 n. 381, 116–20.

[26] *Italia Pontificia* 8, 26 (n. 83).

[27] H.-W. Klewitz, *Reformpapsttum und Kardinalkolleg* (Darmstadt, 1957) pp. 135–205.

tories, their prelates were left unmolested if they acknowledged the primacy of the pope. Hence two Greek prelates from the Norman south – the archbishops of S. Severino and Rossano – attended the Lateran council of 1112.[28] Elsewhere the pattern was for the newly created bishoprics to be given to churchmen who enjoyed the confidence of the Norman princes. However, it was also possible for confidants of the pope to become bishops in southern Italy. For example, the archbishopric of Reggio in Calabria was occupied from 1091 to 1095 by the cardinal priest Rangerius of S. Susanna, the trusted agent of Urban II; and his successor, Roger, cooperated closely with Paschal II.[29]

The conquest of Sicily restored this former Byzantine, subsequently Moslem, island to Roman obedience. It was this conquest which enabled the Norman historians Amatus of Monte Cassino and Geoffrey Malaterra to present the Hauteville dynasty as the instrument of God's vengeance on the Saracens. Amatus, rewriting history, claimed that the Normans had originally come to Italy to fight the holy war against the infidels.[30] Three-quarters of a century after the Norman conquest Roger II could still declare, in propaganda addressed to Eugenius III in 1151, that 'when the Church of God had lost Sicily to the invading Saracens for many centuries, she was restored to the faith by [Roger's] valour and that of his predecessors'.[11] The part played by Roger II's father, 'the great count' Roger I, in this restoration of Sicily to Christendom was rewarded with the famous privilege of 5 July 1098, which conferred on him the office of papal legate in his own territories. The 'special and dearest son of the universal Church' was granted this privilege because he had 'enlarged the Church of God exceedingly in the territory of the Saracens'.[32] There is no reason to doubt this statement of motive in Urban II's privilege of 1098; even though historians have occasionally interpreted the privilege as a tactical surrender of Gregorian principles in order to appease an overmighty ally whose military aid

---

[28] W. Holtzmann, 'Papsttum, Normannen und griechische Kirche', *Miscellanea Bibliothecae Hertzianae* (Munich, 1961) p. 70 n. 8.

[29] R. Hüls, *Kardinäle, Klerus und Kirchen Roms 1049–1130* (Tübingen, 1977) pp. 207–9; Servatius, *Paschalis II.* p. 97.

[30] Amatus, *Historia Normannorum* I.30 (n. 19) pp. 17–19. See C. Erdmann, *Die Entstehung des Kreuzzugsgedankens* (Stuttgart, 1935) p. 121.

[31] John of Salisbury, *Historia pontificalis* c. 34 (n. 7) p. 69.

[32] Urban II, *JL* 5706; Geoffrey Malaterra, *De rebus gestis Rogerii* IV.29 (n. 19) p. 108. See E. Caspar, 'Die Legatengewalt der normannisch-sicilischen Herrscher im 12. Jahrhundert', *QFIAB* 7 (1904), 218–19. See above p. 176.

was indispensable.[33] Roger I intended to maintain a firm control over the church in his lands; but this did not rule out cooperation with the pope in the organisation of the Sicilian church. The language of Roger I's diplomas is certainly that of harmonious cooperation: 'I have built churches in various suitable places; at the command of the supreme apostolic pontiff I have placed bishops in them and the same pontiff of the Roman see has approved, has given permission and has consecrated those bishops.'[34] The count founded monasteries 'having received the command from holy mother Church and having been advised by the supreme pontiff'.[35]

The cooperative attitude of the princes of the house of Hauteville in the period 1080–1127 must have been inspired at least partly by an external factor. The military expeditions of the German king and emperor in Italy in these years were a threat not only to the reform papacy but also to its Norman vassals. For since the middle of the tenth century Ottonian and Salian emperors had regarded southern Italy as part of their *imperium*; and in the first half of the eleventh century emperors had invested native claimants with the titles of prince of Capua and duke of Apulia. These precedents were not forgotten at the imperial court. In the 1080s Bishop Benzo of Alba addressed to Henry IV a manual of political advice, reminding the emperor that his predecessors Charlemagne, the Ottos and his own father, Henry III, had ruled Apulia and Calabria, and urging him to expel the Norman intruders and resume control of what was rightfully his.[36] When Henry V came to Rome to be crowned emperor in 1111, it was believed in his entourage that the Apulians 'wish to be subjected to the king according to his will'.[37] There is no doubt that even after the papal investiture of the prince of Capua and the duke of Apulia in 1059, these provinces continued to be regarded at the Salian court as imperial fiefs. The investitures of 1059 were probably regarded in Rome not as a papal usurpation of an imperial function – so Paul

---

[33] E.g. N. Cantor, *Church, kingship and lay investiture in England, 1089–1135* (Princeton, 1958) pp. 117–19, whose interpretation is challenged by J. Deér, 'Der Anspruch der Herrscher des 12. Jahrhunderts auf die apostolische Legation', *AHP* 2 (1964), 129–30.

[34] Diploma of 26 April 1092, founding the bishopric of Catania: Klewitz, *Reformpapsttum* (n. 27) p. 179.

[35] Diploma of 1092 for S. Angelo in Val Demone: *ibid.*, p. 179 n. 191.

[36] Benzo of Alba, *Ad Heinricum IV imperatorem* I.13, 15; III.15–17, 19, 25; VII.8, *MGH SS* 11, 603–5, 628–9, 631, 681.

[37] Burchard of Aachen, *Epistola* ed. W. Holtzmann, 'England, Unteritalien und der Vertrag von Ponte Mammolo', *NA* 50 (1933), 282–301.

Kehr (1934) and Josef Deér (1972) have argued – but as the papal exercise of an imperial vicariate, necessitated by the special circumstances of Henry IV's minority.[38] Nicholas II's action harked back to the days of the German popes (1046–57) who had acted as imperial representatives with special responsibility for southern Italian policy. There is an echo of this attitude as late as 1073, in the oath which Richard I of Capua swore to Gregory VII: 'I shall swear fealty to King Henry when I am admonished by you or by your successors to do so, nevertheless saving my fealty to the holy Roman church.'[39] The idea of a joint papal-imperial jurisdiction over southern Italy which seems to survive in this oath has vanished from the oaths administered to Jordan I of Capua and Robert Guiscard in June 1080.[40] The imperial vicariate of 1059 gave way on the outbreak of papal-imperial hostilities to a papal usurpation of imperial claims in southern Italy. The descent of Henry IV into Italy to reclaim his rights forced the Norman princes to choose between contending feudal lords. Jordan of Capua chose in 1082 to be the vassal of the emperor and 'oath-breaker to St Peter'.[41] The direct relationship between Capua and the Roman church was not restored until 1118, in the pontificate of Gelasius II.[42] The house of Hauteville, however, preferred a papal to an imperial overlord. Robert Guiscard was called upon by Henry IV in 1076 to do homage for his duchy. According to the elaborate account of Amatus of Monte Cassino, Guiscard replied that he recognised only the lordship of God and SS. Peter and Paul, by whose grace he had conquered that land; but if Henry would grant him other lands, he would do homage for them.[43] Like any ambitious vassal, Robert Guiscard no doubt preferred a powerless ecclesiastical lord to a potentially meddlesome secular lord; but he seems also to have been won over by the strategy adopted by the pope in the early 1080s. Gregory VII wooed his powerful vassal by encouraging and legitimising his military adventures in the Byzantine empire.[44]

The two succeeding dukes of Apulia, Guiscard's son and grand-

[38] Kehr, *Belehnungen* (n. 2) pp. 15–19 (the case of Capua); Deér, *Papsttum* (n. 2) pp. 87–90.
[39] Gregory VII, *Registrum* I.21a, p. 36.
[40] *Registrum* VIII.1a, pp. 514–15; Deusdedit, *Collectio canonum* III.289 ed. V. Wolf von Glanvell (Paderborn, 1905) p. 396.
[41] Gregory VII, *Registrum* IX.27, p. 610.
[42] Deér, *Papsttum* (n. 2) pp. 146–7.
[43] Amatus, *Historia Normannorum* VII.27 (n. 19) pp. 320–1.
[44] Gregory VII, *Registrum* VIII.6, pp. 523–4.

son, Roger Borsa (1085–1111) and William (1111–27) not only proved consistently loyal to their lord, the pope, but also revealed a personal piety quite different from that of their predecessor. They showed themselves 'humble to the priests of Christ, fervently honouring clerks';[45] but above all they were devoted to the reform papacy. There was little exaggeration in Urban II's praise of Roger Borsa, who 'always faithfully obeyed the apostolic see'.[46] This devotion is stamped on the coins minted by Roger Borsa and William, which bear the head of St Peter.[47] The crucial development in this period of friendly relations was the direct involvement of the popes in the government of the duchy of Apulia. This was the papal response to the political disintegration of the duchy after the death of Robert Guiscard: a disintegration resulting not necessarily from the ineptitude of Guiscard's heirs, but rather from the fissile feudal structures of Apulia. The Norman counts holding the great Apulian fiefs had always conspired to free themselves from ducal control. Guiscard had ruled by offering the bribe of further territorial acquisitions at the expense of Byzantium; but at the end of his life the emergence of Emperor Alexius I Comnenus (1081–1118) at the head of a reinvigorated Byzantine empire scotched the immediate possibility of further Norman expansion. Guiscard's heirs reaped the whirlwind of constant baronial rebellions. The reform popes (for whom Apulia had become the principal refuge when Rome was too dangerous) responded by establishing a spiritual protectorate over their vassal state.[48] Papal intervention most frequently took the form of peace councils, in which rebels were induced by spiritual sanctions to respect 'the peace of God' (*pax Dei*). The most important such occasion was Paschal II's council of Troia in August 1115, at which a three-year peace was agreed with the Apulian barons.[49]

The pontificate of Paschal II witnessed an intensification of papal involvement in southern Italy because it coincided with the minorities of all three Hauteville princes – William of Apulia, Simon of Sicily (and subsequently his younger brother, Roger II) and Bohemund II of Tarento – whose regent-mothers had need of papal

---

[45] Romuald of Salerno, *Annales* 1111, 1127 (n. 10) pp. 414, 418.

[46] Urban II, *JL* 5070, *MPL* 151, 508A.

[47] *Corpus Nummorum Italicorum* 18: *Italia meridionale continentale* (Rome, 1939) p. 320 n. 1, plate *xx*.2; Deér, *Papsttum* (n. 2) p. 145.

[48] F. Chalandon, *Histoire de la domination normande en Italie et en Sicile* 1 (Paris, 1907), 308–26; Deér, *Papsttum* (n. 2) pp. 146, 151–3.

[49] *Italia Pontificia* 8, 29 (no. 101); Servatius, *Paschalis II.* p. 92. For the papal promotion of the 'peace of God' see above p. 326.

support. It was for this reason that in 1111, when Henry V marched into Italy, Paschal II could not summon the aid of his Hauteville vassals. (An army of 300 men was sent by Robert I of Capua, the only surviving Norman prince of mature years; but his force was obliged to retreat by the overwhelming strength of Henry V's army.)[50] In this situation of extreme weakness the pope was obliged to concede the imperial demands in the treaty of Ponte Mammolo (13 April 1111); but he nevertheless succeeded in winning from the emperor recognition of the rights of the Roman church in southern Italy.[51] The measures taken by Paschal II in the last years of his pontificate suggested a new means of enforcing these rights in Apulia. The investiture of the young Duke William during the council of Ceprano in October 1114 was a traditional way of demonstrating papal overlordship.[52] However, the peace negotiations with the counts of Loritello and Ariano and with other barons at the council of Troia in August 1115 suggested an innovatory papal policy which was to be implemented in the years 1118–28: the vassals of the duke of Apulia became the vassals of the pope also. Gelasius II, Calixtus II and Honorius II established direct feudal relations with the local magnates, the 'captains' (*capitanei*), barons and counts. Paul Kehr's analysis (1934) of this process suggests that the papal curia deliberately sought 'to loosen or even to dissolve the tight structure of Robert Guiscard's Apulian vassal-state'.[53] However, it is more likely that the purpose of these feudal ties was the same as that of the papal peace councils: to check rebellion and to hinder the political disintegration which was entirely inimical to papal interests. This papal concern with the preservation of Apulia culminated in 1120 with Duke William, on the occasion of his journey to Constantinople, placing his duchy under the protection of Calixtus II.[54] The papal letters of this year emphasise the importance of this demonstration of papal overlordship and indicate that the pope was tightening his control over the duke's vassals.[55] It was a necessary measure, if he was to defend Apulia against the opportunistic attacks of Roger II of Sicily.

The 'feudal policy' of the papal curia in the period 1118–28 played

[50] *Chronica monasterii Casinensis* IV.39 (n. 19) p. 507.
[51] Holtzmann, 'Ponte Mammolo' (n. 37) pp. 282–301. See below pp. 428–9.
[52] Romuald of Salerno, *Annales* 1115 (n. 10) p. 415, emphasises the traditional nature of the ceremony.
[53] Kehr, *Belehnungen* (n. 2) p. 36. Cf. Deér, *Papsttum* (n. 2) pp. 162–3.
[54] Pandulf, *Vita Calixti II: Liber pontificalis* 2, 322–3.
[55] Calixtus II, *JL* 6877, *MPL* 163, 1190D–1191B; *JL* 6892: *NA* 3 (1878), 180.

a constructive part in preserving the inheritance of the Apulian Hautevilles. When, however, the duchy came into the hands of the detested Sicilian Hauteville, Roger II of Sicily, the curia realised the destructive potential of its 'feudal policy'. Between 1128 and 1139 the papacy at last adopted that strategy which Paul Kehr attributed to it in the previous decade: the pope used his feudal links with the under-vassals of Apulia 'to loosen or even to dissolve' the political structure of the duchy. Roger II of Sicily was unacceptable as duke of Apulia above all because he would never permit the papal inter-ference in the duchy which had become normal in the reign of his pious cousin. As count of Sicily he had been the vassal of the duke of Apulia, from whom he had extorted the province of Calabria after four years of intermittent warfare.[56] It was hardly to be expected that his conduct towards his new lord, the pope, would be any better. Moreover since the pontificate of Paschal II Roger had often been reproved by the curia for his tyrannical treatment of the Sicilian church, but had ignored all reproofs.[57] It is not surprising, therefore, that the accession of Roger II caused a revolution in papal–Norman relations. What is surprising, however, is that this volte-face was so extreme as to go against established papal interests in an apparently reckless manner. After a decade of preserving the integrity of Apulia, the papal curia set about encouraging the duke's vassals to rebel. After half a century of defending the principle of papal overlordship of southern Italy against imperial claims – a principle maintained even in the dark days of Ponte Mammolo in 1111 – the curia appealed for imperial intervention in southern Italy to depose Roger II. For this appeal to be effective, it was necessary to admit that southern Italy was a territory within the jurisdiction of the emperor. When Bernard of Clairvaux called upon Emperor Lothar III to assist Innocent II against Roger in 1134/5, he reminded the emperor that 'without doubt he who makes himself king in Sicily opposes Caesar'.[58] Similarly the Apulian nobles who allied with the pope and were consequently expelled by Roger, sought the aid of the emperor, 'declaring that Apulia and Sicily belonged to his imperial jurisdiction'.[59] Lothar III's subsequent expedition to southern Italy in

[56] Falco of Benevento, *Chronicon* 1122 in *Cronisti e scrittori sincroni napoletani editi e inediti* ed. G. del Re 1 (Naples, 1845), 186; Romuald of Salerno, *Annales* 1125 (n. 10) p. 418.
[57] Paschal II, *JL* 6562: *Liber Censuum* 2, 125–6; *Chronica monasterii Casinensis* IV.49, p. 516.
[58] Bernard of Clairvaux, *Epistola* 139, *MPL* 182, 294B.
[59] Romuald of Salerno, *Annales* [1135?] (n. 10) p. 421.

1137 is represented in the chronicle of the imperial historian, Otto of Freising not only as a response to the pope's appeal but also as an imperial reconquest of lands previously lost to the empire.[60] The papal measures against Roger II, therefore, ensured that Lothar III and his Staufen successors would take an active interest in southern Italy, as a province of their empire.[61]

The situation of the papacy in the 1120s was precisely the reverse of that during the Investiture Contest, when the hostility of the emperor had forced the pope to seek the aid of the Normans. Now the enemy was Roger II of Sicily. The concordat of Worms of 1122 brought about a reconciliation of pope and emperor, which after the election of Lothar III in 1125 grew into a close relationship. This change in political circumstances prompted the most influential group in the papal curia of the 1120s to campaign vigorously against the Norman alliance.[62] The beginnings of the new curial policy and the formation of the group which was to implement it can be traced to 1121, a critical year in papal–Norman relations. In September 1121 Calixtus II came to the fortress of Rocca Niceforo to persuade Roger II to give up his invasion of Apulia. While Roger prevaricated, the papal entourage was struck by an epidemic which killed 'almost all the abler cardinals . . . and the great Hugh [of SS. Apostoli], the noble and industrious cardinal' and left the pope himself 'only half alive'.[63] Perhaps the shock of this disaster – to which the duplicity of Roger II had obviously contributed – first prompted the new policy of the papal curia.[64] Certainly the disaster of 1121 enforced the reconstruction of the college of cardinals and this seems to have brought into the curia new enemies of Roger II. By 1123 Calixtus II had created sixteen new cardinals.[65] The little biographical information which is available suggests that the new cardinals were drawn pre-

---

[60] Otto of Freising, *Chronica sive Historia de duabus civitatibus* VII.19, *MGH SS rer. Germ.*, 1912, p. 337. Cf. Deér, *Papsttum* (n. 2) p. 42. See below p. 450.

[61] P. Rassow, *Honor Imperii. Die neue Politik Friedrich Barbarossas 1152–1159* (Munich–Berlin, 1940) p. 60; H. Wieruszowski, 'Roger II of Sicily, Rex-Tyrannus, in twelfth-century political thought', *Speculum* 38 (1963), 53–64; Deér, *Papsttum* (n. 2) p. 43.

[52] F.-J. Schmale, *Studien zum Schisma des Jahres 1130* (Cologne-Graz, 1961) pp. 81–2. See above pp. 48–9, 67–8.

[63] Pandulf, *Vita Calixti II*: (n. 54) p. 323. See Hüls, *Kardinäle* (n. 29) pp. 151–2.

[64] Deér, *Papsttum* (n. 2) pp. 172–4.

[65] Hüls, *Kardinäle* pp. 116–17, 142–3, 149, 152–4, 162, 164, 183–4, 193, 196, 199, 205, 220–1, 225–6, 230–6, 238, 240–3.

dominantly from northern Italy and France[66] – as though the pope was creating a counterweight to the Roman and southern Italian cardinals who still favoured an alliance with Roger II. This trend no doubt continued in the succeeding pontificate of Honorius II.[67]

The most important of the new cardinals of the 1120s was the Burgundian Haimeric, cardinal deacon of S. Maria Nuova, chancellor and dominant curial politician for nearly two decades.[68] As we have already seen, it was Haimeric who ensured the continuity of Calixtus II's policy by organising the succession – against fierce opposition – of Honorius II in 1124 and Innocent II in 1130. The most obvious qualification of these two candidates, Cardinal bishop Lambert of Ostia and Gregory, cardinal deacon of S. Angelo in Pescheria, was the fact that in September 1122 they had negotiated with the emperor the concordat of Worms, the agreement which made possible the anti-Norman strategy.[69] The principal opponent of the new strategy of the 1120s was Peter Pierleone, cardinal deacon of SS. Cosma e Damiano and subsequently cardinal priest of S. Maria in Trastevere. He was a member of the powerful Roman family of Pierleone, who had enjoyed close relations with the Sicilian Hautevilles since the days of the 'great count' Roger I.[70] Elected as Anacletus II in the double election of 1130, Peter Pierleone received Roger II as his closest ally, issuing the privilege which transformed the Hauteville principalities into the 'kingdom of Sicily and Calabria'. In a sense this alliance of 1130–8 was simply the culmination of the old alliance of the Pierleoni and the Sicilian Hautevilles. (The papal privilege of 1130 creating the new kingdom was subscribed by nine members of the Pierleone clan and by only one other witness.)[71] It is possible, however, that the alliance with Roger II was

---

[66] Cardinal bishop Giles of Tusculum (Toucy, near Auxerre): Hüls, pp. 142–3; Gerard of S. Croce in Gerusalemme (Bologna): Hüls, p. 164; Petrus Rufus of SS. Martino e Silvestro (Bologna): Hüls pp. 193, 220; Haimeric of S. Maria Nuova (Burgundy): Hüls p. 236; Hubert of S. Maria in Via Lata (Pisa): Hüls pp. 162, 238.

[67] Information is scarcer in the case of Honorius II's eighteen appointments: Hüls, *Kardinäle* pp. 96–9, 108, 128–9, 138, 149, 154–5, 158, 162–3, 168, 183, 196, 211, 230–1, 239, 243, 248, 253. Cf. Schmale, *Schisma* pp. 52–7.

[68] Schmale, *Schisma* (n. 62) pp. 91–191. See above pp. 67–74, 94–5.

[69] O. Schumann, *Die päpstlichen Legaten in Deutschland zur Zeit Heinrichs IV. und Heinrichs V. (1056–1125)* (dissertation: Marburg, 1912) p. 117. See below p. 437.

[70] Hüls, *Kardinäle* (n. 29) pp. 189–91, 225; J. Deér, *The dynastic porphyry tombs of the Norman period in Sicily* (Dumbarton Oaks Studies 5: Cambridge, Mass., 1959) pp. 121–2.

[71] Deér, *Normannenstaaten* (n. 16) pp. 62–4 (no. XVII.2); *idem*, *Papsttum* (n. 2) pp. 212–14.

welcomed by those cardinals – a slight majority of the college – who in February 1130 elected Anacletus II and rejected Cardinal Haimeric's candidate, Innocent II. If this was so, the political strategy of Calixtus II and Haimeric – the abandonment of the Norman alliance created by the reform papacy – must have been a major issue in the papal schism of 1130.

The new papal strategy became fully operational on the death of Duke William of Apulia (25 July 1127). Roger II, claiming Apulia as his inheritance, was excommunicated by Honorius II 'because he seized the title of duke, to which he had no right, without consulting the Roman pontiff'.[72] Once more the archaic feudal theory of the papal curia was advanced to counter a Norman claim based on hereditary right. The proceedings of Honorius II in 1127–8 and those of Innocent II in the 1130s derived their legal justification from Gregory VII's formulation of the pope's feudal rights in southern Italy: papal investiture alone could confer possession of a principality and investiture would be refused to a candidate who was morally unworthy. According to this view, on the death of Duke William his duchy escheated to the Roman church. Honorius II 'went down to Apulia, summoned by the barons of that land, which belongs to the jurisdiction of St Peter, to protect and defend it from the Sicilian count Roger, who had invaded it'.[73] The pope considered Roger II to be 'an enemy of St Peter' and therefore unworthy of investiture.[74] Honorius constructed an alliance of Roger's opponents in order to drive out the usurper; but the alliance disintegrated without fighting a battle. The pope was left with no alternative but to invest the 'enemy of St Peter' with the duchy of Apulia on 22 August 1128. The oath of fealty sworn at this investiture contained a promise not to seize Benevento or Capua.[75] Even in defeat Honorius still struggled to avert the ultimate catastrophe of the union of all the southern Italian principalities under the rule of Roger II. His efforts were vain. In the autumn of 1129 Robert II of Capua, prompted by 'sheer terror', became Roger's vassal.[76] Early in 1130 Roger was called on by the pope himself to intervene in Benevento to prevent the formation of a commune there.[77]

---

[72] Romuald of Salerno, *Annales* 1127 (n. 10) p. 418.
[73] Boso, *Vita Honorii II: Liber pontificalis* 2, 379.
[74] Falco of Benevento, *Chronicon* 1127 (n. 56) p. 196.
[75] *Ibid.*, 1128, p. 200.
[76] Alexander of Telese, *De rebus gestis Rogerii Siciliae regis* 1.24 in *Cronisti e scrittori* (n. 56) 1, 101.
[77] Falco of Benevento, *Chronicon* 1129 (n. 56) p. 201.

The papal schism of 1130 set the seal on Roger's triumphs. So dependent was Anacletus II on his Norman ally that he conceded all Roger's demands: a 'kingdom of Sicily, Calabria and Apulia' which included the principality of Capua and the duchy of Naples as vassal dependencies, together with the right to demand the aid (*auxilium*) of the Beneventans against his enemies.[78] These sweeping concessions inspired the rumour among the supporters of the rival pope that Anacletus had granted to Roger 'Rome itself and all the land from there as far as Sicily'.[79] It was at least true that Anacletus II's privilege of 27 September 1130 conceded territorial rights which no predecessor would ever have contemplated – notably in the case of Benevento. Here the papal interests built up for the past eighty years had to give way before the need to placate Anacletus' only ally.[80] Anacletus also surrendered the constitutional principle on which his predecessors had insisted since 1059: he accepted Roger's claim that he owed his kingdom to hereditary right, not to papal investiture. The privilege of 1130 states that Roger and his successors owed homage and fealty to Anacletus and his successors; nevertheless, if for any reason homage and fealty was not performed, the Norman kings 'shall suffer no diminution of their honour or territory'. Here is a complete reversal of the principle in the oath of fealty formulated by Gregory VII in 1080, which assumed that the pope could deny possession to an unsuitable vassal by refusing him investiture. According to Anacletus' privilege, even if the pope refused investiture to an heir of the Sicilian Hautevilles, his refusal could not prevent the prince's accession. Roger and his heirs received the kingdom 'to be held by a perpetual right, to be ruled in perpetuity'.[81]

King Roger's triumph was threatened by the machinations of Anacletus' rival, Innocent II, who by 1132 had convinced most of western Christendom of the righteousness of his cause. Innocent II's attitude towards Roger in the years 1130–9 was the same as that of Honorius II in 1127–8. This 'enemy of St Peter' was in unlawful possession of a fief which had escheated to the Roman church, and for which the pope had yet to choose a worthy tenant. Innocent gave a practical demonstration of the papal feudal theory in August 1137,

---

[78] Anacletus II, *JL* 8411, *MPL* 179, 715D–717A. See Deér, *Papsttum* (n. 2) pp. 204–7.

[79] *Codex Udalrici* 259 ed. P. Jaffé, *Bibliotheca rerum germanicarum* 5 (Berlin, 1869), 443–4.

[80] O. Vehse, 'Benevent als Territorium des Kirchenstaates bis zum Beginn der avignonesischen Epoche', *QFIAB* 22 (1930–1), 142–3.

[81] Deér, *Papsttum* (n. 2) pp. 209–11.

when the duchy of Apulia was conferred on his chosen candidate, Count Rainulf of Alife, Roger's ambitious vassal. This demonstration was made possible by the intervention of Innocent II's ally, the German king Lothar III, whom he had crowned as emperor in June 1133. The papal–imperial cooperation against Roger II in 1137 seemed to be the successful culmination of the new papal policy inaugurated by the concordat of Worms in 1122. In the event, however, it provided Innocent II with an ambiguous victory. Lothar III entered southern Italy, intending to reimpose imperial control and therefore he saw the investiture of Rainulf of Alife as an opportunity to demonstrate his authority over the province. Innocent refused to give up the papal claim to be overlord of the southern Italian principalities.

For this reason a very serious quarrel arose between pope and emperor. The pope claimed that the investiture of the duchy of Apulia belonged to the jurisdiction of the Roman pontiff and that this right had for a long time been sedulously maintained by his predecessors. The emperor asserted that on the contrary it belonged to the jurisdiction of the empire . . . However, as they were both travelling and neither party had access to documents or proofs, this disagreement could not be settled; and so by common consent they reached this compromise: that both pope and emperor should invest Count Rainulf with the duchy of Apulia and afterwards at a more appropriate time and place . . . this disagreement would be settled justly. So they invested Count Rainulf with the duchy of Apulia, the pope holding the standard at the top, the emperor holding it below.[82]

Emperor Lothar III died four months after this contentious investiture, having seen Innocent established in Rome. There in April 1139 the impressive attendance at the Second Lateran Council revealed the Church reunited under Innocent's authority.[83] However, the victor of the schism was soon to suffer a bitter defeat at the hands of the one prince who did not acknowledge him as pope. The council excommunicated King Roger, who had now regained control of southern Italy. Innocent relied upon his vassal Rainulf of Alife to expel the invader; but Rainulf died three weeks after the end of the council. Therefore the pope himself led the alliance of Roger's enemies into the field, intending to enforce a settlement by means of a show of strength. Innocent's only recorded demand was for the independence of the principality of Capua; presumably he now

---

[82] Romuald of Salerno, *Annales* 1137 (n. 10) p. 422. See below p. 451.
[83] See above p. 138.

accepted Roger's right to Apulia.[84] Innocent had reverted to the position of Honorius II in August 1128: acceptance of the Hauteville hereditary claim to Apulia, combined with resistance to the unification of the southern Italian principalities. When Roger refused the papal demand, Innocent opened hostilities. He was defeated at Galluccio on 22 July 1139 and was taken prisoner, together with his entourage. Five days later Innocent issued a privilege which contained all the concessions made by Anacletus II's privilege of 1130: a kingdom to be held by 'Roger, illustrious and glorious king of Sicily and his heirs in perpetuity', which 'they are to hold without diminution' even if they fail to do homage to the pope.[85] Roger's territories are described in the privilege of 1139 as 'the kingdom of Sicily, the duchy of Apulia and the principality of Capua'. This careful distinction of *regnum*, *ducatus* and *principatus* was reflected in the investitures performed by Innocent on 25 July 1139. The pope gave to the king a banner representing Sicily, to his eldest son, Roger, a second banner representing Apulia and to his third son, Anfuso, a third banner representing Capua.[86] Historians have interpreted the symbolism of the three banners as a Norman concession to the papal principle that southern Italy should never be united under a single ruler. 'Innocent II maintained his old standpoint and gained an advantage which should not be minimised: the king accepted or seemed to accept the fictitious independence of the three feudal territories.'[87] However, Josef Deér (1972) has now shown that this territorial division was a dynastic arrangement created by Roger himself in the 1130s and imposed on Innocent as part of the package of 1139.[88]

Galluccio was a total defeat for the curial policy first formulated *ca.* 1122. The most that could be done to save face in the privilege of 1139 was to pretend that Anacletus II's creation of the kingdom of Sicily in 1130 had never happened. The papal chancellor, Cardinal Haimeric, the foremost exponent of the strategy which foundered on the field of Galluccio, invented the fiction that Sicily had always been a kingdom ('as is told in ancient histories') and that Honorius II had added Apulia to Roger's kingdom, 'believing [him] to be suitable'.[89] The Gregorian attribute of 'suitability' (*idoneitas*) was now

---

[84] Falco of Benevento, *Chronicon* 1139 (n. 56) p. 245.
[85] Deér, *Normannenstaaten* (n. 16) pp. 74–5 (no. xx.4).
[86] Falco of Benevento, *Chronicon* 1139, p. 246. Cf. *Annales Cavenses* 1138, *MGH SS* 3, 192. See Deér, *Papsttum* (n. 2) pp. 228–9.
[87] Kehr, *Belehnungen* (n. 2) p. 42.   [88] Deér, *Papsttum* (n. 2) pp. 224–30.
[89] Deér, *Normannenstaaten* (n. 16) p. 74 (no. xx.4).

ascribed to the prince whose startling unsuitability had been evident
to the papal curia since 1121. After 1139 King Roger's territorial
ambitions became even more objectionable and dangerous to the
papacy; for he now began to encroach on the Patrimony of St Peter.
In 1140 his sons attacked the southern and eastern edges of the
patrimony; in 1143 the king received the submission of the territory
of Marsia; in 1144 his army plundered Campagna and laid siege to
Terracina. When the papal curia protested, Roger replied that he
'wished only to regain control of lands belonging to his principality'.[90] Once more Innocent II urged Roger's enemies to take the
field against him, appealing to Lothar III's successor, Conrad III, and
to the Byzantine emperor, John II Comnenus; but without success.
The death of Innocent in September 1143 offered the curia a new
sanction against Roger II. Feudal custom required the new pope to
renew the investiture and the privilege of 1139. Roger requested this
confirmation of his rights; but Celestine II 'refused to ratify the
agreement made between Pope Innocent and King Roger, and cast
doubt upon it'.[91] Celestine II was the former cardinal priest Guido of
Castello, one of Honorius II's recruits to the college and a supporter
of Innocent II in the 1130s, when he had played an important part in
negotiations with Roger.[92] During his brief pontificate Celestine
perpetuated the policy of the 1130s; as did his successor, Lucius II,
who had a similar curial background, with experience in southern
Italy.[93] Evidently the college of cardinals was determined to elect to
the papacy only candidates likely to be hostile towards King Roger.
In the event Roger never secured the renewal of investiture and of
Innocent II's privilege.

The papacy in the 1140s and 1150s had to contend not only with
the aggression of the Sicilian Hautevilles, but also with the Roman
revolution which created a commune in the city.[94] It had been papal
insecurity in Rome which had first driven the papacy to make an
alliance with the Normans in 1059; and this new turmoil threatened
to force the curia to seek the protection of Roger II. The years 1143–
56 found the papacy negotiating half-heartedly with the Sicilian king
for aid against the Romans, while appealing wholeheartedly to the
German king to intervene as Lothar III had done in 1137. This was

[90] Falco of Benevento, *Chronicon* 1140 (n. 56) p. 250.
[91] Romuald of Salerno, *Annales* 1143 (n. 10) p. 424.
[92] Hüls, *Kardinäle* (n. 29) p. 239; B. Zenker, *Die Mitglieder des Kardinalkollegiums von 1130 bis 1159* (dissertation: Würzburg, 1964) pp. 83–4.
[93] Hüls, *Kardinäle* p. 164: Zenker, *Mitglieder* pp. 129–31.
[94] See above pp. 13–15.

the attitude of Lucius II, who in 1144 negotiated a seven-year truce
with Roger (the king promising to respect the integrity of the papal
patrimony). It proved impossible to negotiate a permanent peace
'because of the opposition of the cardinals'[95] and because Lucius
adhered faithfully to the pro-imperial policy of Calixtus II, who had
appointed him to the college of cardinals. (As cardinal priest of S.
Croce in Gerusalemme, he had been the architect of the alliance with
Lothar III.)[96] Lucius' successor, Eugenius III, in 1148 actually
received military aid from Roger against the Romans; but still there
was no permanent peace and no renewal of the privilege of 1139.
Reconciliation was hindered by the long-term grievance of Roger's
treatment of the Sicilian church. Appealing to the legatine privilege
granted to his father in 1098, Roger 'did not allow legates of the
Roman church to enter his territory, unless they were summoned by
himself'. Moreover 'he disposed of ecclesiastical offices as if they
were palace appointments'.[97] In 1151 he added the new offence of
having his son crowned 'without consulting the Roman pontiff'.[98]
Eugenius III hoped that this dangerous neighbour could be
restrained by the intervention of the German king: hence his alarm
and indignation when he learned that Bernard of Clairvaux was
attempting to make peace between Roger II and Conrad III.[99]
Eugenius' hopes were realised on 23 March 1153, when his legates
concluded the treaty of Constance with the new German king,
Frederick I. The king swore that he would not make peace with
Roger II or with the Romans without the pope's agreement, that he
would restore the temporal power of St Peter and protect the *honor*
of the papacy. In return the pope would 'increase and expand the
honor of the empire' and would crown Frederick emperor in
Rome.[100]

For three decades the papal curia had been dominated by a party
hostile to the Sicilian Hautevilles and conciliatory towards the
German king. The treaty of Constance was that party's last triumph.
Eugenius III's successor, Anastasius IV, was the last survivor of the

95 Romuald of Salerno, *Annales* 1143 (n. 10) p. 424.
96 Hüls, *Kardinäle* (n. 29) p. 164: Zenker, *Mitglieder* (n. 92) pp. 129–31.
97 John of Salisbury, *Historia pontificalis* c. 32 (n. 7) pp. 65–6.
98 *Ibid.*, c. 34, p. 68.
99 Letter of Guido of S. Grisogono: *Wibaldi Epistolae* 273 ed. P. Jaffé, *Bibliotheca rerum germanicarum* I (Berlin, 1864), 401. See Deér, *Papsttum* (n. 2) p. 241.
100 Treaty of Constance: *MGH Constitutiones* I, 201–3 (nos. 144–5). See Rassow, *Honor Imperii* (n. 61) pp. 60–1, and the criticisms of Deér, *Papsttum* (n. 2) pp. 244–6 n. 1105. See below pp. 461–2.

cardinals created by Calixtus II and Honorius II to ensure support for their strategy.[101] Soon after his death in December 1154 a new party was forming in the curia, favouring an alliance with the new king of Sicily, Roger II's son, William I (1154–66). Its enemies were eventually to label it 'the Sicilian party'.[102] The leader of this party – and the dominant politician in the curia from the mid-1150s – had also been one of the negotiators of the treaty of Constance: Roland Bandinelli, cardinal priest of S. Marco and papal chancellor (1153–9).[103] The beginning of Cardinal Roland's disillusionment with the treaty of Constance can be dated to 1155, shortly after the new pope, Hadrian IV, had renewed the treaty with Frederick I and crowned him emperor according to its terms. At the beginning of his pontificate Hadrian IV vigorously set about implementing the policy which he had inherited, of undermining the power of the Sicilian kingdom. He refused to recognise the title of William I, calling him not 'king' but 'lord of Sicily', since he had been crowned without papal permission. He revived the 'feudal policy' of the years 1118–28, receiving homage from the Apulian barons as their 'principal lord' and promising to restore to Robert II the principality of Capua, from which Roger II had deposed him.[104] The renewal of the treaty of Constance was a crucial part of Hadrian's strategy. As if to underline his dependence on the German king, Norman troops plundered Campagna and laid siege to Benevento even as Frederick I neared Rome in June 1155. However, Frederick failed to aid the pope either against King William of Sicily or against the turbulent Romans. From this failure stemmed both the hostility of Cardinal Roland towards Frederick I and the formation of 'the Sicilian party'; although it required a military disaster on the scale of Galluccio in 1139 to make their policy acceptable to the rest of the curia.

The disappointing outcome of the German alliance caused Hadrian IV to turn to the alternative alliance contemplated in 1142 by Innocent II. In 1155 Byzantine forces held the Adriatic port of Ancona: evidence of the ambition of Emperor Manuel I Comnenus

---

[101] Hüls, *Kardinäle* (n. 29) pp. 128–9, 201; Zenker, *Mitglieder* (n. 92) pp. 46–8.

[102] *Annales Stadenses* 1159, *MGH SS* 16, 344: see Zenker, *Mitglieder* p. 87. Cf. Council of Pavia: *MGH Constitutiones* 1, 259–60 (no. 187). See above pp. 52–3, 79–80, 116–17 and below pp. 470–2.

[103] C. Dunken, *Die politische Wirksamkeit der päpstlichen Legaten in der Zeit des Kampfes zwischen Kaisertum und Papsttum in Oberitalien unter Friedrich I.* (Berlin, 1931) pp. 12–13.

[104] Boso, *Vita Hadriani IV: Liber pontificalis* 2, 393–4. See Deér, *Papsttum* (n. 2) pp. 244–7.

to restore southern Italy to his empire. The Byzantine general, promising a lavish subsidy, sought to persuade the pope to join him in an attack on the kingdom of Sicily. It is not clear whether Hadrian accepted this proposal or whether he planned a simultaneous but independent attack.[105] The chances of victory seemed remarkably favourable: at the end of 1155 King William I became seriously ill; many of his southern Italian vassals rebelled and allied with the Greek forces. The king's chief minister, Maio of Bari, 'emir of emirs', offered the pope fealty and homage, restitution for the recent injuries to the papal patrimony, help against the Romans and 'complete liberty' for the Sicilian church as the price of peace. His terms were rejected by a majority of the cardinals.[106] The pope waged war on his unruly vassal and suffered the fate of Innocent II in 1139. King William recovered from his sickness, defeated his rebellious vassals, expelled the Byzantine army and besieged Benevento, where the pope had his headquarters. The papal defeat resulted in the concessions of the concordat of Benevento of 18 June 1156, which was mainly the work of Maio of Bari and Cardinal Roland, the papal chancellor. The concordat contained a definitive settlement of all the territorial disputes of the years 1139–56, entirely to the advantage of the king of Sicily. 'The unity of the Norman empire was an established fact.'[107] There was no longer any question of restoring the independence of the principality of Capua, as Hadrian IV had sought to do the previous autumn. Moreover the concordat legitimated the conquests made by Roger II and his sons during the 1140s at the expense of the Patrimony of St Peter.[108] King William's territories were listed as 'the kingdom of Sicily, the duchy of Apulia and the principality of Capua, together with all their appurtenances, Naples, Salerno and Amalfi with their appurtenances, Marsia and what lies beyond Marsia'.[109] The ecclesiastical settlement of June 1156 gave the pope far less than Maio of Bari had offered him a few months before. 'Apulia and Calabria and those territories neighbouring on Apulia' could receive papal legates without restriction; but in Sicily there were to be no legations and no appeals without the king's per-

---

[105] Boso, *Vita Hadriani IV* p. 394. See J. G. Rowe, 'Hadrian IV, the Byzantine empire and the Latin orient' in *Essays in medieval history presented to Bertie Wilkinson* ed. T. A. Sandquist and M. R. Powicke (Toronto, 1969) pp. 10–12.

[106] Boso, *Vita Hadriani IV* p. 394. See Deér, *Papsttum* (n. 2) p. 247.

[107] P. Kehr, *Belehnungen* (n. 2) p. 46.

[108] Clementi, 'Sicily and south Italy' (n. 1) pp. 192–7.

[109] Concordat of Benevento: privilege of William I c. 12, *MGH Constitutiones* 1, 590 (no. 413).

mission.[110] The papal surrender was virtually complete: nevertheless the concordat formed the basis of the amicable relationship between the papacy and its vassal kingdom of Sicily from 1156 until 1189, when the Hauteville dynasty died out in the direct male line. Harmony prevailed partly because both the Norman kings and the papacy made only modest demands of each other. Above all there was harmony because the conflict between papacy and empire in the pontificate of Alexander III created a papal dependence on the Normans like that of Gregory VII, Victor III and Urban II.

The schism of 1159 originated, like that of 1130, in a struggle between a curial party dedicated to an alliance with the emperor and a 'Sicilian party' favouring alliance with the Sicilian Hauteville. The most obvious difference between the schisms was that in 1159 it was the pope of 'the Sicilian party', Alexander III, who won recognition in most areas of western Christendom, while his rival was generally regarded as an imperial puppet. This rival was 'Victor IV': Octavian of Monticelli, cardinal priest of S. Cecilia, 'a particular lover of the Germans',[111] employed as a legate to Germany during the 1150s and a negotiator of the treaty of Constance with his kinsman, Frederick I.[112] Alexander III was the former papal chancellor, Cardinal Roland Bandinelli, whom contemporaries believed to be the leader of 'the Sicilian party'. Hostile polemic claimed that the cardinals of this party 'swore that on the death of Pope Hadrian they would elect one of themselves, who would remain true to their designs'.[113] Alexander's dependence on the king of Sicily for financial and military aid was an obvious target for the propaganda of the imperial party.[114] The closeness of this papal-Norman alliance is apparent in the official biography of Alexander III, composed by his confidant, Boso, cardinal priest of S. Pudenziana. In his biography of Hadrian IV Boso presented King William I as a peace-breaker who 'impudently raised his horns against his mother and mistress, the

---

[110] *Ibid.*, c. 4–9, p. 589. Deér, *Papsttum* (n. 2) pp. 258–9 argues that these clauses were a surrender on the part of the king, because they abandoned the principle of the legatine privilege of 1098.

[111] *Gesta Alberonis archiepiscopi, MGH SS* 8, 255.

[112] P. Kehr, 'Zur Geschichte Viktors IV.', *NA* 46 (1926), 55, 84–5. The precise relationship is unknown. See also Dunken, *Legaten* (n. 103) pp. 12–13; J. Bachmann, *Die päpstlichen Legaten in Deutschland und Skandinavien (1125–1159)* (Berlin, 1913) p. 122.

[113] *Annales Stadenses* 1159 (n. 102) p. 344.

[114] E.g. Council of Pavia, *MGH Constitutiones* 1, 258–9 (no. 187).

holy Roman church'.[115] In the biography of Alexander III, however, William I became 'the most Christian king of Sicily, worthy of being remembered', who 'recognised the pontiff as his father and lord from whom he held the patrimony of Sicily and all his other territory'.[116] This eulogy occurs in the narrative of events in November 1165, when the king provided Alexander with a galley and escort for his journey from Messina to Ostia. William I's death the following May inspired a tribute from Boso. 'The faithful and devout son of the Roman church, William, illustrious and glorious king of Sicily – whose soul we commit to the Lord – departed in peace in Palermo. His elder son, William [II], succeeded, at the command of the Lord, both to his kingdom and to his fidelity and devotion.'[117]

The importance of this alliance with William I and William II (1166–89) for the survival of Alexander III's cause during the schism is underlined by the evidence of Alexander's itinerary in the 1160s and 1170s. Alexander spent the first two years of his pontificate in papal strongholds on the frontier of the Sicilian kingdom. When a rebellion of William I's vassals rendered this region unsafe, the king sent galleys to bring the pope to Genoa. After an exile of three-and-a-half years in France, Alexander returned to Rome; but the arrival of Emperor Frederick I in July 1167 forced him to flee. Once again Sicilian galleys brought him to safety, this time to Benevento, where he remained for two-and-a-half years as the guest of William II (1167–70). Alexander spent the last seven years of the schism in papal fortresses situated between Rome and the Sicilian border.[118] The material aid which the kings provided during the schism was considerable: Norman troops fought for the pope against the imperial forces in 1165 and 1176. The kingdom paid an annual feudal *census* of 1,000 gold *squifati* and there were additional gifts of money: for example, that made by William I on his deathbed, which one contemporary estimated at 40,000 silver marks.[119] Good relations between the Sicilian court and the curia were maintained by Alexander's expert on Sicilian affairs, John of Naples, cardinal priest

---

[115] Boso, *Vita Hadriani IV* (n. 104) p. 389.

[116] Boso, *Vita Alexandri III* : *Liber pontificalis* 2, 412.

[117] *Ibid.*, p. 414. See H. Enzensberger, 'Der "böse" und der "gute" Wilhelm. Zur Kirchenpolitik der normannischen Könige von Sizilien nach dem Vertrag von Benevent (1156)', *DA* 36 (1980), 386–96.

[118] P. Jaffé, *Regesta pontificum Romanorum* 2, 147–55, 205–302.

[119] John of Salisbury, *Letter* 168 ed. W. J. Millor and C. N. L. Brooke 2 (Oxford, 1979), 116; Boso, *Vita Alexandri III* (n. 116) pp. 416–17. See Chalandon, *Histoire* (n. 48) 2, 301, 375. On the feudal *census* see above p. 273.

of S. Anastasia. A native of the Sicilian kingdom, John undertook three legations there, in 1160, 1166 and 1169. His duties were mainly diplomatic in character and he evidently gained the confidence of William I, since the king entrusted him with his deathbed gift to the pope. Another member of the curia who promoted the Sicilian alliance was Cardinal bishop Hubald of Ostia (the future Lucius III), who had been one of 'the Sicilian party' who favoured an alliance with the Sicilian king in 1156. He undertook a legation to the Sicilian kingdom in 1166–7.[120] The minority of the boy-king William II (1166–71) witnessed a degree of papal and royal cooperation in the administration of the southern Italian church unprecedented since the reign of Duke William of Apulia. The precarious hold of the regency government on power in these years caused it to tolerate such a direct papal intervention in the Sicilian church as Alexander's deposition of Bishop William I of Caiazzo on the grounds of simony (1168).[121] Letters of Alexander III are extant from the period of William II's majority, in which the pope complained of abuses in the Sicilian church; but there is also evidence that the royal government responded positively and speedily to such complaints.[122] The principal evidence that papal–royal cooperation survived the end of William II's minority and also the end of the papal schism is the impressive southern Italian attendance at Alexander's Third Lateran Council in 1179. Seventy-three southern Italian bishops were present at the council.[123]

William II's premature death (18 November 1189) was a severe shock for the papacy. The childless king had acknowledged as his successor his aunt, Constance, the posthumous daughter of Roger II, who in 1186 had married the son of Emperor Frederick I, Henry VI, king of the Germans (1190–7). The threat of an imperial-Norman alliance, which had troubled Gregory VII in 1076 and Eugenius III in 1150, was now transformed into the much more fearsome prospect of 'the union of the kingdom with the empire' (*unio regni ad imperium*). Emperor Frederick's first attempt to negotiate a Staufen-

---

[120] Chalandon, *Histoire* 2, 354–5; Zenker, *Mitglieder* (n. 92) pp. 73–5; 23–4.

[121] Boso, *Vita Alexandri III* (n. 116) p. 419.

[122] Alexander III, *JL* 13101: S. Loewenfeld, *Epistolae pontificum Romanorum ineditae* (Leipzig, 1885) pp. 159–60; *JL* – : W. Holtzmann, 'Kanonistische Ergänzungen zur Italia Pontificia', *QFIAB* 38 (1958), 122–3. See G. A. Loud, 'Royal control of the church in the twelfth-century kingdom of Sicily', *Studies in Church History* 18 (Oxford, 1982), 147–59; idem, *Church and society in the Norman principality of Capua, 1058–1197* (Oxford, 1985) p. 190.

[123] Mansi, *Sacra Concilia* 22, 213–14.

Hauteville marriage had been made in 1176, in the last months of the papal schism. It was one of Frederick's ploys to divide the members of the anti-imperial coalition; but it had been foiled by the statesmanship of Alexander III.[124] In 1184 the emperor finally succeeded in negotiating a marriage between his son and Constance of Sicily. The attitude of the new pope, Lucius III, to this match is not known. Some historians have guessed that he was an active participant in the negotiations, in the interests of the peace of Christendom.[125] However, the part which he had played, as Cardinal bishop Hubald of Ostia, in promoting the papal-Sicilian alliance, argues against this view. The earliest evidence that the papal curia was responding to the danger presented by William II's childless state and the marriage of his heir presumptive to the German king comes from the year 1188. In the summer of that year Clement III arranged for William II to swear an oath of fealty to St Peter, the Roman church and the pope in the presence of the papal legates, Cardinal Albinus of S. Croce and Cardinal Peter of S. Lorenzo in Damaso. It was the first occasion since the treaty of Benevento in 1156 that the pope had requested the oath from the king of Sicily and there can be little doubt that the request was connected with the threat of 'the union of the kingdom with the empire'. For William II's oath differed in one significant respect from the oath, formulated by Gregory VII in 1080, which had been taken by his predecessors. The oath of 1188 bound not only William II himself but also his heirs to observe fealty to the pope. A letter of Clement III of the same date underlined this obligation on the part of William II's heirs.[126]

In 1188 the papal curia, facing the possibility that William II would die childless, emphasised the principle of the feudal dependence of the kingdom of Sicily on the Roman church by reviving the oath of fealty sworn by the Sicilian king to the pope. A little more than a year later, on the death of William II, the curia took the decisive measure of reviving the papal strategy of 1127–8 and 1130–9: that is, of using the pope's feudal authority to prevent the succession of an unsuitable

---

[124] Romuald of Salerno, *Annales* [1176] (n. 10) p. 441.

[125] So J. Haller, 'Heinrich VI. und die römische Kirche', *MIÖG* 35 (1914), 414; P. Munz, *Frederick Barbarossa* (London, 1969) pp. 367–8; but see G. Baaken, 'Unio regni ad imperium. Die Verhandlungen von Verona 1184 und die Eheabredung zwischen König Heinrich VI. und Konstanze von Sizilien', *QFIAB* 52 (1972), 219–97. See below p. 501.

[126] Oath of William: *MGH Constitutiones* I, 591–2: for the date of the oath see Baaken, 'Unio regni' p. 267; but see also Deér, *Normannenstaaten* (n. 16) p. 93. Clement III, *JL* 16375, *MPL* 204, 1486AC. See Kehr, *Belehnungen* (n. 2) pp. 49–50.

candidate to the throne. The papal curia seized the opportunity offered by the Sicilian opponents of the succession of Constance. At the end of 1189 a faction led by Matthew of Ajello (who had served the late king as head of his chancery) organised the election of Count Tancred of Lecce, William II's cousin, to the kingship. (Tancred was the illegitimate son of William I's brother, Duke Roger of Apulia.)[127] No papal letters concerning Sicily survive for the crucial months December 1189 and January 1190; so the papal reaction has to be reconstructed from the narrative sources. The annalist of Monte Cassino claimed that Tancred was elected with the consent of Clement III. Another chronicler from the same region, Richard of San Germano, wrote of 'the Roman curia giving its consent' to Tancred's coronation. The German chronicler Arnold of Lübeck wrote that Tancred was crowned 'with the consent and favour of the Roman church'.[128] Tancred's oath of fealty to the pope is extant, recording the investiture of the new king by Celestine III with 'the kingdom of Sicily, the duchy of Apulia and the principality of Capua' (May 1192).[129] Like Honorius II in 1127–8 and Innocent II in 1130–9, Clement III and Celestine III countered the claim of an Hauteville candidate based on hereditary right with a papal claim to feudal overlordship. The argument used to reject the claim of Roger II was revived in order to reject the claim of his daughter, Constance: the pope invoked the principle of 'suitability' (*idoneitas*). As superior feudal lord of Sicily, the pope rejected Constance and accepted her nephew, Tancred, because he was more suitable to serve as the papal vassal in the Sicilian kingdom.

King Tancred (1190–4), strengthened by an alliance with King Richard I of England (brother-in-law of the late William II), imposed his authority on the Apulian barons. His rival's husband, Emperor Henry VI, was forced to abandon his first attempt to conquer the Sicilian kingdom in the summer of 1191, when his army was hit by an epidemic. Thereafter the emperor was detained in Germany for more than two years by rebellions in Saxony and in the Rhineland. In June 1192 Tancred, evidently securely in control of his kingdom, rewarded the pope for his support. The reward was the concordat of Gravina, a revised version of the concordat of Benevento of 1156.

---

[127] Richard of San Germano, *Chronica* 1190, *MGH SS* 19, 234. See Chalandon, *Histoire* (n. 48) 2, 121–3.

[128] *Annales Casinenses* 1190, *MGH SS* 19, 314; Richard of San Germano, *Chronica* 1190, p. 234; Arnold of Lübeck, *Chronica Slavorum* v. 5, *MGH SS* 21, 182.

[129] Oath of Tancred: *MGH Constitutiones* 1, 592–3.

The new concordat dropped the distinction made in 1156 between Sicily and the mainland: the right of appeal to Rome was now extended to 'the whole kingdom of Sicily'. Papal legates could now enter Sicily once every five years and when 'evident necessity demands it'.[130] Papal authority was extended over the churches of Sicily for the first time since the Norman conquest of the island. As the price of the papal legitimation of his title, Tancred surrendered the legatine privilege of 1098 to which his grandfather and great-grandfather had clung so tenaciously. The reign of King Tancred was, however, only a temporary reprieve for the papacy. Both the king and his eldest son, Roger, died suddenly, early in 1194. Emperor Henry VI then had no difficulty in seizing the kingdom from Tancred's widow and his infant son, William III. Henry VI was crowned king of Sicily on Christmas day 1194 in Palermo and the succession was assured when on the following day Empress Constance gave birth to a son, the future Frederick II. The Staufen regime had no reason to conciliate the papacy. The empress wrote to Celestine III in October 1195, repudiating the concordat of Gravina on the grounds that it had been conceded by a usurper. The ecclesiastical customs of Roger II were restored.[131] The public response of the papal curia to this débâcle was to complain about Henry VI's refusal to do homage to the pope for the kingdom of Sicily and about his treatment of the Sicilian church. The private response of the curia was allegedly to conspire with the Sicilian opponents of the Staufen regime. The great rebellion of the Sicilian barons against Henry VI in May 1197 took place 'with the connivance . . . if it is permissible to believe it, of Pope Celestine himself'.[132]

The Staufen conquest of Sicily deprived the papacy of far more than the concessions of Gravina. Since the pontificate of Gregory VII the papal curia had sought security by playing off the Norman princes against the emperor. During the Investiture Contest and again during the schism of 1159–77 popes had sought refuge in southern Italy and used the financial and military resources of the Norman princes to defeat the emperors. In the period between the concordat of Worms and the concordat of Benevento popes had sought the aid of emperors to check the growing power of Roger II.

[130] Concordat of Gravina: privilege of Tancred c. 3, 4, MGH Constitutiones 1, 593.
[131] Constance, letter to Celestine III, ed. P. Kehr, 'Das Briefbuch des Thomas von Gaeta', QFIAB 8 (1905), 50.
[132] Annales Marbacenses 1196, MGH SS rer. Germ., 1907, p. 69. See G. Baaken, 'Die Verhandlungen zwischen Kaiser Heinrich VI. und Papst Coelestin III. in den Jahren 1195–1197', DA 27 (1970), 498–505.

The union of the kingdom of Sicily with the empire deprived the papacy of room for manoeuvre. The strategy of both parties in the papal curia, the Sicilian and the imperial, suddenly became irrelevant. A new strategy must be found. The sudden death of Emperor Henry VI on 28 September 1197 and the election of Pope Innocent III on the day of the death of Celestine III, 8 January 1198, marked the beginning of the search for such a strategy.

PAPACY AND EMPIRE

_____ • _____

THE INVESTITURE CONTEST

Four months after his accession Pope Gregory VII wrote to the powerful German prince, Rudolf of Rheinfelden, duke of Swabia and kinsman by marriage of King Henry IV, about the means

by which the empire is ruled more gloriously and the strength of holy Church is confirmed: namely, that priesthood and empire are joined in the unity of harmony. For just as by means of two eyes the human body is ruled by temporal light, so by means of these two dignities, agreeing in pure religion, the body of the Church proves to be ruled and illuminated by spiritual light.[1]

This idea was drawn from the most influential of early medieval statements of the relations of empire and papacy, the writings of Pope Gelasius I (492–6). 'The world is chiefly governed by these two: the sacred authority of pontiffs and the royal power.' 'Christ . . . separated the offices of both powers according to their proper activities and their special dignities.' The emperor's office is to 'rule over the human race in dignity'; but he must 'devoutly bow the neck to those who are placed in charge of religious matters and seek from them the means of [his] salvation'. Papacy and empire were a divinely ordained duality, governing the Christian people side by side, each with a distinct function but dependent on the other, 'so that Christian emperors need pontiffs in order to attain eternal life

[1] Gregory VII, *Registrum* I.19, p. 31.

and pontiffs have recourse to imperial direction in the conduct of temporal affairs'.[2] This necessary cooperation between empire and papacy – 'the imperial majesty and the gentle power of the apostolic see' – is the theme of a letter written by Gregory VII to Henry IV on 7 December 1074. Gregory contemplated leading an expedition to the east to liberate 'the church of Constantinople' from the Saracens and he therefore sought Henry's counsel and aid: 'I leave the Roman church to you, after God, to protect her as a holy mother and to defend her honour.'[3] The approval with which Gregory wrote of the *imperatoria maiestas* of 'the glorious King Henry' in December 1074 is in stark contrast with the pope's most famous statement on royal authority, written in March 1081 after his second excommunication and deposition of Henry IV. 'Who does not know that kings and dukes are descended from those who, in disregard of God, through arrogance, plunder, treachery, murder, finally through almost all crimes, prompted by the prince of this world, the devil, strove to dominate their equals, that is, [their fellow] men, in blind greed and intolerable presumption.'[4] The conventional statement of the divine origin of royal authority gave way, after six years of dealings with Henry IV, to an innovatory statement of the diabolic origin of kingship. Between 1074 and 1081 there was a revolution in the political thinking of the curia, the consequences of which were to be felt long after the deaths of Gregory VII and Henry IV.

Gregory VII became pope at a moment of tension in the relations of the papacy and the German court: the reform papacy's first attack on the customs by means of which the Salian monarch controlled the churches in his empire (the so-called 'imperial Church system'). The papacy had firm evidence that in recent years the king had used his right of investiture to appoint prelates who had paid him for their ecclesiastical offices. A few weeks before Gregory VII's accession the papal synod of March 1073 had excommunicated a number of the king's counsellors who were held responsible for the simoniacal practices of the court. Since Gregory's predecessor, Alexander II, was mortally ill at the time of the synod, no doubt Gregory himself

[2] Gelasius I, *Epistola* 12, ed. A. Thiel, *Epistolae Romanorum pontificum genuinae* I (Braunsberg, 1868), 350; *idem, Tractatus* IV.11, *ibid.*, p. 567. See L. Knabe, *Die gelasianische Zweigewaltentheorie bis zum Ende des Investiturstreits* (Historische Studien 292: Berlin, 1936) p. 154.

[3] Gregory VII, *Registrum* II.31, pp. 166–7. See H. E. J. Cowdrey, 'Pope Gregory VII's "crusading" plans of 1074', in *Outremer. Studies in the history of the crusading kingdom of Jerusalem presented to Joshua Prawer* (Jerusalem, 1982) pp. 27–40.

[4] *Registrum* VIII.21, p. 552.

(who, as Archdeacon Hildebrand, was Alexander's principal adviser) had played a major part in these proceedings. Gregory was perhaps already convinced that the practice of lay investiture was the most potent cause of simony: the practice had indeed been condemned by his former mentor, Cardinal Humbert of Silva Candida, in a polemic composed *ca.* 1060.[5] This conviction would eventually inspire the papal decrees against lay investiture, Gregory VII's most radical challenge to the 'imperial Church system'. However, in the short term the tension between the papacy and the German king was dissipated by the 'suppliant letter' which Henry IV sent to Gregory VII in September 1073. The king confessed that he had 'sold' churches to simoniac clerks under the influence of his evil counsellors; he requested 'the counsel and aid' of the pope, especially in the case of the archbishopric of Milan, 'because we cannot restore order in the churches without your authority'.[6] Gregory's response was enthusiastic: 'King Henry has sent us words full of sweetness and obedience, such as we recall neither him nor his predecessors ever sending to Roman pontiffs.'[7] The following March papal legates were sent to Germany to restore order to the Church and in their presence on 27 April at Nuremberg the king did penance[8] – the first of the series of penitential acts by means of which Henry IV sought to repair his relationship with the reform papacy at moments of crisis in his reign. It was the crisis of the Saxon rebellion which had compelled him to send his 'suppliant letter' of September. As Gregory observed later, after being undeceived: Henry had submitted 'when the cause of the Saxons began more and more to threaten the king and he saw that the military strength of the kingdom was in most cases ready to desert him'. When in June 1075 Henry crushed the rebellion at the battle of Homburg,

---

[5] C. Schneider, *Prophetisches Sacerdotium und heilsgeschichtliches Regnum im Dialog 1073–1077* (Munich, 1972) p. 42. On Humbert's condemnation of lay investiture see most recently B. Szabó-Bechstein, *Libertas Ecclesiae. Ein Schlüsselbegriff des Investiturstreits und seine Vorgeschichte*, SG 12 (1985), 130–7. On the 'imperial Church system' see most recently T. Reuter, 'The "imperial church system" of the Ottonian and Salian rulers: a reconsideration', *Journal of Ecclesiastical History* 33 (1982), 347–74; J. Fleckenstein, 'Problematik und Gestalt der ottonisch-salischen Reichskirche' in *Reich und Kirche vor dem Investiturstreit. Vorträge beim wissenschaftlichen Kolloquium aus Anlass des 80. Geburtstags von Gerd Tellenbach* ed. K. Schmid (Sigmaringen, 1985) pp. 83–98.

[6] Henry IV, *Epistola* 5, MGH Dt. Ma. 1, 8–9.

[7] *Registrum* I.25, p. 42.

[8] C. Erdmann, *Studien zur Briefliteratur Deutschlands im elften Jahrhundert* (Schriften der MGH 1, 1938) p. 238.

the thank-offerings which he made to God for the victory which he obtained were that he immediately broke the promises of amendment which he had made . . . He did not cease until he had made a shipwreck of the faith in Christ of almost all the bishops in Italy and of as many as he could in Germany, forcing them to deny the obedience which they owed to St Peter and the apostolic see.[9]

After a year of uninhibited papal intervention in the imperial church – culminating in the summoning of eight bishops to answer charges in the papal synod of Lent 1075 – Henry IV was enabled by his suppression of the Saxon rebellion to resume the traditional royal control of the Church.

Henry's most controversial action was the investiture of his chaplain Tedald as archbishop of Milan, ignoring the claims of the archbishop elect recognised by the papacy. Henry seized the opportunity presented by the defeat of the pro-papal Milanese reform party, the Pataria, and the death of its leader, Erlembald (18 June 1075), to secure control of the great metropolitan see and of the rest of the kingdom of Italy.[10] In summer or autumn 1075 Henry sent his adviser Count Eberhard (one of the excommunicated counsellors of 1073) to restore order in Lombardy, evidently in preparation for a royal progress through the kingdom – the first since his accession in 1056.[11] Simultaneously he sent a letter (no longer extant) to the pope, to which Gregory replied early in September 1075: 'I am prepared to open the bosom of the holy Roman church to you and to receive you as lord, brother and son and to give you what help is necessary.' Since the letter describes Henry as 'you whom God has placed on the highest summit of things', it is reasonable to suggest that this correspondence concerned Henry's wish to be crowned emperor in Rome and that Gregory's letter of September contains his acquiescence.[12] Gregory's next letter to the king, dated 8 December 1075, reveals a

---

[9] Gregory VII, *Epistolae Vagantes* 14, ed. H. E. J. Cowdrey (Oxford, 1972) p. 36 (summer 1076). On the rebellion of the nobility of East Saxony and Thuringia see most recently K. Leyser, 'The crisis of medieval Germany', *Proceedings of the British Academy* 69 (1983), 409–43.

[10] H. E. J. Cowdrey, 'The papacy, the Patarenes and the church of Milan', *TRHS* 5th ser., 18 (1968), 25–48; H. Keller, 'Pataria und Stadtverfassung, Stadtgemeinde und Reform: Mailand im "Investiturstreit"', in *Investiturstreit und Reichsverfassung* ed. J. Fleckenstein (Sigmaringen, 1973) p. 346. On the Pataria see also G. Miccoli, 'Per la storia della pataria milanese', in *idem, Chiesa gregoriana* (Florence, 1966) pp. 101–60.

[11] G. Meyer von Knonau, *Jahrbücher des Deutschen Reiches unter Heinrich IV. und Heinrich V.* 2 (Leipzig, 1894), 571.

[12] *Registrum* III.7, p. 257. See Meyer von Knonau 2, 566–7.

change of heart, prompted by Henry's attempt to secure control of his Italian kingdom and especially the appointment of Tedald: 'How you have kept the promises which you had made to us in the case of Milan . . . and in what spirit you made the promises, the event itself makes clear.' Until the king amends his conduct 'we shall remain silent about what is in your letter'. This is presumably a reference to Henry's coronation as emperor, as is also the remark, 'we particularly desire, and it would very much become you, that just as you are superior to other men in glory, honour and valour, so you should excel also in devotion to Christ', and the wish that Henry 'recognise the *empire* of Christ above you'. The letter of 8 December warned the king that the imperial coronation promised three months before would only take place 'if he obeys the apostolic see'.[13] The three envoys whom Henry had sent to Rome to negotiate the details of his coronation, returned bearing this papal letter, together with a warning not included in the letter, 'that on account of [his sins] not only should he be excommunicated . . . but he should be deprived of all the dignity of kingship'.[14] The letter and this additional message reached Henry on 1 January 1076 in Goslar, where he was celebrating Christmas with unusual splendour. At this moment the king seemed to be more powerful than at any previous time in his reign: he had defeated the Saxon rebels and at Christmastide 1075 he had secured from the princes the recognition of his son Conrad as the future king.[15] By contrast Gregory's situation appeared at this moment to be extremely vulnerable. His reforming methods had created many enemies in the imperial territories and he seemed to be insecure even in Rome: on Christmas day 1075 he was held prisoner, though only for a few hours, by his enemy Cencius son of the prefect Stephan.[16] It is not surprising, therefore, that in January 1076 Henry IV dropped the conciliatory mask which he had been compelled to wear since September 1073. He now took to their logical conclusion his efforts to control the kingdom of Italy by attempting to depose the pope. At the synod of Worms on 24 January, attended by twenty-four of the thirty-eight bishops in the German kingdom, Henry persuaded or compelled his bishops to renounce their obedience to the pope.[17] The

---

[13] *Registrum* III. 10, pp. 263–7.   [14] *Epistolae Vagantes* 14 (n. 9) p. 38.

[15] Meyer von Knonau (n. 11) 2, 583–4, 611.

[16] *Ibid.*, pp. 586–90; G. B. Borino, 'Cencio del prefetto Stefano l'attentatore di Gregorio VII', *SG* 4 (1952), 373–440.

[17] H. Zimmermann, 'Wurde Gregor VII. 1076 in Worms abgesetzt?', in *Heinrich Appelt zum sechzigsten Geburtstag gewidmet von Kollegen und Schülern (MIÖG* 78 (1970)) pp. 121–31.

king then sent a letter to 'the monk Hildebrand' demanding his abdication and another letter to 'all the clergy and people of the holy Roman church', calling on them to depose the pope. 'Rise up against him, most faithful ones, and let the foremost in the faith be the first to condemn him.'[18]

Henry IV's explanation of the causes of the conflict of 1076 is found in his letter to 'Hildebrand' of 24 January. The pope had 'snatched away all the hereditary dignity which was owed to me by that [Roman] see' and had 'tried to alienate the kingdom of Italy'. He had 'not feared to lay hands on the most reverend bishops' (presumably by supporting the violent tactics of the Pataria in the archdiocese of Milan and by summoning eight imperial bishops to answer charges in Rome). Finally, he was determined 'to rob me of my soul and my kingdom or die in the attempt'.[19] In short, Henry's royal authority was being undermined by Gregory's brand of reform. He could no longer afford the alliance with the pope which he had continued during 1075 in order to make sure of the imperial coronation. Gregory VII's explanation of the conflict appears in the excommunication and deposition of the king, pronounced in the Roman synod of February 1076, and in the letter sent the following summer to his supporters in the German kingdom. Henry had 'risen up against [St Peter's] church with unheard-of arrogance'.[20] He 'refused to abstain from contact with those who were excommunicated for sacrilege and the crime of simoniacal heresy'; he would not promise to do penance 'for the guilty actions of his life' and 'he was not afraid to rend . . . the unity of holy Church'.[21] Henry's attitude towards the Church in the kingdom of Italy showed that the alliance on which Gregory had counted in 1074–5 – that union of 'the imperial majesty and the gentle power of the apostolic see' – was an illusion.

While there were many obvious precedents for Henry IV's attempt to depose the pope – the most recent being the proceedings of his father, Henry III, at Sutri (1046) – it was unprecedented for a pope to use the power of binding and loosing to depose a king and absolve his vassals from their fealty to him. During the summer of 1076 Gregory despatched to the German kingdom letters of unusual length, intended to 'satisfy the misgivings of those who think that we seized the spiritual sword rashly'. The misgivings of Bishop

[18] Henry IV, *Epistolae* 10, 11 (n. 6) pp. 12–15.
[19] *Ibid.*, 11, pp. 14–15. The last two charges are elaborated in *Epistola* 12 (pp. 15–17), intended for a German audience.
[20] *Registrum* III.10a, p. 270.   [21] *Epistolae Vagantes* 14 (n. 9) pp. 38–40.

Herman of Metz were extinguished by a papal letter full of historical examples refuting 'those who say that a king ought not to be excommunicated'.[22] The claim that the pope 'can absolve subjects from fealty to evil men' was made in the *Dictatus pape*, the brief statements about papal authority which Gregory caused to be compiled *ca.* 1075; but like some of the other statements in the compilation, this claim was entirely 'lawless'. Gregory's legal advisers could have found no backing for the claim in their canon law books.[23] The charge that Gregory had 'violated the sanctity of the oath' was to pursue him for the rest of his pontificate.[24] Nevertheless, unprecedented though his measures were, the events of 1076 were to show that it was not the pope but his antagonist who had overestimated his authority. During the spring and summer the German episcopate distanced itself from the court and sought reconciliation with Rome. The Saxon nobility renewed their rebellion under their former leader, Otto of Northeim, and a conspiracy was formed against the king by those south German princes whose support had given him his victory in June 1075.[25] The papal and the princely opposition to Henry IV coalesced in October at the diet of Tribur. Here the papal legates Sigehard, patriarch of Aquileia and Altmann, bishop of Passau joined in the debates of the princes concerning the future of the kingship and subsequently negotiated between the princes and the king, who had arrived at Oppenheim, on the opposite bank of the Rhine. Henry made large concessions, the most important of which are contained in 'the *promissio* of Oppenheim', addressed to the pope. The king promised 'to maintain the obedience in all things due to the apostolic see and to you, Pope Gregory'. Since he was accused of plotting against the apostolic see, he undertook either to prove his innocence or to perform an appropriate penance.[26] This declaration was followed by a manifesto to his subjects in which the king announced that 'it has pleased us, on receiving sounder counsel, to change our mind and, following the custom of our predecessors and ancestors, to maintain in all things the obedience due to that holy see

---

[22] *Ibid.*, p. 34; *Registrum* IV.2, p. 294.

[23] *Dictatus pape* 27: *Registrum* II.55a, p. 208. See H. Fuhrmann, ' "Quod catholicus non habeatur, qui non concordat Romanae ecclesiae". Randnotizen zum Dictatus Papae' in *Festschrift für Helmut Beumann zum 65. Geburtstag* ed. K.-U. Jäschke and R. Wenskus (Sigmaringen, 1977) pp. 263–87.

[24] Wido of Ferrara, *De scismate Hildebrandi* I.7, *MGH Libelli* I, 539–40. Cf. Wenrich of Trier, *Epistola* c. 6, *ibid.*, pp. 293–4; Henry IV, *Epistola* 17, p. 25.

[25] Meyer von Knonau, *Jahrbücher* (n. 11) 2, 671–5, 681–2, 713–15.

[26] *Promissio: MGH Dt. Ma.* 1, 69.

and to the lord Pope Gregory, who is known to be at its head'.[27] The abandonment of the stance of 24 January at the synod of Worms was the sole means by which Henry could prevent his deposition by the princes at Tribur. Henry had seriously misjudged the situation. He had tried to depose the pope without leaving Germany, relying on the Romans to enforce his decision; but the incident of Christmastide 1075, when the pope had been kidnapped by Cencius, had served only to strengthen Gregory's hold on the loyalty of the Romans.[28] The rapid growth in the prestige and influence of the papacy since 1046 meant that it was no longer so easy to depose a pope as in the reign of Henry III. Incidents such as the sudden death of Bishop William of Utrecht (27 April 1076) one month after he had pronounced the excommunication of the pope and the destruction of his cathedral by lightning immediately after the king had celebrated Easter there (27 March) were recognised as confirming the authority of the pope and served to undermine support for the king.[29]

Among the princes at Tribur there were irreconcilable enemies of Henry IV, determined to depose and replace him. Momentarily foiled by the moderate counsels of the papal legates and the timely concessions of the king, they regained the initiative by securing the princes' consent to a declaration that if Henry had not gained absolution by the end of a year from the date of his excommunication, they would no longer recognise him as their king. The princes invited the pope to come in person to Germany to judge between Henry and his accusers at the diet they had arranged for 2 February 1077 in Augsburg.[30] Henry's response to this new development was to send envoys to the pope, requesting that Gregory absolve the king in Rome or at least delay his journey to Germany. 'The many and great debates with the king's envoys' left Gregory committed to the alliance with the princes.[31] Clearly the princes' invitation to judge their dispute with the king had caught the pope's imagination: they had gained his confidence by seeming to share his vision of the vicar of St Peter as arbiter of secular affairs. The only way in which Henry could prevent the conjunction of his enemies and the pope at the diet of Augsburg was to outbid the princes at the same game; which is what he did at Canossa. Henry won absolution from the pope by an

---

[27] Henry IV, *Epistola* 14, p. 21. [28] Meyer von Knonau 2, 588–9.
[29] *Ibid.*, pp. 660–2, 669–70.
[30] See most recently H. Beumann, 'Tribur, Rom und Canossa' in *Investiturstreit und Reichsverfassung* (n. 10) pp. 33–60; E. Hlawitschka, 'Zwischen Tribur und Canossa', *HJb* 94 (1974), 25–45, with references to the earlier literature.
[31] *Epistolae Vagantes* 17 (n. 9), p. 48.

explicit acceptance of the papal role of judge in temporal as well as spiritual matters. Crossing the Alps into northern Italy, Henry intercepted the pope at Canossa, the fortress of Countess Matilda of Tuscany (Gregory's ally and Henry's kinswoman and vassal). Gregory was waiting for the German princes to send escorts to accompany him to Augsburg: the news of Henry's approach caused him to seek refuge at Canossa. The princes of northern Italy (including Adelaide of Turin, countess of Savoy, Henry's mother-in-law) had come to welcome the pope when he crossed the Appenines. They now began to intercede with Gregory for their overlord, the Salian king. Henry's godfather, Abbot Hugh of Cluny, added his prayers to those of Countess Matilda and the other mediators. 'For three days [25–27 January 1077] he remained before the castle gate, without any royal ornament, pitiful in appearance, barefoot and clad in woollen garments, and he continued tearfully to beg for apostolic help and consolation.' Thus Gregory himself described the king's penance. 'Overcome at last by the earnestness of his penitence and by the prayers of all who were present, we released him from the bonds of excommunication and received him into the grace of communion and into the bosom of holy mother Church.'[32]

In restoring Henry to communion, did Gregory also restore him to the kingship? Historians are divided on this question.[33] The simplest answer is that the two protagonists came away from Canossa with different ideas of what had been decided there. A papal letter, written immediately after the absolution, stated that 'the whole business has so far been suspended', evidently referring to the oath which Henry had taken at Canossa: 'I will do justice according to [Gregory's] judgement or make an agreement according to his counsel concerning the complaints which . . . the princes of the kingdom of the Germans have made against me, before the date which the lord Pope Gregory has fixed.'[34] Gregory's intention was that Henry would be restored to the kingship after order and justice had been restored to Germany by a council held by the pope. 'Our coming [to Germany] and your unanimous advice seem extremely necessary', Gregory wrote to the princes on 28 January. For three years he sent

[32] *Registrum* IV.12, p. 313.
[33] A. Fliche, 'Grégoire VII, à Canossa, a-t-il réintégré Henri IV dans sa fonction royale?', *SG* 1 (1947), 373–86; H.-X. Arquillière, 'Grégoire VII, à Canossa, a-t-il réintégré Henri IV dans sa fonction royale?', *SG* 4 (1952), 1–25; G. Miccoli, 'Il valore dell' assoluzione di Canossa' in *idem, Chiesa gregoriana* pp. 203–23; K. F. Morrison, 'Canossa: a revision', *Traditio* 18 (1962), 121–48.
[34] *Registrum* IV.12, 12a, pp. 313, 314–15.

letters and legates to urge the rival parties in Germany to participate in this council. When in March 1080 Gregory was at last convinced that Henry was preventing this council from meeting, he excommunicated Henry again, recalling that in January 1077 he had 'restored to him communion alone, but I did not install him in the kingship . . . And I kept him in this condition so that I might do justice and make peace between him and the bishops and princes beyond the mountains.'[35] Henry IV, however, had left Canossa in the belief that he was fully restored to the kingship, that he had outmanoeuvered the princes and rendered their plans for a diet irrelevant.

The price which Henry IV paid for the tactical success of Canossa was the public acceptance of the unprecedented claims which Gregory VII had made for the papal office. A year ago Henry had boasted of 'the royal power conceded to us by God' and had declared, 'Our Lord Jesus Christ called us to the kingship, but he did not call [Hildebrand] to the priesthood.'[36] His penance at Canossa suggested that the pope could dispose of the kingship as he wished. Nevertheless Henry achieved his immediate purpose: a breach in the alliance of the pope and the German princes. Henry's enemies among the princes had from the beginning of the crisis of 1076 sought nothing less than Henry's deposition and the election of a new king. The alliance with the pope was the means by which the princes hoped to legitimise the deposition: the absolution at Canossa was, therefore, a serious set-back to their plans. Gregory was aware that his action would damage his alliance with the princes. The letter which he sent them immediately after the absolution is a vigorous exercise in self-exculpation: the encounter with the king had occurred because of the princes' failure to send the promised escort; the absolution had been extorted by the pleading of the mediators ('some exclaimed that we were showing not the gravity of apostolic severity but rather the cruelty of tyrannical ferocity').[37] The rebel princes resolved to behave as though the absolution at Canossa had never happened. In March 1077 they met at Forchheim and elected a new king, Rudolf of Rheinfelden, duke of Swabia, who immediately wrote to the pope promising his obedience. The election of the duke of Swabia was an attempt by the princes to repair their alliance with the pope and to ensure his support for their action. The rebels chose Rudolf – rather than a more powerful prince like Otto of Northeim

---

[35] *Ibid.*, VII.14a, p. 484.
[36] Henry IV, *Epistola* 12, p. 16.   [37] *Registrum* IV.12, pp. 312–13.

– because his close association with ecclesiastical reform would recommend him to Gregory VII. Rudolf was the patron of the monastery of St Blasien in the Black Forest.[38] (He was to owe his later reputation of a model Christian prince fighting against the tyranny of Henry IV, to a monk of St Blasien, the chronicler Bernold.)[39] Moreover Gregory had written to Rudolf, 'dearest son of St Peter', in January 1075, exhorting him to assist the campaign against simony and clerical marriage in Germany.[40]

The election of Rudolf as king in March 1077 was confirmed by Gregory's legates, Cardinal deacon Bernard and Abbot Bernard of St Victor in Marseilles, but not by Gregory himself. 'The bishops and princes beyond the mountains . . . elected Duke Rudolf as their king without my advice, as [St Peter and St Paul] are my witnesses', Gregory declared in March 1080, looking back on his relations with the rival parties in Germany in the past three years.[41] During those years he rejected Henry's repeated requests that he excommunicate Rudolf, but he likewise refused the demands of the rebel princes that he recognise Rudolf as king in Henry's place. Gregory clearly wished to retain for as long as possible the role of mediator in the politics of the German kingdom: he continued to favour the idea of a council, over which he would preside, to judge between the rival kings.[42] While the pope adhered to a policy of strict neutrality, his legate, Cardinal deacon Bernard became a partisan of the rebels and excommunicated Henry IV in November 1077. Gregory's refusal to sanction this sentence created serious tension between the pope and the princes. The rebels began to fear that he had been taken in by Henry's 'shameful deceits'. 'Do not appease men of this sort', they urged in the summer of 1078, 'and bring your holy name into ridicule.'[43] On 7 August 1078 Henry defeated the anti-king at Mellrichstadt and it

---

[38] H. Jakobs, *Der Adel in der Klosterreform von St Blasien* (Cologne-Graz, 1968) pp. 40–2, 232–5; *idem*, 'Rudolf von Rheinfelden und die Kirchenreform' in *Investiturstreit und Reichsverfassung* (n. 10) pp. 87–115.

[39] Bernold, *Chronicon* 1080, *MGH SS* 5, 436.

[40] *Registrum* II.45, pp. 182–5.

[41] *Registrum* VII.14a, p. 484. Cf. *Registrum* IX.29, p. 613. On Forchheim see W. Schlesinger, 'Die Wahl Rudolfs von Schwaben zum Gegenkönig 1077 in Forchheim' in *Investiturstreit und Reichsverfassung* (n. 10) pp. 61–85, with references to the earlier literature.

[42] I. S. Robinson, 'Pope Gregory VII, the princes and the *pactum*, 1077–1080', *EHR* 94 (1979), 728–35, 754–6.

[43] Bruno of Merseburg, *Saxonicum bellum* c. 110, *MGH Dt. Ma.* 2, 99–101. See O.-H. Kost, *Das östliche Niedersachsen im Investiturstreit. Studien zu Brunos Buch vom Sachsenkrieg* (Göttingen, 1962) pp. 114–15.

began to seem likely that 'the business of the kingship' might be settled by Henry's annihilation of his rival's power. Gregory might after all be compelled by Henry's military successes to recognise him as king. It was in this context that the Roman synod of November 1078 formulated the most innovatory decree of Gregory's pontificate. 'We decree that no clerk may receive investiture of a bishopric, abbey or church from the hands of emperor or king or any lay person, male or female.'[44] In a recent study Rudolf Schieffer has argued convincingly that this decree of 1078 was the *first* of the series of decrees against lay investiture which dominated the relations of empire and papacy until 1122.[45] The investiture decree of 1078 was the culmination of Gregory VII's campaign against simony in the imperial Church. The campaign which had begun with the disciplinary measures of 1074–5 against suspected simoniacs, now developed into an attack on the monarch's right to appoint prelates – an attempt to undo royal control of the Church. Seen in the context of Gregory's handling of 'the business of the kingship' in autumn 1078, the investiture decree looks like an insurance policy. If (as seemed increasingly likely) the pope had to recognise Henry IV as king, the new decree would protect the imperial Church from any future relapse into simony on his part.

Gregory's refusal to confirm the election of 1077 was consistent with his warning of September 1076 that the rebel princes must not proceed to a new election without papal advice and consent.[46] The princes' disobedience contrasted sharply with the demonstration of obedience by their enemy, Henry IV, at Canossa. Conversely, the recognition which Gregory at last accorded to Rudolf in March 1080 was the result of his own 'obedience' and Henry's 'disobedience'. The pope was now convinced that Henry was responsible for the failure of his favourite scheme – the council to settle 'the business of the kingship' over which the pope himself was to preside. 'Henry . . . not fearing the danger of disobedience, which is the crime of idolatry, by preventing [the holding of] the assembly, has incurred excommunication.'[47] Gregory dealt with the uncooperative German king in the same way in which, earlier in his pontificate, he had dealt

---

[44] *Registrum* VI.5b, p. 403.

[45] R. Schieffer, *Die Entstehung des päpstlichen Investiturverbots für den deutschen König* (Schriften der *MGH* 28, 1981) pp. 153–73. The author refutes the suggestion that an investiture decree had already been issued by the Roman council of Lent 1075: pp. 114–52. But see also the review of Schieffer's work by F. Kempf, *AHP* 20 (1982), 409–15.

[46] *Registrum* IV.3, p. 299.   [47] *Registrum* VII.14a, p. 486.

with uncooperative bishops – by commanding their subjects to disobey them: 'We command you in no way to obey them . . . even as they do not obey the commands of the apostolic see.'[48] According to Gregory VII, the first duty of a king, as of a bishop, was *oboedientia*: the penalty for *inoboedientia* was deposition. Gregory's experience of 'the business of the kingship' in the years 1076–80 had the effect of clarifying his political ideas. His letter of 15 March 1081 to Herman of Metz, a 3,000-word defence of the second excommunication of Henry IV, reveals the new emphasis. Here is found the startling idea that kingship originated in the prompting of the devil, in 'blind greed and intolerable presumption' and the desire to dominate others.[49] The institution of monarchy predated Christianity: only the Church could convert monarchy from a satanic to a Christian institution. The implications of this conversion are underlined in one of the historical examples cited in the letter: the deposition of the Frankish king Childeric III in 751 at the command of Pope Zacharias. Gregory had used this example once before, in his letter of 1076 to Herman of Metz; but now he gave it a new twist: 'Another Roman pontiff deposed a king of the Franks from the kingship, not so much because of his iniquities as *because he was not useful enough* to hold such great power.'[50] A king must be 'useful' (utilis) as well as obedient, the pope being the judge of his usefulness.

Gregory was given a new opportunity of exercising his judgement only seven months after confirming Rudolf as king; for Rudolf died on 15 October 1080 of wounds received in the battle on the Elster.[51] The election of a new king is the subject of Gregory's letter of March 1081 to his most trusted supporters in Germany, Bishop Altmann of Passau and Abbot William of Hirsau. The princes must find 'a suitable king for the honour of holy church', even if their search involved long delays; for 'unless he is obedient, humbly devoted and useful to holy Church – just as a Christian king ought to be and as we hoped of Rudolf – then beyond a doubt holy Church will not only not countenance him but will oppose him'. The successful candidate must take an oath of fealty to St Peter and his vicar:

---

[48] *Epistolae Vagantes* 11 (n. 9), p. 26. See I. S. Robinson, '"Periculosus homo": Pope Gregory VII and episcopal authority', *Viator* 9 (1978), 103–31.

[49] *Registrum* VIII.21, p. 552.

[50] *Ibid.*, p. 554; cf. *Registrum* IV.2, p. 294. See W. Affeldt, 'Königserhebung Pippins und Unlösbarkeit des Eides im Liber de unitate ecclesiae conservanda', *DA* 25 (1969), 313–46.

[51] Meyer von Knonau, *Jahrbücher* (n. 11) 3, 644–52.

From this hour onwards I shall be the vassal in good faith of the blessed apostle Peter and of his vicar who now lives in the flesh, Pope Gregory; and whatever the pope commands me with the words 'in true obedience' I shall faithfully comply with, as a Christian ought . . . I shall, with Christ's help, pay to God and St Peter all due honour and service; and on the day when I shall first come into the pope's presence, I shall become St Peter's knight and his by an act of homage.[52]

This oath, to be administered to the new king by the papal legate, seems to be modelled on the oaths sworn to the pope by his vassals, the Norman princes of southern Italy – except that the oath of 1081 makes more sweeping demands for obedience. This oath and this letter of March 1081 contain the final version of Gregory's political thought. The king must be 'suitable' (*idoneus*) for the duties prescribed by the Church; he must be 'obedient, humbly devoted and useful to holy Church'; he must serve the pope as his feudal lord. In the event, the rebel princes ignored Gregory's prescriptions for king-making: no papal legate was present at the election of their new anti-king Herman of Salm and the new king did not take the Gregorian oath of fealty.[53] Nevertheless Gregory's vision of politics – the king of the Germans as vassal of the pope – would continue (albeit inter-mittently) to influence the curia's view of the relations of empire and papacy throughout the Middle Ages.

Gregory's second excommunication of Henry IV – in total con-trast to that of 1076 – prompted the majority of the German and Italian bishops to side with the king. Councils of bishops in Bamberg (12 April), Mainz (31 May) and Brixen (25 June 1080) acquiesced in Henry's deposition of Gregory; and the council of Brixen elected a new pope, 'Clement III' – Wibert of Parma, archbishop of Ravenna.[54] Wibert was a member of the imperial aristocracy with a distinguished record of service to the imperial court as chancellor for Italy. He was no enemy of reform – there is some evidence that in the early 1070s Gregory VII regarded him as an ally – but he had become the enemy of Gregory when the latter began to attack the indepen-dence of his archbishopric of Ravenna.[55] At the council of Brixen Wibert became the figurehead of Henry IV's attempt to control not only the episcopate of his German and Italian kingdoms but also the

[52] *Registrum* IX.3, pp. 575–6.
[53] Meyer von Knonau 3, 417–18.
[54] J. Vogel, *Gregor VII. und Heinrich IV. nach Canossa* (Berlin–New York, 1983) pp. 198–219.
[55] I. S. Robinson, 'The friendship network of Gregory VII', *History* 63 (1978), 4–5.

Roman church. No longer did Henry intend (as in January 1076) to depose the pope from a distance: he would make his long-deferred expedition to Italy to claim the crown of that kingdom, enthrone his pope in Rome and receive from him the imperial crown. Henry's success in achieving these objectives by 1084 suggested to contemporaries that he had God's approval[56] – a suggestion which Henry's propagandists were not slow to exploit. 'God . . . shows daily that he has ordained [us]: for anyone may see how he has guarded us from the snares of Hildebrand and his supporters.' 'In Rome . . . the Lord performed for us with ten men . . . what our predecessors could only have done with ten thousand.'[57] When Henry entered Italy, Gregory's Norman vassals offered no resistance: Robert Guiscard was absent on campaign against the Byzantine emperor. The most reliable supporter of the reform papacy throughout the reign of Henry IV was Countess Matilda of Tuscany; but she was defeated by Henry's Lombard supporters even before the king entered Italy.[58] After two years of campaigning, in June 1083 Henry had occupied the Leonine city and by the end of March 1084 the pope's hold over Rome was reduced to the single fortress of Sant'Angelo. Gregory's refusal to negotiate with the king had prompted many of the Romans and twelve of his own cardinals to desert him early in 1084. On 24 March 'Clement III' was enthroned in St Peter's and on Easter day (31 March) he officiated at the imperial coronation of Henry IV.[59] Three months after the coronation the emperor had already returned to his German kingdom. He left Rome on 21 May, immediately before the arrival of the army of Robert Guiscard, who (extricating himself momentarily from his Byzantine adventures) came at last to the aid of his lord. Gregory was freed from his virtual imprisonment in the Castel Sant'Angelo; but the devastation caused in Rome by his Norman liberators created such revulsion against the pope among the Romans that it was not safe for him to remain there. He was therefore taken by his liberators into southern Italy.[60]

Gregory spent the last eleven months of his pontificate in Salerno.

[56] E.g. Lanfranc of Canterbury, *Letter* 52 ed. H. Clover and M. Gibson (Oxford, 1979) pp. 164–6.
[57] Henry IV, *Epistolae* 17, 18 (n. 6), pp. 25, 27.
[58] D. B. Zema, 'The houses of Tuscany and Pierleone in the crisis of Rome', *Traditio* 2 (1944), 157–69: here p. 164.
[59] Meyer von Knonau, *Jahrbücher* (n. 11) 3, 474–8, 523–6, 529–35; H. E. J. Cowdrey, *The age of Abbot Desiderius* (Oxford, 1983) pp. 138–70.
[60] Meyer von Knonau 3, 551–7; Cowdrey, *Desiderius* pp. 171–2.

Here in July 1084 he held his last council, in which he renewed his excommunication of the emperor, his antipope and their party.[61] Here he issued his last encyclical 'to all the faithful in Christ who truly love the apostolic see', reminding them that 'the holy Roman church is the mother and mistress of all the churches'. The emperor is not mentioned by name in this letter, which speaks instead of Satan having 'armed his members against us' and having injured the apostolic see more seriously than at any time since the reign of Constantine I.[62] On his death-bed on 25 May 1085 Gregory embraced the role of the martyr persecuted for righteousness' sake: 'I have loved righteousness and hated iniquity – therefore I die in exile.'[63] In one version of this death-bed scene 'a venerable bishop' responds to these last words with a Gregorian statement of papal authority: 'You cannot die in exile, lord, because you have received the nations as your inheritance and the ends of the earth as your possession, as the representative of Christ and his apostles.'[64] It was an empty claim; for at the time of Gregory's death the authority of the antipope Wibert of Ravenna was recognised not only in the imperial territories but in Hungary and Croatia and perhaps also in England and southern Italy.[65] The cause of 'Clement III' inevitably profited from the delay in electing a successor to Gregory VII and from the reluctance of the eventual successor, Victor III, to assume office. Victor III – Abbot Desiderius of Monte Cassino – ruled for only seven months after finally being pressed by his allies to accept the papal office. His attitude to the conflict with the emperor which he had inherited is hard to determine. He had negotiated with the excommunicate Henry IV in April 1082 and perhaps obtained from him a privilege for Monte Cassino. Five years later Victor's principal opponent inside the Gregorian party, Archbishop Hugh of Lyons, claimed that Desiderius-Victor had incurred 'Pope Gregory's excommunication for a whole year and more' because of this contact

[61] J. Vogel, 'Gregors VII. Abzug aus Rom und sein letztes Pontifikatsjahr in Salerno' in *Tradition als historische Kraft. Festschrift für Karl Hauck* ed. N. Kamp and J. Wollasch (Berlin–New York, 1982) pp. 341–9.

[62] *Epistolae Vagantes* 54 (n. 9) pp. 128–34.

[63] Hannoversche Briefsammlung 35 in *Briefsammlungen der Zeit Heinrichs IV.*, MGH *Briefe der deutschen Kaiserzeit* 5, 75–6. See P. E. Hübinger, *Die letzten Worte Papst Gregors VII.* (Opladen, 1973).

[64] Paul of Bernried, *Vita Gregorii VII* c. 110, ed. J. M. Watterich, *Pontificum Romanorum Vitae* I (Leipzig, 1862), 540.

[65] P. F. Kehr, 'Zur Geschichte Wiberts von Ravenna (Clemens III.)', *SB der preussischen Akademie der Wissenschaften, 1921* (Berlin, 1921) pp. 356–8.

with the emperor.[66] There is no other evidence of this excommunication; but the negotiations of 1082 are an important clue to Victor's attitude towards Henry IV. Those negotiations had taken place at the urgent insistence of the Norman prince and papal vassal Jordan of Capua; and it was Jordan who in March 1087, at a synod in Capua, overcame Victor's reluctance to act as pope. The desire of Jordan of Capua for reconciliation with the emperor is the clue to the conduct of his neighbour, the abbot of Monte Cassino. In 1082 Jordan had evidently opened negotiations against the will of his feudal lord, the pope: in 1087, now that he had become the most effective of the vassals of the papacy, Jordan ensured the election of a conciliatory pope.[67] That Victor's attitude towards Henry IV was conciliatory is suggested by the proceedings of his synod of Benevento (August 1087). Here the Gregorian decrees against simony and lay investiture were restated and likewise the excommunication of the 'heresiarch' Wibert of Ravenna; but there was no mention of excommunicating the emperor.[68]

If Victor III desired reconciliation with Henry IV, his successor, Urban II (elected on 12 March 1088 after a six-months' vacancy) immediately announced a return to the attitude of Gregory VII. The new pope had direct experience of the conflict in Germany; for in 1084–5, as Cardinal bishop Odo of Ostia, he had had the thankless task of papal legate, responsible for rallying the shattered papal party in the German kingdom.[69] Urban declared himself to be a Gregorian in the letter announcing his election to the south German bishops and princes: he desired 'to follow entirely in [Gregory's] footsteps'.[70] However, the early months of Urban's pontificate showed that his veneration for Gregory VII and his adherence to his reform programme did not entail a policy of irreconcilable opposition to the anti-Gregorian party. Unlike his predecessor, Urban confirmed the excommunication of both the antipope and the emperor at his first synod, in Melfi (September 1089); but he accompanied this sentence with offers of reconciliation to the clergy and laity of their party. Urban's first notable convert was Archbishop Anselm III, whom the emperor had invested with Milan in 1086. The Milanese church had

---

[66] Hugh of Flavigny, *Chronicon* II, *MGH SS* 8, 466–8. See T. Leccisotti, 'L'incontro di Desiderio di Montecassino col re Enrico IV ad Albano', *SG* I (1947), 307–19; Cowdrey, *Desiderius* (n. 59) pp. 156–65, 245–6.

[67] Meyer von Knonau, *Jahrbücher* (n. 11) 3, 441–6; 4, 180. But see Cowdrey, *Desiderius* p. 192.

[68] *Chronica monasterii Casinensis* III.72, *MGH SS* 34, 453–5.

[69] Becker, *Urban II.* 1, 62–77.　　　　　[70] Urban II, *JL* 5348: *MPL* 151, 284A.

become disillusioned with the emperor and his antipope; for 'Clement III' used the papal office to elevate his archbishopric of Ravenna at the expense of its old rival, Milan. Urban relaxed the strict Gregorian line on investiture and brought into his obedience in 1088 the proud metropolitan see of Lombardy which for the past generation had been the bitter enemy of the reform papacy.[71] Milan, crucial to the emperor because she dominated communications between his German and Italian kingdoms, now became the key to the diplomacy of Urban II. In 1089 that diplomacy succeeded in welding his north Italian and south German allies into a dynastic alliance which seriously threatened the integrity of Henry IV's empire. Urban negotiated a marriage between his most reliable supporter in Italy, Matilda of Tuscany, and Welf V, son of the most powerful of the pro-papal princes in Germany, Duke Welf IV of Bavaria.[72] Urban's experience as legate in Germany in 1084–5 had suggested that the south German princely families were the papacy's most valuable supporters in the kingdom. His permanent legate and vicar in Germany was a member of such a family: Gebhard of Zähringen, whom he had consecrated as bishop of Constance in 1084 – the brother of Welf IV's ally Berthold II of Zähringen. With the help of this legate Urban was able to achieve one of the political objectives of Gregory VII and to enlist the two south German princes as vassals of St Peter. In 1093 'Gebhard, bishop of Constance and legate of the apostolic see, received the homage of duke Welf of Bavaria as a vassal, as he had previously done with his own brother Duke Berthold of Swabia'.[73] The practical significance of this vassalage of St Peter is not clear; but it must at least have entailed a close alliance with the papacy and the defence of papal interests in Germany.[74]

The value to the papacy of these alliances with the south German princes, the countess of Tuscany and the archbishop of Milan was demonstrated in the dangerous crisis which overtook the emperor in 1093. The first five years of Urban's pontificate had been a period of uninterrupted success for Henry IV. He had come to terms with the

---

[71] H. E. J. Cowdrey, 'The succession of the archbishops of Milan in the time of Pope Urban II', *EHR* 83 (1968), 285–94.

[72] Meyer von Knonau, *Jahrbücher* (n. 11) 4, 273–4.

[73] Bernold, *Chronicon* 1093 (n. 39) p. 457. See A. Becker, 'Urban II. und die deutsche Kirche' in *Investiturstreit und Reichsverfassung* (n. 10) pp. 245, 267–8. Cf. Gregory VII, *Registrum* IX.3, p. 574.

[74] H. Maurer, 'Ein päpstliches Patrimonium auf der Baar', *Zeitschrift für die Geschichte des Oberrheins* 118 (1970), 43–56.

Saxon rebels and had strengthened the hold of his dynasty on the German kingship by having his son Conrad crowned in Aachen in 1087. Re-entering Italy in the spring of 1090, he defeated the vassals of Matilda of Tuscany and captured Mantua, while the imperial forces in Rome became for the first time masters of the entire city. The antipope Clement III was able to return to Rome from Ravenna, which had been his headquarters for most of his reign; while Urban took refuge with his Norman vassals.[75] The victories of 1090–2 suggested that the emperor would deal with Urban II as he had dealt with Gregory VII in 1081–4. The rapid reversal in Henry's fortunes was the result of the appearance of an anti-king – a rival more dangerous than Rudolf of Swabia had been, because he was the heir to the throne. 'The emperor's son . . . persuaded by Matilda (for whom may not female guile subvert and deceive?) joined his father's enemies, had himself crowned, usurped the kingship, profaned law, confused order, fought against nature . . . '[76] The true motive for the rebellion of the twenty-year-old Conrad is not clear; although a clue is provided in the chronicle of Ekkehard of Aura. Here Conrad is described as 'thoroughly catholic and most obedient to the apostolic see; more given to religion than to government and arms, but possessing more than enough strength and boldness, he preferred to spend his leisure time in reading than in games'.[77] According to Ekkehard, therefore, Conrad rebelled against his father not as the opportunistic ally of the papal party, but as the pious champion of the Church. Urban II's ally, Archbishop Anselm of Milan, crowned him king of Italy and the kingdom of Italy rallied to him and to the papal allies, Matilda and the Welfs. The emperor was left without allies in Italy and, since his enemies controlled the Alpine passes, he was cut off from the German kingdom.[78]

The years 1093–6 saw the reform papacy at the height of its political influence in Italy. The submission of the Lombard church to the apostolic see – which Gregory VII, using the innovatory method of alliance with the Pataria, had failed to achieve – was attained by means of a more traditional device, the reforming council. The council of Piacenza (March 1095), better attended than any previous reforming council, saw the culmination of the papal policy of recon-

[75] Meyer von Knonau 4, 333–8.
[76] *Vita Heinrici VI imperatoris* c. 7, *MGH SS rer. Germ.* (1899) p. 26.
[77] Ekkehard, *Chronica* 1 (Ausgewählte Quellen zur deutschen Geschichte des Mittel-alters 15: Darmstadt, 1972) p. 128.
[78] Meyer von Knonau 4, 393–6, 416–17.

ciling former Henrician churchmen to the reform papacy, while confirming Gregorian legislation.[79] The triumph of Piacenza and the
reconciliation of Lombardy were possible because of the political
ascendancy of Conrad and his allies. Urban's alliance with the anti-
king was confirmed by a meeting one month after the council of
Piacenza. 'King Conrad . . . met Pope Urban as he came to Cremona
and performed the office of groom on 10 April.' The anti-king performed the *stratoris officium* which, according to the forged 'Donation
of Constantine', the first Christian emperor had performed for Pope
Sylvester I (314–35), holding the bridle of his horse. Conrad's performance of this ceremony demonstrated that he recognised Urban's
claim to be pope. At a second meeting on 15 April Conrad swore
fidelitas to the pope 'concerning life and limbs and the Roman papacy'
– presumably the conventional oath of security sworn by a king
coming into the papal presence.[80] Neither the oath nor the ceremony
of the *strator* transformed Conrad into a papal vassal on the lines
required by Gregory VII of the anti-king in 1081.[81] The importance
of this agreement between Urban and Conrad lies in the demand that
the anti-king obey 'the apostolic decrees' and specifically that against
investiture. The heir to the Salian empire accepted the Gregorian
reform programme in return for a papal promise of 'counsel and help
. . . to obtain the crown of the empire'. This papal 'counsel and help'
took the immediate form of negotiating a marriage between Conrad
and the daughter of the papal vassal Count Roger I of Sicily.[82]
Urban's diplomacy seemed likely to create a family alliance of
Norman prince and Salian king of Italy which would encircle Rome
and the papal patrimony. There is, however, no indication that the
papal curia in 1095 felt any of the anxiety that was to wrack it a century later when a similar encirclement was achieved. The Norman-
Salian marriage seemed the surest means of consolidating the
alliances on which papal security depended. Under the protection of
these alliances, Urban continued the Gregorian campaign against
investiture. A decree of his council in Clermont (November 1095)
elaborated and extended the original investiture decree of 1078: the
prohibition on investiture was accompanied by a prohibition on the

---

[79] *MGH Constitutiones* I, 560–3.
[80] Bernold, *Chronicon* 1080 (n. 39), p. 463; *Urbani II. et Conradi regis conventus* in
MGH Constitutiones I, 564. See Becker, *Urban II.* I, 133–6.
[81] Gregory VII, *Registrum* IX.3, pp. 575–6. See above p. 411.
[82] W. Holtzmann, 'Maximilla regina, soror Rogerii regis', *DA* 19 (1963), 149–67.

performance of homage by bishops and abbots, so that the Church would 'be free of every worldly power'.[83]

The journey of Urban II through Lombardy, into southern France and back again to Rome (September 1094–December 1096) resembled the progress of a victorious warlord. Of particular significance was the number of disputed episcopal elections referred to the pope during this journey: two while en route from Piacenza, five during and after the council of Clermont – an index of the restored authority of the reform papacy as striking as the large attendance at the councils.[84] A further sign that the curia had recovered from the disasters of the 1080s was the ease with which Urban's successor was elected. On 13 August 1099, only fifteen days after Urban's death, Rainer, cardinal priest of S. Clemente was elected. His choice of the name Paschal II was perhaps intended to recall the success of Pope Paschal I in securing the confirmation of his rights from Emperor Louis I in 817, the new pope's name suggesting a determination to assert the rights of the reform papacy against Henry IV.[85] In the first synod which he was able to hold in Rome, in March 1102, Paschal identified himself with the attitude of his predecessors in confirming the excommunication of the emperor.

Because he has not ceased to rend the tunic of Christ, that is, the Church . . . he was excommunicated and condemned for his disobedience, firstly by Pope Gregory of blessed memory, then by the most holy Urban, my predecessor; and we also in our last synod, by the judgement of the whole Church, consigned him to perpetual anathema.

Moreover 'the schism of our time' caused by Henry's disobedience 'is counted among the principal heresies'.[86] In this Lateran council of 1102 the papal line had hardened: the emperor and his supporters, by promoting schism, were guilty not simply of disobedience but also of heresy. By 1102 the foremost schismatic, Gregory VII's and Urban II's rival, the antipope Wibert of Ravenna was dead. Never-

---

[83] R. Somerville, *The Councils of Urban II* I: *Decreta Claromontensia* (Annuarium Historiae Conciliorum, supplementum 1: Amsterdam, 1972) p. 90.

[84] R. Crozet, 'Le voyage d'Urbain II et ses négociations avec le clergé de France (1095–1096)', *Revue historique* 179 (1937), 272–310.

[85] So Servatius, *Paschalis II.* pp. 36–7. Alternatively, Rainer could have been thinking of the influential treatise against simony attributed in many manuscripts to Paschal I: in which case, in assuming the name Paschal II he was declaring his determination to extirpate simony. See *Epistola Widonis, MGH Libelli* 1, 1–7; J. Gilchrist, 'Die Epistola Widonis oder Pseudo-Paschalis', *DA* 37 (1981), 576–604.

[86] Ekkehard, *Chronica* I (n. 77), p. 180.

theless, after his death in September 1100 the Wibertine party among the Roman nobility elected two further antipopes, perhaps with the support of the emperor: Theoderic of Albano (1100) and Albert of Silva Candida (1102). Again in 1105 the emperor's allies in Rome elected a short-lived antipope, Maginulf, archpriest of S. Angelo ('Sylvester IV').[87] The imperial party in the city ensured that Rome remained as insecure a residence for Paschal II as it had been for the earlier reforming popes.

At no point in his pontificate did Paschal II enjoy the security and influence afforded to Urban II by his system of alliances. The coalition of princes which had once made King Conrad formidable, had already begun to crumble in 1095. The refusal of Matilda of Tuscany to yield control of her lands to her husband, Welf V, caused the breakdown both of their marriage and of the alliance of the houses of Welf and Canossa. Welf IV abandoned the anti-king and was reconciled with the emperor, who was thereby enabled at last to return to his German kingdom (spring 1097). An imperial diet in Mainz (May 1098) deposed Conrad (who died forgotten in 1101) and replaced him with his younger brother, Henry V.[88] The emperor's pacification of the German kingdom was followed by an attempt at reconciliation with the reform papacy. 'In 1102 Emperor Henry held a conference with the princes and announced that he would set out for Rome and summon a general council there around 1 February, in order that his own cause and that of the pope could be discussed according to canon law and catholic unity be confirmed between the royal and the priestly power, which had been divided for so many years.'[89] The emperor realised that there could be no lasting peace in the empire as long as he was at odds with the papal curia. There was still a papal party in south Germany, led by the papal legate, Bishop Gebhard of Constance, which commanded considerable support among the nobility. Any prince who rebelled against Henry IV in the name of 'the freedom of the Church' was likely to be aided by this party: hence the emperor's attempts to conciliate Paschal II in the last six years of his life. In January 1103 Henry made the last of the gestures of penitence which characterised his policy towards the reform papacy: he declared himself ready 'to yield up the government to his son, King Henry, and visit the Lord's Sepulchre' in

---

[87] Servatius, *Paschalis II.* pp. 69–72; R. Hüls, *Kardinäle, Klerus und Kirchen Roms 1049–1130* (Tübingen, 1977) pp. 92–3, 136–7, 269–70.

[88] Meyer von Knonau, *Jahrbücher* (n. 11) 4, 447–8, 477–9; 5, 26–7.

[89] Ekkehard, *Chronica* I, p. 178.

Jerusalem.[90] The emperor looked to the enterprise which had so redounded to the prestige of Urban II – the crusade – as a means of reconciliation with the papacy; but his gesture met with no response. Henry's attempts to negotiate with the papal curia were vain because they were based on his retention of investiture. In the opinion of Paschal II, investiture and its 'ancestor', Simon Magus, were the principal dangers to the freedom of the Church.[91] The failure of these negotiations was easily exploited in the rebellion of Henry V which swept the emperor from power in 1105–6. Henry V 'declared that henceforth he would have nothing to do with [his father] because he was excommunicate; and so he furthered his own cause under the pretence that it was the cause of God'.[92]

During the rebellion of 1105–6 both the young king and the emperor attempted to gain the support of the pope. Henry IV offered peace and friendship 'just as our grandfather and father and our other predecessors had, preserving the honour of the apostolic dignity . . . just as our predecessors preserved it in the case of your predecessors and we preserved it' in the case of Nicholas II and Alexander II. The emperor's letter of 1105 to the pope attacked the memory of Gregory VII and Urban II, who 'seemed to persecute us out of hatred and anger rather than zeal for righteousness'.[93] Henry IV offered a peace settlement based on the situation before 1073: after thirty years of struggle he still regarded the Gregorian papacy as an aberration. Henry V, however, 'condemned the heresy' of schism and 'promised due obedience' to the pope. The synod of Nordhausen, which (on the advice of the legate, Gebhard of Constance) he summoned in May 1105, condemned 'simoniacal heresy' and clerical marriage.[94] The sudden death of Henry IV (7 August 1106) left as the legitimate ruler of the empire a champion of important aspects of the Gregorian reform programme. Not all, however: for Henry V had not renounced his father's claim to investiture. The new king sent envoys to Paschal's synod of Guastalla (October 1106), which reconciled those imperial churchmen ordained in simony (but not themselves guilty of simony) – so continuing the work of Urban II's councils.[95] The business of Henry V's envoys at Guastalla, how-

---

[90] *Ibid.*, p. 182.
[91] Paschal II, *JL* 6050: *MPL* 163, 174D–175D. See Servatius, *Paschalis II*, pp. 153–8.
[92] *Vita Heinrici IV* (n. 76) c. 9, p. 30.
[93] Henry IV, *Epistola* 34 (n. 6), pp. 43–4.
[94] Ekkehard, *Chronica* I (n. 77), p. 190. See Servatius, *Paschalis II*. pp. 186–9.
[95] Ekkehard, *Chronica* III, pp. 290–2.

ever, was to demand 'that the right of the kingship (*ius regni*) be granted to him'. In return for this *ius* the king promised to submit 'as to a father'.[96] A full statement of this *ius* and of the papal reaction to it is first found in the negotiations between the king's representatives and the pope at Châlons-sur-Marne in May 1107. The leader of the German delegation, Archbishop Bruno of Trier, defined the royal rights in episcopal election. The king approved the candidate before the election and after the elect had been consecrated 'freely and without simony', he was brought back to the king 'for the *regalia*, so that he may be invested with ring and staff and perform fealty and homage: and no wonder, for otherwise he must not take possession of the cities and castles, margraviates, tolls and whatever belongs to the imperial dignity'. The attitude of Henry V proved, therefore, to be that of his father: the fact that the imperial bishops enjoyed such extensive political power compelled the monarch to control episcopal appointments by means of investiture. Paschal II's response at Châlons-sur-Marne was couched in the language of Gregory VII and Urban II. The demands of the German king would reduce the Church to slavery: investiture with staff and ring was a usurpation of the rights of God himself; homage – bringing a priest's hands into contact with 'the hands of a layman, made bloody by [the use of] the sword' – was a derogation of the priesthood.[97] A few days later, at the synod of Troyes (23 May) Paschal renewed his earlier decrees against investiture: 'Whoever henceforward receives from a layman investiture of a bishopric or an ecclesiastical dignity must be deposed; and likewise he who consecrates the candidate.'[98]

Of the many issues dividing Henry IV from the reform papacy, that of lay investiture survived to dominate the relations of Henry V with the papacy in the years 1106–22. The label 'Investiture Contest', too narrow to be an accurate description of the conflict of empire and papacy in the years 1076–1106, is much more appropriate when applied to Henry V's attempts to extort recognition of his *ius* from the papacy. It was precisely at the time that Henry V was beginning this campaign that the papacy reached a settlement of the issue of lay investiture with the French and English kings. In the English kingdom the papal prohibition had been upheld by Archbishop Anselm of Canterbury (1093–1109) against the determination of King Henry

---

[96] So Donizo, *Vita Mathildis* II.17, *MGH SS* 12, 400. See Servatius, *Paschalis II.* pp. 101–2.

[97] Suger of St Denis, *Vita Ludovici grossi regis* c. 10 ed. H. Waquet (Paris, 1929) p. 58.

[98] Council of Troyes c. 1, *MGH Constitutiones* 1, 566.

I (1100–35) to retain his predecessors' strict control over the English church. The issue of investiture had never arisen in Anselm's bitter quarrels with Henry I's elder brother, King William II (1087–1100), a violent opponent of ecclesiastical reform, because Anselm remained unacquainted with the relevant papal decrees until he was driven into exile and took refuge in the reforming circles of Lyons and Rome (1097–1100). In Urban II's Roman synod of 1099 Anselm had heard the pope confirm the decrees prohibiting lay investiture and the performance of homage by bishops and abbots. Invited to return to Canterbury in 1100 by Henry I, Anselm had refused investiture and homage to the new king. He subsequently refused also to consecrate clerks whom Henry had invested with bishoprics. Anselm's championship of the papal decrees resulted in his second exile in 1103. A compromise eventually proved possible because of the political needs of the king and the pope. Henry I could not afford conflict with the Church and possible excommunication because he was planning the conquest of the duchy of his brother, Robert II of Normandy. Paschal II was embroiled in the German investiture dispute and could not risk losing the friendship and the financial aid of the English king. After a conciliatory meeting between the king and Archbishop Anselm in Laigle (July 1105) Paschal was ready to provide a solution. He wrote to Anselm on 23 March 1106, permitting him to consecrate bishops appointed 'without investiture, even though they have done homage to the king, until by the grace of almighty God the king's heart is softened by the showers of your preaching to give this [homage] up'. The king's heart was never softened and this compromise – the royal renunciation of investiture and the papal concession of homage – was confirmed in a royal council in London (August 1107) and became the definitive solution of the investiture issue in the Anglo-Norman lands. The controversial ceremony of investiture was abandoned but the king retained control of ecclesiastical appointments: the election of bishops and abbots continued to take place in the king's chapel and the elect must do homage to the king in order to receive the temporal possessions and rights of their churches.[99]

A similar settlement seems to have been negotiated in the Capetian

---

[99] Paschal II, *JL* 6073: *MPL* 163, 186C–187D = Anselm of Canterbury, *Opera omnia* ed. F. S. Schmitt 5 (Edinburgh, 1951), 340–2. See R. W. Southern, *Saint Anselm and his biographer* (Cambridge, 1963) pp. 150–80; N. F. Cantor, *Church, kingship and lay investiture in England 1089–1135* (Princeton, 1958) pp. 63–87, 109–30, 146–67, 197–201, 253–73.

kingdom in 1106–7; but the sources offer no precise details. In France there had been no sustained investiture dispute like that between Anselm and Henry I in England: the conflict of King Philip I (1060–1108) with Urban II and Paschal II was mainly the result of his matrimonial adventures. However, the case of the disputed episcopal election at Beauvais in 1100 had occasioned a clash between Philip and Paschal II on the issue of royal control over ecclesiastical appointments. That this single dispute at Beauvais did not develop into a prolonged 'investiture contest' is generally attributed by historians to the influence of the ideas of the canonist Ivo of Chartres. Ivo, bishop of Chartres (1090–1115) sought a solution to the dispute about lay investiture by emphasising the distinction between the spiritual and the temporal aspects of the office of bishop. He was not the first author to point out that eleventh-century bishops had acquired a double role, as secular administrators and royal servants as well as pastors; but Ivo's was the most learned and influential exposition of this idea. In a widely disseminated letter of 1097 to the intransigent Gregorian, Archbishop Hugh of Lyons (the papal legate in France), Ivo argued that a large part of the temporal possessions and rights enjoyed by bishops were *regalia*: that is, property and jurisdictional rights conferred by the king in respect of their governmental duties. Bishops therefore undoubtedly had feudal obligations to the king and it was this fact that was symbolised in the ceremony of investiture: 'kings do not claim to give anything spiritual' when investing bishops.[100] Ivo's argument did not diminish the papal hostility towards investiture; but his clarification of the royal position may well have contributed to the settlement of the problem. Between 30 April and 3 May 1107 Paschal II was the guest of Philip I and his son King Louis VI in the abbey of St Denis. An eyewitness, Abbot Suger of St Denis, reported (nearly forty years later) that the pope 'conversed familiarly with [the kings] concerning the condition of the Church' but he recorded no details of this conversation. His

---

[100] Ivo of Chartres, *Epistola ad Hugonem archiepiscopum Lugdunensem*, MGH *Libelli* 2, 644–5. See A. Becker, *Studien zum Investiturproblem in Frankreich. Papsttum, Königtum und Episkopat im Zeitalter der gregorianischen Kirchenreform (1049–1119)* (Schriften der Universität des Saarlandes: Saarbrücken, 1955) pp. 99–104, 143–51; H. Hoffmann, 'Ivo von Chartres und die Lösung des Investiturproblems', *DA* 15 (1959), 393–400. On the stature and influence of Ivo see R. Sprandel, *Ivo von Chartres und seine Stellung in der Kirchengeschichte* (Stuttgart, 1962). For the contemporary debate on the investiture issue see Z. N. Brooke, 'Lay investiture and its relation to the conflict of empire and papacy', *Proceedings of the British Academy* 25 (1939), 217–47.

account suggests an informal agreement rather than a concordat. The surviving accounts of episcopal elections in France at the beginning of the twelfth century are equally uninformative. The Capetian king had renounced investiture but it is not clear whether he had also given up demanding homage from bishops elect or whether the papal settlement with the French kingdom exactly resembled that with England.[101]

Immediately after his meeting with the Capetian kings at St Denis, Paschal II was escorted by the kings and many French prelates to Châlons-sur-Marne to negotiate with the representatives of the German king. This unsuccessful meeting was followed by twelve years of equally fruitless negotiations with Henry V. The reason for this failure to reach an agreement with the German ruler along the lines of the French and English settlements was the refusal of Henry V to contemplate the renunciation of investiture. His stance provoked a similar intransigence on the part of the papal curia. 'This quarrel will be settled not here but at Rome with swords,' the king's envoys allegedly declared, 'grinding their teeth with German impetuosity' after the meeting at Châlons-sur-Marne.[102] For three years Henry V was prevented from carrying out this threat by unrest in Germany and wars with his eastern neighbours. However, early in 1110 he announced to the princes that he wished to 'obtain the imperial blessing from the supreme pontiff . . . bring the broad provinces of Italy into the community of the German kingdom . . . and show his readiness to perform whatever is demanded by the defence of the Church, according to the will of the apostolic father'.[103] The response of Paschal II was to renew his investiture decree in the Lateran synod of March 1110 and to obtain promises of support against Henry both from his Norman vassals and from the Roman nobility. When, however, in the autumn of 1110 Henry V entered Lombardy with an army allegedly 30,000 strong, none of the promised help appeared, except for a token force of 300 men commanded by the Norman prince Robert of Capua, which rapidly withdrew from the path of the oncoming German army. Matilda of Tuscany, hitherto the staunchest ally of the reform papacy, in 1110 (and for the remaining five years of her life) adopted a neutral attitude

---

[101] Suger, *Vita Ludovici* c. 10 (n. 97), p. 54. See A. Fliche, 'Y a-t-il eu en France et en Angleterre une querelle des investitures?', *Revue Bénédictine* 46 (1934), 283–95; Becker, *Investiturproblem* (n. 100) pp. 111–23.

[102] Suger, *Vita* c. 10, p. 60.   [103] Ekkehard, *Chronica* III (n. 77), p. 298.

towards the plans of her distant kinsman, the German king.[104] Paschal was therefore left defenceless when Henry V reached Rome in February 1111.

It is by no means certain, however, that the agreement reached between the papal and royal envoys in Rome on 4 February was extorted from the defenceless pope. For the terms of the settlement accepted on 4 February were those first suggested by Paschal; and the subsequent failure of that settlement was the result – so the evidence suggests – of deliberate sabotage by Henry V.[105] The agreement reached on 4 February in the church of S. Maria in Turri and confirmed five days later at Sutri was that

the king will renounce all investiture of all churches . . . on the day of his coronation . . . He will set the churches free, together with the offerings and possessions which manifestly do not belong to the royal power (*regnum*) . . . The lord pope will command the bishops present on the day of the [imperial] coronation to give up to the king the *regalia* which belonged to the royal power in the time of Charles, Louis, Henry and his other predecessors.[106]

This agreement was to be announced during the imperial coronation ceremony on 12 February; but in the event the ceremony was broken off in disorder and the agreement was never ratified. Instead Henry V took prisoner the pope and sixteen cardinals. Two conflicting explanations of this interruption survive. A letter issued in justification of Henry V's conduct claims that the interruption was caused by a general objection to the papal renunciation of the *regalia*: 'All resisted [Paschal] – namely the bishops and abbots, both on his side and on ours, and all the sons of the Church – and denounced his decree as evident heresy.' However, the more detailed account preserved in the register of Paschal II states that the coronation was broken off because the king, on the advice of 'his bishops and princes', refused to ratify the agreement of S. Maria in Turri.[107] This is also the version of events found in the majority of the narrative sources, those authors most favourable to Paschal alleging that Henry had never any intention of fulfilling the agreement. 'A wolf in sheep's clothing, he kissed the feet of the lord pope . . . then took

---

[104] Servatius, *Paschalis II.* pp. 102, 216–18.

[105] Ekkehard, *Chronica* III, p. 302; *Disputatio vel defensio Paschalis papae, MGH Libelli* 2, 660. See U.-R. Blumenthal, '*Patrimonia* and *regalia* in 1111', in *Law, church and society. Essays in honor of Stephan Kuttner* ed. K. Pennington and R. Somerville (Pennsylvania, 1977) pp. 12–16.

[106] Agreement of S. Maria in Turri: *MGH Constitutiones* 1, 137–8.

[107] Henry V, Encyclical: *ibid.*, p. 151; Paschal II, *Relatio: ibid.*, p. 148. See Blumenthal, '*Patrimonia*' pp. 13–15.

captive the pope, our head . . . and violently dragged him from the basilica.'[108]

The aspect of these events of February 1111 which has most preoccupied historians is the papal renunciation of the *regalia* – 'duchies, marches, counties, mints, tolls, markets, advowries belonging to the kingdom, the rights of estate administrators and law courts which manifestly belong to the kingdom, together with their property, knight-service and castles belonging to the kingdom'.[109] Historians in the 1960s unanimously agreed that Paschal II's privilege of February 1111 sought to impose poverty on the Church: in return for recovering her liberty, the Church would renounce riches. This was Paschal's personal solution to the problem of investiture (anticipating the theme of renouncing the world which would dominate the writings of Bernard of Clairvaux); but it was universally rejected because it was too revolutionary for his contemporaries.[110] The research of the 1970s, however, overturned this interpretation. M. J. Wilks' study of Paschal's renunciation of the *regalia* concludes: 'there was nothing novel or revolutionary involved: and no connection with theories of apostolic poverty or monastic withdrawal from the world'. Paschal's privilege of February 1111 would not have impoverished the Church, since his renunciation did not include the possessions and rights with which benefactors had from early times endowed the Church – the possessions and rights which the eleventh century called *ecclesiastica*.[111] Paschal's privilege specifies that the churches must retain 'the offerings and hereditary possessions which manifestly did not belong to the kingdom'.[112] Moreover the renunciation did not apply

---

[108] *Disputatio* (n. 105) p. 660. Cf. *Chronica monasterii Casinensis* IV.36 (n. 68), p. 503. See Meyer von Knonau, *Jahrbücher* (n. 11) 6, 369–90.

[109] Agreement of S. Maria in Turri (n. 106) pp. 138–9; Paschal II, privilege of 12 February 1111: *MGH Constitutiones* I, 141.

[110] P. Zerbi, 'Pasquale II et l'ideale della povertà della chiesa', *Annuario dell' Università Cattolica del S. Cuore 1964–5* (Milan, 1965) pp. 207–29; G. Miccoli, *Chiesa gregoriana* (n. 10) p. 277; B. Tierney, *The crisis of church and state 1050–1300* (Englewood Cliffs, N.J., 1964) pp. 87–8. This interpretation was also accepted by the Marxist historian, E. Werner, *Zwischen Canossa und Worms. Staat und Kirche 1077–1122* (3rd edition: Berlin, 1978) p. 169. See G. M. Cantarella, 'Le vicende di Pasquale II (1099–1118) nella recente storiografia', *Rivista di storia della chiesa in Italia* 35 (1981), 486–504.

[111] M. J. Wilks, '*Ecclesiastica* and *regalia*: papal investiture policy from the Council of Guastalla to the First Lateran Council, 1106–23' in *Councils and assemblies* (Studies in Church History 7: Cambridge, 1971) pp. 84, 81.

[112] Paschal II, privilege of 12 February 1111 (n. 109) p. 141.

to the Patrimony of St Peter, the lands which the papacy had allegedly received from Emperor Constantine I. U.-R. Blumenthal has pointed out that a recurrent theme of the negotiations of 1111 was the promise of Henry V to 'restore and grant the patrimonies and possessions of St Peter, as was done by Charles, Louis, Henry and the other emperors'.[113] Her interpretation of the negotiations of February 1111 is that Paschal drove a hard bargain. Henry V was to receive the *regalia* in return for renouncing investiture *and* regaining control of the Patrimony of St Peter for the pope, for which the reform papacy had been striving since the mid-eleventh century.[114] This interpretation throws into doubt the claim in Henry V's propaganda that Paschal's own supporters rejected the papal initiative of 4 February 'as evident heresy': the fulfilment of two of the major objectives of the Gregorian papacy would surely not have been opposed by members of the papal party. The true reason for the failure to reach an agreement on 12 February has been uncovered by Johannes Fried's study of the concept of *regalia*. Negotiations broke down because the two parties interpreted the term *regalia* in opposite ways. Henry V and his advisers did not recognise the distinction in Paschal's privilege between the property and rights 'which manifestly belong to the kingdom' and 'the offerings and hereditary possessions which manifestly did not belong to the kingdom': these *ecclesiastica* seemed to the Germans to be part of the *regalia*.[115] Having accepted the papal solution presented at S. Maria in Turri on 4 February, Henry V went back on the agreement when the papal proposals were spelled out in full in the privilege of 12 February.

Paschal II's motive for renouncing the *regalia* is stated clearly in his privilege of 12 February.

In [Henry V's] kingdom bishops and abbots are so preoccupied with secular responsibilities that they are compelled to attend the [royal] court continually and to perform military service . . . Ministers of the altar have become ministers of the court . . . Hence the intolerable custom has developed in the Church that bishops elect do not receive consecration until they have first been invested by the hand of the king. For this reason the evil practice of simoniacal heresy has sometimes so prevailed that bishoprics have been seized without any election taking place . . . Therefore, we command that the *regalia* be given up to the kingdom . . . For, once released from

---

[113] Agreement of S. Maria in Turri (n. 106) p. 137.
[114] Blumenthal, '*Patrimonia*' (n. 105) pp. 9–12.
[115] J. Fried, 'Der Regalienbegriff im 11. und 12. Jahrhundert', *DA* 29 (1973), 478–9, 505–6.

secular responsibilities, bishops should occupy themselves with the care of their people and should no longer be absent from their churches.[116]

The purpose, therefore, was not the imposition of poverty on the Church but the fulfilment of the campaign of the reform papacy for the eradication of simony and the freeing of the Church from lay control. The privilege is careful to emphasise that Paschal was 'following the footsteps' of his 'predecessors Gregory VII and Urban II, popes of happy memory'. Nevertheless Paschal's initiative marked a significant departure from the attitude of Gregory VII. Both popes were agreed on the need to abolish lay investiture; but Gregory VII seems to have envisaged bishops and abbots elected without investiture but continuing to exercise their secular functions. Paschal realised that it was impossible for kings to relinquish control of the appointment of churchmen holding *regalia*. The credit for convincing Paschal of this fact is generally given by historians to the *Treatise on the investiture of bishops* composed *ca.* 1109 at the request of Henry V (perhaps by the monk Sigebert of Gembloux). The treatise is a justification of the royal right of investiture which was perhaps brought to Rome by Henry's envoys in 1109 and which seems to have influenced the wording of the papal privilege of February 1111.[117] The treatise argues that 'it is fitting and reasonable that the king . . . should invest and enthrone the bishop . . . to whom he entrusts his city, since he has transferred his own rights into [the bishop's] house'.[118] Paschal's response to this argument, in his privilege of 12 February, was that the king should recover his rights: there would then be no further need for him to invest bishops.

Henry V neither accepted the papal definition of *regalia* nor believed in the ability of the pope to implement his privilege.[119] Having taken prisoner the pope and many of his entourage, he tried to impose a simpler solution: papal acceptance of the royal right of investiture. After two months of captivity Paschal was compelled by 'the calamities of the captives . . . the desolation of the Roman church . . . the very grave danger of schism' to submit to Henry's demands.[120] Paschal obtained his release by crowning Henry

---

[116] Paschal II, privilege of 12 February 1111 (n. 109) p. 141.
[117] Meyer von Knonau, *Jahrbücher* (n. 11) 6, 105–11; Servatius, *Paschalis II.* pp. 228–30; Fried, 'Regalienbegriff' (n. 115) pp. 467–72; J. Krimm-Beumann, 'Der Traktat *De Investitura episcoporum* von 1109', *DA* 33 (1977), 37–83.
[118] *Tractatus de investitura episcoporum, MGH Libelli* 2, 502; Krimm-Beumann p. 79.
[119] Henry V, Encyclical (n. 107) p. 150.
[120] Papal account of the events of February–April 1111: *MGH Constitutiones* 1, 149.

emperor (13 April) and agreeing to his demands in the treaty of Ponte Mammolo (11 April): 'When a bishop or abbot has been freely elected without simony and with the king's consent, the lord king shall invest him with the ring and the staff.'[121] After receiving the imperial crown and the papal privilege granting him investiture, Henry returned to Germany, leaving the pope to face the indignation of the reform party. Paschal II's betrayal of the stand of Gregory VII and Urban II against lay investiture was denounced in Rome by the cardinals who had escaped capture on 12 February – notably by John of Tusculum, Leo of Ostia and Bruno of Segni – and by influential churchmen north of the Alps, most prominently Archbishop Guido of Vienne (the papal legate for eastern France and Burgundy), Archbishops Josceran of Lyons and Adalbert of Mainz and the papal legate Cardinal bishop Cuno of Palestrina.[122] The hostility of these critics gave rise to the rumour that 'a synod is to be held in Rome, in which they say that Pope Paschal is to be deposed and another elected'.[123] When that synod met in March 1112, however, Paschal appeased his critics by revoking his 'evil privilege' (*pravilegium*) of April 1111 and making a profession of his faith, including his adherence to 'the decrees of my lord Pope Gregory and of Pope Urban of blessed memory'.[124]

For the remaining six years of his pontificate Paschal resisted the demands of his supporters for the excommunication of Henry V. The pope evidently considered himself bound by the oath which he had taken at Ponte Mammolo never to excommunicate Henry.[125] Papal legates, however, ignored the papal attitude. Archbishop Guido of Vienne excommunicated the emperor at a synod in Vienne (16 September 1112) and 'turning to the German kingdom, stirred

---

[121] Treaty of Ponte Mammolo: *ibid.*, p. 142.

[122] R. Hiestand, 'Legat, Kaiser und Basileus: Bischof Kuno von Praeneste und die Krise des Papsttums von 1111/1112' in *Aus Reichsgeschichte und Nordischer Geschichte. Karl Jordan zum 65. Geburtstag* ed. H. Fuhrmann, H.-E. Mayer and K. Wriedt (Kieler Historische Studien 16: Stuttgart, 1972) pp. 141–52; S. Chodorow, 'Ideology and canon law in the crisis of 1111' in *Proceedings of the Fourth International Congress of Medieval Canon Law* (Monumenta Iuris Canonici series C, subsidia 5: Vatican City, 1976) pp. 55–80: U.-R. Blumenthal, 'Opposition to Pope Paschal II: some comments on the Lateran Council of 1112', *Annuarium Historiae Conciliorum* 10 (1978), 82–98; M. Stroll, 'New perspectives on the struggle between Guy of Vienne and Henry V', *AHP* 18 (1980), 97–115.

[123] Bishop Azo of Acqui to Henry V: *Codex Udalrici* 161 ed. P. Jaffé, *Bibliotheca rerum germanicarum* 5 (Berlin, 1869), 288.

[124] See above p. 129.

[125] Treaty of Ponte Mammolo (n. 121) pp. 142–3.

up the princes . . . against him'.[126] In the years 1112–15 Henry V faced political problems like those which had overtaken his father – rebellion in Saxony, a conspiracy of princes, civil war. The pope made no attempt to profit by his weakness to obtain a favourable settlement of the question of investiture; but papal legates sought to exploit the situation. Both Cuno of Palestrina and Theoderic, cardinal priest of S. Grisogono excommunicated the emperor (1115) and tried to construct an alliance between the German rebels and the papacy; but Paschal showed no readiness to revert to the political methods of Gregory VII. Challenged by Cuno of Palestrina in the Lateran synod of 1116, Paschal would not repudiate his legates' actions; but nor would he pronounce the excommunication in the synod.[127] Negotiations between pope and emperor were resumed in 1116 on the initiative of Henry V, employing Abbot Pontius of Cluny as a mediator. When Henry made his second visit to Rome (March–May 1117) to pursue these negotiations, he found that the pope 'had withdrawn, for fear of the Roman people'.[128] Paschal had indeed lost control of Rome during the faction-fighting of the summer and autumn of 1116; but his withdrawal to Benevento early in 1117 was motivated by fear not of the Roman people but of a repetition of the events of February–April 1111.[129] No doubt Henry V's anxiety to negotiate with the pope was prompted by political difficulties in Germany similar to those which beset Henry IV in his last years; but this weakness did not make the emperor more conciliatory towards the pope. At the end of his pontificate Paschal was faced with the same demand which the emperor had forced him to concede in the *pravilegium* of 1111 and which his own supporters had compelled him to repudiate in the synods of 1112 and 1116: 'that it is our right to grant our *regalia* to any one by means of staff and ring'.[130] Henry V refused to relinquish the claims of Henry IV; while Paschal, although personally inclined to compromise, was constantly under pressure from the curia to imitate the rigour of Gregory VII. Paschal's official biography gives him an orthodox Gregorian death-

---

[126] Suger, *Vita Ludovici* (n. 97) c. 10, p. 68. See Servatius, *Paschalis II*. pp. 320–4.
[127] Ekkehard, *Chronica* III (n. 77) pp. 322–4. See Hiestand, 'Legat' (n. 122) pp. 141–52; Servatius, *Paschalis II*. pp. 325–9.
[128] Henry V: *Codex Udalrici* 178 (n. 123) pp. 314–15.
[129] P. Partner, *The lands of St Peter* (London, 1972) pp. 152–3; but see Servatius, *Paschalis II*. pp. 79–81 and n. 161, 332.
[130] Henry V (n. 128) p. 315.

bed scene (21 January 1118): summoning the clergy 'he charged them to follow him in constancy to the faith, in adherence to the truth . . . in cursing German iniquity'.[131]

During the one-year pontificate of Gelasius II (24 January 1118–29 January 1119) the relations of empire and papacy deteriorated even further. The new pope, John of Gaeta, cardinal deacon of S. Maria in Cosmedin and chancellor in the two previous pontificates (1089–1118), was as much inclined to compromise as Paschal II. He had indeed been Paschal's principal adviser, 'the support of his old age in all things', who had shared his captivity in 1111 and drafted the papal part of the treaty of Ponte Mammolo.[132] In the opinion of the staunch Gregorian, Archbishop Conrad of Salzburg, 'none of them was more worthless than John' because of his willingness to conciliate the emperor.[133] The worsening of papal-imperial relations occurred because Henry V 'cruelly revived the schism'.[134] Henry entered Rome without warning on the night of 2 March 1118, hoping to take the pope elect by surprise; but Gelasius was able to escape to Gaeta. Henry declared that 'if [the pope] observed the treaty which Pope Paschal had made with the emperor', he would guarantee the pope's security; 'but otherwise he would enthrone another pope in the Roman church'.[135] The emperor was still bent on obtaining papal approval of the *pravilegium* of April 1111. On Gelasius' refusal to negotiate on these terms – he declared instead his intention of referring the dispute between empire and papacy to a council in Lombardy in October[136] – Henry carried out his threat. On 8 March the emperor created as his antipope 'Gregory VIII' a prelate from Spain, Archbishop Maurice of Braga. Maurice had come to Rome in 1117 on the business of his church and when Paschal II had fled at the approach of Henry V, Maurice had been the only churchman prepared to collaborate with the emperor. He had crowned the emperor in St Peter's on Easter day and been excommunicated for his presumption by Paschal. Now he began an

---

[131] *Vita Paschalis II: Liber pontificalis* 2, 305.

[132] *Vita Gelasii II: ibid.*, pp. 311–12. See J. Ramackers, 'Das Alter des Kaiserkrönungsordo Cencius II.', *QFIAB* 37 (1957), 45–6; Servatius, *Paschalis II.* pp. 59, 246, 337.

[133] *Vita Theogeri abbatis S. Georgii et episcopi Mettensis, MGH SS* 12, 470.

[134] Ekkehard, *Chronica* IV (n. 77) p. 338.

[135] *Chronica monasterii Casinensis* (n. 68) IV.64, p. 526. See Meyer von Knonau, *Jahrbücher* (n. 11), 7, 60–4.

[136] Gelasius II, *JL* 6635: *MPL* 163, 489AD.

inglorious career as imperial antipope (1118–21), recognised only in the rebellious areas of Rome and the papal patrimony.[137]

The creation of the antipope at last provoked the papal excommunication which had been withheld since 1111: Gelasius excommunicated 'the king together with his idol' on Palm Sunday (7 April) at Capua.[138] The task of rallying the German church to the pope was entrusted to the energetic legate Cuno of Palestrina (who had already excommunicated the emperor on his own initiative in 1115). Cuno, with the help of Archbishop Adalbert of Mainz, was effective enough to provoke Henry's hasty return to Germany. Gelasius was now free to return to Rome; but after two months the violence of the rival noble clans forced him to 'flee from Sodom, from Egypt, from the new Babylon' to France (September 1118).[139] Three months after his arrival in France he was brought, mortally ill, to Cluny. The chronicle of Falco of Benevento contains an account of Gelasius' settlement of the papal succession on his deathbed – a story which is partially corroborated elsewhere. 'Feeling plainly that he was seized by a serious attack of sickness, he commanded that the bishop of Palestrina should be summoned and he strove to impose on him the highest honour of the Roman see.' Cuno of Palestrina, however, declining the honour, advised that the current danger of the Church demanded 'the prudent mind' and 'secular virtues' of Archbishop Guido of Vienne; and Gelasius accordingly agreed with the cardinals and bishops to send for Guido.[140] Having abandoned the conciliatory measures of 1111–18 in favour of a policy of Gregorian rigour, Gelasius II became dependent for its successful implementation on those men – Cuno and Guido – who had been his sternest critics when he was the principal adviser of Paschal II's last years. The reversal of the conciliatory policy of 1111–18 seemed complete when, on 2 February 1119 in Cluny, Guido of Vienne was elected to succeed Gelasius, as Calixtus II.

In the pontificate of Calixtus II the stalemate of the past decade was

---

[137] C. Erdmann, 'Mauritius Burdinus (Gregor VIII.)', *QFIAB* 19 (1927), 205–61; P. David, *Etudes historiques sur la Galice et le Portugal du VIe au XIIe siècle* (Coimbra, 1947) pp. 441–501.

[138] Gelasius II, *JL* 6642 (to Cuno of Palestrina): (n. 136) 493B.

[139] *Vita Gelasii II* (n. 132) pp. 316–17. See Meyer von Knonau, *Jahrbücher* (n. 11), 7, 73–85; O. Schumann, *Die päpstlichen Legaten zur Zeit Heinrichs IV. und Heinrichs V.* (Marburg, 1912) pp. 102–4.

[140] Falco of Benevento, *Chronicon* 1119 (see above p. 64). Cf. Calixtus II, *JL* 6682: *MPL* 163, 1093AB (= Ekkehard, *Chronica* IV, p. 340). See Meyer von Knonau 7, 105–6; Hüls, *Kardinäle* (n. 87) p. 114.

overcome: the antipope 'Gregory VIII' was forced to submit by the pope's Norman vassals and the emperor at last consented to renounce investiture. The narrative sources emphasise Calixtus' preeminent qualifications for his office. He was 'born of royal stock, the brother of dukes, the kinsman of kings and emperors': son of the count of Burgundy and kinsman of Henry V, of the queen of France, the kings of Castile and England, of the marquess of Montferrat and the counts of Savoy and Flanders.[141] Moreover he was a staunch Gregorian who had led the opposition to the *pravilegium* of April 1111 and he had excommunicated the emperor in his legatine council in Vienne (1112). Henry V had therefore declared Guido to be a destroyer of peace and concord and clearly regarded him as a dangerous enemy.[142] Nevertheless it was this pope of unimpeachable Gregorian credentials who settled the investiture question with the emperor in September 1122 by means of a compromise – and a compromise which aroused the anger of intransigent Gregorians at the First Lateran Council (March 1123).[143] How was the uncompromising Guido transformed into the conciliatory Calixtus II? A recent study has suggested that Guido's uncompromising stance in 1112 was the result less of conviction than of opportunism, dictated by the need to safeguard the interests of his family in Burgundy against the emperor. Guido's opposition to lay investiture and his excommunication of the emperor were simply ways of weakening Henry's hold over Burgundy. After Guido became pope, Burgundy ceased to be his primary concern and it became easier for him to reach a compromise on investiture.[144] It is important, however, not to overlook Calixtus' own explanation of the compromise of 1122 to his Gregorian critics in the First Lateran Council (as recorded by the theologian Gerhoch of Reichersberg). The pope 'was able to appease [his critics] by explaining that in order to restore peace it was necessary not to approve but to tolerate' the compromise.[145] In the opinion of Calixtus, the agreement finally reached with the emperor, the concordat of Worms (23 September 1122), was imperfect, a temporary solution concluded only 'to restore peace'. Paschal II had spoken in the same way of the agreement on investiture reached with the king of England in 1107, which

---

[141] Orderic Vitalis, *Historia ecclesiastica* XII. 9, 24, ed. M. Chibnall 6 (Oxford, 1978) pp. 211, 283. See Meyer von Knonau 7, 109 n. 15, 117.

[142] Meyer von Knonau 6, 247–8; 7, 108.

[143] Gerhoch of Reichersberg, *Libellus de ordine donorum Sancti Spiritus*, MGH Libelli 3, 280.

[144] Stroll, 'Guy of Vienne' (n. 122) pp. 97–115.   [145] Gerhoch, *De ordine* p. 280.

was to be a model for the concordat of 1122.[146] The temporary character of the agreement of September 1122 is underlined by the form of the privilege which Calixtus conferred on the emperor. It is addressed to his 'beloved son Henry, emperor augustus of the Romans', with no reference to his successors: the privilege would cease to be valid on the death of Henry V.[147] The papal curia continued to insist that the privilege 'was given for the sake of peace to [Henry] alone and not to his successors'.[148] If Calixtus regarded the concordat of 1122 as a temporary expedient, to be renegotiated on the death of Henry V, there is no reason to suppose that he ever abandoned the strict Gregorian line which he had followed in 1112. It was not a change in the attitude of Guido-Calixtus towards lay investiture, but a sudden opportunity of peace which prompted the negotiations of 1119–22.

The opportunity was created by the weakness of Henry V in Germany. The emperor faced rebellion in Saxony and war on the Hungarian border; but his most serious problem was the hostility of the German church. A series of episcopal elections in 1118–19 (Metz, Münster, Merseburg, Hildesheim, Osnabrück, Liège and Magdeburg) demonstrated the progress of the papal reform programme in Germany: churchmen demanded canonical elections and rejected investiture by the emperor.[149] 'Henry was compelled by the envoys of the priests and princes of the whole kingdom to agree to the holding of a diet at Tribur, where . . . he promised to be present [in a synod] for the purpose of reconciliation with the universal Church.' The emperor tacitly abandoned his antipope and recognised Calixtus II as the lawful pope.[150] In autumn 1119 the papal envoys Abbot Pontius of Cluny and William of Champeaux, bishop of Châlons met the emperor in Strassburg and found him concili-

---

[146] Paschal II, *JL* 6073: (n. 99).

[147] Concordat of Worms: *MGH Constitutiones* I, 161. See A. Hofmeister, 'Das Wormser Konkordat. Zum Streit um seine Bedeutung' in *Forschungen und Versuche zur Geschichte des Mittelalters und der Neuzeit. Festschrift Dietrich Schäfer* (Jena, 1915) pp. 64–148; R. L. Benson, *The Bishop-Elect. A study in medieval ecclesiastical office* (Princeton, 1968) pp. 229–30; Wilks, '*Ecclesiastica*' (n. 111) pp. 77–9; P. Classen, 'Das Wormser Konkordat in der deutschen Verfassungsgeschichte' in *Investiturstreit und Reichsverfassung* (n. 10) pp. 413–22.

[148] Otto of Freising, *Chronica sive historia de duobus civitatibus* VII.16, *MGH SS rer. Germ.* (1912) p. 331.

[149] Meyer von Knonau, *Jahrbücher* (n. 11) 7, 79–80, 88–9; 86–7, 98, 99–102.

[150] Ekkehard, *Chronica* IV (n. 77) pp. 340–2. See H. Büttner, 'Erzbischof Adalbert von Mainz, die Kurie und das Reich in den Jahren 1118 bis 1122' in *Investiturstreit und Reichsverfassung* (n. 10) p. 401.

atory and ready to meet the pope during the forthcoming council of Rheims. The learned bishop of Châlons, who played a major part in the negotiations of 1119, could speak authoritatively about the compromise which the papacy had already reached with the French king concerning investitures. 'If you desire to have a true peace', Bishop William told the emperor,

you ought to give up entirely the investiture of bishoprics and abbacies. That you may be sure that you would suffer no loss of royal authority by this [renunciation], you should know that when I was elected bishop in the kingdom of the French, I received nothing from the king's hand either before or after consecration. Nevertheless I serve [him] faithfully . . . in all things which belonged in ancient times to the state but which were given by Christian kings to the Church of God, just as the bishops in your kingdom serve you . . .

'Indeed!' cried Henry V, 'then so be it. I require no more.'[151] On the basis of these negotiations in Strassburg the papal legates Cardinal bishop Lambert of Ostia and Gregory, cardinal deacon of S. Angelo drew up a draft treaty with Henry and arranged for a meeting between pope and emperor on 24 October 1119. In the interval between the second and third session of the council of Rheims (22–26 October) Calixtus travelled to Mouzon (in the Ardennes) to keep this appointment; but pope and emperor never met. Papal representatives, including Lambert of Ostia, John of Crema (cardinal priest of S. Grisogono) and the bishop of Châlons, brought to Henry a version of the draft treaty 'diligently revised' by the pope's advisers. After the emperor had twice postponed the ratification of the treaty (24–25 October), the papal party broke off negotiations and returned to Rheims. 'Having taken great pains to reach this man, I find no desire for peace in him', said Calixtus.[152] In its last session (30 October) the council of Rheims prohibited lay investiture and excommunicated Henry V.[153]

Any account of the negotiations of October 1119 must be based largely on the *Narrative of the council of Rheims* written by Hesso, master of the cathedral school of Strassburg. It is a tendentious narrative with two main preoccupations: to emphasise the importance of the bishop of Châlons (who may have commissioned the work and supplied Hesso with information) and to attribute to the emperor the

[151] Hesso, *Relatio de concilio Remensi, MGH Libelli* 3, 22.
[152] *Ibid.*, p. 26. See T. Schieffer, 'Nochmals die Verhandlungen von Mouzon (1119)' in *Festschrift Edmund E. Stengel* (Münster-Cologne, 1952) pp. 324–41.
[153] Hesso, *Relatio* p. 28. See above p. 133.

blame for the failure of the negotiations.[154] Because of the character of the principal source, it is difficult to explain the breakdown of negotiations at Mouzon. Historians have concentrated on the role of William of Champeaux, bishop of Châlons and have suggested that his account of the renunciation of investiture in the French kingdom may have misled the emperor. Henry was evidently satisfied with the papal proposals as William presented them in Strassburg; but once the proposals had been 'diligently revised' at Mouzon, the emperor realised that he had been under a misapprehension. The problem may have arisen from differences in French and German feudal practice.[155] Alternatively William may have misled the emperor by an omission in his account of his own episcopal election: for in Hesso's account he says nothing of doing homage to the French king for the *regalia* of his bishopric, which was perhaps the practice in France, as in England, after the agreement reached with Paschal II.[156] The question of the unsuccessful negotiations at Mouzon is best approached by considering the related question of the reasons for the success of the negotiations in Worms three years later. In 1122, as in 1119, the negotiations were forced on the emperor by the rebellious German princes. The price of ending the civil war in Germany was the acceptance of the demands of the princes, as formulated in the diet of Würzburg (September–October 1121):

The emperor shall obey the apostolic see. In the case of the complaint which the Church has against him, a settlement shall be made between him and the pope with the advice and the help of the princes and there is to be a true and lasting peace, so that the emperor may have what belongs to him and to the kingship and the churches and every one retain his possessions in peace and quiet.[157]

Calixtus responded with an affectionate letter to 'his kinsman' the emperor (19 February 1122), assuring him that 'the Church seeks to claim none of your rights: . . . let the Church obtain what is Christ's,

---

[154] This second preoccupation is also found in the account of Orderic Vitalis, *Historia ecclesiastica* XII.21 (n. 141), p. 266, with its echoes of the events of 1111. See Hoffmann, 'Ivo von Chartres' (n. 100) pp. 425–9.

[155] H. Mitteis, *Lehnrecht und Staatsgewalt. Untersuchungen zur mittelalterlichen Verfassungsgeschichte* (Weimar, 1933) p. 229.

[156] Hoffmann, 'Ivo von Chartres' pp. 425–6.

[157] *Annalista Saxo* 1121, *MGH SS* 6, 757; *MGH Constitutiones* I, 158. See Meyer von Knonau, *Jahrbücher* (n. 11) 7, 166–75.

let the emperor have what is his'.[158] Seven months later three papal legates – Lambert of Ostia, Gregory of S. Angelo and Saxo, cardinal priest of S. Stefano – negotiated a settlement with the emperor at Worms. No detailed account of these negotiations survives: the chronicler Ekkehard of Aura simply remarks that 'there was a struggle for peace and harmony for a week or more'.[159] The settlement finally adopted on 23 September 1122 resembled that already reached in England in 1107. The emperor renounced 'all investiture with ring and staff' and conceded that 'there is to be canonical election and free consecration in all the churches which are in my kingdom and empire'. In return the pope conceded that elections of German bishops and abbots should take place 'in your presence, without simony or any violence'. In addition the monarch could confer the *regalia* on the elect with a touch of his sceptre and could receive the homage of the elect.[160]

Most historians agree that the concordat of Worms 'put into effect the canonical theories of Ivo of Chartres'.[161] It is obviously no coincidence that Ivo's letter of 1097 is found in numerous German manuscripts concerned with the problem of investiture and notably in the most important of the manuscripts containing the *Treatise on the investiture of bishops* commissioned by the emperor himself.[162] However, the dissemination of the ideas of Ivo of Chartres in Germany does not wholly explain the success of the negotiations at Worms after the failure three years before. The most significant difference between the concordat of Worms and the draft treaty of 1119 lies in the concessions made by the pope. In 1122 Calixtus conceded that episcopal and abbatial elections should take place 'in [the emperor's] presence' – that is, at the imperial court – and that 'the elect shall receive the *regalia* from [the emperor] by the sceptre and shall perform what he owes to [the emperor] by right in respect of

---

[158] Calixtus II, *JL* 6950: (n. 140) 1232B–1233B.

[159] Ekkehard, *Chronica* IV (n. 77), p. 356. See Schumann, *Legaten* (n. 139) pp. 116–17.

[160] Concordat of Worms (n. 147) pp. 159–61. See Classen, 'Das Wormser Konkordat' (n. 147) pp. 422–31.

[161] A. Fliche, *La réforme grégorienne et la réconquête chrétienne (1057–1123)* (Histoire de l'Eglise 8: Paris, 1950) p. 388. See also E. Bernheim, *Zur Geschichte des Wormser Konkordats* (Göttingen, 1878) p. 12; Hoffmann, 'Ivo von Chartres' (n. 100) pp. 393–440; Classen, 'Das Wormser Konkordat' pp. 420–1. For a different view see Cantor, *Church, kingship and lay investiture in England 1089–1135* (n. 99) pp. 202–16.

[162] Bamberg, Staatsbibliothek Can. 9. See Krimm-Beumann, 'Traktat' (n. 117) pp. 44 n. 32, 49–56 and above p. 428.

[the *regalia*]' – presumably including homage.[163] In 1119 the papal privilege had offered no more than 'true peace' to the emperor and his supporters.[164] In September 1122 the emperor obtained better terms only after long hesitation on the part of the legates, who feared 'the censure of the Church'.[165] What Henry V obtained at Worms were the 'customs' current in the English church after Henry I made peace with Paschal II in 1107 – customs with which the emperor, as son-in-law of the English king, must have been acquainted.[166] Calixtus had declined to make similar concessions to the emperor in 1119 and it was evidently this refusal which caused the breakdown of negotiations at Mouzon. However, it was not the case that Calixtus was attempting to deny to the emperor concessions which he was prepared to permit to other rulers: 'election in the king's chapel' (*electio in capella regis*) and homage were as objectionable to the papacy in England as in Germany. There is no evidence that Paschal II approved these customs in 1107: he regarded them as evils which must be tolerated 'until the king's heart is softened . . . to give [them] up'.[167] Hence the refusal of the papal legates in 1119 to concede the English customs to Henry V and the failure of William of Champeaux to describe in full the similar French customs in his interview with the emperor. In 1122 the legates were forced to admit that there could be no peace unless these customs were expressly conceded to Henry V. Calixtus II, unlike Paschal II in 1107, was obliged to spell them out in a privilege – albeit a privilege which was intended to last only for the lifetime of Henry V and which avoided the offensive word 'homage'.

The emperor's renunciation of investiture was celebrated in the papal curia as a victory. A mosaic was set up in the Lateran palace, which depicted Henry V giving his privilege, the text clearly legible, to Calixtus II. There was no sign of the papal privilege for the emperor.[168] Likewise the biography of Calixtus by Cardinal Boso

---

[163] Concordat of Worms (n. 147) p. 161. See Hofmeister, 'Konkordat' (n. 147) pp. 87–94; Classen, 'Das Wormser Konkordat' (n. 147) pp. 422–31; Benson, *Bishop-Elect* (n. 147) pp. 230–2.

[164] Hesso, *Relatio* (n. 151) p. 24; *MGH Constitutiones* 1, 158.

[165] Adalbert of Mainz to Calixtus II, ed. Jaffé (n. 123) p. 519.

[166] K. J. Leyser, 'England and the Empire in the early twelfth century', *TRHS* 5th ser., 10 (1960), 61–83.

[167] Paschal II, *JL* 6073 (n. 99). See Leyser pp. 72–3.

[168] *Vita Calixti II: Liber pontificalis* 2, 322. See G. B. Ladner, *Die Papstbildnisse des Mittelalters* 1 (Vatican City, 1941), 199 and plate XIX; Classen, 'Das Wormser Konkordat' (n. 147) p. 416.

quotes the imperial privilege and ignores that of the pope.[169] With the greatest reluctance Henry V had surrendered the practice of investiture in a permanent grant 'to God and the holy apostles of God, Peter and Paul, and the holy catholic Church'. Nevertheless to critics of the concordat at the First Lateran Council it seemed that Calixtus had surrendered important principles for which Gregory VII and Urban II had fought. The imperial privilege promised 'canonical election and free consecration'; but the papal privilege allowed the elections of German prelates to take place in the emperor's presence, gave him a decisive role in settling disputed elections and permitted the emperor to grant the *regalia* before the elect had been consecrated. Clearly neither the papal nor the imperial party could claim the concordat of Worms as a total victory. As Calixtus explained at the Lateran Council, it was a compromise which the curia was forced to tolerate 'in order to restore peace' – a truce which was possible only because it made no attempt to tackle the causes of the fifty-year conflict of papacy and empire.

The concordat of 1122 'reconciled the point of view of the Roman church and that of the German monarch' and (wrote Augustin Fliche) 'inaugurated an essentially peaceful period which was to last for thirty years', until the accession of Frederick I Barbarossa.[170] This thirty-year peace between empire and papacy began with the pontificates of two popes who, as cardinals, had been responsible for negotiating the concordat of Worms: Honorius II (1124–30), the former Lambert of Ostia, and Innocent II (1130–43), the former Gregory of S. Angelo.[171] During their pontificates the papal curia showed no inclination to disturb the peace; but it was not unwilling to exploit the ambiguities in the concordat of 1122. The terse phrases of the papal privilege – no doubt deliberately – left much unsaid. For example, in the case of German prelates it was conceded that the elect should receive the *regalia* from the emperor before receiving consecration. Did this mean that by withholding the *regalia* from a candidate of whom he disapproved, the emperor could exercise a veto; or did the 'free consecration' promised in the imperial privilege mean that the metropolitan could consecrate the elect even if the emperor

---

[169] Boso, *Vita Calixti II: Liber pontificalis* 2, 378.

[170] A. Fliche, R. Foreville and J. Rousset de Pina, *Du premier Concile du Latran a l'avènement d'Innocent III (1123–1198)* (Histoire de l'Eglise 9: Paris, 1948) p. 43.

[171] The third negotiator of the concordat, Cardinal Saxo of S. Stefano was almost elected pope instead of Lambert in 1124, according to *Vita Honorii II: Liber pontificalis* 2, 327. See above p. 66.

had refused to confer the *regalia* on him? During the reign of Henry V's successor, Lothar III (1125–37) on at least two occasions the elect was consecrated without having first received the *regalia*: in March 1132 Pope Innocent II consecrated the archbishop of Trier and the following August the staunch Gregorian, Archbishop Conrad of Salzburg, consecrated the bishop of Regensburg.[172] Given the opportunity, the pope and the papal party in Germany were prepared to ignore the custom conceded to the emperor in 1122.

Their opportunism, however, did not permanently erode the imperial claim to the customs granted in the concordat of Worms. Bishop Otto of Freising, chronicler and kinsman of the Staufen kings, described in 1156 the rights which the concordat gave the crown in the case of a disputed episcopal election. 'It belongs to the monarch's authority to appoint the bishop whom he wishes, on the advice of his magnates; and no [bishop] elect is to be consecrated before he receives the *regalia* from his hand by the sceptre.'[173] Unlike Lothar III, his Staufen successor, Conrad III (1138–52) tried to insist on the observance of all the customs conceded in 1122, including that of the homage of prelates, which Lothar had waived.[174] Conrad's successor, Frederick I (1152–90) achieved a formidable lordship over the German church, based on the feudal obligations of prelates towards the emperor. Frederick sought to impose the German customs on the bishops of his Italian kingdom – a significant extension of the imperial rights in the concordat.[175] In the late twelfth century it was the imperial, rather than the papal interpretation of the concordat of Worms which found general acceptance in the German church. When in 1186 Pope Urban III imitated the conduct of Innocent II half a century before and consecrated Folmar of Trier before he had received the *regalia* from the emperor, the pope was rebuked by eminent German prelates. 'The empire seems to have suffered dismemberment and extreme diminution of its rights,' wrote Archbishop Wichman of Magdeburg, 'especially because the most careful record of former times never mentions that this was done by any of your predecessors to any of [the emperor's] predecessors . . . '[176] Thirty years of Frederick Barbarossa's firm govern-

---

[172] Hauck, *Kirchengeschichte Deutschlands* 4, 149–52.

[173] Otto of Freising, *Gesta Friderici I imperatoris* II.6, *MGH SS rer. Germ.* (1884) pp. 85–6.

[174] Classen, 'Das Wormser Konkordat' (n. 147) p. 433.

[175] *Ibid.*, pp. 436–7, 442–3; Benson, *Bishop-Elect* (n. 147) pp. 284–91.

[176] *MGH Constitutiones* 1, 445. Cf. Archbishop Adalbert of Mainz and his suffragans to the cardinals: *ibid.*, p. 447.

ment had obliterated the memory of Innocent II's attempt to reinterpret the concordat. In the last year of Innocent II's pontificate Gerhoch of Reichersberg had been encouraged by the pope's attitude to hope for the revision of the concordat in the sense desired by the Gregorians at the First Lateran Council. 'The concession which was extended [in 1122] . . . has now partly been cancelled out, since – thanks be to God – the elections of bishops take place outside the king's presence. We hope that in the near future that evil [of homage] may be removed from our midst . . . '[177] These hopes were frustrated by Frederick I's vigilant control of episcopal elections, which with few exceptions produced a German episcopate ready to accept the emperor's interpretation of his rights over the Church.[178]

THE THIRTY-YEAR PEACE, 1122–1152

The thirty-year peace following the concordat of Worms began with a triumph for the Gregorian party in Germany. On the death of the childless Henry V (23 May 1125), Archbishop Adalbert of Mainz (the pope's standing legate) secured the election by the princes, not of Henry V's heir, his nephew Frederick II of Staufen, duke of Swabia, but of the candidate most closely associated with the papal party. This was Lothar of Supplinburg, duke of Saxony, the enemy of the Salian emperors since his rebellion, as a youth, against Henry IV in 1088 and the ally of Adalbert of Mainz since 1112.[179] The election of Lothar on 30 August 1125 in Mainz resembled in many ways that of the anti-king Rudolf of Rheinfelden at Forchheim in 1077, which may indeed have been in the minds of Adalbert and his supporters. Lothar's election demonstrated the principle first stated at Forchheim, 'that the royal power [might be ceded] to no one by heredity'.[180] In 1125, as in 1077, two papal legates *a latere* were present – Gerard, cardinal priest of S. Croce in Gerusalemme (the future Pope Lucius II) and Romanus, cardinal deacon of S. Maria in Porticu – who played a decisive part in securing a unanimous decision in favour of Lothar III.[181] Again as in 1077, the new king

---

[177] Gerhoch, *De ordine* (n. 143) p. 280.

[178] Benson, *Bishop-Elect* (n. 147) pp. 288–90.

[179] Hauck, *Kirchengeschichte Deutschlands* 4, 116–21; H. Stoob, 'Zur Königswahl Lothars von Sachsen im Jahre 1125' in *Historische Forschungen für Walter Schlesinger* ed. H. Beumann (Cologne-Vienna, 1974) pp. 438–61.

[180] Bruno, *Saxonicum bellum* (n. 43) c. 91, p. 85. See above p. 407.

[181] *Narratio de electione Lotharii* c. 1, MGH SS 12, 510; Anselm, *Continuatio chronicorum Sigeberti* 1125, ibid., 6, 380. See J. Bachmann, *Die päpstlichen Legaten in Deutschland und Skandinavien 1125–1159* (Berlin, 1913) p. 5.

sought confirmation of his election by the pope, Honorius II.[182]
According to the *Narrative of the election of Lothar* (perhaps the work
of an eyewitness), immediately after the election the new king agreed
with his electors 'what liberty the priesthood ought to have'. He
renounced two of the rights guaranteed in the concordat of Worms:
'the presence of the king' at the elections of prelates and the conferring of the *regalia* before consecration.[183] The value of the *Narrative*
as a source has been much disputed.[184] Perhaps the author misunder-
stood the proceedings which he witnessed or perhaps he wrote as a
partisan of the Gregorians: certainly his account of Lothar's renunciation is not corroborated by any other source. However, even if the
reign did not begin with a spectacular rejection of the customs recognised in 1122, during the early years of Lothar's reign there was a
definite slackening of royal control over episcopal elections. For
example, in 1126 the king accepted the decision of the papal legate,
Cardinal Gerard of S. Croce in Gerusalemme, when he approved the
election to the archbishopric of Magdeburg of Abbot Norbert of
Prémontré and rejected the candidature of Conrad of Querfurt,
Lothar's kinsman. The king likewise acquiesced in the deposition by
Pope Honorius II of the bishops of Würzburg (1126) and Halberstadt
(1128).[185] In return, the German church rallied to Lothar's cause
when his enemies elected Conrad of Staufen (brother of Duke
Frederick II of Swabia) as anti-king (December 1127). The bishops
excommunicated Conrad and the pope seems to have followed their
example. When in 1128 Conrad invaded Lombardy and was
crowned king of Italy by the archbishop of Milan, Honorius' legate
excommunicated the archbishop at a synod in Pavia.[186]

The alliance of the pope and the king of the Germans, fore-
shadowed in the pontificate of Honorius II, became of greater
importance to the papacy in the pontificate of Innocent II. During the
eight-year schism which followed the double election of 14 February
1130 Innocent II was unable to establish himself in Rome against his
rival, Anacletus II. Innocent turned for help to Lothar III, who
responded with an expedition to Italy in 1133 – during which the

[182] Innocent II, *JL* 7413: *MPL* 179, 56C.
[183] *Narratio* (n. 181) c. 6, p. 511.
[184] E.g. Hauck, *Kirchengeschichte Deutschlands* 4, 118–20; Classen, 'Das Wormser
     Konkordat' (n. 147) pp. 423–4.
[185] Hauck, *Kirchengeschichte Deutschlands* 4, 126–33.
[186] *Annalista Saxo* 1128 (n. 157), p. 765; *Annales Magdeburgenses*, *MGH SS* 16, 183;
     Otto of Freising, *Chronica* (n. 148) VII.17, pp. 333–4. See R. Somerville, 'Pope
     Honorius II, Conrad of Hohenstaufen and Lothar III', *AHP* 10 (1972), 341–6.

pope crowned him emperor – and a second expedition in 1136–7. The documents in which Innocent and his most influential supporter, Bernard of Clairvaux, sought this help and in which Lothar responded to their appeal, all speak the same language: the traditional papal language defining the duties of an emperor towards the Roman church. Innocent commanded the German princes to 'help your mother, the holy Roman church, since she is in the greatest need . . . and incite our son, King Lothar, to our honour and service . . . and bring him to our presence next winter'.[187] Bernard reminded Lothar that 'it is the business of the advocate of the Church to prevent the fury of the schismatics from troubling the Church'.[188] Lothar himself announced on the eve of his imperial coronation that as it had pleased God 'to appoint us patron and defender of the holy Roman church, therefore it is necessary for us to labour the more willingly for her liberation'.[189] In Cardinal Boso's biography of Innocent II in the *Liber pontificalis* Lothar is presented as 'the most Christian emperor, fired with zeal for God and the Christian faith, like a catholic advocate of the Church'.[190] The emperor as the *advocatus*, *patronus* and *defensor* of the Roman church had been a familiar theme in Rome since Carolingian times. The reappearance of this traditional language in the 1130s bears witness to a major development in papal policy: the abandonment of the political attitudes of the Investiture Contest and the restoration of the emperor to the role of defender of the papacy.

This development was already beginning at the time of the negotiation of the concordat of Worms and it was accelerated by the emergence of a formidable new opponent of the papacy, Roger II of Sicily. Reliance on the Norman vassals of the Roman church had been an important aspect of the policy of the reform papacy since 1059, especially after the outbreak of the war with Henry IV. However, precisely at the moment when, in 1122, the pope made peace with the emperor and therefore had less need of his Norman vassals, the dangerous ambitions of Count Roger of Sicily prompted the formation of an anti-Norman party in the papal curia.[191] In the First

---

[187] Innocent II, *JL* 7413 (n. 182), 57A.   [188] Bernard, *Epistola* 139, *MPL* 182, 294A.
[189] Lothar III, *Encyclica: MGH Constitutiones* 1, 167.
[190] Boso, *Vita Innocentii II: Liber pontificalis* 2, 383. On this terminology see W. Ullmann, *The growth of papal government in the Middle Ages* (3rd edition: London, 1970) pp. 69, 137, 162, 224, 296, 298, 432.
[191] F.-J. Schmale, *Studien zum Schisma des Jahres 1130* (Cologne-Graz, 1961) pp. 81–2; J. Deér, *Papsttum und Normannen* (Studien und Quellen zur Welt Kaiser Friedrichs II. 1: Cologne-Vienna, 1972) pp. 173–4.

Lateran Council in March 1123 critics of the peace with the emperor tried unsuccessfully to secure the rejection of the concordat of Worms. During the next few months Calixtus II appointed ten new cardinals, who seem to have been men mainly of north Italian or French origin. These appointments suggest a conscious policy of countering the influence of the Roman and south Italian cardinals who opposed the concordat with the emperor and favoured the continuance of the Norman alliance. The new cardinals formed the core of the anti-Norman party, strengthened by similar appointments in the pontificate of Honorius II.[192] Their leader was Haimeric, cardinal deacon of S. Maria Nuova, whom Calixtus appointed in 1123 to the key office of chancellor. His eighteen years in this office, during which he became the most influential politician in the curia, were devoted to the implementation of the new policy: peace with the German king and resistance to the attempts of Roger II of Sicily to acquire the mainland territories of his dynasty. It was Haimeric and the anti-Norman party who secured the election of their candidate, Honorius II, in December 1124, outwitting their principal opponent, Peter Pierleone, who commanded the support of a majority of the cardinals – and nearly provoking schism. During Honorius' pontificate the opponents of Haimeric's party lost their influential positions in the curia and ceased to be appointed to important legations.[193] On the death of Honorius the struggle of the two parties for the succession provoked the schism of 1130. The opponents of Haimeric, still a majority of the cardinals, elected Peter Pierleone as Anacletus II, relying on the strength of his family, the Pierleoni, in Rome and on their close association with Roger II and the Normans. The election of Haimeric's candidate, Innocent II, preceded that of Anacletus by a few hours.

By midsummer 1130 each pope had sent letters and legates to the German kingdom, denouncing his rival and seeking the support of King Lothar III. Anacletus was the more conciliatory, offering the imperial crown and announcing that he had excommunicated Lothar's enemy, Conrad of Staufen, as an illustration of the principle that 'the royal power and holy Roman authority ought to respond to each other with mutual diligence'.[194] The only extant letter of

[192] See above pp. 48–9, 67–8; 381–2 and nn. 66–7.
[193] H.-W. Klewitz, 'Das Ende des Reformpapsttums' in *idem*, *Reformpapsttum und Kardinalkolleg* (Darmstadt, 1957) pp. 247–50; F.-J. Schmale, 'Papsttum und Kurie zwischen Gregor VII. und Innocenz II.', *HZ* 193 (1961), 278; *idem*, *Schisma* (n. 191) pp. 72–3, 120–3, 136–8, 143–4.
[194] Anacletus II, *JL* 8388: *MPL* 179, 707AC. Cf. *JL* 8389: *ibid.*, 707D–708C.

Innocent is a brusque command to the German bishops and princes to 'incite' Lothar to fulfil his obligations to the Roman church.[195] Anacletus was secure in Rome, while Innocent had been forced to seek refuge in Pisa. Nevertheless it was Anacletus who sought from Lothar recognition of his title, while Innocent simply demanded the 'service' which he regarded as due from the German king to the Roman church. Innocent's confidence was in fact justified; for there was little likelihood of Lothar's recognising Anacletus or even of his trying to act as arbiter in the papal schism. By midsummer 1130 Innocent had already been recognised as pope by many influential reforming circles: by Bernard of Clairvaux and the Cistercians, the Premonstratensians and Cluny, by the church in Spain and by the archdiocese of Ravenna. In Germany Archbishop Norbert of Magdeburg (the founder of the Premonstratensian order) and Archbishop Conrad of Salzburg were prominent supporters of Innocent II. All the German archbishops were convinced reformers – except Adalbero of Hamburg, an appointee of Henry V and partisan of Anacletus in 1130 – and in the early years of Lothar's reign the episcopate had acquired a reforming complexion.[196] If Lothar had supported Anacletus, he would have made enemies of the most distinguished reformers in western Christendom and of a significant part of the German episcopate. He would risk pushing Innocent and the German reformers into the arms of the Staufen anti-king (who was remaining ostentatiously aloof from Anacletus). The problem of the schism was referred to 'a council of sixteen bishops' at Würzburg, in the presence of Innocent's legate, Archbishop Walter of Ravenna (October 1130), and Innocent was unanimously recognised as pope.[197]

At the pope's request, Lothar and Innocent met at Liège on 21 March 1131. On the pope's arrival Lothar 'offered himself most humbly as a groom and hastened to him on foot in the midst of the holy procession: holding in one hand the staff to defend him and in the other the rein of his white horse, he led him as if [Innocent] was

---

[195] Innocent II, *JL* 7413 (n. 182), 57A. F.-J. Schmale, 'Die Bemühungen Innozenz' II. um seine Anerkennung in Deutschland', *ZKG* 65 (1954), 240–69 has identified the letters attributed to Innocent II, *JL* 7403–4, 7411, in *Codex Udalrici*, as forgeries.

[196] Hauck, *Kirchengeschichte Deutschlands* 4, 134–5, 144–5; Schmale, *Schisma* (n. 191) pp. 200–1.

[197] *Annalista Saxo* 1130 (n. 157), p. 767; *Annales Palidenses* 1130, *MGH SS* 16, 78. See Hauck 4, 146–7.

his lord'.[198] According to this report by Abbot Suger of St Denis, Lothar performed the *stratoris officium* which the 'Donation of Constantine' supposed Constantine I to have performed for Pope Sylvester I. Abbot Suger seems, however, to have misinterpreted this ceremony, suggesting that the *stratoris officium* acknowledged that the king was the vassal of the pope. It is more likely that the ceremony retained the meaning which it had had on the last occasion of its performance, when the anti-king Conrad performed the office of groom for Urban II in 1095. In 1131, as in 1095, the ceremony amounted to recognition of the pope's title and rejection of the claims of the antipope.[199] That Lothar was far from accepting the status of vassal of the Roman church is suggested by two other accounts of the meeting at Liège. The chronicler Otto of Freising recorded that when Innocent 'summoned King Lothar to the defence of the holy Roman church, the latter did not hesitate in promising his aid . . . First, however, he modestly explained how much his kingdom was weakened by its love for the churches and at what cost to itself it had given up the investiture of churches'.[200] The second account, that of Ernald of Bonneval in his biography of Bernard of Clairvaux, represents Lothar's 'explanation' as a demand. 'Believing that the time was opportune, the king churlishly urged that the investitures of bishops – which the Roman church had obtained from his predecessor, Emperor Henry, by means of the greatest efforts and many dangers – should be restored to him.' Lothar was compelled to withdraw his demand only by the eloquence of Bernard of Clairvaux.[201] According to these two independent accounts of the meeting in Liège, therefore, Lothar requested, as the price of his military support, a return to the customs of the Salian church before the concordat of Worms.

It is not known why Lothar had come to believe that his kingdom had been 'weakened by its love for the churches'. A zealous reformer like Conrad of Salzburg may have consecrated a bishop without first receiving royal approval; or perhaps the proceedings of the council of Würzburg in October 1130 had revealed the unprecedented independence of the episcopate. There is no doubt, however, that a year after his meeting with Innocent at Liège, Lothar suffered infringe-

---

[198] Suger, *Vita Ludovici* (n. 97) c. 32, pp. 260–2. Cf. *Gesta abbatum Lobbiensium* c. 23, *MGH SS* 21, 325.

[199] See above p. 417.

[200] Otto of Freising, *Chronica* (n. 148) VII.18, p. 335.

[201] Ernald of Bonneval, *Vita prima sancti Bernardi* II.5, *MPL* 185, 271C–272A.

ment of the rights guaranteed by the concordat of Worms. Two German prelates were consecrated before they had received the *regalia* from the king: Bishop Henry of Regensburg, consecrated by Conrad of Salzburg, and Archbishop Albero of Trier, consecrated by Innocent himself.[202] 'The development is clear,' wrote Albert Hauck: 'while Lothar sought to recover the influence over episcopal elections which the concordat of Worms gave to the king, the leaders of the ecclesiastical party proceeded to break the rule which had been observed in the first years of his reign.'[203] Innocent's action and that of his supporter, Conrad of Salzburg, may have been intended as a riposte to the claims made by Lothar at Liège. Perhaps their actions were a reminder that the papal concessions made at Worms in 1122 were for the lifetime of Henry V only and had not descended to his successor.[204] Certainly the papal breach of the concordat in 1132 ensured that the complaints made by Lothar in Liège in 1131 would be resumed in Rome in 1133.

In late summer 1132 Lothar 'led an army into Italy, albeit a small force, because of the discord in the [German] kingdom'. His principal adviser on this expedition was Archbishop Norbert of Magdeburg, whom he had recently appointed chancellor for the Italian kingdom. Resisting a final attempt by Anacletus II to secure his support, Lothar joined Innocent at Viterbo and they eventually reached Rome on 30 April 1133.[205] The royal army was not strong enough to dislodge Anacletus from the Leonine city and from St Peter's, where imperial coronations traditionally took place. Lothar was crowned, therefore, in the Lateran basilica on 4 June 1133. Immediately after the coronation – according to the anonymous *Life* of Norbert of Magdeburg – Lothar renewed the demands which he had made two years before in Liège. 'When he had been crowned, the emperor unadvisedly requested that the investiture of bishoprics – which is as much as to say, the freedom of the churches – should be surrendered to him by the lord pope, for the honour of the empire

---

[202] Balderic, *Gesta Alberonis archiepiscopi* c. 12–13, *MGH SS* 8, 250; J. Bauermann, 'Die Frage der Bischofswahlen auf dem Würzburger Reichstag von 1133' in *Kritische Beiträge zur Geschichte des Mittelalters. Festschrift für Robert Holtzmann* ed. M. Lintzel (Historische Studien 238: Berlin, 1933) p. 132.

[203] Hauck, *Kirchengeschichte Deutschlands* 4, 152. See also Benson, *Bishop-Elect* (n. 147) pp. 267–81.

[204] See above p. 434.

[205] Otto of Freising, *Chronica* (n. 148) VII.18, p. 335; *Vita Norberti archiepiscopi Magdeburgensis* c. 21, *MGH SS* 12, 701. See Hauck, *Kirchengeschichte Deutschlands* 4, 152–3.

and to strengthen the alliance which he had concluded with the pope.' Innocent was prevented from conceding this demand only by the intervention of Norbert, who reproved him for wishing to reduce the Church to slavery. At Norbert's rebuke 'the emperor gave up his irregular request and the pope his unlawful concession'.[206] So closely does this anecdote resemble Ernald's account of the intervention of Bernard of Clairvaux at Liège in 1131, that we might suppose that Norbert's biographer had appropriated the Bernardine story to his own hero. However, there is no doubt that the issue of investiture was renegotiated in Rome in 1133; for there survives a papal privilege, dated 8 June 1133, which defines Lothar's rights in episcopal elections. 'Wishing not to diminish but rather to increase the majesty of empire', Innocent's privilege confirmed 'the due and canonical customs'. This privilege of 1133 is in most respects less specific, but in one respect much more specific than the privilege of Calixtus II in 1122. Instead of restating the terms of the concordat of Worms, Innocent used the vague expression 'due and canonical customs'. However, the final sentence of Innocent's privilege added a new concession to those of 1122. The pope forbade anyone elected bishop or abbot 'to usurp or seize the *regalia* before requesting them from [Lothar] and performing to Your Magnificence what is rightfully owed to you in respect of them'.[207] This is surely a reference to the controversial cases of Archbishop Albero of Trier and Bishop Henry of Regensburg in 1132; both had administered the *regalia* before seeking Lothar's permission.[208] Innocent's privilege suggests a less dramatic version of events than that in the *Life* of Norbert of Magdeburg: namely, that at the time of the imperial coronation Lothar complained about the breach of the 'canonical customs' of the German church and the pope promised redress. Three months later, after his return to Germany, the emperor proclaimed at a diet at Würzburg the rights newly guaranteed him by the pope. Lothar confirmed the election of Bishop Henry of Regensburg, but he rebuked Archbishop Conrad of Salzburg for consecrating a bishop who had not yet received the *regalia*. The emperor 'said that the bishopric of Regensburg belonged to him'.[209] As far as Lothar was concerned, therefore, his negotiations with Innocent had restored royal control over the Church.

---

[206] *Vita Norberti* c. 21, p. 702.
[207] Innocent II, *JL* 7632: *MGH Constitutiones* I, 168–9. See Benson, *Bishop-Elect* (n. 147) pp. 256–63.
[208] Benson pp. 263–81.   [209] Bauermann, 'Würzburger Reichstag' (n. 202) p. 132.

The day on which Innocent issued his privilege, 8 June 1133, witnessed the settlement of another contentious issue. The pope issued a second privilege, conferring on Lothar the allodial property of Countess Matilda of Tuscany. The great countess had bequeathed her property to St Peter in a testament drawn up in 1079/80 and renewed in 1102; but soon after her death (24 July 1115) her distant kinsman, Emperor Henry V had seized her lands, claiming to be her heir. Since 1116 the papacy had been unable to secure the inheritance. Finally, three years after the accession of Lothar III, the interests of both papacy and empire had been threatened by the attempt of the anti-king Conrad of Staufen to seize the Matildine lands as a power base for his war against Lothar.[210] For their mutual security, therefore, Innocent invested Lothar with Matilda's property for an annual payment of 100 pounds of silver, with the proviso that the property should return to the lordship of the Roman church on the emperor's death. The fief was regranted to Lothar's daughter and son-in-law, the Welf prince Henry the Proud, duke of Bavaria, on condition that the duke perform homage and fealty to St Peter and to Innocent. No homage or fealty was demanded from the emperor, 'the most special defender of the Church'.[211] Three years passed before Lothar and his son-in-law, the new papal vassal, could take an active part in the politics of the papal schism. The emperor returned to Germany immediately after his coronation and Innocent was soon forced to flee from Rome to Pisa, while his enemy, Roger II of Sicily, assumed control of the Norman lands of southern Italy. Since Lothar was detained in Germany by the continued rebellion of the Staufen, Innocent sought to reconcile the warring parties. In 1135 Cardinal bishop Theodwin of S. Rufina (the only German in the college) was sent to Germany as papal legate and, together with Cardinal Gerard of S. Croce in Gerusalemme, played a decisive role in the pacification of the kingdom.[212] In February or March of the same year Bernard of Clairvaux travelled to Germany on the same errand, perhaps also sent by the pope. 'At the intervention of Bernard' the rebels were reconciled to the emperor at the diet of Bamberg (17 March 1135)

---

[210] P. Scheffer-Boichorst, 'Zu dem mathildinischen Schenkungen', *MIÖG* 9 (1888), 177–91; Servatius, *Paschalis II.* pp. 101–3; W. Bernhardi, *Lothar von Supplinburg* (Jahrbücher der deutschen Geschichte: Leipzig, 1879) pp. 206–7, 481–5.

[211] Innocent II, *JL* 7633: *MGH Constitutiones* I, 169–70.

[212] Bachmann, *Legaten* (n. 181) pp. 46–9.

and promised to accompany Lothar on an expedition to Italy the next year.[213]

In a letter of 1134/5 Bernard exhorted the emperor to fulfil his duty to the Roman church.

It is not my business to summon you to battle: nevertheless (I can safely say) it is the business of the advocate of the Church to prevent the fury of the schismatics from troubling the Church; it is the business of Caesar to claim his own crown from the Sicilian usurper. For . . . without doubt he who makes himself king in Sicily opposes Caesar.[214]

According to Bernard, therefore, Lothar must return to Italy not only to restore Innocent II to Rome but also to vindicate the rights of the emperor over Sicily against the usurper Roger II. Lothar's second expedition to Italy was to show that while he himself took these rights very seriously, his ally the pope was loath to recognise them. His campaign of 1136–7 seemed to the admiring chronicler Otto of Freising to be a triumphant reconquest of long lost imperial territories. 'The emperor performed such mighty deeds in Apulia and Campania as no king of the Franks is known to have achieved from Charlemagne up to that time.'[215] The enemies of Roger II among the Apulian nobility saw Lothar's campaign in the same light and acknowledged that 'Apulia and Sicily belonged to his imperial jurisdiction'.[216] Lothar's military success compelled even Roger II – as a Saxon chronicler believed – to recognise the suzerainty of the emperor. After Lothar had captured Bari (May 1137) 'Roger sent envoys, seeking the emperor's grace, and promised him unlimited money and his son as a hostage, if he would confer the principality of Apulia on his other son'.[217] The claim that the Norman lands belonged to the *imperium* ran directly counter to papal theory and practice, which since 1059 had assumed that Apulia and Sicily were fiefs held of the papacy. The official papal view was that Lothar had come to Italy 'as the catholic advocate of the Church' to vindicate the rights of St Peter and that his victories were gained 'through the merits of St Peter'.[218] These rival claims to suzerainty produced

[213] Otto of Freising, *Chronica* (n. 148) VII. 19, p. 336; *Annalista Saxo* 1135 (n. 157), p. 770; *Annales Magdeburgenses* 1135 (n. 186), p. 185. See E. Vacandard, *Vie de Saint Bernard Abbé de Clairvaux* I (Paris, 1910), 369–72.

[214] Bernard, *Epistola* 139 (n. 188), 294A.

[215] Otto of Freising, *Chronica* VII.19, p. 337.

[216] Romuald of Salerno, *Annales* [1135?], *MGH SS* 19, 421. See Deér, *Papsttum und Normannen* (n. 191) pp. 42–3.

[217] *Annalista Saxo* 1137 (n. 157), p. 774.

[218] Boso, *Vita Innocentii II* (n. 190) p. 383. See above p. 443.

open conflict as soon as Roger was defeated. Count Rainulf of Alife was to be invested with Apulia in place of the usurper (August 1137); but both pope and emperor claimed the right to invest the new duke, 'each declaring that the duchy of Apulia belonged to his juris-diction'.[219] The dispute could not be settled satisfactorily, 'as they were both travelling and neither party had access to documents or proofs'. They therefore adopted the temporary solution of a joint investiture: 'they invested Count Rainulf with the duchy of Apulia, the pope holding the standard at the top, the emperor holding it below'.[220] The dispute was to be settled 'at a more appropriate time and place'; but these further negotiations never took place. Lothar died four months after the investiture, while on the return journey to Germany (3–4 December 1137). His claim to the Norman lands sur-vived him: it was to recur in the propaganda of his Staufen successors until Henry VI successfully united Apulia and Sicily with the empire, fifty-seven years after the investiture of Rainulf.

Lothar III was revered in reforming circles as 'a God-fearing emperor, a vigorous warlord, distinguished in arms, prudent in counsel, terrible to the enemies of God, the friend of justice, the enemy of injustice'.[221] Lothar was 'useful and suitable for the honour of the empire', according to Petrus Diaconus, chronicler of Monte Cassino, reviving the terms in which Gregory VII had judged monarchs.[222] Lothar was the only emperor of the central Middle Ages whose attitude seemed to approximate to the papal interpret-ation of the imperial office and the role of *advocatus*, *patronus* and *defensor* of the Roman church. Nevertheless he was not the *Pfaffen-könig*, weakly dependent on the Church, that has sometimes been suggested.[223] He extorted from the pope confirmation of his rights over the German church in 1133; and he used the opportunity of his second Italian expedition to strengthen his hold over the kingdom of Italy. Hence the contentious investiture of August 1137; hence also the election of an imperial churchman, Abbot Wibald of Stablo and Malmédy, as abbot of Monte Cassino in September 1137 and the

---

[219] Otto of Freising, *Chronica* VII.20, pp. 338–9.

[220] Romuald, *Annales* 1137 (n. 216), p. 422. See above p. 385.

[221] *Vita Norberti* (n. 205) c. 21, p. 702. See Bernhardi, *Lothar* (n. 210) p. 794 n. 16; Hauck, *Kirchengeschichte Deutschlands* 4, 122.

[222] *Chronica monasterii Casinensis* (n. 68) IV.87, p. 548. See above pp. 315, 411.

[223] See, for example, K. Hampe, *Germany under the Salian and Hohenstaufen emperors* (English translation of 12th German edition: Oxford, 1973) pp. 124–5; J. W. Thompson, *Feudal Germany* (Chicago, 1928) p. 161; G. Barraclough, *The Origins of Modern Germany* (2nd edition: Oxford, 1947) pp. 156–7.

subsequent investiture of Lothar's son-in-law, Henry the Proud, with the margraviate of Tuscany.[224] In these instances Innocent II found the emperor's conduct far from satisfactory; but after Lothar's death the pope presented a version of his relations with Lothar far more to his liking.

Innocent's interpretation took the form of a mural of the imperial coronation of Lothar III in the St Nicholas chapel of the Lateran palace, no longer extant but known to us from sketches made in the sixteenth and seventeenth centuries and from descriptions given by four German authors writing in the reign of Emperor Frederick I. These German accounts were all written after the mural had aroused Frederick's anger and prompted the German bishops to write to Pope Hadrian IV early in 1158, demanding its removal. 'A serious disagreement arose between the pope and the lord emperor. For Pope Innocent had once caused to be painted on a wall in Rome both himself seated on the papal throne and Emperor Lothar in his presence with hands folded, bowing down to receive the crown of the empire.'[225] All the German accounts give a feudal interpretation of the mural: namely, that Lothar was represented as receiving the imperial crown from the pope as a vassal receives a fief from his lord. The most explicit account – that of Frederick I's biographer, Rahewin – records the inscription which accompanied the mural: 'The king . . . becomes the vassal of the pope and takes the crown which he gives.' Modern discussions of the lost mural have focussed on this inscription and its portrayal of the emperor as a papal vassal – the only precedent for which was the demand of Gregory VII in 1081 that the German anti-king swear an oath of fealty to the pope.[226] It has been suggested that in commissioning the mural, the papal curia amalgamated Lothar's imperial coronation with the investiture of the Matildine lands four days later and so created the impression

---

[224] *Chronica monasterii Casinensis* IV. 124, p. 599. See J. Haller, *Das Papsttum. Idee und Wirklichkeit* 3 (2nd edition: Basel, 1962), 46–7; K. Jordan, *Heinrich der Löwe. Eine Biographie* (Munich, 1979) p. 22.

[225] *Chronica regia Coloniensis, MGH SS rer. Germ.* (1880) p. 93. See also the letter of the German bishops to Hadrian IV: *MGH Constitutiones* I, 234; Rahewin, *Gesta Friderici imperatoris* III.10, *MGH SS rer. Germ.* (1884) p. 141; Gerhoch of Reichersberg, *De investigatione Antichristi, MGH Libelli* 3, 392–3; idem, *De quarta vigilia, ibid.*, pp. 511–12. See most recently F. Kempf, 'Kanonistik und kuriale Politik im 12. Jahrhundert', *AHP* I (1963), 23–5; A. Frugoni, '*A pictura cepit*', *BISI* 78 (1967), 123–35; W. Heinemeyer, '*Beneficium – non feudum sed bonum factum*. Der Streit auf dem Reichstag zu Besançon 1157', *Archiv für Diplomatik* 15 (1969), 183–97.

[226] See above p. 411.

that the empire was a papal fief.[227] However, the surviving sketches of the Lateran mural – in sharp contrast to the German accounts and particularly to Rahewin's reported inscription – do not show any feudal ceremony.[228] It is possible indeed that the inscription was not part of Innocent II's original conception and represents a later 'escalation' of papal claims. Nevertheless, even without the feudal inscription, the mural remains a striking statement of the relations of papacy and empire. The pope appears enthroned, crowned and wearing ceremonial garments; he raises up the kneeling Lothar, who is uncrowned and simply clad. It is clear that Innocent enjoys the highest authority on earth: he condescends to the German king, who humbles himself before the papal throne, and raises him to the imperial dignity. Even if Innocent did not apply the feudal language used by Gregory VII in 1081, his conception of papal-imperial relations was thoroughly Gregorian.

Lothar III was long remembered in the papal curia (perhaps because of Innocent II's mural) as a model prince.[229] His successor, Conrad III, could not match his achievements as a defender of the Roman church. He was the first German king since the mid-tenth century who failed to be crowned emperor by the pope (although the journey to Rome was planned shortly before his death). The papacy, however, urgently needed another Lothar. For lack of such an ally Innocent II was defeated and taken prisoner by Roger II of Sicily and compelled to recognise his royal title and his possession of Apulia and Calabria (25 July 1139). For the remaining fifteen years of Roger's reign the curia watched helpless while the Sicilian king encroached upon the papal patrimony. The helplessness of the papacy was increased by the appearance of an enemy even nearer home. In the last months of Innocent's pontificate 'the Roman people, lovers of novelty, set up a senate in the Capitol against his will'.[230] The creation of the Roman commune seemed likely to compel Innocent's successors – Celestine II (1143–4), Lucius II (1144–5), Eugenius III (1145–53) and Anastasius IV (1153–4) – to seek the protection of the king of Sicily. In 1144 and again in 1148 the curia

---

[227] K. Jordan, 'Lothar III. und die frühe Stauferzeit' in B. Gebhardt, *Handbuch der deutschen Geschichte* I (8th edition: Stuttgart, 1954) 289; M. Maccarrone, *Papato e impero dalla elezione di Federico I alla morte di Adriano IV (1152–1159)* (Rome, 1959) pp. 132–7.

[228] G. Ladner, 'I mosaici e gli affreschi ecclesiastico-politici nell' antico palazzo Lateranense', *Rivista di Archeologia Christiana* 12 (1935), 281–90.

[229] Innocent III, *Registrum de negotio imperii* c. 32, *MPL* 216, 1035C.

[230] Boso, *Vita Innocentii II* (n. 190) p. 385. See above p. 13.

negotiated a short-term alliance with Roger II; but a permanent alliance proved impossible 'because of the opposition of the cardinals'.[231] The anti-Norman party in the curia, formed in the pontificates of Calixtus II and Honorius II, continued to dominate papal policy even after the death of its leader, the chancellor Haimeric, in 1141. Three of Innocent's successors were veterans of Haimeric's party. Celestine II (Guido, cardinal deacon of S. Maria in Via Lata) had been appointed to the college by Honorius II. Anastasius IV had entered the college as Conrad, cardinal priest of S. Pudenziana in the pontificate of Paschal II and had been promoted to the cardinal bishopric of Sabina by Honorius II. Lucius II, the former Gerard, cardinal priest of S. Croce in Gerusalemme, had been the appointee of Calixtus II and the successor of Haimeric as chancellor.[232] Cardinal Gerard served both Honorius II and Innocent II as their expert in German affairs: he was the principal negotiator of the papal alliance with Lothar III during the six legations which he undertook to Germany between 1125 and 1136. The theologian Gerhoch of Reichersberg recalled the legate Gerard 'bearing peace and illuminating [Germany], bringing joy to cities and monasteries'.[233] As pope, Lucius II, like his former colleagues, Guido-Celestine and Conrad-Anastasius, continued to prefer a German to a Sicilian alliance. He 'sent a humble letter to King Conrad . . . summoning him to the defence of the Roman church'.[234] The only pope of the second quarter of the twelfth century who was not a member of Haimeric's anti-Norman party was Eugenius III (the former Cistercian abbot of SS. Vincenzo e Anastasio alle Tre Fontane, outside Rome). In Eugenius' case the influence of his mentor, Bernard of Clairvaux, and the strength of the anti-Norman party in the curia perpetuated the desire for a German alliance, despite the pope's alleged dislike of the Germans.[235]

Conrad III (the former anti-king, excommunicated for his opposition to Lothar) owed his election as king to the conspiracy of two papal legates: the recently appointed permanent legate in Germany,

[231] Romuald, *Annales* 1143 (n. 216), p. 424. See above pp. 116, 388.
[232] Celestine II: Hüls, *Kardinäle* (n. 87) p. 239; B. Zenker, *Die Mitglieder des Kardinalkollegiums von 1130 bis 1159* (dissertation: Würzburg, 1964) pp. 83–4. Lucius II: Hüls p. 164; Zenker pp. 129–31. Anastasius IV: Hüls pp. 128–9, 201; Zenker pp. 46–8.
[233] Gerhoch, *De investigatione Antichristi* (n. 225) p. 358. See Bachmann, *Legaten* (n. 181) pp. 10–49.
[234] Lucius II, *JL* 8684: Otto of Freising, *Chronica* (n. 148) VII.31, p. 358.
[235] The allegation is found in John of Salisbury, *Historia pontificalis* c. 38, ed. M. Chibnall (London, 1956) p. 76. See Zenker, *Mitglieder* (n. 232) pp. 253–5.

Archbishop Albero of Trier, and Cardinal bishop Theodwin of S. Rufina. In order to prevent the succession of Lothar's heir, the Welf prince Henry the Proud, Archbishop Albero and his adherents proceeded to elect the Staufen prince Conrad at an assembly in Coblenz on 7 March 1138, eleven weeks before the date agreed by the other princes for the election. Cardinal Theodwin was present at the election and crowned Conrad a week later in Aachen. A Liège annal claims that this coronation took place 'according to the will and command of Pope Innocent'; while the chronicle of Otto of Freising records that at Conrad's election Theodwin 'promised the consent of the supreme pontiff and all the Roman people and of the cities of Italy'.[236] Innocent's attitude to the election is, however, not clear. He may have been opposed to the election of Henry the Proud, with whom he had recently had 'a great quarrel' concerning the booty taken at Viterbo during the campaign of 1137.[237] It is likely that the precipitate action of his legates left the pope no choice in the matter. Albero of Trier desired a king less dangerous than the Welf candidate; Theodwin was prompted by his friendship with Conrad. 'On the friendliest terms with King Conrad', the German cardinal Theodwin devoted the rest of his career to the king's interests, living in Conrad's entourage for most of the 1140s.[238]

Early in the new reign Bernard of Clairvaux wrote to Conrad, urging him to 'show reverence to the supreme and apostolic see and to the vicar of St Peter'. Again in 1146 Bernard summoned the king, just as he had summoned his predecessor, to take the field against the pope's enemies: 'Gird your sword on your thigh and let Caesar restore to himself what is Caesar's and to God what is God's. Certainly it is important for Caesar both to protect his own crown and to defend the Church: the former is the duty of the king, the latter of the advocate of the Church.'[239] Conrad was prevented from performing these roles of emperor and advocate of the Church by his war against the Welfs in Germany. The conflict was unleashed by the king's attempt at the diet of Würzburg (July 1138) to deprive Henry the Proud of his two duchies of Bavaria and Saxony. The subsequent war continued for the rest of the reign, with a single respite in

---

[236] *Annales sancti Jacobi Leodensis* 1138, *MGH SS* 16, 640; Otto of Freising, *Chronica* (n. 148) VII.22, p. 343. See Hauck, *Kirchengeschichte Deutschlands* 4, 158–60.
[237] *Annalista Saxo* 1137 (n. 157), p. 773.
[238] *Annales Palidenses* 1151 (n. 197), p. 85. See Bachmann, *Legaten* (n. 181) pp. 59–79; Zenker, *Mitglieder* (n. 233) pp. 26–8.
[239] Bernard, *Epistolae* 183, 244 c. 3 (n. 188), 345BC, 442A.

1147–8. This respite was obtained by Bernard of Clairvaux, not however for the purpose of an expedition to aid the pope, but for the Second Crusade. Bernard recruited the king to the crusade (27 December 1146) and likewise the leader of the Welf party, Welf VI (brother of the deceased Henry the Proud) and other prominent princes.[240] The attitude to this development of the new pope, Bernard's pupil, Eugenius III, is not known. It has been conjectured that Conrad's recruitment to the crusade was unwelcome to Eugenius because it distracted the king from his duties in Italy.[241] The only surviving papal letter on this subject is, however, congenial. It is addressed to Conrad's ten-year-old son Henry, elected king on the eve of his father's departure (March 1147). 'Bearing in mind [Conrad's] devotion to St Peter and the holy Roman church', the pope promised aid and counsel to the young king during his father's absence.[242]

Conrad's friendship with the curia was threatened not by his decision to take the cross so much as by the alliance which he made during the crusade. While wintering at the Byzantine court in 1147–8 Conrad agreed with Emperor Manuel I Comnenus on joint military action against Roger II of Sicily. This alliance endangered papal interests because it involved a promise of restitution to Byzantium of part of the Norman territories.[243] The papal reaction to the German–Byzantine alliance is recorded in the correspondence of Conrad's chief adviser, Abbot Wibald of Stablo-Malmédy and of Corvey, with his friends in the curia. 'A certain rumour had disturbed both the lord pope and his curia, namely that our most serene lord Conrad, king of the Romans was said to have concluded a treaty with the emperor of the Greeks so that he might contrive to weaken and injure the holy Roman church.' Guido the chancellor, on behalf of the pope, exhorted Wibald to use his influence against this alliance; and in spring 1150 Wibald could report to the curia: 'We have done what he commanded . . . by long dwelling together and by incessant conversation we have instilled in [Conrad] the good of

---

[240] For Conrad's motives see A. Cosak, 'Konrads III. Entschluss zum Kreuzzug', *MIÖG* 35 (1914), 278–96. Cf. V. G. Berry, 'The Second Crusade' in K. M. Setton (ed.), *A history of the crusades* 1 (Wisconsin, 1969), 473–9.

[241] H. Gleber, *Papst Eugen III. (1145–1153) unter besonderer Berücksichtigung seiner politischen Tätigkeit* (Jena, 1936) p. 38.

[242] Eugenius III, *JL* 9084: *MPL* 180, 1300A.

[243] H. Vollrath, 'Konrad III. und Byzanz', *Archiv für Kulturgeschichte* 59 (1977), 321–65.

humility and obedience.'[244] It was evidently thanks to Wibald that neither the joint military expedition against Roger II nor the Byzantine reconquest of southern Italy ever took place. Abbot Wibald was truly (as Conrad described him to Eugenius III in 1151) 'most faithful in all things both to you and to our holy mother the Roman church'.[245] The triangular relationship of Conrad, Wibald and the papal curia has prompted historians to regard Conrad III (like Lothar III) as a *Pfaffenkönig* whom 'the curial party surrounded like a ring of iron', prompting him to pursue a papal rather than a 'German' policy.[246] Such a judgement does not take into account the attitudes of the curial and German statesmen who had grown up during the thirty years' peace of 1122–52. The settlement of the question of investitures, the cooperation of Lothar III and Innocent II, above all the career of the overmighty Roger II of Sicily had accustomed papal and royal advisers to assume that whatever was in the interests of the papacy must also be in the interests of the German kingdom and vice versa.[247] This supposed identity of interests was symbolised by the careers of Wibald of Stablo, the royal adviser 'most faithful to the Roman church' and Theodwin of S. Rufina, the papal legate devoted to the interests of the king. This identity of interests is the theme of the letters sent to Conrad by Bernard of Clairvaux and by his pupil, Eugenius III. In January 1152 Eugenius greeted Conrad's announcement of his long deferred Italian expedition with the classic *sententia* of Pope Gelasius I. ' "The world is chiefly governed by these two: the sacred authority of pontiffs and the imperial power." . . . If they are in agreement, religion is safely preserved in holy Church . . . and the Christian people is governed soundly.'[248]

In Albert Hauck's indispensable study of the ecclesiastical history of Germany the chapter on the period 1125–52 is entitled 'The elimination of royal influence and papal government in the Church', while that on the subsequent four decades is called 'Reaction under

---

[244] Wibald, *Epistola* 252, ed. P. Jaffé, *Bibliotheca rerum germanicarum* 1 (Berlin, 1864), 377. See Vollrath, 'Konrad III.' p. 330 n. 33.
[245] Conrad III, letter to Eugenius III: *MGH Constitutiones* 1, 188.
[246] H. Zatschek, 'Wibald von Stablo', *MIÖG* Ergänzungsband 10 (1928), 416. Cf. Hauck, *Kirchengeschichte Deutschlands* 4, 165.
[247] F.-J. Schmale, 'Lothar III. und Friedrich I. als Könige und Kaiser' in *Friedrich Barbarossa* (Wege der Forschung 390: Darmstadt, 1975) p. 127.
[248] Eugenius III, *JL* 9541 (n. 242), 1501BC. Cf. Gelasius I, *Epistola* 12 (n. 2). See also Bernard, *Epistolae* 244 c. 1, 361 (n. 188), 440D, 563A–564B; Robert Pullen, *Sententiae* VI.56; VII.7, *MPL* 186, 905D–906A, 919C. See Zenker, *Mitglieder* (n. 232) pp. 89–92.

Frederick I'. It is an exaggeration to speak of royal influence being 'eliminated' from the German church in the reigns of Lothar and Conrad; but there is no doubt that papal involvement in the affairs of the Church increased rapidly during these years and receded just as rapidly in the reign of Frederick Barbarossa. The most obvious index of this papal involvement is the activity of legates *a latere*. In the quarter-century after 1125 scarcely a year passed when there was not at least one Roman legate in Germany and in some years as many as four were simultaneously active in the kingdom. At the beginning of the papal schism 1131 brought four Innocentine legates (Gerard of S. Croce in Gerusalemme, Matthew of Albano, Anselm of S. Lorenzo in Lucina and Obert of Cremona) and 1132 brought four more (William of Palestrina, Guido of S. Maria in Via Lata, John of Crema and Azo of Aqui). The crusading year 1147 also brought four Roman legates (the chancellor Guido, the subdeacon John, the chaplain *Raim[undus?]* and Master Grecus).[249] The legates of these years had a political role: in 1131–2 to win support against the party of Anacletus II; in 1147 to pacify the kingdom in the interests of the crusade. More characteristic of legatine activity in this quarter-century – and more significant for the penetration of papal influence in the Church – were the interventions of the legates in ecclesiastical matters. For example, in 1127 Peter, cardinal deacon of S. Maria in Via Lata held two legatine synods, in Toul and in Worms, where he helped the enemies of Archbishop Godfrey of Trier to compel that prelate's abdication. Similarly in 1131 Cardinal bishop Matthew of Albano, presiding over a synod in Mainz, received the abdication of the bishop of Strassburg.[250] Increasingly Roman legates involved themselves in episcopal elections, securing the acceptance of papal supporters such as Norbert of Magdeburg (against a rival who was the nephew of Lothar III) and Albero of Trier.[251] In 1132 three legates participated in the election of Archbishop Bruno of Cologne and one of their number, William of Palestrina, consecrated him.[252]

The pope was also prepared to intervene directly in the German church without the mediation of legates. Innocent II reminded the German clergy of 'the general law of the Church' 'that the more

---

[249] Hauck, *Kirchengeschichte Deutschlands* 4, 169 n. 3; Bachmann, *Legaten* (n. 181) pp. 21–116, 156.

[250] L. Spätling, 'Kardinallegat Petrus im Pontifikat Honorius' II.', *Antonianum* 38 (1963), 162–92; Bachmann pp. 27–30.

[251] Hauck 4, 126, 151–2; Bachmann pp. 10, 27.

[252] Mansi, *Sacra Concilia* 21, 479.

important cases (*maiores causae*) are referred to the apostolic see for examination and all the oppressed may appeal to her without fear'.[253] This statement was occasioned by a case in which Innocent gave a striking demonstration of the 'general law': the deposition of Bishop Alexander of Liège at the council of Pisa (30 May 1135), on the basis of the accusations of Nicholas, canon of Liège.[254] The situation in Liège – an alliance of the curia with the local accuser of a simoniacal bishop – recalls the methods of Gregory VII; and the sequel was authentically Gregorian: Alexander sickened and died shortly after his deposition. Equally Gregorian was the action of Eugenius III when, 'prompt to punish all disobedience', he suspended the archbishops of Mainz and Cologne 'and all who had been summoned to the council [of Rheims, 1148] and had not attended'.[255] Where these papal interventions in the German church differed from those of Gregory VII in 1074–5, however, was in the general response which they received from churchmen. The available evidence – appeals to Rome, prelates seeking consecration in Rome, religious houses placing themselves under papal jurisdiction – indicates a positive response.[256] In the period 1125–52 the German church felt the same centripetal attraction as the other churches of western Christendom.

The 'reaction' which is evident after the accession of Frederick I was not only the reaction of a king determined to maintain control of the Church nor only a by-product of the renewed conflict of empire and papacy (1159–77). Even before Frederick's relations with the curia became hostile, the German church had lost most of those prelates sympathetic to papal objectives who had been her leaders during the thirty years' peace. The most effective of them, Albero of Trier, had died shortly before Conrad III. Conrad's closest adviser, Wibald of Stablo and Corvey, 'most faithful to the Roman church', was retained by Frederick as an adviser, but by 1157 he had retired from the court, unable to make his counsel prevail against that of the new chancellor, Rainald of Dassel. The episcopal elections of the new reign – over which Frederick generally exercised an influence greater than that envisaged in the concordat of Worms – produced an episcopate who had more confidence in the protection of the emperor than that of the pope.[257] A survivor like Bishop Eberhard of

---

[253] Innocent II, *JL* 7696 (n. 182), 226C.

[254] *Gesta abbatum Trudonensium* XIII.1, *MGH SS* 10, 312.

[255] John of Salisbury, *Historia pontificalis* c. 4 (n. 235), p. 10.

[256] Hauck, *Kirchengeschichte Deutschlands* 4, 172–8.

[257] *Ibid.*, 4, 206–10; P. Munz, *Frederick Barbarossa. A study in medieval politics* (London, 1969) pp. 127–8; Benson, *Bishop-Elect* (n. 147) pp. 284–91. For Frederick I's

Bamberg (another of Conrad III's advisers) found it impossible to adapt to the new regime. 'I am being led where I do not wish to go', he wrote to Archbishop Eberhard of Salzburg in 1159.[258] It was in fact only in Salzburg that the loyalties of the thirty years' peace survived intact. During the archiepiscopates of Eberhard (1147–64), Conrad II (1164–8) and Adalbert (1168–74), Salzburg was (as it had been during the Investiture Contest) an island of fidelity to the papacy and opposition to the emperor; and her archbishops became the permanent legates of the pope in Germany.[259] The curia's reliance on native legates rather than on legates *a latere* in Germany is an important index of the diminishing of papal influence. It marks a reversion to the practice of the late eleventh century. Once more the legates assumed the political role of rallying the isolated supporters of the embattled pope, rather than the ecclesiastical role of the years 1125–52: that involvement in ecclesiastical government which promoted the centralisation of the Church.[260] Frederick I meanwhile insisted that the prelates of his empire were office-holders, owing fidelity and service to the *imperium*. On the occasion of the royal progress in the kingdom of Burgundy in 1157 the archbishops of Vienne and Lyons and the bishops of Valence and Avignon 'performed fealty and homage to Frederick and reverently received their fiefs from his hand', 'which no one now alive can remember ever happening before'.[261] On the same occasion he reminded bishops that their possession of *regalia* imposed on them obligations towards the emperor, 'since those things which are held of the empire are held according to feudal law'.[262] The willingness of the majority of imperial churchmen to accept this definition of their role forced the papal curia to revise its policy towards the Empire.

THE PAPACY AND THE STAUFEN, 1152–1198

The elections of Lothar III and Conrad III had resembled those of the anti-kings of the Investiture Contest; but the election of Conrad's

---

attitude to the German church see F. Opll, 'Amator ecclesiarum. Studien zur religiösen Haltung Friedrich Barbarossas', *MIÖG* 88 (1980), 70–93.

[258] Rahewin, *Gesta* (n. 225) IV.34, p. 219.

[259] W. Schmidt, 'Die Stellung der Erzbischöfe und des Erzstiftes von Salzburg zu Kirche und Reich unter Kaiser Friedrich I. bis zum Frieden von Venedig (1177)', *Archiv für österreichische Geschichte* 34 (1865), 3–144.

[260] M. Pacaut, 'Les légats d'Alexandre III (1159–1181)', *RHE* 50 (1955), 821–2, 824–6.

[261] Rahewin, *Gesta* III.12, pp. 143–4.

[262] Frederick I, *Sententia de feudis imperii non alienandis: MGH Constitutiones* 1, 236.

nephew, Frederick III of Staufen, duke of Swabia – King Frederick I Barbarossa – on 4 March 1152 was of a different character.[263] Firstly, Frederick had no plausible rival. Secondly, no papal legate was present either at his election or at his coronation, although the legate Jordan, cardinal priest of S. Susanna, was currently in the kingdom. Frederick simply announced his election to the pope: unlike his two predecessors, he sought the confirmation neither of the pope nor of his legates. It is tempting to interpret this omission as the first sign of Frederick's 'reaction' against the policy of his predecessors: Frederick I refused to give way to the pressure from the papal curia to which Lothar and Conrad had succumbed. However, it is likely that the pressure on Lothar and Conrad to seek papal confirmation came not from the curia itself, but from the pro-papal politicians to whom they owed their election to the kingship. In the context of the faction strife of 1125 and 1138 papal confirmation strengthened the position of the king elect; but in 1152 Frederick, accepted by the two main princely factions, the Staufen and the Welfs, had no need of this additional sanction. Eugenius III's letter of 17 May 1152, replying to Frederick's announcement of his election, has been interpreted as an attempt to confer the papal confirmation which the king elect had not sought.[264] In fact this letter does not use the word 'confirm', but says: 'We approve with the beneficent favour of the apostolic see.' The term 'apostolic favour' (*favor apostolicus*) was used half a century later by Innocent III with the definite implication that the papal favour could make or unmake a king; but Innocent III found himself in the situation of a contested election to the German throne. There is no reason for supposing that Eugenius III, in the very different situation of 1152, meant to express anything more than approval and good will towards the king elect.[265] The letter indeed records his joy at the news that Frederick intends to fulfil 'the good promise made to us and the Roman church by your uncle and predecessor' – the expedition to the aid of the pope.

By the end of the first year of Frederick's reign, Eugenius had secured that alliance with the German king for which he had striven throughout his pontificate: the treaty of Constance, concluded by

---

[263] Maccarrone, *Papato* (n. 227) pp. 11–39; Munz, *Barbarossa* (n. 257) pp. 44–6.
[264] Eugenius III, *JL* 9577 (n. 242), 1522D–1523C = *MGH Constitutiones* 1, 194. See Hauck, *Kirchengeschichte Deutschlands* 4, 198.
[265] F. Kempf, 'Der "favor apostolicus' bei der Wahl Friedrich Barbarossas und im deutschen Thronstreit (1198–1208)' in *Speculum historiale. Geschichte im Spiegel von Geschichtsschreibung und Geschichtsdeutung* ed. C. Bauer, L. Boehm and M. Müller (Freiburg–Munich, 1965) pp. 469–78.

the king with the papal legates on 23 March 1153. The treaty defined
the duties of the king in Italy, in return for which he would receive
the imperial crown: to restore the *regalia* – the temporal power – of
St Peter, to protect the 'honour' (*honor*) of the papacy, to make no
peace with the Romans or the king of Sicily without the pope's
approval. Both king and pope agreed to 'grant no land to the king of
the Greeks on this side of the sea' – a reference to Conrad III's Byzantine alliance, which had alarmed the curia in 1150. Eugenius also
agreed to 'increase and expand the *honor* of the empire' and to excommunicate the king's enemies.[266] In the final months of his pontificate
Eugenius' legates furthered the alliance by two timely concessions to
Frederick: the annulment of his first marriage and the deposition of
four unsatisfactory bishops.[267] Eugenius' shortlived successor,
Anastasius IV made the further concession (which Eugenius had
refused) of permitting the translation of Frederick's candidate,
Bishop Wichmann of Zeitz, to the archsee of Magdeburg.[268]

The alliance survived the deaths of Eugenius III (8 July 1153) and
Anastasius IV (3 December 1154) and into the pontificate of the
English pope, Hadrian IV. Three weeks after his accession in
December 1154 Hadrian sent legates – two of whom, Bernard, cardinal priest of S. Clemente and Octavian, cardinal priest of S. Cecilia,
had participated in negotiating the treaty of Constance – 'to treat
with [Frederick] about the *honor* and the exaltation of the Roman
church and the welfare of the kingdom'. Simultaneously Hadrian
wrote to the royal adviser Wibald, bidding him raise the problems of
the Church with the king as soon as possible.[269] The new pope, like
his five predecessors, was hardpressed both by the Romans and by
the king of Sicily. The Roman commune had found an able leader in
Arnold of Brescia, reforming preacher and critic of the papacy. In the
Sicilian kingdom Roger II's successor, William I, had assumed the
title of king without seeking the permission of his feudal lord, the
pope (Easter 1154). When Hadrian refused to recognise him as king,

---

[266] *MGH Constitutiones* 1, 201–3. See W. Ohnsorge, *Abendland und Byzanz*
(Darmstadt, 1958) pp. 411–33; P. Rassow, *Honor Imperii. Die neue Politik Friedrich
Barbarossas 1152–1159* (2nd edition: Darmstadt, 1961) pp. 60–5; Maccarrone, *Papato*
(n. 227) pp. 50–1, 79–80; Munz, *Barbarossa* (n. 257) pp. 64–5.

[267] Hauck, *Kirchengeschichte Deutschlands* 4, 203–5; Munz pp. 66–9.

[268] Hadrian IV, *JL* 9966: *MPL* 188, 1372BC. See G. Dunken, *Die politische Wirksamkeit
der päpstlichen Legaten in der Zeit des Kampfes zwischen Kaisertum und Papsttum in
Oberitalien unter Friedrich I.* (Historische Studien 209: Berlin, 1931) p. 12.

[269] Otto of Freising, *Gesta Friderici* (n. 173) II.10, p. 89; Frederick I, letter to Otto,
ibid., p. 1. See Hauck, *Kirchengeschichte Deutschlands* 4, 199–202, 205, 211–12.

William's army began in the summer of 1155 to attack the Patrimony of St Peter. By this time Hadrian had already hastened to renew the treaty of Constance with Frederick I (? January 1155).[270] Frederick had begun his first progress of his Italian kingdom in October 1154; in June 1155 he reached Rome. As a gesture of good will towards the pope he had taken prisoner the fugitive Arnold of Brescia and handed him over to the Roman prefect for execution.[271]

Frederick I and Hadrian IV met first at Sutri on 9 June and nine days later the imperial coronation was performed in St Peter's. The ceremony triggered off riots in Rome which were brutally suppressed by the German army. In the days after the coronation Frederick withdrew northwards, Hadrian and the cardinals accompanying him as far as Tivoli, where pope and emperor celebrated together the feast of SS. Peter and Paul (29 June). Soon afterwards, fearing that the unwholesome climate would cause disease in the army, Frederick ordered a return to Germany without venturing an expedition against Sicily. The papal and German sources agree on this bare outline of the events of June 1155, but in matters of detail they differ considerably. The 'official' German version is found in the letter of Frederick to his uncle, the chronicler Bishop Otto of Freising, summarising events early in his reign, and at greater length in Book II of Otto's biography of his nephew. This version claims that on 9 June at Sutri Hadrian was received by the king 'with the honour due to his office', that king and pope enjoyed many 'pleasant conversations' and that Frederick rejected a suggestion from the Romans that he receive the imperial crown from their hands in return for a payment of 'a very great sum of money' and his swearing an oath to the commune.[272] The papal version, the biography of Hadrian IV by Boso, cardinal deacon of SS. Cosma e Damiano, says nothing of this Roman offer and presents a very different account of the relations of Frederick and Hadrian. When on 9 June the pope rode into Frederick's camp at Sutri (according to Boso), the king refused to perform the ceremonial 'groom's office' (*stratoris officium*). The cardinals accompanying the pope deduced from this refusal that the king's intentions were hostile and fled in terror, leaving the pope, 'astonished and perturbed and uncertain what would be done to him', to negotiate with Frederick. The king

---

[270] This is the date suggested by L. Weiland: *MGH Constitutiones* 1, 213–14. See Rassow, *Honor Imperii* (n. 266) pp. 66–8.
[271] Otto of Freising, *Gesta* II.28, p. 107.
[272] Frederick I, letter to Otto, pp. 2–3; Otto, *Gesta* II.28–30, pp. 106–11.

was willing to kiss the pope's feet, but Hadrian refused him the kiss of peace until he had shown 'that accustomed and due honour' which 'the orthodox emperors' had always shown to the popes, the *stratoris officium*. Frederick spent the next day consulting 'old records' and 'the more ancient princes and especially those who had come with King Lothar to Pope Innocent'. Persuaded by their advice, Frederick met Hadrian next day at Nepi and performed the ceremony.[273] While the German version of the events of June 1155 presents a picture of harmony and emphasises Frederick's willingness to cooperate, the papal version describes a tense situation caused by Frederick's unwillingness to respect the *honor* of the papacy. Both versions were written with hindsight and with a polemical intention: the German version, to conceal the emperor's failure to fulfil the terms of the treaty of Constance; the papal version, to blame Frederick for the deterioration in papal–imperial relations which had occurred by the end of Hadrian's pontificate. There is, however, some evidence to support Boso's version of a tense encounter. The chaplain of Otto of Freising, Rahewin, who continued the biography of Frederick after Otto's death (1158), supplied a detail which Otto had omitted. In June 1155 Frederick had delivered 'a friendly reproach' to the pope about the picture of Lothar III in the Lateran and the inscription calling him 'the vassal of the pope', and Hadrian had agreed to remove the picture and the inscription.[274] It seems likely that Frederick objected to the *stratoris officium* for the same reason that he objected to the picture of Lothar III: both contained the unacceptable implication that the emperor was the pope's vassal. Nevertheless in June 1155 neither Frederick nor Hadrian desired a quarrel; and Boso's account concedes that the imperial coronation restored harmony. Emperor and pope, 'both wearing their crowns', celebrated the feast of SS. Peter and Paul together, 'for it was entirely fitting that the two foremost princes of the world should celebrate the solemnities of those two princes of the apostles with delight and great joy'.[275]

The breach between Hadrian and Frederick occurred, firstly, because the emperor failed to fulfil the terms of the treaty of

---

[273] Boso, *Vita Hadriani IV* (n. 190) pp. 391–2. See Munz, *Barbarossa* (n. 257) pp. 80–3.

[274] Rahewin, *Gesta Friderici* (n. 225) III.10, p. 141. See above pp. 452–3.

[275] Boso, *Vita* p. 393. On the events of June 1155 see W. Ullmann, 'The pontificate of Adrian IV', *Cambridge Historical Journal* 11 (1955), 239–42, who argued that Hadrian introduced modifications into the imperial coronation ceremony, so as to emphasise papal superiority to the emperor. For a different view see Munz, *Barbarossa* p. 86 n. 1.

Constance after his coronation and, secondly, because the pope took measures to protect himself from his enemies which ultimately involved him in breaking the treaty. Frederick returned to Germany in the summer of 1155 without having restored papal authority over Rome or the Patrimony of St Peter: neither the Roman commune nor the king of Sicily had been subdued. Immediately after the emperor's departure, however, William I of Sicily suffered a setback, a rebellion of prominent vassals, which Hadrian was tempted to exploit. One party of Norman rebels received the formidable support of Byzantine forces, a military mission sent by Emperor Manuel Comnenus to seize Ancona, perhaps with the objective of reconquering southern Italy. In September 1155 the pope allied with the Norman rebels Robert II of Capua and Andrew of Rupecanina against King William. It is not clear whether Hadrian also allied with the Greek army in Ancona.[276] In the event the pope proved to have miscalculated: William I defeated the hostile coalition and Hadrian was forced to make peace on the king's terms. The concordat of Benevento (18 June 1156) confirmed papal suzerainty over the kingdom of Sicily; but it also legalised the conquests recently made by the Sicilian king at the expense of the Patrimony of St Peter.[277] A year later a treaty was concluded between William I and Emperor Manuel Comnenus, in which Byzantium recognised William's title to Sicily and southern Italy. The pope may have acted as mediator in this peace.[278] Both concordat and treaty appeared at the imperial court to be directed against the emperor. The imperial chaplain and panegyrist Godfrey of Viterbo claimed that Hadrian had broken the treaty of Constance not once but twice: by making peace both with the Normans and with Byzantium. '[The pope] wishes to be regarded as Caesar's enemy. Our agreement is undone: the Greek will be his friend. The Roman bishop has joined the enemies of the empire; he makes treaties with the Sicilians and likewise with the Greeks.'[279]

In a letter of 19 January 1157 to Wibald of Stablo and Corvey Hadrian sought to soften the impact of the concordat of Benevento on the imperial court. He had heard that 'there are about the emperor

[276] J. G. Rowe, 'Hadrian IV, the Byzantine empire and the Latin orient' in *Essays in medieval history presented to Bertie Wilkinson* ed. T. A. Sandquist and M. R. Powicke (Toronto, 1969) pp. 9–12.
[277] Concordat of Benevento: *MGH Constitutiones* I, 588–91. See above p. 390.
[278] Rowe, 'Hadrian IV' p. 13.
[279] Godfrey of Viterbo, *Gesta Friderici* 10, *MGH SS* 22, 313.

. . . certain men who strive by all means to extinguish devotion for the holy Roman church in his mind'. He therefore commanded Wibald that he 'advise the emperor to remain a venerator of the apostolic see, so that he is not moved from the good and right frame of mind by the suggestions of any man'.[280] The enemy of the Roman church at the imperial court, of whose malign influence Hadrian had heard rumours was Rainald of Dassel, provost of Hildesheim, who had been appointed imperial chancellor a month before the concordat of Benevento. Rainald soon ousted the advisers whom Frederick had inherited from Conrad III – Wibald and Eberhard of Bamberg – and for the next eleven years remained the emperor's closest adviser, as chancellor (1156–9) and archbishop of Cologne (1159–67).[281] It is evident from the papal letter of January 1157 that seven months after the concordat of Benevento Hadrian was attempting to counter the influence of Rainald of Dassel and to maintain friendly relations with the emperor. Indeed since the beginning of his pontificate he had sought to win friends in Germany who might defend papal interests at the imperial court. At the time of the imperial coronation he had sought the friendship of the mighty Welf prince, Henry the Lion.[282] Immediately after the concordat of Benevento he appointed Archbishop Adolf of Mainz as papal legate, seizing the opportunity to praise Mainz's distinguished record of obedience to the Roman church.[283] If Hadrian's intention was to use these friends as a papal party in Germany – a pressure group such as Gregory VII had created in the 1070s – he was disappointed. In the quarrel of pope and emperor which flared up in October 1157 no party of bishops and princes emerged to oppose Frederick I.

This quarrel was initially concerned with the case of Archbishop Eskil of Lund. Eskil, visiting Rome at the beginning of 1157, received from Hadrian the primacy of the Swedish church. On his return journey he was captured by brigands in Burgundy and held to ransom. Hadrian called upon the emperor to secure Eskil's freedom; and when Frederick did not respond, the pope sent legates to the imperial diet at Besançon (October 1157) with a letter of rebuke to

---

[280] Hadrian IV, *JL* 10246 (n. 268), 1493B.

[281] K. Zeillinger, 'Friedrich Barbarossa, Wibald von Stablo und Eberhard von Bamberg' *MIÖG* 78 (n. 17), 210–23; R. M. Herkenrath, *Rainald von Dassel, Reichskanzler und Erzbischof von Köln* (dissertation: Graz, 1962).

[282] Helmold of Bosau, *Chronica Slavorum* 1.81, *MGH SS rer. Germ.* (1868) pp. 154–5. See Hauck, *Kirchengeschichte Deutschlands* 4, 218–20.

[283] Hadrian IV, *JL* 10201: P. Jaffé, *Bibliotheca rerum germanicarum* 3, 404.

the emperor. This papal letter now became the subject of contention and the case of Archbishop Eskil (who was freed soon after the diet) was forgotten. The suddenness with which Eskil disappeared from the scene has suggested to many historians that the archbishop's imprisonment was simply the pretext used by the papal curia for an attack on the emperor.[284] However, there is good reason for supposing that Hadrian took the case of Eskil of Lund very seriously; and certainly the case involved issues of importance both to the papacy and to the empire. Firstly, Eskil had been a loyal agent of the papacy since the period of the legation of Cardinal bishop Nicholas of Albano (the future Hadrian IV) in Scandinavia (1152–3). In January 1157 he became a papal legate and on receiving the pallium as primate of Sweden, he swore fidelity to the Roman church: on both counts he enjoyed the special protection of the papacy. Secondly, Eskil was an enemy of King Swein Grathe of Denmark and supported his rival for the throne, Knut Magnusson. Swein had obtained the Danish kingdom through his willingness to accept it as a fief from Frederick Barbarossa (1152). Swein's most enthusiastic supporter was his kinsman by marriage, Archbishop Hartwig of Bremen, who was in turn the enemy of Eskil; for Hartwig sought (with the support of the emperor) to subject Lund to the metropolitan jurisdiction of Bremen. When Eskil came to Rome in January 1157, it was in order to seek papal protection against both King Swein and Hartwig of Bremen.[285] There was ample material for papal-imperial conflict in the case of Eskil of Lund. As far as the curia was concerned, Eskil was a faithful agent on whom depended the success of papal plans for the reorganisation of the Scandinavian church. He was also a protégé of the Roman church who was apparently being victimised because of his opposition to the emperor's friends. In Frederick's eyes Eskil was a political enemy who was using his close relationship with the papacy to frustrate the legitimate claims of a loyal imperial bishop and to counter imperial influence in Denmark. In Eskil's case the aspirations of empire and papacy in the northern world came into direct confrontation.

The quarrel was directed into a new channel by Hadrian's letter of rebuke, issued on 20 September and delivered to the diet of Besançon

[284] For the literature on the diet of Besançon see Heinemeyer, '*Beneficium*' (n. 225) pp. 155–60.
[285] W. Seegrün, *Das Papsttum und Skandinavien bis zur Vollendung der nordischen Kirchenorganisation (1164)* (Quellen und Forschungen zur Geschichte Schleswig-Holsteins 51: Neumünster, 1967) pp. 149–50, 171–7.

by his legates, Roland, cardinal priest of S. Marco and chancellor, and Bernard, cardinal priest of S. Clemente. The papal letter attributed Frederick's 'dissembling and neglect' to 'the suggestion of a wicked man', prompting the emperor to anger against the Roman church. The emperor was reminded of the debt of gratitude which he owed to the Roman church, which had 'conferred on [him] the fullness of dignity and honour' and 'the sign of the imperial crown'. 'We do not regret that we fulfilled your will and desire: indeed if Your Excellency had received greater *beneficia* (if it were possible) from our hands, we should rightly rejoice . . . '[286] It was the statement that the pope 'conferred' the imperial dignity and the use of the word *beneficia* which caused the 'incident' at Besançon. According to Frederick's biographer, Rahewin, the papal letter was translated into German in the diet by the chancellor Rainald of Dassel; and he interpreted the offending passage as meaning that Frederick had 'received the imperial crown as a fief (*pro beneficio*) from the lord pope'. This translation caused 'tumult and uproar among the magnates of the kingdom', which was worsened by the rejoinder of one of the legates: 'From whom does he hold the empire, if not from the lord pope?' The legate's remark provoked Otto of Wittelsbach, count palatine of Bavaria, to threaten him with his sword; but the emperor intervened to prevent bloodshed. Frederick ordered the legates 'not to wander here and there in the territories of bishops and abbots' but immediately 'to return to the City by the direct route'. The legates were pursued by an imperial letter refuting the notion that the empire was a papal fief and calling on the pope 'to grieve at so great a dishonour to us and to the empire'.[287] Hadrian responded with an appeal to the German bishops to 'perform a service pleasing to St Peter, prince of the apostles, and preserve your own liberty and that of your churches' by striving 'to lead [Frederick] back to the right way as soon as possible'.[288] This Gregorian language had no effect on the German bishops. In their answer to Hadrian's letter they declared themselves to be 'weak and fainthearted' and terrified at the prospect of conflict between pope and emperor: 'We humbly ask and beseech Your Holiness to spare our infirmity and like a good shepherd calm the high spirits of your son [the emperor] with a letter

---

[286] Hadrian IV: *JL* 10304: Rahewin, *Gesta Friderici* III.9 (n. 225), pp. 139–40; *MGH Constitutiones* I, 229–30.
[287] Rahewin, *Gesta* III. 10–11, pp. 140–3.
[288] Hadrian IV, *JL* 10321 (n. 286), pp. 148–9; 232–3.

sweetening your former writing.'[289] No pressure-group appeared in Germany to support the papal stand. Hadrian therefore (in Rahewin's words) 'changed his purpose for the better and sent envoys to calm [Frederick's] spirit'. The legates Henry, cardinal priest of SS. Nereo e Achilleo and Hyacinth, cardinal deacon of S. Maria in Cosmedin brought to an imperial diet at Augsburg (June 1158) the conciliatory letter which the bishops had requested.[290]

Hadrian's letter of June 1158 offered a minimising interpretation of the papal letter of the previous September.

Among us *beneficium* means not a fief but a good deed . . . and Your Magnificence obviously acknowledges that we placed the sign of the imperial dignity on your head in so good and honourable a manner that it may well be considered by all to have been a good deed . . . By this term 'we conferred [the crown]', we meant nothing other than . . . 'we placed [the crown on your head]'.

Some historians have accepted this explanation.[291] Others have argued that the papal letter of September 1157 had indeed claimed that the imperial dignity was a fief conferred by the pope and that the letter of June 1158 marked a retreat from the earlier claim, forced on Hadrian by the attitude of the German bishops. 'What was [Hadrian's earlier letter]', asked Albert Hauck, 'if not an attack, cleverly thought out and boldly resolved upon? It had nothing to do with the interests of the Church and of religion: instead it originated in the Gregorian idea of the world dominion of the papacy.'[292] Did Hadrian intend to revive Gregory VII's conception (1081) of the German king as a vassal of the pope? This was how Rainald of Dassel and other imperial advisers interpreted the letter: hence the imperial propaganda of 1157 is devoted to proving the independence of the 'holy empire' (*sacrum imperium*) bestowed by God on Frederick.[293] Certainly the German bishops were justified in complaining of 'the unfortunate ambiguity of meaning' in the letter. For while in France, Burgundy and Italy the term *beneficium*, in the sense of 'fief', had

---

[289] Rahewin, *Gesta* III.17, pp. 149–51.

[290] Hadrian IV, *JL* 10386 (n. 286), pp. 156–7; 234–5.

[291] W. Ullmann, 'Cardinal Roland and Besançon', *Miscellanea Historiae Pontificiae* 18 (1954), 107–25; *idem*, 'Adrian IV' (n. 275) pp. 243–4. Cf. R. Foreville and J. Rousset de Pina, *Du premier Concile du Latran* (n. 170) pp. 40–3.

[292] Hauck, *Kirchengeschichte Deutschlands* 4, 225. Cf. Pacaut, *Alexandre III* pp. 92–3; Munz, *Barbarossa* (n. 257) pp. 140–3, 186, 189.

[293] The term *sacrum imperium*, closely associated with Rainald of Dassel, first began to be used in imperial documents in 1157: see R. M. Herkenrath, 'Rainald von Dassel als Verfasser und Schreiber von Kaiserurkunden', *MIÖG* 72 (1964), 54–60.

been displaced before the mid-twelfth century by *feudum*, in Germany *beneficium* remained the technical term for a feudal holding into the thirteenth century.[294] It is difficult to believe that the papal curia was not aware of this. Even if Hadrian himself did not revive the feudal terminology of Gregory VII, other members of the curia seem to have recalled it. There is the evidence of the 'feudal' inscription added to Innocent II's mural of the imperial coronation of Lothar III;[295] and the evidence of Rahewin concerning the retort of the papal legate at Besançon: 'From whom does [Frederick] hold the empire, if not from the lord pope?' Some members of the curia were prepared to use the Gregorian language of papal suzerainty over the empire; and it is reasonable to identify these 'Gregorians' with the anti-German party in the curia which came into existence in the years 1156–9.

The enemies of this party called it 'the Sicilian party' and identified as its leader the chancellor, Roland, cardinal priest of S. Marco, who on the death of Hadrian IV (1 September 1159) was elected as Pope Alexander III by a majority of the cardinals.[296] Both hostile and friendly sources (all written after the outbreak of the schism of 1159) connect the origins of the party with the treaty of Benevento (18 June 1156). Those cardinals who rejected Alexander III declared in their manifesto of October 1159:

From the time when friendship was established at Benevento between the lord Pope Hadrian and William of Sicily, contrary to the honour of God's Church and of the empire, great division and discord have arisen (not without cause) among the cardinals. We . . . in no way consented to the friendship, which had been contracted to the detriment of the Church and the empire; but others, blinded by money and many promises and firmly bound to the Sicilian, wickedly defended the treaty . . . and attracted very many others to share their error.

According to this manifesto, Hadrian IV was the dupe of the Sicilian party, who sought 'to induce and deceive the lord pope with all their cunning' to adopt their anti-imperial policy.[297] However, in his biography of Hadrian, Cardinal Boso – himself a member of the Sicilian party – claimed that the party came into being in order to implement Hadrian's own policy. When at the end of 1155 King

[294] Heinemeyer, *'Beneficium'* (n. 225) pp. 160, 235.
[295] See above pp. 452–3.
[296] W. Madertoner, *Die zwiespältige Papstwahl des Jahres 1159* (dissertation: Vienna, 1978) pp. 21–52.
[297] Rahewin, *Gesta* (n. 225) IV.62, pp. 241–2.

William I of Sicily had offered advantageous terms to avoid conflict with the papacy, Hadrian had wished to accept 'so useful an agreement', but his wishes were overruled by the cardinals: 'the greater part of the brethren . . . refused to consent'. In the summer of 1156, when the victorious king of Sicily had the papacy at his mercy, the pope 'sent the greater part of his brethren into Campania and he remained with a few of them in Benevento'. Three of the cardinals who remained in Benevento – the chancellor Roland and Hubald, cardinal priest of S. Prassede, the future Pope Lucius III (both of whom had participated in the negotiation and renewal of the treaty of Constance), together with Julius, cardinal priest of S. Marcello – negotiated the treaty of Benevento, while the politically unreliable majority of the cardinals was kept at a distance.[298] According to Boso, therefore, Hadrian was not the dupe but the ringleader of the Sicilian party. It seems likely enough that Hadrian, although initially anxious to renew Eugenius III's treaty with the German king, soon became dissatisfied with the German alliance. Hadrian's attitude probably resembled that of his chancellor Roland who (in a letter of April 1160) was to date his disenchantment from the imperial coronation in 1155. 'From the time of . . . Pope Hadrian and from the inception of his [imperial] dignity, [Frederick] began, like a tyrant, to oppress and greatly to injure the holy Roman church.' The emperor took prisoner 'archbishops and bishops returning from the apostolic see' and mistreated papal legates. Finaly, at the end of Hadrian's pontificate Frederick 'violently invaded the Patrimony of St Peter'.[299]

The small group of cardinals who formed the nucleus of the Sicilian party in June 1156 made only slow progress in winning over the rest of the curia. Even their attempt to exploit the 'incident' at Besançon as evidence of imperial hostility towards the Roman church merely intensified the division in the curia: a number of cardinals 'favoured the party of the emperor and blamed the negligence and inexperience' of the legates at Besançon.[300] The leaders of the imperial party were Octavian, cardinal priest of S. Cecilia and his kinsman, Guido of Crema, cardinal priest of S. Maria in Trastevere, both noblemen with many family connections among the royal and princely houses of the west and both destined to become the antipopes of Frederick I: 'Victor IV' (1159–64) and 'Paschal III' (1164–8).

[298] Boso, *Vita* (n. 273) pp. 394–5.
[299] Alexander III, *JL* 10627–8: *MPL* 200, 89BC, 91AB.
[300] Rahewin, *Gesta* III.16, p. 147.

Both owed their prominence in the curia to Eugenius III and their careers illustrate the importance which Eugenius had attached to the German alliance. Both were regarded in the curia as experts in German affairs: Octavian in particular was regarded by contemporaries as 'a special lover of the Germans' and 'the advocate of the Germans in the curia'.[301] Both had participated in the negotiation of the treaty of Constance and were determined that the curia should keep the treaty. It is a measure of their continuing influence that in the last year of Hadrian's pontificate Octavian and Guido were sent on a legation to the emperor to request the renewal of the treaty (April 1159). Frederick, however, refused the request. He reproached the pope for his violation of the treaty and for the 'very harsh terms' which Hadrian now sought to impose, directed against Frederick's policy of restoring imperial control over the kingdom of Italy, recently inaugurated at the diet of Roncaglia (November 1158).[302] While the leaders of the imperial party were carrying out their fruitless mission, Hadrian was conducting other negotiations which make it clear that he, no less than Frederick, considered that the papal–German alliance was at an end. In June 1159 Hadrian withdrew from Rome to Anagni with Roland and twelve other cardinals who now comprised the Sicilian party. There the pope negotiated an alliance with the cities of Milan, Brescia, Piacenza and Crema – the Lombard cities which were resisting the imposition of the imperial decrees issued at Roncaglia and which were soon to be at war with the emperor. According to the pro-imperial chronicles, the papacy was responsible for fomenting the rebellion in Lombardy. In these hostile accounts the papal–Milanese alliance is represented as the work of Roland, who is wrongly identified as Milanese (he was of the noble family of Bandinelli in Siena). 'The chancellor Roland, a Milanese by birth . . . turned all whom he could into enemies of the emperor and aroused the envy of the Milanese, among whom he himself originated, against [Frederick].'[303] By the time of Hadrian's death the Sicilian party had openly aligned itself with the emperor's enemies.

---

[301] Balderic, *Gesta Alberonis* c. 23 (n. 202), p. 255; John of Salisbury, *Historia pontificalis* c. 38 (n. 235), pp. 75, 77. See Zenker, *Mitglieder* (n. 232) pp. 56–9, 66–70; Madertoner, *Papstwahl* (n. 296) pp. 90–108, 111–14.

[302] Rahewin, *Gesta* IV.34–5, pp. 219–21. See Munz, *Barbarossa* (n. 257) pp. 194–200; Partner, *Lands of St. Peter* (n. 129) pp. 197–202.

[303] *Annales Stadenses* 1159, *MGH SS* 16, 344. Cf. Rahewin, *Gesta* IV.21, p. 208; Godfrey of Viterbo, *Gesta* 11 (n. 279), p. 314. See Madertoner, *Papstwahl* (n. 296) pp. 37–42.

The faction struggle which had preoccupied the curia since 1156 culminated in the papal election of 4–7 September 1159, which plunged the western Church into an eighteen-year schism. The Sicilian party, thirteen strong in Anagni in June 1159, seems to have attracted the support of ten previously uncommitted cardinals for the candidature of the chancellor Roland as Pope Alexander III. His rival Octavian, as Victor IV, may initially have had the support of nine cardinals, but their numbers rapidly dwindled to five. Both parties were guilty of some irregularity of conduct during the election. The Sicilian party, assured of a majority, hastened to install its candidate as pope, ignoring the electoral agreement made by the college of cardinals before the election, which required the electors to reach a unanimous decision. The imperial party resorted to violence to prevent Roland's installation as pope.[304] Each party was to accuse the other (with some justification) of having plotted the succession of its candidate during the lifetime of Hadrian IV. Frederick I denounced the Sicilian party in a manifesto of February 1160: 'lest [their] evil faction should perhaps vanish because of the death of Pope Hadrian, they imposed an oath upon each other that on the death of the pope, no other should replace him except a member of their conspiracy [with William of Sicily and the Lombard cities]'.[305] Alexander III presented the counter-charge in a series of letters in April 1160. 'During [Hadrian's] lifetime [Frederick] planned, if the opportunity arose, to appoint as pope (or rather as apostate) Octavian, who was always the secret enemy of the Church.'[306] This accusation is supported by two pieces of evidence: firstly, the emperor's relations with the house of Monticelli, the family of Octavian; and secondly, the fact that Frederick's envoy was in Rome at the time of the election – Otto of Wittelsbach, who had attacked the papal legates at Besançon in 1157. The envoy had come to Rome in the summer of 1159 to negotiate with the pope and the Romans. The negotiations with the pope were fruitless, but those with the Romans were so successful that after the disputed election the Romans supported Victor IV. Alexander III, after spending a week besieged in Castel Sant'Angelo, was forced to flee the city. There is, however, no evidence that Otto of Wittelsbach tried to influence the election: his violent intervention occurred immediately after the

---

[304] Madertoner pp. 48–52, 120–8.
[305] Rahewin, *Gesta* IV.79, p. 263. Cf. Council of Pavia (1160) c. 6: *MGH Constitutiones* I, 259. See Madertoner pp. 43–7.
[306] Alexander III, *JL* 10627–8 (n. 299), 89C, 91C.

election, when he sought to make the Patrimony of St Peter subject to Victor IV.[307] The emperor's relations with the house of Monticelli seem superficially to offer less ambiguous evidence of Frederick's determination to raise his kinsman Octavian to the papacy. Four months before the election Frederick had conferred on Octavian's brothers, as an imperial fief, the city and county of Terni, which the papacy claimed as part of the Patrimony of St Peter.[308] However, in the context of the events of May 1159 this investiture was probably a measure intended to win friends in Rome in the event of a showdown with Hadrian IV. There is no firm evidence that Frederick plotted to make Octavian pope; although it is clear that once Octavian was elected, the emperor devoted himself wholeheartedly to his cause.

According to the practice of recent centuries, a papal schism was usually ended by a council summoned by the emperor. On two occasions during the early history of the reform papacy the imperial government had convoked such a council (Sutri in 1046 and Mantua in 1064). At the beginning of the schism of 1130 Anacletus II had appealed to Lothar III to recognise his title, while Innocent II had brusquely summoned Lothar to his aid. Lothar had responded by referring the rival claims to a council of bishops at Würzburg. Frederick I determined to resolve the schism of 1159 by the same means: a council 'to reform the unity of the Church', which was to meet in Pavia early in 1160. The emperor summoned the churchmen 'of our whole empire and other kingdoms, namely England, France, Hungary and Denmark', together with 'the chancellor Roland and the other cardinals who elected him Roman pontiff'.[309] The council of Pavia (5–11 February 1160) was attended by nearly fifty prelates, predominantly from the imperial territories and by the envoys of the kings of France and England and perhaps also of Denmark, Hungary and Bohemia. Given Frederick's own attitude, it is not surprising that his council recognised the title of Victor IV and rejected that of Alexander III; but many imperial churchmen had not come to Pavia as committed supporters of Octavian. They were persuaded by the

---

[307] Madertoner pp. 131–41. See the letter of the Alexandrine cardinals to Frederick I: W. Holtzmann, 'Quellen und Forschungen zur Geschichte Friedrich Barbarossas (Englische Analekten I)', *NA* 48 (1930), 398–400.

[308] P. F. Kehr, 'Zur Geschichte Viktors IV. (Oktavian von Monticelli)', *NA* 46 (1926), 53–85; K. Zeillinger, 'Zwei Diplome Barbarossas für seine römischen Parteigänger (1159)', *DA* 20 (1964), 568–81; H. Schwarzmeier, 'Zur Familie Viktors IV. in der Sabina', *QFIAB* 48 (1968), 64–79; Madertoner pp. 131–41.

[309] Council of Pavia (n. 305) pp. 253–6.

evidence produced at the council – notably the evidence of Alexander's alliance with Sicily and the Lombard cities.[310] The council heard no detailed defence of Alexander's claim. He was represented by one of his electors, William, cardinal priest of S. Pietro in Vincoli, whose silence during the council was interpreted as consent by the Victorines and as treachery by at least one of Alexander's supporters.[311] Cardinal William's silence at Pavia was, however, justified by the attitude of his pope. Alexander denounced the emperor's summoning of a council – 'in which he seems to have departed entirely from the custom of his predecessors and to have overstepped the limits of his dignity'. Alexander's response to the council of Pavia was to restate the privilege of the Roman church, which judged the cases of all other churches but 'never submitted to the judgement of any other'.[312] Alexander was to give the same Gregorian response to the emperor's second attempt to resolve the schism by means of a general council, this time at St Jean de Losne (7–8 September 1162).[313]

Frederick's conciliar solution to the schism persuaded neither 'the party of the chancellor Roland' nor the greater part of western Christendom. Neither Louis VII of France nor Henry II of England accepted the decision of the council of Pavia and four months later they formally recognised Alexander III as pope at a council in Beauvais.[314] In August 1160 the emperor declared that 'many kingdoms – Spain, Hungary, Denmark, Bohemia – and also the count of Barcelona and the count of St Gilles with the whole of Provence and Burgundy obey [Victor IV] and [his cause] gains in strength from day to day'. In fact, however, of these territories only Provence and Burgundy proved consistently obedient to Victor: the others were either Alexandrine or divided in their loyalties between a Victorine prince and an Alexandrine episcopate.[315] By January 1161 Alexander

---

[310] Madertoner pp. 142–82.

[311] John of Salisbury, *Letter* 214, ed. W. J. Millor, H. E. Butler and C. N. L. Brooke 1 (London, 1955), 210–11. See Zenker, *Mitglieder* (n. 232) p. 119.

[312] Alexander III, *JL* 10597: Boso, *Vita Alexandri III: Liber pontificalis* 2, 401–2; *MGH Constitutiones* 1, 256–7.

[313] W. Heinemeyer, 'Die Verhandlungen an der Saône im Jahre 1162', *DA* 20 (1964), 155–89.

[314] F. Barlow, 'The English, Norman and French councils called to deal with the papal schism of 1159', *EHR* 51 (1936), 264–8; M. G. Cheney, 'The recognition of Pope Alexander III: some neglected evidence', *ibid.*, 84 (1969), 474–97.

[315] Frederick I, mandate to the patriarch of Aquileia: *MGH Constitutiones* 1, 274. See Hauck, *Kirchengeschichte Deutschlands* 4, 256; Foreville and Rousset de Pina (n. 170) pp. 57–9.

could make a more impressive and rather more accurate counter-claim. 'The eastern Church in a council solemnly celebrated in Nazareth in the presence of the illustrious king of Jerusalem, the French, the English, the Spanish and the whole western Church' had condemned Octavian and recognised Alexander.[316] The pope's Anglo-Norman supporter Bishop Arnulf of Lisieux simultaneously assured the Alexandrine cardinals that the recognition of King Henry II would automatically entail that of 'the kingdom of the French, the English, the Spanish, the Irish and . . . Norway'.[317] The success of the Alexandrine cause in 1160–1 faced the emperor with a twofold task: to defeat the pope's allies in Italy – the Lombard cities and the king of Sicily – and to detach from Alexander's obedience his two most important supporters in northern Europe, the kings of France and England. Frederick forced the surrender of Milan in March 1162. His total destruction of the city terrified the rest of Lombardy into submission. While the imperial adviser Rainald of Dassel proceeded to reorganise the administration of Tuscany and the emperor pre-pared an expedition against Sicily, Alexander sought safety in France.

During the pope's three-year sojourn in France imperial diplomacy concentrated on winning over Louis VII and Henry II to the party of the antipope. In the spring of 1162 Frederick tried to exploit the French king's unwillingness to offer asylum to Alexander and momentarily persuaded Louis to accept his plan for a general council. Louis was to compel Alexander's attendance at a meeting of the two monarchs and the two popes at St Jean de Losne on the Saône: there Frederick could complete what was begun at Pavia.[318] Imperial diplomacy was continually directed also to dislodging Henry II from the Alexandrine obedience. In May 1165 Rainald of Dassel (who had been negotiating matrimonial projects with the English royal family) announced that Henry II was now prepared to recognise the antipope.[319] However, both the manoeuvre of 1162 and that of 1165 proved unavailing since the French and English churches remained convinced of the legality of Alexander's claims. The kings might yield to the emperor's persuasion but their bishops and clergy declined to follow them. What these churchmen knew or

---

[316] Alexander III, *JL* 10645 (n. 299), 102C.
[317] Arnulf of Lisieux, *Letter* 29, ed. F. Barlow (Camden Society 3rd ser., 61: London, 1939) p. 49.
[318] Heinemeyer, 'Verhandlungen' (n. 313) pp. 155–89; Munz, *Barbarossa* (n. 257) pp. 228–35.
[319] Foreville and Rousset de Pina (n. 291) pp. 78–9, 105; Munz pp. 239–40.

suspected of Frederick's political designs and his attitude towards the papacy turned them resolutely against the emperor and his antipope. It was rumoured that after the failure of Louis VII to produce Alexander at St Jean de Losne, Rainald of Dassel had bitterly denounced 'the temerity of the provincial kings' who dared to meddle in the emperor's affairs. 'If the emperor wished to pronounce judgement on a dispute concerning a bishopric which had arisen in the states [of the French and English kings], no doubt they would regard this as a serious injustice; yet they are trying to do the same thing in the city of Rome.'[320] The propaganda of the Alexandrine party in France and England emphasised the contempt of the emperor and his advisers for the *provinciales reges* and Frederick's intention of treating the Roman church as an imperial bishopric. Arnulf of Lisieux warned the English church that Frederick wished to imitate his predecessors who 'had aspired to subject the Roman church to their dominion and had always raised up or encouraged schismatics against her . . . so as to subordinate her to their will'.[321] John of Salisbury, Alexander's most fervent supporter in Canterbury, declared that it had been Frederick's plan since the pontificate of Eugenius III 'to reform the government of the whole world and to subject the world to the city' of Rome. 'Who has subjected the universal Church to the judgement of a particular church? Who has made the Germans the judges of the nations?'[322]

The themes of this propaganda were borrowed from the letters which Alexander himself issued after the council of Pavia. There Frederick is denounced as a tyrant who 'follows the most wicked footsteps of his forefathers'. An emperor 'ought to be the special protector and defender' of the Roman church, but Frederick is her oppressor.[323] Frederick had rejected the example of his predecessor, Lothar III, in favour of that of his great-grandfather, Henry IV. The principal theme of Alexander III's propaganda is found also in the papal polemics of the Investiture Contest: the emperor and his antipope 'strive to tear in pieces the seamless tunic of Christ', that is, the unity of the Church. The first letters of his pontificate take up this image. 'The eternal and unchangeable providence of the Creator willed that from her foundation the holy and immaculate Church

---

[320] Saxo Grammaticus, *Gesta Danorum* XIV, MGH SS 29, 114.

[321] Arnulf, *Letter* 28 (n. 317), p. 40.

[322] John of Salisbury, *Letter* 124 (n. 311), p. 206.

[323] Alexander III, *JL* 10627, to Arnulf of Lisieux (n. 299), 88A–90C; *JL* 10628, to Archbishop Eberhard of Salzburg and his suffragans, 90D–92D; *JL* 10629, to Archbishop John of Toledo: *NA* 6 (1880), 369.

should be governed by a system, so that there is one shepherd and teacher, to whom the prelates of all the churches are irresistibly subject': this 'miraculous unity' is now threatened by 'the apostate and schismatic Octavian'.[324] The antipope was excommunicated one week after Alexander's consecration (27 September 1159); Frederick was excommunicated six months later (24 March 1160), after the council of Pavia. The emperor's offence was 'that he has received Octavian and obstinately presumes to adhere to him'. Frederick, 'as it is said', had invested Octavian with the papacy 'by means of a ring' (the accusation was false). 'He is seen to subject the Church of God to his rule' and 'he intends to subject to himself the kings and princes of various regions by means of both the spiritual and the material sword'. If he succeeded in imposing his antipope on the Church, it would be impossible to prevent his extending his dominion over the other secular rulers.[325]

Immediately after the council of Pavia Alexander's legate in Milan, John of Anagni, cardinal deacon of S. Maria in Porticu, excommunicated the schismatics and their supporters and declared that all Frederick's acts were null and void 'until he had made peace with the Church'.[326] Simultaneously Alexander absolved all Frederick's subjects from the fealty which they had sworn to him and commanded them 'for the remission of sins' to offer the tyrant no counsel or aid.[327] This was done (claimed the pope's biographer, Cardinal Boso) 'according to the ancient custom of his predecessors'[328] – that is, of Gregory VII and his successors, who had excommunicated Henry IV and Henry V. However, a comparison of these Gregorian condemnations with the sentence pronounced by Alexander on Frederick reveals an important difference. Firstly, unlike Gregory VII, Alexander did not combine sentence of *deposition* with his excommunication of the emperor. There was no word of depriving Frederick of 'the government of the whole kingdom of the Germans and of Italy' in the sentence of March 1160 nor in the renewal of the excommunication of 'the schismatic Octavian

[324] Alexander III, *JL* 10584, to the archbishop of Genoa; *JL* 10587, to the bishop, canons and masters of Bologna: *JL* 10589, to the bishop and clergy of Paris; *JL* 10590, to the archbishop of Canterbury; *JL* 10591 (fragment), to Henry II of England; *JL* 10592, to the archbishop of Salzburg: (n. 299) 69A–73C; *NA* 3 (1878), 146.

[325] Alexander III, *JL* 10627: 90BC.

[326] Cardinal John of Anagni, letter to the Milanese: *Italia Pontificia* 6, 9 (no. 37), 11 (no. 174).

[327] Alexander III, *JL* 10628: 92CD.   [328] Boso, *Vita Alexandri III* (n. 312) p. 403.

and all his supporters' in the papal council of Montpellier on 17 May 1162.[329] When the excommunication was again renewed at the council of Tours (19 May 1163), Frederick's name was omitted. A Norman chronicler attributed to Alexander the statement, 'We exclude the emperor, whom we wish to reconcile to us on these matters'; and in the sermon opening the council Arnulf of Lisieux prayed that Frederick 'will be converted and live, since he is laudable among earthly princes for prudence and virtue'.[330] The emperor did not respond to this attempt at conciliation. When Victor IV died (20 April 1164), instead of opening negotiations with Alexander, Frederick recognised the new antipope, Paschal III, elected by the Victorine cardinals. Alexander seems to have renewed the excommunication of the emperor in 1167, when the rebellious north Italian cities hostile to the emperor organised themselves into the Lombard League. It is at this point that the papal deposition of the emperor is mentioned for the first and only time in the sources. In a letter written late in 1167 John of Salisbury claimed that Alexander had 'taken away the royal dignity from [Frederick] and anathematised him', following the example of Gregory VII. John repeated this claim on a number of occasions between December 1167 and March 1170.[331] The most likely explanation is that John's extreme hostility towards the emperor, his polemical intention in these letters and the scarcity of information from Italy caused him to exaggerate the severity of the papal sentence. Certainly the only extant papal document referring to the sentence of 1167, a letter to the consuls of Brescia (31 May), instructs them not to obey the emperor; but it says nothing of his deposition.[332] The decisive evidence is the description given both by Alexander and by Cardinal Boso of the final reconciliation of pope and emperor in Venice in July 1177. When Frederick

[329] *Ibid.*, p. 405; Alexander III, *JL* 10719: 144C (cf. Gregory VII, *Registrum* III.10, p. 271). See Pacaut, *Alexander III* p. 178 and the review by C. R. Cheney, *EHR* 73 (1958), 288.

[330] Stephen of Rouen, *Draco Normannicus* III.15, *RS* 82/2 (1885), 751; Arnulf of Lisieux, *Sermo: MPL* 201, 158B. See R. Somerville, *Pope Alexander III and the Council of Tours (1163)* (Los Angeles, 1977) pp. 63–7.

[331] John of Salisbury, *Letter* 242, ed. W. J. Millor and C. N. L. Brooke 2 (Oxford, 1979), 474. Cf. *Letters* 236, 239, 240, 272–4, 298, pp. 446, 454, 458, 553, 572, 574, 690.

[332] P. F. Kehr, 'Nachträge zu den Papsturkunden Italiens', *Nachrichten von der Königlichen Gesellschaft der Wissenschaften zu Göttingen, phil.-hist. Klasse* 1912, pp. 32–3 (no. 11). See Hauck, *Kirchengeschichte Deutschlands* 4, 288 and n. 4; Pacaut, *Alexandre III* p. 178; T. A. Reuter, 'John of Salisbury and the Germans' in *The world of John of Salisbury* ed. M. Wilks (Studies in Church History, subsidia 3: Oxford, 1984) pp. 416–18.

had renounced the antipope and 'promised obedience to the venerable Pope Alexander, as to the catholic prince, and to his canonically
elected successors', the cardinals 'both absolved him from the
sentence of excommunication and readmitted him to catholic
unity'.[333] Pope and biographer alike ignored the distinction between
restoration to communion and restoration to kingship which
Gregory VII had made a century before.

During the schism of 1159–77 Alexander III avoided the
Gregorian language not only of deposition but also of the superiority
of papal to imperial authority. The claims of Gregory VII – that 'the
priests of Christ are the fathers and masters of kings and princes and
all the faithful' and that the pope can therefore dismiss a useless king
and replace him with a useful one – do not reappear in Alexander's
propaganda. The theory of the pope's supremacy over the emperor
had continued to be insinuated in the propaganda of Innocent II and
Hadrian IV: the 'incident' at Besançon was provoked by Hadrian's
alleged revival of the Gregorian notion of the emperor as vassal of the
pope. The 'incident' at Besançon was the last official appearance
during the twelfth century of the theory of papal supremacy over the
empire. Historians usually assume (although without any firm evidence) that the chancellor Roland was the legate responsible for the
remark which infuriated the princes at Besançon: 'From whom does
[the emperor] hold the empire, if not from the lord pope?'[334] After he
became pope, however, Roland-Alexander seems never to have
reverted to this argument. The Gregorian concept of papal
supremacy is certainly found in the polemical literature of the schism
of 1159–77. The poet Walter of Châtillon, for example, wrote that
'the pope is supreme and the emperor is beneath him . . . Caesar
receives the temporal power from him who possesses the pastoral
care'.[335] No such claim is found in papal letters concerning the
schism. Here the emphasis is not on the authority of the pope but on
the crimes of the emperor which have earned him excommunication. Frederick was excommunicated not because he was disobedient towards the pope (Henry IV's offence) but because he was
'a violent persecutor of the Church'. His subjects were absolved
from fealty to him not because he had been deposed by the pope but
because in persecuting the Church he had ceased to fulfil the principal

---

[333] Boso, *Vita* (n. 312) p. 439. Cf. Alexander III, *JL* 12891 (n. 299), 1131B.

[334] C. R. Cheney, review of Pacaut, *Alexandre III* (n. 329) p. 288; Maccarrone, *Papato*
(n. 227) pp. 213–16. See above p. 468.

[335] Walter of Châtillon, *Carmina* II, *MGH Libelli* 3, 559–60.

function of his office. He was no longer 'the advocate and defender of the Church' and therefore 'should be called tyrant rather than emperor'.[336]

Frederick's supporters countered this papal argument with the idea, central to Staufen political thought, that the imperial authority was instituted by God: 'the kingship and the empire are ours from God alone through the election of the princes.' Staufen propagandists sought to emphasise the continuity between the pagan Roman empire and that of Frederick, the implication being that, as God had created the empire before he created the papacy, the former could owe none of its authority to the latter.[337] In the papal letters of the schism there was no attempt to refute this argument by means of Gregorian theories of the origins of the two powers and their relationship. Not even the ending of the schism prompted the victorious Alexander to make claims of papal supremacy. The imperial document confirming the Peace of Venice (July 1177) seized the opportunity to restate the Staufen conception of the 'holy empire'. 'Since the imperial majesty has been ordained on earth by the King of kings so that by its efforts the whole earth may rejoice in the increase of peace, we whom God has placed on the throne of the Roman empire must and will embrace [peace] the more diligently and maintain it the more fervently.'[338] For Alexander the Peace of Venice was an opportunity to reiterate the papal view of the schism, with only a passing reference to papal authority. The emperor, instead of defending the Church, had attacked it so that 'the dignity of the Roman church has almost perished and she who had been the mistress of the nations and the prince of provinces has been subjected to tribute'. Now, however, 'he who could not listen to a word of peace has been changed into another man': consequently he has been absolved from excommunication.[339]

This restraint shown by Alexander III in proclaiming his cause against the emperor is the most striking feature of the intellectual history of the second conflict of empire and papacy. Not only did Alexander not use the language of Gregory VII: he also ignored the elaborations of Gregorian theory presented by influential authors of

[336] Alexander III, *JL* 10655–6; 10644–5: 108A, 108D; 100B, 102B.
[337] Rahewin, *Gesta* (n. 225) III.11, pp. 142–3. See H. Appelt, 'Die Kaiseridee Friedrich Barbarossas', *SB der Akademie der Wissenschaften in Wien* 252 Abh. 4, phil.-hist. *Klasse* (Vienna, 1967); F. Kempf, 'Kanonistik' (n. 225) p. 39.
[338] Boso, *Vita* (n. 312) p. 442.
[339] Romuald of Salerno, *Annales* 1177, *MGH SS* 19, 444–5. See Pacaut, *Alexandre III* p. 180; Cheney, review (n. 329) p. 288.

the early twelfth century such as Bernard of Clairvaux, Hugh of St Victor and the encyclopaedist Honorius Augustodunensis.[340] Marcel Pacaut's study of Alexander III's conception of papal authority (1956) identifies Alexander as the disciple of Master Gratian of Bologna, 'the father of canon law', whose *Decretum* (*ca.* 1140), a private compilation of canons, rapidly became the standard textbook of students of canon law. Pacaut's analysis of Alexander's pronouncements on the freedom of the Church, the spiritual preeminence of the pope and the role of the secular power, suggests that Gratian's *Decretum* was 'the principal source of the thought of Alexander III'.[341] Master Gratian borrowed much from the late eleventh-century canonists whose writings were intended to justify the actions of Gregory VII; but he did not accept the Gregorian conception of the supremacy of the pope in secular affairs. Gratian preferred the Gelasian idea of two independent powers, spiritual and secular, with distinct functions. 'There are two persons by whom this world is ruled, namely the royal and the priestly. Just as kings are preeminent in the affairs of the world, so priests are preeminent in the affairs of God.'[342] The subsequent generation of canonists – the 'Decretists', whose writings took the form of commentaries on Gratian's *Decretum* – did not all agree with this view. During the 1160s two groups emerged among the Decretists with directly opposite answers to the question, 'from whom does the emperor obtain his sword' (that is, his authority)? The Decretists who accepted Gratian's solution gave the Gelasian (or 'dualist') answer: 'from God'; while their opponents gave the Gregorian (or 'hierocratic') answer: 'from the pope'.[343]

Alexander III's conflict with Frederick I had evidently provoked a debate among canonists about the relations of papacy and empire. Alexander's own pronouncements on this subject studiously avoided answering the question, 'from whom does the emperor obtain his sword?' Was the pope keenly aware of the canonists' debate: was he in fact taking up a 'dualist' position in that debate? Historians have long claimed Alexander as a former professor of

---

[340] Ullmann, *Papal government* (n. 190) pp. 414–19, 426–41.

[341] Pacaut, *Alexandre III* pp. 318–34.

[342] Gratian, *Decretum* c.2 q.7 *dictum post* c. 41. See Kempf, 'Kanonistik' (n. 225) pp. 26–35.

[343] F. Kempf, *Papsttum und Kaisertum bei Innocenz III. Die geistigen und rechtlichen Grundlagen seiner Thronstreitpolitik* (Miscellanea Historiae Pontificiae 19: Rome, 1954) pp. 199–252. See above pp. 299–301.

canon law in Bologna, a pupil of Master Gratian and one of the earliest Decretists; but this identification is far from certain. No contemporary source connects Alexander with Bologna: his biographer, Cardinal Boso, described him as a native of Siena who made his reputation as 'a clerk in the church of Pisa'.[344] The connection with Bologna was originally suggested by the fact that one of the Decretists was undoubtedly named 'Master Rolandus of Bologna'. There is, however, no firm evidence to identify this Master Rolandus with Roland Bandinelli, the future pope.[345] Nor can we be certain that Alexander had studied Gratian's *Decretum*: his letters never refer specifically to the *Decretum* when citing canon law. (The first unambiguous evidence of the use of the *Decretum* in the papal curia comes from the pontificate of Clement III, six years after Alexander's death. In the last decade of the century the *Decretum* finally became the canon law book of the curia, consulted in all matters of difficulty.)[346] However, even if Alexander was not himself a canonist, some of his cardinals are known to have studied law. His trusted adviser, the chancellor Albert of Morra, cardinal priest of S. Lorenzo in Lucina (the future Pope Gregory VIII) was reputed to have taught in Bologna and to have composed a commentary on the *Decretum* in which he took a 'dualist' view of the emperor's authority.[347] In addition, six of the cardinals whom Alexander recruited to the curia have been identified as canonists: the Spaniard Petrus de Cardona, cardinal priest of S. Lorenzo in Damaso, the Frenchman Matthaeus, cardinal priest of S. Marcello, the cardinal priest Vivian of S. Stefano in Celio monte, the cardinal deacon Gratian of SS. Cosma e Damiano, Lombardus of Piacenza and most important, the Decretist Laborans, cardinal priest of S. Maria trans Tiberim.[348] Their knowledge of the *Decretum* and of the current debate of the Decretists may well have had a moderating influence on the curia's policy towards the empire. (Albert of Morra indeed was regarded by

[344] Boso, *Vita* (n. 312) p. 397.

[345] J. T. Noonan, 'Who was Rolandus?' in *Law, church and society. Essays in honor of Stephan Kuttner* ed. K. Pennington and R. Somerville (Pennsylvania, 1977) pp. 21–48.

[346] W. Holtzmann, 'Die Benutzung Gratians in der päpstlichen Kanzlei im 12. Jahrhundert', *Studia Gratiana* I (1953), 323–49.

[347] P. F. Kehr, 'Papst Gregor VIII. als Ordensgründer' in *Miscellanea Francesco Ehrle* 2 (Studi e Testi 38: Rome, 1924) p. 250; Pacaut, *Alexandre III* p. 356. See below p. 506.

[348] Holtzmann, 'Benutzung Gratians' p. 328; Pacaut, *Alexandre III* pp. 271, 275; B. Smalley, *The Becket conflict and the schools* (Oxford, 1973) p. 143.

Frederick as sympathetic to imperial interests; but he did not on this account forfeit Alexander's trust.)[349]

The presence of these canonists in the curia offers a partial explanation of the restrained tone of the claims of the papacy vis-à-vis the secular power in the years 1159–77. The rest of the explanation is surely to be found in the curia's urgent need of financial and political support from the secular rulers outside the empire. Alexander's survival depended on the aid of the Sicilian kings William I and William II, of the unpredictable Henry II of England and above all of Louis VII of France, 'the sole defender of the Church after God'.[350] All these kings insisted, like Frederick I, that their kingship was 'ordained on earth by the King of kings'. All would have been alienated from the papal cause, had Alexander used Gregorian 'hierocratic' arguments against the emperor. The papal primacy, as R. W. Southern has pointed out, 'would never have been effective if lay rulers had not found that, even if it offered them nothing, it took almost nothing from them'.[351] During the schism Alexander, vulnerable and poverty-stricken, was never in a position to assert the primacy of the pope in secular affairs and the papal right to depose disobedient kings. The details of his itinerary underline Alexander's constant dependence on his secular allies. The first two years of the pontificate were spent on the frontier of the Norman kingdom of Sicily, in Terracina and Anagni, until a rebellion of King William I's vassals compelled withdrawal (with the aid of Sicilian galleys) to Genoa. From March 1162 until August 1165 Alexander took refuge in France, wandering from Henry II's duchy of Aquitaine to the Capetian citadel of Paris (February–April 1163) and to Henry II's county of Anjou, where he held his impressive council in Tours (May 1163) and finally establishing the curia for one-and-a-half years in Sens, in Capetian territory (September 1163–April 1165). An improvement in the fortunes of the Alexandrine party in Rome, coinciding with a sharp deterioration in the relations of the French and English kings, prompted Alexander's return to Rome in November 1165. The curia was once more established in the Lateran until the emperor again installed himself in Rome in July 1167. Then Alexander fled (again with the help of Sicilian galleys) to the kingdom of William II of Sicily, where he stayed for two-and-a-half years

---

[349] Robert of Auxerre, *Chronicon, MGH SS* 26, 252. See Kehr, 'Gregor VIII.' p. 252.
[350] Alexander III, *JL* 10773: 180A.
[351] R. W. Southern, *Western society and the Church in the Middle Ages* (Harmondsworth, 1970) p. 127.

in Benevento (August 1167–February 1170). For the remaining seven years of the schism he sheltered in various strongholds between Rome and the Sicilian frontier: Tusculum (October 1170–January 1173), Segni (March 1173), Anagni (March 1173–March 1174 and again October 1175–November 1176), Ferentino (November 1174–July 1175).[352]

The dilemma faced by the fugitive pope during these years is most clearly articulated in his famous letter of June 1165 to a fellow exile, Archbishop Thomas Becket of Canterbury.

Since the days are evil and many things must be endured because of the nature of the time, we beseech Your Discretion, we warn, we counsel, we urge that in dealing with your own affairs and with those of the Church you show yourself to be cautious, farsighted and circumspect and do nothing in haste or rashly but with mature reflection and gravity so that as far as possible – saving the freedom of the Church and the dignity of your office – you may strive and labour by all means to regain the grace and good will of the illustrious king of the English.[353]

Alexander was obliged to take up the cause of the persecuted archbishop and the threat to the liberty of the English church at precisely the same time as the emperor's adviser, Rainald of Dassel, was negotiating the marriage of a daughter of Henry II with a son of the emperor. Alexander's defence of Becket seemed likely to convert the English king into a supporter of the antipope. Henry II wrote to Rainald: 'I have long desired a lawful opportunity for withdrawing from Pope Alexander and his treacherous cardinals, who presume to support that traitor Thomas, formerly archbishop of Canterbury, against me.'[354] The pope's hasty attempts to conciliate the king and restrain the archbishop from further acts of provocation drew a stern rebuke from Becket: 'Not for us, father, but in the name of our Lord Jesus Christ, earn for yourself a great name, restore your glory and recover your reputation.' An English visitor observed that although everyone in Alexander's curia praised the courage of Becket, no one there showed a trace of that courage: they all feared Frederick more than God.[355] Alexander never indulged in a reckless stand like that of Thomas Becket (or Gregory VII). The caution, the avoidance of hasty action which Alexander recommended to Becket was the

---

[352] P. Jaffé – S. Loewenfeld, *Regesta pontificum Romanorum* 2, 240–302.
[353] Alexander III, *JL* 11207 (n. 299), 377A = *Materials for the history of Thomas Becket, archbishop of Canterbury* 5, *RS* 67/5 (1881), 179–80.
[354] Henry II: *ibid.*, 5, 428.
[355] Becket to Alexander III: *ibid.*, 6, 155; Becket's envoy to Becket: *ibid.*, 5, 59.

hallmark of his own policy. 'The Lord will grant better times and both you and we can pursue this matter in greater safety.'

The twelfth-century papacy did not possess the material resources to defeat an opponent as powerful as Frederick Barbarossa. The Alexandrine curia of 1159–77, often lacking even the conventional resources of the twelfth-century papacy, was more than usually at the mercy of events. Cardinal Boso, keenly aware of this fact, invariably attributed papal successes and imperial setbacks to the intervention of 'the Lord, who does not abandon those who set their hopes in him and destroy the wicked counsels of princes'. In July 1167, for example, the emperor, making his fourth Italian expedition, was at the height of his power in the Italian kingdom. He established himself in Rome, compelled Alexander to flee and installed the new antipope Paschal III; but he did not long enjoy his triumph. God 'sent so great a plague of sudden death on his army that within the space of seven days almost all the greater of his princes who were attacking the Church with him were struck down by sudden death and died miserably'. Similarly God assisted Frederick's enemies, the Lombard cities, to drive out 'the schismatics and intruders' from the bishoprics of Lombardy. In the winter of 1174–5 during his fifth Italian expedition Frederick besieged Alessandria, the city founded by the Lombards in 1168 and named in honour of the pope. Once again 'almighty God miraculously resisted his wicked plan' by sending a flood. The last of these divine interventions was the defeat of the emperor at Legnano (29 May 1176), which finally compelled Frederick to seek peace with the pope. 'The Lord rendered the League of the Lombards so strong and bold against the Germans that as soon as they joined battle with those barbarians, they were victorious at the first onset.' In Boso's narrative a convention of historical writing which derived ultimately from the Old Testament is combined with a realistic appraisal of Alexander's vulnerability and his dependence on his allies.[356] This vulnerability made Alexander cautious and willing to compromise: it did not, however, render him inactive. If his survival depended on the victory of the emperor's enemies, the pope must ensure that those enemies remained friends of the curia and that their hostility towards Frederick did not abate. Hence the most important institution of papal government during the schism of 1159–77 was the papal legation. Papal legates kept Alexander in touch with the princes – and equally necessarily, with the clergy – of the territories

[356] Boso, *Vita* (n. 312) pp. 407, 418, 414, 427, 433.

in his obedience; they coordinated the opposition to the emperor; they raised money for the needy Alexandrine curia. They might also be concerned with questions of reform and the discipline of the clergy; but their major preoccupations – and here they differed most from their predecessors of the second quarter of the twelfth century – were political. The combined circumstances of a wandering curia and an unstable political situation increasingly placed the details of policy-making in the hands of the legates.[357] Three series of papal legations in particular played a vital role in the politics of the schism: the missions to Germany, Byzantium and most importantly, Lombardy.

The legates in Germany had the twofold function of strengthening the Alexandrine party and negotiating peace with the imperial party. At the beginning of the schism only south-eastern Germany – the jurisdiction of Archbishop Eberhard of Salzburg and of his suffragans – recognised Alexander. In February 1163 Eberhard was given the title of legate, with the duty of resisting the schismatics by all possible means; but soon afterwards he was attempting to negotiate a settlement with the imperial court. In the course of the summer of 1163 these negotiations were taken in hand by an impressive legation which included Cardinal Albert of S. Lorenzo in Lucina (the future Gregory VIII, whom Frederick regarded as sympathetic) and which met the emperor in Nuremberg.[358] The death of the antipope Victor IV (20 April 1164) seemed likely to end the schism, even though Rainald of Dassel on his own initiative hastened the election of a successor, the antipope Paschal III. In the months following Victor's death some of the most influential German prelates announced their conversion to the Alexandrine party. Bishop Conrad of Passau, formerly a Victorine, became a supporter of Alexander on succeeding Eberhard as archbishop of Salzburg (September 1164). (He was elected by the canons of Salzburg 'on condition that, like his predecessor, he would stand with Pope Alexander', even though the emperor would refuse him the *regalia*.)[359] The most dangerous defection from the imperial party was that of Archbishop Conrad of Mainz, who used the opportunity of a pilgrimage to St James of

---

[357] W. Ohnsorge, *Die Legaten Alexanders III. im ersten Jahrzehnt seines Pontifikats (1159–1169)* (Historische Studien 175: Berlin, 1928); Dunken, *Die politische Wirksamkeit der päpstlichen Legaten* (n. 268); Pacaut, 'Les légats d'Alexandre III' (n. 260) pp. 821–38. See above pp. 166–7.

[358] Alexander III, JL 10824 (n. 299), 197D–198B. See Hauck, *Kirchengeschichte Deutschlands* 4, 270–1. See below pp. 505–6.

[359] *Annales Reicherspergenses* 1164, *MGH SS* 17, 471. See Hauck 4, 274.

Compostela in autumn 1164 to submit to Alexander. (Conrad was the brother of the emperor's staunch supporter, Otto of Wittelsbach, and owed his archbishopric to the emperor's intervention; but he was also a former canon of Salzburg and his 'conversion' perhaps reflects the influence of Eberhard on his circle.) The defection of Conrad of Mainz was followed by that of two other metropolitans, Hillin of Trier and Wichman of Magdeburg.[360] Early in 1165 the Alexandrine curia boasted that the only supporters left to the antipope were the emperor, Rainald and Henry the Lion, duke of Saxony and Bavaria;[361] but their rejoicing was premature.

Frederick responded to this challenge to his authority with the harsh measures of the diet of Würzburg (23 May 1165). The emperor swore never to recognise the schismatic Roland nor any successor elected from his party and he bound his own successor by this oath. The same oath was to be taken by the German princes and prelates, those absent from the diet being given six weeks to fulfil their obligation on pain of deposition, confiscation or banishment. The resolutions of the diet were rigorously carried out. Conrad of Wittelsbach was deposed from the archbishopric of Mainz and replaced by Frederick's chancellor, Christian of Buch (who was as well hated by the Alexandrine party as his predecessor, Rainald of Dassel). Conrad of Salzburg was outlawed for his refusal to take the oath.[362] The final stage in this reassertion of imperial authority over the German church and kingdom came seven months later: the canonisation of Charlemagne by the antipope (29 December 1165). The reputation of the great emperor, to whom the German church had owed so much, now conferred the aura of sanctity on Frederick's emperorship and reminded his subjects of their obligations to the divinely ordained monarch.[363] The imperial measures were entirely successful. Alexander responded by giving the papal party in Germany a new leader in the person of Conrad of Wittelsbach, appointed cardinal and legate in Bavaria. Papal letters urged the faithful to resist the schismatic prelates whom the emperor had imposed on the Church; but there were no more defections to the Alexandrine party. At the end of the schism, as at the beginning, only Salzburg recognised

---

[360] Hauck 4, 274–5.
[361] Cardinal Otto to Thomas Becket: *Materials* (n. 353) 5, 158–9. See K. Jordan, 'Heinrich der Löwe und das Schisma unter Alexander III.', *MIÖG* 78 (n. 17), 224–35.
[362] *MGH Constitutiones* 1, 314–21. See Hauck 4, 276–82.
[363] Hauck 4, 282–3; R. Folz, *Le souvenir et la légende de Charlemagne dans l'Empire germanique médiévale* (Paris, 1950) pp. 159–237.

Alexander and even Salzburg was hardpressed to remain loyal in the archiepiscopate of Adalbert (1168–74), a nephew of the emperor (and son of the king of Bohemia) but Alexandrine in sympathy.[364] Alexander and his legates never came near to creating in Germany a party of princes and bishops on the scale of that which had crippled Henry IV in the days of the Gregorian papacy.

The refusal of the western emperor to negotiate with the Alexandrine party prompted the pope to seek recognition from the eastern emperor. Manuel I Comnenus had already shown his willingness to intervene in Italy when in 1154 he had sent the expedition which captured Ancona. The papal schism now seemed to offer him a favourable opportunity of recovering former Byzantine territory in the west and of solving what modern historians call 'the two-emperor problem' by destroying the rival empire of Frederick Barbarossa.[365] The six papal legations which Alexander sent to Constantinople between 1160 and 1168 had the task of exploiting Manuel's ambitions in the interests of the Alexandrine party. In Frederick's entourage it was assumed in 1161 that the pope had initiated the negotiations with Byzantium: 'that wretched Roland, like someone writhing in agony and seeking aid everywhere in a ridiculous manner, has written to [the emperor] of Constantinople, promising him the vanity of vanities'.[366] Cardinal Boso's biography presents an exactly opposite version of events. Manuel 'knowing of the insults and injuries which Frederick was trying to inflict on the venerable Pope Alexander' sent an envoy to the latter with a twofold proposition. 'The emperor wished to unite his Greek church with the holy Roman church . . . [and] he also asked that the crown of the Roman empire should be restored to him by the apostolic see since he declared that it belonged to his own jurisdiction and not to that of Frederick the German.'[367] As far as these secret negotiations can be reconstructed, it seems that Manuel's original intention in 1163 was an alliance with Louis VII of France against Frederick and that it was at Louis' insistence that the pope and the king of Sicily were included in the alliance. As Louis VII showed increasing reluctance to accept

---

[364] Alexander III, *JL* 11365, 12483 (n. 299), 525BC, 1022D–1023B. See Hauck 4, 293, 296–7.

[365] H.-D. Kahl, 'Römische Krönungspläne im Komnenenhause? Ein Beitrag zur Entwicklung des Zweikaiserproblems im 12. Jahrhundert', *Archiv für Kulturgeschichte* 59 (1977), 282–315.

[366] F. Güterbock, 'Le lettere del notaio imperiale Burcardo intorno alla politica del Barbarossa nella schisma ed alla distruzione di Milano', *BISI* 61 (1949), 57.

[367] Boso, *Vita* (n. 312) p. 415.

the Byzantine plan, Manuel relied more and more on Alexander to bring the alliance into being. The reunion of the Greek and Latin churches was the reward which Manuel offered the pope in 1167 and again in 1168, if in return he would legitimate the reunion of the eastern and western empires.[368] Subsequently Frederick I at a diet in Worms in 1172 publicly accused Alexander and his supporters of planning 'to confer the crown of the Roman empire on the Greek'.[369] There is good reason to believe, however, that the plan was Manuel's alone and that ultimately it foundered because of Alexander's unwillingness to recognise Manuel as emperor of the west. Boso's version of the papal reply to the Byzantine envoy in May 1168 may well be accurate:

What [Manuel] demands is very far-reaching and extremely complicated and since the statutes of the holy Fathers forbid such things because of their difficulty, we cannot and must not consent to such an agreement; for according to the office committed to us by God we should be the author and guardian of the peace.[370]

Such a reply is consistent with Alexander's attitude towards Frederick I throughout the schism: his refusal to depose the emperor and his reticence on the subject of the authority of the pope vis-à-vis the emperor. Alexander's rejection of the Byzantine proposals is a further indication that the pope and his advisers were strongly influenced by those 'statutes of the holy Fathers' which respected the independence and autonomy of the secular sphere – that is, by the 'dualist' trend in canon law.

As with Manuel I Comnenus, so also with the Lombard cities: the strategy of the Alexandrine curia was to exploit hostility towards Frederick I in the interests of resolving the schism in Alexander's favour. Alexander's relationship with the Lombards dated from the alliance concluded by the papacy with Milan, Brescia, Piacenza and Crema in the last months of Hadrian IV's pontificate and intended to resist Frederick's attempts to impose imperial control on the kingdom of Italy. The chancellor Roland had been regarded as the initiator of this alliance and it was given prominence in the imperial propaganda against his election.[371] At the beginning of the schism Milan was the most active of the emperor's opponents. Her

---

[368] Ohnsorge, *Legaten* (n. 357) pp. 69–86; Kahl, 'Römische Krönungspläne' (n. 365) pp. 283–95.

[369] *Chronica regia Coloniensis* 1172 (n. 225), p. 121.

[370] Boso, *Vita* p. 420. See Ohnsorge, *Legaten* pp. 85–6.

[371] See above p. 472.

surrender after a year-long siege (1 March 1162) and her total destruction by the emperor cowed the other hostile cities into submission and prompted the flight of the Alexandrine curia into France. The first successful Italian resistance to Frederick came in 1164 from the north-east, where Verona and her neighbours Padua, Vicenza and Treviso formed a league, of which the great maritime city of Venice subsequently became a member. Effective resistance in Lombardy began in 1167, stimulated by the disaster which befell Frederick's army in August. Frederick's fourth expedition to Italy culminated in the defeat of the Romans at Tusculum (29 May), the flight of the Alexandrine curia and the installation of the antipope Paschal III in Rome. But the emperor's greatest triumph in Italy was followed immediately by his worst catastrophe: an outbreak of malaria in his army claimed 2,000 victims, the most illustrious being the emperor's chief adviser, Rainald of Dassel. The disaster gave immediate encouragement to the efforts of the four Lombard cities – Cremona, Mantua, Bergamo and Brescia – which in March 1167 had formed a league against the emperor. By the end of the year the emperor's enemies in northern Italy had organised themselves into a Lombard League of sixteen cities.[372]

The purpose of the formation of the Lombard League was *not* the defence of Alexander III and his claim to the papacy. Cardinal Boso accurately identified the motives of the Lombards in 1167: 'The cities of Lombardy, which had had long experience of [Frederick's] hostility and cruelty, seeing that his mind and will were kindled against them even more fiercely than usual, debated together and decided that they must drive him out of Lombardy, since he was striving to reduce all Italy to shameful servitude.'[373] The purpose of the League was to destroy the system of government which the emperor had introduced at Roncaglia in 1158. Nevertheless the Lombards' successes automatically strengthened the Alexandrine cause. Among the earliest actions of the League members was the expulsion from their territories of those bishops who adhered to the emperor and the antipope, replacing them with supporters of Alexander. In August 1168/9 the pope was already rejoicing that Lombardy had been emptied of excommunicates and schismatics.[374]

---

[372] *Popolo e Stato in Italia nell' età di Federico Barbarossa. Alessandria e la Lega Lombarda* (Turin, 1970), with details of the earlier literature.

[373] Boso, *Vita* p. 418.

[374] Alexander III, *JL* 11572, 11580 (n. 299), 556D–557C, 561CD. See Hauck, *Kirchengeschichte Deutschlands* 4, 287.

The systematic deposition of imperialist churchmen by the League ensured that Frederick could not create in the Lombard church such another power base as he possessed in the church in Germany. The symbol of the Lombard-papal alliance was the new city founded by the League in May 1168 in the plain of Marengo and 'named Alessandria out of respect for St Peter and Pope Alexander'. The city was to be the property of the Roman church and was to pay an annual tribute. It was even rumoured that the pope intended to settle there.[375] During the last ten years of the schism the Lombard alliance was the cornerstone of Alexander's diplomacy and the continuance of the League, the key to his survival. 'We must watch over their unity with careful vigilance and forethought', he told Conrad of Wittelsbach in January 1172. To the members of the League he wrote that the Lombard struggle for liberty against the emperor and the struggle for the freedom of the Church were one and the same: 'we know that you are united with the Church as sharers in good and ill'.[376]

The emperor was equally anxious to divide the allies; and this was the hidden purpose behind the peace negotiations which he inaugurated in 1169. His first intermediaries were the abbots of Cîteaux and Clairvaux, chosen because of the devotion of their order to the Alexandrine cause (for which Cistercian houses in Germany had paid dearly). The peace talks were then taken up by Bishop Eberhard of Bamberg, another Alexandrine sympathiser, who met the pope at Veroli in March 1170. Negotiations were broken off when Alexander insisted that the Lombards be included in the peace proposed by the emperor. Frederick's response, pronounced at a diet in Fulda (8 June 1170) was a repetition of the declaration made five years before at Würzburg, never to recognise Alexander as pope.[377] The emperor's fifth Italian expedition, beginning in September 1174, attempted to solve the dual problem of the schism and the Lombard rebellion by means of a decisive military victory. Frederick met with immediate success in western Lombardy; but his progress was halted by the stubborn resistance of Alessandria, which he besieged throughout the winter of 1174–5. At Eastertide 1175 he abandoned

[375] Boso, *Vita* pp. 418–19; John of Salisbury, *Letter* 276 (n. 331), p. 589. See *Popolo e Stato* (n. 372).

[376] Alexander III, *JL* 12137 (n. 299), 770C–771A; *JL* 11747: J. F. Böhmer, *Acta Imperii selecta* 2, ed. J. Ficker (Innsbruck, 1870), 600.

[377] M. Preiss, *Die politische Tätigkeit und Stellung der Cisterzienser im Schisma von 1159–1177* (Historische Studien 248: Berlin, 1934) pp. 113–28; T. Reuter, 'Das Edikt Friedrich Barbarossas gegen die Zisterzienser', *MIÖG* 84 (1976), 328–36.

the siege and a truce was agreed with the Lombards at Montebello (10 April). The imperial tactic in these new negotiations was to detach the League from the Alexandrine curia; but the Lombards made Frederick's recognition of Alexander a condition of the peace.[378] Frederick then turned again to the curia, negotiating at Pavia with the three most prominent Alexandrine cardinals, Hubald of Ostia (the future Pope Lucius III), Bernard of Porto and William, cardinal priest of S. Pietro in Vincoli. Frederick wished to make a separate peace with Alexander: the cardinals insisted on bringing the Lombards into the negotiations. The cardinals broke off the negotiations, according to Cardinal Boso, because of the emperor's extreme demands. 'He required from the Church in spiritual matters what can never be found to have been granted to a layman' – presumably that the schismatic imperial bishops be permitted to retain their sees – 'and he demanded from the Lombards more than that with which the Emperors Charles, Louis and Otto had been content.'[379] The emperor resumed his war against the League in autumn 1175 and the following spring he decided to attack Milan. North-west of the city at Legnano he was opposed by a League army outnumbering his own forces. Frederick nevertheless gave battle and was defeated (29 May 1176). The battle of Legnano hastened the peace settlement in Italy and the end of the schism. The victory of the League was also Alexander's victory – the reward for nine years of rigid adherence to the Lombard allies.

The direction and maintenance of the papal–Lombard alliance was mainly in the hands of five very able papal legates, who must be numbered among the most important contributors to the Alexandrine victory: William of S. Pietro in Vincoli (later cardinal bishop of Porto), the cardinal deacon Odo of S. Nicola in carcere Tulliano, the cardinal deacon Manfred of S. Giorgio in Velabro (later cardinal priest of S. Cecilia and cardinal bishop of Palestrina) and above all Archbishop Galdin of Milan and Hildebrand, cardinal deacon of S. Eustachio (subsequently cardinal priest of SS. Apostoli). William of S. Pietro in Vincoli had appeared in papal documents of the pontificate of Hadrian IV with the title 'legate of the whole of Lombardy' and 'vicar of the pope in Lombardy': he was presumably one of the architects of the controversial papal–Lombard alliance of 1159. He attended the emperor's council of Pavia (1160) as observer on behalf of the Alexandrine party and reappeared in

[378] W. Heinemeyer, 'Der Friede von Montebello (1175)', *DA* 11 (1954), 101–39.
[379] Boso, *Vita* (n. 312) p. 431.

northern Italy as a legate in 1164 and 1169. He was involved both in the unsuccessful negotiations with the emperor in 1175 and in the negotiations of February 1177 which led to the Peace of Venice.[380] Cardinals Odo and Manfred were active in the archdiocese of Ravenna after the retreat of the imperial army in 1167, assisting Hildebrand of SS. Apostoli in winning north-eastern Italy for the Alexandrine obedience. Between 1170 and 1172 Manfred collaborated with Hildebrand in advising the Lombard League.[381] Galdin was one of the saints of the Alexandrine party, his sanctity and his practical abilities proving of equal value to the cause in Lombardy. He was Milanese by birth and served as archdeacon and chancellor of the church of Milan until at the outbreak of the schism he followed his Alexandrine archbishop, Hubert, into exile in France. There he met Alexander, who appointed him cardinal priest of S. Sabina (1165), then archbishop of Milan in succession to Hubert (1166) and legate in Lombardy, charged with the rebuilding of Milan and encouraging Lombard resistance to the emperor.[382] The Bolognese Hildebrand of SS. Apostoli, protégé both of Eugenius III and of Hadrian IV, was sent in 1159 to defend the Alexandrine cause in Venice, where he remained as papal vicar during Alexander's sojourn in France. Between 1166 and his death in 1178, with the exception of 1175, he served as 'legate in the whole of Lombardy'. Hildebrand was the principal specialist in Lombard politics in the Alexandrine curia and the chief papal adviser to the League.[383] It was the task of these five legates 'to strengthen and preserve the unity' of the League,[384] to keep open the lines of communication between the curia and the Lombards and to ensure that the Alexandrine cause benefited from the League's political and military successes.

The peace negotiations which followed the Lombard victory at Legnano began in October 1176 but were protracted until the following July. In the preliminary peace of Anagni (November) the imperial plenipotentiaries and the Alexandrine curia both conceded the points which they had hitherto rejected utterly. The imperial party accepted Alexander's title: the papal party recognised the orders of the German bishops appointed during the schism. The

---

[380] Dunken, *Die politische Wirksamkeit der päpstlichen Legaten* (n. 268) pp. 20–1, 169, 171; Pacaut, 'Les légats' (n. 260) pp. 832–3; Zenker, *Mitglieder* (n. 232) pp. 118–23.

[381] Dunken pp. 169–71.

[382] *Ibid.*, pp. 79–80, 168–71; Pacaut, 'Les légats' pp. 834–5.

[383] Dunken pp. 70–1, 83–4, 110–11, 166, 169–71; Pacaut, 'Les légats' pp. 833–4; Zenker pp. 107–9.

[384] Alexander III, JL 12737 (n. 299), 1082B = *MGH Constitutiones* I, 581.

imperial negotiators at Anagni also conceded the restoration to the pope of the long contested Matildine lands in Tuscany. Subsequently, however, the emperor was able to renege on this concession, when he blackmailed the pope into granting him the revenues of the Matildine lands for fifteen years in return for accepting Alexander's proposals for peace with the papal allies, the Lombard cities and the king of Sicily.[385] The peace of Anagni seemed at first to have achieved the emperor's objective of separating the pope from his allies: the rumour spread even as far as France that Alexander had made peace without including the Lombards. Alexander travelled to Ferrara (April 1177) to reassure the League, the foremost defenders of 'the greatness of the Church and the liberty of Italy', and to agree the details of the peace conference.[386] The conference began on 10 May in Venice (the site on which the emperor now insisted, in preference to Bologna, which had been agreed at Anagni). For over two months the plenipotentiaries tried in vain to make peace between the Lombards and the emperor, who refused to moderate the demands which he had first made in Roncaglia in 1158. Finally the parties accepted the compromise devised by the pope: the emperor was to observe a permanent peace with the Roman church, a peace of fifteen years with the king of Sicily and a truce of six years with the Lombards. Unknown to Archbishop Christian of Mainz and the other imperial plenipotentiaries, Frederick at the eleventh hour contemplated the use of force to impose his own terms on the other parties. His plot is described in the chronicle of Archbishop Romuald of Salerno, who was present in Venice as a Sicilian plenipotentiary. During the negotiations the emperor had moved from Pomposa to Chioggia, where he was invited by a group of Venetian conspirators to come to their city at once without Alexander's permission. The rumour of his coming caused the Lombard negotiators to withdraw to Treviso and the Sicilians to prepare to disembark their galleys, urging the pope to accompany them. According to Romuald, the conspiracy was foiled by the doge of Venice, who feared reprisals by King William II of Sicily against Venetians in his dominions, and also by the emperor's advisers, who refused to go back on the agreements.[387] The emperor was therefore compelled to

---

[385] P. F. Kehr, 'Der Vertrag von Anagni im Jahre 1176', *NA* 13 (1888), 75–118; K. Leyser, 'Some reflections on twelfth-century kings and kingship' in *idem, Medieval Germany and its neighbours 900–1250* (London, 1982) pp. 259–61.

[386] Alexander III, *JL* 12821 (n. 299), 1108D–1109D. Cf. Romuald of Salerno, *Annales* 1177 (n. 339), p. 445.

[387] Romuald, *Annales* 1177, pp. 449–52. See Leyser, 'Reflections' (n. 385) p. 261.

ratify the agreements. He came to Venice for the solemn celebration of the peace and was absolved from his eighteen-year excommunication (24 July 1177). The next day Frederick performed for Alexander the 'groom's office' (*stratoris officium*), the ceremony which he had hesitated to perform for Hadrian IV in 1155, but which he had since performed for the antipope Victor IV after the council of Pavia (1160). The *stratoris officium* on 25 July 1177 (as in 1095 and 1131) signified not the feudal dependence of the emperor upon the pope, but the emperor's recognition of the pope's title and his rejection of the antipope. Finally on 1 August the emperor, in the pope's presence, swore to observe the peace and the truce; and on 14 August he participated in the papal council which excommunicated schismatics who failed to become reconciled to the Church.[388]

The end of the second conflict of empire and papacy, according to Cardinal Boso, saw 'Emperor Frederick prostrate at the feet of Pope Alexander'; while Romuald of Salerno wondered at 'the spectacle of an old priest, unarmed, repelling the German fury'.[389] In the matter of the schism Alexander was undoubtedly the victor. The Alexandrine party prevented the accession of a pope who was the candidate of only a minority of the cardinals, but whose strength lay in the support of the emperor. Alexander's resistance forestalled the restoration of an imperial control over papal elections like that of Emperor Henry III in the mid-eleventh century. His victory was consolidated in the first canon of the Third Lateran Council of 1179, which ruled that in future papal elections only a candidate supported by at least two-thirds of the cardinals would be recognised as pope.[390] In other respects the settlement at the end of the schism was much more moderate than, for example, that which followed Innocent II's victory in 1139.[391] The last of the antipopes of the schism, Calixtus III (1168–77, formerly Abbot John of Strumi), on renouncing the title of pope, was to be given an abbey. His 'so-called cardinals' were to retain the dignities which they had possessed at the beginning of the schism. (Calixtus at first resisted the settlement which had been made without consulting him; he was outlawed by the emperor and finally submitted to Alexander on 29 August

---

[388] Boso, *Vita* (n. 312) pp. 439–41. Peace of Venice: *MGH Constitutiones* 1, 360–4. See H. Zimmermann, 'Canossa 1077 und Venedig 1177 und Jahrhunderte danach' in *Studi Matildici. Atti e Memorie del III Convegno di Studi Matildici Reggio E. 1977* (Deputazione di storia patria per le antiche provincie modenesi, Biblioteca, N.S. 44: Modena, 1978) pp. 183–216.

[389] Boso, *Vita* p. 445; Romuald, *Annales* 1177, p. 445.

[390] See above pp. 84–5.   [391] See above p. 138.

1178.)[392] The fate of the clergy ordained during the schism was in many cases left to be decided by the Third Lateran Council. Following the precedents of the two most recent schisms, the conciliar fathers ruled that ordinations made by the antipopes or by those consecrated by the antipopes were invalid; but that ordinations made by schismatics who were formerly catholics – that is, properly consecrated before the schism – were valid.[393] However, the German episcopate had already been exempted from this rule during the preliminaries of the peace of 1177.

The moderation of the settlement probably reflects the personality of Alexander himself; but it may also reflect the war-weariness of the Alexandrine curia and the tensions created in the papal–Lombard alliance by the peace of Anagni. In his eagerness for peace Alexander was ready to forego the guarantees of Anagni, to sacrifice fifteen years of revenues from the Matildine lands and to leave unsettled the question of the proprietorship of the Matildine inheritance. Nor was this the only important territorial question left unsettled by the Peace of Venice. The peace of Anagni had guaranteed that the Roman church would recover 'the *regalia* of St Peter' – the term first used by the reform papacy for its lordship in the papal patrimony. The Peace of Venice does not mention 'the *regalia* of St Peter', but refers only to the mutual obligation of papacy and empire to restore and protect each other's possessions and rights. Here again Alexander seems to have permitted a diminution of the original obligations of Anagni in his anxiety to achieve peace.[394] The settlement in the German church most clearly illustrates the limitations of Alexander's victory. In the case of the archbishopric of Mainz the Alexandrine claimant Conrad of Wittelsbach, deposed in 1165 for his opposition to the emperor, was obliged in 1177 to give way to the imperialist intruder Christian of Buch. As compensation Conrad was promised the next vacant archbishopric, which proved to be Salzburg. The Alexandrine Adalbert was forced to give up his claim to Salzburg because he did not possess the emperor's confidence: Conrad, however, was acceptable to Frederick. The disputed election to the archbishopric of Hamburg-Bremen was referred to the Third Lateran Council: it was settled by the pope in a manner approved by the emperor.[395] In

---

[392] Peace of Anagni: *MGH Constitutiones* 1, 349–54. See G. Domenici, 'L'antipapa Callisto III', *Scuola cattolica* 43 (1915), 199–216, 456–71.

[393] III Lateran Council c. 2: *Conciliorum Oecumenicorum Decreta* pp. 211–12.

[394] Anagni c. 3, p. 350; Venice c. 3, p. 362. See Fried, 'Regalienbegriff' (n. 115). pp. 521–2.

[395] Hauck, *Kirchengeschichte Deutschlands* 4, 304–5, 307–9.

1177 Frederick broke the oath which he had devised at the diet of Würzburg in 1165, never to accept Alexander as pope; but his reconciliation with the papacy seems to have left him as firmly in control of the German church as he had been during the schism.

During the last four years of his pontificate Alexander strove to maintain peace with the empire. He remained, as he assured Frederick in 1179, ever vigilant 'for the honour of the emperor and the empire, according to the duties of his office'.[396] When, for example, negotiations between the Lombards and the emperor broke down, Alexander sent Cardinal Laborans as legate to restore peace.[397] Where Germany was concerned, the pope made no attempt to undermine the emperor's mastery of the Church. He summed up Frederick's position in the words, 'the more a man cannot be judged by another, the more strictly he must judge himself'. Frederick was evidently virtually exempt from judgement: the pope could only advise and exhort him.[398] Alexander did not resist Frederick's assumption of the right (which he had already claimed during the schism) to appoint his own candidate in the case of a disputed episcopal election. Frederick filled the bishopric of Brixen in 1178 and the archbishopric of Hamburg-Bremen in 1180; and the pope confirmed the latter appointment through his legates. Like his conception of the duties of prelates, Frederick's conception of the nature of church property was preeminently feudal. He therefore claimed as among 'the rights of the empire' the 'right of *regalia*' – the seizure of the revenues of a bishopric or abbacy during a vacancy – and the 'right of *spolia*' – the seizure of the property of a prelate on his death.[399] Frederick's insistence on the feudal character of the German church went unchallenged by the pope. For Alexander the preservation of the hard-won peace of 1177 was of more immediate importance than 'the freedom of the Church' in Germany.

The death of Alexander III (30 August 1181) did not mean the end of the policy of conciliation of 1177–81. Of Alexander's five successors in the years 1181–98, four were former members of the Alexandrine curia: three were close collaborators of the pope during the schism and the fourth owed to Alexander his rapid promotion in the college of cardinals. Alexander's immediate successor, Lucius III

---

[396] Alexander III, *JL* 13019: *MGH Constitutiones* 1, 585.
[397] F. Güterbock, 'Kaiser, Papst und Lombardenbund nach dem Frieden von Venedig', *QFIAB* 25 (1933–4), 177–81.
[398] Alexander III, *JL* 13611: *Regesta pontificum Romanorum* 2, 359.
[399] Hauck 4, 311–14.

(1181–5), was the most important figure in the Alexandrine curia: Hubald Allucingoli, cardinal bishop of Ostia. Recruited to the college by Innocent II, he owed his further promotion to Hadrian IV, in whose curia he had been, like Roland-Alexander, a member of 'the Sicilian party'. He had taken part in the negotiation of the treaty of Benevento in 1156 and, twenty-one years later, of the Peace of Venice.[400] Alexander's third successor, Gregory VIII (1187), was Albert of Morra, cardinal priest of S. Lorenzo in Lucina, recruited to the college by Hadrian IV and subsequently Alexander's chancellor.[401] Alexander's fourth successor, Clement III (1187–91), was Paul Scolari, cardinal bishop of Palestrina, whom Alexander had recruited to the college and who had rapidly come to prominence in the curia during the last three years of the pontificate.[402] Finally Celestine III (1191–8) was the veteran Hyacinth Bobo, cardinal deacon of S. Maria in Cosmedin, who could boast of sixty-five years of service in the curia before his accession to the papacy.[403] These four old men pursued during their pontificates the same policies which they had carried out as Alexander's agents. Conciliatory by temperament, they were the more inclined to peace by the war-weariness and poverty which followed the schism – and perhaps above all by the Peace of Constance (1183), which transformed the Lombard cities from a hostile League into loyal subjects of the emperor. The exceptional figure among the popes of the late twelfth century was Lucius III's successor, Urban III (1185–7). Hubert Crivelli had not been a member of Alexander's curia: he entered the college as cardinal priest of S. Lorenzo in Damaso in 1182. During the schism he had been archdeacon of Bourges and a member of the circle of the exiled Thomas Becket of Canterbury. Subsequently he had returned to his native Milan, as archdeacon and later as archbishop (1185).[404] Urban III's attitude to the emperor differed sharply from that of his immediate predecessors and successors; and his pontificate witnessed the last conflict of Frederick Barbarossa with the papacy.

---

[400] Zenker, *Mitglieder* (n. 232) pp. 22–5, 153; V. Pfaff, 'Sieben Jahre päpstlicher Politik. Die Wirksamkeit der Päpste Lucius III., Urban III., Gregor VIII.', *ZSSRG KA* 67 (1981), 173–4.

[401] Zenker pp. 125–9, 153–4; Pfaff p. 177. See above pp. 94, 483.

[402] P. Zerbi, *Papato, impero e 'respublica christiana' dal 1187 al 1198* (Pubblicazioni dell' Università Cattolica del S. Cuore, N.S. 55: Milan, 1955) pp. 15–16; V. Pfaff, 'Papst Clemens III. (1187–1191)', *ZSSRG KA* 66 (1980), 261–2.

[403] Zerbi pp. 65–81; V. Pfaff, 'Papst Coelestin III.', *ZSSRG KA* 47 (1961), 109–10.

[404] Pfaff, 'Sieben Jahre' (n. 400) pp. 175–6.

The pontificate of Lucius III witnessed both the attempted settlement of the questions left unresolved in the Peace of Venice and the dismantling of the alliances on which the Alexandrine victory had depended. In 1183 the six-year truce arranged in Venice between the emperor and the Lombard cities came to an end and was replaced by a permanent peace negotiated in Constance (June 1183). Frederick at last renounced the governmental measures introduced at the diet of Roncaglia in 1158: the cities' right of self-government was recognised in return for the payment of an annual tribute and recognition of the emperor's suzerainty. The city of Alessandria lost the name conferred 'out of respect for St Peter and Pope Alexander' and was refounded with the name Caesarea.[405] After the conclusion of the Peace of Constance some of the Lombard cities formed alliances with the emperor, including his former inveterate enemy, Milan (1185). Meanwhile the peace between the emperor and the king of Sicily, on which the pope had insisted in 1176–7, was strengthened in the course of 1183–4 by a marriage alliance. On 29 October 1184 Frederick's son, Henry VI, was betrothed to Constance, posthumous daughter of King Roger II and aunt of the reigning King William II.

The attitude of the papacy to this betrothal is not known. The project of a German–Sicilian marriage had first been broached a decade before, when Frederick had offered his daughter Sophia to William II, whose hopes of a Byzantine bride had been disappointed in 1173. The project had been scotched by Alexander III, who in the spring of 1176 had replaced Sophia with an English princess, Joanna, daughter of Henry II.[406] In the dangerous years 1173–6 Alexander dared not permit an alliance between his vassal and his enemy; but by 1184 the situation was changed. Frederick was not the enemy of Lucius III: indeed Frederick's servant, Archbishop Christian of Mainz, formerly the bitter enemy of the Alexandrine curia, proved himself the loyal ally of Lucius in his struggle against the rebellious Romans. In 1184 it was impossible for the curia to foresee that the thirty-year-old William II of Sicily and his eighteen-year-old queen would have no children and that William would die prematurely, naming as his heir the aunt who was the wife of Henry VI. The betrothal of 1184, instead of conjuring up the vision of the future

---

[405] *Reconciliatio Alexandriae: MGH Constitutiones* 1, 407–8; Peace of Constance: *ibid.*, pp. 408–18.
[406] Romuald of Salerno, *Annales* [1176], p. 441. See F. Chalandon, *Histoire de la domination normande en Italie et en Sicile* 2 (Paris, 1907), 376–9.

union of the kingdom of Sicily with the empire, may have seemed to Lucius III the natural consequence of the peace of 1177. Given that the pope, as suzerain of the king of Sicily, should have been consulted about this marriage, is it likely that (as Johannes Haller argued) Lucius himself instigated the marriage alliance, in the interests of peace and of the crusade? Could a former member of 'the Sicilian party' in the curia have contemplated such a step? The only twelfth-century text which claims that Lucius initiated the marriage is the panegyric of Henry VI composed by Peter of Eboli a decade after the betrothal. The poet identified Lucius as the 'bridesman' (*pronuba*) in the nuptials of Constance and Henry; and added: 'Lucius joined them and Celestine anointed them' – that is, Celestine III subsequently crowned them as emperor and empress (1191).[407] Peter of Eboli brought the names of these two popes into his narrative with the propagandist purpose of suggesting that the papacy approved the claim of Constance and Henry VI to the kingdom of Sicily, which was a serious distortion of the facts. Moreover Peter's reference to Lucius associates him not with the betrothal but with the wedding of the royal couple – which actually took place in the pontificate of Urban III (on 27 January 1186) and from which the pope was conspicuously absent. Peter's statement, therefore, throws no real light on Lucius' attitude to the German–Sicilian alliance.

The most contentious matter left unresolved since 1177 was the proprietorship of the Matildine lands. Lucius and Frederick met to settle this and other pressing problems in October–November 1184 in Verona (where the curia settled between 1184 and 1186). Pope and emperor had no difficulty in agreeing on the launching of a new crusade to assist the kingdom of Jerusalem and on new measures against the spread of heresy. No agreement was reached, however,

---

[407] Peter of Eboli, *Liber ad honorem Augusti* v.22–3, *Fonti per la storia d' Italia* 39 (1906), 5. See J. Haller, 'Heinrich VI. und die römische Kirche', *MIÖG* 35 (1914), 414–37; idem, *Das Papsttum* 3 (n. 224), 191, 203; K. Wenck, 'Die römischen Päpste zwischen Alexander III. und Innocenz III. und der Designationsversuch Weihnachten 1197' in *Papsttum und Kaisertum. Forschungen zur politischen Geschichte und Geisteskultur des Mittelalters. Paul Kehr zum 65. Geburtstag dargebracht* ed. A. Brackmann (Munich, 1926) pp. 423–4; Munz, *Barbarossa* (n. 257) pp. 367–8. Haller's arguments were questioned by H. Kauffmann, *Die italienische Politik Kaiser Friedrichs I. nach dem Frieden von Constanz 1183–1189* (Greifswalder Abhandlungen zur Geschichte des Mittelalters 3: Greifswald, 1933) p. 36; Foreville and Rousset de Pina (n. 291) p. 193. The most detailed discussion is that of G. Baaken, 'Unio regni ad imperium. Die Verhandlungen von Verona 1184 und die Eheabredung zwischen König Heinrich VI. und Konstanze von Sizilien', *QFIAB* 52 (1972), 219–97.

on the subject of the Matildine inheritance. The solution desired by the emperor was that the pope should renounce all claim to the inheritance and in return the emperor would pay to the pope one-tenth and to the cardinals one-ninth of all his Italian revenues, present and future. Alternatively a joint papal–imperial commission of enquiry would investigate the rival claims. Lucius presumably rejected the first suggestion because it would have made the papacy too dependent on the empire; and the alternative suggestion produced no mutually acceptable solution.[408] By the time that pope and emperor met at Verona two new problems had arisen to trouble the peace of empire and papacy. The first was Frederick's wish to have his son, Henry VI, crowned co-emperor during his own lifetime. (Henry had been elected king of the Germans by the princes in 1169.) The proposal was firmly rejected by the cardinals and Lucius replied to the emperor's request that it was 'not fitting that two emperors should rule the Roman empire'.[409] The second problem was the disputed election to the archbishopric of Trier. The opposition of a rival faction in the cathedral chapter to the election of Folmar (May 1183) gave Frederick the opportunity to reassert his right to settle a disputed election. He obtained from the princes in the diet of Constance the judgement 'that if [the electors] disagreed in an election, the emperor on the advice of the princes might substitute whatever suitable person he desired'. He then proceeded to a new election, in which Rudolf of Wied, provost of Trier, was elected by Folmar's opponents. Folmar then appealed to the pope, while his partisans occupied the cathedral of Trier. At their meeting in Verona Frederick called on Lucius to recognise Rudolf as archbishop; but the pope instead responded to Folmar's appeal and took the case into his own hands, summoning the two candidates to the curia.[410] In the last months of Lucius' pontificate the emperor acted vigorously to enforce his own settlement of the disputed questions. Imperial agents occupied the Matildine lands; Henry VI intervened in Trier to confiscate the property of Folmar's supporters; the emperor

---

[408] Frederick I, letter to Lucius III: *MGH Constitutiones* 1, 420–1. See Foreville and Rousset de Pina (n. 291) pp. 191–2; Pfaff, 'Sieben Jahre' (n. 400) pp. 164–5.
[409] Arnold of Lübeck, *Chronica Slavorum* III.11, *MGH SS* 21, 156. See W. Ohnsorge, 'Das Mitkaisertum in der abendländischen Geschichte des frühen Mittelalters', *ZSSRG GA* 67 (1950), 330; Baaken, '*Unio regni*' (n. 407) pp. 238–43.
[410] *Gesta Trevirorum, Continuatio* III.6, *MGH SS* 24, 383–4. See Hauck, *Kirchengeschichte Deutschlands* 4, 316–17; Wenck, 'Päpste' (n. 407) p. 423; Pfaff, 'Sieben Jahre' (n. 400) p. 165.

threatened dire consequences if Lucius dared to consecrate Folmar as archbishop.

On his deathbed (25 November 1185) Lucius III exhorted his successor not to crown Henry VI. Urban III needed no urging. Elected in haste on the day of Lucius' death by a conclave of only eleven cardinals (eight of them north Italians), Urban's most obvious qualification was that he was the bitterest opponent of the Staufen in the curia. His influence may have been responsible for the curia's resistance to the emperor's demands at Verona. He was of the noble Milanese family of Crivelli, who had suffered much when Frederick I had captured the city in 1162. A newcomer to the college of cardinals, he had served Lucius as papal legate in Lombardy and he had been elected archbishop of Milan in January 1185.[411] On his accession to the papacy Urban refused to renounce the archbishopric of Milan, in order to deprive the emperor of the right of *regalia* during the vacancy. The emperor's response was equally provocative. It was in Milan on 27 January 1186 that the wedding of Henry VI and Constance took place, followed by their coronation, both performed by the patriarch of Aquileia. These proceedings were a violation of Urban's rights as archbishop of Milan and the pope was not slow to discipline the bishops who participated in the ceremonies.[412] Whether the coronation of 1186 was also a violation of Urban's rights as pope – an attempt to deprive the pope of his traditional function of crowning the emperor – is by no means clear. Historians have interpreted the coronation variously as Henry VI's accession as king of Italy, as no more than a ceremonial crown-wearing and as the crowning of a co-emperor which Frederick had proposed in 1184. Urban, like his predecessor, had been asked to crown Henry emperor, but had declined to do so unless Frederick first renounced the imperial crown. Did Frederick nevertheless proceed with the coronation of his son as co-emperor? The crucial evidence is that of the contemporary chroniclers who claim that during the coronation of 1186 Frederick himself invested Henry with the title of *Caesar*. These accounts undoubtedly recall the Byzantine ceremony in which the reigning emperor appointed his successor as co-emperor. The chroniclers may of course have conflated their accounts of the coronation with their knowledge of Frederick's attempts to have his son crowned co-emperor and in so doing, have exaggerated the import-ance of the ceremony. If their accounts are accurate, we must con-

---

[411] Hauck 4, 318; Wenck p. 426; Pfaff pp. 175–6.
[412] *Continuatio Sigiberti Chronici* 1186, *MGH SS* 6, 423–4.

clude that the coronation in Milan had a distinctly imperial character and that it therefore threatened the right of the pope to transmit the imperial dignity.[413]

The escalation of the dispute from the spring of 1186 onwards suggests that Urban himself interpreted the coronation as a threat. He attempted to mobilise the Lombard cities against the emperor, but they refused to break the peace of 1183.[414] Simultaneously Urban denounced Frederick's conduct towards the German church, particularly his imposition of the 'right of *spolia*'. In May 1186 the pope announced his decision in the case of the Trier election, which was in favour of Folmar and against the imperial candidate Rudolf. On 1 June, despite a promise given some months before to the emperor's envoys, Urban consecrated Folmar archbishop of Trier. The imperial response was the occupation of the Patrimony of St Peter by the army of Henry VI. The papal curia in Verona was under siege, cut off from contact with the rest of Christendom.[415] Urban deliberately sought confrontation with the emperor, doubtless partly inspired by his family's hostility towards the Staufen. He may also have felt impelled to imitate the stand for the freedom of the Church taken by Thomas Becket, to whose circle he had belonged during Becket's exile. Equally influential, however, was Urban's assessment of the political situation of Germany in 1186. Urban counted on achieving what Alexander III had failed to achieve: the creation of a strong papal party in Germany. His hopes were centred on Philip of Heinsberg, archbishop of Cologne (1167–91). Philip had served the emperor well as chancellor and as archbishop and he had been richly rewarded when the emperor contrived the downfall of Henry the Lion (1180): Archbishop Philip had been invested with the newly created duchy of Westphalia. But unlike his predecessor, Rainald of Dassel, Philip's ambitions as an independent Rhineland prince brought him into conflict with the imperial dynasty. The former opponent of Alexander III now became the ally of Urban III, who in 1186 appointed him papal legate in Germany. Philip's influence drew

---

[413] *Annales Romani* 1186, *ibid.*, 5, 479; Ralph de Diceto, *Ymagines historiarum* 1186, *RS* 68 (1876), 39. Cf. Arnold of Lübeck, *Chronica* (n. 409) III.17, p. 158. See Hauck 4, 319; Kauffmann, *Die italienische Politik* (n. 407) pp. 88–101, 171–4; H.-W. Klewitz, 'Die Festkrönungen der deutschen Könige', *ZSSRG KA* 28 (1939), 61; Ohnsorge, 'Mitkaisertum' (n. 409) pp. 330–9.

[414] *MGH Constitutiones* 1, 445, 447. See Hauck 4, 320; Pfaff, 'Sieben Jahre' (n. 400) p. 164.

[415] Arnold of Lübeck, *Chronica* III.17–18, pp. 158–9; *Gesta Trevirorum, Continuatio* (n. 410) III.8, pp. 385–6. See Hauck 4, 319–21.

other bishops, notably Berthold of Metz, into the papal party.[416] Frederick I dealt with the papal party in 1186 in the same way in which he had countered the desertion of the prelates in 1165. He summoned the bishops to the diet of Gelnhausen (28 November 1186), at which (according to the chronicler Arnold of Lübeck) the emperor himself expounded his case against the pope. A majority of the German episcopate accepted his claim that the rights of the empire and of the German churches were threatened by papal presumption. The bishops sent letters to the pope, supporting the emperor's complaints and accusing Urban of disturbing the peace of the Church. The bishops' letter to the cardinals spoke in harsher language of 'the intolerable injustice' which Urban had inflicted on the empire.[417] After this show of strength the emperor sent a new embassy to the papal curia; but Urban evaded it by escaping from Verona and making for Venice. The pope had hitherto been prevented from excommunicating the emperor by the intervention of the citizens of Verona. He evidently intended to pronounce the excommunication in Venice; but he travelled no further than Ferrara, where he died during the night of 19–20 October 1187.

The election of a successor in Ferrara on 21 October revealed how little sympathy the cardinals had with Urban III's stand against the emperor. The cardinals considered three possible candidates, each of whom would restore peace with the emperor: Cardinal bishop Henry of Albano (the Cistercian Henry of Marcy), Cardinal bishop Paul Scolari of Palestrina and the chancellor, Cardinal Albert of Morra. Henry of Albano refused the papal dignity; Paul Scolari's ill health seemed to disqualify him; and so the chancellor Albert was elected, taking the name Gregory VIII.[418] The new pope had opposed his predecessor on the crucial issue of the consecration of Folmar of Trier.[419] 'Emperor Frederick rejoiced exceedingly when he heard of [Gregory's] elevation,' wrote the chronicler Robert of Auxerre, 'because he knew him to be a discreet man, zealous for justice and well disposed towards [the emperor] himself.' According to Canterbury gossip, the cardinals elected Gregory because he stood

---

[416] Hauck 4, 319–20.

[417] Letter of the German bishops to Urban III: *MGH Constitutiones* 1, 444–6; letter of the German bishops to the cardinals: *ibid.*, pp. 446–8. Cf. Arnold of Lübeck, *Chronica* III.19, pp. 160–1. See Hauck 4, 321–2.

[418] Peter of Blois, letter to Archbishop Baldwin of Canterbury: *Epistolae Cantuarienses* in *Chronicles and Memorials of the reign of Richard I* 2, RS 38/2 (1865), 107–8. See Wenck, 'Päpste' (n. 407) pp. 428–9.

[419] Gregory VIII, *JL* 16075: *MPL* 202, 1560AB.

high in the favour of the emperor, to whom he had betrayed the secrets of the curia in the past.[420] Nevertheless, despite his reputation as a friend of the emperor, Gregory was still influenced by the passions of the Alexandrine schism: one of the last actions of his life was to disinter and scatter the remains of the antipope Octavian–Victor IV (buried in the cathedral of Lucca), because he had died excommunicate.[421] 'No one knows the customs and rights of the Roman church as he does,' Henry of Albano said of Gregory at his election. He obeyed the canon law concerning excommunicates and schismatics with extreme rigour; but concerning the relations of empire and papacy he adopted a Gelasian or 'dualist' position. A gloss attributed to him as a canonist in Bologna reads: 'The emperor does not hold the power of the sword from the pope.'[422] Above all Gregory was dedicated to the reform of the Church and to the launching of a crusade to Outremer: for both these aims peace with the empire was indispensable. The papal letter of 29 November to the emperor was therefore full of good will and the desire for harmonious cooperation.[423] The emperor responded by lifting the siege of the papal curia and placing an escort at the pope's disposal. The threat of a renewed schism was removed; but before contentious issues could be settled, Gregory VIII died (17 December 1187) after a pontificate of only fifty-seven days.

On the day of Gregory's funeral (19 December) the cardinals elected as his successor the candidate whom two months before they had rejected as 'seriously ill and entirely unequal to such a burden' – Paul Scolari, cardinal bishop of Palestrina, who took the name Clement III.[424] The curia urgently desired to return to Rome and Clement III's family connections with prominent Roman clans may therefore have been the qualification which overrode considerations of health and secured his election. The most solid political achievement of his pontificate was indeed the papal treaty with the Roman senate (31 May 1188), which restored papal lordship over the city after forty-five years of strife with the Roman commune.[425] Once reestablished in Rome the curia faced the task of carrying out the

[420] Robert of Auxerre (n. 349) p. 252; Gervaise of Canterbury, Chronica 1187, RS 73/1 (1879), 388. See P. Scheffer-Boichorst, Kaiser Friedrichs I. letzter Streit mit der Kurie (Berlin, 1866) p. 146 n. 2.

[421] Continuatio Sigiberti (n. 412) p. 474.

[422] Pacaut, Alexandre III p. 356.

[423] Gregory VIII, JL 16071 (n. 419), 1558AD.

[424] Peter of Blois (n. 418) p. 108. See Pfaff, 'Clemens III.' (n. 402) pp. 262–3.

[425] See above p. 16.

measures initiated by Gregory VIII in the interests of the Third Crusade: the pacification of Christendom and securing the cooperation of the Italian cities and the western monarchs. The emperor was the first to pledge his participation in the crusade: he took the cross at the imperial diet of 27 March 1188, 'the diet of Christ' (*curia Christi*), which he and Cardinal Henry of Albano, the official preacher of the crusade, had summoned to Mainz.[426] During the following months the papal legates in Germany – Jordan, cardinal priest of S. Pudenziana, Peter, cardinal priest of S. Pietro in Vincoli and Soffred, cardinal deacon of S. Maria in Via Lata – negotiated the settlement of the dispute with the emperor. In the matter of the archbishopric of Trier the curia abandoned Folmar, whom Urban III had consecrated, and the rival candidate, Rudolf, was also set aside. In a new election in the presence of the emperor and the legate, Cardinal Soffred, the archbishopric was conferred on the imperial chancellor, John. The general agreement between the legates and the emperor was concluded in Strassburg on 3 April 1189. In return for Clement III's promise to crown Henry VI emperor, Frederick restored the Patrimony of St Peter to the lordship of the pope, insisting however on the reservation 'saving the right of the empire'. Nothing was said of the Matildine lands.[427] From this last conflict of Frederick I with the papacy the emperor therefore emerged victorious. The resolution of the Trier dispute confirmed him in that control of the German church for which he had striven throughout his reign. The curia must console itself with the reflection that the concessions of 1189 and the retreat from the stand made by Urban III were the price to be paid for the successful launching of the Third Crusade. In May 1189 Frederick set off on crusade, the first reigning emperor to participate in the papal holy war.

Frederick Barbarossa never returned from this expedition: he drowned in the River Saleph in Cilicia (10 June 1190). Half-a-year before this accident, another royal death had occurred, of even greater significance for the development of papal–imperial relations: the premature death of William II of Sicily (18 November 1189). Since William died childless, the legitimate heir to his kingdom was his aunt, Constance, wife of Henry VI, to whom the pope had just promised the imperial crown. For the rest of the century (and indeed

---

[426] I. Friedländer, *Die päpstlichen Legaten in Deutschland und Italien am Ende des 12. Jahrhunderts (1181–1198)* (Historische Studien 177: Berlin, 1928) p. 39.

[427] *MGH Constitutiones* I, 460–1. See Zerbi, *Papato* (n. 402) pp. 22–8; Pfaff, 'Clemens III.' (n. 402) pp. 275–6.

until the extinction of the Staufen dynasty) the political calculations of the curia were dominated by 'the union of the kingdom with the empire'. The shock with which the curia received the first news of William's death is apparent in the letter which Clement immediately sent to his closest adviser, John of Anagni, cardinal priest of S. Marco, bidding him break off his legation to England and return at once to Rome.[428] The problem of the Sicilian succession had, however, already been preoccupying the curia for over a year at the time of William's death. In the summer of 1188 Clement had obtained from William his oath of fealty as the vassal of St Peter – the first time since the concordat of Benevento (1156) that the pope had demanded the oath from the Norman king. In addition a papal letter of 1188 had reminded William that his heirs would owe fealty and homage to the popes in the future. This emphasis on the role of the pope as feudal overlord of Sicily, to whom William II's heir would be subject, was the curia's response to the threat posed by William's childlessness and the marriage of the heir presumptive to Henry VI.[429] Perhaps the curia had already decided in 1188 that the feudal authority of the pope would be used to prevent the succession of an unsuitable claimant. The opportunity came soon after William's death, when Sicilian rebels refused to recognise the hereditary right of Constance and elected as king, Tancred, count of Lecce, the illegitimate cousin of William II. Both south Italian and German chronicles agree that Tancred's coronation (January 1190) took place 'with the consent and favour of the Roman church'.[430] The curia, exercising the rights of suzerainty restated in 1188, denied the succession to Constance and accorded it to Tancred, so as to prevent 'the union of the kingdom with the empire'. Less than a year after the conclusion of peace at Strassburg, therefore, the papacy was prepared to risk the renewal of conflict with the Staufen. Nevertheless the curia sought to prevent, or at least to delay, the opening of hostilities. When in January 1191 Henry VI marched into Italy to claim both the imperial crown and his wife's inheritance, Clement held to his promise (April 1189) to crown him and sent two cardinals

[428] Clement III, *JL* 16544: *Epistolae Cantuarienses* (n. 418) p. 321.
[429] P. Kehr, *Die Belehnungen der süditalienischen Normannenfürsten durch die Päpste (1059–1192), Abhandlungen der Preussischen Akademie der Wissenschaften 1934, phil.-hist. Klasse* 1, 49–50. See above p. 394.
[430] *Annales Casinenses, MGH SS* 19, 314; Richard of S. Germano, *Chronica* 1190, *ibid.*, p. 324; Arnold of Lübeck, *Chronica* (n. 409) v. 5, p. 182.

to welcome him.[431] But before Henry reached Rome, Clement had died (probably on 10 April 1191).[432]

Clement III's pontificate had witnessed the last large-scale recruitment to the college of cardinals of the twelfth century. In March 1188 Clement had created twelve new cardinals; in May 1189 he had appointed more; finally in October 1190 eleven more cardinals had been created. The effect of Clement's appointments was that, firstly, the college was considerably enlarged (from an estimated nineteen at his accession to thirty-one at his death) and, secondly, that the college was given a strongly Roman character. Most of Clement's new cardinals were connected with the more powerful Roman families (the most famous being Lothar of the Conti family – the future Innocent III – who despite his youth was made cardinal deacon of SS. Sergio e Baccho in 1190); so that at his death the Roman cardinals numbered eighteen, almost three-fifths of the college.[433] Clement evidently intended to strengthen the links between the curia and the city, so as to safeguard his treaty with the Roman senate (May 1188) and spare the curia the hardship of another exile. He must also have intended to wean the Roman nobility from their alliance with the emperor, which had developed during the schism. In the summer of 1167 Frederick I had made a treaty with the Roman senate and this document became the basis of the treaty which the senate concluded with Clement twenty-one years later.[434] The large-scale creation of cardinals, which occurred just when the curia was becoming preoccupied with the Sicilian succession, may have been intended in part as an insurance policy. If the worst befell in the kingdom of Sicily – 'the union of the kingdom with the empire' – the 'Romanization' of the sacred college might secure Rome as a safe citadel for the papacy. However, in the short term Clement's appointments created serious tensions within the college. Once again, as in the pontificates of Honorius II and Hadrian IV, the college contained cardinals with sharply opposed attitudes to the emperor. Clement's appointee, Peter, cardinal priest of S. Cecilia, was in 1192 to assist Henry VI by raising money from the north

[431] Pfaff, 'Clemens III.' (n. 402) p. 278.
[432] The date is uncertain: see Zerbi, *Papato* (n. 402) pp. 61, 65; V. Pfaff, 'Feststellungen zu den Urkunden und dem Itinerar Papst Coelestins III.', *HJb* 78 (1959), 132–4.
[433] Pfaff, 'Clemens III.' pp. 263, 269, 280–4; Wenck, 'Päpste' (n. 407) pp. 440–1; H. Tillmann, *Pope Innocent III* (English translation: Amsterdam, 1980), pp. 5–6.
[434] J. Petersohn, 'Der Vertrag des Römischen Senats mit Papst Clemens III. (1188) und das Pactum Friedrich Barbarossas mit den Römern (1167)', *MIÖG* 82 (1974), 289–337.

Italian cities for the emperor's campaign against Tancred; while
Albinus, whom Clement promoted to be cardinal bishop of Albano,
was described by Tancred in a diploma of 1190 as his dearest
friend.[435]

How could an enlarged college of cardinals, deeply divided on
fundamental issues of papal policy, full of ambitious men, many of
whom had powerful families close at hand to forward their
ambitions – how could the college avoid schism in April 1191? It was
presumably the imminent arrival in Rome of Henry VI which forced
the college into a unanimous election. Avoiding the dangerous
choice of a cardinal of the Sicilian or German faction, the cardinals
elected their most senior colleague, the eighty-five-year-old Cardinal deacon Hyacinth of S. Maria in Cosmedin, who took the name
Celestine III. 'Hyacinth reluctantly consented to be made pope . . .
lest a sudden schism arise in the church of God', explained the
English chronicler Ralph de Diceto.[436] As a member of the noble
Roman family of Bobo–Orsini, Celestine was acceptable to the
Roman majority in the college: he could be expected to pursue the
Rome-centred strategy of Clement III. The reputation for moderation acquired during his sixty-five years in the service of the curia
also augured well for continuity. Perhaps it was assumed in April
1191 that Celestine's great age would – like Clement III's chronic
illness – leave much of the decision-making in the hands of papal
advisers. In the event Celestine seems to have retained his control of
affairs until the last year of his pontificate. He possessed a temperament appropriate to the head of a divided curia: he was a 'stubborn
temporiser'.[437]

Celestine was consecrated pope on Easter Sunday (14 April) 1191
and the following day he crowned Henry VI emperor. As in the cases
of the other imperial coronations of the twelfth century, the details
of the coronation of 1191 are difficult to reconstruct and to interpret.
The anecdote of the English chronicler Roger of Hoveden must
surely be discounted. He recorded that the pope, seated on his

---

[435] V. Pfaff, 'Das Papsttum in der Weltpolitik des endenden 12. Jahrhunderts, *ibid.*,
360; Friedländer, *Legaten* (n. 426) pp. 119–23.

[436] Ralph de Diceto, *Ymagines historiarum* (n. 413) p. 89.

[437] W. Holtzmann, 'Imperium und Nationen' in *Relazioni del X Congresso Internazionale di Scienze storiche 3: Storia del Medioevo* (Florence, 1955), 300. On the
personality of Celestine III see Wenck, 'Päpste' (n. 407) pp. 442–54, who presents
Celestine as a weak personality. For the opposite view see Haller, 'Heinrich VI.'
(n. 407) pp. 567–71, 658–62; Pfaff, 'Coelestin III.' (n. 403) pp. 110–14; Zerbi,
Papato (n. 402) pp. 77–81.

throne, held the imperial crown between his feet and when the emperor knelt to receive the crown, the pope kicked it away from him. The cardinals recovered the crown and placed it on the emperor's head. Celestine 'thereby signified that he had the power to topple him from the empire if [Henry] acted contrary to his duty'. Roger's account is contradicted by Celestine himself in his letter to Henry VI of 1195: 'we placed the imperial crown on your head with our own hands'.[438] More instructive, but still problematical, are the comments of Henry VI and of Celestine's successor, Innocent III. A letter of Henry VI to Celestine (29 February 1192) speaks of the 'mutual understanding' felt by pope and emperor at the coronation, 'especially because we were then prepared . . . to perform what must have been pleasing to the pope'.[439] Innocent III referred to the coronation of 1191 in a memorandum concerning the election of Henry's successor, the theme being that the emperor can receive his office only from the pope, 'when he is blessed by him, crowned and invested with the empire'. 'Henry knew this very well and having received the crown from our predecessor Pope Celestine of good memory, after he had withdrawn a little, he finally returned and begged to be invested by him with the empire by means of a golden orb.'[440] Innocent III's memorandum clearly speaks of two ceremonies: firstly, Henry was crowned; then after an interval he was 'finally' (*tandem*) invested with an orb. But how long was this interval? Johannes Haller in his study of Henry VI's relations with the Roman church (1914) argued that five-and-a-half years elapsed between the imperial coronation and Henry's request 'to be invested with the empire'. According to Haller, the request mentioned by Innocent III was part of the negotiations of 1196 in which Henry sought to introduce radical constitutional changes: the pope was asked to permit the imperial crown to become, like the Sicilian crown, hereditary in the Staufen dynasty and in return the emperor would acknowledge himself the vassal of the pope.[441]

However, if Innocent III's description is juxtaposed to Henry VI's

[438] Roger of Hoveden, *Chronica*, RS 51/3 (1870), 102–3; Celestine III, *JL* 17226; *MPL* 206, 1089C. See P. E. Schramm, *HZ* 135 (1927), 464 (Review of G. Laehr, *Die Konstantinische Schenkung*).

[439] Henry VI, letter to Celestine III: *MGH Constitutiones* 1, 490.

[440] Innocent III, *Registrum de negotio imperii* (n. 229) c. 29, 1025B. See G. Baaken, 'Die Verhandlungen zwischen Kaiser Heinrich VI. und Papst Coelestin III. in den Jahren 1195–1197', *DA* 27 (1970), 459–60 and n. 18.

[441] Haller, 'Heinrich VI.' (n. 407) pp. 647–59; *idem, Das Papsttum* 3 (n. 224), 213–16, 384–8.

letter of 1192, stating that during the coronation the emperor performed 'what must have been pleasing to the pope', a different
interpretation is suggested. The interval between the crowning of
Henry VI and his request to be invested with the orb was a matter of
minutes rather than of five-and-a-half years: for what Innocent III
described was an interrupted coronation ceremony on 15 April 1191.
After Celestine had crowned Henry, he tried to confer on him also a
golden orb, the symbol of the universal monarchy of the emperor;
but since this part of the ceremonial was unfamiliar to Henry, 'he
withdrew a little' – presumably to consult his advisers – and being
reassured that his dignity would not be undermined by this investiture, 'he finally returned' and agreed to receive the orb. According to
this interpretation there was no question of the emperor acknowledging himself the vassal of the pope – merely the introduction of a
new ceremonial into the imperial coronation.[442] A further interpretation emerges if Innocent III's memorandum is compared with the
letters which Henry VI and his father sent to Clement III in 1189,
when the coronation was still being planned. Both letters insist on a
traditional ceremony 'according to what law and custom have laid
down from antiquity up to these times'. This insistence on a traditional ceremony, combined with Innocent III's statement that
Henry 'begged to be invested . . . with the empire by means of a
golden orb', might suggest that investiture with the orb was an
ancient ceremonial, fallen into disuse in the twelfth century but
restored in 1191 at the request of the emperor.[443] As for Henry VI's
statement of 1192, that on the occasion of the coronation he had performed 'what must have been pleasing to the pope', many interpretations suggest themselves: for example, the emperor's surrender of
Tusculum (demanded by the Romans as the price of his coronation)
or a promise by the emperor to withdraw his troops from the

---

[442] E. Jordan, 'Henri VI a-t-il offert à Célestin III de lui faire hommage pour
l'Empire?' in *Mélanges d'Histoire du Moyen Âge offerts à Ferdinand Lot par ses amis et
ses élèves* (Paris, 1925) pp. 285–306; E. Eichmann, *Die Kaiserkrönung im Abendland*
1 (Würzburg, 1942), 229–30; P. Zerbi, 'Un momento oscuro nella incoronazione
romano di Enrico VI (a. 1191)' in *Miscellanea Giulio Belvederi* (Collezione 'Amici
delle catacombe' 23: Rome, 1954) pp. 517–28. See also P. E. Schramm, *Sphaira-
Globus-Reichsapfel. Wanderung und Wandlung eines Herrschaftszeichens von Caesar bis
zu Elisabeth II.* (Stuttgart, 1958) pp. 91–3.

[443] Frederick I, letter to Clement III: *MGH Constitutiones* 1, 462; Henry VI, letter to
Clement III: *ibid.*, p. 463. See V. Pfaff, *Kaiser Heinrichs VI. höchstes Angebot an die
römische Kurie (1196)* (Heidelberger Abhandlungen zur mittleren und neueren
Geschichte 55: Heidelberg, 1927) pp. 19–26.

Patrimony of St Peter. In short, we are not compelled to take literally Innocent III's description of Henry VI being 'invested with the empire' and to assume that at the coronation of 1191 the emperor acknowledged himself the vassal of the pope. For Innocent III's description of the coronation is written in 'hierocratic' (or Gregorian) language, the language of those canonists who regarded the empire as subordinate to the papacy. But Celestine III and his closest advisers still used the 'dualist' (or Gelasian) language customary in the curia of Alexander III. When Celestine wrote to Henry on 27 April 1195, after a four-year breakdown in papal–imperial relations, he rebuked the emperor for his transgressions, but rebuked him in Gelasian language. In future Henry must be guided entirely by God, 'in whose dominion are the powers and jurisdictions of all kingdoms . . . who gives salvation to kings and causes emperors to walk in the royal way and to reign happily'.[444]

Soon after the coronation the emperor marched south to conquer the kingdom of Sicily, 'despite the prohibition and resistance of the pope'.[445] This first expedition was a failure: an outbreak of malaria forced the imperial army to abandon the siege of Naples; the emperor himself fell seriously ill and a false report of his death prompted the city of Salerno to hand over the empress to her enemy and nephew, King Tancred. By the end of 1191 Henry had returned to Germany, where the news of his grave illness was stimulating unrest in Saxony. For the next two-and-a-half years rebellions and princely conspiracies throughout Germany prevented the launching of a second Sicilian expedition. Henry's difficulties enabled Tancred to strengthen his hold on the kingdom of Sicily, aided by an alliance with the emperor's enemy, King Richard I of England. Meanwhile in the three years following the imperial coronation the papacy pursued an ambiguous policy. The pope seized every opportunity of allying with the German rebels; he recognised Tancred as king of Sicily; but simultaneously he attempted to negotiate peace with the emperor. The papal measures of 1191–4 suggest less a consistent policy towards Henry VI than an attempt to satisfy the rival demands of the German and Sicilian factions in the curia. It is very significant, for example, that the decision to invest Tancred with the Sicilian kingdom was taken when almost half the cardinals were absent from the curia (March–May 1192) – including Staufen sympathisers like

---

[444] Celestine III, *JL* 17226 (n. 438), 1089D.
[445] Richard of S. Germano, *Chronica* 1191 (n. 430), p. 325. Cf. *Annales Casinenses* (n. 430) p. 314; Arnold of Lübeck, *Chronica* (n. 409) v. 5, p. 182.

Peter of S. Cecilia.[446] The negotiations with the Sicilian king were entrusted to Tancred's sympathisers, Albinus and Gregory, cardinal deacon of S. Maria in Aquiro. Presumably the Sicilian faction in the curia also influenced the decision to grant to the emperor's enemies, the Welf princes Henry the Lion and his son, Henry of Brunswick, the papal privilege of 5 August 1191, granting them immunity from all excommunication except that pronounced by the pope or his legate.[447] The same circle of advisers probably influenced the handling of the case of the bishopric of Liège. The emperor intervened in a disputed election in Liège to impose his own candidate; but the candidate elected by the majority of the chapter, Albert of Brabant, appealed to the pope, who ratified his election (July 1192). No sooner had Albert been consecrated by the archbishop of Rheims, than he was murdered by *ministeriales* of Liège (24 November 1192). The murder was widely believed to have been instigated by the emperor and it sparked off a rebellion of almost all the secular princes and prince-bishops of the lower and middle Rhineland, led by Duke Henry of Brabant, the brother of the deceased bishop. According to the chronicler Gislebert of Mons, the Rhenish princes 'ingratiated themselves with the lord Pope Celestine and made an alliance with him'.[448]

Each of these measures invited the renewal of conflict with the empire; but these hostile manoeuvres were accompanied by attempts to make peace, doubtless spurred on by the German faction in the curia. Early in 1192 Celestine sent the Cistercian abbot of Casamari to negotiate a truce between the emperor and Tancred, but without success. The following summer, after investing Tancred with Sicily, Celestine secured the release of Empress Constance, intending 'to negotiate an agreement with her in Rome'; but she refused his request.[449] The same conciliatory spirit is evident in the curia's response to the imprisonment of the English king in Germany (December 1192–February 1194). It was on his homeward journey from the Third Crusade that Richard I was taken prisoner by Duke Leopold of Austria, to avenge an insult inflicted at the siege of Acre.

---

[446] V. Pfaff, 'Die Kardinäle unter Papst Coelestin III. (2. Teil)', *ZSSRG KA* 52 (1966), 342–4.

[447] Celestine III, *JL* 16736 (n. 438), 892C–893A.

[448] Gislebert of Mons, *Chronicon Hanoniense*, *MGH SS* 21, 582. See V. Pfaff, 'Die deutschen Domkapitel und das Papsttum am Ende des 12. Jahrhunderts', *HJb* 93 (1973), 36–8; Zerbi, *Papato* (n. 402) pp. 98–9.

[449] *Annales Casinenses* (n. 430) p. 316. See Pfaff, 'Weltpolitik' (n. 435) pp. 355–6, 358–9.

On 14 February 1193 the king was surrendered to the emperor, whose grievances against Richard were the aid which he had given to the Sicilian usurper and the money which he had extorted from the Sicilian treasury in repayment of the dowry of his sister Joanna, the widow of King William II. The ransom which the emperor demanded for Richard's release was intended as compensation for this extortion; and the delay in paying the ransom enabled the emperor to increase the price of Richard's freedom: 150,000 marks instead of 100,000 and the demand that the king accept England from the emperor as a fief of the empire. As a crusader and pilgrim Richard had the right to expect papal protection and in Rome his queen, Berengaria, and his sister, Joanna, pressed the pope to secure his release. Celestine excommunicated Leopold of Austria and placed his territory under an interdict; but he was reluctant to resort to firm measures against the emperor. This papal reluctance was denounced as scandalous cowardice by the dowager Queen Eleanor of England in the letters written on her behalf by Peter of Blois.[450] The moderation which Eleanor deplored reflected the internal politics of the curia. The pope's handling of the case of Richard I's imprisonment coincided with a period (March–May 1193) when almost all the cardinals were present in Rome and when, therefore, the rival factions in the college had each to be appeased.[451] The cardinals who favoured the excommunication of Henry VI were in a minority; while a majority of the cardinals feared that if the curia took firm measures to secure Richard's release, they would only have the effect of strengthening the alliance between the emperor and Richard's even greater enemy, his feudal lord, King Philip II of France.

For three years the curia pursued the incompatible policies of preventing 'the union of the kingdom with the empire' and seeking peace with Henry VI: then suddenly the death of Tancred (20 February 1194) left the papacy with no more room for manoeuvre. Soon after Tancred's death Henry was able to restore peace to Germany. His second Sicilian expedition, financed by the ransom of Richard I and supported by a Genoese–Pisan fleet, was a complete success. On 20 November 1194 Henry entered Palermo; on Christmas day he was crowned king of Sicily. The day after the coronation the Staufen succession was assured when the empress

---

[450] Eleanor of Aquitaine, *Epistolae* 1–3 (= Peter of Blois, *Epistolae* 144–6): *MPL* 206, 1262C–1272D. See Pfaff, 'Weltpolitik' pp. 360–2; J. Gillingham, *Richard the Lionheart* (London, 1978) pp. 217–40.

[451] Pfaff, 'Kardinäle' (n. 446) pp. 347–50.

gave birth to a son, the future Frederick II. In the months following his triumph it was Henry who reopened negotiations with the curia, addressing pope and cardinals with the project of a new crusade. The emperor had secretly received the cross from the bishop of Sutri, a suffragan of the pope (31 March 1195); he had then proclaimed the crusade in Germany: now he asked the pope to send legates to preach the crusade in the German kingdom.[452] Celestine's response was the letter of 27 April 1195 announcing the legation to Germany of Cardinal Peter of S. Cecilia and Gratian, cardinal deacon of SS. Cosma e Damiano. When the decision was taken to send this letter and this legation, all except one of the cardinals were present in the curia; and the language of the letter reflects the attitude of the majority of the cardinals to Henry VI in his hour of triumph. The letter is addressed to 'the dearest son in Christ Henry, illustrious emperor of the Romans and ever augustus'; but it denies Henry the title 'king of Sicily', which he had added to his imperial title since Christmas 1194. It is largely a letter of reproof, referring obliquely to the scandals of the murder of Albert of Brabant and the imprisonment of Richard I, rebuking the emperor for failing to punish his delinquent followers, reminding him of the duties of an emperor and hoping for his amendment.[453] While refusing to recognise him as king of Sicily and showing no immediate enthusiasm for his crusading project, the curia nevertheless complied with his request for a legation and significantly chose in Peter of S. Cecilia the cardinal most sympathetic to the Staufen cause. The rival factions in the curia pressed the pope at once to defy and to conciliate the emperor.

Negotiations began in the summer of 1195, conducted principally by Cardinal Peter of S. Cecilia in Germany and by Bishop Wolfger of Passau in Rome. The search for a settlement continued for two years, until shortly before Henry's premature death; but without reaching agreement. In midsummer 1196 the emperor crossed the Alps with a small entourage, wishing to hasten the progress of negotiations by his presence in northern Italy. In November he moved to the neighbourhood of Rome. The original project of the crusade had now been assimilated in Henry's plans to assure the imperial succession for his son. The Annals of Marbach (composed by a chaplain of Henry VI) record that 'the emperor began to negotiate an agreement with the pope, desiring that [Celestine]

---

[452] Baaken, 'Verhandlungen' (n. 440) pp. 478–88.
[453] Celestine III, *JL* 17226 (n. 438), 1089C–1091A. See Baaken, 'Verhandlungen' p. 482; Pfaff, 'Kardinäle' p. 358.

would baptise his son, for he had not yet been baptised, and that he would anoint him king. Had [the pope] done this, [the emperor], so it is believed, would have received the cross from him publicly' – so committing himself to the crusade definitively.[454] During his last sojourn in Germany (July 1195–June 1196) Henry had been pre-occupied with winning the support of the princes for his plan to make the imperial crown hereditary in the Staufen dynasty. At the diet of Würzburg (31 March 1196) 'the emperor wished to confirm with the princes a decree new and unheard-of in the Roman king-dom: that in the Roman kingdom, as in that of France and the other kingdoms, kings should succeed each other by hereditary right'.[455] The majority of the princes at Würzburg accepted the plan; but it was opposed by a group of princes from the lower Rhineland and Westphalia, led by Archbishop Adolf of Cologne. Their attitude gained ground among the German princes during Henry's absence in Italy; and at a diet in Erfurt (October 1196) the princes withdrew their support for the succession plan.

Meanwhile Henry tried to persuade the pope to crown the infant Frederick II and so put the succession question beyond doubt. The best-informed chronicler, the Marbach annalist, wrote simply that the pope was requested to 'anoint [Frederick] king', without specify-ing the title which was to be conferred on the child. The likeliest explanation is that Henry VI revived Frederick I's proposal of 1184, to have his son crowned *emperor* during his own lifetime: the pro-posal which Lucius III had rejected, since it was 'not fitting that two emperors should rule the Roman empire'. Had Celestine accepted such a proposal in 1196, his action would have been tantamount to ratification of Henry's succession plan and would have undermined the growing opposition of the German princes.[456] Instead the curia set aside the proposal and insisted on discussing the accumulated grievances of Henry VI's regime in Sicily and Italy: Henry's alleged rights over the Sicilian church, his refusal to do homage to the pope

---

[454] *Annales Marbacenses* 1196, *MGH SS rer. Germ.* (1907) p. 68. See Baaken, 'Verhandlungen' pp. 481, 502–3. On the author of the annals – probably Frederick, provost of St Thomas, Strassburg and chaplain of Henry VI – see W. Wattenbach – F.-J. Schmale, *Deutschlands Geschichtsquellen im Mittelalter. Vom Tode Kaiser Heinrichs V. bis zum Ende des Interregnum* I (Darmstadt, 1976), 122–3.

[455] *Annales Marbacenses* 1196, p. 68. See E. Perels, *Der Erbreichsplan Heinrichs VI.* (Berlin, 1927).

[456] C.-E. Perrin, 'Les négociations de 1196 entre l'empereur Henri VI et le pape Célestin III' in *Mélanges d'histoire du moyen âge dédiés à la mémoire du Louis Halphen* (Paris, 1951) p. 566. See above p. 511.

for the Sicilian kingdom, the depredations of Henry's brother, Philip of Swabia, duke of Tuscany, against churchmen and church property. Finally in mid-November 1196 a formal delegation from the curia – the most senior cardinals, Octavian of Ostia and Peter of S. Cecilia, and the chamberlain Cencius – announced to the emperor the papal rejection of the request to crown his son.[457] Henry withdrew to his Sicilian kingdom; but on 10 February 1197 he sent a last letter to the pope, requesting him to send 'your and our beloved cardinals' Octavian, Peter and Pandulf, cardinal priest of SS. Apostoli, to continue negotiations.[458] No record survives of these final negotiations: presumably they were overtaken by the great rebellion of the Sicilian baronage against the emperor (May 1197), in which even Empress Constance was involved. Henry put down the rebellion with terrifying severity; but he did not long survive his victory: he became seriously ill at the beginning of August and died on 28 September 1197 in Messina. A single chronicler – the imperial chaplain who wrote the Annals of Marbach – claimed that the papal curia was privy to the conspiracy which had threatened the emperor in the last months of his life. The rebels had acted 'with the connivance, so it is said, of the Lombards and the Romans and even – if it is permissible to believe it – of Pope Celestine himself'.[459] There is no evidence to corroborate this claim; but the ambiguous policy suggested by the Marbach annalist – simultaneously negotiating with the emperor and conspiring with the Sicilian rebels – is at least consistent with the papal policy of the years 1191–4. For Celestine III and his closest advisers the first consideration of papal policy seems always to have been the independence of the kingdom of Sicily.

Historians' interpretations of the negotiations between pope and emperor in 1196 have always focussed on an intriguing passage in a letter of Henry to Celestine dated 17 November 1196. Referring to the negotiations of the preceding summer and autumn, the emperor stated that he had been willing to make certain concessions in order to secure a firm peace between empire and papacy.

In reverence for God, for the salvation of our soul, from love of your person, whom we hold dear and likewise for the profit and honour of the Roman church, we offered such things as were never offered by our father of happy

---

[457] Baaken, 'Verhandlungen' (n. 440) pp. 498–505; Pfaff, 'Weltpolitik' (n. 435) pp. 368–73.
[458] *MGH Constitutiones* 1, 514. See Baaken, 'Verhandlungen' pp. 464–77, 505–6.
[459] *Annales Marbacenses* 1196 (n. 454), p. 69.

memory, Frederick, formerly most invincible emperor of the Romans, nor by any of our predecessors to any of your predecessors.[460]

What unprecedented offer did Henry VI make to Celestine III in 1196? Johannes Haller argued in 1914 that Henry offered to become the vassal of the pope if in return Celestine would crown the infant Frederick II. Haller's thesis was based (as we have seen) on his interpretation of Innocent III's reference to Henry having 'begged to be invested by [Celestine] with the empire by means of a golden orb'.[461] No other document, however, suggests that Henry was willing in 1196 to hold the empire as a fief from the pope. Nor is there any clear indication in Innocent III's memorandum that he was referring to a proposal made in 1196: the passage in question seems rather to refer to the imperial coronation of 1191. Moreover in 1196 Henry VI refused fealty and homage to Celestine in respect of his kingdom of Sicily, even though they had undoubtedly been conceded to the pope by previous Sicilian kings. Is it likely that an emperor who refused to recognise the feudal rights of the papacy even where they were customary, would welcome a feudal relationship with the pope where it was a startling innovation?

Haller also drew attention to a text of a later date which he likewise related to the negotiations of 1196: a passage in the *Speculum Ecclesiae* of the Welsh author, Giraldus Cambrensis, composed after 1215. According to Giraldus, Henry VI had wished to free the Roman church from her poverty, but he died before he could implement his plan. He had proposed to confer on the pope a prebend in each of the metropolitan churches and each of the richer bishoprics of his empire, while the cardinals and other members of the curia would receive prebends in the lesser bishoprics.[462] The notorious eccentricities of Giraldus' historical writings and the late date of this particular work immediately raise doubts; although the author's long sojourn in Rome in the pontificate of Innocent III would have given him the opportunity to learn about Henry's relations with the papacy. The imperial proposal described by Giraldus clearly resembles the proposal made by Frederick I to Lucius III in 1184: that the emperor would pay to the pope one-tenth and to the cardinals

---

[460] Henry VI, letter to Celestine III: *MGH Constitutiones* I, 525. On the date see Baaken, 'Verhandlungen' pp. 467–77.

[461] Haller, 'Heinrich VI.' (n. 407) pp. 647–57. See above p. 511. Haller's interpretation has recently been defended by Baaken, 'Verhandlungen' pp. 509–13.

[462] Giraldus Cambrensis, *Speculum Ecclesiae* IV.19, *RS* 21/4 (1873), 302. See Haller, 'Heinrich VI.' pp. 641–4; Pfaff, *Angebot* (n. 443) pp. 18, 39; Perrin, 'Négociations' (n. 456) pp. 565–72.

one-ninth of all his Italian revenues, if in return the pope renounced his claim to the Matildine lands.[463] Was Henry VI's unprecedented offer to the pope, therefore, a more generous version of the proposal of 1184? The story is told only in the *Speculum Ecclesiae* and it lacks a context: the emperor's offer is not linked with the negotiations of 1196 and the request to crown Frederick II. It is possible indeed that Giraldus was thinking of Frederick I's offer of 1184 and attributed it to the wrong emperor. Giraldus' story must, therefore, be regarded with some suspicion. Perhaps the true explanation of Henry VI's unprecedented offer to the pope is that given by the annalist of Marbach: that the emperor would make a public commitment to the crusade if in return the pope would anoint his son king. There was of course nothing unprecedented about an emperor's participation in a crusade: Henry's father had commanded a crusading army only seven years before. But what was unprecedented about Henry's crusading preparations – as revealed in the crusading summons to the Germans (12 April 1195) – were the financial obligations to which he committed himself. The emperor undertook to furnish a crusading army entirely at his own cost.

We have decided to send for the recovery of [Jerusalem] 1,500 knights and the same number of foot-soldiers at our own expense in March and for a year thereafter and we have promised to give to each knight 30 ounces of gold and provisions sufficient to feed him and two servants for a year, and to each foot-soldier, ten ounces of gold and provisions sufficient to feed him for a year.[464]

This might fairly be described as an offer made 'in reverence for God, for the salvation of our soul . . . for the profit and honour of the Roman church', such as was 'never offered by our father . . . nor by any of our predecessors'.

The only firm conclusion that can be drawn from an analysis of the negotiations of 1196 is that Henry VI, in order to secure the succession of his son to the empire, was prepared to make concessions far more expansive than anything offered by Frederick I, when he negotiated the succession of *his* son in 1184. What raised the price of Frederick II's coronation in 1196 was Henry's absolute commitment to 'the union of the kingdom with the empire'; while the pope, the feudal lord of Sicily, was equally committed to the independence of the kingdom. The succession of Frederick II and the union of Sicily and the empire are the themes of the surviving fragments of the will

[463] See above p. 502.
[464] *MGH Constitutiones* 1, 514. Cf. *Annales Marbacenses* 1196 (n. 454), p. 68.

of Henry VI – a document which, however, has been challenged as at least partly inauthentic. The will instructed the empress and her son to 'confer on the lord pope and the Roman church all the rights which they were accustomed to have from the kings of Sicily' – including the homage and fealty which Henry had always refused in his negotiations with Celestine. 'Concerning the empire we ordain that the lord pope and the Roman church shall confirm that it is our son's'; in return for which the papacy was to recover those parts of the Patrimony of St Peter currently under military occupation, together with the greater part of the Matildine inheritance.[465] These death-bed concessions, if they are authentic, presumably reflected the most important demands which the curia had made during the negotiations of 1196. (The papacy had been defrauded of the Matildine lands in the peace negotiations of 1176–7 and had made repeated efforts to recover them.) Before the representatives of the three-year-old Frederick II could offer these new terms to the curia, Celestine had died, aged ninety-two (8 January 1198). According to the chronicle of Roger of Hoveden, soon after the death of the emperor Celestine became so seriously ill that at Christmastide 1197 he attempted to resign his office in favour of John of St Paul, cardinal priest of S. Prisca; but the cardinals rejected his innovatory proposals. There is no corroboration for this story in any other source; and Roger of Hoveden's accompanying account of the undignified scramble for the papal dignity on the death of Celestine III is undoubtedly inaccurate.[466]

It is certainly true that by the beginning of 1197 John of St Paul had become the pope's most trusted adviser, constantly at his side; and since Celestine was indeed incapacitated during the last months of his pontificate, John of St Paul must have been the dominant figure in the curia.[467] These last months witnessed a sudden upsurge of purposeful activity: the emperor's death released the curia from the posture of 'stubborn temporising' into which it had been frozen for the past six years. The German faction and the conciliators lost their

---

[465] *MGH Constitutiones* I, 530–1. On the authenticity of the will (which survives as a quotation in the *Gesta Innocentii III*) see the negative conclusions of V. Pfaff, 'Die Gesta Innocenz' III. und das Testament Heinrichs VI.', *ZSSRG KA* 50 (1964), 78–126.

[466] Roger of Hoveden, *Chronica* (n. 438) pp. 4, 32. See above p. 89.

[467] Wenck, 'Päpste' (n. 407) pp. 456–74; Pfaff, 'Coelestin III.' (n. 403) p. 114. On Celestine's illness see his letter to the bishop, consuls and people of Ascoli (23 December 1197): P. F. Kehr, *Nachrichten der Göttinger Gesellschaft, phil.-hist. Klasse* (1898) pp. 43–4.

influence and the opponents of the Staufen were free to exploit the opportunities of the interregnum. The most important initiative was that of the legates Pandulf, cardinal priest of SS. Apostoli and Bernard, cardinal priest of S. Pietro in Vincoli, who on 11 November 1197 formed a league of the Tuscan cities Lucca, Florence, Siena, San Miniato, Prato, Volterra and later Arezzo. (They tried unsuccessfully to force Pisa to join the league by placing her under an interdict.) The Tuscan League swore to recognise no lord and to make no alliance without the approval of the Roman church. The strategy of Cardinals Pandulf and Bernard was firmly in the tradition of papal policy during the Alexandrine schism and the pontificates of Alexander III's successors. It is therefore particularly significant that one of the earliest actions of the new pope, Innocent III, was the condemnation of the Tuscan League as neither useful nor honourable, since the lordship of Tuscany belonged to the Roman church.[468] Innocent III could well afford to abandon the strategies of his predecessors and to impose 'hierocratic' ideas on a curia accustomed for forty years to more moderate attitudes. For Innocent inherited in 1198 a political situation far more favourable than any of his predecessors had known since the beginning of the papal reform movement: 'the union of the kingdom with the empire' apparently ended, a disputed royal election in Germany, Henry VI's succession plan forgotten, almost all the papal territorial claims in Italy vindicated. Now at last it was practicable to adopt the theory of papal–imperial relations which Gregory VII had developed in the later years of his pontificate; to speak of the pope's 'investing' the emperor with the empire; to attribute to the pope the right to depose a monarch and to choose his successor according to the principle of 'suitability' (*idoneitas*).

There is a striking contrast between the regime of Innocent III and that of the later twelfth-century popes. The election of 1198 initiated a period of self-confident innovation in some ways reminiscent of the Gregorian reform of the late eleventh century. Innocent III's new measures radically affected all the areas of papal policy covered by this book. The papacy became actively involved in the founding of religious orders of startlingly novel appearance. The curia took decisive measures to combat the heretical movements, translating

---

[468] R. Davidsohn, *Geschichte von Florenz* I (Berlin, 1896), 612–14, 622; Wenck p. 464. See V. Pfaff, 'Der Vorgänger: das Wirken Coelestins III. aus der Sicht von Innozenz III.', *ZSSRG KA* 60 (1974), 121–67.

the twelfth-century papal and conciliar decrees into action. The crusading bulls of Innocent III emphatically reclaimed the direction of the crusade for the papacy. With the *Compilatio tertia* of 1209 the pope for the first time assumed responsibility for the compilation of a collection of papal decretals. Simultaneously Innocent III aggressively asserted his lordship over the Patrimony of St Peter; while his interventions in the secular politics of western Christendom were unprecedented in their range and vigour. There can be no doubt of Innocent III's determination to distance himself from the attitudes and policies of the later twelfth-century papacy. It is significant that the only twelfth-century predecessor whom he revered – reserving for him alone the epithet 'of *holy* memory' – was Innocent II. (The memory of Innocent II may indeed have prompted Cardinal Lothar of SS. Sergio e Baccho to choose the pontifical name 'Innocent'.) Innocent II had been unusually successful in his relations with the empire and he had also been a thorough 'Gregorian' in his interpretation of the relations of papacy and empire. Perhaps these were the reasons for Innocent III's approval.[469]

As we have seen, it was the premature death of Emperor Henry VI which gave Innocent III his unprecedented freedom of action. For the past century-and-a-quarter every papal regime had been forced into an alliance either with the emperor or, more frequently, with the emperor's enemies and in particular with the Norman ruler of southern Italy and Sicily. However, the papal curia had rarely been unanimous in its approval of either of these alliances; so that an important feature of curial politics in the twelfth century was the conflict between a Sicilian faction and an imperial faction of cardinals. We have seen that this faction struggle could influence papal elections, could contribute in 1130 and 1159 to papal schism and could paralyse the decision-making processes of the curia. For most of the pontificate of Innocent III the king of Sicily, Frederick II, was a minor and therefore the ward of his feudal lord, the pope; while there was no generally acknowledged candidate for the imperial crown. There was no need, therefore, for an imperial or a Sicilian alliance and equally no need for an imperial or Sicilian faction of cardinals.[470] The freedom from political threats and from internal

---

[469] See above pp. 452–3. On Innocent III's attitude to Innocent II see Schmale, *Schisma* (n. 191) p. 286 n. 4.
[470] On the college of cardinals in Innocent III's pontificate see W. Maleczek, *Papst und Kardinalskolleg von 1191 bis 1216* (Vienna, 1984).

faction explains the self-confidence and energy of the new regime of 1198. The contrast between the new and the old regime serves to remind us of the vital role which the relationship with the empire played in papal history between 1073 and 1198.

APPENDIX
A LIST OF POPES, 1073–1198

The dates given are those of the election, consecration and death of the pope. Details of the antipopes are given in italics.

Gregory VII, *e.* 22 April 1073, *c.* 29/30 June 1073, *d.* 25 May 1085
  Clement III (Wibert of Ravenna), e. 25 June 1080, c. 24 March 1084, d. September 1100
Victor III, *e.* 24 May 1086, *c.* 9 May 1087, *d.* 16 September 1087
Urban II, *e., c.* 12 March 1088, *d.* 29 July 1099
Paschal II, *e.* 13 August 1099, *c.* 14 August 1099, *d.* 21 January 1118
  Theoderic, c. September 1100, expelled December 1100
  Albert, e. February 1102, deposed March 1102
  Sylvester IV (Maginulf), e. 18 November 1105, deposed 12 April 1111
Gelasius II, *e.* 24 January 1118, *c.* 10 March 1118, *d.* 29 January 1119
  Gregory VIII (Burdinus), e., c. 8 March 1118, deposed April 1121
Calixtus II, *e.* 2 February 1119, *c.* 9 February 1119, *d.* 13 December 1124
Honorius II, *e.* 16 December 1124, *c.* 21 December 1124, *d.* 13/14 February 1130
Innocent II, *e.* 14 February 1130, *c.* 23 February 1130, *d.* 24 September 1143
  Anacletus II, e. 14 February 1130, c. 23 February 1130, d. 25 January 1138
  Victor IV, e. 15 March 1138, resigned 29 May 1139
Celestine II, *e., c.* 26 September 1143, *d.* 8 March 1144
Lucius II, *e.* 12 March 1144, *d.* 15 February 1145

Eugenius III, *e.* 15 February 1145, *c.* 18 February 1145, *d.* 8 July 1153

Anastasius IV, *e.* (*c.*) 12 July 1153, *d.* 3 December 1154

Hadrian IV, *e.* 4 December 1154, *c.* 5 December 1154, *d.* 1 September 1159

Alexander III, *e.* 7 September 1159, *c.* 20 September 1159, *d.* 30 August 1181

   Victor IV, e. 7 September 1159, c. 4 October 1159, d. 20 April 1164

   Paschal III, e. 2 April 1164, c. 26 April 1164, d. 20 September 1168

   Calixtus III, e. September 1168, resigned 29 August 1178

   Innocent III, e. 29 September 1179, deposed January 1180

Lucius III, *e.* 1 September 1181, *c.* 6 September 1181, *d.* 25 November 1185

Urban III, *e.* 25 November 1185, *c.* 1 December 1185, *d.* 20 October 1187

Gregory VIII, *e.* 21 October 1187, *c.* 25 October 1187, *d.* 17 December 1187

Clement III, *e.* 19 December 1187, *c.* 20 December 1187, *d.* 10 April 1191

Celestine III, *e.* 10 April 1191, *c.* 14 April 1191, *d.* 8 January 1198

INDEX

527